Great Thinkers in Economics

Series Editors
John King
School of Humanities and Social Sciences
La Trobe University
Melbourne, Australia

Alexander Millmow
Federation Business School
Federation University
Mt Helen, Australia

The famous historian, E.H. Carr once said that in order to understand history it is necessary to understand the historian writing it. The same could be said of economics. Famous economists often remark that specific episodes in their lives, or particular events that took place in their formative years attracted them to economics. Great Thinkers in Economics is designed to illuminate the economics of some of the great historical and contemporary economists by exploring the interaction between their lives and work, and the events surrounding them.

Paolo Paesani

Richard F. Kahn

An Intellectual Biography

palgrave
macmillan

Paolo Paesani
Department of Literature, Philosophy and Art History
University of Rome Tor Vergata
Rome, Italy

ISSN 2662-6276 ISSN 2662-6284 (electronic)
Great Thinkers in Economics
ISBN 978-3-032-09122-2 ISBN 978-3-032-09123-9 (eBook)
https://doi.org/10.1007/978-3-032-09123-9

This Palgrave Macmillan imprint is published by the registered company Springer Nature Switzerland AG.
The registered company address is: Gewerbestrasse 11, 6330 Cham, Switzerland

To the memory of my father Mario Paesani

Preface

This book stems from my interest in Cambridge economics. This interest began more than thirty years ago at Sapienza University of Rome, where, as an undergraduate student, I attended lectures by professors who had studied at Cambridge in the 1960s before returning to Italy. I particularly remember Pierangelo Garegnani, Fernando Vianello, Mario Nuti, Mario Mellano and, above all, Marcello de Cecco, my undergraduate thesis advisor and first mentor, who had Richard Kahn as his own supervisor at Cambridge. During my postgraduate studies at Bocconi University in Milan and the European University Institute in Florence, I did not have many opportunities to explore Cambridge economics further. However, I promised myself that I would return to it as soon as possible. More recently, together with friends and colleagues including Annalisa Rosselli, Maria Cristina Marcuzzo, Carlo Cristiano and many others I have devoted a significant part of my research to different aspects of Cambridge economics. In 2022, Maria Cristina Marcuzzo and I co-edited a second collection of Kahn's writings based on guidelines entrusted to Marcuzzo by Kahn himself.

Rome, 31 July 2025

Rome, Italy
Paolo Paesani

List of Archives Consulted

Cambridge, King's College Archive Centre (and microfilms in Library of Banca d'Italia, Rome)

1. Papers of Richard Ferdinand Kahn (RFK)
2. Papers of John Maynard Keynes (JMK)
3. Papers of Joan Violet Robinson (JVR)
4. Papers of Nicholas Kaldor (NK)

Cambridge, Marshall Library of Economics (and microfilm of EAGR in Library of Banca d'Italia, Rome)

5. Personal papers of Austin Robinson (EAGR)
6. Papers of the Marshall Society (Marsoc)

Cambridge, Churchill College Archives Centre

7. Papers of Austin Robinson (ROBN)
8. Papers of David Howell (Lord Howell of Guildford) (HWLL)

London, London School of Economics Library, Archives and Special Collections

9. Papers of James Edward Meade (MEADE)
10. Papers of Lionel Robbins (ROBBINS)

Other archives in the UK, USA and Italy

11. The National Archives (TNA), London
12. Papers of Hugh Gaitskell (at UCL), London
13. Papers of Piero Sraffa (SP) (online archive), originals at Trinity College, Cambridge
14. Papers of Dennis H. Robertson (online archive), originals at Trinity College, Cambridge
15. Papers of Raffaele Mattioli, Milan
16. Papers of Luigi L. Pasinetti, Milan
17. Saint Paul's School Archives, London
18. Archivio Intesa San Paolo, Milan
19. The Papers of Marjorie S. Turner. Special Collections & University Archives

San Diego State University Library

Acknowledgements

My first thanks go to Wyndham Hacket-Pain for his advice, constant support and great patience over the four years it took me to write this book. Thanks also go to Ms Karthika Devi and the team at Palgrave Macmillan.

I would like to thank Dr Patricia McGuire and Tom Davies for their assistance during my time at the King's College Archive Centre. Thanks also go to Dr Maria Grazia Masone and her staff at the Paolo Baffi Library (Bank of Italy), Dr Paola Chiapponi (Archivio Intesa San Paolo), Clare Trowell and Simon Frost of the Marshall Library, Jessica Saunders of the Churchill Archive Centre, Kelly Strickland of St Paul's School, and the archivists of the London School of Economics, the National Archives, and the Gaitskell Archive at University College London. I would also like to thank Dr Paola Coppola, Director of the School of Economics Library at the University of Rome Tor Vergata, and her staff. I am particularly indebted to Daniela Ficini for her constant, kind assistance.

Susan Howson kindly answered my questions about Richard Kahn and James Meade. I would like to thank her for sharing her memories of Kahn, for reading and commenting on the manuscript, and for her generous help and support in general. Any remaining errors are my responsibility. David and Sarah Papineau, Richard Kahn's nephew and niece, also generously provided me with information about the Kahn family and Kahn's time in Cambridge in the 1970s. Their help is kindly acknowledged and greatly appreciated.

Alexandra Saunders proofread and edited my English with great care, professionalism and efficacy. I thank her for help in deciphering Kahn's difficult-to-read handwriting, for the information she provided me with about Kahn and Cambridge, and for her kindness. I look forward to our future cooperation. As on previous occasions, Iolanda (Dina) Sanfilippo was a great help in finalising the manuscript, providing reassurance throughout. I thank her for kindly agreeing to help me, despite her many other commitments. The help of Patrizia Marta and Giuseppe Barbieri is also greatly appreciated.

Maria Cristina Marcuzzo believed in this project from the outset and encouraged me to develop it. I benefited from her constant support, advice, suggestions and careful reading of the manuscript. I would like to thank her for sharing her recollections of Richard Kahn with me, for her scholarly work, and her efforts to preserve and enhance Kahn's legacy.

Throughout this project, Annalisa Rosselli provided invaluable advice and support. I thank her for this, for carefully reading the draft manuscript. I would also like to thank Annalisa for encouraging me many years ago to specialise in the history of economic thought and for our work together on the theory of speculation in the spirit of Marshall, Keynes and Kahn. Without her guidance and support, this book would not exist.

Marco Dardi, the editor of the Italian edition of Kahn's Fellowship Dissertation and author of illuminating studies on various aspects of Kahn's scholarly work, generously offered to share his recollections and insights on Richard Kahn in an interview featured in the final chapter of this book. I greatly appreciated our conversations and his helpful suggestions.

Carlo Cristiano read the first draft of this book with great attention and patience. His knowledge of Marshall, the Marshallians and Keynes, as well as his advice, was invaluable in helping me refine my arguments, both in this case and in our previous joint work. I thank him for his help, his generosity and above all his friendship.

Massimo Di Matteo read the entire manuscript with great care and patience. I am deeply grateful for his thoughtful suggestions and advice, and for our many stimulating conversations about Italian economists at Cambridge and Oxford. Daniela Felisini read the final version of the manuscript and provided useful advice. I thank her for this and her encouragement. I would also like to thank Fabrizio Bientinesi, who agreed to read the manuscript after we discussed the project on several occasions. Giulio Cifarelli was a valuable source of information about Cambridge in the 1970s. I am grateful to him for sharing this knowledge, for reading parts of the manuscript and for his irreverent wit.

Many other colleagues have provided me with useful advice and suggestions, memories of Kahn and Cambridge, support ideas and patient listening. I would like to thank: Angela Ambrosino, Mario Amendola, Tony Aspromourgos, Michaël Assous, Michele Bagella, Enrico Bellino, Anna Carabelli, Mario Cedrini, Pierluigi Ciocca, Ghislain Deleplace, Maxime Desmarais-Tremblay, John Eatwell, Luca Fantacci, Tom Ferguson, Saverio M. Fratini, Maurizio Franzini, Giacomo Gabbuti, Alfredo Gigliobianco, Nicola Giocoli, Rebeca Gomez-Betancourt, Harald Hagemann, Giorgio La Malfa, Ivo Maes, Roberto Marchionatti, Fabio Masini, Ugo Pagano, Antonella Palumbo, Ilaria Pasotti, Lorenzo Pecchi, Gustavo Piga, Constantinos Repapis, Alessandro Roncaglia, Elisa Rossi Danelzik, Claudio Sardoni, Bertram Schefold, Eleonora Sanfilippo, Annamaria Simonazzi, Antonella Stirati, Teodoro Dario Togati, Paolo Trabucchi, Manuela Mosca and Giandomenica Becchio. Thanks go to the participants in the annual conferences of Italian Association for the History of Political Economy (STOREP), the Italian Association for the History of Economic Thought (AISPE), and the European Society for the History of Economic Thought (ESHET), the PhD students at Scuola Superiore Sant'Anna, and the attendees of the Summer School in the History of Economic Thought in Turin in 2023, who listened to parts of this work.

In thanking those who read all or part of the manuscript and gave me advice, I wish to emphasise that I am solely responsible for any errors, omissions or shortcomings in the final text.

During the summer of 2024, which I spent between London and Cambridge, I was generously hosted by Dr Saneya Iskander, a wise, caring and intelligent woman. She was eager to read this book, but sadly passed away unexpectedly in April 2025. I will always remember her with gratitude and affection, as well as her children, my friend Waleed Gumaa, his sister Randa Gumaa and their families.

In Cambridge I had a chance encounter with Joan Harcourt, which turned into two weeks of pleasurable conversations and memories about Geoff Harcourt, Richard Kahn, Joan Robinson, and Cambridge life. I thank her for this, and for her infectious good humour. I would also like to express my gratitude to Professor Julia Bamford de Cecco for taking the time to share her memories of Kahn, Joan Robinson and Cambridge with me.

I would like to thank my family and friends for their constant support.

One final thought, in loving memory of Marilisa Di Febio Sillano.

Competing Interests The author has no competing interests to declare that are relevant to the content of this manuscript.

Praise for *Richard F. Kahn*

"This masterly intellectual biography finally reveals the profile of the economist who Samuelson described as the 'elusive figure who hides in the preface of Cambridge books'. It is a must reading for anyone interested in the Cambridge tradition in economics and in one of its more important protagonists."

—Maria Cristina Marcuzzo, *Sapienza, Università di Roma and Accademia Nazionale dei Lincei*

"As a long-awaited intellectual biography of one the most ubiquitous yet cautious and discrete Cambridge economists, and based on an admirable knowledge of unpublished archives and correspondence, this remarkable book is a meticulous reconstruction of the incremental changes brought by Kahn to his initial Marshallian up bringing both in economic theory and policy while always keeping Cambridge at the centre. Scrupulously fair with his treatment of Kahn, the author offers an extremely well-balanced appreciation of the progressive fragmentation of the Cambridge tradition. This highly readable, well-written and thoughtful intellectual biography demonstrates with great care that Kahn's reluctance to squarely face up the dominant non-Cambridge neoclassical synthesis seems to have somewhat precipitated the fall of the "Keynesian citadel" he was otherwise so keen to defend."

—Pascal Bridel, *Centre Walras-Pareto, Université de ausanne, Switzerland*

"Paolo Paesani's readable and richly-documented intellectual biography of the great Cambridge economist Richard Kahn is an indispensable contribution to understanding three major developments in 20th century economics: Keynes's revolutionary breakthrough in macroeconomics, the emergence of imperfect competition, and Post-Keynesian growth and development theory. Anyone with any interest in any of these three upheavals in economic theory or in wartime and postwar British economic policymaking should read this book, and will enjoy doing so."

—Prof. Robert Dimand, *Professor of Economics, Brock University, Ontario, Canada*

Contents

About the Author

Paolo Paesani is full professor of the History of Economic Thought at the Department of Literature, Philosophy and Art History at the University of Rome Tor Vergata. He is visiting professor at both the University of Lyon 2 and the Riga Graduate School of Law. He holds a Bachelor's degree in Economics from Sapienza University (Rome, 1997), a Master's degree in Economics from Bocconi University (Milan, 1998) and a PhD in Economics from the European University Institute (Florence, 2005). His main research interests include the history of macroeconomic analysis between the 1930s and 1970s, speculation theory, and the European economy. He is an active member of the Italian Association for the History of Political Economy (STOREP) and the European Society for the History of Economic Thought (ESHET), holding positions on their governing bodies.

CHAPTER 1

Introducing Richard Kahn

Anyone approaching the study of Richard F. Kahn (1905–1989) is confronted with an enigma. Witnesses agree in describing Kahn as a man of great analytical ability, firm convictions and strong opinions. For years he was regarded as the doyen of Keynesian economics, an eminent figure at the University of Cambridge, one of the world's leading centres for economic studies between the 1920s and the 1970s, a famous economist active in national and international institutions and in British economic debates (Dardi, 1990; Pasinetti, 1991; Harcourt, 1991; Marcuzzo, 2012).

> There was a time at which, as Chairman of the Economics Faculty, Professorial Fellow and Fellowship Elector at King's, convener of the so called 'Secret Seminar', he seemed to have the whole of the Cambridge economics thought process rotating around him. The teaching of economics in Cambridge was re-shaped under his initiative. The 'Secret Seminar' [...] was a post-war version of the early 'Cambridge Circus'. It was held in Kahn's rooms in Webb's Court. There it was that the major contributions generated by the Cambridge Keynesian school of economics took shape. (Pasinetti, 1991, p. 430)

In the face of such fame, particularly in Cambridge circles, reference to Kahn's work in the post-war economic literature is very limited. Most of the secondary literature, with few notable exceptions, focuses on the 1930s and Kahn's role in the Keynesian revolution and the development

P. Paesani, *Richard F. Kahn*, Great Thinkers in Economics,
https://doi.org/10.1007/978-3-032-09123-9_1

of the theory of imperfect competition. Similar considerations apply to the literature on post-war British economic history.

After the war and until the early 1980s, largely but not exclusively as a result of his position at Cambridge and his elevation to the House of Lords in 1965, Kahn was a recognised member of the British establishment. As such he had direct contact with, and on some occasions influence over, economic policy-making in Britain. However, in reconstructions of various aspects of the British post-war economy and economic policy, Kahn's name is absent or relegated to footnotes. The same is true, with few exceptions, of his involvement with supranational institutions including the Organisation for European Economic Cooperation (OEEC, 1955 and 1959–1960), the Food and Agriculture Organisation (FAO, 1950s) and the United Nations Conference on Trade and Development (UNCTAD, 1960s).

Kahn wrote a lot but published few important works, even by the standards of his time, which were so different from ours (Kahn, 1972).[1] Articles and entire books remained unpublished or were published late, when the chances of influencing the issues they addressed had diminished. Kahn's participation in the British economic policy debate was constant but discreet, often in the form of short letters to *The Times* or *The Economist* or articles aimed mainly at a selected British audience. In his twenty-four years in the House of Lords, between 1965 and 1989, Kahn spoke a total of twenty times, and his interventions were modest in their impact. Only in the last years of his life did Kahn decide to talk about himself and his contribution to economics and even then he carved out for himself the role of Keynes's faithful disciple, committed to revisiting and defending the ideas of the master.

Many reasons have been put forward to explain Kahn's reluctance to publish and, more generally, his attitude and preference for avoiding the limelight: modesty, meticulousness, extreme precision, horror at seeing his name associated with an error, a willingness to maintain very high standards in his own work, onerous academic commitments, a certain penchant for secrecy. Each of these elements helps to explain the enigma, but so far there has been no overall reconstruction that would allow these elements to be placed in the context of Kahn's intellectual biography and linked to his relationship with institutions in Britain and internationally. Such a reconstruction has now been attempted, and this introduction aims

[1] Appendix A contains Kahn's complete bibliography.

to summarise its main findings and what they reveal about the enigma surrounding Kahn's name.

In attempting this task, I would like to begin with an observation that plays an important role in my reconstruction of Kahn's intellectual biography. Between the 1930s and 1940s, Kahn acquired a set of beliefs about economic theory and policy and a 'view of the world' that remained essentially unchanged over the following decades. This consistency was both Kahn's strength and his weakness; strength because it provided him with a firm frame of reference within which he could defend his views in a way that was recognisable to 'friends and foes' alike; weakness because, as economic theory and policy changed, Kahn chose not to change and thus became increasingly marginalised in the post-war economic debates and their subsequent reconstructions.

Kahn adopted a similar attitude in his relationship with the institutions with which he came into contact during his life. The war years, when Kahn left Cambridge to work for various administrations as a temporary civil servant, were crucial for his formation and left him with a strong desire to make a positive impact on society, in the spirit of the mission that Marshall had imagined for Cambridge economics graduates. Kahn had more than one opportunity to do so, but these attempts were rarely successful. On several occasions, and for various reasons, which I reconstruct in detail, Kahn faced with resistance at the political level or among senior civil servants. On these occasions, after trying to persuade his counterparts, he chose to reiterate his point of view and avoid further confrontation rather than curry the opinion of his political interlocutors. This attitude helped to limit his concrete influence and, as a consequence, his visibility. Even when his opinions were listened to, as in the case of the Radcliffe Committee, this was only partially the case.

Kahn's consistency is intertwined with his commitment to cultivating deep personal and intellectual relationships with economists in Cambridge and beyond. My research documents the care and attention Kahn gave to his relationship with John Maynard Keynes from 1927, when Keynes became his tutor at Cambridge (together with Gerald Shove), until 1946, the year of Keynes's death. To the already known facts about this relationship, my research adds information about Keynes's role in guiding the young, inexperienced Kahn through the world of British institutions, about the role Kahn played in providing information and advice to Keynes during the war and, most importantly, about the fact that the relationship between Keynes and Kahn during the war, while remaining close, changed significantly from what it had been in the 1930s.

Equally important, and much longer, was Kahn's relationship with Joan Robinson. This relationship began in 1928 and continued uninterrupted until Robinson's death in 1983. Going beyond the personal dimension, my study shows how the basis of this relationship was the intellectual admiration that each felt for the other. The public tributes that Joan Robinson paid to Kahn in her published works and the private tributes to Robinson that emerge from Kahn's correspondence (in particular with Nicholas Kaldor) bear testimony to this. Whereas much attention has been paid to the Kahn–Robinson relationship in the 1930s, less is known about the post-war decades. With this in mind, my research focuses on the role that Kahn and Robinson played in the Faculty of Economics and Politics at Cambridge in the 1950s and 1960s and on the similarities and differences between their analytical approaches and interests. Equally long but more complicated was Kahn's association with Kaldor. Here, too, my research aims to expand on what is already known on this subject, in particular by focusing on the confrontations between Kahn and Kaldor on various issues from the commodity-based international reserve currency to the well-known controversy between the Old and New Cambridge Schools in the 1970s.

Keynes, Joan Robinson and Kaldor are the three main nodes in a wide network of relationships that Kahn established at Cambridge, from the 1930s onwards, and that includes Austin Robinson, Piero Sraffa, James Meade, Ruth Cohen, Brian Reddaway and Noel Annan, among Kahn's own generation, and Geoffrey Harcourt, Luigi Pasinetti, Richard Goodwin, Frank Hahn, John Eatwell and many others, among younger economists. Each of them, and Kahn's many other correspondents, played a role in the development of Kahn's ideas and in his commitment to building and consolidating the Keynesian citadel at Cambridge.[2]

These initial remarks should not lead to believe that my research aims to present an idealised image of Kahn. At various times in his life, Kahn demonstrated a strongly partisan attitude, occasionally bordering on intolerance. In the second half of the 1930s, he played a leading role among the 'Young Turks' who fought alongside Keynes against Pigou and the neoclassical (Marshallian) tradition in which Kahn himself had been

[2] Appendix C provides brief biographical profiles of some of the individuals with whom Kahn interacted during his professional career.

trained and which, as we shall see, continued to exert a strong influence on him. In the 1950s and 1960s, when he was at the height of his influence and academic power, Kahn often adopted a belligerent and uncompromising attitude, fighting at the head of the Keynesian party against opponents with the Faculty of Economics such as D. Robertson and R. Stone.

Teaching was an essential part of Richard Kahn's work. From 1931 until his retirement in 1972, he devoted himself to it constantly, with interruptions caused by the war (1939–1946) and institutional commitments, such as in 1955.[3] My research reconstructs this aspect of Kahn's career, also making use of unpublished notes from his lectures. As a teacher, Kahn seems not to have been particularly gifted. Those who attended his lectures, especially when he was in later years, remember a shy man, who spoke in a low voice, often uncomfortable in front of his students, capable of projecting an image that was at once distant and intimidating, at least in the eyes of the younger generation. These elements, together with others related to his complex personality, and in particular the distance between the often aloof, rigid and intellectually haughty 'public Kahn' and the kind, attentive and caring 'private Kahn', help us to understand why Kahn did not succeed in setting up a school or attracting young theoretical economists with whom he could collaborate in spreading his ideas. It seems that no one played the same role with Kahn as Kahn did with Keynes, and even if someone had tried, Kahn probably would not have accepted them.

When Kahn did develop closer relationships with younger scholars, in his maturity, he preferred to associate with economists, such as Kenneth Berrill and Michael Posner, or with scholars with a strong interest in the history of economics, and in particular Donald Moggridge.[4] Kahn was also close to John Eatwell, who, along with Moggridge, persuaded him to publish his collected essays and took care of preparing the manuscript for publication, as Kahn acknowledged. In the 1970s, after his retirement, Kahn was more often critical than supportive of the young radical heterodox economists at Cambridge, such as Domenico Mario Nuti, Ajit Singh and Robert Rowthorn, as evidenced by his attitude to the founding of the *Cambridge Journal of Economics* and other episodes analysed by A. Saith

[3] Appendix B lists all the courses Kahn taught at Cambridge from 1931 to 1972.

[4] On Kenneth Berrill, Michael Posner and Donald Moggridge, see Appendix C.

in his recent impressive work on the twilight of heterodox economics at Cambridge (Saith, 2022).

Kahn, perhaps as a result of his lifelong love for Italy, also collaborated, appreciated and was in close contact with Italian scholars, many of whom had been students at Cambridge in the 1950s and 1960s (Baranzini & Mirante, 2016). The name of Luigi Pasinetti, with whom Kahn maintained a long friendship, stands out, together with those of Beniamino Andreatta, Luigi Spaventa, Marcello de Cecco and Michele Salvati, among others. To this must be added Kahn's friendly acquaintance with Giacomo Becattini and Marco Dardi, who edited the Italian translation (and first publication) of Kahn's Fellowship Dissertation, and with Maria Cristina Marcuzzo, who conducted a lengthy biographical interview with him (Marcuzzo, 2020) and played a crucial role in preserving his papers and, more generally, keeping the Kahn legacy alive over the years.

Richard Kahn's intellectual life as Cambridge economist began in 1927, when having completed his studies in mathematics and physics, with good but not brilliant results; he moved to economics under the guidance of Keynes and Shove. It ended in 1989, the year of his death, with the publication in English of his Fellowship Dissertation. Within these sixty-two years my research identifies three periods of more intense activity, interspersed with two long interruptions.

The first phase of maximum creativity lasted about eleven years, from 1928, when Kahn began work on the Fellowship Dissertation, to 1939, when he left Cambridge to work as a temporary civil servant until 1946. The 1930s were the 'years of High Theory' and the two Cambridge revolutions: imperfect competition and the Keynesian revolution, in which Kahn played a major role along with Keynes, Sraffa, Joan Robinson and others.[5] The Fellowship Dissertation on the *Economics of the Short Period* that won him early fame among the Cambridge economists and a Fellowship at King's College, his trip to the United States during which he made contacts with leading figures in the US academic world (including Joseph Schumpeter, Frank Taussig, Edward Chamberlin), his participation as assistant secretary of the Committee of Economists of the Economic Advisory Council with Keynes and Arthur C. Pigou, his pivotal role in the 'Cambridge Circus', in the development of the *General Theory* and in the Cambridge controversies that followed it, his early exchanges with

[5] The third Cambridge revolution, that of the capital critique, came later and Kahn did not take part in it.

non-Cambridge economists (Friedrich von Hayek, Gottfried Haberler, Michal Kalecki), his articles on the multiplier, on optimal output and on duopoly, all helped to make the name and reputation of the young Kahn as a gifted economist. He became a University Lecturer in 1933 and a member of the King's economics teaching staff in 1936.

All this is well known and has been studied extensively as Chap. 2 and the first part of Chap. 3 in my research document. Less well known, and considered in Chap. 2, are the essays that Kahn wrote, as a student, in response to questions posed to him by Keynes and Shove. These essays document the quality and intensity of Kahn's Marshallian training, as well as his precocious interest in certain theoretical concepts that would be of great importance in his contribution to the elaboration of the *General Theory*. Equally little known, are Kahn's unpublished early writings on international economic issues—such as the transfer problem and post-war recovery.

Kahn's first period of creative intellectual activity was interrupted by the outbreak of the Second World War. Like other young economists of his generation, he was recruited as a temporary civil servant, first at the Board of Trade (1939–1941), and then in Middle East Supply Centre in Cairo (1941–1942) and back in London in various other Ministries (Production, Supply). He carried out this job with dedication and passion for seven years, during which time he was physically (but not emotionally) removed from Cambridge and from developments in economic theory.

During the war, Kahn was confronted with problems to which he would return in later years as part of his commitment to developing the Keynesian apparatus and its policy implications. I refer in particular to the issues of direct control over firms and rationing, which had already been hotly debated during the First World War and to the problem of how to reconcile full employment with the control of inflation and the balance of payments, the management of scarce resources (raw materials, skilled labour), the stabilisation of prices and wages, nationalisation. At the personal level, Kahn made important contacts during the war, which contributed to establish his position as a respected member of the British establishment. At the same time, Kahn strengthened his relationship with other Cambridge economists who, like him, were civil servants and who would become his allies in the battles within the Faculty of Economics in the years to come (in particular Austin Robinson, Brian Reddaway and Ruth Cohen). The second part of Chap. 3 focuses on these aspects.

Returning to Cambridge in September 1946, Kahn immersed himself again in academic life. He was no longer a young lecturer busy building an academic reputation under Keynes's protective wing, but an experienced man with a strong desire to exert a positive influence as he had done during the war. At Cambridge, where he became Professor in 1951, Kahn's interest in policy and applied issues gradually took precedence over economic theory, in which he remained nonetheless active until the 1960s. This interest was reconciled with his commitment to the consolidation of the Keynesian citadel of Cambridge and the academic battles that this entailed. To what is already known about this, my research adds the 'inside' reconstruction, based on original and partly unexplored archival material, of some particularly important episodes, linking them to Kahn's modus operandi and the development of his economic ideas.

In the second phase of his creative activity, from 1946 to the early 1960s, Kahn, together with Joan Robinson, Kaldor, and many others, developed Post–Keynesian growth and distribution theory along lines different from those of the neoclassical synthesis. In the 1950s, the focus of Kahn's interest shifted from imperfect competition and industrial economics to monetary issues and portfolio theory, inflation, the relationship between prices and wages, commodity prices and balance of payments problems. The main results of his intellectual activity were the re-elaboration of the notion of liquidity preference, with a focus on the link between speculative and precautionary motives, the testimony to the Radcliffe Committee, the analysis of the concept of the wage–wage spiral, the analysis of the British and international payments problems and his studies on commodity price stabilisation and buffer stocks. In addition to these more important writings, many of which were related to Kahn's activities in connection with institutions in Britain (Board of Trade, National Coal Board) and abroad (OEEC, FAO), there are other writings of a more ephemeral nature.

Among the channels through which Kahn disseminated his ideas during his second phases of more intense intellectual activity (1947–1965), we find *The Listener* and Bank reviews such as the *Westminster Bank Review*. The main significance of these venues lay in the identity of their audiences: the public listening to BBC radio broadcasts in the case of *The Listener*, and mainly members of the British financial community and political establishment in the case of the Bank reviews. Kahn chose these venues to discuss Keynes's ideas and emphasise their continued relevance to current economic policy debates. Kahn also maintained a discreet but constant presence in the public debate through letters to *The Times*, *The Financial Times* and *The Economist*. From 1965, this activity was supplemented by the speeches in the House of Lords. A recurring theme in Richard Kahn's intellectual contributions was his engagement with questions of international economics. These included the regulation of global trade, the stabilisation of commodity prices at a supranational level through buffer stock mechanisms and the regulation and governance of foreign exchange markets. At the heart of these discussions lies his consistent reliance on the principles established by Keynes at Bretton Woods, particularly the emphasis placed on creating institutions and rules that allow countries to maintain autonomy in developing their economic policies while encouraging the gradual liberalisation of trade and capital movements. Chapters 4, 5, 6, and 7, which form the core of this research, are devoted to all these aspects as well as to Kahn's other activities at Cambridge and beyond.

The 1960s coincided with the second interruption in Kahn's scholarly output. Throughout the decade, Kahn did not publish any significant work, limiting himself to few writings on contingent issues and to participating in four UNCTAD commissions that drafted as many reports. The only theoretically important work on the valuation ratio and the growth of firms, which he wrote between 1964 and 1965, remained unpublished until 1972, when it was included in Kahn's first collection of essays. If the interruption of Kahn's scholarly production in the 1940s can be explained by his wartime activities, the silence of the 1960s is more problematic as Kahn was still at the centre of academic life and in full possession of his intellectual faculties at a time when, particularly in Cambridge, a new phase of great theoretical ferment was beginning.

On the basis of the evidence presented in my research, I interpret Kahn's silence as a manifestation of the growing incompatibility between his approach to economic analysis and the trends prevailing at the time. By the start of the 1970s, Kahn's preference for qualitative over quantitative analysis; his attention to the complex of motivations underlying liquidity preference and investment decisions (conjectures and opinions, different perceptions of risks of different types, uncertainty), but without reference to utility functions; his insistence on the margins of indeterminacy surrounding the key economic relations defined within the Keynesian theoretical framework (liquidity preference, investment function, relationship between employment, money wages and prices); his almost sociological approach to the description of categories of economic agents or of the wage setting process in Britain, set Kahn's approach to economics apart both from mainstream economics (general equilibrium, mathematisation, econometrics) and, less obviously, from the heterodox economics and heterodox interpretations of Keynes that were prevailing at Cambridge at the time (Sraffian, neo-Marxist, Kaleckian economics).

Kahn's growing incompatibility with the various strands of economic heterodoxy at Cambridge was also political. In the 1970s, while many of the young heterodox Cambridge economists were adopting politically radical left-wing positions, Kahn moved in the opposite direction. His long-standing affiliation to the Labour Party and his generally left-of-centre political orientation gave way to an increasingly critical attitude towards the Wilson and Callaghan Labour governments and the trade unions that supported them, paving the way to Kahn's decision to leave the Labour Party and join the more moderate Social Democratic Party.

Kahn's response to his progressive isolation at Cambridge in the 1970s characterised the third and final phase of active intellectual life. While continuing to take an interest in the life of the Faculty of Economics, he returned to actively participating in British economic debates, as he had done in the 1950s, and giving lectures and seminars, also abroad, more frequently than in the past (Chap. 8). In this context, Kahn repeatedly defended Cambridge Keynesianism and his own role as a leading exponent of that approach against criticism from various fronts, including the British monetarists and former Cambridge graduates who were no longer part of the Keynesian citadel. In parallel, Kahn returned to intervene in the policy debate, with a focus on inflation and unemployment in Britain, reiterating his long-standing criticism of the quantity theory of money, which monetarism was trying to revive. Revisiting ideas expressed in the 1950s, Kahn emphasised the link between wages and prices, the impossibility of distinguishing precisely between demand-pull and cost-push inflation, the superiority of incomes policy as a means of controlling inflation without renouncing high and stable employment, the need to restore a system of fixed but adjustable exchange rates, after the 1971 Bretton Woods crisis.

These activities ran parallel to Kahn's commitment to promoting the legacy of Keynes while at the same time revisiting his works (Chap. 9). The publication of the *Collected Writings of John Maynard Keynes*, of which Kahn was the literary executor, was a very important moment in this respect. In the same years, Kahn gave a series of lectures on Keynes which gave him the occasion to revisit some key aspects of the *General Theory*, highlighting the links with Keynes's earlier work, as well as its strengths and weaknesses. In the same spirit, Kahn contributed to the Canterbury Keynes seminar with an important article on Keynes's role in the establishment of the International monetary system and with his reminiscence of the Cambridge Circus. On this occasion, Kahn reserved for himself the credit of having rejected the quantity theory of money before Keynes and of having developed a vision of the simultaneous determination of the prices and output, extending to the macroeconomic level the concepts of supply and demand price and of supply function. Chapter 9 also documents Kahn's decision, inspired by his contacts with Giacomo Becattini and Marco Dardi, to publish his Fellowship Dissertation, ideally ending his intellectual journey at the point where it had begun sixty years earlier. The fact that this publication appeared first in Italian, in 1983, the year of the deaths of Piero Sraffa and Joan Robinson, and then in English in 1989, the year of Kahn's own death, seems highly symbolic in this respect.

Chapter 10 reflects on Richard Kahn as Cambridge economist, on his views on teaching economics, on his ideas about the relationship between economic theory and policy, on his place in the History of Economic Though and his legacy. The chapter, enriched by two interviews with Maria Cristina Marcuzzo and Marco Dardi, characterises Kahn as the most Marshallian of the great Cambridge Keynesians, the one on whom Marshall's legacy, filtered through Pigou, Shove and Keynes (as a pupil of Marshall, friend of Shove and antagonist of Pigou), had a stronger and more lasting influence than on Joan Robinson, who came from the same tradition but moved away from it, or Kaldor, who did not share that tradition at all. I regard this characterisation as crucial for understanding the enigma surrounding Richard Kahn's name.

References

Baranzini, M., & Mirante, A. (2016). *A compendium of Italian economists at Oxbridge*. Palgrave Macmillan.

Dardi, M. (1990). Richard Kahn. *Studi Economici, 41*, 3–86.

Harcourt, G. C. (1991). R.F. Kahn: A tribute. *BNL Quarterly Review, 176*, 15–30.

Kahn, R. F. (1972). *Selected essays on employment and growth*. Cambridge University Press.

Marcuzzo, M. C. (2012). The elusive figure who hides in the preface of Cambridge books: An appraisal of Richard Kahn's contributions. In N. Salvadori,

C. Gehrke, I. Steedman, & R. Sturn (Eds.), *Classical political economy and modern theory: Essays in honour of Heinz Kurz* (pp. 185–206). Routledge.

Marcuzzo, M. C. (2020). Richard Ferdinand Kahn: A disciple of Keynes. *History of Economics Review, 76*, 1–57.

Pasinetti, L. L. (1991). Richard Ferdinand Kahn 1905–1989. *Proceedings of the British Academy, 76*, 423–443.

Saith, A. (2022). *Cambridge economics in the post-Keynesian era: The eclipse of heterodox traditions.* Springer.

CHAPTER 2

Kahn Rising

2.1 Early Years and Marshallian Imprint

Richard Ferdinand Kahn was born on 10 August 1905 in London from a bourgeois cultured family of strict Jewish observance. His father, Augustus Kahn (1868–1944), was born in Germany and came to England at the age of four. Augustus graduated in mathematics from St John's College, Cambridge, and was a teacher and headmaster before becoming a government inspector of schools. Richard Kahn's mother, Regina Rosa Schoyer (1879–1964), was born in Germany and came to England, where the wedding took place on 14 April 1904, as a young woman.

According to the 1921 census,[1] the Kahn household resided at 26 Fairhazel Gardens, South Hampstead, NW London[2] and was composed of the two parents and seven children: Richard (15 years old at the time), Doris (14), Margaret (12), Beatrice (10), Wilfred (7), Harold (6) and Constance (3). Only Richard, Doris, Beatrice and Constance survived into adulthood. Harold and Wilfred died of whooping cough in their teens while at school (St Paul's like Richard). Margaret also died in her teens after suffering from an eating disorder. Beatrice and Doris both emigrated to Palestine/Israel—Beatrice before the Second World War, Doris after.

[1] See https://ancestors.familysearch.org/en/LVVX-FSQ/baron-richard-ferdinand-kahn-1905-1989

[2] I am indebted to Alexandra Saunders for this information.

P. Paesani, *Richard F. Kahn*, Great Thinkers in Economics,
https://doi.org/10.1007/978-3-032-09123-9_2

Beatrice (1910–2000) married Aba Lanzkron and had children and grandchildren (probably numbering about 100 now), Doris married David Slutzkin and had no children. Constance (1918–1985) married Owen C. Papineau and lived in England, Italy and South Africa. The couple had three sons and a daughter.[3]

Kahn was educated at St Paul's School, London, where he entered in the spring of 1918 and left in July 1924, having completed the Science Form. In October 1922, he was recorded as a member of the editorial board of *The Pauline*, the main school magazine, and was also a member of the school debating society.[4] His 1918 exam records indicate that Kahn was a very proficient student. In that year he was first in his class in Mathematics and Classics. He appears to have been slightly less gifted in English, Divinity, Drawing and French. Over the following five years his performance remained satisfactory.[5]

Upon leaving St Paul's, Kahn won a scholarship to King's College, Cambridge, where he arrived in the autumn of 1924. At Cambridge Kahn read Mathematics, and was placed in the First Class in the Tripos Part I (in 1925). He went on to study Physics, graduating in 1927 with somewhat disappointing results (a Second-Class degree in the Natural Sciences Tripos). Faced with the choice of finding a job or taking full advantage of his scholarship and spending a fourth year at Cambridge, Kahn chose to stay on and devote himself to the study of economics, under the supervision of Keynes and Gerald Shove. Shove was Kahn's first supervisor and in some respects the most important one. In his entry for the *Palgrave Dictionary of Economics*, written many years later, Kahn recalled that Shove was a superb teacher, an original, dauntless thinker and a source of inspiration for his students.[6]

[3] I am indebted to Sarah Papineau and David Papineau for this information. On Kahn's family background and early years, see Harcourt (1991, pp. 15–16), Pasinetti (1991, pp. 425–426).

[4] Four articles published in *The Pauline* in November 1922, December 1922, March 1923 and October 1923 mention Kahn's name, while the June 1924 issue announced that Kahn had won a special science prize.

[5] Ref. Saint Paul's School Archives.

[6] On this, see Kahn (1987). On Shove and his scholarly contribution, see Sardoni (2004, 2017). On the relationships between Shove, Keynes and the other Cambridge economists, including Kahn, in the first forty years of the twentieth century, see Carabelli (2005) and Rosselli (2005a).

If Kahn and Shove met on a weekly basis, the supervisions with Keynes took place fortnightly in Term with other undergraduate students. Marcuzzo (2002a, 422–423, 2005a, 21–22) provides a wealth of evidence of Keynes's high regard for the young Kahn and his talent for economics. Keynes wrote in the margin of a paper by Kahn of 4 November 1927 that 'I think you have a real aptitude for Economics'. A few months later, on 27 April 1928, commenting on an essay, he wrote: 'Very good—almost a perfect answer'. Two days later he wrote to his wife, Lydia, 'Yesterday my favourite pupil Kahn wrote me one of the best answers I ever had from a pupil—he must get a first class'. On the publication of the Tripos results,[7] where Kahn was placed in the First Class, Keynes wrote: 'My dear Kahn, very warm congratulations that all was, after all, well in the exams—though, as you know, I expected it'. On 4 June 1928, Keynes wrote to Pigou in support of Kahn's candidature for a Wrenbury student scholarship, which Kahn eventually won.[8]

Kahn's archive contains a great deal of information about his economic studies in 1927–1928, both in the form of lecture notes and in the form of answers to questions put to him by Keynes and Shove as part of their supervisory activities (ref. RFK/3/3). This includes lecture notes, as well as his responses to questions posed by Keynes and Shove (see Table 2.1). The teachers whose names Kahn mentions in his notes, apart from Shove and Keynes, are Dennis H. Robertson (monetary economics and banking), Arthur C. Pigou (principles of economics), Piero Sraffa (advanced theory of value), Maurice Dobb (distribution theory, labour market), plus a course given by Werner Sombart at the London School of Economics on the theory and history of capitalism.[9]

The questions Keynes and Shove put to Kahn reflected the content of the courses and were designed to test Kahn's understanding of the main

[7] On the Cambridge Economics Tripos between 1903 and 1955, see Tribe (2000).

[8] On this, see Bridel and Ingrao (2005, p. 152) and *The Historical Register of the University of Cambridge, Supplement, 1921–1930* (78; available here https://ia801308.us.archive.org/6/items/historicalre192130univuoft/historicalre192130univuoft.pdf). In the following year Kahn also received the Adam Smith prize (ibid., p. 79).

[9] The list of courses intended for candidates for the Economics Tripos Part II included: Structure and Problems of Industry (Pigou), Distribution and Labour (Dobb), Theory of Money (Keynes), Public Finance (Tappan), Money, Credit and Prices (Robertson), Theory of Population (Shove), Advanced Theory of Value (Sraffa), Theory of Statistics (Yule), International Law (Pearce Higgins), France before the Revolution (Clapham), Political Theory (Passant), Political Science (Simpson) (source: *Cambridge University Reporter*, 4 October 1927, 67).

Table 2.1 Richard F. Kahn as a student of Economics: list of lecture notes and essays

Archival reference	*Type*	*Date*	*Topic*	*Related person*	*Content and comments by related person*
3/3/1	N	1927–1928	Value of money	Robertson	Elaborations on Cambridge equation, forces governing k, and T, effects of motion of P
3/3/12	Q	16.10.1927	Quantity theory of money	Shove	Elaborations on MV + M′V′ = Pt, half of the essay is devoted to the objections to the QTM and the idea that P affects Md and therefore M, separate discussion of Bank money
3/3/20	N	NI	UK monetary system (gold and silver)	NI	Comparison between UK system and Ireland (free state), Germany, France, USA, Indian Currency
3/3/44	N	NI	Value of money—meaning of gold standard	NI	Four definitions of gold standard
3/3/50	Q	9.11.1929	Effects of gold discovery: good or bad?	Shove	
3/3/53	N	NI	Banking	NI	Banking in England (history, central bank business, data on deposits) and the USA (same data)
3/3/72	Q	3.03.1928	Effect of rise in US discount rate on world conditions	Keynes	
3/3/75	N	NI	German banking	NI	History, data, focus on war
3/3/81	N	NI	Comparison between British and German banking practices in relation to industry	Robertson	Paper opens with apologies and reference to Robertson lecture
3/3/110	N	NI	Comparison of banking systems: South Africa, Australia, Japan, India	NI	Data and mostly on structure and key events
3/3/119	N	NI	Various topics	NI	Theory of monetary savings, government inflation, effects of increased loans by banks, effect of growth of population and total output, variation of QTM

3/2/139	N	NI	Foreign exchanges	NI	Mechanism of London market, connections between exchanges and balance of payments, topics in international trade
3/3/165	N	NI	Disordered business	NI	Root cause government inflation, cross country comparison France, Belgium, Italy, Russia, India, Japan, England
3/3/178	N	1926	Banking policy and the price level	Robertson	Discussion of Robertson concepts
3/3/186	N	NI	Banking (JMK Mich. 1929)	Robertson	Analysis of bank balance sheet items
3/3/195	N	NI	Consequences to society of changes in the value of money	Robertson	Reference to *A Tract on Monetary Reform*
3/3/203	N	NI	Various topics related to monetary theory	Robertson	Reference to Fisher (1913), purchasing power parity theory
3/3/262	N	1927–1928	Principles of economics	Pigou	National dividend
3/3/264	Q	3.2.1928	Demand and supply elasticity; consumer surplus	Keynes	Keynes's comment: I think that Marshall never, or scarcely ever, mentions elasticity of supply—a sure sign that he thought it a conception too dicky (unreliable) for general use. A good answer
3/3/270	N	1927–1928	Principles of economics	Pigou	Demand, elasticity of demand
3/3/274	Q	2.12.1927	Elasticity of demand (price of beer)	Keynes	Comment by Keynes: Fallacies: elasticity applies to small changes, demand for beer in reality is non linear; moreover it shifts over time due to changing population and substitution effects
3/3/276	N	1927–1928	Principles of economics	Pigou	Consumer's surplus
3/3/277	Q	13.11.1927	Consumer's surplus: concept and measure	Shove	Comment by Shove: You should have defined consumer surplus as well as saying how to measure it
3/3/276	N	1927–1928	Principles of economics	Pigou	Supply (complications), short and long run
3/3/277	Q	16.10.1927	Elasticity of demand	Shove	Focuses on market, short period, long period and secular prices. No comments by Shove

(*continued*)

Table 2.1 (continued)

Archival reference	*Type*	*Date*	*Topic*	*Related person*	*Content and comments by related person*
3/3/276	N	1927–1928	Principles of economics	Pigou	Markets and prices
3/3/277	Q	13.11.1927	Effect of specific tax on price of a commodity	Shove	Comment by Shove: Elasticity of supply is a slippery concept
3/3/289	Q	2.12.1927	Joint production: effect of tax on A on price of B	Keynes	No comments by Keynes
3/3/292	Q	23.10.1927	Difference between rent as a surplus and interest and profit	Shove	Comment by Shove: Good so far but more wanted
3/3/293	Q	21.10.1927	Rent of land	Keynes	Good
3/3/296	N	NI	Monopoly	NI	Bilateral, simple, discriminatory monopoly
3/3/299	Q	23.10.1927	Value of the commodity under (a) monopoly and (b) monopsony	Shove	Comment by Shove: You have not got the point of (b) (Beta ++)
3/3/302	Q	13.11.1927	Effect of different sales taxes on monopoly	Shove	(Alpha)
3/3/305	Q	17.02.1928	Welfare impact of discriminatory monopoly	Keynes	Comment by Keynes: You don't explicitly (?) consider the case probably the most important practically—of the unit of production very large in relation to consumer demand (e.g. the country doctor, the country railway); though I daresay it is covered up under one or other of your cases. Your answer is a bit too abstract
3/3/310	Q	2.03.1928	Welfare impact of price discrimination in the case of electricity	Keynes	Alpha – good
3/3/315	Q	23.11.1927	Discuss criteria to set railway fares	Shove	Comment by Shove: All wrong. I don't think you've understood the question B+
3/3/317	N	NI	Internal and external economies	NI	General discussion plus graphical analysis

3/3/320	Q	12.02.1928	Impact of total output of own industry or of other industries on a firm's costs	Shove	Comment by Shove: g so far (?) more concrete treatment Alpha—Kahn expresses regret for hurried answer
3/3/323	Q	2.12.1927	Relationship between price and marginal costs and the marginal firm	Keynes	uncorrected
3/3/324	N	NI	Distribution of national dividend among factor and people	NI	Pareto's law, reference to demand price and supply price
3/3/329	Q	12.02.1928	Supply price of (a) capital, (b) labour, (c) land	Shove	Alpha –
3/3/331	Q	27.04.1928	Condition that justify gov. subsidy on particular branches of production	Keynes	Comment by Keynes: Very good—Almost a perfect answer—a + minor comments
3/3/336	N	NI	Population, demographic growth and diminishing returns	NI	Effect of changes of population on production and vice versa, age distribution, rate of natural increase, refer to Malthus and Shove
3/3/343	N	1928–1929	Cost, demand and supply	Sraffa	Discussion of relationship between costs and supply for firm and industry under different returns
3/3/369	N	NI	External economies	Pigou?	No comments
3/3/371	Q	NI	Three questions on supply, cost and process	Sraffa?	Two pencilled comments probably by Sraffa
3/3/382	N	NI	Demand curves and consumer surplus	NI	Analysis of demand, consumer surplus, price elasticity
3/3/389	N	NI	Indifference curves	NI	Graphs and comment
3/3/393	N	Lent 1928	Theory of distribution	M. Dobb	Full course
3/3/412	Q	20.11.1927	Link between inheritance and inequality	Shove	B ++
3/3/414	N	NI	Loose sheet	NI	Part of a bigger document

(*continued*)

Table 2.1 (continued)

Archival reference	*Type*	*Date*	*Topic*	*Related person*	*Content and comments by related person*
3/3/4125	N	NI	Wages	NI	Trade unionism, difference between labour power and commodities
3/3/421	Q	4.11.1927	Marshall's theory of normal wages	Keynes	Alpha – Comment by Keynes: You don't bring the second part of the answer in close contact with the first
3/3/425	Q	26.10.1927	Obstacles to labour mobility	Shove	Alpha pencilled comments very difficult to read
3/3/428	Q	23.10.1927	Lower competition in labour market and obsolescence of the classical theory of wages	Shove	Beta ++; g [good]
3/3/430	Q	4.11.1927	Relationship between individual's income and economic service to the community	Keynes	Alpha – Comment by Keynes: In my opinion the discrepancies between income and service in the higher ranks are very great; in the lower less. I think you have a real aptitude for economics
3/3/435	Q	22.01.1928	Determinants of the earnings of barristers	Shove	Beta – f [fair?]
3/3/437	Q	5.02.1928	Meaning of exploitation of labour	Shove	Beta
3/3/440	Q	4.03.1928	Differences between earning of different grades and groups of workers	Shove	Alpha/Alpha +; pencilled comments hard to read
3/3/446	Q	18.11.1927	Pros and cons of legal eight hours day	Keynes	Beta +; pencilled comments on individual aspects of the answer
3/3/451	Q	4.03.1928	Welfare effects of restrictions on output by groups of workpeople on the country	Shove	Alpha/Alpha +

3/3/453	N	NI	Two sheets on Beveridge on population and on wage policy	ND	No comments
3/3/455	Q	23.11.1927	Effects of social insurance on wages	Shove	Beta Alpha
3/3/458	Q	16.10.1927	Ambiguities of the phrase 'a living wage'	Shove	Alpha Beta
3/3/460	Q	19.02.1928	Manual obligations rising over the life of a workers for a constant wage	Shove	Alpha Beta
3/3/463	Q	27.04.1928	Principles to determine the salary of a woman teacher	Keynes	Alpha +
3/3/465	Q	27.04.1928	Principles to construct the ideal wage index for an industry	Keynes	Alpha +; two questions related to the contents of the answer
3/3/467	N	NI	Methods of trade unions (full course)	Dobb	General considerations, analysis of British labour market and the institutions that regulate the wage setting process
3/3/550	N	13.03.1928	The theory and history of capitalism	Sombart	Typewritten with the indication, course of two lectures given at the London School of Economics
3/3/559	N	NI	Railways (Stamp)	NI	Spatial aspects of the division of labour
3/3/561	Q	19.02.1928	Prospect of profits of British railways	Shove	Alpha Beta g [good]
3/3/564	Q	18.11.1927	Discuss salient characteristics of motor industry in the UK and US	Keynes	Beta +; pencilled comments
3/3/572	N	March 1928	Data on coal industry and agriculture	NI	No comments

(*continued*)

Table 2.1 (continued)

Archival reference	*Type*	*Date*	*Topic*	*Related person*	*Content and comments by related person*
3/3/574	Q	30.10.1927	Likely movement of agricultural prices in 20 or 30 years	Shove	Beta ++; g [good]
3/3/576	Q	26.10.1927	Compare difficulties of cotton industry, coal mining, agriculture	Shove	Alpha very satisfactory and promising, g
3/3/578	Q	30.10.1927	Justifications and consequences of an import duty on iron and steel	Shove	Beta ++
3/3/581	Q	9.11.1927	Postwar industrial revolution in Britain?	Shove	Beta +; comment by Shove: Something wanted about postwar changes in industry
3/3/583	Q	6.11.1927	Changes in standards of living and poverty in Britain	Shove	Alpha –: g; minor pencilled comments
3/3/586	Q	30.10.1927	Relationship between unemployment, high wages and over-population	Shove	Beta + +; minor comments
3/3/589	Q	17.02.1928	Relationship between production and distribution in the short run	Keynes	Main comment by Keynes: I think the main point is that production is subject to increasing returns and distribution to decreasing returns and that the two influences are fighting against each other
3/3/592	N	NI	Foreign trade and miscellaneous	NI	Plenty of notes on statistics
3/3/616	Q	26.02.1928	Difficulties in enforcing prohibitionism in the US and consumer surplus	Shove	Alpha, g [good]

3/3/618	Q	26.02.1928	Classical doctrine that rent does not enter into the cost of production	Shove	Alpha, g [good]
3/3/619	Q	26.02.1928	Relationship between marginal cost and marginal firm	Shove	Alpha, not quite so g [good]
3/3/621	Q	26.02.1928	Equality between a worker's earnings and his net product as a theory of wages	Shove	Alpha, g
3/3/623	Q	26.02.1928	Welfare analysis of restriction on new workers entering an occupation	Shove	v.g. [very good]
3/3/625	Q	NI	Impact of poll tax on employment at the industry and aggregate level	Shove	g. [good]
3/3/627	Q	End of Lent term	Economics Part II, public finance	Shove	Review questions (with limited comments)
3/3/640	Q	4.05.1928	Economics Tripos Part II, June 1927, distribution and labour	Keynes	Review questions (with limited comments)
3/3/652	Q	11.05.1928	Money, credit and prices	Keynes	Review questions (with limited comments)
3/3/666	Q	NI	Principles	Keynes	Review questions (with limited comments)
3/3/681	N	NI	Miscellaneous material	NI	Mostly quantitative data and statistics

N = lecture notes; Q = review question; NI = non indicated

Source: Kahn Papers RFK 3/3

theoretical concepts, his ability to apply these concepts to concrete situations and his knowledge of real facts, particularly in relation to various aspects of the British economy. The topics ranged from whether the discovery of gold deposits is good or bad for a country (Shove) to the analysis of the price elasticity of demand for beer (Keynes), from the conditions justifying the introduction of a government subsidy in favour of a particular industry (Keynes) to the profit prospects of the English railways and the criteria to set fares (Shove), from the comparative analysis of the difficulties of the cotton and coal industries (a subject to which Kahn would return in his fellowship Dissertation, Shove) to the prohibitionism in the United States (Shove), from the effects of a tariff on the import of steel and iron (Shove) to the consequences of the introduction of the eight-hour day (Keynes). The more strictly theoretical questions revolved around the key concepts according to the Marshallian approach to economics: supply and demand, consumer surplus, elasticity, the notion of the normal wage, the relationship between output and costs, the relationship between unemployment, wages and population.

On 3 February 1928, for example, Keynes asked Kahn to provide 'a precise treatment of the concepts of the elasticities of demand and supply and of the consumer surplus, with particular reference to the limits of their usefulness'. In his reply (Ref. RFK/3/3/264–270), Kahn begins by introducing the concept of the demand function as a relationship between the quantity purchased x and the price y, and clarifies that the function $y = f(x)$

> is only of universal significance when every point on it refers to a steady state, i.e. where the price has remained at the level y for a sufficient period of time and there is no expectation of it changing within the sufficiently remote future. […] An added difficulty is caused through such changes in consumption that result from modifications of habits and fashion induced by a change in price. […] In cases where this factor is an important one, y can no longer be treated as a pure determinate function of x, and the conception of a demand curve loses much of its significance. We have rather to consider a whole series of demand curves, each relevant to a particular condition of fashion and habits.

With these and other caveats in mind, Kahn goes on to explain the formula for price elasticity of demand, stressing that its application is limited to short sections of a hypothetical demand curve and that the numerical estimate is in any case subject to considerable uncertainty. The same caveats apply to the determination of consumer surplus by integrating the demand function. From here, Kahn moves on to the supply curve and the price elasticity of supply.

Kahn argues that, although the elasticity of supply is derived in a similar way to that of demand, it is far more complex due to the slower pace of changes in production conditions. In the short term, when capital and organisation are fixed, producers adjust their output in order to maximise quasi-rent, producing up to the point at which marginal cost equals price. As the price falls, output contracts sharply, particularly when it no longer covers average costs. However, estimating short-run elasticity is highly uncertain as it relies on past conditions and future expectations. In the long run, supply is more elastic, as firms can enter or exit the market and adjust their production scale. They cluster around a 'representative firm' that earns normal profits. Nevertheless, Kahn acknowledges that long-run elasticity is largely theoretical, given that economic change is neither perfectly reversible nor easily measurable in practice.

Despite the many caveats Kahn had in mind, Keynes urged him not to put too much faith in the concept of elasticity of supply. At the end of Kahn's reply, Keynes pencilled: 'I think that Marshall never, or hardly ever, mentions elasticity of supply—a sure sign that he thought the concept too dicky [unreliable] for general use' (RFK/3/3/270). A similar warning about the 'slippery nature' of the concept of elasticity of supply can be found in a comment by Shove at the end of Kahn's answer to a question of 3 November 1927 on the effect of a specific tax on the price of a commodity.[10] Despite these warnings, however, Kahn remained attached to the notion of the elasticity of supply as a part of his understanding of the idea of the supply function at the firm, industry and aggregate level. The supply function would recur in many of Kahn's theoretical contributions in later years, albeit in different forms.

[10] To get an idea of the reasons behind Keynes's and Shove's perplexity about the notion of elasticity of supply in the context of the economic literature of the early 1930s, see Schultz (1927), where this concept is linked to Pigou (1920) and the notion of marginal supply price and Bittermann (1934).

2.2 Kahn at Cambridge Between the Late 1920s and the Early 1930s

Kahn's economic apprenticeship at Cambridge took place in a context marked by the development of Marshallian studies, Sraffa's critique of Marshall (and Pigou) and the beginning of the Keynesian revolution. Within the Marshallian camp, we can distinguish two main approaches, both of which influenced Kahn's early work.[11]

The first approach, mainly associated with Pigou, focused on the development of analytical tools useful for transforming Marshall's *Principles* into an instrument for solving policy problems. This included the idea of measuring fluctuations in social welfare through changes in the size, distribution and composition of national income, emphasis on supply functions, the reinterpretation of Marshall's representative firm to make it compatible with the idea of competitive equilibrium, the notion of externality and of internal and external economies, the identification of a system of taxes and subsidies as a means of redistributing resources with a view to increasing social welfare and efficiency. On the methodological level, the 'Pigou approach' invited one to focus on the identification of static competitive equilibriums with the aid of mathematical and graphical tools.

The second approach, which we can ideally associate with Shove, emphasised various aspects of Marshall's legacy: attention to the interdependence (and mutual influence) of demand and costs in determining production at the firm and industry levels, attention to the heterogeneity of firms within an industry (and of economic agents in general) and attention to the time dimension of economic phenomena. Methodologically, where the differences between the two approaches were most marked, the 'Shovian' approach concentrated on a rough and ready indication of the

[11] On Cambridge economics after Marshall, see Maloney (1985), Collard (1990), Cristiano (2010), Groenewegen (2012), Hart (2012, 2013), Knight (2018), Marchionatti (2021, pp. 21–90), Robinson A. (1990), among many others. In particular, Hart focuses on the presence and interweaving of two different perspectives in Marshall's thought: the equilibrium perspective and the evolutionary perspective. In Kahn's work from the 1930s, the equilibrium perspective is absolutely prevalent. Traces of the evolutionary perspective—which views the economic system as an organism that changes and evolves based on internal dynamics—intertwined with the equilibrium perspective can be seen in Kahn's mature work. For more on Marshall's evolutionary economics in relation to his early studies in psychology and subsequent theoretical development, see Raffaelli (2003).

forces at work in determining real phenomena, showing a certain reluctance to use methods that, in the name of accuracy, took the analysis to an overly abstract or overly complicated level.

Alongside these two approaches stood the critique of Marshall (and Pigou) by Sraffa, whose lectures he and Joan Robinson attended in 1928 and with whom Kahn later became friends. As is well known, this critique was first formulated in Italian (Sraffa, 1925) and subsequently in English in an article that Sraffa published in the *Economic Journal* in 1926 at Keynes's invitation (Sraffa, 1926). In this article, Sraffa criticised the traditional theory of returns to scale under perfect competition, arguing that increasing and diminishing returns have different origins and cannot be unified into a single supply curve. Internal economies of scale undermine perfect competition, while external economies have a minimal effect on firm costs. To maintain competitive conditions, Sraffa proposed to assume constant unit costs for small changes in output, implying that prices are determined by production costs rather than by supply and demand. His critique thus challenged, in particular, Pigou's version of Marshallian economics, which as we saw above was at the heart of Kahn's economic education.

By 1930–1931, Pigou, Shove and Sraffa were three of the thirteen members of the entire graduate staff of the Faculty of Economics and Politics at the University of Cambridge, with Pigou the only Professor and Shove and Sraffa two of the ten lecturers.[12] And then there was Keynes in his unique insider–outsider position. Outsider in that he was external to the Faculty and had no official academic position. Insider in that he was a Fellow of King's College, of which he was also First Bursar (with Kahn as Second Bursar from 1935 until 1946 when he succeeded Keynes), a mentor to students (as he had been to Kahn), organiser of the Political Economy Club, holder of a course in monetary theory and, above all, the main driving force behind the Keynesian revolution that was to break out against the Marshallian (Pigouvian) orthodoxy, in which both Keynes and Kahn had been trained.

[12] The others lecturers where Evans and Burns (Economic history), Alston and Thatcher (engaged in pass degree teaching), Claude Guillebaud, Maurice Dobb (Labour economics), Austin Robinson (lecturing on industry and industrial organisation), Marjorie Tappan Hollond (lecturing on public finance and economic fluctuations) and Humphrey Mynors (assistant lecturer, also teaching on industry and industrial organisation). Robertson was the only reader. On Keynes and his Cambridge colleagues in the 1930s, see A. Robinson (1977) and Johnson (1977). On Kahn at Cambridge in the 1930s, see A. Robinson (1994).

After impressing Keynes with his powers of reasoning and his aptitude for economics and after successfully completing Part II of the Tripos, Kahn, who had decided to stay on at King's to compete for a college fellowship, soon became part of Keynes's inner circle.

> When Kahn first met Keynes at the age of twenty-two he was a slight, serious, rather beautiful young man, with masses of thick, black hair. He spoke with an air of quiet authority, which contrasted oddly with extreme nervousness about his health—a lifelong obsession. Of German ancestry, he remained an orthodox Jew all his life. [...] He was a much better mathematician than most of those in Keynes's circle; [...] His mind was remarkably meticulous and he took great pains to help his friends. His relationship with Keynes was a prototype of the other important relationships of his life, particularly that with Joan Robinson. He was the self-effacing backroom boy rather than the star of the show; an excellent listener, with a hardcore of analytical power. (Skidelsky, 2003, p. 399)

> Before August 1929, [...] [Kahn] had become closely involved in Keynes's intellectual life. He was to remain so until the war, eventually completely displacing Dennis Robertson. To Keynes's work, as well as to his own and others', especially that of Joan Robinson, Kahn brought a powerful mind with a flair for a fruitful simplification and an emphasis on the bare bones of an argument. (Moggridge, 1992, p. 480)

One way of reconstructing the relationships between Kahn, Keynes and some of the economists with whom they were in close contact at Cambridge and beyond in the 1930s is to read the correspondence that they exchanged on a daily basis. In a world in which few articles were written, in which there were few scholarly journals and few conferences, the study of correspondence offers a privileged perspective for placing an author's ideas in the time and context in which they took shape, and for exploring the links between that author and the people with whom he or she lived in close contact in a country where the postal system was particularly efficient.[13]

This was particularly true at Cambridge in the 1930s, where the supervisory activity took place in the colleges, the lectures were held in different parts of the town, faculties were often located in a different place from where the lectures were held and telephone communication was still quite rare (Marcuzzo et al., 2008). In this spirit, M.C. Marcuzzo and A. Rosselli,

[13] On this aspect, see Marcuzzo and Rosselli (2005, p. 2).

together with a number of colleagues, have reconstructed all the available letters exchanged between Keynes, Kahn and eight other economists (Harrod, Hayek, Kaldor, Pigou, Robertson, Joan Robinson, Shove and Sraffa) between 1907 and 1946 (Marcuzzo & Rosselli, 2005).[14] Reading Kahn's letters from the 1930s,[15] the image that emerges is that of a young scholar eager to be part of Keynes's inner circle, watchful to cultivate his privileged relationship with him, jealous of that relationship when he had reason to believe that anything might threaten it.[16] Kahn generally maintained a calm and courteous tone in his letters, moving carefully among the members of the Faculty of Economics and Politics.[17]

Of all the relationships that Kahn established in Cambridge in the early 1930s, the most important, along with that with Keynes, was the one with Joan Robinson. This relationship, which began in 1928 when they had both attended Sraffa's lectures, was one of the cornerstones of Kahn's life and continued uninterrupted until Joan Robinson's death in 1983. Especially in the early stages, as different sources indicate, this relationship was based on an intellectual partnership in which Joan Robinson's enthusiasm and creative impulses were combined with Kahn's meticulousness, logical abilities and mastery of mathematical tools. During the 1930s, the relationship between Kahn and Robinson was tinged with a sentimental element, which played a very important role for a time and then turned

[14] One of the merits of this research is to show how, in interwar Cambridge, many new ideas emerged from dialogue and daily confrontation, making it difficult to attribute precise authorship of an idea. On this way of 'doing economics' in Cambridge, with a focus on Pigou, see Knight (2018, pp. 115–149 in particular). On Marcuzzo and Rosselli (2005), see Review Symposium (2007).

[15] Of the 2855 letters analysed, about 40% concern exchanges between Keynes and Kahn and between Kahn and Joan Robinson. On this, see Marcuzzo et al. (2005) and Rosselli (2005b).

[16] A significant episode in this respect is Kahn's reaction to Keynes's decision to entrust Kaldor, then at the LSE, rather than Kahn or anyone else at Cambridge, with the task of commenting on Pigou (1937), which had been received negatively by Keynes and his young students. On this episode, see also Sect. 6.3.

[17] On the correspondence between Hayek and Cambridge economists, see Ingrao and Ranchetti (2005). On Hayek's feelings towards Kahn in Cambridge in 1931, Caldwell and Klausinger (2022, p. 497) recall that 'Hayek did not find many companions at King's. Keynes's circle did not extend a welcome [...] and about Richard Kahn said that "he clearly avoided me, which I did not regret"'. Kahn and Hayek met during seminars but made no 'friendly' acquaintance. On the reception of the seminar Hayek gave in Cambridge in 1931, see Kahn (1984, p. 184); Robinson (1978, pp. 2–3); Caldwell and Klausinger (2022, pp. 281–282).

into a deep and intense friendship, of which esteem and intellectual exchange remained the cornerstones.[18]

In the early 1930s both Kahn and Joan Robinson wrote important works, important both in terms of establishing their reputation as Cambridge economists and for the impetus they gave to the introduction of the concept of imperfect competition into the theoretical debate of the time. In the case of Kahn, it was the fellowship Dissertation on the *Economics of the Short Period*, to which the following section is devoted; in the case of Joan Robinson it was *The Economics of Imperfect Competition* of 1933. It is in this book, much more than in Kahn's Dissertation, that the first fruits of the Kahn–Robinson partnership and Kahn's influence can be seen, as Robinson herself acknowledged in the preface to her book.[19]

> In particular I have had the constant assistance of Mr. R. F. Kahn. The whole technical apparatus was built up with his aid, and many of the major problems—notably the problems of Price Discrimination and of Exploitation—were solved as much by him as by me. He has also contributed a number of mathematical proofs which I should have been incapable of finding myself. (Robinson, 1933, p. xiii)

The Economics of Imperfect Competition, in the elaboration of which Austin Robinson too played an important role, provides a systematic analysis of market structures that deviate from perfect competition and introduces the concept of imperfect competition, where firms face downward sloping demand curves that allow them to set prices above marginal cost, which equals marginal revenue. Robinson formalises the relationship between marginal revenue and demand elasticity and shows that firms in imperfectly competitive markets restrict output to maximise profits, leading to welfare losses. She also develops the theory of monopsony and criticises neoclassical distribution theory, arguing that factor rewards depend

[18] On the beginning of the Kahn–Robinson relationship, see Rosselli (2005b, p. 260, fn. 2), Harcourt and Kerr (2009, pp. 15–16), Aslanbeigui and Oakes (2009, pp. 51–87). See also Marcuzzo (2003, 2005b) and Marcuzzo (1991) on Joan Robinson's role in the establishment of the Cambridge school.

[19] In the same Foreword, Joan Robinson also mentions her debt to Marshall and Pigou and acknowledges her use of work of Sraffa, Austin Robinson and Shove. On the relationship between Kahn and Joan Robinson around the publication of *The Economics of Imperfect Competition*, see Aslanbeigui and Oakes (2009, pp. 89–139). See also Marcuzzo (1996a, 2005b).

on market power rather than marginal productivity.[20] In their correspondence (Rosselli, 2005b), we see Kahn following Robinson step by step in the formalisation of these concepts, teaching her the necessary mathematical tools and walking with her along the path that led to the extension of the Marshallian analytical apparatus to imperfect competition, the same path he had taken less than two years earlier in writing his fellowship Dissertation.

Cambridge received Robinson's book, to which Kahn had contributed so much, favourably but with some caution. Asked by the publisher Macmillan to comment on the book, Keynes recommended its publication, but emphasised that it contained the development of ideas that were not only present in published works but had also been discussed orally at both Oxford and Cambridge. In the case of Pigou, who was soon to become the main target of Keynes's criticism, with the support of Kahn and Joan Robinson, we see the oscillation between a cautious, not uncritical appreciation of Joan Robinson's work and a defence of Marshall.[21]

Already at the time of its publication, and even more so in the years that followed, Robinson's book was seen as a further development of a Marshallian and Pigouvian theoretical apparatus, in which the innovative elements, also developed in response to Sraffa's criticism of Marshall, were grafted onto a conventional theoretical framework. A similar argument can be made for Kahn's fellowship Dissertation, written four years before Robinson (1933) and entitled *The Economics of the Short Period*, to which we now turn.

[20] On *The Economics of Imperfect Competition* in connection with Kahn's work, see Harcourt and Kerr (2009, pp. 15–21), Marcuzzo (1996a) and Dardi (1996) who emphasise the links between Joan Robinson's book and the Marshallian–Pigouvian approach, and how Robinson's treatment of imperfect competition can be understood as a generalisation of that approach. On the 'discovery' of the concept of marginal revenue in 1930 as the starting point for the economics of imperfect competition, see A. Robinson (1977). On the attribution to Kahn of the tangency between the demand curve and the decreasing average cost curve as a condition defining the long-run equilibrium of a firm under conditions of imperfect competition, see Shove (1933). This article is also important as an example of Shove's vision of the complex relationship between supply and demand. According to Shove, without prior knowledge of the characteristics of demand, it is not possible to determine the cost curve and hence supply, and vice versa. On this point, and on the distance between Shove and Robinson, see Dardi (1983, p. 18, fn. 16).

[21] The same ambivalent attitude can be seen in Shove's review of *The Economics of Imperfect Competition* for the *Economic Journal* (Shove, 1933).

2.3 The Fellowship Dissertation: Content, Reactions, Developments

After successfully completing his year in economics (1927–1928), Kahn, encouraged by Keynes, Shove and Sraffa, decided to apply for a fellowship at King's College. Initially, Keynes suggested that he could work on a monetary topic using data from the Midland Bank. This would probably have meant relying on some version of the quantity theory of money, which was still dominant at Cambridge and about which Kahn was sceptical, as he would be all his life.[22] To Kahn's relief the plan failed, due to the opposition of A.W. Crick, Head of the Intelligence unit of the Midland Bank, who refused to share the bank's statistics with Kahn.[23] As Kahn recalled retrospectively,

> Keynes then left me to choose my own subject, and, under the influence of Marshall's *Principles*, I chose the economics of the short period. In making my choice I was encouraged by Shove, and by Piero Sraffa. Keynes happily acquiesced. Neither he nor I had the slightest idea that my work on the short period was later on going to influence the development of Keynes's own thought. But there are no traces of Keynes's thought in the dissertation itself. (Marcuzzo, 2020, p. 8)

The chronology of the Dissertation is easily summarised.[24] In September 1928, Kahn began his research. Partly with the help of Keynes, who was involved with the British cotton industry in the 1920s (Marchionatti, 1995), Kahn collected a large amount of data and literature on his subject.[25] This included newspaper articles, trade journals and interviews with

[22] On Kahn's early 'prejudice' towards the QTM, see Kahn (1984, pp. 52–53). On the role played by Kahn and Joan Robinson on Keynes's rejection of the QTM in the *General Theory*, see Marcuzzo (2002b, 2017).

[23] On this, see RFK/3/6 and Kahn ([1929] 1989, pp. x–xi)

[24] On the chronology and main contents of Kahn's fellowship Dissertation, see Maneschi (1988), Marris (1992), O'Shaughnessy (1994), Marcuzzo (1994), Aslanbeigui and Oakes (2011).

[25] Reflecting on Kahn's strategy to gather research material for the Dissertation, partly through visiting industrial establishments and seeking direct contact with entrepreneurs and managers in the cotton and coal industries (see, e.g., the manuscript contained in RFK/3/10/56–65 that contains a piece on short-term equilibrium with reference to the cotton industry, finally framed as a letter to the Cotton Yarn Association, 20 February 1929) one is tempted to draw comparisons with a similar activity undertaken by Marshall (Matsuyama, 2022).

industry representatives.[26] In October 1929 Kahn submitted an essay with the same title as the Dissertation for the Adam Smith Prize at Cambridge University and won the prize with Pigou's praise (Moggridge, 1979, p. 4). On 7 December 1929 he presented the Dissertation to the Fellowship Committee, which included Keynes, Pigou and Robertson and which approved it in March 1930.

The main reason for Kahn's interest in the economics of the short period was the limited space that Marshall and the Marshallians had devoted to the subject.[27] As he approached the subject and collected relevant data, moreover, Kahn noticed a discrepancy between reality and economic theory that invited investigation. While economic theory predicted that competition would eliminate less efficient firms, leaving the most efficient free to produce at maximum capacity, the reality Kahn observed was very different, as more and less efficient firms coexisted, all producing below capacity. In his search for an explanation of this discrepancy, Kahn formulated the most innovative concepts of his Dissertation.

In the Introduction (Kahn, [1929] 1989, p. xxiii), Kahn discusses the limited space Marshall devoted to the short run in his *Principles*, Marshall's difficulties in drawing a clear boundary between the long and the short run and the connection between Marshall's long run and the conditions of economic expansion that prevailed throughout most of the nineteenth century.[28] By 1928, stagnation had set in and many British staple industries were struggling to survive, with a given organisation and a given (and partially idle) productive capacity which justified Kahn's choice of the short run as a reference for analysing their behaviour.

For Kahn the determination of the respective duration of the short and the long term cannot be made on the basis of abstract considerations, but only by observing data and the behaviour of entrepreneurs. In the short run the equipment and organisation of all (or almost all) firms in the same industry can be assumed to be constant. It follows that part of the total costs are invariant and independent of output, while the rest vary with it. The duration of the short run varies greatly depending on the circumstances. In times of prosperity plants can be improved, expanded and

[26] This material is collected in RFK/3/7 to RFK/3/13. See also RFK/2/7.

[27] On the contributions to industrial economics by other Marshallians, older than Kahn, see and Raffaelli (2004) and Groenewegen (2012).

[28] For an overview of the challenges associated with defining the distinction between short-term and long-term perspectives within the context of Marshall's concept of equilibrium, refer to the work of Italian economist A. Da Empoli (Di Matteo, 2012).

made more efficient relatively quickly and without particular difficulty. In periods of stagnation the rate of decline can be very slow, especially if entrepreneurs expect a rapid return to prosperity.[29] In this case, the one relevant to Kahn's Dissertation, the short run can last a very long time.

In order to analyse the behaviour of firms in the short run, it is, first of all, essential to define the characteristics of the market in which they operate. Two criteria stand out in this case: the difference between perfect and imperfect markets, and between perfect competition and polypoly, a curious term that Kahn traces back to the Italian economist Umberto Ricci (see Kahn, [1929] 1989, p. 2, fn 2). Referring to Pigou's *The Economics of Welfare* for a similar taxonomy, Kahn identifies the three conditions that must be met simultaneously in order to have perfect competition.

> (a) There must be a large number of separate firms, each producing an output which is small in relation to the aggregate output.
> (b) There must be no agreement, however informal, among producers controlling a substantial portion of the aggregate output; and, in the absence of such an agreement, individuals must act each for himself, devoid of all feeling of corporate responsibility and business convention.
> (c) The market in which the output of the industry is sold must be perfect. A perfect market is one in which differences of price (after costs of transport have been allowed for) cannot persist over an appreciable period of time. If a single firm raises its price in a perfect market, either its output is rapidly reduced to zero or the other firm or firms raise their price. (Kahn, [1929] 1989, pp. 12–13)

If only conditions (a) and (b) are met, the industry is a polypoly. Condition (c) alone defines a perfect market, while conditions (a) and (c) together define an imperfect market. Based on these definitions and the initial assumption of perfect competition, Kahn analyses the supply and cost curve at the firm and industry level (Chaps. 2, 3, 4, 5, and 6), noting:

[29] An anticipation of this idea can be found in a paper Kahn read to Keynes's Political Economy Club on 12 November 1928. 'While long period economics deals with things as they should be, and never are, short period economics is concerned with things as they are,— and, we fear, usually never should be. By a short period we mean one in which the stock of fixed plant is appreciably constant and the [?] on which depends the organisation is fixed. There is not time for the stock of fixed plant to decline and such additions, as are made, are negligible in relation to the whole. It follows that, as Mr. Robertson has aptly put it, "the short period is not the same length at both ends and never has been".' (RFK/3/18/1/1). For a reference to Robertson's statement, see Harcourt (2017).

> [It] is clear that in the short period prime cost is a major factor and fixed cost a very minor factor, so far as effects on output and price are concerned. [...] But we can go even further in separating the factors that are available to operate on price and output in the short period. Prime cost consists very largely of the costs of wages and raw material. Now raw material is either imported, in which case its cost must be regarded as outside the sphere of national influences, or it is derived, directly or indirectly, from industries whose prime costs consist almost entirely of wages. It may, therefore, be concluded that on the side of supply the only factor that in the short period can have a substantial influence on the price and magnitude of the national output is the level of money wages. (On the side of demand there are, of course, such very important influences as the rates of credit creation, of investment, and of saving, tariffs, the rate of exchange, and the repercussions of an alteration in the level of unemployment.) (Kahn, [1929] 1989, p. 43)

We see here, for the first time, the formulation of the causal relationship between nominal wages and prices, on which Kahn would insist repeatedly over the following decades. In the Dissertation Kahn focuses on part of this relationship that appears on the supply side. In subsequent work, he also analysed the influence of wages on prices via the demand side. This would eventually become an important element of the theory of prices, set out in the *General Theory*, as Keynes (1939, p. 39, fn. 1) himself recognised: 'It was Mr. Kahn who first attacked the relation of the general level of prices to wages in the same way as that in which that of particular prices has always been handled, namely as a problem of demand and supply in the short period rather than as a result to be derived from monetary factors'.[30]

Firms operate to maximise profits defined as the difference between sale proceeds and total costs. Total costs are equal to the sum of fixed overhead costs and prime costs, defined as the sum of running overhead costs and variable costs (also referred to as direct costs). On the basis of these definitions, Kahn discusses the relationship between prime costs and the individual firm's supply curve, focusing on the case where revenues do not cover prime costs and the reasons why a firm chooses to produce at a

[30] An early example of the idea that nominal wages determine the prices of all goods, at least in the short run—an idea to which Kahn would return several times in the following decades—is found in a note by Kahn entitled 'The Effect on Employment of a Reduction of Wages in a Closed System'. The note, dating from the early 1930s, has been analysed by O'Shaughnessy (1994, pp. 49–52).

prime loss, as many of the firms observed by Kahn did. These reasons include the desire to maintain business contacts, the desire not to lose valuable employees, the desire not to show signs of weakness and thus to preserve the firm's reputation, the attempt not to lose their income (in the case of managers) even if this is to the detriment of shareholders and the desire not to risk having their credit lines cut when production resumes (as it is expected to do).

At this point, the contradiction between economic theory and reality mentioned above becomes relevant. While theory predicts that perfect competition should drive the least efficient firms, which incur the greatest losses, out of the market, allowing the most efficient firms to produce at capacity, the reality that Kahn observes is a very different one. Under stagnating conditions more and less efficient firms coexist, all of them producing at a loss and below capacity. Kahn's explanation is that firms want to minimise losses and experiment with different strategies to do so, at least as long as they expect a recovery and provided they can withstand the negative cash flow.

The result of this process is that firms shut down plants for a few days each month and operate at full capacity on other days. Representing this choice in terms of cost curves, Kahn concludes that firms operate along an inverted L-shaped unit prime cost curve, flat at a constant unit cost below capacity, vertical after that point. This curve is the first major theoretical innovation in Kahn's Dissertation, with respect to the standard practice of assuming U-shaped average cost curves.[31]

> The essential feature of such a curve is that it does not begin to rise until the point of capacity output is reached. As a determinant of output it loses most of the significance which we have hitherto attached to the marginal prime cost curve. If the price is greater than the average prime cost (denoted by the horizontal part of the curve), we should expect that under conditions of perfect competition, the output would be equal to the capacity output. [...] If this were so we should find that the only firms that work below capacity are the inefficient firms whose prime costs are greater than the price; which are therefore losing more than their fixed costs and would lose less if they were to produce less or nothing at all. But it happens to be a fact that short-time working is not confined to these firms. [...] It is on this Scylla that the assumptions of perfect competition come to grief and precipitate us into the

[31] On Kahn's inverted L curve and the role of this cost curve as a microfoundation of non-mainstream macroeconomics, see Marcuzzo (1996b).

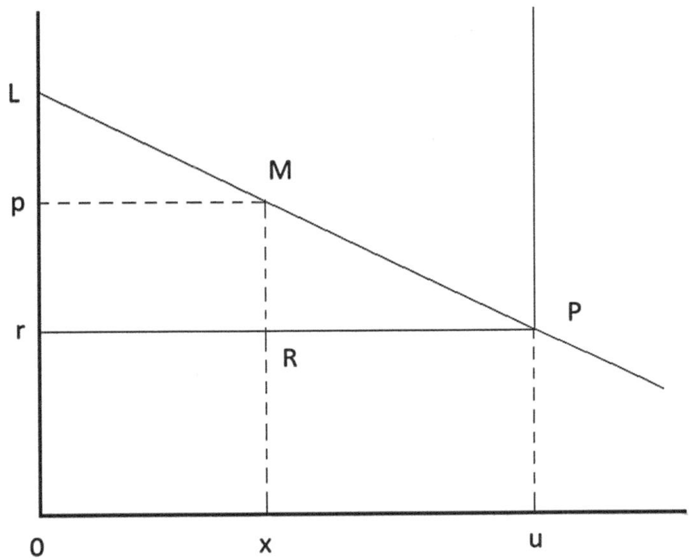

Fig. 2.1 Annihilation coefficient and equilibrium of the single firm in an imperfect market

> Charybdis, I am afraid, of subsequent chapters: no *via media* is open. (Kahn, [1929] 1989, p. 59)

Charybdis is the imperfect market in which each firm faces a negatively sloping demand curve. This curve, which Kahn assumes to be linear, lies to the left of the vertical slope of the inverted L-shaped supply curve and the point of maximum profit will be characterised by a level of output below capacity and a price above the unit cost of production (Fig. 2.1). To find the optimal price-output combination, Kahn introduces a new concept, the annihilation coefficient *q*,[32] which is the second major theoretical innovation of his Dissertation after the inverted L-shaped cost curve. This coefficient

[32] On the link between the concept of the coefficient of annihilation and the concept of the mark-up on the unit cost of production as developed by M. Kalecki, see Dardi (1983, p. 18, fn. 17).

> is a measure of the imperfection of the market, and it is under this guise that the imperfection of the market will usually enter into our equations and into the discussions to which they will give rise. q will often be referred to as the 'annihilation coefficient'. The choice of this name is related to the fact that, in the case where the individual demand curve is a straight line through its length, q is the increase of price that would be necessary to reduce the firm's output by an amount equal to its capacity output. (Kahn, [1929] 1989, p. 121)

To understand how Kahn used the annihilation coefficient to identify the equilibrium of the individual firm (see Fig. 2.1), we follow his notation and indicate by

- p the price set by the firm,
- r the given prime unit cost of production, corresponding to the horizontal section of the firm's supply curve,
- x the level of output chosen by the firm for a given demand and price p,
- *tanθ* the tangent of the angle θ formed by firm's demand and supply curves,
- u the given capacity output,
- f the ratio of the chosen output to the capacity output ($f = x/u$),
- q the product of the capacity output and *tanθ* ($q = u\tan\theta$).

Representing these elements in Fig. 2.1, and assuming for simplicity that the *LMP* linear demand curve intersects the supply curve at output equal to production capacity u, the annihilation coefficient q is equal to the length of the segment *Lr* and the ratio between this and capacity output, that is q/u, is equal to $\tan\theta$. In equilibrium, given that the length of the segment $rR = x$ is equal to *RP* by ordinary monopoly considerations, the relationship between the excess of the optimal price over the constant unit cost ($p - r$) and the optimal output chosen by the firm is equal to

$$p - r = x\tan\theta = (fu)(q/u) = fq \quad (2.1)$$

While the prime profit, which the firm aims to maximise, is equal to

$$\text{Prime profit} = (p - r)x = (fq)(fu) = f^2qu \quad (2.2)$$

Based on these concepts, Kahn analyses how firms and industries respond to a change in demand (Kahn, [1929] 1989, pp. 123–124). He does so starting with the simplest case (identical firms with identical cost curves), considering a single firm and assuming that *q* and *r* are constant. On these assumptions, a change in demand will result in the following effects:

$$\Delta p = q \Delta f \tag{2.3}$$

Taking (2.1) into account, Eq. (2.3) can be rewritten as

$$\frac{\Delta p}{p - r} = \frac{\Delta f}{f} \tag{2.4}$$

where the proportional increase in output, measured as a fraction of the capacity output, is equal to the ratio between the change in price and the excess of price over *r*. This means that a 10% increase in output is associated with a price increase of 10% of its excess over prime cost, while the elasticity of supply of the individual firm, on the value of which the changes in price and quantity caused by the change in demand depend, varies inversely with the annihilation coefficient (other things equal) and is equal to

$$\frac{\Delta f}{f} / \frac{\Delta p}{p} = \frac{p}{p - r} = \frac{p}{fq} \tag{2.5}$$

While the absolute change in prime profits, which the change in demand originates, is equal to

$$\text{Absolute change in prime profits} = 2 fqu \Delta \mathrm{f} \tag{2.6}$$

and the proportional change in prime profits is equal to twice the change in optimal output

$$2 fqu \Delta \mathrm{f} / f^2 qu = 2 \frac{\Delta f}{f} \tag{2.7}$$

From here Kahn moves on to analyse increasingly complex cases (Chaps. 8, 9, 10, and 11), combining mathematical and geometric analysis and comparing his theoretical results with the empirical evidence on the cotton and coal industries. In doing so he focuses on the factors that in reality prevented entrepreneurs from lowering prices in the face of weak and declining demand, as would be expected in a competitive, albeit imperfect, market. These factors include the fear of spoiling the market, the possibility that a price cut would create the expectation of further cuts and thus reduce sales, the fear that buyers would lose confidence in a producer who offered them goods at sharply reduced prices, which might hinder the possibility of raising prices again at a later date, the force of tradition, implicit collusion and the esprit de corps among entrepreneurs. We see here the origins of Kahn's later analysis of duopoly and oligopoly.

In arriving at these conclusions, and more generally, Kahn's Dissertation shows the influences of all three approaches present in Cambridge in the 1920s: Pigou's formalism, Shove's orthodox Marshallianism and Sraffa's critique.[33] Kahn's attention to the exact determination of equilibria at the firm and industry level under static conditions and perfect competition, in line with Pigou's approach, is combined with his awareness of the dependence of costs, and hence of the supply decision, on changing demand conditions and the heterogeneity of firms, as Kahn had learnt from Shove (Kahn, [1929] 1989, p. 165).

The same analysis is then extended from perfect to imperfect competition, inspired by Sraffa (1926), but based on novel analytical tools (inverted L-shaped cost curve, annihilation coefficient) and arriving at different results from Sraffa regarding the effects of imperfect competition on optimal price and quantities. The main difference between Kahn and Sraffa in the Dissertation concerns the effect of imperfect competition on the equilibrium price. While Sraffa was convinced that even a small imperfection would lead firms to set the price at the monopoly level, Kahn came to a different conclusion. The price in an imperfectly competitive market lies between the monopoly price and the perfectly competitive price, and

[33] In fact, Kahn's Dissertation precedes by only one year the 1930 Symposium on the representative firm and increasing returns, in which the three approaches appeared in the exchange between Robertson, Sraffa and Shove. For the original debate, see Robertson et al. (1930). On the relevance of this debate in the context of the great controversies during the interwar period, see Marchionatti (2021, pp. 343–368).

the closer to one extreme or the other, the greater (lesser) the degree of market imperfection.[34]

Taken as a whole, Kahn's Dissertation appears as a work of great ingenuity, based on a meticulous analysis of data and the ability to innovate a pre-existing analytical apparatus, once it was recognised that this apparatus was inadequate to explain the real economic situation of a set of industries composed of firms heterogeneous in size and efficiency and trapped in a persistent stagnation. In presenting his innovations, Kahn emphasises the 'incremental' aspect of his discoveries, the debt to others (Marshall, Pigou, Shove and Sraffa) and the continuity in the transition from the old to the new ideas rather than the rupture. Nevertheless, the fact remains that the Dissertation is indeed a seminal contribution to the development of the theory of imperfect markets in the Anglo–Saxon academic tradition, and an extraordinary achievement given that Kahn achieved it after only three years of economics study.

This fact was noted favourably by the two reviewers of the Dissertation, Pigou and Robertson (ref. RFK/2/8/1–12). Pigou praised Kahn for his 'truly remarkable power of analysis, his independence of mind, his extraordinary tenacity'. On the specific analytical points, in addition to expressing his dissatisfaction with the lack of references to the representative firm, the main criticism concerns the inverted L-shaped cost curve contained in Chap. 5 of the Dissertation, which in Pigou's view was the least satisfactory part of the essay. For Pigou, Kahn's discussion of the various strategies adopted by firms to reduce losses in the face of weak demand does not justify the idea of an inverted L-shaped average cost curve, either theoretically or empirically.[35]

> It may well be, indeed, that in many industries there is, for a typical firm, a considerable range of output, in respect of which average prime cost per unit is approximately constant. But it is ridiculous to suppose that there suddenly comes a point at which this cost bounds up to infinity. If by 'capacity output' we mean maximum possible output, then it is certain that average prime

[34] On this point, which Kahn recalls in the introduction to the Dissertation and illustrates in Chap. 7, par. 7, taking his cue from Sraffa (1926), see Marcuzzo (2001, pp. 87–89 in particular) and Dardi (2001).

[35] In Kahn's disagreement with Sraffa, Pigou sided with Kahn, but emphasised that he did not attach sufficient importance to the instability of prices and output when there are only a few sellers, because of 'the uncertainty and change of opinion on the part of each of them as to the way in which the others are likely to act'.

cost will have risen steeply for some time before that output is reached; if we mean optimum output, in the sense of that output at which average prime cost plus overhead costs are at a minimum, it is certain that the average prime cost does not rise to infinity immediately after that output is exceeded. (RFK/2/8/4)

An equally positive judgement can be found in Robertson's report, which, after summarising Kahn's two main theses (the almost total irrelevance of fixed costs in determining the optimal level of output and the short-run price, and the possibility that an output level below capacity can be optimal), focuses on the novelty of the annihilation coefficient, thanks to which 'Mr. Kahn has fought his way successfully through an exceedingly difficult and tangled field, and has shed a flood of light on that vast and dim terrian [sic], of high importance in practical affairs, which lies between the brightly-lit but narrow areas of perfect monopoly and perfect competition' (ref. RFK/2/8/10).

After becoming a fellow of King's College, Kahn considered publishing a reworked version of the Dissertation, which however remained unpublished.[36] As Kahn himself recalled in later years:

In the course of the following three or four years I did rewrite seven chapters, intending them for publication. On looking at them I am amazed to find that they are almost entirely confined to conditions of perfect competition; whereas the importance of my dissertation largely rested on its treatment of imperfect competition, and of the particular case of duopoly. [...] Among the fragments of my abortive book there is one important passage, extracts from which I can usefully quote, because its argument is not to be found in the dissertation:

The whole usefulness of the device of the Short Period is based on the fact that the life of fixed capital is considerably greater than the period of production, greater that is to say than the life of working capital. It cannot be too strongly emphasised that this is a *fact*, which could not be deduced by *a priori* reasoning. In a different kind of world in which, for example, the

[36] Opinions differ as to why this manuscript, and the Dissertation in general, remained unpublished in spite of the positive reports. Marcuzzo (1994) mentions Pigou's criticism of the inverted L-shaped cost curve and the concomitant discovery of the marginal revenue which displaced the annihilation coefficient as possible reasons. Aslanbeigui and Oakes (2011) discuss Kahn's decision not to publish his early work in connection with his relationship with Joan Robinson.

> plough wore out after a single season's use (or, better still, in which crops took as long to reach fruition as ploughs to reach decrepitude), quite a different kind of analysis would be appropriate. (Kahn, [1929] 1989, pp. xii–xiii)

These words provide an important retrospective clue to Kahn's willingness, in the early 1930s, when he was assisting Keynes in the formulation of the *General Theory*, to downplay the innovation of imperfect competition in favour of other aspects of his analysis, and in particular the very definition of the concept of the short period. At this stage, Kahn's idea seems to have been that imperfect competition should be seen as an intermediate case between perfect competition and monopoly, more general and realistic than either, but not fundamentally different in terms of the possibility of analysing it with the tools of marginal analysis. It is in the concept of the short period, its precise definition and the distinction with respect to the long run (the importance of which is downplayed), that Kahn sees the real novelty of his contribution.

A further indication that this might indeed be the case can be found in the lectures on the Economics of the short period that Kahn gave for the first time in the Lent Term of 1931.[37] A testimony to these lectures is provided by the notes taken in the Michaelmas term of 1932 by Lorie Tarshis, who sent them to Kahn in the 1970s.[38] After introducing the course, citing Marshall as his main source of inspiration (Lecture 1), and illustrating the concepts of national dividend and national income (Lecture 2), Kahn gets to the heart of the matter, clarifying (Tarshis's words):

> In order to draw a useful supply curve—assume 1) situation of industry is determined by the present state of the demand. The slow change presents no problem but the fast change makes difficulties. Legitimate to assume that given the stereotyped features of an industry you can draw a supply curve since the output of an industry depends entirely on the demand curve of the moment. Does not depend on the past or expectations of the future. [...] The decision as to how much to produce depends only on demand conditions [...]. And also the decision as to <u>how</u> to produce it since the <u>how</u> is dependent on the <u>how much</u>. In the long run the 'past' is a most important factor—as is the expectation of the future—then slow changes. But the rapid

[37] RFK/4/13 contains autograph manuscript lecture notes on the short period (first given to Cambridge University in Lent Term 1931). See Appendix B on this.

[38] Ref. RFK/4/15/1–10. On Tarshis, see Harcourt (1995).

changes can be regarded as being uniquely determined by current conditions. (RFK/4/15/3)

Underlining the role of demand, with somewhat more emphasis than in the Dissertation, Kahn goes on to recall the objective factors (time and cost of adapting facilities and organisation) and subjective factors (expectations of recovery, optimism, tenacity, inertia), which together determine the length of both the short and the 'middle' periods, the latter defined as the state in which irretrievably loss-making firms have exited the market but before the single normal rate of profit has been established across sectors.

In analysing the short-run equilibrium of the firm under conditions of perfect and imperfect competition, Kahn's lectures make no use of the two main innovations of the Dissertation. Instead of the inverted L-shaped unit prime cost curve we find a marginal cost function described in these terms (Tarshis's words): 'MC is likely when businesses are working under capacity to equal Average Direct Cost. As you approach capacity MC will begin to increase' (ref. RFK/4/15/11). This is essentially identical to that proposed by Pigou in his report on the Dissertation. In the same vein, the lecture notes contain no trace of the annihilation coefficient, as its role in determining the equilibrium is entirely taken over by the new (for the time), and more pliable,[39] concept of marginal revenue. Kahn associates this new concept with the names of Gifford, Sloan, Harrod, Mather, Viner and Mr. Robinson (RFK/4/5/7), and clarifies that it can be either increasing or decreasing in relation to output, depending on the characteristics of the relevant market.[40]

Building on Tarshis (1979, pp. 367–376 in particular), we can retrace the path traced by Kahn's lectures to construct the aggregate supply curve starting from the profit maximisation of the i-th firm. By denoting by p_i the price set by the i-th firm, by O_i the quantity produced, by $TC_i(O_i)$ the

[39] Whereas the annihilation coefficient is constant and linked to the assumption of a linear demand function, the marginal revenue is neither.

[40] Shackle (1967) provides the classical account of the emergence of the notion of marginal revenue and of its role in connection with the imperfect competition. On this, see also A. Robinson (1992). On the possibility that the introduction of the concept of marginal revenue provided an easier way of determining the equilibrium of imperfect competition, effectively displacing the annihilation coefficient and the method outlined above, see Maneschi (1988) and O'Shaughnessy (1994). On the origins, results and implications of monopolistic competition, see also Keppler (1994).

total cost function and by $p_i = p_i(O_i)$ the demand function faced by the ith firm, the profit maximisation problem can be written as follows:

$$\max_{O_i}\left[p_i O_i - TC_i(O_i)\right];\text{subject to}\, p_i = p_i(O_i) \tag{2.8}$$

Replacing the constraint in the objective function and substituting K_i for the price elasticity of demand ($K_i = p_i' O_i / p_i$), the optimal quantity is calculated by equating marginal cost $MC_i(O_i)$ with marginal revenue $\left(p_i + p_i' O_i\right)$ (Eq. 2.9), while the optimal price set by the firm is equal to the product of marginal cost and the profit margin ($K_i/K_i - 1$) (Eq. 2.10).

$$p_i + p_i' O_i = MC_i(O_i) \tag{2.9}$$

$$p_i = \left(\frac{K_i}{K_i - 1}\right) MC_i(O_i) \tag{2.10}$$

Based on these elements, Kahn defines the supply function of the *i*th firm as follows:

$$Z_i(O_i) = p_i O_i = \left(\frac{K_i}{K_i - 1}\right) MC(O_i) O_i \tag{2.11}$$

And the aggregate supply function, assuming that there are M firms in the economy, becomes

$$Z(O) = \sum_{i=1}^{M} p_i O_i = \sum_{i=1}^{M}\left(\frac{K_i}{K_i - 1}\right) MC(O_i) O_i \tag{2.12}$$

As Marcuzzo observes, commenting on Tarshis (1979):

> It is worth noticing that the above is a *general* formulation, which does not require special assumptions about market form or the shape of the marginal cost curve. Specific assumptions are reflected in the shape of the supply curve and in the value of its elasticity. According to Tarshis, the different possibilities were discussed in Kahn's lectures (Tarshis, 1979, 369n). [...] The importance of the aggregate supply curve, drawn in the expected

> proceeds-aggregate output space, is that the derivation from it of the 'level of prices' is straightforward: for each level of output, it is given by the ratio of expected proceeds to output. This means that the level of prices can be determined by the same forces as the level of output and not by the Quantity of Money. This was an important step in the development of Keynesian ideas, as Joan Robinson reminded as years later: 'A short period supply curve relating the level of money prices to the level of activity (at given money-wage rates) led straight from Marshall to the General Theory'. (Marcuzzo, 1996a, p. 15)

Both the Dissertation and Kahn's lecture notes provide the first important evidence of the tension between tradition and innovation which, as we show in this research, characterises Kahn's whole contribution to economic analysis. On the side of tradition, we find the Marshallian approach, the reference to supply and demand as 'the two influences which affect the question of what happens to prices' (RFK/4/15/12), the idea that the behaviour of firms should be analysed in the light of the profit-maximisation and the marginal principle, attention to conventional elements and corporate spirit influences entrepreneurs' behaviour, leading them to keep prices unchanged even when it would seem inconvenient to do so. On the innovation side, we find the annihilation coefficient, the inverted L-shaped cost curve, the idea (later left in the background) that imperfect competition is the norm rather than the exception, and the notion of demand and supply can be extended from the industry to the macroeconomic level.

2.4 The Multiplier

A few months after becoming a Fellow of King's College, Kahn was coopted by Keynes as assistant secretary of the Committee of Economists of the Economic Advisory Council, established in 1930 by Prime Minister Ramsay MacDonald to address the prolonged stagnation of the UK economy aggravated by the Great Depression.[41] Among the various solutions presented to the Council was, as is well known, the possibility of using public works to reduce unemployment.

In Britain, interest in this idea had grown during the transition from the Victorian to the Edwardian era and even more so in the 1920s, as a

[41] On the Committee of Economists of the Economic Advisory Council, see Howson and Winch (1977, pp. 46–81 in particular).

result of stagnation and mass unemployment.[42] Proponents of public works recognised that hiring unemployed people (primary employment) would bring additional benefits as the newly employed began to spend their earnings (secondary employment). On the other hand, they did not know how to calculate these benefits, nor how to deflect criticism from those who, espousing the Treasury view, believed that crowding out of private investment and possibly inflation would be the only lasting consequences of public works.[43]

In the run-up to the 1929 election the Liberal Party's campaign to 'defeat unemployment', and in particular the publication of the pamphlet *Can Lloyd George Do It?* written by Keynes and Hubert Henderson, had made the issue of public works highly topical (Sloman, 2015). In this context, Kahn's article on the multiplier took shape (Kahn, 1931). This article, on which Kahn's fame depends to the present day, provides the first formal derivation, published in a scientific journal,[44] of the relationship between the increase in primary and secondary employment made possible by public investment, expressing the total increase in employment as the sum of a convergent geometric series. This is why Kahn's article is so important, and why it has earned him his place in the history of twentieth-century macroeconomics.[45]

There are differing opinions on Kahn's motives for becoming interested in the topic of public works. On the one hand Joan Robinson argued that this interest was the result of Keynes's request to look into the relationship between primary and secondary employment. On the other hand, according to Moggridge (1973a, p. 74, fn. 7), Kahn took an independent interest in the problem, and 'was particularly puzzled by the statement on page 31 (*Essays in Persuasion*, London, 1972, 112) that "nearly a *half* of

[42] There is a large and varied literature on this, and on Keynes's role in the public works debate, which it is not possible to review here. Some relevant contributions to this literature include Glynn and Booth (1987), Tomlinson (1987), Clarke (1988), Peden (1988), Garside (1990).

[43] On the Treasury view, the doctrine held by the British Treasury during the 1920s and 1930s, asserting that government borrowing for public works would displace private sector investment, and the political and administrative dimension of the debate on public expenditure and unemployment in interwar Britain, see Peden (1984) in addition to the reference mentioned in the footnote above.

[44] For a qualification of this statement, see Dimand (1994). See also Marcuzzo (2014, particularly 158, fn 5).

[45] On the development of the multiplier in a historical perspective with a focus on the antecedents of Kahn's analysis, see Dimand (2019).

the *capital* cost would be recovered *at the time*" (in italics in the original). He started with a hunch that it must be the *whole*'.

The article originated as a revision of a paper on 'The Relationship Between Primary and Secondary Employment' that Kahn had prepared for the Committee of Economists of the Economic Advisory Council in the summer of 1930.[46] Kahn's first contribution to the work of the Committee, consisted of a set of discussion topics and questions circulated in preparation for the first meeting, scheduled for 10 September 1930.[47] Analysis of this document reveals the strong influence of Keynes's *Treatise on Money* in the way Kahn treated the problem of unemployment and possible ways of dealing with it (Howson & Winch, 1977, p. 49). In addition, in the document we find references to issues that Kahn had already addressed in his fellowship Dissertation. These include the problem of excess capacity, the need to consider the likely duration of unemployment in determining the most appropriate policy to deal with it and the consequent reaction of trade unions.

A careful reading of Kahn (1931) is important from both a theoretical and a methodological point of view. At the theoretical level, the article contains a number of ideas with which Kahn had begun to familiarise himself in his Dissertation, and which would later influence Keynes as he developed his *General Theory*. I refer in particular to the short-run supply function for an aggregate of goods, to the idea of demand as a limiting factor on output and to the idea that, for a given state of supply and demand, prices depend mainly on nominal wages. On the methodological level, the article reveals Kahn's preference for reasoning based on the consideration of static and dynamic aspects within the framework of equilibrium reasoning schemes, together with his attention to distinguishing between the primary causes of an economic phenomenon and the effects of retroaction.

The article consists of seventeen paragraphs, which can be divided into four parts. The first part (paragraphs I–V) clarifies the purpose of the study, the basic assumptions and the meaning of some frequently recurring expressions (e.g. saving on the dole). Kahn assumes that investment

[46] The early version of the multiplier idea circulated among the members of the Committee of Economists can be found in the Keynes archive (Keynes papers EA/4 'Relation between Primary and Secondary Employment').

[47] Ref. Cab. 58/150, E.A.C. (E) t, 'Draft Heads for Discussion', 6 September 1930, 207–216.

is financed by issuing public debt, with the 'intelligent cooperation' of the central bank. The possible increase in taxation to finance investment, or the adoption of a restrictive monetary policy for fear of inflation, triggered by the rise in public spending, may dampen/eliminate the expansionary effect. Kahn also assumes that monetary wages do not rise in response to rising employment (given high initial unemployment), that prices can rise as a result of the economy moving up along the supply function (for a given level of nominal wages) and that public investment does not affect labour productivity.

The second part of the article (Sections VI–X) deals with the problem of the possible increase in the cost of living as a result of increased public investment. In discussing this problem, Kahn introduces the concept of a supply and demand curve for an aggregate of consumer goods, thereby projecting to the level of the economy as a whole concepts originally conceived at the microeconomic level, in continuity with the ideas he was developing in his lectures.[48]

> The price-level and output of home-produced consumption-goods, just like the price and output of any single commodity, are determined by the conditions of supply and demand. If the conditions of supply, can be regarded as fixed, both the price-level and the output are determined by the demand; and there is a unique correlation between price-level and output. (Kahn, 1931, p. 177)

Based on this approach, which allows the level of prices and employment to be determined simultaneously without reference to the quantity theory of money, the cost of living will rise, remain constant or fall depending on whether the supply curve of consumer goods as a whole is positively, horizontally or negatively sloped. On the other hand, as demand rises, price increases are physiological and not to be feared.[49] On the basis of these considerations and the assumption of an infinitely elastic supply curve, Kahn bases the calculation of the secondary employment generated

[48] As Kahn recalled on several public and private occasions in the 1970s, he regarded this is as the main theoretical innovation of his 1931 article, an innovation whose Marshallian origin cannot be ignored (see Chaps. 8 and 9).

[49] The price rises would occur even if the expansion took place in the context of a global economic recovery without any government intervention. The rise in prices would even be stronger because direct demand for consumer goods from abroad would increase and the prices of imported food and raw materials would rise.

by the hiring of a person through the public works programme on the following elements: W = wage of the new hire, P = additional profit generated by his activity,[50] R = value of additional imports induced by his activity, thus

$$W + P + R = \text{value of output generated by a new person hired through the public works programme} \quad (2.13)$$

indicating by

$$mW = \text{net increase in the rate of expenditure on home} - \text{produced consumption} - \text{goods out of additional wage earned } (0 < m < 1) \quad (2.14)$$

and with

$$nP = \text{net increase in the rate of expenditure on home} - \text{produced consumption} - \text{goods out of additional profit earned } (0 < n < 1) \quad (2.15)$$

The increase in employment in the consumer goods sector induced by the employment of an additional worker in the capital goods sector is

$$(mW + nP)/(W + P + R) = k < 1 \quad (2.16)$$

This increase, in turn, generates a series of subsequent increases as the new employees spend their income, creating new job opportunities for others.[51] The total effect of this expansion in secondary employment is given by

[50] W and P are assumed to be the same for primary and secondary employment.

[51] In a footnote, Kahn points out that in reality the multiplier process takes place over time, but states that he does not want to go into the question of time lags and therefore considers the final position of equilibrium when everything has settled down (Kahn, 1931, 183, fn. 2).

$$k + k^2 + k^3 + \ldots = k/(1-k) \tag{2.17}$$

Taking into account the fact that the worker hired through the public works programme earns *W* but loses the subsidy *U*, the increase in final consumption should be written as

$$m'(W-U) = mW \text{ where } m = m'(1-U/W) \tag{2.18}$$

from which (2.16) becomes

$$k = m'(1-U/W)(W/W+P+R) + n(P/W+P+R) \tag{2.19}$$

Based on data supplied to him by Colin Clark,[52] and assuming that the shares of *W*, *P* and *R* out of (*W* + *P* + *R*) are 7/10, 2/10, 1/10, respectively, and that *m*′ is equal to 5/6, Kahn proposes a series of numerical estimates of (*k*/1 − *k*), ranging from a 0.56 (if *U*/*W* = ½ and *n* = 1/3) to 0.92 (if *U*/*W* = 3/7 and *n* = 3/4).[53]

The last part of the article (paragraphs XIII–XVII) is devoted mainly to 'Mr Meade's relation' and the demonstration that new investment generates an equal flow of additional financial resources. In this part of the article, Kahn, building on ideas discussed with James Meade, whose name will reappear in several parts of this research,[54] shows how an increase in

[52] For Clark's involvement in the work of the EAC and for Kahn's role in the publication of Clark's article 'The Determination of the Multiplier from National Income Statistics' (Clark, 1938), see Millmow (2021, pp. 31–37). For an example of the figures provided by Clark to Kahn, see (RFK/1/1/96–101). Kahn's calculations on the possible value of the multiplier, estimated between 2.1 and 2.4, can be found in RFK/2/6/6–7.

[53] For these estimates, see Kahn (1931, p. 186). Assuming a positively sloping rather than an infinitely elastic aggregate supply curve, the increase in prices caused by the increase in demand requires a reduction of the multiplier by less than 1/5 (assuming that the price elasticity of demand is 1). Kahn admits that this reduction may be overestimated if one takes into account that the price increase increases profits and the demand for consumer goods by profit-takers.

[54] On the origins of the cooperation between Kahn and Meade leading to the definition of 'Mr Meade's relation' as part of Meade's lifetime contribution, see Howson (2000, pp. F123–124) and Atkinson and Weale (2000, pp. 476–477). On Mr. Meade's Relation, Kahn's Multiplier and the Chronology of the *General Theory*, see Dimand (1994) and the reply by Patinkin (1994). James Meade and Richard Kahn first met in the 'Keynes's Circus' discussion group at Cambridge in the 1930–1931 academic year. Meade joined the group, which met

public investment leads to an equal increase in the resources needed to finance it and could therefore be regarded as self-financing. As Kahn puts is

> For each man placed in employment the saving on the dole is U, the increase in imports of raw materials and unfinished goods is R in value, the increased imports of finished goods that result from the newly-employed man's expenditure are $(1 - m')(W - U)$ in value, and the sum of the increase in unspent profits and of the increase in imports of finished goods to which the newly-accruing profits are devoted is $(1 - n)P$. (Kahn, 1931, p. 188)

Using Kahn's notation, the total sum of these elements is equal to

$$\begin{aligned} U + R + (1 - m')(W - U) = +(1 - n)P &= (W + P + R) - (mW + nP) \\ &= (W + P + R)(1 - k) \end{aligned} \tag{2.20}$$

Based on Eq. (2.20), Kahn concludes:

> If N men are placed in primary employment, the total increase in employment is $N/(1 - k)$. It follows that the sum of these items is $N(W + P + R)$, which is precisely the value of the product of the primary employment, *i.e.* the cost to the State of the roads. We have then the following relation: Cost of investment = saving on dole + increase in imports + increase in unspent profits. (Ibid., p. 188)

Having shown, contrary to the Treasury's view, that an increase in public spending on investment would generate the additional resources needed to finance this increase, Kahn moves on to discuss the benefits of coordinating public investment internationally in terms of additional expansion. To these benefits must be added the possible productivity gains from new investment. Among the drawbacks, Kahn highlights loss of interest on foreign loans caused by the increase in imports and the consequent reduction in the current account surplus, and the possible negative effects that public works policies may have on the state of confidence in the economy, with the result of weakening the expansive effect of the public works.

in Kahn's rooms at King's College, at this time. The two men quickly formed a lasting intellectual friendship, as detailed elsewhere in this research.

> There is strong justification for concluding on *a priori* grounds that the inauguration of an active economic policy would promote confidence rather than upset it. But this is not a valid reason for disbelieving the warning, so frequently put forward at the present time, that an extensive policy of public works would promote a feeling of distrust. For the state of confidence is a function of what people are thinking, even though their thinking may be completely irrational, and therefore only those who are in touch with the minds of the people are competent to pass judgment on this question. A lowering of confidence may operate in two ways. It may, in the first place, reduce people's willingness or ability to carry on real investment at home. But also of great importance is its effect in increasing people's desire to hold their money abroad rather than at home. (Ibid., p. 197)

In terms of the distributional effects of public investment, the unemployed and the business community gain, while rentiers and those already in work lose as a result of rising prices. Looking at workers as a whole, it is very likely that their overall income will rise in nominal and real terms (unless the supply curve of consumer goods is so steep that it causes a very sharp rise in the prices of consumer goods, reducing income in real terms).

From a general perspective, the 1931 article offers additional evidence, following his Dissertation, of the young Kahn's capacity to reconsider pre-existing theoretical concepts in an innovative way and to distinguish primary causes from feedback effects (secondary causes). Moreover, by taking into account price fluctuations, the balance of payments and the budgetary consequences of an increase in public investment, Kahn's multiplier allows us to pay regard to aspects that the standard Keynesian multiplier relegates to the background.

On a different level, the multiplier article reveals Kahn's attention to address the doubts and concerns of those who viewed public works with suspicion, doubts that were present in the minds of Treasury officials, some leading members of the Conservative and Labour parties and important sections of the public.[55] In the early 1930s, these doubts outweighed the strength of Keynes's and Kahn's argument and the option of using public works to combat unemployment was not taken up, leaving the task of doing so to local authorities, expansionary monetary policy after the abandonment of the gold standard in 1931, protectionism and, later, to

[55] On the importance of Treasury officials' perceptions of financial and administrative obstacles to the implementation of Keynesian 'New Economics' see Middleton (1982), in addition to the reference mentioned in the previous footnotes.

the rearmament. The issue of public works, however, did not vanish from the British government's agenda and returned to prominence with the publication of the White Paper on Employment in 1944, as we discuss below.

After 1931 Kahn returned to the subject of the multiplier several times, either in response to critical comments or for other reasons. A first opportunity was provided by the need to respond to an article by the Danish economist J. Warming (1932), who, while confirming Kahn's estimates, had accused him of underestimating the importance of the additional savings brought about by the increase in national income.[56] Kahn (1932) reiterated that the theme of the dispersion of the new purchasing power created by public investment policy was present throughout his paper and explicitly recognised that saving was related to income.

In 1933, during his trip to the United States, Kahn returned to the link between the multiplier and saving. In his speech to the American Statistical Association in December 1932, Kahn for the first time used the marginal propensity to save to describe the multiplier process (Kahn, 1933). On the same occasion he reiterated that in assessing the potential inflationary effects of a public works policy, the slope of the supply curve for aggregate output must be taken into account. In a situation of high unemployment and idle capacity, this curve is very elastic and the rise in prices associated with an increase in output is minimal. On the other hand, if the inflationary effect of a given expansionary measure is to be reduced, the measure can be applied more sparingly. Moreover, the fear that an expansionary policy financed by recourse to banks and/or the central bank will have greater inflationary effects than a debt-financed policy is unfounded, even if it is widespread. In an expanding economy, it is physiological for the money supply to increase.

A third opportunity to defend his ideas came in 1936, a few months after the publication of *The General Theory* (Kahn, 1936). Here Kahn responded to criticisms of the German economist Hans Neisser,[57] in particular the idea that there was a fundamental similarity between the process of the multiplier and the effects of an increase in the money supply as predicted by the quantity theory of money. Kahn responded by accusing Neisser of confusing money and income, of ignoring 'Mr Meade's

[56] On Warming and his role in the development of the multiplier theory, see Boserup (1969) and Cain (1979), in addition to Dimand (1994).

[57] On Neisser's contribution and his exchange with Kahn, see Hagemann (1990).

relation', which predicts that savings increase with income and thus provide the additional resources needed to finance public works even with the same quantity of money, and of arguing in a world where Say's Law and the Quantity Theory apply, and that is not the world Kahn has in mind.

In drawing a final assessment of the genesis and immediate impact of the article on the multiplier, we can follow Shackle (1951) when he recalls:

> In his famous article, one of the great landmarks of economics and of the Economic Journal, which published it, Mr. Richard Kahn made (I give his own words) "no claims of originality." It is, I think, only on a very narrow and impoverished definition of originality that this disclaimer can be accepted. Important advances in any branch of knowledge are almost necessarily founded on pre-existing, though perhaps vaguely formulated, ideas. The originality of those who make such advances consists in the power to imagine new *structures* composed of old ideas whose connectibility has not been recognised; and in the effort of mind by which they bring vague ideas to a sharp focus and give them precise expression. (Shackle, 1951, p. 241)

These words very aptly describe Kahn's lifelong modus operandi, both in terms of his ability to rework existing concepts in an original, creative and innovative way and in terms of his refusal to take credit for everything, putting tradition first. Indeed, these merits are there and should be acknowledged.

Many years after the article on the multiplier was published, Kahn revisited it (Kahn, 1984, pp. 91–118). He recalled beginning work on the article in August 1930. He retraced the main stages of the formulation of the article, including his collaboration with Colin Clark and James Meade, the criticism he received from Pigou and Henderson and Warming's contribution. Kahn also took the opportunity to respond to two subsequent criticisms: that of Patinkin, who accused him of neglecting the dynamics of the multiplier; and that of Robertson, who claimed that the transmission mechanism could be traced back to the quantity theory of money. Kahn replied that he had deliberately adopted a comparative statics approach, contesting the equivalence between money creation and output growth while admitting that monetary financing could reinforce the expansionary effects of investment. In the same lecture, Kahn recalled the role of the Cambridge Circus (1930–1931), a group of young scholars who criticised Keynes's *Treatise on Money* in particular regarding the assumption a rigid supply hypothesis.[58] Finally, he revisited some of the key stages in the development of the *General Theory* and of his collaboration with Keynes, the topic to which we now turn.

2.5 The Collaboration Between Keynes and Kahn from the *Treatise on Money* (1930) to the *General Theory* (1936)

The relationship between Keynes and Kahn in the second half of the 1930s has been the subject of intense research, aimed, among other things, at clarifying Kahn's contribution to the genesis of the *General Theory*. There are very different views on this issue. On the one hand, there are those who have gone so far as to consider Kahn almost as a co-author of the *General Theory* (Schumpeter, 1954, p. 1172), a view that Kahn always rebutted, or at any rate as Keynes's 'main pillar support' (Harrod, 1951, p. 451). On the other hand, Patinkin (1976) has sought to downplay the importance of the contribution to the development of Keynes's ideas, and in particular to the notion of effective demand, given by Kahn and the other members of the 'Cambridge Circus', the group of economists who read, commented and criticised the *Treatise on Money* and assisted Keynes in the formulation of the *General Theory*.[59]

Given the breadth of the existing literature on the subject of the Keynes–Kahn collaboration in the years leading up to the publication of the *General Theory*, this section will confine itself to reconstructing a hopefully complete picture of the salient stages of this collaboration and the main analytical innovations to which it led.[60]

The story begins with the publication of the *Treatise on Money* on 31 October 1930. Kahn himself dates the beginning of his involvement in the writing of the *Treatise* to January 1930, one month after the delivery of

[58] The group included Kahn, Joan and Austin Robinson, Piero Sraffa and James Meade. There is a vast literature on the Circus and its role in the genesis of the *General Theory* and on Kahn's pivotal role in this context. Recent reference on the Cambridge Circus includes Aslanbeigui and Oakes (2002) and Marcuzzo (2023).

[59] On the evolution of Patinkin's thought on Keynes, see Hartwig (2022).

[60] The main references for this section, apart from volume XIII of the *Collected Writings* of Keynes, are Wright (1956), Moggridge (1973a), Harcourt (1994), Patinkin (1993, 1994) and Marcuzzo (2002a). Rymes's lecture notes (Rymes, 1989) provide a 'live' perspective on the transition from the *Treatise* to the *General Theory*. Clarke (1988), Laidler (1999) and Skidelsky (2003, pp. 481–482) complete the picture.

the fellowship Dissertation.[61] In fact, there are two pieces of evidence of earlier involvement, the draft preface to the *Treatise* of 1 September 1929 with Keynes's thanks to Kahn (Moggridge, 1973b, p. 83) and letters from Kahn to Keynes between September 1929 and March 1930 (JMK L/K, 28).[62]

This was followed by the article on the multiplier, which had an important influence in persuading Keynes to abandon the Quantity Theory of Money and the simplifying assumption of a given level of output in favour of a theory of the joint determination of the general level of prices and output based on the notions of aggregate supply and demand.

> Thus, in these particular ways did Kahn help to clear the way for Keynes to liberate himself from Say's Law and the quantity theory, to reintroduce aggregate demand and the concept of effective demand into economic analysis (together with an old friend in a new guise, aggregate supply), to create the consumption function and relate it to the multiplier, to formulate a new monetary theory of the determination of the money rate of interest which was to rule the roost, to transform the real rate of interest into the marginal efficiency of capital, and to provide a simple short-period Marshallian account of the general price level in which the money-wage played a central role—in short, to write *The General Theory*. (Harcourt, 1994, p. 18)

Between late 1930 and the first half of 1931, as the multiplier article was taking its final shape, Keynes discussed the *Treatise* with Robertson, Hayek and Pigou and with the members of the Cambridge Circus that included Kahn, Austin and Joan Robinson, James Meade and Piero Sraffa. From January until March 1931, the Circus met weekly to read, comment on and criticise the *Treatise*. It was Kahn's job to report the results of these discussions to Keynes and to inform the other members of the Circus of Keynes's reactions. A series of seminars followed between March and May in which other faculty members and some of the best third-year students also participated.

[61] Ref. Letter from Kahn to Patinkin (Patinkin & Leith, 1977, p. 148) and Kahn (1984, p. 175).

[62] Moggridge (1994) interprets Kahn's 'forgetfulness' as a desire to distance himself from the *Treatise*, emphasising its role in the gestation of the new Keynesian ideas that would emerge in the *General Theory*. Marcuzzo (2002a), re-reading the correspondence between Keynes and Kahn, suggests that the two initially discussed general problems of monetary theory, and only from 1930 onwards how to complete the *Treatise*.

The main focus of the Circus discussions concerned three matters, all three of which are related to Kahn's early work. The first matter pertains to the possibility that a discrepancy between investment and saving leads to changes in the level of national output and not only in the prices of consumer and investment goods, as is the case in the *Treatise*, where Keynes assumes that the level of national output is given. The second matter relates to 'Mr Meade's relation' (see above) and the demonstration of the way in which the change in investment generates a compensating change in saving. The third matter concerns the relationship between the price of consumer goods P and the price of investment goods P'. In the *Treatise*, Keynes treats P and P' as independent of each other, with P depending on the unit cost of production and the gap between I' (cost of production of capital goods) and S (savings = income less windfall profits or losses — expenditure on consumer goods) relative to output, and P' depending on how savers allocate the resources at their disposal, on the lending decisions of banks, on the spread between I (value of capital goods) and I'. Between April and September 1931, Kahn urged Keynes that P and P' were directly linked and that only if profits were not spent on the purchase of consumer goods could the independence of P and P' be justified.[63]

With these ideas in mind, Keynes left for the United States in June 1931 to deliver a series of lectures at the Harris Foundation. The text of these lectures reveals the development of Keynes's ideas on the effects of fluctuations in investment on output and employment rather than on prices, and on the possibility of the economic system operating below full employment. In these lectures we find references to the short run and the aggregate supply curve, both central to Kahn's early work.

> The analysis I shall try to outline is not merely my own; it is due to a young English economist, Mr R.F. Kahn. [...] let us consider the totality of industries. You have over a short period something of the nature of a supply curve which tells you that for a given level of prime profit [i.e., the difference between gross receipts and prime costs] there will be a given level of output, that if you have a certain amount of prime profits, that would be sufficient to bring certain quantity of potential output over the prime cost level. Every increase in aggregate prime profit will enable somebody to expand, because he will just get over the price cost point, and every diminution will knock

[63] On this point in particular, see Moggridge (1973a, p. 73). On the macroeconomics of the *Treatise on Money*, see Dimand (1986).

> someone out, so if you have a supply curve which is valid over the short period only, so that for every quantity of aggregate prime profit you have a given quantity of output, you could only increase employment and output by increasing prime profit. (Keynes, 1973, p. 368)

In the weeks following the Harris Foundation Lectures, Keynes continued to question the relationship between changes in investment, profits and output. In a letter from Keynes to Kahn dated 20 September 1931 (Marcuzzo, 2002a, p. 432), Keynes discussed the possibility that an increase in investment raises profits and that this increase has a positive effect partly on saving and partly on output (along the aggregate supply curve), which then induces a further increase in saving that counteracts the initial increase in profits.

Kahn responded to these remarks by raising a number of doubts, which added to Keynes's own. Largely because of these, Keynes decided to postpone his university lectures from the autumn of 1931 to the spring of 1932. Keynes's lectures delivered in the Easter term of 1932 still bear the title 'The Pure Theory of Money', the same as those delivered in 1929. The content, however, was very different and again we see here the effects of the influence of Kahn and others, including Robertson and Joan Robinson, on Keynes's evolving thinking.

After a first lecture, delivered on 25 April 1932, and devoted to clarifying some general points of definition and method, in the second lecture, given on 2 May 1932, Keynes proposed a new transmission mechanism from investment to output and profits. This mechanism states that increased investment increases output, employment and saving, while profits move in the opposite direction. After they had heard these early lectures, Kahn and Joan Robinson, together with Austin Robinson, wrote a document known as the *Trumpington Road Manifesto*, after the street where the Robinsons lived. In this document, the three proposed to Keynes the description of an alternative mechanism to explain the link between variation in investment and variation in output, different from the one originally envisaged by Keynes.[64]

Between the autumn of 1932 and Easter of the following year, the development of the *General Theory* took another important step. In

[64] The manifesto can be found in Keynes (1979, pp. 42–45). See Rymes (1989, pp. 27–44) for an account of the relationship between Kahn's multiplier arguments and the exchanges with Keynes over the *Trumpington Road Manifesto*.

December 1932, as discussed in more detail in Sect. 3.1, Kahn went to the United States on a Rockefeller Foundation Fellowship. The same month, he presented a paper entitled 'Public Works and Inflation', in which he referred to his article on the multiplier and the concepts of supply and demand for output as a whole. Between December 1932 and April 1933 the collaboration with Keynes was by correspondence. In England, meanwhile, Keynes presented the multiplier in an article for the *New Statesman* on 1 April 1933 and in a series of articles for the *Times* that would become the essay *Means to Prosperity*. Kahn read and commented on these articles, giving Keynes further food for thought.

It was from this elaboration that the notion of effective demand was born in 1933. In the Michaelmas 1933 lectures Keynes focused on the analysis of the movements of employment and output in response to changes in investment, the critique of the 'classical theory' of the labour market, and introduced the concept of involuntary unemployment. The various elements that make up the *General Theory* began to take shape.

Between the spring of 1933 and the beginning of 1934, Keynes submitted the manuscript of the future *General Theory* to the 'strict supervision' of Kahn (Moggridge, 1973b, p. 422), who repeatedly read, commented on and criticised the various chapters of the manuscript. In September 1934 Keynes instructed the editor to begin preparing proofs for the lectures scheduled for the Michaelmas term of 1934. These proofs began to circulate and were read and commented on, in particular by Robertson, who expressed dissatisfaction with the choice of the Kahn–Keynes short-run method of analysis (Moggridge, 1973b, p. 497). Kahn's assistance to Keynes continued uninterrupted until the summer of 1935, when the *General Theory* was completed.

> [T]he repeated consultations, the long weeks of supervisions at Tilton, the disciplining of Keynes's intuitive grasp of the subject into more refined channels and the repeated drafts of the definitional chapters of the book all emphasize the extent of Kahn' influence. (Moggridge, 1973a, p. 88)

On the basis of the evidence proposed in this section, I would like to emphasise two points that are well known and that the present research hopes to corroborate.[65] First, there are a number of elements in the

[65] On Marshallian microeconomics as part of the theoretical framework of the *General Theory*, in particular with regard to the short-run aggregate supply function at the level of

General Theory, the origin of which can be traced back to the Marshallian tradition at Cambridge, to which both Keynes and Kahn belonged. Second, the presence of these elements, in particular the aggregate supply function and the extension of the supply and demand framework to the macroeconomic level (both present in Kahn's early work), is largely due to Kahn's influence on Keynes, combined with Keynes's well-known desire to write a book in the language of his likely opponents.

The idea that the *General Theory* could be better understood as an extension of the demand for and cost of production of a single product to the analysis of the demand for global production and its production costs had been emphasised since the first debates after the *General Theory* (e.g. Robinson, 1951), and it was Keynes himself who acknowledged to Kahn that he had been the first to move in this direction.[66] This is not to diminish the innovative significance of the *General Theory*, nor to ignore the fact that many, starting from Keynes himself, Kahn and Joan Robinson, regarded the publication of this book as a revolutionary act.

My purpose here is only to underline the possibility of linking the *General Theory* to the Cambridge Marshallian tradition, in which both Keynes and Kahn (albeit at different times) had been trained, and to indicate Kahn's contribution as essential in this respect, in particular regarding three aspects: the notion of aggregate supply function, the possibility of extending the notions of supply and demand price from the industry to the aggregate level and the application of these concepts to the definition of the multiplier. If the desire to revolutionise the conclusions emerging from the Marshallian tradition prevails in Keynes, Kahn, in his own works

firms, industries and the economy as a whole, see Asimakopulos (1982) and more generally Asimakopulos (1991). On the Marshallian elements underlying the principle of effective demand, and more generally on Kahn's influence on Keynes, see Kregel (1980). On Kahn's role in promoting a conventional view of supply and equilibrium in his contribution to the genesis of the *General Theory*, see Tonveronachi (1983). I would like to thank Alessandro Roncaglia for this valuable insight. On the elements of continuity and rupture between Keynes and Marshall, see also the essays in Ridolfi (1984).

[66] That Patinkin and others in the mid-1970s could doubt the importance of the influence of the Cambridge Circus and Kahn on Keynes can be explained by two factors to which we shall return in Chap. 9. On the one hand, the distance between the reinterpretation of Keynes from the perspective of general economic equilibrium proposed by Patinkin and others, which had little or nothing to do with Kahn's approach. On the other hand, a certain reluctance on the part of Kahn, at least until the late 1970s, to claim the importance of his influence on Keynes.

of the second half of the 1930s, adopted, as we shall see, a more cautious approach.

2.6 Kahn's Early Unpublished Writings on International Economic Issues

Between 1929 and 1931, in parallel with his other activities, Kahn devoted himself to the study of some relevant international economic issues. The main fruits of this activity, little known to the present day, are three unpublished papers preserved in the Kahn archives. These works deal respectively with international economic cooperation, the newly established Bank for International Settlements and the Transfer problem. The fact that Kahn decided not to publish these works should make us approach them with caution. However, as they are complete works, we cannot ignore them nor can we ignore the links between these works and the theoretical framework and the ideas about economic policy set out by Kahn in his Dissertation and article on the multiplier.

The first paper, entitled 'The Possibility and Effects of United States Cooperation',[67] contains the text of a talk given by Kahn on 23 January 1929 to the Monetary Policy Group of the Marshall Society, of which Kahn was a member.[68] This paper is important for its analysis of the factors on which the effectiveness of monetary policy depends and the advantages and difficulties associated with coordinating monetary policies at the international level. These factors include the state of confidence of the banks, the morphology of the financial system, the determination with which the monetary authorities carry out their monetary manoeuvres, the way in which traders perceive these manoeuvres.[69]

[67] The article was found in the archives at the Marshall Library by Prof Marco Dardi and sent to Kahn, who had no recollection of it, in 1988 (RFK/3/4/1). The text of the article can be found in RFK/3/4/2–23.

[68] The Marshall Society is the Economics society of the University of Cambridge, named after Alfred Marshall. To this day it serves as a platform for students interested in economics, organising talks, debates, and networking events with prominent economists. The society also publishes an annual journal and hosts competitions to encourage academic discussion and research in economics.

[69] These elements are present, in varying degrees, in the analysis of money and the business cycle that came to influence Kahn from Marshall and Pigou via Keynes and Robertson. On the monetary theory of Marshall and the Cambridge School, see Eshag (1963). On Keynes's changing views on monetary policy between 1910 and 1946, see Moggridge and Howson (1974).

Kahn begins by asking whether a recovery of the British economy, stagnant since the return to the gold standard in 1925, could be triggered by persuading the United States, with its huge gold reserves and sophisticated financial system, to adopt an expansionary monetary policy. Kahn outlines the two main ways through which an expansionary US monetary policy could benefit British industry, referring to concepts (the supply and demand curve for output as a whole) and economic mechanisms (increased consumption induced by increased investment) similar to those that would soon appear in the article on the multiplier.

> (a) The 'general' remedy is the improvement of the general world conditions of demand for the products of the staple industries, so as to lead to increased production. Of such an increase in production a fair share may be expected to accrue to this country.
> (b) The 'particular' remedy is the improvement of the relative position of England at the expense of the rest of the world, by raising the cost of production in other countries.
>
> In both cases, the prices of the products of our staple industries are raised, so that it becomes possible for us to produce more: in the case of the 'general' remedy this is due to the world's demand curve being raised, while in the case of the 'particular' remedy it is due to the supply curves of some of our competitors being raised,—so that they [in the original] produce less. (RFK/3/4/3–4)

The effectiveness of the general remedy, assuming that the United States can be persuaded to adopt expansionary monetary measures, depends on two factors: (a) the ability of domestic banking systems to sustain the economic recovery induced by the US expansion; (b) the impact of the recovery on prices and wages in the various countries. In both cases, Kahn highlights the risk that the fear of importing inflation from the United States, while trying to maintain the gold standard, will lead the Bank of England to hinder the transmission of the expansionary monetary impulse and the benefits that might flow from it in terms of increased production, consumption and investment.

> Here again it all depends on central bank's policy. It is reasonable to suppose (and history supports the supposition) that a lowering of the Federal Reserve Rates, leading to imports of gold into this country, would be followed by a lowering of the Bank Rate. But it by no means follows that any substantial

> expansion of credit will result. Owing to the necessity of maintaining a conventional ratio of cash to deposits, the joint stock banks can only expand credit if the Bank of England allows their cash to expand. (RFK/3/4/12)

Before the First World War this would have happened almost automatically, but after the war the Bank of England discovered the possibility of neutralising the effects of gold inflows and outflows on domestic circulation by sterilisation operations.[70] In this new context, there is no longer any guarantee that domestic credit will increase as a result of the Bank of England's increased gold reserves, and Kahn fears that the Bank of England's caution and the fear of importing inflation may neutralise the benefits of US monetary expansion for British industry. The fear that nominal wages and prices in Britain will rise rapidly in response to the rise in the price of imported raw materials, favoured by the global recovery, makes this possibility very real.

Having emphasised the presence of this second obstacle, in addition to the Bank of England's caution, dictated by the need to maintain the gold standard, Kahn devotes the last part of his talk to discussing the possibility of Great Britain playing ahead of the game 'coercing an unwilling America into involuntary cooperation. Our weapon would be a flow of gold to New York. This could be promoted by lowering our rates of interest. Our hope would be that the gold would provide the basis for an expansion of credit in the United States' (RFK/3/4/18).

Realistically, Kahn recognises that the chances of this manoeuvre succeeding are very slim, both because 'the supply of ammunition available for a bombardment of New York would be exhausted before the plan of attack was well under way' (ibid.), and because the Federal Reserve would intervene against an undesirable expansion of credit in the United States as a result of the influx of gold and capital from Britain. On this last aspect, and in general on the United States pursuing an expansionary monetary policy that would allow gold to reach the United Kingdom regardless of the reasons that may have determined this policy, Kahn underlines two additional obstacles

[70] Sterilisation operations in monetary policy refer to central bank actions aimed at offsetting the impact of foreign exchange interventions on the domestic money supply. This is typically done by buying or selling government securities to neutralise changes in liquidity. The goal is to maintain monetary stability without affecting exchange rate policies.

(i) The first is a psychological rather than an economic factor. In fact it is a superstition. An extended drainage of gold from New York will not only be deeply resented by the average American, but will actually curb the business men's optimism and prevent that expansion of American trade which forms an element in the course of treatment we are prescribing.
(ii) The second factor may be regarded as pseudo-economic. Whatever may be the nature of popular prejudice, it is a fact, recently mentioned by the Governor of the Federal Reserve Board, that interest rates have been kept down in the United States in order to aid the process of European recovery. But in recent months the boom in industrial shares has been regarded as causing a diversion of credit from productive to speculative purposes, and as necessitating a policy of dear money. [...] As long as the Federal Reserve authorities feel it to be their duty to keep share prices down at a reasonable level, there can be little hope of cooperation with this country. (RFK/3/4/19–20)

The cooperation between central banks at an international level, the advantages that can derive from it and the possible obstacles are the focus of the second unpublished writing which Kahn devoted to international economic issues in 1930, focusing on the newly established Bank for International Settlements (henceforth BIS) (RFK/2/1–34). After recalling the reasons for the establishment of the BIS as part of Young's plan to deal with the German war reparations,[71] Kahn elaborates on the possible auxiliary functions of the new institution, and in particular on the possibility that the BIS might become a real bank, capable of granting loans to the various nations, and not merely an intermediary passively fulfilling the role of certifying the transfer of payments from Germany to the creditor nations.

In discussing this possibility, Kahn emphasises how the bank's limited resources mean that the benefit that a single country can derive by employing the credit facilities of the Bank is measured by the degree to which other countries are not at the same time employing those credit facilities; and that to the extent to which this country employs them, a certain burden is imposed on the rest of the world. This fact can lead to conflicts

[71] The Young Plan (1929–1930) restructured Germany's First World War reparations, reducing the total amount owed and establishing fixed annual payments to be made over a period of 59 years. It also ended foreign economic controls and led to the establishment of the Bank for International Settlements. However, the plan collapsed amid the Great Depression and had been abandoned by 1932.

between nations and prevent the BIS from fulfilling its primary function: to promote cooperation between central banks.

> The function of the Bank which will suffer most if there is a lack of harmony at meetings of its Board is its function of promoting co-operation between Central Banks. [...] If the Bank does nothing else, it will at least provide a regular meeting place for the heads of Central Banks. That this will be a praiseworthy achievement is generally admitted, though some critics have pointed out that the Bank is a somewhat cumbrous piece of mechanism to set at work to attain so simple an end. For instance a monthly game of poker, if only attendance were de rigueur, would be just as effective. Indeed I am prepared to defend the view that it would be more effective. The formalities which are in an integral part of the meetings of the Board of Directors tend often to become the source of irritation at international gatherings. [...] The question that we have to face is whether such an attitude of mind will be compatible with fruitful discussion at meetings of the International Bank. (RFK/2/1/5–6)

In expressing these doubts, Kahn does not deny the importance of cooperation between central banks, especially in view of the serious monetary problems of the day, from the shortage of gold reserves to the high level of interest rates. However, he fears the risks that can derive from entrusting the solution of these problems to the new institutions

> By exchanging its own resources for a deposit at the International Bank, a Central Bank is put in a position to sell the currency of any country it likes at any moment it likes and at as great a rate as it likes until its deposit is exhausted. The possibilities are alarming—or at any rate will appear alarming to the cautious minds of Central Bankers. Reliance cannot here be paid on the good sense of an international body. (RFK/2/1/14)

> The political difficulties will predominate, and there will always be an inducement to refrain from any positive course of action which might lead to frictions at future meetings of the Board. Mr. Paul Einzig, in his recent book on the Bank of International Settlements, lays considerable emphasis on the difficulties that may arise in this way. "If Bulgaria gets a loan", says Mr. Einzig, "Yugoslavia may threaten to withdraw unless she gets a similar loan; while Austria may be offended when she gets credits simultaneously with Hungary". It is obvious that there will be no point in lending to all countries. A loan will be only useful to a country if, and to the extent that, there are other countries which are not at the same time receiving loans.

> Unable, for this reason, to lend to everyone, the International Bank may be tempted to lend to none. (RFK/2/1/21-22)

If these reasons lead Kahn to doubt that the BIS could rapidly become a real bank, further doubts are raised by the new BIS prerogatives in the clearing of international payments. The possibility that different nations could settle their credit and debit balances with each other by transferring reserves from one correspondent account to another within the BIS system, 'eliminating the costs and risks now incurred and the shipping and re-shipping of gold', is a cause for concern for Kahn. The main risk he sees in this possibility, and in facilitating the virtual movement of gold reserves from one country to another, is that the gold points will move closer together, fuelling destabilising speculation in the foreign exchange market.

> It is this gap between the gold points which, by affording speculative attractions to those who operate in foreign currencies, provides the element of elasticity which is so essential to the smooth working of the gold standard. When a currency becomes cheap, there are always people who will buy it in the expectation that it will soon become dearer; the assistance of which it stands in need is thereby automatically provided and the need for gold movements is lessened. The smaller the gap between the gold points, the less can be the assistance that speculators will provide; and the greater, and the more rapid, are the repercussions of a chance breath of wind on the surface of international finance. [...] By eliminating the necessity for the transshipment of gold, the International Bank will provide the possibility of closing up the gold points; but it will not reduce the seriousness of a transfer of resources from one central bank to another. (RFK/2/1/24–26)

Attention to the advantages and obstacles along the path of international monetary cooperation and to the risks of relying on internal deflation to improve one's balance of payments, in the absence of a better alternative, are at the centre of the third unpublished paper that Kahn devoted to international economic problems in the early 1930s.

This paper, entitled 'The Transfer Problem', was written by Kahn in the context of the well-known debate between J.M. Keynes and B. Ohlin in the pages of the *Economic Journal*.[72] In this debate, Keynes had argued

[72] Source RFK/2/2–24. The article on the transfer problem is accompanied by a typewritten letter from Keynes dated 29 July 1931, in which Keynes raises a series of detailed analytical points and recommends that Kahn send the paper to an Austrian Journal (RFK/2/2/1).

that in order to continue to pay for reparations, once international loans were no longer available, Germany would have to undergo drastic internal deflation in order to boost her exports and draw the necessary resources from there. Against this position, Ohlin argued that the resources transferred from Germany to the creditor nations would increase their purchasing power, with beneficial effects on German exports, without the need for a severe internal deflation.

Kahn's essay opens with the observation that the difference between Keynes's and Ohlin's positions can be traced back to a fundamental difference in the way they conceive of the transfer problem. Keynes has in mind a country that is already paying for the reparations and has already benefited as much as possible from the increase in the purchasing power of the creditor nations made possible by the reparations. Ohlin, on the other hand, has in mind a country that has not yet begun to pay reparations and is suddenly in a position to do so. To ignore this distinction, and to ignore the fact that Germany is paying reparations with the help of international loans, is to overestimate its ability to continue to pay once those loans are stopped. This is the main flaw Kahn sees in the argument of Ohlin and his supporters.

To clarify his own argument, Kahn imagines a world divided into two countries: Germany and Otherland. If the loans that enabled reparations to be paid are cut off and Germany is forced to replace these funds by resorting to internal deflation to boost its exports, this does not necessarily benefit Otherland. The influx of cheap goods from Germany will reduce the profits of Otherland businesses, with negative effects on employment, income and wages there. In this case, the risk is the export of deflation from Germany to other countries and it is not certain that the payment of reparations will trigger the increase in demand for German goods in the rest of the country that Ohlin predicted.

> Any reduction in Germany's wages will set up a tendency for wages to fall all over the world, and Germany's difficulties in securing a sufficient reduction in her real wages will be aggravated. (RFK/2/2/14–15)

Even excluding direct interventions aimed at reducing German wages and prices in order to generate the increase in the surplus necessary to pay the reparations and compensate for the loss of foreign loans, it is not certain that the risk of generalised deflation has been completely averted. Assuming that the reparations have not yet been paid and that the two countries (Germany and Otherland) are in a state of initial equilibrium (the Ohlin hypothesis), if the payment leads to an increase in taxes (and a decrease in consumption and imports) in Germany and a decrease in taxes (and an increase in consumption and imports) in Otherland, it is possible, but unlikely, that the terms of trade will improve in Germany's favour. The increase in demand for German goods by the citizens of Otherland would have to exceed the decrease in demand for German goods by the German citizens themselves.

If, on the other hand, we assume that Germany is already paying the reparations (thanks to international loans from Otherland) and has not yet achieved a sufficient external surplus to do without these loans (Keynes's hypothesis), then achieving equilibrium will certainly require an increase in Germany's external surplus (and hence in Otherland's deficit) and a worsening of Germany's terms of trade which will necessitate further restrictions on the German economy. In both cases, therefore, and in particular in the second one, forcing Germany to compensate by immediately and fully drawing on its own internal resources will push not only Germany but the whole world into a situation of deflation and crisis.

Kahn's concern about the risks of deflation at the international level, as described in the essay on the transfer problem and in the lecture to the Marshall Society, is combined with an awareness of the difficulty of countering these risks through the adoption of measures to support demand and international cooperation, including through new institutions such as the Bank for International Settlements. Hence the need to find solutions that, on the one hand, allow different nations to maintain external equilibrium without resorting to deflation and, on the other hand, allow these same nations to cooperate with each other in a flexible manner while retaining the maximum possible autonomy.

References

Asimakopulos, A. (1982). Keynes's theory of effective demand revisited. *Australian Economic Papers, 21*(38), 18–36.

Asimakopulos, A. (1991). *Keynes's General Theory and Accumulation*. Cambridge University Press.

Aslanbeigui, N., & Oakes, G. (2002). The theory arsenal: the Cambridge circus and the origins of the Keynesian revolution. *Journal of the History of Economic Thought, 24*(1), 5–37.

Aslanbeigui, N., & Oakes, G. (2009). *The Provocative Joan Robinson. The Making of a Cambridge Economist.* Duke University Press.

Aslanbeigui, N., & Oakes, G. (2011). Richard Kahn's fellowship Dissertation: The fate of 'The Economics of the Short Period'. *European Journal of the History of Economic Thought, 18*(3), 381–405.

Atkinson, B. A., & Weale, S. (2000). James Edward Meade. *Proceeding of the British Academy, 105*, 473–500.

Bittermann, H. J. (1934). Elasticity of supply. *American Economic Review, 24*(3), 417–429.

Boserup, M. (1969). A Note on the prehistory of the Kahn multiplier. *Economic Journal, 79*(315), 667–669.

Bridel, P., & Ingrao, B. (2005). The correspondence between Keynes and Pigou. In M. C. Marcuzzo & A. Rosselli (Eds.), *Economists in Cambridge: A Study through their Correspondence, 1907–1946* (pp. 149–166). Routledge.

Cain, N. (1979). Cambridge and its revolution: a perspective on the multiplier and effective demand. *Economic Record, 55*, 108–117.

Caldwell, B., & Klausinger, H. (2022). *Hayek: A Life, 1899–1950.* University of Chicago Press.

Carabelli, A. (2005). A lifelong friendship. The correspondence between Keynes and Shove. In M. C. Marcuzzo & A. Rosselli (Eds.), *Economists in Cambridge: A study through their correspondence, 1907–1946* (pp. 196–215). Routledge.

Clark, C. (1938). Determination of the Multiplier from National Income Statistics. *Economic Journal, 48*(191), 435–448.

Clarke, P. (1988). *The Keynesian Revolution in the Making.* Clarendon Press.

Collard, D. (1990). Cambridge after Marshall. In J. K. Whitaker (Ed.), *Centenary Essays on Alfred Marshall* (pp. 164–192). Cambridge University Press.

Cristiano, C. (2010). Marshall at Cambridge. In T. Raffaelli, G. Becattini, K. Caldari, & M. Dardi (Eds.), *The Impact Of Alfred Marshall's Ideas* (pp. 17–39). Edward Elgar.

Dardi, M. (1983). Introduzione. In R. F. Kahn (Ed.), *L'Economia del Breve Periodo* (pp. 9–30). Bollati Boringhieri.

Dardi, M. (1996). Imperfect competition and short-period economics. In M. C. Marcuzzo, L. L. Pasinetti, & A. Roncaglia (Eds.), *The Economics of Joan Robinson* (pp. 29–35). Routledge.

Dardi, M. (2001). Why did Sraffa lose interest in imperfect competition? A comment on Marcuzzo. In T. Cozzi & R. Marchionatti (Eds.), *Piero Sraffa's Political Economy: A centenary estimate* (pp. 128–135). Routledge.

Di Matteo, M. (2012). Concorrenza ed equilibrio. La concezione innovativa di Attilio da Empoli. In M. Di Matteo & E. Longobardi (Eds.), *Attilio da Empoli (1904–1948): Un Economista Partecipe del suo Tempo* (pp. 81–100). Franco Angeli.

Dimand, R. (1986). The Macroeconomics of the Treatise on Money. *Eastern Economic Journal, 12*(4), 431–450.
Dimand, R. (1994). Mr Meade's relation, Kahn's multiplier and the chronology of the General Theory. *Economic Journal, 104*(426), 1139–1142.
Dimand, R. (2019). The Multiplier. In R. W. Dimand & H. Hagemann (Eds.), *The Elgar Companion to John Maynard Keynes* (pp. 210–217). Edward Elgar.
Eshag, E. (1963). *From Marshall to Keynes: An Essay on the Monetary Theory of the Cambridge School.* Clarendon Press.
Garside, W. R. (1990). *British Unemployment 1919–1939.* Cambridge University Press.
Glynn, S., & Booth, A. (Eds.). (1987). *The Road to Full Employment.* Allen and Unwin.
Groenewegen, P. (2012). *Minor Marshallians and Alfred Marshall.* Routledge.
Hagemann, H. (1990). Neisser's 'The wage rate and employment in market equilibrium': An introduction. *Structural Change and Economic Dynamics, 1*(1), 133–139.
Harcourt, G. C. (1991). R.F. Kahn: A Tribute. *Banca Nazionale del Lavoro Quarterly Review, 44*(176), 15–30.
Harcourt, G. C. (1994). Kahn and Keynes and the making of the General Theory. *Cambridge Journal of Economics, 18*(1), 11–23.
Harcourt, G. C. (1995). Lorie Tarshis, 1911–1993: In Appreciation. *Economic Journal, 105*(432), 1244–1255.
Harcourt, G. C. (2017). Marshall's Principles as seen at Cambridge through the eyes of Gerald Shove. In D. Robertson, J. Robinson, & I. C. Sardoni (Eds.), *On Political Economists and Modern Political Economy: Selected Essays of G. C. Harcourt* (pp. 265–277). Routledge.
Harcourt, G. C., & Kerr, P. (2009). *Joan Robinson.* Palgrave Macmillan.
Harrod, R. F. (1951). *The Life of John Maynard Keynes.* Macmillan.
Hart, N. (2012). *Equilibrium and Evolution.* Palgrave Macmillan.
Hart, N. (2013). *Alfred Marshall and Modern Economics.* Palgrave Macmillan.
Hartwig, J. (2022). The evolution of Patinkin's interpretation of Keynes' principle of effective demand. *European Journal of the History of Economic Thought, 29*(3), 505–522.
Howson, S. (2000). James Meade. *Economic Journal, 110*(461), F122–F145.
Howson, S., & Winch, D. (1977). The Economic Advisory Council. In *1930–1939.* Press.
Ingrao, B., & Ranchetti, F. (2005). Hayek and Cambridge: dialogue and contention. The correspondence with Kahn, Kaldor, J. Robinson and Sraffa. In M. C. Marcuzzo & A. Rosselli (Eds.), *Economists in Cambridge: A study through their correspondence, 1907–1946* (pp. 392–413). Routledge.

Johnson, H. G. (1977). Cambridge as an academic environment in the early 1930s: A reconstruction from the late 1940s. In D. Patinkin & J. C. Leith (Eds.), *Keynes, Cambridge and 'The General Theory'* (pp. 98–114). Macmillan.

Kahn, R. F. ([1929] 1989). *The economics of the short period.* Macmillan.

Kahn, R. F. (1931). The relation of home investment to unemployment. *Economic Journal, 41*(162), 173–198.

Kahn, R. F. (1932). The Financing of Public Works. A Note. *Economic Journal, 42*(167), 492–495.

Kahn, R. F. (1933). Public Works and Inflation. *Journal of the American Statistical Association, 28*(181), 168–173.

Kahn, R. F. (1936). Dr Neisser on secondary employment: a note. *Review of Economics and Statistics, 18*(3), 144–147.

Kahn, R. F. (1984). *The Making of Keynes's General Theory.* Cambridge University Press.

Kahn, R. F. (1987). Shove, G.F. In J. Eatwell, M. Milgate, & P. Newman (Eds.), *The New Palgrave: A Dictionary of Economics* (Vol. IV, pp. 327–328). Macmillan.

Keppler, J. H. (1994). *Monopolistic Competition Theory: Origins, Results, and Implications.* John Hopkins University Press.

Keynes, J. M. (1939). Relative Movements of Real Wages and Output. *Economic Journal, 49*(193), 34–51.

Keynes, J. M. (1973). *The Collected Writings of John Maynard Keynes. Vol. XIII, The General Theory and After: Part I, Preparation.* Cambridge University Press.

Keynes, J. M. (1979). *The Collected Writings of John Maynard Keynes. Vol. XXIX, The General Theory and After: A Supplement.* Cambridge University Press.

Knight, K. L. (2018). *A.C. Pigou and the 'Marshallian' Thought Style.* Palgrave Macmillan.

Kregel, J. A. (1980). I fondamenti marshalliani del principio della domanda effettiva. *Giornale degli Economisti e Annali di Economia, 39*(3/4), 153–168.

Laidler, D. (1999). *Fabricating the Keynesian Revolution: Studies of the inter-war literature on money, the cycle, and unemployment.* Cambridge University Press.

Maloney, J. (1985). *Marshall, Orthodoxy and the Professionalization of Economics.* Cambridge University Press.

Maneschi, A. (1988). The Place of Lord Kahn's The Economics of the Short Period in the theory of imperfect competition. *History of Political Economy, 20*(2), 155–171.

Marchionatti, R. (1995). Keynes and the collapse of the British cotton industry in the 1920s: A Microeconomic Case against Laissez-Faire. *Journal of Post Keynesian Economics, 17*(3), 427–445.

Marchionatti, R. (2021). *Economic Theory in the Twentieth Century, An Intellectual History—Volume II 1919–1945.* Palgrave Macmillan.

Marcuzzo, M. C. with Besomi, D., & Ranchetti, F. (2005). Kahn and the Correspondence with Sraffa, Harrod and Kaldor. In M. C. Marcuzzo & A. Rosselli (Eds.), *Economists in Cambridge: A Study through their Correspondence, 1907–1946* (pp. 149–308). Routledge.

Marcuzzo, M. C. (1991). Joan Robinson e la formazione della Scuola di Cambridge. In J. Robinson (Ed.), *Occupazione, distribuzione e crescita* (M.C. Marcuzzo, Ed., XIX–LXV). Il Mulino.

Marcuzzo, M. C. (1994). R.F. Kahn and imperfect competition. *Cambridge Journal of Economics, 18*(1), 25–39.

Marcuzzo, M. C. (1996a). Joan Robinson and Richard Kahn: The origin of short-period analysis. In M. C. Marcuzzo, L. L. Pasinetti, & A. Roncaglia (Eds.), *The Economics of Joan Robinson* (pp. 11–28). Routledge.

Marcuzzo, M. C. (1996b). Alternative microeconomic foundations for macroeconomics. *Review of Political Economy, 8*(1), 7–22.

Marcuzzo, M. C. (2001). Sraffa and Cambridge economics, 1928–1931. In T. Cozzi & R. Marchionatti (Eds.), *Piero Sraffa's Political Economy: A Centenary Estimate* (pp. 81–99). Routledge.

Marcuzzo, M. C. (2002a). The Collaboration between J.M. Keynes and R.F. Kahn from the *Treatise* to the *General Theory*. *History of Political Economy, 34*(2), 421–448.

Marcuzzo, M. C. (2002b). The Demise of the Quantity Theory of Money. *History of Economic Ideas, 10*(1), 49–62.

Marcuzzo, M. C. (2003). Joan Robinson and the three Cambridge revolutions. *Review of Political Economy, 15*(4), 545–560.

Marcuzzo, M. C. (2005a). Keynes and his favourite pupil. The correspondence between Keynes and Kahn. In M. C. Marcuzzo & A. Rosselli (Eds.), *Economists in Cambridge: A Study through their Correspondence, 1907–1946* (pp. 21–56). Routledge.

Marcuzzo, M. C. (2005b). Robinson and Sraffa. In B. Gibson (Ed.), *Joan Robinson's Economics. A Centennial Celebration* (pp. 29–42). Edward Elgar.

Marcuzzo, M. C. (2014). Whatever Happened to the Keynesian Multiplier? In R. Baranzini & F. Allisson (Eds.), *Economics and Other Branches—In the Shade of the Oak Tree: Essays in Honour of Pascal Bridel* (pp. 157–168). Pickering & Chatto.

Marcuzzo, M. C. (2017). The 'Cambridge' critique of the quantity theory of money: A note on how quantitative easing vindicates it. *Journal of Post Keynesian Economics, 40*(2), 260–271.

Marcuzzo, M. C. (2020). Richard F. Kahn: A Disciple of Keynes. *History of Economics Review, 76*(1), 2–57.

Marcuzzo, M. C. (2023). Cambridge 'Circus'. In L. P. Rochon & S. Rossi (Eds.), *Elgar Encyclopedia of Post-Keynesian Economics* (pp. 37–38). Edward Elgar.

Marcuzzo, M. C., Naldi, N., Sanfilippo, E., & Rosselli, A. (2008). Cambridge as a Place in Economics. *History of Political Economy, 40*(4), 569–593.

Marcuzzo, M. C., & Rosselli, A. (Eds.). (2005). *Economists in Cambridge. A Study through their Correspondence, 1907–1946*. Routledge.

Marris, R. L. (1992). R.F. Kahn's fellowship Dissertation: A Missing Link in the History of Economic Thought. *Economic Journal, 102*(414), 1235–1243.

Matsuyama, N. (2022). The direct impact of Alfred Marshall's American trip in 1875 on his economic analysis of industrial development. *History of Economics Review, 83*(1), 24–39.

Middleton, R. (1982). The Treasury in the 1930s: political and administrative constraints to acceptance of the 'new' economics. *Oxford Economic Papers, 34*(1), 48–77.

Millmow, A. (2021). *The Gypsy Economist: The Life and Times of Colin Clark*. Palgrave Macmillan.

Moggridge, D. (1973a). From the Treatise to the General Theory: An exercise in chronology. *History of Political Economy, 5*(1), 72–88.

Moggridge, D. (Ed.). (1973b). *The Collected Writings of John Maynard Keynes. Vol. XIII, The General Theory and After: Part I, Preparation*. Cambridge University Press.

Moggridge, D. (Ed.). (1979). *The Collected Writings of John Maynard Keynes. Vol. XXIX, The General Theory and After: A Supplement*. Cambridge University Press.

Moggridge, D. (1992). *Maynard Keynes: An Economist's Biography*. Routledge.

Moggridge, D. (1994). Richard Kahn as an historian of economics. *Cambridge Journal of Economics, 18*(1), 107–116.

Moggridge, D. E., & Howson, S. (1974). Keynes on Monetary Policy, 1910–1946. *Oxford Economic Papers, 26*(2), 226–247.

O'Shaughnessy, T. J. (1994). Kahn on the economics of the short period. *Cambridge Journal of Economics, 18*(1), 41–54.

Pasinetti, L. (1991). Richard Ferdinand Kahn. 1905–1989. *Proceedings of the British Academy, 76*, 423–433.

Patinkin, D. (1976). *Keynes' Monetary Thought: A Study of Its Development*. Duke University Press.

Patinkin, D. (1993). On the chronology ofThe General Theory. *Economic Journal, 103*(418), 347–363.

Patinkin, D. (1994). Mr Meade's relation, Kahn's multiplier and the chronology of the General Theory: Reply. *Economic Journal, 104*(426), 1143–1146.

Patinkin, D., & Leith, J. C. (Eds.). (1977). *Keynes*. Macmillan.

Peden, G. C. (1984). The 'Treasury View' on Public Works and Employment in the Interwar Period. *Economic History Review, 37*(2), 167–181.

Peden, G. C. (1988). *Keynes, The Treasury and British Economic Policy*. Palgrave.

Pigou, A. C. (1920). *The Economics of Welfare*. Macmillan.

Pigou, A. C. (1937). Real and money wage rates in relation to unemployment. *Economic Journal, 47*(187), 405–422.
Raffaelli, T. (2003). *Marshall's evolutionary economics*. Routledge.
Raffaelli, T. (2004). Whatever happened to Marshall's industrial economics? *European Journal of the History of Economic Thought, 11*(2), 209–229.
Review Symposium. (2007). *Journal of the History of Economic Thought, 29*(2), 251–261.
Ridolfi, M. (1984). *Alfred Marshall e John M. Keynes: Rottura o continuità? Atti del convegno di studi Perugia, 18–19 giugno 1979*. Maggioli Editore.
Robertson, D. H., Sraffa, P., & Shove, G. F. (1930). Increasing returns and the representative firm. *Economic Journal, 40*(157), 79–116.
Robinson, A. (1977). Keynes and his Cambridge colleagues. In D. Patinkin & J. C. Leith (Eds.), *Keynes, Cambridge and The General Theory* (pp. 25–38). Palgrave Macmillan.
Robinson, A. (1990). Prologue. In R. McWilliams Tullberg (Ed.), *Alfred Marshall in Retrospect*. Edward Elgar.
Robinson, A. (1992). My Apprenticeship as an Economist. In M. Szenberg (Ed.), *Eminent Economists. Their Life Philosophies*. Cambridge University Press.
Robinson, A. (1994). Richard Kahn in the 1930s. *Cambridge Journal of Economics, 18*(1), 7–10.
Robinson, J. V. (1933). *The Economics of Imperfect Competition*. Macmillan.
Robinson, J. V. (1951). *Collected Economic Papers* (Vol. I). Basil Blackwell.
Robinson, J. V. (1978). *Contributions to Modern Economics*. Academic Press.
Rosselli, A. (2005a). The defender of the Marshallian Tradition. Shove and the Correspondence with Kahn, J. Robinson and Sraffa. In M. C. Marcuzzo & A. Rosselli (Eds.), *Economists in Cambridge: A Study through their Correspondence, 1907–1946* (pp. 350–370). Routledge.
Rosselli, A. (2005b). An enduring partnership. The correspondence between Kahn and J. Robinson. In M. C. Marcuzzo & A. Rosselli (Eds.), *Economists in Cambridge: A Study through their Correspondence, 1907–1946* (pp. 257–291). Routledge.
Rymes, T. K. (1989). Keynes's Lectures. 1932–35. In *Notes of a Representative Student*. University of Michigan Press.
Sardoni, C. (2004). The contribution of Gerald Shove to the development of Cambridge Economics. *Review of Political Economy, 16*(3), 361–375.
Sardoni, C. (2017). Gerald Frank Shove (1887–1947). In R. A. Cord (Ed.), *The Palgrave Companion to Cambridge Economics* (pp. 541–554). Springer.
Schultz, H. (1927). Theoretical considerations relating to supply. *Journal of Political Economy, 35*(4), 437–464.
Schumpeter, J. A. (1954). *A History of Economic Analysis*. Oxford University Press.
Shackle, G. L. S. (1951). Twenty years on: a survey of the theory of the multiplier. *Economic Journal, 61*(242), 241–260.

Shackle, G. L. S. (1967). *The Years of High Theory.* Cambridge University Press.
Shove, G. F. (1933). *The Economics of Imperfect Competition* by Joan Robinson [Review]. *Economic Journal, 43*(172), 657–661.
Skidelsky, R. (2003). *John Maynard Keynes: Economist, Philosopher, Statesman.* Penguin Books.
Sloman, P. (2015). Can we conquer unemployment? The Liberal party, public works and the 1931 political crisis. *Historical Research, 88*(239), 161–184.
Sraffa, P. (1925). Sulle relazioni fra costo e quantità prodotta. *Annali di Economia, 2*(1), 277–328.
Sraffa, P. (1926). The laws of returns under competitive conditions. *Economic Journal, 36*(144), 535–550.
Tarshis, L. (1979). The aggregate supply function in Keynes's General Theory. In M. J. Boskin (Ed.), *Essays in Honor of Tibor Scitovsky* (pp. 361–392). New York Academic Press.
Tomlinson, J. (1987). *Employment Policy: The Crucial Years, 1939–1955.* Oxford University Press.
Tonveronachi, M. (1983). *J.M. Keynes: Dall'instabilità ciclica all'equilibrio di sottoccupazione.* La Nuova Italia Scientifica.
Tribe, K. (2000). The Cambridge Economics Tripos 1903–55 and the training of economists. *Manchester School, 68*(2), 222–248.
Warming, J. (1932). International difficulties arising out of the financing of public works during Depression. *Economic Journal, 42*(166), 211–224.
Wright, A. L. L. (1956). The genesis of the multiplier theory. *Oxford Economic Papers, 8*(2), 181–193.

CHAPTER 3

For King's and Country

3.1 Kahn in America

Between 1932 and 1939, having become a fellow of King's College, a place to which he would remain attached for the rest of his life, Kahn took his first steps on the road to a successful academic career. At Cambridge, he lectured on the economics of the short period[1]—the subject of his fellowship Dissertation—and began supervising students and participating in the life of the Faculty of Economics and Politics.[2] Between December 1932 and April 1933, he travelled to the United States and Canada on a Rockefeller Foundation Fellowship reserved for foreign scholars. During this time, he gave lectures and seminars at various universities and had the opportunity to meet prominent American economists.

Kahn's early letters from the United States convey the image of an eager young economist, convinced of the importance of spreading the 'Cambridge gospel' to the American heathens.[3] He would soon be disappointed to find that the heathens, or at least the most prominent among them, were not really interested in what he had to say. This contributed to

[1] Appendix B reconstructs the courses Kahn taught at Cambridge from the 1930s until his retirement in 1972.

[2] Some recollections of this part of Kahn's career can be found in interviews with B. Reddaway and others in Tribe (1997).

[3] On this, see Rosselli (2005, pp. 261–251) and Aslanbeigui and Oakes (2009, pp. 120–136).

P. Paesani, *Richard F. Kahn*, Great Thinkers in Economics,
https://doi.org/10.1007/978-3-032-09123-9_3

the sense of frustration that emerges from his correspondence, along with his dislike of all things American. Kahn's first impression of the United States was disastrous and did not change much during his stay. He did not like the people, their habits and their way of life, especially in the universities. He endorsed neither the research organisation nor the teaching methods, feeling that too much money went on providing professors with secretaries and research assistants and too little on creating an environment that would favour the exchange of ideas (Rosselli, 2005, p. 262).

After a good reception for his paper on 'Public Works and Inflation', presented on 30 December 1932 at the meeting of the American Statistical Association in Cincinnati, the trouble began. Kahn spent January 1933 in Chicago, where he was confronted with the almost complete lack of interest of the two most prominent economic theorists there, Theodore Schulz and Jacob Viner, in Cambridge economics. Viner claimed he barely read *The Economic Journal*, while Schultz prided himself on ignoring it entirely. Kahn realised he could not persuade them of Cambridge's contributions, including theories on imperfect competition, as they believed such ideas were either outdated or already developed at the University of Chicago. In view of this situation, Kahn sought support from graduate students and the business school faculty, hoping to influence the next generation of economists. He strategically promoted Joan Robinson's work on imperfect competition, distributing her articles and book proofs to gain traction (Aslanbeigui & Oakes, 2009, pp. 121–125). Kahn combined this tactic with that of presenting his own ideas, choosing a particularly congenial terrain—the critique of the quantity theory of money.

This was the subject of a lecture given to the Graduate Club of the University of Chicago in January 1933. The lecture notes (ref. RFK/4/17/1–4), written in Kahn's already cramped handwriting, are interesting because they contain early evidence of the arguments behind his hostility to the quantity theory of money and to the possibility of this theory becoming embedded in policy. Kahn does not dispute the validity of the identity between the product of the money supply and the velocity of circulation and the value of transactions in nominal terms ($MV = PT$). He questions the idea that an identity can be used to justify the existence of a unidirectional causal link from the money supply to the price level. His own reading is that the identity determines the amount of money needed to finance a given flow of transactions at a given velocity.[4] Ignoring this fact and applying a mistaken theory to economic policy risks justifying the adoption of measures that are harmful to the economy.

> Quantity theory. Do not deny truth. Truism. So is most economics. Causation significance. This is where I differ. [...] Causal implications all wrong. Quantity of money purely an effect determined by individual decisions. What quantity theory does is to lay bare what determines quantity of money. Depends. But to regard *M* as determining prices and output hopeless line of approach. *M* is quantity demanded. (RFK/4/17/1)

Kahn qualifies this statement by noting that, in some cases, money has an indirect causal role on prices. For example, in a primitive community where the amount of coinage is fixed and no other forms of money exist, an excess of exports over imports will cause an influx of coinage from abroad ('e.g. inflow of silver into China'). In this case money and prices rise simultaneously and it is possible to claim that '*M* causes in a formal sense and not in a mechanistic sense' prices to rise (RFK/4/17/2). Formal causation is the idea that the form, structure or organisation of something determines its behaviour or properties. It explains causation in terms of the patterns, frameworks or principles that shape an outcome. For instance, the structure of a market can formally cause different pricing and production behaviour. Mechanistic causation, on the other hand, refers to a direct, step-by-step and often physical process by which one event or entity causes another. It is typically associated with scientific and empirical explanations, in which a system operates like a machine with identifiable causal links. As he would on many occasions in subsequent years, Kahn insists that the quantity theory of money lacks a clear explanation of the direct causal (or transmission) mechanism whereby changes in the money supply directly cause equivalent changes in the price level.

In more modern societies, where the quantity of money remains somewhat related to the quantity of gold via the Gold Standard, the money supply can still play a causal role in prices, at least in a formal sense. If, for some reason, bankers become convinced of the need to maintain a certain quantity of money in circulation, and they perceive that this quantity must be in some proportion to the quantity of gold reserves, then a change in

[4] Early published evidence of Kahn's criticism of the quantity theory of money as a causal relationship from money to prices, and of his device to express this criticism can be found in Robinson (1933, pp. 23–24).

gold reserves will cause a parallel change in bank money, credit and prices, but only as a reflection of misguided thinking.

> But so long, as bankers, for irrational reasons, desire to see a certain quantity of money in circulation [...], that quantity then is of importance as providing representation of the effects of wrongheaded thinking. (RFK/4/17/2)

If, in order to arouse the interest of the Chicago students, Kahn had chosen to present himself as critic of the quantity theory of money, which was an important part of the economics teaching at that university, in the speech he delivered at the University of Toronto he chose the equally congenial subject of public works and their use against unemployment. The text of this speech provides an early example of Kahn's commitment to promoting the new Keynesian ideas that he himself had helped to clarify with his work on the multiplier.[5]

Kahn began by arguing that there is no structural flaw in developed economic systems that condemns them to remain in a prolonged depression. The remedies are there, and the only obstacle may be the unwillingness or weak leadership on the part of bankers and governments, or fundamental flaws in the ideas that guide them. It is wrong to describe the stagnation that affects many countries in the world, in terms of general overproduction. It is the lack of demand, not the excess supply, that is the problem and if the private sector is not spending enough, the government should intervene. One way to do so is to resort to public works aimed at reviving the construction sector, whose situation is made more difficult by the high level of interest rates on bank loans and corporate bonds. It is wrong to fear such measures because of their short-term impact on public finances and investor confidence. Confidence depends on the actual performance of the economy, and when that performance improves, confidence improves.

On the other hand, it cannot be ignored that when a government acts unilaterally, perhaps with the best of intentions, those who hold liquid assets in the country, fearing the inflationary consequences of these actions, may decide to take their capital abroad, cancelling out the beneficial effects of the government's measures. This is also why it is important for nations to act in concert by adopting expansionary policies at the same time, a

[5] There are two slightly different versions of this speech in Kahn's archive: one handwritten and two typewritten (RFK/4/18).

subject to which Kahn had dedicated part of his 1929 lecture to the Marshall society discussed above.

If this is the way to kick-start the global economy, then the calls for balanced budgets go in exactly the opposite direction and exemplify those fundamental policy errors that prevent recovery from taking place. The same applies to the fear that the national debt will rise as a result of public investment. This fear is misplaced for a number of reasons. When people find jobs, through public works, spending on unemployment benefits decreases. Moreover, once the economic recovery kicks in, the government can begin to reduce public spending, relying on the strength of the multiplier. Emphasising this point, Kahn ended his Toronto speech by reiterating his opposition to the idea of adopting conservative fiscal measures in the face of the crisis, making a prophecy that would tragically come true a few years later.

> Most people, believe it is the duty of governments, at the present time, to reduce expenditure with a corresponding reduction in taxation. As long as that represents the people's belief, as long as governments act accordingly, I can see no hope of recovery until something happens that forces governments to spend money whether that be something catastrophic in the nature of a war or an earthquake (applause). (RFK/4/18/19)

Kahn's choice to present himself as the bearer of new ideas at Chicago and Toronto was the same he made when he travelled to Harvard, in February 1933, where he met Schumpeter and Chamberlin.[6] Schumpeter, who had met him at Cambridge,[7] held Kahn in high esteem, hosted him, helped him secure additional funding and generally advised him on how to navigate the Harvard academic environment.[8] Kahn, on the other hand, seems to have had an ambivalent attitude towards his host. On the one hand, he could not help but acknowledge Schumpeter's generosity; on the other, his letters contain more than one cause for complaint. In particular, Kahn resented Schumpeter's treatment of Keynes and the *Treatise on Money*, having had the opportunity to attend some of his lectures. The relationship with Chamberlin, with whom Kahn had been in contact since his Dissertation (ref. RFK/1/13/19, 22–23), was more strained, as

[6] On this, see Aslanbeigui and Oakes (2009, pp. 125–137).
[7] On this, see McCraw (2007, p. 234).
[8] On this, see Aslanbeigui and Oakes (2011, pp. 390–397).

Chamberlin was about to publish a book on imperfect competition, the same subject as Joan Robinson's forthcoming book.

All in all, Kahn's time at Harvard seems not to have been particularly successful, especially as it ended with a failed attempt to get a paper published in the *Quarterly Journal of Economics.* As Marcuzzo and Paesani (2022, pp. 7–8) reconstruct, Kahn took this paper with him to the United States, having completed a draft few weeks before his departure from England. The article, entitled 'Imperfect Competition and the Marginal Principle', was based on what was to be Chapter VII of Kahn's book on *The Economics of the Short Period*, which he never published. Kahn presented his article in Chicago, Toronto and finally to 'some 100 students and faculty' at Harvard (15–21 February 1933, RFK/13/90/1/131–8).[9]

Kahn's paper begins with the claim that the recent discovery of the new concept of marginal revenue makes it possible to formulate a unified theory of firm behaviour that transcends the traditional dichotomy between perfect competition and monopoly. He pays tribute to Sraffa, citing his 1926 article in the *Economic Journal* as the main inspiration for the new approach to market analysis, and to the early work of Joan Robinson as the first systematic application of this approach. Based on it, comparison between the marginal cost and the marginal revenue curves makes it possible to determine exactly the optimal quantity and price at the point where the two curves meet. This is the marginal principle to which Kahn attached so great an importance for its generality.

> The proposition that the marginal cost of each individual producer is equal to his marginal revenue is fundamental to economic theory. (Kahn, [1933a] 2022, p. 36)

Unlike in perfect competition, where firms are price-takers facing perfectly elastic demand and where price equals marginal revenue, most real-world firms operate in imperfect markets with downward-sloping demand curves. These curves reflect entrepreneurs' expectations about

[9] RFK/2/5 includes two typed copies of the paper on the marginal principle with different annotations. The second copy contains a reference to Kahn's previous presence at Harvard. The deal with Harvard, brokered with Schumpeter's help, was for Kahn to receive $50 for this lecture and another $50 to publish an article in the *Quarterly Journal of Economics*, of which Taussig was editor. The paper was published for the first time in Italian in 1999, in a collection of essays by Kahn translated into Italian and edited by M.C. Marcuzzo for the publishing house Il Mulino, and in English in Marcuzzo and Paesani (2022, pp. 35–50).

competitors' behaviour, shaping marginal revenue and strategic decisions. Through trial and error, firms aim to maximise profits, but they typically settle below maximum efficiency. They reach an equilibrium point where marginal revenue equals marginal cost, and in the long run, where the demand curve is tangent to the average cost curve.

After presenting his article at Harvard, Kahn gave it to Frank W. Taussig for publication in the *Quarterly Journal of Economics.* However, after a rather tense discussion between Taussig and Kahn, the article was not accepted in its original form, as Kahn wrote to Joan Robinson.

> He [Taussig] felt that the thing was quite suitable as a 'talk', which was in fact the primary purpose that it was designed to serve, but it was too "thin" as an article. [...] And then he felt that I might have gone deeper. For instance, instead of just defining marginal revenue, and assuming that the reader knew all about it, I might have gone into the thing and draw some charts. [...] I was given to understand that the whole thing was rather superficial and casual. [...] Taussig expressed himself as doubtful whether the assumption of imperfect competition or that of perfect competition was nearer the facts. [...] It was obvious too that he was under the impression that a great deal of my stuff could only be properly applied to the short period and that he resented my refusal, implicit in my article, to admit this. And he very much resented my abrasive attitude towards the business man. [...] He also very much disliked the impertinent formula on p. 16 [price = marginal cost × elasticity/elasticity minus one ...] He was appalled to imagine that a young man should imagine that he could venture to advise the experienced business man. This cocksure attitude was typical of the Keynesian school, but was particularly deplorable in the young. (RFK/2/5/43–44)

In spite of this damning verdict, Kahn chose to submit his article in its original form rather than tighten it up to meet Taussig's objections and the *Quarterly Journal*'s standards. This led to the inevitable rejection.[10] On this as on other occasions, Kahn chose to 'stick to his guns' and, after trying to persuade the other party, preferred to back down rather than seek a compromise or accommodate the interlocutor's demands. While it is possible that Schumpeter's assurances induced him to do so, Kahn's

[10] On Taussig's economic ideas and his role as editor of the *Quarterly Journal of Economics*, see Schumpeter et al. (1941).

choice seems to be indicative of a self-confidence that, while dented after his stay in Chicago and Harvard, was still fundamentally intact.

Kahn's interest in the American economic situation continued after his return to England, as evidenced by a letter to Meade dated 3 November 1933. In this letter, Kahn expresses his scepticism about Meade and Harrod's idea of writing a letter to *The Times* in support of Roosevelt's New Deal, his doubts about these policies and the economic theories on which they were based (e.g. 'the foolish quantity theory outlook, the fantastic notion of a relationship between the gold value of the dollar and the price level'). On another level, and in agreement with Joan Robinson, Kahn warns Meade of the possibility that the 'pundits' might not sign the letter. Kahn's letter ends with a series of constructive suggestions for overcoming the impasse and with a polite refusal of Meade's invitation to give a lecture at Oxford because of the heavy teaching and other commitments that had accumulated during his trip to America (ref. Meade/2/4).

3.2 The Cautious Young Cambridge Scholar: Ideal Output and Duopoly

On his return from the United States, at the end of April 1933, Kahn plunged back into the Cambridge milieu. His scholarly contributions, during this period, consist of a limited number of articles and short notes, mostly published in the *Economic Journal* and the newly established *Review of Economic Studies.* These articles deal with a variety of theoretical issues generally related to the analysis of industries and markets and the welfare implications of different equilibria; their topics include the financing of public work (Kahn, 1932a), decreasing costs and the notion of elasticity of substitution (Kahn, 1932b, 1933b, 1933c, 1933d, 1935a), ideal output (Kahn, 1935b) and the analysis of duopoly (Kahn, 1937a).

In analysing these subjects, Kahn generally starts from a theoretical concept developed by others,[11] and goes on to examine it in detail, testing its robustness against various hypotheses, and extending it as far as possible. This methodological choice, a mixture of caution, meticulousness and modesty that would characterise his scholarly output for years to come, can be interpreted as reflecting three concurrent motivations. First, Kahn's desire to highlight his best qualities. Others may have been more creative,

[11] In this context, the names of Harrod, Hicks, Allen, Pigou, Shove, Sraffa, Joan and Austin Robinson are particularly relevant.

but Kahn had the gift of precision, logical clarity and a dogged determination to leave no stone unturned. Second, academic honesty (together with the implicit desire to protect himself from the accusation of appropriating others' ideas) in a context where the collegial elaboration of new ideas through daily informal discussion among colleagues, so typical of the Cambridge way of 'doing economics', was beginning to clash with a different approach more oriented towards the recognition of individual contributions. Third, the desire to present his contribution as an incremental innovation rather than a break, and thus to place it within an already established tradition. This approach is particularly evident in the 1935 article on ideal output, where Kahn investigates the welfare impact of external economies and diseconomies and imperfect competition.

> The methods employed are those of Professor Pigou. For the extension of the subject-matter I have drawn largely on the teachings of Mr. Shove (a small portion of which is to be found in his article on "Varying Costs and Marginal Net Products," ECONOMIC JOURNAL, June 1928, pp. 258 ff., though the further elaboration of the matter, deferred for "another occasion" (*ibid.*, p. 265), has never yet been published), and on Mrs. Robinson's chapter on "A World of Monopolies" (*Economics of Imperfect Competition*, Chap. 27), while I have also taken much from Mrs. Robinson's reply to Mr. Fraser, *Review of Economic Studies*, February 1934, pp. 137 ff. (Kahn, 1935b, 1, fn. 2)

After summarising Pigou's thesis on the existence of a limited number of industries characterised by a difference between their private marginal product (PMP) and social marginal product (SMP), and on the advisability of subsidising (taxing) industries where SMP exceeds (falls below) the PMP, with the aim of increasing social welfare, Kahn qualifies and extends this result in two directions.

Unlike Pigou, who regarded the presence of external economies and diseconomies as an exception, Kahn assumes that it is the rule and that it is possible to rank the different industries from those in which external economies are stronger to those in which they are weaker or in which there are external diseconomies. On this hypothesis, he argues that increasing social welfare requires subsidising only those industries with above-average external economies and taxing both industries with below-average external economies and those with diseconomies of scale.

The objective is to reallocate resources in a way that favours (penalises) industries that make a relatively greater (lesser) contribution to social welfare, until a situation is reached where the (positive) difference between SMP and PMP is the same in all industries. From here, Kahn broadens his analysis to include imperfect competition. He focuses on the difference between price and marginal cost as an indicator of market power and the degree of imperfect competition. The originality of Kahn's article primarily lies in its analysis of the shift from perfect to imperfect competition, its adaptation of Pigouvian ideas on taxes and subsidies from correcting externalities to imperfect competition and its implications for welfare.

If the relationship between price P, marginal cost MC (equal to marginal revenue MR) and the price elastic of demand k that defines the firm's equilibrium is $P = MC\ (k/k - 1)$, then the relative mark-up, defined as $(P - MC)/P$, is equal to the reciprocal of the price elasticity of demand $1/k$. This is important when deciding which industries to subsidise or tax. Other things equal, the lower the price elasticity of demand for the goods produced by a given industry, the greater the market power that firms in that industry can exercise by setting a price well above the marginal cost of production, to their advantage and to the detriment of consumers and owners of the factors of production used in that industry. In this context, Kahn argues:

> [I]t is socially desirable to expand those industries in which competition is more imperfect than the industries with which they compete for their factors of production and to contract those in which the opposite condition prevails. The analogy with the type of interference which is called for by the existence of external economies is complete: the degree of imperfection of competition takes the place of the amount of external economies. [...] All industries are to be arranged in descending order of degree of imperfection of competition. Then it is socially desirable to expand those industries which lie above the "average" industry and to contract those which lie below. It is not the absolute degree of imperfection of competition (of "monopoly") but the deviation from the norm which determines the direction and magnitude of the deviation from ideal output. If competition were everywhere equally imperfect there would be no case for interference. (Kahn, 1935b, pp. 21–22)

The intuition behind this result and the gist of Kahn's argument can be illustrated as follows. If the degree of imperfection differs across sectors, what is gained by subsidising the output of less competitive industries exceeds what is lost by taxing the industries where the degree of competitive imperfection is lower. Thus, firms in the subsidised sectors grow in terms of size and output, making initially scarcer goods more abundant. In parallel, firms in the taxed sectors shrink in terms of size and output. Over time, this reallocation should lead to the ideal output.

> The ideal situation of an industry is attained when its size and organisation are exactly such as would prevail if it were subject under conditions of laissez-faire to that degree of imperfection of competition which exists on the average over industry as a whole. While it is desirable in the case of industries in which competition is abnormally imperfect to increase the size of the firm—to raise it closer to the optimum—for industries in which competition is subnormally imperfect, the opposite procedure is called for. Too large an output is here produced by too few firms in the absence of interference, and it is socially desirable to have more firms, each producing on a smaller scale. [...] The reproduction of the conditions of the average degree of imperfection of competition is what is required. (Ibid., p. 29)

Commenting on this result, in one of the first works inspired by Kahn's ideas on ideal output,[12] James Meade observes:

> It may at first appear paradoxical to conclude that there should be *fewer* [in the original] firms in the *more* [in the original] monopolistic industries, since monopoly is naturally considered to exist only when the number of independent sellers is too few. But it must be remembered that this argument is based on the assumption that all factors of production including management are free to move to the industries where they earn most. (Meade, 1937, p. 158)

In imperfectly competitive markets, where there is varying degrees of competition across industries, income distribution favours managers in less competitive sectors. Here, high price-cost margins allow managers to earn above-average returns at the expense of factor owners, who earn less than their marginal productivity. In more competitive sectors, the reverse is true: managers earn less, while factor owners receive relatively higher compensation. Kahn's proposed policy of subsidising less competitive industries and taxing more competitive ones reduces these disparities. It

[12] For a discussion and critique of Kahn's conclusions on ideal output, see Samuelson (1994, pp. 55–58).

narrows the income gap between managers and factor owners by redistributing surplus: rationalisation in subsidised sectors reduces managerial rents and benefits factor owners, while fragmentation in taxed sectors increases managerial pay and decreases returns to factor owners. Overall, this rebalancing promotes greater equity and collective welfare, provided the gains exceed the losses.[13]

Two years after the notes on ideal output, Kahn returned to analyse imperfect competition in the second of his main articles written in the second half of the 1930s. The article on duopoly, a rewriting of Chapter VII of his Dissertation, was written in the context of the recognition of conjectures, beliefs, expectations and uncertainty as important determinants of economic behaviour and as a consequence of the effort to extend the notion of static equilibrium to a multiperiod setup (Giocoli, 2003, p. 175). Kahn's article, in particular, took shape in the context of the debate raised by the idea of modelling the Cournot duopoly by including in the response function of each duopolist the conjecture about the reaction of the other to its actions and imposing a consistency condition on the firms' conjectures, namely that each conjectural variation must coincide with the actual reaction of the rival, on the assumption that the firms have perfect foresight and neglecting the analysis of the movement towards equilibrium (Giocoli, 2005). Once again, true to his cautious approach, Kahn makes it clear:

> The solution that I put forward in this article shows considerable resemblance to various solutions which have been published in the last two or three years by some of that vast host who have gathered in this field. The resemblance is, I think, not quite as close as may superficially appear. [...] A general acknowledgment must here suffice. [I might, however, mention that the characteristic of my solution is asymmetry and that asymmetry has been imported into the theory of duopoly by Professor Pigou (Economics of Stationary States, p. 92), by Dr. von Stackelberg (*Marktform und Gleichgewicht*), by Mr. Coase ("The Problem of Duopoly Reconsidered,"

[13] Thus, Kahn's ideas on ideal output in the presence of imperfect competition became integrated into welfare economics and, as such, were acknowledged in subsequent years for their implications on the allocation of productive factors (Bain, 1941), the treatment of decreasing cost industries (Ruggles, 1949), the application of the distinction between rational and irrational preferences (Johnson, 1960), Kahn's debt to Stackleberg (Thomas, 1963). More recently, see Medema (2017) for a discussion of Kahn (1935b) in the context of the early literature on external economies.

Review of Economic Studies, February 1935), and doubtless by others.] (Kahn, 1937a, p. 1)

Kahn criticises traditional duopoly models (Cournot and Bertrand) as unrealistic, instead introducing two more plausible scenarios—the Bertrandesque and the Cournotesque—to describe how firms behave in response to price changes. In the Bertrandesque case, a firm initially keeps its price unchanged after a competitor lowers theirs, but may adjust it later. In the Cournotesque case, a firm keeps its sales unchanged, but may revise its output later. Kahn applies these concepts to both perfect and imperfect markets, considering the Bertrandesque case to be the most realistic. He demonstrates that any price change by one firm results in a reactive adjustment by the other, which often makes both firms worse off. Consequently, both firms tend to maintain their initial positions, only changing them if external conditions shift.

In this argument, which Kahn had anticipated in his Dissertation (Kahn, [1929] 1989, p. 103), we find one of the origins of the idea of the kinked demand curve (Heller, 1998; Rothschild, 2010). This consists in the idea a firm's demand curve has a 'kink' at the current market price. This kink arises from competitors' asymmetric reactions to price changes: they are unlikely to follow price increases, resulting in highly elastic demand above the kink, but they are likely to match price decreases, resulting in relatively inelastic demand below the kink. Consequently, the marginal revenue curve features a discontinuity, meaning that prices remain stable even amid fluctuations in marginal cost. This model effectively explains price stability in oligopolistic industries.

Faced with these conditions, Kahn argues that the only possible equilibrium is an asymmetric one. One of the two firms (the price leader) sets the optimal price and the other firm (the price follower) sets a slightly lower price at which it produces its optimal output. In a perfect market, the demand curve on the basis of which the price leader sets the optimal price is equal to the market demand curve minus the marginal cost curve of the follower along which its output is placed, which coincides with its supply function. In an imperfect market, the demand curve on which the price leader sets the optimal price is estimated taking into account the price set by the competitor. Asymmetric equilibrium is the only condition in which neither the price leader nor the price follower has an incentive to move; the latter because it is maximising profits, the former because it knows that any movement would put it in a worse position. The process by which firms reach equilibrium is one of trial and error, based on knowledge rather than belief about the rival's reaction, in other words, a return to a kind of 'objective' equilibrium, independent of the firms' expectations and conjectures (Giocoli, 2005, p. 613).

As part of this process, each firm, faced with the actions of the other, experiences small fluctuations in price or quantity, moving in the direction in which it sees its profits increasing and away from the opposite direction. The end result of this process is that prices settle and occasionally fluctuate in a range between the monopoly price and the perfectly competitive price. Higher than the perfectly competitive price, because the limited number of firms allows them to exercise market power, and lower than the monopoly price, because if there were a monopoly price, one of the two would want to lower it and the other would follow. It is often an accident of history that determines who is the leader and who is the follower, especially if the two companies are very similar. If they are not, one will find the role of leader more comfortable and the other that of follower. Only if the two companies are very similar will both find it more comfortable to be followers.

As Aslanbeigui and Oakes (2011) argue, by 1937 Kahn's duopoly analysis, while still valid, was no longer particularly innovative. Others were working on the same topic with results not too dissimilar to Kahn's, and in some cases more advanced. In this context, Kahn gradually lost interest in imperfect competition, which had been a major focus of his research for almost ten years. The main reason to explain this choice, indirectly confirmed by Kahn ([1929] 1989, p. xviii), is related to the possibility that Kahn felt he had reached the limit of what could be said about imperfect competition, remaining within the confines of a Marshallian–Pigouvian approach, renewed in the light of Shove's ideas and Sraffa's critique. Remaining faithful to profit maximisation and the marginal principle (Pigou), to a realistic description of competition capable of taking into account the heterogeneity of firms and the interdependence of supply and demand factors at the industry level (Shove), and to the idea of imperfect competition as a general case (Sraffa), Kahn could not really do much more.

Moreover, by the end of the 1930s, the Marshallian approach to the study of price-setting processes under imperfect competition, based on the application of the marginal principle, the equilibrium of supply and demand and time analysis, was being challenged in particular by a group of Oxford economists who produced important and innovative results.

> An even more fundamental challenge to the Marshallian supply and demand framework emerged even earlier, in the 1930s at Oxford. With the publication of the first three volumes of the *Oxford Economic Papers* in 1938, 1939 and 1940, economists were treated to two very tantalizing but highly upsetting conclusions: (1) investment decisions were not responsive to changes in interest rates, and (2) businessmen did not set prices in accordance with marginalist principles. Each of these conclusions arose from the research undertaken by a group of Oxford economists under the tutelage of Sir Hubert Henderson and each conclusion implied that the Marshallian framework was inconsistent with the empirical evidence. (Lee, 1981, p. 339)

The passing of the baton from Cambridge to Oxford as centres for reflection on price-setting under imperfect competition is linked to the intellectual and human story of Kalecki. He arrived in London in April 1936, having left Poland and the Warsaw Institute of Research on Business Cycles and Prices. Kalecki then moved to Cambridge, where he was warmly welcomed by the community of young economists associated with Keynes. In particular, Joan Robinson and Kahn made great efforts to help him find a job. Ultimately, these efforts resulted in Kalecki being employed as a statistician on a research project investigating various aspects of the British economy.

Launched in 1938, the project was based at the University of Cambridge and funded by the National Institute of Economic and Social Research. Keynes was chairman and Austin Robinson was secretary, while Richard Kahn, Joan Robinson, Piero Sraffa and David Champernowne were participants. After the first year there had been a rift between Keynes and Kahn, on the one hand, and Kalecki, on the other, with Kahn ending up taking somewhat more orthodox positions than Kalecki, on the issue of the relationship between mark-ups and market power of companies and on other aspects of Kalecki's statistical analysis of sales proceeds, prime costs, output and other aspects of a set of relevant industries.[14] In 1939, after a year with the Cambridge Research Scheme, Kalecki presented his findings but faced strong criticism from Keynes, Kahn and, to a lesser extent, Robinson. Disheartened, Kalecki resigned and moved to the University of Oxford, still funded by the National Institute of Economic and Social Research.[15]

[14] On this, see Kahn's letters to Kalecki (ref. RFK/5/1/159–162 and RFK/5/1/146–147).

[15] On Kalecki in Cambridge and Kahn's role, see Toporowski (2013, pp. 92–151) and Marcuzzo (2020a).

3.3 Cambridge Fault-Lines: Keynes, Kahn and the 1937 'Pigou Affair'

If caution and an emphasis on incremental innovation rather than rupture characterises the scientific production of Richard Kahn in the mid-1930s, the same is only partly true of his role in defending and enhancing Keynesian ideas within the Faculty of Economics at Cambridge and beyond. In this context, the first signs of division emerged between the Keynesian camp, led by Keynes, Kahn and Joan Robinson, and those who, starting with Pigou and Robertson, remained unconvinced by Keynes's new ideas and tended to view them critically.

Sanfilippo (2005) reconstructs how Keynes and Robertson's relationship evolved from close and friendly collaboration in the 1920s to a period of escalating communication issues, ultimately culminating in their estrangement in the 1930s. After a fruitful collaboration on monetary issues in the 1920s, the debate over the definition of savings and the *Treatise on Money* marked the beginning of their differences, aggravated by Robertson's exclusion from the Cambridge Circus. The publication of the *General Theory* exacerbated this disagreement, leading to a critical review by Robertson (Robertson, 1936) where his differences with Keynes focused on three key points: the method (sequential for Robertson, static for Keynes), the theory of the interest rate (loanable funds vs. liquidity preference) and the nature of economic stagnation (cyclical for Robertson, structural for Keynes).[16]

Something similar occurred between Robertson, Kahn and the other Keynesians. Naldi (2005a) stresses how Robertson was initially willing to exchange views with his younger colleagues. His correspondence with Kahn in the late 1920s and 1930s, in particular, begins with a few letters containing brief comments and corrections to the text of the Fellowship Dissertation, which were set aside when Kahn decided not to publish it. These were followed by Kahn's comments on two of Robertson's papers, in which Kahn expressed doubts about the concepts of saving and the treatment of wages introduced by Robertson. In general, these exchanges give the impression of a potentially fruitful collaboration between the two, hampered by an increasing difficulty in communication.

[16] On Robertson's intellectual biography, see Fletcher (2007).

A similar pattern characterises the interaction between Pigou and the new generation of Cambridge economists (Naldi, 2005b).[17] He first met Joan Robinson, who had studied economics at Cambridge between 1922 and 1925.[18] Then he met Sraffa and Kahn almost simultaneously in 1927, when Kahn was beginning his economics studies and Sraffa had been hired as a lecturer. It was only later that Pigou came into contact with Kaldor. His relationship with Kahn was quite direct. Their correspondence in the early 1930s dealt with theoretical issues related to perfect competition and monopoly, with particular attention to the paradoxes of these market structures and with Pigou's *Theory of Unemployment* (Knight, 2014; Di Matteo, 2016).

Keynes's choice to cite Pigou's *Theory of Unemployment* as an example of the classical theory that the *General Theory* intended to criticise and redefine as a particular case and Pigou's harsh review of Keynes's book (Pigou, 1936), combined with Robertson's criticisms, certainly contributed to creating a rift within the post-Marshallian guild of Cambridge (Aslanbeigui & Oakes, 2007a), already shaken by Sraffa's criticism and the differences of opinion that had emerged around the cost controversy. It was in this tense context that the 'Pigou affair' broke out in the second half of 1937 (Aslanbeigui & Oakes, 2007b).

In the summer of that year, while Keynes was recovering from a heart attack, Pigou submitted an article to the *Economic Journal* entitled 'Real and Money Wage Rates in Relation to Unemployment' (Pigou, 1937). The article, written on the occasion of Pigou's appointment as President of the Royal Economic Society and approved by Robertson, dealt with the relationship between wages and unemployment. In this article, Pigou reaffirmed the validity of the idea that the fall in nominal wages would lead to the reabsorption of unemployment through the consequent fall in real wages (and rise in profits), rather than through the fall in the transaction demand for money and the interest rate—as envisaged, albeit with considerable doubts, by Keynes—which would have had (at most) transitory

[17] On Pigou's intellectual biography, see Aslanbeigui and Oakes (2009). On the relationship between Keynes and Pigou, see also Bridel and Ingrao (2005).

[18] In subsequent years, Pigou maintained an attitude of cautious appreciation towards Joan Robinson, although he did not spare criticism of her work and of her way of teaching. He vigorously defended Marshall's legacy against her objections and urged her to apply the models presented in *The Economics of Imperfect Competition* to reality. After 1933, Pigou became increasingly critical of Robinson's Keynesian proselytising, particularly its impact on the teaching of economics at Cambridge.

benefits. In this way, Pigou's article, although never explicitly mentioning Keynes and the *General Theory*, 'as he thought it was unfair to bother a sick man',[19] appeared to be a critique of one of the main conclusions of that book.

Pigou may have thought that this was Keynes's argument, but Keynes certainly had many doubts about the possibility that a fall in nominal wages could lead to full employment, even taking into account the possible effects on interest rates, both because the effects were uncertain and because of the well-known doubts about the positive influence of lower interest rates on investment in periods of depression. By not mentioning Keynes, Pigou was able to attribute and criticise a thesis that Keynes himself would not have fully endorsed.

In his immediate and strongly critical reaction to Pigou's article, Keynes enrolled Austin Robinson, Kahn and Kaldor in devising a strategy to neutralise Pigou. Kahn was not particularly pleased with Kaldor's arrival on the scene or Keynes's decision to entrust him rather than Kahn or one of the other Cambridge Keynesians with the task of defending the Keynesian point of view. In a letter to Keynes dated 22 October 1937 (Moggridge, 1973, p. 260), Kahn, although he had not read Kaldor's article in response to Pigou, was sure that its publication would 'darken council. After all we could all of us write replies to Pigou if you wanted them and I do not see why Kaldor should thus be favoured'.[20]

Pigou's response, and the part played by Robertson and Champernowne in assisting him to refine his initial ideas, the picture that emerges is one of an environment rife with conflict and growing misunderstandings.[21] Focusing on Kahn's role in the 'Pigou affair', Aslanbeigui and Oakes (2007b, p. 23) describe him as 'adjutant, tactician, informer and informant, agent provocateur, and keeper of the flame', revolutionary and secret agent, 'the most committed and ruthless proponent of Keynes's attack on Pigou'.

Beyond the choice of terms, this characterisation should be considered carefully. On the one hand, it captures an aspect of Kahn's modus operandi, the tendency to operate behind the scenes, combining caution and

[19] Letter from Kahn to Keynes, 18 October 1937, in Moggridge (1973, p. 259).

[20] Perhaps, out of respect for Pigou, Keynes did not want a young Cambridge economist to criticise him too severely, and so he chose Kaldor, who was approaching Keynesian economics but had not studied at Cambridge.

[21] The reference to the 'Pigou affair' in Keynes's *Collected Writings* is in Moggridge (1973, pp. 235–268). On the role of Champernowne in the 'Pigou affair', see also Boianovsky (2020).

firmness in defending his ideas, which has been documented by others more or less sympathetic to Kahn (e.g. Pasinetti, 1987; Goodhart, 1997) and which this research documents in more detail below. On the other hand, however, Aslanbeigui and Oakes leave in the background the scientific reasons which, beyond partisanship, may have motivated Kahn's criticism of Pigou. Highlighting these reasons is important in order to fully understand Kahn's attitude.

In the part of Pigou's article that Kahn was most critical of (sections 7 and 8), Pigou attributed a direct causal role to the quantity of money and the velocity of circulation in the determination of income (Pigou, 1937, p. 26), an idea that Kahn had already radically rejected in 1933. Moreover, Kahn's belief in the existence of a direct proportional relationship between nominal wages and prices cast doubt on the possibility that a fall in monetary wages would be followed by a fall in real wages. Finally, Kahn, following Keynes, was very sceptical about the merits of reviving the idea that the main way to return to full employment was through wage and price deflation.

Given these elements, it is not surprising that Kahn encouraged Keynes to demolish Pigou's argument by pointing out its fundamental inconsistency. A destructive intention, no doubt, but limited to the macroeconomic sphere. Moreover, the fact that both Shove, who considered Pigou's article the worst he had ever read (Moggridge, 1973, p. 258), and Sraffa, who agreed with Shove's verdict (ibid., p. 259) and even went so far as to criticise Pigou's treatment of interest rates, must have confirmed Kahn in his strongly negative judgement. These considerations aside, the fact remains that by the end of the 1930s the common theoretical reference to Marshall's *Principles* and Pigou's work as the basis of Cambridge economics had given way to a split between different approaches. This fragmentation, and the personal tensions it created, inevitably affected the life of the Faculty of Economics, the organisation of courses and examinations and the selection of new members of the teaching staff, even if not to the point of jeopardising Cambridge's primacy as the centre of economic knowledge production in Britain.[22]

[22] On the role of the University of Cambridge, and in particular Marshall and Pigou, in the formation of economics, see Tribe (2022, pp. 75–172) and Aslanbeigui and Oakes (2023), which contain further relevant information on the fractured state of the Cambridge Faculty of Economics at the end of the 1930s.

3.4 The Keynesian Partisan: Kahn Versus Haberler Around the Years of the *General Theory*

In the second half of the 1930s, apart from the works on ideal output and duopoly, Kahn published relatively little. His record for this period is limited to seven reviews of varying length, six of which were devoted to books and one to the Report of the Committee of Investigation for England on Complaints made by the Central Milk Distributive Committee and the Parliamentary Committee of the Co-operative Congress as to the Operation of the Milk Marketing Scheme.[23] The topics of the books reviewed were at the intersection of his research interests and the most pressing economic problems of the day: instability, unemployment and policies to restore economic progress. The review of *Prosperity and Depression* by Gottfried Haberler is particularly important in this respect and in the context of Kahn's efforts in defence of the new Keynesian ideas.

Haberler's book, published in 1937, was the result of a five-year research project on business cycles, launched by the League of Nations in 1933 with funding from the Rockefeller Foundation. As part of this project, in his capacity as a member of the Economic and Financial Organisation of the League of Nations, Haberler analysed existing theories of the business cycle, followed by a 'synthetic exposition' of the causes and nature of fluctuations.[24] In the first part of the book, Haberler critically reviewed classical and neoclassical theories of business cycles, providing a broad perspective on the subject and focusing on monetary (credit and interest rates) and non-monetary influences (e.g. technological change and external shocks). He devoted little space to the theories of the Scandinavian economists, and even less to the *General Theory*, which appeared in February 1936, by which time the bulk of the first part of Haberler's volume had already been written. In the second part of the book, Haberler integrated insights from the different theories and discussed the policy

[23] To this one should add the English translation of K. Wicksell, *Geldzins und Guterpreise* (*Interest and Prices: A Study of the Causes Regulating the Value of Money*. London: Macmillan). On this translation and its great value, see Moggridge (1994, pp. 107–108). For an early review of Wicksell's translated book, see Howey (1936).

[24] Laidler (1999) contextualises and discusses Haberler's book together with Kahn's review, which Laidler describes as 'rather weak'. On Haberler's project, see Boianovsky and Trautwein (2006), with reference to Keynes's criticism of Haberler's project and of the exchange between Haberler and Kahn. On the friction between Haberler and the Cambridge Keynesians, see also Samuelson (1996).

implications of his analysis, suggesting possible fiscal and monetary interventions to manage and stabilise economic fluctuations. On 20 August 1934, Haberler sent a draft of the first part of his report to various economists who were experts on the subject of economic fluctuations, including Kahn, with the request that they 'look through it and send me any comments or criticism that it may suggest to you'.[25]

This led to a correspondence between Kahn and Haberler that developed at a time when the main ideas behind the *General Theory* had already taken shape but were not yet widely known outside Cambridge. What was known about Keynes's views on economic fluctuations came mainly from the *Treatise on Money*, with its peculiar definitions of income, saving and investment. It was known, and Haberler knew it, that Keynes was about to publish a new book, the contents of which however were unknown. These factors contributed to the difficulties of communication between Haberler and Kahn and made the confrontation between the two essentially sterile (ref. RFK/13/57/98–111).

In particular, Kahn and Haberler clashed on three points: the definition of savings and investment, the possibility of a divergence between the two quantities and the role of changes in investment in determining the economic cycle. On the one hand, Kahn—already reasoning with the theoretical framework of *General Theory* in mind—insisted on the equality of investment and savings, with the former determining the latter, and on the impossibility of constructing a theory of the business cycle based on the divergence between the two. On the other hand, Haberler, also citing Robertson's authority,[26] rejected the idea that saving and investment were the same thing and pointed out that his study devoted a great deal of space to investment-based theories of the business cycle (Spiethoff, Hansen, Hayek, Cassel).

[25] Letter from Haberler to Kahn, 20 August 1934 (RFK/13/57/111). In 1932, Haberler had spent a month at King's College at Keynes's invitation, also attending the Political Economy Club seminar, as he himself testified (Source: https://mises.org/austrian-economics-newsletter/between-mises-and-keynes-interview-gottfried-von-haberler). It was probably on this occasion that he met Kahn.

[26] Haberler refers to Robertson (1934). As Boianovsky and Presley (2009) observe, Robertson's article introduced the diagrammatic representation of the market for loanable funds and brought out for the first time in the literature the connection between the twin notions of a natural rate of interest and a natural (or normal) rate of unemployment, which equilibrate the market for goods (i.e. saving = investment) and the market for labour, respectively.

In light of this exchange, it must have seemed natural for Keynes, in his role as editor, to ask Kahn to review Haberler's book for the *Economic Journal* when it was published. This gave Kahn the opportunity to reiterate his criticisms, taking them out of the sphere of private correspondence and into the public domain, and to highlight the limitations and contradictions of Haberler's analysis with respect to the new ideas set out in the *General Theory* (Kahn, 1937b).

The first problem Kahn finds with Haberler's analysis is his definition of savings, which includes both sums of money used to repay loans and hoarded in the form of cash or idle deposits. Both actions, according to Haberler, are manifestations of an excess of saving over investment. However, Kahn notes that when loans are repaid with savings, bank deposits are reduced by an equal amount. There is no possibility here of 'savings going to waste'. Nor can there be any 'excess of investment over savings'. Moreover, Kahn observes that 'the theory of the business cycle proposed by Haberler is based on adherence to the quantity theory of money and the idea that MV is another aspect of total demand for goods'.

According to this approach, which Kahn rejects, any discrepancy between saving and investment has as its counterpart variations in bank credit and hence in the money supply. Thus, investment can exceed savings if there is a parallel creation of bank credit and an increase in the money supply and in prices. Similarly, an excess of saving over investment leads to the repayment of loans and a reduction in the money supply and in prices. Against this view, Kahn observes:

> There is no room in this analysis for the simple-minded view that when bricklayers are thrown out of work because the demand for houses is becoming saturated, they buy fewer shirts, thus causing unemployment among shirtmakers. (Kahn, 1937b, p. 672)

Nor is there room for the concept of liquidity preference, nor for the idea that a change in the active circulation of money can be the consequence, rather than the cause, of a change in prices and output. Haberler's claim that autonomous changes in investment and saving directly impact the quantity of money leads him to claim that the rate of interest is determined by the intersection of the demand for savings with a newly defined supply curve of loanable funds, which is the sum of savings, new creations of money and dishoarding. Here, Kahn warns, there is a danger of confusing flows with stocks. It is total money supply and total hoarding that one must look at to determine the monetary rate, not changes in them. Haberler's theory, Kahn concludes, does not provide clear policy indications whether we need to save less or save more in order to get out of a depression. Equally open remains the question of the usefulness of public works, which Haberler seems to cautiously recommend, as long as a way is found to finance them without creating inflation or destabilising the confidence of investors.

In the face of this damning criticism, the *Economic Journal* offered Haberler the possibility of a rejoinder (Haberler, 1938).[27] Haberler took it, accusing Kahn of ignoring that for those who believe in the quantity theory of money, a rise in hoarding implies a decrease in the velocity of circulation and in someone's nominal income, not necessarily a change in the quantity of money. Furthermore, Kahn's definitions of saving and investment indeed imply the identity between the two quantities, as in the *General Theory*.

Haberler, however, adopts Robertson's definition, according to which saving is the bridge between income paid intermittently and expenditure paid continuously, and in this case S can differ from I. When investment exceeds saving, the gap is filled by loans that increase MV, and this increase can well be called inflationary, without giving the word a negative meaning, as Kahn seems to believe. Haberler then dismisses all of Kahn's other criticisms, accusing him of distorting his ideas and of making an improper use of quotations. Kahn (1938a) replied briefly, admitting that he had made a mistake on the question of the definitions of hoarding, but reiterating:

> The problem of trade cycle theory is to discover *what governs* PT, and on this problem Professor Haberler's concepts of hoarding and inflation can, by his own admission, throw no light whatsoever. They might possibly be useful in the realm of descriptive economics, but they can play no part in economic theory. (Kahn, 1938a, pp. 334–355)

[27] In a letter, dated 5 March 1938 (RFK/13/57/290), Keynes informed Kahn of the fact that Haberler 'would prefer that your reply, if any, should appear in a subsequent number of the Journal. 'One reason' he says 'for this is that he hopes to come to England next June, and may have the chance of discussing the matter with you personally'. In the end, Haberler's request was not granted and both his rejoinder and Kahn's reply appeared in the May 1938 issue of the Journal.

On the question of how the interest rate is determined, Kahn reiterates his concern about the risk of confusing flows and stocks,[28] and takes Haberler to task for failing to answer the question of whether it is more efficient to finance a public investment programme with money or with securities. As his reply to Haberler shows, Kahn based his dialectical strategy on drawing the opponent into his own camp by translating the opponent's arguments into his own definitions in order to show the inconsistency between the two. In this strategy, the desire to win outweighs the desire to compromise, together with the determination and ability to develop clever arguments and counter-arguments to advance one's ideas against the opposition. With the outbreak of the Second World War in September 1939, as Kahn left Cambridge to work as a temporary civil servant, these qualities would be put to the test in a very different context.

3.5 Kahn's Early Wartime Activities (1939–1941): Board of Trade and Point Rationing

After the stagnation of the 1920s, aggravated by the deflationary effects of the return to the Gold Standard in 1925, which were the background to the Dissertation and the article on the multiplier, the British economy had experienced a significant recovery in the second half of the 1930s (also thanks to the devaluation of sterling and the consequent reduction in interest rates after the crisis of 1931).[29] By 1939, when the war broke out, the economy was growing at 4.6%, with unemployment at around 9% and inflation at around 2.5%. The demands of war and mobilisation necessitated the introduction of a wide range of direct controls on all economic activity.[30]

During the Second World War Britain was transformed from a predominantly market economy to a planned economy, as it moved from a peacetime base to one of full-scale war mobilisation. Expenditure on war-related activities rose from around 7% of net national expenditure in 1938 to 53% in 1941, peaking at 55% in 1943, when it totalled £4512 million.

[28] Kahn expressed similar concerns in his 1938 review of the book *Studies in the Theory of Economic Expansion* by the Swedish economist, E. Lundberg (Kahn, 1938b).

[29] On the British economy between the wars, see Eichengreen (2004) and Howlett (2004), among many others. The primary reference on the role of low interest rates is Howson (1975).

[30] For a recent brief introduction to the British war economy, see Edgerton (2020) and the reference cited therein. On the British war economy, the standard reference is Hancock and Gowing (1975). On this, see also Howlett (1993).

This increase was achieved by a substantial curtailment of private investment and a sharp reduction in the growth of consumption of non-war goods and services. The latter had stood at £4090 million in 1938, but despite the rapid wartime growth of the economy it had reached only £4526 million by 1943 (Howlett, 2004).

In this context, the British government recruited a number of economists and statisticians to the War Cabinet Offices and the various government departments.[31] Their task was to collect data and information on available human and material resources, advise on their efficient use and contribute to the organisation of wartime production and distribution activities. This played a crucial role in the professionalisation of economists in Britain, connected to the government's growing economic influence and, in subsequent years, the gradual adoption of Keynesian ideas in economic policymaking.[32] Apart from Keynes and H. Henderson, who had already worked as government advisers during the First World War, the first Cambridge economist to be involved in these activities was Dennis Robertson in September, followed by Austin Robinson in December.[33] Kahn followed in the winter of 1939, serving as temporary administrator in various government agencies until mid-1946. In this context, as Harcourt recalls,

> [Kahn] took to life in Whitehall like a duck to water, firing off volleys of minutes and memoranda in all directions defending his ideas in committees,

[31] In particular, I refer to the Central Economic Intelligence Service, which operated from 1939 to 1940, before being replaced by the Economic Section and the Central Statistical Office in January 1941. On this, see Booth (1986), Cairncross (1995), Howlett (1993).

[32] On the professionalisation of economists in Britain the reference studies are Winch (1969), Middleton (1998), Peden (1991), Tribe (2022). On the expansion of the British government, see Middleton (1996). On the wartime activities of British economists, see also Cairncross (1995). An important early source on this is Chester (1951), which brings together essays arising from the involvement of economists in British public administration during the Second World War. Kahn was to be one of the contributors to the book, based on a provisional table of contents held in the Robbins Archives at the LSE (ROBBINS/3/2/10). In the end, Kahn did not participate in the project.

[33] Some LSE economists were also recruited immediately on the outbreak of the war in the Treasury and elsewhere. Austin Robinson's official papers, held in the archives at Churchill College, Cambridge, provide a complete picture of his many wartime activities. On Austin Robinson's wartime activities, see Cairncross (1993, pp. 78–96).

conspiring with fellow economists in other departments to promote his policies. (Harcourt, 1991, p. 22)[34]

During the war years Kahn honed his skills in analysing concrete economic problems, finding technically acceptable solutions and devising strategies to put them into practice. He worked closely with Austin Robinson and other Cambridge economists (e.g. Ruth Cohen, Brian Reddaway), cementing friendships and alliances that would be very important in subsequent years. Joan Robinson, Piero Sraffa and Nicholas Kaldor were, for different reasons, either related to their personal condition (Joan Robinson was a married woman with two children) or related to the fact of not being British citizens (Kaldor), kept away from direct involvement. At the same time, Kahn acquired important contacts in the British establishment, a fact that helped to increase his influence in post-war policy-making in Britain.

The relationship between Kahn and Keynes remained strong even if it changed with respect to the 1930s. As the correspondence between them shows, each relied on the other for information, advice and support. Keynes turned to Kahn for comment on the memoranda he was writing or whenever he needed detailed information on the issues on which Kahn was working. Meanwhile, he watched over Kahn's progress, supporting him and helping him navigate the complex machinery of government. For his part, Kahn readily provided Keynes with the information he needed, commented on his drafts and acted as a liaison between Keynes and the various offices in which Kahn worked. Occasionally, Kahn sought Keynes's help in advancing his own and his superiors' ideas, both in the Treasury, where Kahn had no direct access, and with public opinion. At the same time, Keynes and Kahn moved in different spheres. On the one hand, Keynes was constantly at the centre of the most pressing problems, working closely with the Treasury. On the other hand, Kahn was kept away from major financial issues and high politics at the Board of Trade and in the other administrations in which he worked.

In 1939, when Kahn started to work for the Board of Trade, Keynes had just written two articles for *The Times* where, based on approximate estimates of British GDP and the various components of aggregate demand, he set out his ideas on how to finance Britain's war by deferred

[34] On Kahn's entry into the civil service, see also Moggridge (1992, p. 627) and Skidelsky (2003, p. 584).

consumption, compulsory saving and increased taxation with the aim to prevent inflation. The ideas published in these two articles, and then in the subsequent pamphlet entitled *How to Pay for the War*, represent one of the first applications of the Keynesian model to a situation of full employment and excess demand pressure.[35]

As Spahn (2019) recalls, in *How to Pay for the War*, Keynes introduced a concept similar to a full-employment multiplier, which converted excess demand into rising wages and prices. Rather than increasing interest rates or taxes, in order to prevent an inflationary scenario, Keynes proposed a mandatory savings plan, extended to the entire working class. From a political and reformist perspective he viewed this as beneficial, as workers would accumulate wealth post-war. However, he failed to persuade the Labour Party and trade unions. Following the 1941 budget, the government adopted some of Keynes's ideas set out in *How to Pay for the War*, particularly with regard to using the new national income estimates to calculate the inflationary gap and determine the appropriate taxation to offset it.[36] In this context, as Hancock and Gowing (1975, pp. 325–343) illustrate, rationing and price controls were secondary.

Keynes's commitment to promoting *How to Pay for the War* did not prevent him from dealing with other matters, in particular exchange controls (Moggridge, 1978, p. 156). At the outbreak of war, non-residents were allowed to convert their sterling holdings into foreign currencies free of exchange controls, and British exporters to invoice their sales in sterling. Non-residents could thus exchange their pounds with other non-residents, who could in turn use those pounds to buy British products. In this way it became possible to take foreign currency out of Britain without it being offset by export earnings denominated in a foreign currency. Initial attempts to close the gap had been unsuccessful, and the matter had become quite pressing. Kahn's first letter to Keynes after starting his new job at the Board of Trade refers to this problem, as well as offering some interesting insights into Kahn's assessment of his new role.

[35] On this, see Moggridge (1978, pp. 40–155, 1992, pp. 627–649) and Skidelsky (2003, pp. 587–598).

[36] In *How to Pay for the War*, Keynes defined the inflationary gap as the excess of aggregate expenditure or purchasing power over the value of output at full employment, a condition arising when wartime mobilisation fixes real output while incomes and spending continue to rise. The concept underpinned his advocacy of compulsory saving and taxation to withdraw surplus demand. On *How to Pay for the War*, Spahn (2019). For an early discussion of the notion of inflationary gap, see Salant (1942), Friedman (1942) and Turvey (1948).

> There is, I think, no danger of my being treated as a mere advisory economist. I am reading my way into the machine and shall, I expect, get thoroughly absorbed. There is, I suppose, a danger of becoming a mere cog (my rank, does not, in itself, entitle me to much initiative). But I think that is a danger on the right side. I am prepared to suffer some boredom and degradation if it will save me from the feeling of frustration that a merely advisory position must almost inevitably engender. [...] Meanwhile ideas for a comprehensive memorandum on the whole situation buzz round in my head but it is my intention to let them buzz until I am well embedded in the machine. In addition to taking my place in the I[ndustrial] S[upplies] Dept. (the main function of which is to ballyrag with the Ministry of Supply on behalf of exporters) I am to be directly available to anybody in the B. of T. (principally I imagine the permanent head) for advice on economic questions.[37]

In mid-March 1940 Kahn's first attempt to mobilise Keynes's support in the interest of the Board of Trade took place. Since the Treasury had instructed the Ministry of Supply not to pay for its purchases with 'blocked' (i.e. inconvertible) sterling, for fear of triggering the liquidation of pre-existing sterling balances, this meant that Britain was paying for its imports with convertible sterling, which was then sold in New York, widening the discount with respect to the official rate of $4.03. Kahn saw this as 'absolute madness' and turned to Keynes, suggesting to publicly 'explode the myth' that a heavy discount on sterling in New York was 'anything but beneficial' to Britain (by discouraging sterling holders from selling abroad).[38]

> It will be disastrous if public feeling in the matter will deter the Treasury from going any further in the direction of ensuring that export proceeds come home to us.[39]

[37] Letter from Kahn to Keynes, 17 December 1939 (ref. JMK/L/K/122–123).

[38] As Kanago and McCormick (2013) recall, between 25 August 1939 and 7 June 1940, there was a free market for British pounds in New York. German success at the outset of the Second World War caused the value of free sterling to fall relative to the official exchange rate, making it more difficult and expensive for Britain to finance the war. Eventually, Britain chose to abolish convertibility, even at the expense of tarnishing the reputation of London's financial markets.

[39] Letter from Kahn to Keynes, 14 March 1940 (Keynes papers, JMK/W/3/56).

While acknowledging the validity of Kahn's argument, Keynes proposed a different strategy, at the same time imparting to Kahn a lesson in political communication and strategy.

> The more I think about it and the more extensive the information which reaches me, the more convinced I am that you are right. [...] All the same, I am much perplexed as to how best attack it controversially. The matter is frightfully technical, of a kind which you cannot possibly expect the public to understand or form a judgement on. [...] Also, in matters of detail, it is extraordinarily difficult to be quite sure of one's facts. And I have learned to be cautious about public controversy unless I feel that I know the other fellow's case beforehand better than he knows it himself. [...] I believe that the best chance would be to take it up with the Bank of England [...] as a result of the deferred pay proposal, I am personally reconciled with the Governor [...] with the result that, after an interval of some years, I have been again given free entry to the Bank.[40]

The issue of exchange controls resurfaced in May 1940 when Keynes sent Kahn a draft memorandum on exchange policy and asked for comments (in Moggridge, 1978, pp. 163–171), 'particularly on questions of fact' relating to the introduction of blocked sterling accounts, about which Keynes was ambivalent and therefore prepared to propose a gradual approach.[41] Keynes's proposal consisted of a series of restrictions on the sale of sterling assets and sterling loans to foreigners, and the introduction of various controls on imports, but did not go so far as to forbid the sale of sterling in all cases. Echoing concerns he had expressed in March, Kahn replied:

> I think this is very good. My main criticism is that you omit to deal with the effect of your proposals on the free rate. It is a question of weighing up the effects of "blocking" foreign [?] securities (but not balances) against the effect of comprehensive "dollar invoicing". I imagine it is quite clear that the net effect would be a heavy fall in the New York value of sterling.[42]

In the end, in June 1940, the government further tightened exchange controls in response to the fall of France, introducing more stringent

[40] Letter from Keynes to Kahn, 16 March 1940 (JMK/W/3/57–58).
[41] Letter from Keynes to Kahn, 22 May 1940 (JMK/W/3/231).
[42] Letter from Kahn to Keynes, 24 May 1940 (ref. JMK/W/3/246).

restrictions on the use of sterling by non-residents and additional requirements for obtaining licences for foreign currency transactions. Thus, after an initial phase of low awareness, especially on the part of public opinion between September 1939 and April 1940 (the Phoney War), the climate began to change, before the abrupt awakening of the disasters of May and June, especially Dunkirk. Between May and June 1940, Kahn continued to discuss exchange controls with Keynes, only to find out:

> The Treasury (in the shape of an official of the Establishment Dep[artmen]t—not Sir Horace Wilson agreed to my affiliation here only on condition that I have nothing to do with currency questions! W.B. let this out after a very large number of drinks at the Strand. [...] He also said that if I thought I could be more good ballyragging at the Treasury then I am at B/T I could regard myself as sacked. His kind offer is worth bearing in mind. What is more immediate, however, is whether I can really be useful at B/T if I have to keep off "currency questions".[43]

In the end, Kahn chose to remain at the Board of Trade and focus on how 'to prevent the demands of the War from encroaching on the availability of labour and productive capacity for production of goods for export' (Marcuzzo, 2020b, p. 14). This meant radical and innovative measures, which Kahn helped to formulate and argue for, to reduce the consumption of consumer goods in order to free up resources for munitions and services. These measures would inevitably lead to a temporary increase in unemployment and the risk of both demoralising and antagonising public opinion. It was probably with this risk in mind that Keynes had expressed his doubts about direct controls on consumption, prompting Kahn's reply on 30 May 1940.

> If you dislike the creation of unemployment why do you favour your plan, the virtue of which is to be found precisely in its having that effect.[44]

[43] Letter from Kahn to Keynes, 30 May 1940 (ref. JMK/W/3/302). I have been unable to trace exactly who W. B. is. I would like to thank Susan Howson for suggesting that W. B. stands for William Brian Reddaway.

[44] Letter from Kahn to Keynes, 30 May 1940 (ref. JMK/A/40/9). On Keynes's differences with Labour, see Toye (1999), in addition to the general reference mentioned above. On the Labour Party and Keynes from a more general perspective, see Toye (2007). On rationing, controls and consumption in Britain from 1939 to 1955, see Zweiniger-Bargielowska (2002).

Keynes and Kahn did not share the same views on the question of direct controls on private consumption and on rationing in general. While Keynes's plan in *How to Pay for the War* was to temporarily deprive consumers of some of their purchasing power through the mechanism of deferred savings, with the intention, among other things, of avoiding inflation and the need to introduce direct controls, Kahn, in line with the views of the Labour Party, clearly favoured direct controls (also in the name of fairness) and the consequent reduction of consumption through rationing. Keynes replied two days later, making it clear that his main concern was not with the merits of the measure but with the risks of too hasty an implementation.

> Dear Alexander, I am not at all against your policy of creating unemployment. Far from it. It is a question of pace; and also I was talking in the context of creating unemployment to the detriment of exports, which is rather different thing from home consumption. I am all for your policy, so far as the home consumer is concerned. Indeed, I think it might be worth a letter to the press, to emphasise the importance of individual initiative in this direction. A man, who is at the disposal of the Labour Exchange ought, in present circumstances, to get a job pretty soon.[45]

Reassured by having Keynes on his side, Kahn agreed that a letter to the press would have been most helpful, not only for its impact on public opinion, but also and more importantly as a means of strengthening the Board of Trade's hand against the opposition of the Ministry of Labour.

> Our object is quite definitely to ginger up the Min[istr]y of Labour, for whom nobody (from Sir W.B. [William Beveridge] downward) has a good word. Whatever the extent may turn out to be to which we are permitted to go the officials of B/T would have preferred a more ruthless policy, designed primarily to provoke such a scandal that the Min[istr]y of Labour would have been obliged to reform their ways. Far too many officials (in the Min of Supply and of Aircraft production as well as in the Min of Labour) have a vested interest in labour shortages as an excuse for incompetence and inertia. What you say about the difficulty of dragging men from one job to another exactly expresses our views.[46]

[45] Letter from Keynes to Kahn, 2 June 1940 (ref. RFK/13/57/462). Alexander is the name Keynes and his wife, Lydia Lopokova, sometimes used to refer to Kahn.

[46] Letter from Kahn to Keynes, 3 June 1940, (ref. JMK/A/40/13–14).

And so the letter to *The Times* took shape,[47] marking a further step towards the extension of wartime controls on the allocation of human and physical resources. In this letter Keynes observed that the Ministry of Supply had the machinery to absorb the unemployed, but not to 'draw men out of their present unessential jobs' into more useful ones. For this to be possible, the Ministry of Labour should collect data on the immediately available able-bodied workers, including those who had lost their jobs as a result of rationing, and transmit them promptly to the Ministry of Supply. This was a matter of interdepartmental cooperation in which 'a high number of available unemployed would be the test of success for the Ministry of Labour and a low number a test of success for the Ministry of Supply'. At the same time, the public should not fear the rise in unemployment that would result from the curtailment of superfluous consumption, but should realise that this was what Britain needed at the moment (ref. JMK/A/40/15–16).

Between the summer of 1940 and the spring of 1941, Keynes's main task was to help draw up the new budget for 1941 with Kingsley Wood, Chancellor of the Exchequer (Moggridge, 1978, pp. 195–354; Skidelsky, 2003, pp. 605–609). As Moggridge (1978, p. 325) recalls, 'The 1941 budget, as well as being notable for its use of a national accounting analytical framework, also saw the publication with the Budget of a White Paper providing the relevant figures for a pre-war year and the previous year'.[48] This analytical framework, one of the first contributions to the development of modern national accounting, was developed by James Meade, who had also joined the Economic Section in June 1940 (and remained in it until 1947), and Richard Stone (Meade & Stone, 1941). The Treasury did not immediately favour Meade and Stone's ideas, so Kahn, whose friendship with Meade dated back to the 1930s, sought Keynes's help.

> My dear Maynard, quite clearly your proper course is to see Meade, letting him know that I have dropped you a hint and that he should be perfectly

[47] The text of the letter, published on 5 May 1940 and devoted to the subject of manpower control, and Beveridge's subsequent reactions to others can be found in Moggridge (1978, pp. 184–187). Keynes, briefed by Kahn, returned to the question of manpower in his exchanges with Professor Lindemann, Churchill's adviser, in the summer of 1940 (Moggridge, 1978, pp. 187–190).

[48] On the penetration of Keynesian ideas within the British Treasury in the 1940s and 1950s, see, in addition to the sources mentioned above, Peden (1990) and, more recently and in greater detail, with particular reference to the war years, Peden (2000, pp. 303–359).

open with you. I can only pass on what he has told me. [...] The only actual instance of positive obstructionism which I can call to mind takes the form of an instruction (subsequently, I believe, withdrawn as a result of protest) by the Treasury to the Registrar-General to withdraw certain information. What is more serious is that rightly or wrongly (I believe rightly but that is neither here nor there) Meade believes that his activities enjoy Treasury opposition.[49]

Apart from this letter, communication between Keynes and Kahn between the end of 1940 and the first part of 1941 does not appear to have been particularly intense.[50] By the spring of 1941, Kahn's correspondence with Austin Robinson[51] provides further evidence of Kahn's awareness of interdepartmental conflict as a potential obstacle to the successful implementation of the measures recommended by the Board of Trade, as there had been with Meade and the Treasury in the previous months. On 20 May 1941, for example, Kahn replied to a note from Robinson on the retail margins applied by small grocers, expressing his concern about the conflict between the Board of Trade and the Ministry of Food over this issue.

I wish I could feel more convinced in my own mind that in action the Ministry of Food are quite so ready to be ruthless as your Note suggests. I have seen something of them in connection with the Schedule of Reserved Occupation, during discussions about which we could never get them to recognise the possibility of a reduction in the numbers, say, of separate milk roundsmen serving a particular street or the number of bakers, even in the evacuation area.[52]

[49] Letter from Kahn to Keynes, 4 November 1940, (Moggridge, 1978, pp. 327–328).
[50] On this, see Marcuzzo (2005, Table 1.1).
[51] Austin Robinson worked in the Economic Section until 1942. He then moved to the Ministry of Production, where he was an economic adviser and Head of the Programmes Division. Following the war, he joined the Board of Trade. See Cairncross (1993, pp. 78–109).
[52] Letter from Kahn to Austin Robinson, 20 May 1941, (ref. ROBN/1/5/3). The reserved (or scheduled) occupation scheme was a complicated one, exempting certain key skilled workers from conscription and covering five million men in a wide range of occupations. These included railway and dock workers, miners, farmers, agricultural workers, teachers and doctors.

Once again, the problem was the conflict between the Board of Trade's conviction of the need to extend the rationing and the reluctance of other departments to adopt measures that would prove unpopular and difficult to implement. However, in the summer of 1941, after some hesitation, the idea was finally adopted. As Kahn recalled in later years:

> The Board of Trade had to decide the character of the rationing scheme. The Head of the Department was in favour of a strict allocation to each person of the various articles of clothing; for example, each year one pair of shoes, two shirts and so on, and perhaps a new suit every three years. I pointed out that different people had different requirements. I learnt about the German 'points' system as a result of reading in the Economic Journal the reviews of German press statements and articles by Hans Singer (April 1941, pp. 30–31). I strongly advocated such a point system. [...] We called in to our help my Cambridge colleague, Brian Reddaway. He worked out a system of points aimed at securing a pattern of consumption which did match the pattern of available productive capacity. (Marcuzzo, 2020b, pp. 14–15)

The point systems, one of the various methods of implementing rationing, was meant to be applied to groups of commodities in which it was desirable and practicable to allow freedom of choice to consumers in purchasing individual items within the group while restricting total consumption of the whole group. In Britain this meant clothes and certain kinds of canned foods, with a specified number of coupons corresponding to each item within the corresponding group. During the first full year of clothing rationing, which ended on 31 May 1942, each person was allotted 66 coupons, which could be used in any quantity at any time, except that 20 coupons were reserved for use after 1 January 1942.[53]

Kahn's arguments in favour of the points system and how to ensure its successful implementation are set out in a letter to Austin Robinson dated 2 July 1941.

> Obviously one of the virtuous of a point system is that the forces of laissez-faire can come back into their own—production can be allowed to follow demand and we shall do what we can to enable it to do so. We are not,

[53] On the rationing and the points system, as one of the outstanding examples of the influence of economists on policymaking in wartime Britain, see Booth (1985), which includes interesting reference to Kahn.

however, so foolish as to suppose that all we now have to do is to sit back, fold our hands and watch the machine work. For a considerable time, and to some extent indefinitely, there are bound to be some things which consumers will want to buy against coupons and fail.[54]

The primary objective of the points system, and the sign of its success, according to Kahn, was the absence of acute shortages within certain categories of goods. To achieve this, in the case of clothing and footwear, the first items to be rationed, it was essential to ensure, at least initially, that there were large stocks of cheap, durable clothing in the main categories, leaving silk and linen items, which were made available in very small quantities, in the background. While rationing food may seem more difficult than rationing clothing, Kahn noted that the scope for substituting one food item for another was greater than in the case of clothing.

If a man needs a pair of socks, it is not much consolation to tell him that while there are no socks there are plenty of shirts. But if I want a tin of pineapple and you tell me that I must have some ground rice instead, you are not really outraging me. (Ibid.)

This is also why Kahn felt it was important to use all the flexibility that the organisation of textile production allowed. The other factor on which the success of the scheme depended was the possibility of the flow of raw materials largely following the flow of vouchers. Here again, the spontaneous operation of market forces should have been complemented by careful monitoring of registered traders and producers in the retail and wholesale sectors, and by the discretionary use of final licences and direct control of the nature of the product and its origin.

When all is said and done, what is the alternative to our system? I take it that there is no need to discuss the advantages of some kind of rationing over nothing at all. [...] Group rationing is essentially a matter of curtailing the purchasing power directed to a particular range of commodities. In a war it is not possible that every individual taste will be catered for. But the curtailment of purchasing power does make it very much easier to ensure that everybody obtains a reasonable amount of something. (Ibid.)

[54] Letter from Kahn to Austin Robinson, 2 July 1941, (ref. ROBN/1/10/3).

By the end of 1941, the problem of ensuring the flexible and efficient use of scarce resources concerned both the availability of civilian consumer goods and the shipping space in which to transport them as Britain was largely dependent on foreign imports of food and raw materials. In this context, Kahn turned his attention to international trade issues, again seeking the advice of Keynes and at the same time offering to act as a liaison officer between him and the Board of Trade, acting in the interests of all the parties.

> My dear Maynard, it would be rather convenient if you were able to say whether you think there will be a chance of discussing the post-war trade problems in the course of the weekend of the 30th August. [...] There appears to be some sort of idea that I may be able to act as a kind of bridge, and if that does not seem to you a good idea, I may as well know it. I have taken a considerable part in discussions here and it seems to me to be very possible that the people here have a somewhat exaggerated idea of your own views, while, for your own part, you may very probably credit the Board of Trade with more extreme views that the facts justify. [...] I believe that when analysed it will be found that the only fundamental issue is what degree of American co-operation would be necessary in order to justify a return to what might be called a liberal economic system.[55]

The disagreement reflected the particular friction between some elements of the Board of Trade, which favoured a liberal approach to international trade, and the more cautious stance held by Keynes and the British Treasury.[56] These differences came to a head in Britain after the US Congress enacted the Lend-Lease Act in March 1941.[57] This measure, as is well known, allowed the United States to provide military aid to its allies, including Britain, without direct payment, in exchange for strategic bases or the transfer of other resources. There were differing views within the British government on this, and more generally on economic

[55] Letter from Kahn to Keynes, 19 August 1941, (Keynes papers, JMK/L/K/135).

[56] On this, see Eichengreen (1984, pp. 367–368 in particular).

[57] On Keynes's role in relation to the Lend-Lease Act and more generally on the problems of external war financing and on the disagreements within the British government, the main references are Moggridge (1979), Pressnell (1986, pp. 28–65), Peden (2000, pp. 330–337), Skidelsky (2003, pp. 613–639). It is interesting to note that in Moggridge (1979) the only references to Kahn are to Middle Eastern issues, which we will discuss in the next section. This is another sign of the partial distance that had opened up between Keynes and Kahn during the war years.

cooperation between Britain and the United States. Some, including Henry Clay, economic adviser to the Board of Trade, saw Lend-Lease as a vital lifeline to support the war effort and the commitment to liberalise trade after the war as a way of improving and strengthening relations with the United States. Others, including Hubert Henderson at the Treasury,[58] were more concerned about the long-term implications for British sovereignty and dependence on the United States.

These debates within the British government, in particular around Article VII of the UK-US mutual aid agreement, reflected the tension between securing immediate military support and maintaining Britain's economic and financial autonomy. In this context, the Treasury was immediately aware of the financial abyss opening up with the war and the pressure from the United States for a free trade policy, while the United Kingdom sought to protect itself by maintaining the sterling area. These tensions are confirmed by a second letter in which Kahn, reporting to Keynes on his attendance at a meeting chaired by A.E. Overton, Permanent Secretary of the Board of Trade from 1941 to 1945, commented:

> Overton realises that the post war position is too horrible to contemplate and he reluctantly accepts the view, so far as I can judge (though he would probably prefer not to be pressed on this point), that very probably the things you advocate (deficit?) will be necessary. But he still wants to feel that there is a chance of avoiding them.[59]

To which Keynes replied:

> I am not seriously worried by the rather unexpected apparent strength of the laissez-faire school. For I have not the slightest doubt that we shall start in practice de facto with a control and that what actually happens will be evolved from that in a direction which is extremely unlikely to be laissez-faire. [...] My aim will be [...] to aim at putting the practical problem in its true light and then concentrate on technical means of solution without bothering myself about ideals, which, whether right or wrong, are in the actual circumstances pure fantasy. [...] For one thing, you will be able to tell me what views people in the Board of Trade suppose me to hold.[60]

[58] On this, see Eichengreen (1984, p. 369, fn. 17).
[59] Letter from Kahn to Keynes, 19 August 1941, (JMK/L/K/136–137).
[60] Letter from Keynes to Kahn, 21 August 1941, (JMK/L/K/138–139).

Keynes's pragmatic approach to the regulation of international trade reflected two motivations: on the one hand, the urgent problem of financing the war and containing Britain's foreign debt; on the other, the typically Keynesian idea that each country should retain a margin of autonomy in defining its own economic policy, and that it was the external dimension that had to adapt to the needs of domestic economic policy. In 1941, at the height of the Second World War, the first consideration was clearly much more urgent than the second, which would instead be central to Keynes's contribution to the creation of the Bretton Woods system, and would also have a considerable influence on Kahn's own ideas about international trade and exchange rates.

3.6 Cairo and the Middle East Supply Centre: 1941–1943

In the summer of 1941, Kahn's involvement with Keynes in discussing the future of international trade was linked to the problem of organising shipping and coordinating supplies, particularly of raw materials, between the different areas of the Empire and Britain. This activity was carried out under the general direction of Oliver Lyttelton, who had become President of the Board of Trade in October 1940 and a member of the Food Policy Committee in 1941.[61]

When Oliver Lyttelton was appointed Minister of State for the Middle East in June 1941, with a seat in the War Cabinet and responsibility for the Middle East Supply Centre, he moved to Cairo and suggested to Kahn that he should follow him.

> My dear Maynard, Oliver, before leaving, sent me a message that he would probably want me. You were not available for consultation and I gave way without hesitation to my natural instincts and said I should love it. [...] He has in mind some kind of economic-statistical dep[artmen]t to deal with civil requirements. It seems most unsuitable for me but I want to go. I feel rather bad about you and the College, I have done practically nothing for either for a long time but I suppose having me in the background is some slight safeguard.[62]

[61] See Appendix C for a brief biography of Oliver Lyttelton. See also Moggridge (1979, p. 316, fn. 1) and Commons and Lords Hansard website https://api.parliament.uk/historic-hansard/people/mr-oliver-lyttelton/index.html

[62] Letter from Kahn to Keynes, 21 August 1941, (JMK/L/K/140–141).

To which Keynes replied:

> I am much interested and not greatly surprised at Oliver's demand. [...] I expect you will greatly enjoy the trip, but whether the gain to the Middle East will be equal to the loss of the Board of Trade I am not sure. [...] Assuming you do go out, I should have thought you ought to have a more substantial job than the particular thing which Oliver proposes to invent for you. I hope I shall not be indiscreet if I have a word about this in the Treasury.[63]

And so Kahn followed Lyttelton to Cairo, where he remained from October 1941 to January 1943, first as Economic Adviser and then, from January 1942, as Deputy Director-General of the Middle East Supply Centre. As Lloyd (1956) recounts in his research on the Middle East Supply Centre, Kahn chaired the Middle East Agricultural Conference in Cairo on 14 and 15 May 1942. He also contributed to the formulation of a plan to sell official gold stocks at market prices in the Middle East and India to reduce inflationary pressures. Kahn is cited as the main inspiration for this idea based on three arguments: (1) the influx of gold and its subsequent conversion into coins and jewellery would absorb some of the purchasing power that would otherwise have been directed towards the purchase of commodities; (2) the proceeds from the sale of gold stocks would help cover some of the war expenses, thus reducing the need to issue paper money; and (3) the probable fall in the price of gold due to the increase in sales would encourage a fall in other prices.[64]

When Kahn arrived in Egypt the region was facing severe economic difficulties. Initially, during 1939–1941, wartime disruptions and slow troop deployment kept inflation low. However, from spring 1941 the situation worsened, due to increased military activity, rising local military expenditures and import cuts. A poor harvest in summer 1941 led to food shortages, aggravated by hoarding and a lack of goods, fuelling inflation and urban discontent. Britain feared political instability as the war approached, but local governments, with full treasuries and little war interest, resisted tax increases, bond issuance or price controls. Instead, military spending was funded by increasing Egyptian sterling balances in

[63] Letter from Keynes to Kahn, 24 August 1941, (JMK/L/K/142–143).

[64] Kahn's ideas appear to be a development of the proposals contained in a 1941 memorandum written by Col. R.A. Harari and entitled 'A Gold Policy for M.E.' (Moggridge, 1979, p. 318, fn. 3).

London, which escalated as prices and wages rose. A shortage of shipping further led to a balance of payments surplus with the sterling area, also financed through rising sterling balances (Moggridge, 1979, pp. 316–317).

Against this background, the correspondence between Keynes and Kahn between October 1941 and March 1942 shows the same pattern as in Kahn's early years at the Board of Trade. Each man relied on the other as a privileged source of information and clarification. Subjects raised included the question of the Egyptian balances in London,[65] the development and improvement of railways in the Middle East and Persia,[66] the Harari Memorandum of 1942 which outlined British policy towards Saudi Arabia and the implication of the Lend-Lease act for the Middle East,[67] the financing of war expenditure in the Middle East and its potential inflationary consequences.[68]

In Cairo, Kahn's main operative task was to organise and coordinate the shipping of agricultural and mineral products between Britain, the Middle East and the other areas of the Empire. Kahn undertook this task with some trepidation about the relevance of his work.

> My dear Maynard, I am just off to Syria, to keep an eye on our wheat campaign (we are conducting a bear operation against the bulls)—my only genuine preoccupation (and I cannot pretend that it has taken up much of my time) since I arrived here. […] It is very hard to tell how useful I am going to be on the basis of two months' experience. […] Unfortunately the Minister has little time for economic questions and there are already some vested interests in the field.[69]

[65] In a letter dated 31 October 1941, Keynes (Moggridge, 1979, pp. 317–318) drew Kahn's attention to the problem of Egypt's growing positive balances in the London clearing system and asked him to inform Lyttelton of the problem and of the need to stop treating the Egyptians 'as impoverished relations entitled to call on their rich uncle for anything that costs anything'. In reply to this letter, on 15 December 1941, Kahn sent Keynes a series of proposals for reducing the pressure of demand for raw materials in Egypt, based on a memorandum from the Chief Economic Adviser for the Middle East, Colonel R.A. Harari (see the previous note above). The issue remains on the table, even if London is reluctant to part with its gold reserves. On the second memorandum, Harari and the end of the affair, see Moggridge (1979, pp. 320–323).

[66] Letter from Keynes to Kahn, 31 October 1941, (JMK/L/K/147–156).

[67] Letter from Kahn to Keynes, 10 January 1942, (JMK/L/K/170) and Keynes to Kahn, 12 January 1942, (JMK/L/K/163–167).

[68] Letter from Kahn to Keynes, 30 March 1942 (JMK/L/K/174).

[69] Letter from Kahn to Keynes, 17 December 1941, (JMK/L/K/161).

One of the main tasks of the Middle East Supply Centre was to match the surpluses and deficits that emerged in the different regions. An official report on the issue of export surpluses had been prepared by the Secretariat of the War Cabinet's Ministerial Sub-Committee on Export Subsidies in November 1940.[70] Reading Kahn's recollections of how he dealt with the problem of the barley surplus in Iraq, or with an exceptional rice crop in Egypt and the food needs of the workers in the rubber plantations in Ceylon (Marcuzzo, 2020b, pp. 16–18), gives an idea of the complexity of these tasks. It was also during this period that Kahn developed a lasting interest in commodities and the possibility of stabilising their prices through a system of buffer stocks, an idea originally proposed by Keynes in his plans for the post-war monetary and financial system, and first announced to Kahn in the spring of 1942.

> We spend more and more time on post-war questions. So far as external affairs are concerned, I think we have really made some progress. My currency schemes, which you saw in an early version, have gone through a vast number of drafts without, in truth substantial change. [...] [L]ast week they were considered at a special meeting of the War Cabinet, which gave them a general blessing. Now it is a question of capturing American sympathy. [...] I have also prepared a general scheme for the international control of commodities with buffer stocks and price stabilisation. At present this is at an earlier stage of pilgrimage through Whitehall, but seems to be going fairly well.[71]

Kahn replied to this letter, confirming his new appointment as economic advisor to the Minister of State, de facto second in command of the Middle East Supply Centre, but with limited ability to intervene in monetary and financial matters because of opposition from the Treasury, which disliked any interference from the decentralised authorities.

> So far as I can see most financial questions are dealt with, very properly, direct between the Treasury and the territories, the telegrams merely being repeated for information to the Minister of State. On the currency difficulties of Saudi Arabia and Persia, I have regarded my role as confined to that of ensuring that shipping space is not employed merely to assist the solution

[70] A copy of this report is available in Robinson's Official Papers (ref. ROBN/1/3/1).

[71] Letter from Keynes to Kahn, 11 May 1942, (JMK/L/K/184–188). The documents to which Keynes refers in this letter can be found in Moggridge (1980, pp. 105–134).

of currency problems (thus completely reversing the role which was mine in the earlier part of the war).[72]

Despite his promise not to interfere, Kahn continued to take an interest in financial matters during the second half of his tenure in Egypt. This is evidenced, for example, by a letter from Keynes dated 19 June 1942 on the financial situation in Palestine.[73] To this official letter, Keynes added a private one informing Kahn of the Treasury's permission to deal with financial matters and of the arrival of Sir R. Hopkins as Permanent Secretary of the Treasury and head of the Civil Service, replacing Horace Wilson. Despite these reassurances, by mid-August 1942, Kahn had decided that his experience in the Middle East was drawing to an end.

> My dear Maynard, I am ashamed to have to tell you that I am writing to [Sir Arnold] Overton by this bag to enquire whether there is any chance of returning to the Board of Trade. It has been clear that I enjoy the confidence of neither Rucker nor Johnson (the Director General of MESC) and that I have ceased to be allowed any responsibility. The fact is that they are too good to need me except as a Stooge. […] My title as economic Adviser has been a joke. […] I imagine the Board of Trade are pretty well "suited". Have you any alternative suggestion? […] I realise that my wares have suffered from a year's depreciation.[74]

To this Keynes replied, in his usual comforting and optimistic mood:

> I expect you have done all that is possible for you to do there, and I am strongly of your opinion that it would be a good idea to come home, where you are very badly wanted. Overton agrees with this and tells me that a telegram has gone out from the Cabinet offices asking for your return, not for the Board of Trade but for the Ministry of Production, where Oliver

[72] Letter from Kahn to Keynes, 29 May 1942, (JMK/L/K/188–190). In 1941–1942, both Saudi Arabia and Persia faced severe currency difficulties as a result of the global economic disruptions. Saudi Arabia struggled with the depreciation of the riyal, foreign exchange shortages and the challenges of maintaining its currency's value amid declining pilgrimage revenues and disrupted trade. Persia faced similar challenges, compounded by the Allied occupation, rampant inflation and external control over its economy.

[73] Letter from Kahn to Keynes, 19 June 1942, (JMK/L/K/196–197).

[74] Letter from Kahn to Keynes, 16 August 1942, (JMK/L/K/202).

would like to have you and where there is an enormous amount of work to be done of the very first importance.[75]

Reassured about his short-term prospects and aware that he could not leave his position at a moment's notice, Kahn decided to wait.[76] In the autumn of 1942, he first devoted his attention to the operations of the Caisse Centrale in Syria, a financial institution set up by the Free French government under General de Gaulle to manage the finances and economic affairs in the French-controlled territories in the Middle East, particularly Syria and Lebanon, during the Second World War.[77] He then travelled to Teheran and Baghdad, dealing with the provision of wheat and barley. By the end of October, the outbreak of inflation in both countries prompted the Minister of State to press Kahn very strongly to stay on as his Economic adviser without, however, convincing him.[78]

3.7 Back to London: Supply and Production and the 1944 White Paper

On his return to England in January 1943, Kahn spent a year in the Ministry of Supply, using the expertise he had gained in the Middle East to work on the post-war situation of raw materials. There he worked under Oliver Franks,[79] whose expertise in raw materials, planning and pricing was recognised.[80] According to Kahn's own recollections:

> Keynes took an interest in my work at the Ministry of Supply. He was worried that the Ministry under wartime arrangements were selling raw materials to industry through their Controllers at prices unduly low compared with prospective post-War prices. This involved a rather unnecessary and wasteful loss of Exchequer revenue. It brought him into touch with Oliver Franks, the Head of my Department, with useful results. Here, too, I was

[75] Letter from Keynes to Kahn, 28 August 1942, (JMK/L/K/203–205).

[76] Letter from Kahn to Keynes, 14 September 1942, (JMK/L/K/209–212).

[77] Letter from Kahn to Keynes, 15 September 1942, (Keynes papers JMK/L/K/213–214).

[78] Letter from Kahn to Keynes, 28 October 1942, (Keynes papers JMK/L/K/226–228).

[79] See Appendix C for a brief biography of Oliver Franks.

[80] On Franks's expertise on commodities and direct controls, see the text of the three lectures that he delivered at the London School of Economics in 1947 (Franks, 1947). On his experience in the United States, see the Truman Library website https://www.trumanlibrary.gov/library/oral-histories/frankso. Kahn and Franks met again in an official capacity during the work of the Radcliffe Committee in 1958–1959.

> influenced by Keynes's advocacy of buffer stocks. It was a subject which fascinated me, and after my return to Cambridge I wrote a number of papers on the subject. (Marcuzzo, 2020b, pp. 18–19)

An example of this activity is a memorandum on the post-war tin position that Kahn sent to Keynes on 12 April 1944 (ref. JMK/L/K/280–285). Another example is the exchange of correspondence and documents, dated to February–May 1943, between Keynes, Kahn and Martin Eccles, then Director-General of the Iron and Steel Control.[81] In addition to his other tasks at the Ministry of Supply, where he remained until June 1944, Kahn was marginally involved in the final stages of the drafting of the White Paper on Employment Policy, one of the key documents in the establishment of the Keynesian doctrine in economic policymaking.

As Booth (1987, pp. 175–195), Peden (1988, pp. 44–49) and Tomlinson (1987, pp. 45–105) discuss, albeit with different nuances, the White Paper was a compromise document between the Keynesianism of the Economic Section, where James Meade worked; the Treasury's concerns about the impact of a full employment policy on the national debt, the UK balance of payments and investor confidence; and the fears of sections of the British government not to be overtaken by William Beveridge's plan in satisfying the demand for reform emanating from British society.[82]

Proof of this is offered by a letter from Kahn to J.P.R. Maud,[83] who had sent him a revised draft of the White Paper, giving advice on how to redraft the conclusions and 'improve the flavour of the document as a whole'.

[81] Letter from Keynes to Eccles, 25 March 1943 (JMK/L/K/258).

[82] These three papers are part of an intense debate among British economic historians, facilitated by the opening of the official archives 30 years after the events in question, about the actual occurrence of the Keynesian revolution in early post-war British policymaking. Limiting ourselves to the first contributions, Tomlinson (1981), on the one hand, questions the idea of a 'Keynesian revolution' in British economic policy, arguing that it overstates the influence of economic theory. He suggests that the emphasis on policymakers' theoretical commitments, while consistent with socialist views on ideology, leads to a flawed analysis of economic constraints. On the other hand, Booth (e.g. 1983) argues that Keynesian ideas gradually penetrated policymaking between the late 1930s and the 1940s until they were fully accepted in 1947, and that there were no significant differences of opinion between Keynes and the Keynesians working in government. In between these two positions are those of Peden, Howson, Rollings and Winch, among others. For a general assessment of the debate, see Peden (2003). On Keynes's views on the White Paper, see also Clarke (1996, pp. 28–29).

[83] See Appendix C for a brief biography of John Primatt Redcliffe-Maud (see also Jisk Archive Hub website https://archiveshub.jisc.ac.uk/search/archives/e5427a97-0b11-3876-a10a-f7e5c6ea107a)

> Particularly salutary would be the suggestion that the Government is anxious to invite discussion and pooling of ideas. Its attitude—particularly with regard to Beveridge—hitherto adopted, of "Keep off the Grass!" will take some living down; but I think that your conclusion would definitely help. The necessity for the living-down process arises inevitably from the poverty of the Government's contribution to thought; and I am sure that the right course is to acknowledge this with a good grace. The other feature of your conclusion which would, I think be helpful, is the touch of eloquence and the suggestion that the Government is really sincere, and not merely dealing with an issue into which it has unhappily been forced. (RFK/6/1/19–20)

This letter is interesting for what it reveals about Kahn's awareness of two of the main problems affecting the government's employment strategy: the rivalry with Beveridge, regarded by many as the true champion of reform and full employment in Britain, against the scepticism of many in Whitehall,[84] and the reluctant attitude of important sections of the government, and in particular of the Treasury, to accept the idea that the government should take responsibility for 'maintaining a high and stable level of employment'. The letter to Maud is followed by a three-page typed note containing Kahn's comments on the conclusions of the draft White Paper. Kahn's doubts about the compromising nature of the document are evident in this note (RFK/6/1/23–25).

> My feeling is that the public will respond by alleging that the Government is paying not much more than lip-service to the doctrines which it proclaims. It may well be argued that the departments concerned with interests which

[84]On Beveridge, see Harris (1998). The fact that Kahn's name does not appear in this detailed biography of Beveridge is a first indication of the distance between the two. Nor does any evidence of a direct significant relationship with Beveridge emerge from Kahn's Papers. The situation is different for Joan Robinson and Kaldor, who worked on Beveridge's book *Full Employment in a Free Society* (1944) and gave it a Keynesian connotation, as Marcuzzo (2010) has reconstructed by comparing the ideas of Beveridge and Keynes on the subject of full employment and the welfare state. On the other hand, the main objectives of the Beveridge Plan, such as securing full employment over time and fighting the five evils of want, disease, ignorance, squalor and idleness, were the basis for the actions of the Attlee government, with which Kahn worked between 1945 and 1946. On the basis of this and other evidence that we present in the following chapters, it seems plausible to conclude that, while Kahn's insistence on the need to maintain full employment over time, continuously and with all the instruments available to the government brings him closer to the original approach of Beveridge, Kahn's attention to the macroeconomic rather than the social aspects of full employment, and a certain conservatism in his vision, distance him from this approach.

> are anti-pathetic to the main doctrines have succeeded in adequately protecting themselves against a compliance which—from their point of view—might be excessive. (RFK/6/1/23)

Kahn found the paragraph on the timing of public investment 'quite astonishingly apologetic', with more than a hint of defeatism where it mentioned the need to support sound finance. At the same time, he noted a discrepancy between this caution and the progressive tone of the rest of the document and worried that this could confuse the public and increase their scepticism about the real intentions of the Government. With regard to the variable unemployment insurance contribution, a proposal advanced by Meade, Kahn had an ambivalent attitude; while considering it 'extremely valuable', Kahn saw the risk that this measure could be seen as useful for moderating fluctuations in unemployment, but not for preventing it altogether.

> The part to be played by the Central Government as an active spender of money (as opposed to that of an organiser of the expenditure of the other authorities) is remarkably small. [...] But to omit any reference to what the central Government might itself undertake (in addition to the automatic arrangements of variable unemployment insurance contributions) is only to invite criticism. [...] one is of course up against the principle of sound finance, but [...] There is a great deal which only the central Government itself will be able effectively to undertake in the field of those things which become well worth doing as soon as their influence on the level of employment becomes one of the relevant considerations. [...] I believe, myself, that nothing would be so well designed to impress the public with the Government's sincerity, than a frank admission that the doctrine contained in the Treasury contribution to the 1929 White Paper (the reply to: "We Can Conquer Unemployment" by Lloyd George) is repudiated. (RFK/6/1/24–25)

Once again, as he had done on other occasions during the previous years, Kahn sought Keynes's help in promoting his own views, as set out in the letter to Maud. Keynes replied:

> My dear Richard, Yes, I have come into contact with the Full Employment White Paper intermittently and have tried to polish up the last draft a bit. I think you will find that some at least of the points you mention have now been dealt with. (RFK/6/1/18)

Keynes says no more on this point, and if Kahn had any influence on the White Paper, it must have been small, since none of his specific suggestions were accepted in the end. Nevertheless, his involvement in the drafting of the White Paper helped to signal him out as an expert on employment problems when he moved to the Ministry of Production in June 1944. Here Kahn worked alongside Austin Robinson, again under Oliver Lyttelton, with the task to secure coordination between its various departments and to sit on committees dealing with the organisation of supplies to the people of the liberated and conquered territories. At the Ministry of Production Kahn dealt with issues ranging from the use of Italian munitions factories and measures to promote exports (ref. ROBN/2/3/7), to manpower and production (ref. ROBN/3/5/4).

At the same time he continued to be consulted as an expert on employment policy, as evidenced by a document, dated 20 June 1944 and entitled *Notes for Minister's Speech in Debate on Employment Policy.*[85] The document, a briefing for Lyttelton, is in two parts. The first deals with the nature of unemployment and what the government should do about it in the short and long term. The second part contains proposals for specific measures which were under discussion at the time. Robinson and Kahn argue that, in the long run, unemployment can be caused by a structural deficiency in aggregate demand or by technological progress. The measures envisaged by the government are designed to neutralise the first cause and to mitigate as far as possible the effects of the other, in the knowledge that

> [t]he world gets richer through the process of doing with 98 men this year what 100 men did last year. [...] We are seeking to "maintain a high and stable level of employment". [...] It does not mean that we are going to attempt to maintain complete stability of employment in every industry and every firm. Technical progress must continue to mean that some industries grow while others slowly decline. It will still be true that efficient firms will expand, while inefficient will decline. [...] But it does mean we are determined to prevent so far as is possible, the temporary fluctuation in the employment of industries, and of industry as a whole, which arise from the failure of effective demand. (ROBN/2/3/6)

[85] The transcript of the parliamentary debate that took place on 23 June 1944 is here https://api.parliament.uk/historic-hansard/commons/1944/jun/23/employment-policy

In the short term, however, and with the war against Japan still going on, promoting the return of some of the manpower to former occupations will require the maintenance of wartime controls. Moreover, Britain has gone from being the world's largest creditor to the world's largest debtor and whereas before the war interest on foreign assets covered a large part of the cost of imports, after the war this will no longer be possible and exports will have to rise sharply.[86]

> The Battle for Solvency is going to be hard and stern and as vital to the life of this country as the Battle of the Atlantic, and if we do not win it, the maintenance of a high level of employment may elude us. (ROBN/2/3/6)

The other risk, perceived by Robinson and Kahn, to the government's employment policy is that the private sector may revert to the practices of the inter-war period: abrupt and erratic changes in investment and the adoption of cartels and other restrictive practices. The government must be vigilant on both fronts, while preserving the framework of a 'basically free, dynamic and progressive' society. In this context, Kahn continued to think about how to create the right conditions to make a high and stable level of employment sustainable. Again in December 1945, sending Keynes his comments on a draft that Keynes himself had sent to Lionel Robbins, who had become head of the Economic Section, Kahn wrote:

> My dear Maynard, you may like to see the attached information on your minute to Robbins about labour controls. I agree myself very much that we badly need a wages policy and I am inclined also to doubt whether our system is capable of operating successfully except with the aid of more slack, in the shape of unemployment, than is likely to be regarded as reasonable.[87]

The passage highlights a key concern in Kahn's later work—how to reconcile full employment, price stability and balance of payments equilibrium. As post-war economic pressures resurfaced, many economists saw

[86] The issue of how to increase exports and improve the balance of payments returns in a memorandum dated 21 July 1944 to Lyttelton, President of the Board of Trade, which is divided into two parts (ROBN/2/3/6). The first part, written by Robinson, deals with a number of general issues, outlining the urgency of the situation and recalling the need to act simultaneously on trade policy, exchange rates and raw material supplies. The second part, written by Kahn, contains a series of comments on the specific measures then under discussion at the Board of Trade.

[87] Letter from Kahn to Keynes, 31 December 1945, (JMK/L/K/320).

low unemployment as unsustainable and advocated demand restraint. In contrast, Kahn proposed a distinctive approach: controlling inflation through wage policy, managing trade directly and curbing private consumption via targeted fiscal and monetary tools, thus preserving investment rather than restricting it.

The overall picture that emerges from Kahn's wartime activities is that of a man confident in his own abilities and opinions and careful to define the right arguments and strategies for advancing them. Underlying this commitment is Kahn's desire to be useful and a strong sense of responsibility towards the duties of his office, coupled with a legitimate ambition to see his commitment recognised. This attitude is combined with his desire to influence events, including with the help of Keynes. The bond between the two remained strong, even if their relationship changed. Beyond the purely personal aspects, they shared a desire to be kept informed and an awareness that much of the effectiveness of an economic policy measure depended on how it was received by public opinion. Both recognised the importance of 'preparing the ground', of helping the public to form the right convictions, at least on the most important issues, from rationing to employment policy. At the same time, after a decade spent side by side laying the foundations of the Keynesian revolution, the lives of Keynes and Kahn became partly separate, in particular when the Bretton Woods negotiations started.[88] While Keynes was involved in the Bretton Woods negotiations, and once again in close communication with Robertson,[89] the frequency of his communications with Kahn decreased, as Kahn was not directly involved in this part of his work.[90] In this context, Kahn, perhaps partly by choice, partly by circumstance, ended up in a less prominent position.

Despite his commitment to the civil service, Kahn never expressed any desire to remain there after the war. As early as December 1943, while discussing matters relating to the Bursar's activities at King's College,

[88] On Keynes's wartime activities and Bretton Woods, see Moggridge (1992, pp. 627–920) and Skidelsky (2003, pp. 583–707) as a general reference and more recently Bollard (2020, pp. 99–136).

[89] On Keynes and Robertson at Bretton Woods, see Sanfilippo (2008).

[90] In Pressnell (1986) and Gardner (1969), two early reference studies on the external economic policy of the United Kingdom since the war and on the negotiations between the United States and United Kingdom the name of Kahn is virtually absent. In Steil (2013) Kahn is named only as the recipient of Keynes's letters from Bretton Woods.

Kahn manifested his strong desire to return to Cambridge.[91] Almost all the letters between Kahn and Keynes contain references to life at King's College and the Faculty of Economics. While discussing the problems of international trade in the post-war period, the two do not fail to mention the investments to be made on behalf of King's College or the dinner to be held to celebrate the 500th anniversary of its foundation. Many of Kahn's letters to Keynes show that Cambridge and King's College were always at the centre of Kahn's interest and concern. It is therefore not surprising that after the end of the war, and after spending several months working with the Attlee government, as we will document in the following chapters, Kahn chose to return to King's College, which was to remain the centre of his life and intellectual and academic activity until his death in 1989.

References

Aslanbeigui, N., & Oakes, G. (2007a). The twilight of the Marshallian guild: The culture of Cambridge economics circa 1930. *Journal of the History of Economic Thought, 29*(2), 255–261.

Aslanbeigui, N., & Oakes, G. (2007b). The editor as scientific revolutionary: Keynes, the economic journal, and the Pigou affair, 1936–1938. *Journal of the History of Economic Thought, 29*(1), 15–48.

Aslanbeigui, N., & Oakes, G. (2009). *The provocative Joan Robinson: The making of a Cambridge economist*. Duke University Press.

Aslanbeigui, N., & Oakes, G. (2011). Richard Kahn's fellowship dissertation: The fate of 'the economics of the short period'. *European Journal of the History of Economic Thought, 18*(3), 381–405.

Aslanbeigui, N., & Oakes, G. (2023). The 'tragedy of Cambridge economics' and other stories. *History of Political Economy, 55*(4), 773–784.

Bain, J. S. (1941). The profit rate as a measure of monopoly power. *Quarterly Journal of Economics, 55*(2), 271–293.

[91] Letter from Kahn to Keynes, 6 December 1943 (JMK/L/K/265–269). In the same letter Kahn cautiously but clearly expressed the hope of being considered for a professorship, although he was aware of Shove's possible candidacy. Susan Howson pointed out to me that the professorship in question must have been the Chair of Political Economy, as Pigou was about to retire. Keynes was offered the position, but declined, and Robertson was appointed instead. In 1949, the new Chair was first offered to Meade, who declined, and then to Austin Robinson, who was appointed.

Boianovsky, M. (2020). Between Pigou and Keynes: Champernowne on employment and expectations. In A. Arnon, W. Young, & K. van der Beek (Eds.), *Expectations* (pp. 69–85). Springer.

Boianovsky, M., & Presley, J. R. (2009). The Robertson connection between the natural rates of interest and unemployment. *Structural Change and Economic Dynamics, 20*(2), 136–150.

Boianovsky, M., & Trautwein, H.-M. (2006). Haberler, the league of nations, and the quest for consensus in business cycle theory in the 1930s. *History of Political Economy, 38*, 45–89.

Bollard, A. (2020). *Economists at war: How a handful of economists helped win and lose the World Wars*. Oxford University Press.

Booth, A. (1983). The 'Keynesian revolution' in economic policy-making. *Economic History Review, 36*(1), 103–123.

Booth, A. (1985). Economists and points rationing in the second world war. *Journal of European Economic History, 14*(2), 297–317.

Booth, A. (1986). Economic advice at the Centre of British Government, 1939–1941. *The Historical Journal, 29*(3), 655–675.

Booth, A. (1987). The war and the white paper. In Glynn & Booth (Eds.), *The road to full employment* (pp. 175–197). Allen & Unwin.

Bridel, P., & Ingrao, B. (2005). Managing Cambridge economics. The correspondence between Keynes and Pigou. In M. C. Marcuzzo & A. Rosselli (Eds.), *Economists in Cambridge: A study through their correspondence 1907–1946* (pp. 149–173). Routledge.

Cairncross, A. (1993). *Austin Robinson: The life of an economic adviser*. Palgrave Macmillan.

Cairncross, A. (1995). Economists in wartime. *Contemporary European History, 4*(1), 19–36.

Chester, D. N. (1951). *Lessons of the British war economy*. Cambridge University Press.

Clarke, P. F. (1996). The historical Keynes and the history of Keynesianism. In T. C. W. Blanning & D. Cannadine (Eds.), *History and biography: Essays in honour of Derek Beales* (pp. 203–226). Cambridge University Press.

Di Matteo, M. (2016). Towards a rational reconstruction of Pigou's 'Theory of Unemployment'. *Research in the History of Economic Thought and Methodology, 34*, 339–356.

Edgerton, D. (2020). Never alone and always strong: The British war economy in 1940 and after. In M. Harrison & S. Broadberry (Eds.), *The economics of the second world war: Seventy-five years on* (pp. 55–60). CEPR Press.

Eichengreen, B. (1984). Keynes and protection. *Journal of Economic History, 44*(2), 363–373.

Eichengreen, B. (2004). The British economy between the wars. In R. Floud & P. Johnson (Eds.), *The Cambridge economic history of modern Britain* (pp. 314–343). Cambridge University Press.
Fletcher, G. (2007). *Dennis Robertson: Essays on his life and work.* Palgrave Macmillan.
Franks, O. (1947). *Central planning and control in war and peace: Three lectures delivered at the London School of Economics and Political Science on the invitation of the senate of the University of London.* Longmans, Green.
Friedman, M. (1942). The inflationary gap: II. Discussion of the inflationary gap. *American Economic Review, 32*(2), 314–320.
Gardner, R. N. (1969). *Sterling-Dollar diplomacy: The origins and the prospects of our international economic order* (new expanded ed.). McGraw-Hill.
Giocoli, N. (2003). *Modeling rational agents: From interwar economics to early modern game theory.* Edward Elgar Publishing.
Giocoli, N. (2005). The escape from conjectural variations: The consistency condition in duopoly theory from Bowley to Fellner. *Cambridge Journal of Economics, 29*(4), 601–618.
Goodhart, C. A. E. (1997). Whither now? *Banca Nazionale del Lavoro Quarterly Review, 50*(203), 387–430.
Haberler, G. (1938). Some comments on Mr. Kahn's review of prosperity and depression: A comment. *Economic Journal, 48*(190), 322–333.
Hancock, W. K., & Gowing, M. (1975). *British war economy. History of the second world war* (vol. 1, rev. ed.). Her Majesty's Stationery Office.
Harcourt, G. C. (1991). R.F. Kahn: A tribute. *Banca Nazionale del Lavoro Quarterly Review, 44*(176), 15–30.
Harris, J. (1998). *William Beveridge: A biography.* Oxford University Press.
Heller, C. (1998). Richard Kahn's short-term economics and the beginnings of oligopoly theory: A contribution to the history of contemporary economic thought. *Brazilian Journal of Political Economy, 18*(2), 260–277.
Howey, R. S. (1936). [Review of lectures on political economy; interest and prices (Geldzins und Güterpreise): A study of the causes regulating the value of money, by K. Wicksell, L. Robbins, K. Wicksell, & R. F. Kahn]. *American Economic Review, 26*(3), 493–495.
Howlett, P. (1993). New light through old windows: A new perspective on the British economy in the second world war. *Journal of Contemporary History, 28*(2), 361–379.
Howlett, P. (2004). The war-time economy, 1939–1945. In R. Floud & P. Johnson (Eds.), *The Cambridge economic history of modern Britain* (pp. 1–26). Cambridge University Press.
Howson, S. K. (1975). *Domestic monetary management in Britain 1919–1938.* University of Cambridge Department of applied economics occasional papers, no. 48. Cambridge University Press.

Johnson, H. G. (1960). The political economy of opulence. *Canadian Journal of Economics and Political Science/Revue canadienne de economiques et science politique, 26*(4), 552–564.
Kahn, R. F. ([1929] 1989). *The economics of the short period.* Macmillan.
Kahn, R. F. (1932a). The financing of public works: A note. *Economic Journal, 42*(167), 492–495.
Kahn, R. F. (1932b). Decreasing costs: A note on the contributions of Mr Harrod and Mr Allen. *Economic Journal, 42*(168), 657–661.
Kahn, R. F. ([1933a] 2022). Imperfect competition and the marginal principle. First published in English in M. C. Marcuzzo & P. Paesani (Eds.), *Richard F. Kahn: Collected economic essays* (pp. 35–50). Palgrave Macmillan. Translated into Italian by M. C. Marcuzzo and published in R. F. Kahn (1999). *Concorrenza, Occupazione e Moneta* (M. C. Marcuzzo, Ed.). Il Mulino.
Kahn, R. F. (1933b). Public works and inflation. *Journal of the American Statistical Association, 28*(Suppl. 181A)., papers and proceedings of the ninety-fourth annual meeting of the American Statistical Association, 168–173.
Kahn, R. F. (1933c). The elasticity of substitution and the relative share of a factor. *Review of Economic Studies, 1*(1), 72–78.
Kahn, R. F. (1933d). Reply to J.R. Hicks, 'IV—A note on Mr Kahn's paper. *Review of Economic Studies, 1*(1), 80.
Kahn, R. F. (1935a). Two applications of the concept of elasticity of substitution. *Economic Journal, 45*(178), 242–245.
Kahn, R. F. (1935b). Some notes on ideal output. *Economic Journal, 45*(177), 1–35.
Kahn, R. F. (1937a). The problem of duopoly. *Economic Journal, 47*, 1–20.
Kahn, R. F. (1937b). The league of nations enquiry into the trade cycle. *Economic Journal, 47*(188), 670–679.
Kahn, R. F. (1938a). [Some comments on Mr. Kahn's review of prosperity and depression]: A rejoinder. *Economic Journal, 48*(190), 333–336.
Kahn, R. F. (1938b). Review of *studies in the theory of economic expansion*, by E. Lundberg. *Economic Journal, 48*(190), 265–268.
Kanago, B., & McCormick, K. (2013). The Dollar-pound exchange rate during the first nine months of world war II. *Atlantic Economic Journal, 41*, 385–404.
Knight, K. L. (2014). *A.C. Pigou's the theory of unemployment and its corrigenda: The letters of Maurice Allen, Arthur L. Bowley, Richard Kahn and Dennis Robertson.* Department of Economics Discussion Papers series no. 14–08. University of Western Australia, Business School.
Laidler, D. (1999). *Fabricating the Keynesian revolution: Studies of the inter-war literature on money, the cycle, and unemployment.* Cambridge University Press.
Lee, F. S. (1981). The Oxford challenge to Marshallian supply and demand: The history of the Oxford economists' research group. *Oxford Economic Papers, 33*(3), 339–351.

Lloyd, E. M. H. (1956). *Food and inflation in the Middle East, 1940–45*. Stanford University Press.

Marcuzzo, M. C. (2005). Keynes and his favourite pupil. The correspondence between Keynes and Kahn. In M. C. Marcuzzo & A. Rosselli (Eds.), *Economists in Cambridge: A study through their correspondence, 1907–1946* (pp. 21–57). Routledge.

Marcuzzo, M. C. (2010). Whose Welfare State? Beveridge vs Keynes. In R. Backhouse & T. Nishizawa (Eds.), *No wealth but life: Welfare economics and the welfare state in Britain 1880–1945* (pp. 189–206). Cambridge University Press.

Marcuzzo, M. C. (2020a). Kalecki and Cambridge. *Review of Political Economy, 32*(4), 500–510.

Marcuzzo, M. C. (2020b). Richard Ferdinand Kahn: A disciple of Keynes. *History of Economics Review, 76*, 1–57.

Marcuzzo, M. C., & Paesani, P. (2022). *Richard F. Kahn: Collected Economic Essays*. Palgrave Macmillan.

McCraw, T. K. (2007). *Prophet of innovation: Joseph Schumpeter and creative destruction*. Harvard University Press.

Meade, J. E. (1937). *An introduction to economic analysis and policy* (2nd ed.). Oxford University Press.

Meade, J. E., & Stone, R. (1941). The construction of tables of National Income, expenditure, Savings and Investment. *Economic Journal, 51*(202/203), 216–233.

Medema, S. G. (2017). 'Exceptional and unimportant'? The rise, fall, and rebirth of externalities in economic analysis. *SSRN Electronic Journal*. https://doi.org/10.2139/ssrn.3057411

Middleton, R. (1996). *Government versus the market: The growth of the public sector, economic management, and British economic performance, c. 1890–1979*. Edward Elgar.

Middleton, R. (1998). *Charlatans or Saviours? Economists and the British Economy from Marshall to Meade*. Edward Elgar.

Moggridge, D. (Ed.). (1973). The collected writings of John Maynard Keynes, Volume XIV, The general theory and after. Part II*: Defence and Development*. Macmillan.

Moggridge, D. (Ed.). (1978). The collected writings of John Maynard Keynes, Volume XXII, Activities 1939–1945*: Internal War Finance*. Macmillan.

Moggridge, D. (Ed.). (1979) The collected writings of John Maynard Keynes, Volume XXIII, Activities 1940–1943*: External War Finance*. Macmillan.

Moggridge, D. (Ed.). (1980) *The collected writings of John Maynard Keynes*, volume XXVII, *activities 1940–1946: Shaping the post-war world employment*. Macmillan.

Moggridge, D. (1992). *Maynard Keynes: An economist's biography*. Routledge.

Moggridge, D. E. (1994). Richard Kahn as an historian of economics. *Cambridge Journal of Economics, 18*(1), 107–116.
Naldi, N. (2005a). Robertson and the great divide. The correspondence with Kahn, Kaldor, J. Robinson and Sraffa. In M. C. Marcuzzo & A. Rosselli (Eds.), *Economists in Cambridge: A study through their correspondence, 1907–1946* (pp. 371–391). Routledge.
Naldi, N. (2005b). The prof and his younger colleagues. Pigou and the correspondence with Kahn, Kaldor, J. Robinson and Sraffa. In M. C. Marcuzzo & A. Rosselli (Eds.), *Economists in Cambridge: A study through their correspondence, 1907–1946* (pp. 331–349). Routledge.
Pasinetti, L. L. (1987). Kahn, Richard Ferdinand (1905–1989). In J. Eatwell, M. Milgate, & P. Newman (Eds.), *The new Palgrave: A dictionary of economics* (Vol. 3, pp. 1–3). Macmillan.
Peden, G. C. (1988). *Keynes, the Treasury and British economic policy.* Macmillan.
Peden, G. C. (1990). Old dogs and new tricks: The British Treasury and Keynesian economics in the 1940s and 1950s. In M. O. Furner & B. Supple (Eds.), *The state and economic knowledge: The American and British experiences* (pp. 208–238). Cambridge University Press.
Peden, G. C. (1991). *British economic and social policy: Lloyd George to Margaret Thatcher* (2nd ed.). Philip Allan.
Peden, G. C. (2000). *The Treasury and British public policy, 1906–1959.* Oxford University Press.
Peden, G. C. (2003). New revisionists and the Keynesian era in British economic policy: A comment. *Economic History Review, 56*(1), 118–124.
Pigou, A. C. (1936). Mr. J.M. Keynes' general theory of employment, Interest and Money. *Economica, 3*, 115–132.
Pigou, A. C. (1937). Real and money wage rates in relation to unemployment. *Economic Journal, 47*(187), 405–422.
Pressnell, L. S. (1986). *External economic policy since the war, Vol. 1, The Post-war Financial Settlement.* Her Majesty's Stationery Office.
Robertson, D. H. (1934). Industrial fluctuation and the natural rate of interest. *Economic Journal, 44*, 650–656.
Robertson, D. H. (1936). Some notes on Mr. Keynes' theory of employment. *Quarterly Journal of Economics, 51*, 168–191.
Robinson, J. (1933). The theory of money and the analysis of output. *Review of Economic Studies, 1*(1), 22–26.
Rosselli, A. (2005). An enduring partnership: The correspondence between Kahn and J. Robinson. In M. C. Marcuzzo & A. Rosselli (Eds.), *Economists in Cambridge: A study through their correspondence, 1907–1946* (pp. 259–291). Routledge.
Rothschild, R. (2010). Kinked demand curve. In M. Blaug & P. Lloyd (Eds.), *Famous figures and diagrams in economics* (pp. 155–161). Edward Elgar.

Ruggles, N. (1949). The welfare basis of the marginal cost pricing principle. *Review of Economic Studies, 17*(1), 29–46.

Salant, W. S. (1942). The inflationary gap: I. Meaning and significance for policy making. *American Economic Review, 32*(2), 308–314.

Samuelson, P. (1994). Richard Kahn: His welfare economics and lifetime achievements. *Cambridge Journal of Economics, 18*, 55–72.

Samuelson, P. A. (1996). Obituary [Haberler]. *Economic Journal, 106*(439), 1679–1687.

Sanfilippo, E. (2005). Keynes's valuable opponent and collaborator. The correspondence between Keynes and Robertson. In M. C. Marcuzzo & A. Rosselli (Eds.), *Economists in Cambridge: A study through their correspondence, 1907–1946* (pp. 58–91). Routledge.

Sanfilippo, E. (2008). The collaboration between Keynes and Robertson during the second world war: A perspective from the National Archives. In R. Leeson (Ed.), *The Keynesian tradition. Archival insights into the evolution of economics* (pp. 42–64). Palgrave Macmillan.

Schumpeter, J. A., Cole, A. H., & Mason, E. S. (1941). Frank William Taussig. *Quarterly Journal of Economics, 55*(3), 337–363.

Skidelsky, R. (2003). *John Maynard Keynes: 1883–1946: Economist, philosopher, Statesman*. Penguin books.

Spahn, P. (2019). How to pay for the war. In R. W. Dimand & H. Hagemann (Eds.), *The Elgar companion to John Maynard Keynes* (pp. 195–200). Edward Elgar.

Steil, B. (2013). *The Battle of Bretton woods: John Maynard Keynes, Harry Dexter white, and the making of a New World order*. Princeton University Press.

Thomas, M. J. (1963). The problem of duopoly in economic theory. *The American Economist, 7*(1), 54–59.

Tomlinson, J. (1981). Public works, we can conquer unemployment, and the Treasury view. In *Problems of British economic policy, 1870–1945* (1st ed., pp. 1–16). Routledge.

Tomlinson, J. (1987). *Employment policy: The crucial years, 1939–1955*. Clarendon Press.

Toporowski, J. (2013). *Michał Kalecki: An intellectual biography. Volume I: Rendezvous in Cambridge 1899–1939*. Palgrave Macmillan.

Toye, R. (1999). Keynes, the labour movement, and 'how to pay for the war'. *Modern British History, 10*, 255–281.

Toye, R. (2007). The labour party and Keynes. In E. H. H. Green & D. M. Tanner (Eds.), *The strange survival of Liberal England: Political leaders, moral values and the reception of economic debate* (pp. 153–185). Cambridge University Press.

Tribe, K. (1997). *Economic careers: Economics and economists in Britain, 1930–1970*. Routledge.

Tribe, K. (2022). *Constructing economic science. The invention of a discipline 1850–1950*. Oxford University Press.

Turvey, R. (1948). The Inflationary Gap. *Ekonomisk Tidskrift, 50*(1), 10–17.

Winch, D. N. (1969). *Economics and policy: A historical study*. Hodder & Stoughton.

Zweiniger-Bargielowska, I. (2002). *Austerity in Britain: Rationing, controls, and consumption, 1939–1955*. Oxford University Press.

CHAPTER 4

Cambridge Revisited

4.1 Early Post-War

Between 1945 and 1953, the period covered by this chapter, the British economy underwent profound changes as it recovered from the ravages of war. The immediate post-war period was characterised by severe economic difficulties, including heavy national debt, reduced industrial output and widespread shortages of essential goods. To manage these challenges, the government imposed strict austerity measures, continuing rationing into the early 1950s. Consumer goods were scarce as Britain prioritised exports to rebuild its official reserves. The Labour government under Clement Attlee (1945–1951) introduced key welfare reforms aimed at establishing a welfare state. These included the creation of the National Health Service (NHS) in 1948 and the expansion of social security systems, including unemployment benefits and pensions, to protect citizens from economic uncertainty. Furthermore, the Labour government pursued nationalisation, bringing major industries and institutions such as coal, steel, railways and the Bank of England under state control. These measures aimed to stabilise the economy and rebuild critical infrastructure.[1]

The Marshall Plan provided a significant boost to Britain's economic recovery in 1948, with the country receiving approximately $3.3 billion in

[1] On economic policy and the Attlee government, see Tomlinson (1987, 1997) and Thorpe (2015, pp. 119–140).

P. Paesani, *Richard F. Kahn*, Great Thinkers in Economics,
https://doi.org/10.1007/978-3-032-09123-9_4

aid. This capital influx stabilised the economy, assuaged shortages and encouraged industrial modernisation.[2] The Marshall Plan also fostered economic cooperation with European nations, deepening Britain's involvement in international trade with them. However, by the late 1940s, Britain faced a balance of payments crisis due to high import levels and insufficient foreign exchange reserves. In 1947, the introduction of the pound's convertibility into US dollars under American pressure led to the first post-war sterling crisis. A second crisis in 1949 forced the Labour government to devalue the pound by 30%, lowering its value from $4.03 to $2.80 against the US dollar. While this made British exports more competitive, it also triggered inflation and weakened domestic purchasing power.

The outbreak of the Korean War in 1950 stimulated global demand for British-manufactured goods, particularly military supplies, leading to an economic boom marked by increased production and employment. However, higher defence spending strained the budget and contributed to inflation. By 1950–1951, as the economy stabilised, many austerity measures were phased out, and rationing policies were relaxed. In 1951 Winston Churchill and the Conservative Party returned to power, shifting the political focus from Labour's nationalisation policies to promoting private sector growth, while retaining key elements of the welfare state and maintaining high levels of employment. Despite economic growth resulting from the Korean War and Marshall Plan aid, Britain continued to struggle with trade deficits, declining global influence and rising international competition, which shaped its economic policy during this period.

In the transition from the 1940s to the 1950s, some Keynesian ideas took root in official British economic thinking at the Treasury and in other Departments. This included the notion that the government had a responsibility to maintain a high and stable level of employment, as set out in the 1944 White Paper, and to reconcile this with stable prices, equilibrium in the balance of payments and growth through a combination of appropriate budgetary, fiscal and monetary measures aimed at controlling aggregate demand and its components.[3]

[2] For an introduction to the influence of the Marshall Plan and the UK economy in the Attlee years, see Tomlinson (2000a).

[3] On this, see Peden (1990, 2003), Middleton (1998, pp. 201–236), Booth (2001a, 2001b), in addition to the reference mentioned in the previous footnotes.

In the Attlee years, the idea of budgeting on the basis of estimates of macroeconomic aggregates and the inflation gap, combined with a structurally expansionary monetary policy (cheap money policy) in order to limit the burden of public debt and promote investment, was part of the same Keynesian framework. The Conservative victory in 1951 combined a degree of continuity in the areas of budgetary policy and demand management,[4] as exemplified by the 1956 White Paper on the *Economic Implications of Full Employment*, with a change of direction in monetary policy, which, as we shall see, was reactivated in a restrictive manner in the face of rising inflationary pressures.

The penetration of Keynesian ideas into the practice of British economic policy occurred primarily through the activities of the Economic Section of the Cabinet Office, headed first by James Meade (1945–1947) and then by Robert Hall (1947–1961),[5] but also through the activity of the other Keynesian economists working in or close to policy circles, including Richard Kahn, who remained in active government service at the Board of Trade until the autumn of 1946. Between 1945 and 1946 Kahn worked on a wide range of issues, from employment policy to nationalisation and the administration of direct control. Evidence from James Meade's Cabinet diaries and other sources shows that even at this early stage some of Kahn's ideas and his own brand of Keynesianism were not necessarily in line with official opinion.

In this context, Kahn adopted a critical yet measured stance towards certain aspects of the post-war Labour government, particularly its approach to nationalisation. While he was fundamentally supportive of the efficiency and integrity of the Civil Service, as evidenced in a 1946 lecture to the Marshall Society discussed below, he expressed reservations about certain policy directions. These concerns, coupled with his strong desire to return to academia, likely influenced his decision to leave government service and return to Cambridge that same year. However, his departure did not sever his ties with policy circles. Back at Cambridge, Kahn resumed his academic work, producing writings that reflected the influence of his wartime experience. He advocated a proactive governmental role in sustaining post-war employment levels, fostering investment and defending policy autonomy against external pressures. His preferred policy mix

[4] On demand management in the United Kingdom in the 1950s, see Holmans (1999) and the review by Tomlinson (2000b).

[5] On the history of the Economic Section, see Cairncross and Watts (1989).

included low interest rates, fiscal intervention and direct controls on consumption and imports. He also envisaged a cooperative framework in which trade unions would moderate wage demands and accept labour allocation controls in exchange for employment guarantees, while business leaders would avoid destabilising practices and trust in sustained demand. Although he was broadly aligned with the Labour Party's economic agenda, Kahn's emphasis on controls and coordinated restraint was not universally embraced, even within his own party. Following Labour's defeat in the 1951 election, the incoming Conservative government moved away from this framework, favouring liberalisation, reduced controls and the reactivation of monetary policy against inflation.[6] During the 1950s, Kahn's emphasis on cheap money, industrial dirigisme and fine tuning through direct controls rather than demand management found limited support not only at the political level but also among British economists.[7] This did not prevent Kahn from defending his policy views both in private and in public and, in parallel, developing the Keynesian theoretical framework in several directions.

4.2 Kahn's Early Post-War Government Activities and Views on the Civil Service

After the end of the war and the election victory of the Labour Party, under the leadership of Clement Attlee, Kahn remained in the Civil Service for another year, becoming Head of the General Division of the Board of Trade, which had been amalgamated with the Ministry of Production (Marcuzzo, 2020, p. 20). At the Board of Trade, Kahn, together with Austin Robinson and Brian Reddaway, was part of a group of economists

[6]The classical references on the British economy and economic policy between 1945 and the early 1950s are Dow (1964), Worswick and Ady (1952) and Cairncross (1985). Kahn's name is not mentioned by Cairncross, nor by Worswick and Ady, and is mentioned in a footnote by Dow as co-author of a report on the problem of rising prices, which we will consider in Chap. 5. Kahn is also absent from Cairncross (1992) in relation to the period covered by this chapter, from Howson (1993) on monetary policy 1945–1951 and from Tomlinson (1997) on democratic socialism and economic policy in the Attlee years (1945–1951). As Kahn was never involved in formulating monetary or fiscal policy, he was not present in retrospective reconstructions of British policymaking. These areas were the Treasury's exclusive responsibility, and Kahn had no direct contact with them.

[7]For an overview of the policy debate among British economists in the 1950s with numerous references to Kahn, see Hutchison (1968).

and policymakers who favoured an approach to the regulation of the British economy based on planning, long-term targets and controls on the use of real resources and manpower.[8] This approach was supported in particular by Sir Otto Clarke, and to a different extent by Sir Stafford Cripps,[9] head of the Board of Trade and later Chancellor of the Exchequer. It clashed with an alternative approach championed (among others) by the Economic Section, led by James Meade. This alternative approach advocated a gradual return to free trade within the framework of a mixed economy, balanced through automatic stabilisers and fiscal policy.

Evidence of the frictions between the group Otto Clarke labelled 'Thermostatters', favourable to aggregate demand management based on the estimation of the 'inflationary gap',[10] and 'Gosplanners', who favoured more direct physical planning (the term being a reference to the Soviet planning agency), emerges from Meade's Cabinet diaries (Howson & Moggridge, 1990).[11] In particular, in February 1946, Meade records a moment of tension with the small group of Cambridge economists working at the Board of Trade, formed by Austin Robinson, Kahn and Brian Reddaway.

The problem arose from request, originating from the Lord President's Committee,[12] that the calculations within the Economic Survey for 1946 should be repeated on a quarterly basis, that the Survey for 1947 should be brought forward and that the Survey for 1950 should be attempted. In

[8] On this approach and on Austin Robinson's role in this context, with references (to Richard Kahn), see A. Robinson (1986, 1992) and Cairncross (1993). On the attitude of the British Civil Service towards planning and direct controls and on the generational clash between the Civil Service traditional attitude to laissez-faire and 'enthusiasts of economic planning within the civil service [...] individuals who had been brought in since 1939, often from the universities, to assist with the problems of running the wartime economy', see Barker (1986).

[9] On Otto Clarke (1906–1990), see Appendix C and Theakston (1999). On Stafford Cripps, see Appendix C and Schuster (1955, pp. 25–30 in particular).

[10] The concept of the inflationary gap refers to the excess of aggregate demand over an economy's productive capacity at full employment. Meade and the Economic Section emphasised the importance of countercyclical fiscal measures in mitigating inflationary pressures and ensuring macroeconomic stability. As discussed in the previous chapter, Keynes proposed the concept of the inflationary gap in *How to Pay for the War*, and it became part of the toolkit used by the authorities responsible for defining British budgetary policy starting with the 1941 budget.

[11] On the clash between 'Gosplanners' and 'Thermostatters', see Toye (2000a).

[12] For an early description of central economic coordination in the British government, see Taylor (1954).

this context, the Cambridge Group objected to the presentation of the imbalance between demand and available supply in terms of a purely notional 'inflationary gap': they argued 'that for 1946 one should reconstruct not a forecast of departmental requirements and a comparison of these with available supplies, but rather an actual forecast of what is likely to happen in the absence of further ministerial decisions as to how the gap between requirements and availabilities should be closed'.[13] They also argued that 'the highest priority should now be given to a survey for 1950 rather than revised surveys for 1946 and 1947'.

On the first point, Meade and the other members of the Economic Survey Working Party (which included the Economic Section, the Office of Statistics, the Treasury, the Board of Trade and the Ministry of Labour) decided to proceed in a more politically neutral way, without giving the impression that the Economic Section was allocating available resources (Howson & Moggridge, 1990, pp. 210–211). On the side of the Cambridge Three, Austin Robinson wrote to Reddaway (ibid., fn. 2) on 19 February 1946: 'I hope ... the long tiresome meeting at which you, Kahn and I, plus Otto Clarke, fought the combined stupidities of the Cabinet Office and the Central [Statistical] Office was [not] all time entirely wasted'. In the end, the Economic Section's line was adopted on the first point, and on the second the idea of starting work on the 1950 estimates without consulting any departments other than the three involved (Treasury, Board of Trade, Ministry of Labour) was adopted. At the meeting in question, Meade complained: 'We were [...] treated to a disgraceful and clearly prepared filibuster by the three Board of Trade economists'. A few days later, while recording the contents of a conversation with Keynes, Meade had the opportunity to return to the subject of collusion between the Cambridge economists.

> In the course of conversations with Keynes on other matters he has referred again to our estimates of national income for 1946; he is certainly in a much subdued mood and even goes so far as to admit that we have established a number of points! His minute in which he generally condemned our estimates for 1946 and our methods of making those estimates was framed in almost exactly the same words which Kahn used of us in criticising us at the first Economic Survey Working Party referred to above that I suspect some

[13] On this, see Howson and Moggridge (1990, pp. 210–211). See also Toye (2000a, pp. 86–87).

> collusion among the economists at King's College Cambridge! (Howson & Moggridge, 1990, p. 213)

Between 1945 and 1946, in addition to his involvement with the Economic Survey Working Party, Kahn participated as an observer on the committee preparing for the nationalisation of the basic industries, and to the organisation of tripartite working parties to advise on ways of securing improvements in the efficiency of leading British industries other than engineering and steel production, which the Labour government had entrusted to the Ministry of Supply.[14] Kahn's recollection of these episodes, in his interview with M.C. Marcuzzo, offers evidence of his support for the nationalisation of the core industries and direct controls, as well as his criticism of some aspects of the Labour government's handling of nationalisation and of other working parties, established by Stafford Cripps to analyse the structure and methods of select older British industries that required in-depth study to identify necessary measures for their progress and prosperity in the challenging post-war era.

> Even by some members of the Labour Party, it was felt that nationalisation was an act of betrayal; that left in private hands, the same improvements would have been achieved as those achieved by the nationalised industry over the long period during which the industry remained in public ownership. This claim, for my own part, I dispute. But the coal-mining industry provided a much stronger case for nationalisation. The character of the management was revolutionised, partly as a result of radical reform of training facilities for management and the process of selection. [...] In my opinion, the working parties suffered from the defect that the Trades Unions representatives belonged, on the whole, to the old generation: they were stodgy and unimaginative in their outlook. There was a tendency to follow the lead of the employers' representatives, most of whom lacked any spirit of enterprise. I failed to persuade Stafford Cripps to include representatives of the Foremen's Trades Unions. A foreman has reached his position by reason of his abilities, so he could have made a progressive contribution. But, sad to relate, and surprising in view of Stafford Cripps's well-deserved reputation, he allowed himself to be advised by an aged Trades Unions Secretary and by an aged and unenterprising employer. (Marcuzzo, 2020, pp. 20–22)

[14] On nationalisation in the context of British early post-war industrial policy with limited reference on a matter related to Kahn's involvement with the Working Party on the Price Policies of Socialised Industries, see Chick (1998, pp. 110–11 in particular).

Several questions arise from this preliminary evidence about Kahn's early post-war activities in the Attlee government. His position within the government's structure for dealing with economic problems remains unclear. On the one hand we see him involved in various activities as late as 1946, with direct access to Stafford Cripps, but possibly in a secondary position alongside Austin Robinson at the Board of Trade rather than at the forefront (Treasury, Economic Section). On the other hand, his views on economic planning and the opportunity to extend certain wartime controls into the post-war period, an idea supported by others, including many Labour ministers but not by permanent civil servants, may have contributed to his increasing isolation.

However, the question deserves further investigation, particularly in relation to Meade's ideas on the same subject. A first set of clues to help us answer these questions come from the text of an unpublished lecture on 'The Civil Service as Seen by an Economist' delivered by Kahn to the Marshall Society on 22 November 1946. The minutes of the Society, signed by Ruth Cohen and Frances Bettelheim,[15] recorded the lecture as follows:

> On Friday, Nov. 22nd, the meeting was held at 5 pm. Mr. Kahn addressed the society on: 'The Civil Service as seen by an Economist.' Mr. Kahn said that the Civil service had left him with only two feelings: Exhaustion and Admiration. Owing to the large number of decisions to be taken and the

[15] In autumn 1947, Ruth Cohen was involved in drafting a memorandum on resale price maintenance, together with Richard Kahn, Joan Robinson and Brian Reddaway (JVR/iv/7.2/1–11). In 1947, resale price maintenance (RPM) became the subject of public policy debate in Britain, reflecting the wider conflict between post-war economic planning and market liberalisation. RPM, whereby manufacturers imposed minimum resale prices on retailers, was defended by producer groups as a means of protecting profit margins and retail service standards. However, critics including Keynesian economists such as Richard Kahn, Joan Robinson and Brian Reddaway argued that the RPM should be phased out, or at least curtailed, to make retail services less profitable. This would encourage the transfer of scarce resources (including manpower) from the consumer goods sector to the investment goods sector and exports. This debate prompted the Board of Trade, led by Harold Wilson, to launch an official investigation, resulting in the Lloyd-Jacob Report (1949). The report recommended prohibiting the collective enforcement of resale prices, while preserving the right of individual manufacturers to set them. In 1964, Kahn and others published a statement at a time when Wilson's new Labour government was once again facing the problem of regulating prices (Cohen et al., 1964). For a theoretical overview of the issue, within the framework of pricing theories (with references to Kahn, Robinson and Cohen), see Silberston (1973). On Ruth Cohen, see Appendix C, Johnson (1978) and Deane (2018).

> insufficiency of staff, senior officials were confronted with far too much work. The question of priorities was therefore important. The Civil service at present was 'a series of masterly improvisations' and that 'red tape was not available.' The human qualities were superb. For this reason, organisations run on a 'commercial' basis (like the Nationalisation Board and the Working Parties) were not necessarily superior. The co-operation between trained administration and business executive had proved to be of value during the war. Greater co-ordination was needed to make the Civil service fully efficient. A discussion followed and the meeting was closed at 6.45 pm. (Ref. Marsoc 3/282–283)

The manuscript of Kahn's speech in the Kahn Archive (RFK/4/21) provides context for his confidence in the ability of the British public administration to efficiently and flexibly solve the economic problems of the time, including through the use of direct controls. Furthermore, Kahn's lecture is significant because it demonstrates that even in 1946, his views, particularly regarding the management of nationalisation, already diverged from those of key figures within the Labour government. This is one example of the independence of judgement that would often lead Kahn to prioritise consistency with his own ideas over the desire to please his official interlocutors, thereby limiting his chances of exerting concrete influence on policymaking.

In Kahn's recollection the Civil Service appears not as a rational system, but as an organism that adapts and improves in response to new and complex problems. This process is partly spontaneous and partly guided by senior civil servants, whom Kahn likens to academics. Behind this assimilation, with its undertones of elitism, we hear an echo of Marshall's commitment to training 'cold heads and warm hearts'; people selected for their intellectual and moral qualities, entrusted with the task of dealing impartially with domestic and international problems and able to solve them by virtue of their qualities and superior training.

> I suppose that partly it is the very high calibre, both intellectual and, in the widest sense, moral of the more senior permanent civil servant, who, we are apt to forget, is in training and aptitude very close to those who have chosen the academic way of life. But it must also derive from some deeply latent instinct in the pre-war Service of co-operation between Departments and adaptation to changes in conditions. The curious thing is how catching that spirit is. (RFK/4/21/9)

On another level, moving from an assessment of the past to that of the present, Kahn does not hold back in his criticism of Labour's decision to entrust the new nationalised industries to boards of directors rather than to direct control by the Civil Service. Underlying Kahn's scepticism is a concern about the people who will be asked to serve on the Boards in an executive or advisory capacity. Inevitably, most boards will be made up of businessmen from the industries themselves. While this is a good thing, because of the experience that they can bring to the management of nationalised companies, there are considerable risks in entrusting business with tasks of administration and implementation of government policy.

> I am basing my attitude very largely on what we have seen of business men brought into the Civil Service during the war. Let me warn you that this is one of the subjects on which I am notorious for being bigoted. [...] Having warned you on this point I can now safely go on to say that the business men put up a very poor show compared with the academics (and when I speak of academics I am not thinking particularly of economists: in fact the most successful academics are not economists). [...] As experts in their various fields of industrial experience the business men of course had an essential part to play. But in my experience it was the exception only who was a success in dealing with problems of administration or policy. (RFK/4/21/12)

For the cooperation between professional civil servants and business experts to be successful, it is important to find the right balance between them. Civil servants need to 'make up their own minds' about the problems they need to solve and take the relevant decisions about how to solve them. The role of the economic experts is to provide suggestions and advice, especially on long-term planning and forecasting, and to carry out the directives of the civil servants when they are called upon to do so. During the war, the structures organised on the basis of this division of responsibilities proved very successful, and Kahn accuses the Labour government of in some cases dismantling this structure and then trying to rebuild it, and in other cases failing to resist its decay, as in the case of the commodity boards. As on subsequent occasions when Kahn spoke of direct controls, this accusation seems to ignore the fact that the war was an exceptional period in which the normal dialogue between social partners had been suspended in the name of a higher interest. After the war, it seemed perfectly natural for this dialogue to resume.

Kahn identifies similar problems in the organisation of working groups set up to advise on how to improve efficiency. The development of the Civil Service during the war led to the creation of new ministries designed to correspond and interact with different sectors of the economy. Within each of these ministries was a set of competences which, according to Kahn, the Labour government had chosen to essentially ignore. The result had been the creation of the Working Groups, new structures which, by bringing together representatives of industry, trade unions and government in the name of 'commercial' management of economic problems, risked being unwieldy and inefficient.

Kahn acknowledges criticisms of the Civil Service, but argues that keeping ultimate responsibility within a single department ensures accountability and effective decision-making. For multi-departmental issues, he proposes a central planning secretariat to structure complex issues into surveys and programmes, preventing a disconnect between policymaking and implementation. In this context, economists and statisticians have a crucial role to play in preparing analyses, framing problems in terms of scarcity and pricing and providing informed advice. However, Kahn emphasises that practical experience often trumps academic training and that young economists must demonstrate skill, humility and adaptability to succeed in the Civil Service.

> What good then, it may be asked, can a young economist, holding a junior administrative position, hope to exercise? [...] One can scarcely expect—though perhaps one sometimes does—on first entering a strange Dept. to be treated as an oracle. [...] The art of being a successful civil servant is quite largely to appreciate the nature of the eccentricities of the various cogs which comprise the machine. Badly handled the machine jams. The eccentricities must be humoured and played with loving care and attention; to treat the machine as though the cogs are sound is to ask for trouble. But properly handled, with the achievement of a balance of patience and firmness which it is not always easy to strike, the machine does move—not at an even pace certainly it is a rattle of fits and starts—but it does get over a surprising amount of ground. (RFK/4/21/26)

Reading these words, one cannot help but be reminded of the young Kahn's intention to produce a comprehensive plan on the state of the economy once he had settled into the government machinery, of the care with which he built up a relationship with his superiors, of his commitment to being part of the policymaking process in order to be useful and at the same time to have his influence recognised. These elements characterised Kahn's years in the Civil Service and probably played an important part in his decision to extend his association with the Board of Trade on his return to Cambridge in the autumn of 1946.

At the same time, Kahn's view of the Civil Service and economic policy as a commitment to identifying the best technical solution in the public interest and entrusting its implementation to an expert and politically impartial administration seems strongly influenced by the climate of the war years and not very much in tune with the return to partisan politics. On another level, Kahn's position on planning and direct control and his attitude to the Labour government's handling of nationalisation may not have helped to strengthen his position within the British government and with it his ability to exercise real influence. This is clear from the reconstruction of a little-known episode concerning Kahn's participation in 1947–1948 in a confidential study group on the prospects for the British economy in the post-war international trading system.

4.3 The Economists' Committee and the UK Study Group on Customs Unions

By the end of the war Britain had lost much of its overseas assets and the income they generated. This, combined with the country's traditional dependence on imports of food and raw materials and its loss of external competitiveness, left the balance of payments in a very fragile position and made its rebalancing, along with reconstruction, one of the Attlee government's economic priorities. As Tomlinson (1991, p. 47) notes, the balance of payments in the years following the Second World War should not be viewed solely as an economic constraint that dictated unavoidable policy decisions. It also encompassed a significant outflow of government spending abroad, for strategic reasons and international prestige, along with foreign investment.[16]

During the war, Britain relied heavily on US Lend-Lease assistance to support the war effort and Lend-Lease had masked the significance of the balance of payments and the need to earn dollars. At the end of the war,

[16] On this, see Shonfield (1958), among others. For an early discussion of Britain's position in relation to the world's trade situation, see Lidbury (1947). On the UK War economy, see Hancock and Gowing (1949). On UK-US financial and trade diplomacy the standard references are Sayers (1956) and Gardner (1956).

however, Lend-Lease was abruptly terminated, leaving Britain in dire financial straits, with depleted reserves and the threat of economic collapse. In response, the British delegation led by Keynes negotiated a $5 billion loan agreement with the United States and Canada, but the terms of the loan were stringent, notably requiring Britain to make sterling fully convertible into US dollars by mid-1947. This reflected the US objective of strengthening the dollar's dominance as the world's reserve currency. The issue of sterling-dollar convertibility highlighted wider economic tensions between the two nations, with the United States pushing for a dollar-dominated financial system and Britain seeking a more balanced approach. Britain's economic autonomy was increasingly constrained by these external pressures, making the post-war recovery all the more difficult.

Alongside these financial issues, between 1944 and 1947 the United States and the United Kingdom held contrasting views on international trade regulation, reflecting their different economic conditions and strategic priorities. While the United States advocated trade liberalisation and multilateralism, Britain sought to preserve its system of Imperial Preferences. This system was crucial to Britain's economic recovery as it faced a severe dollar shortage and had to prioritise trade within the sterling area. The United States, however, saw these preferential arrangements as discriminatory and pushed for their dismantling in favour of a more open global trading system.

This divergence was particularly evident during the negotiations that led to the approval, but not the ratification, of the International Trade Organisation (ITO) at the Havana Conference in 1947.[17] The United States promoted the ITO as a way to prevent protectionism and ensure fair competition, emphasising the need for non-discriminatory trade policies. The British government supported it too, even pushed strongly for it; after all the idea of an ITO was James Meade's in 1942.[18] At the same time, however, British policymakers feared that sudden trade liberalisation could undermine domestic industries and weaken economic ties with the Commonwealth, further exacerbating the country's fragile economic

[17] A Preparatory Committee was set up in February 1946 and met for the first time in London in October that year to work on the Charter of an International Trade Organisation; work continued from April to November 1947. For the contents of the ITO Charter and an evaluation of these from a US perspective, see Wilcox (1947). For an evaluation of the same contents from a British perspective, see Meade (1950).

[18] I would like to thank Susan Howson for drawing my attention to this point. On the genesis of GATT and the British stance on the ITO proposal, see Irwin et al. (2009).

situation. In January 1947 the British Cabinet had agreed, on condition that it be kept strictly secret, to set up a committee to examine possible alternatives in the event of the total or partial failure of the plans for an ITO. In this context, Kahn was approached by Sir John Henry Woods, Permanent Secretary to the Board of Trade, to become a member of this committee. As Woods told the economists involved, '[I][t would be extremely embarrassing if it became known [...] that we were doing anything which might be regarded as a hedge on the ITO' (RFK/7/2/27).

On 11 February 1947, after consulting with Austin Robinson, Kahn conditionally accepted, agreeing to the suggested participation of Hrothgar J. Habakkuk, an economic historian who was, at the time, a fellow of Pembroke College, Cambridge. Kahn also suggested the name of Donald MacDougall (Wadham College, Oxford), who had worked in the Prime Minister's Statistical Section during the war an expert on foreign trade and data.[19] In his first letter to Woods, we find an example of Kahn's modus operandi and penchant for working behind the scenes that others have noted about him.

> Austin agrees with me that it would place too great a responsibility on the members of the team if they are not able to draw on the knowledge, experience and ideas of certain persons who are not members and who must be kept in ignorance of the nature, and indeed the existence, of the exercise. Some suitable cover would have to be devised and in my case it would help if I might be allowed to announce as the subject of my lectures next term something related to the field of study.[20]

This first letter to Woods, marked confidential, was followed on the same day by a second letter, marked confidential *and personal*, expressing Kahn and Austin Robinson's concern at the possibility of Dennis Robertson being appointed to the ITO Committee.

> Austin and I both feel rather emphatically that the inclusion of Denis as a member of the team would seriously militate against success. On the other hand, we feel that his judgment and experience should if possible be utilised, and what we would like to suggest is that he be made a kind of assessor. [...]

[19] On Donald MacDougall, see Appendix C and MacDougall (1987).

[20] Kahn to Woods, 11 February 1947, (RFK/7/2/30–32). Kahn's proposal was indeed accepted, as confirmed by the Cambridge University Reporter for 1946–1947.

> At the same time, we feel that Denis represents the more liberal attitude in these matters.[21]

As well as confirming the distance between Robertson and the Cambridge Keynesians, this passage is interesting as an indication of Robinson and Kahn's sceptical attitude towards a laissez-faire approach to international trade and is an important element to bear in mind in the reconstruction that follows. Woods' response, on 26 February 1947, made it clear that Robertson would be part of the committee, 'at Treasury instance and, I am sure with the concurrence of the Chancellor'. At the same time, Woods sought to clarify and limit the precise terms of the Committee's mandate, partly to avoid the risk of friction with the Economic Section, still chaired by James Meade.

> It may be, indeed, that we are a little at odds about the form which the enquiry should take. You may be feeling that your business is, having surveyed the ground, to make positive recommendations; and that upon this basis you doubt whether a single set of recommendations could emerge if Denis were in all respects a member of the team. Our conception of the task is significantly different. What we really want is a review of the situation, a formulation of the various possible policies which are open to us, and some statement of the advantages and disadvantages attaching to it. Anything more specific and recommendatory would tend to be embarrassing not only, on my conjecture, from the point of view of the team itself, if it includes Denis, but also from the point of view of the Government machine, and especially I think of the Economic Section.[22]

And so the Economists' Committee, officially appointed on 8 March 1947 (ref. RFK/7/2/147–148), set to work under the leadership of Robertson, for reasons of seniority.[23] In early May, a letter from Kahn to H. Lintott,[24] his closest contact at the Board of Trade at the time, reveals a series of

[21] Kahn to Woods, 11 February 1947, (RFK/7/2/33–34).

[22] Woods to Kahn, 26 February 1947 (RFK/7/2/27).

[23] For a brief reference to this group, which met from March to October 1947 without coming up with a valid alternative to ITO, see Toye (2003, 180, fn. 115). A more detailed description of the group's work is contained in MacDougall (1987, pp. 66–67). Regarding Kahn, MacDougall writes: 'Then there was Richard (later Lord) Kahn, who worked closely for many years with Joan Robinson. During our exercise he wrote lengthy, largely theoretical papers, on, for example, the characteristics of countries that would fit well into a group aiming at free mutual trade. Another member was Austin Robinson. [...] His instinct, and mine, unlike Kahn's—was to look first at the figures'.

[24] Kahn to Lintott, 8 May 1947, (RFK/7/2/20–21). On Henry J.B. Lintott, see Appendix C.

complaints about the lack of progress, the lack of leadership from Robertson and the lack of relevant documentation, as well as an implicit hope for support. This was followed by other letters of the same tenor, indicating not only Kahn's continuing misgivings but also a certain lack of enthusiasm on the part of the 'government machine' for the work of the Committee.

The first output of this work came in the form of a report presented on 8 July 1947. The report consisted of five chapters, covering Britain's problems in securing adequate imports (Chapter I), the obstacles to increasing exports to the level required to match adequate imports and the possibility of reducing these obstacles through participation in an 'economic group' of nations (Chapter II), the position of the British Empire in relation to the notion of an economic group (Chapter III), effects of associating certain Western European countries (starting with Denmark, Holland and Belgium) to the economic group formed by the British Empire (Chapter IV), risks of retaliation (Chapter V) (ref. RFK/7/2/481).

The Committee's analysis of this issue, in the context of the possible failure of the ITO and of the emerging European Customs Union, did not lead to particularly optimistic conclusions. The United Kingdom would struggle to import essential goods due to financial constraints, while tariffs would further limit trade efficiency. Securing foreign currency through exports would be vital to afford necessary imports, making luxury trade exchanges less beneficial. Additionally, worsening terms of trade could force the United Kingdom to prioritise import substitution alongside export promotion to maintain economic stability, pointing to the need to maintain import and exchange controls in the near future.

The discussion of the first report, on 23 July 1947, suggests a degree of disappointment on the part of the government at the pessimistic tone and the pessimistic assumptions on which the report was based, with the risk of upsetting the United States by expressing too strong doubts about British participation in a European Customs Union. In this context Kahn stood out for the precision of his remarks and his cautious attitude towards the notion of a customs union, which he stressed would be discriminatory towards the countries excluded from it and possibly incompatible with the objectives of the ITO. He also highlighted the unknowns of a hypothetical European Customs Union in terms of the behaviour of its potential participants, including Belgium and France, and how it might be advantageous to the world, and particularly the United States, but would most likely be detrimental to the United Kingdom (ref. RFK/7/2/85–90).

At a subsequent meeting, on 2 August 1947,[25] the government asked the Economists' Committee to comment on the implications for the United Kingdom of three possible customs unions: (a) the Benelux countries, France and West Germany; (b) France and Italy; (c) Sweden, Norway and Denmark; and on ways of strengthening the balance of payments in the event of failure of the ITO. The Committee decided to deal with the two questions separately and produced a second and a third report, which were sent together on 23 August 1947. Again the conclusions reflected caution and a certain pessimism, the existence of differing views within the Committee, and awareness of the expectation of the government.

> Although the group made no very specific recommendations, the general tenor of our reports was that, if we could not get an ITO, we should try to get something as like it as possible, under which countries could work towards freer, multilateral, non-discriminatory trade on a worldwide basis, but with let-outs for countries or group of countries in balance of payments difficulties (which we recognised would have to be called in aid by many countries, including Britain, for a considerable period ahead). (MacDougall, 1987, p. 67)

Despite their attempt to be balanced and conciliatory, on 9 October 1947, when the second and third reports were discussed, with R.J. Shackle of the Board of Trade leading the discussion, it was clear that the focus of the discussion was no longer on the Economists' Committee. The establishment of the Committee of European Economic Cooperation and of the UK Study Group, set up to prepare the British response to the Marshall Plan and at the same time to assess the possibility of a customs union between the United Kingdom and the former colonies (or possibly all the Commonwealth countries), took on primary importance.[26]

Again, as the minutes of the October meeting show, we see Kahn pressing the government representatives, pointing out the inconsistencies between the principles of the ITO and those of a customs union, the problems, from the British point of view, in the event of simultaneous participation in a European Customs Union and a Commonwealth

[25] In July 1947 Austin Robinson resigned from the committee to join the Planning Staff under Stafford Cripps in 1947–1948, chiefly engaged in preparing a four-year plan outlining the route to a self-supporting economy by 1952, when Marshall Aid was due to end (Cairncross, 1993, pp. 97–101).

[26] Ref. https://archives.eui.eu/en/isaar/38

Customs Union, the possibility that the United States might reconsider its support for an EU Customs Union if it ended up threatening its interests and the possible security risks (ref. RFK/7/2/41–46). Six days after the discussion of the second and third reports, Robertson announced to Lintott the dissolution of the Economists' Committee.

> If H.M.G. thinks fit to invite any member of the late group to become a member of Shackle's working party, it should be Kahn. But in view of Habakkuk's special knowledge and of the time factor involved in attendance of meetings, we suggest for consideration that Habakkuk should be appointed as his "alternate".[27]

This was followed by a personal letter from Kahn to Lintott, expressing his dismay at the lack of interest in the Economists' reports

> I must say that, on top of the failure of the Treasury to put in an appearance at the meetings of your Committee which were devoted to discussing our Reports, I do feel very dismayed. [...] Personally I feel that I have been wasting my time during the summer [...] the reason we were appointed to do a job that Civil Servants could do far better was that the Civil Servants concerned were so busy, and it seems to me a pity that we could not have been warned that they would remain so busy as to not have time to look at our products.[28]

Despite the apparent lack of impact of the Economists' reports and his misgivings about this fact, Kahn decided to join Shackle's UK Study Group on the Customs Union, with the approval of H.J. Woods (ref. RFK/7/3/63). His participation, however, was not particularly fruitful. The correspondence reveals Kahn's difficulties in obtaining relevant documents, his continuing concerns about the idea of a customs union and his irritation at the official ambivalence on the issue.[29]

> Much more serious is the fact (it would not be generally accepted but I believe it to be a fact) that the mere passage of time is getting us morally

[27] Robertson to Lintott, 13 October 1947, (RFK/7/2/66).

[28] From Kahn to Lintott, 20 October 1947, (RFK/7/2/64–65). In fact, as Toye (2003, p. 180) observes, 'these products were read, but were written in an obscure and involved style [...] too abstract for the ordinary civil servant'.

[29] See, for example, the letter from Kahn to Miss Forsyth (secretary of the UK Group), 13 Mar. 1948, (RFK/7/3/1574–6).

> committed more and more deeply to a policy which it would be disastrous for us to become involved in. I believe strongly that our right course is to work for maximum possible economic cooperation in Western Europe, but not to be forced to give up economic cooperation in other parts of the world in the way in which a commitment to form part of an eventual customs union would certainly tie our hands. [...] I must apologise for worrying you with all this but, as far as I can see, there is nobody in the Board of Trade, apart from Harry Lintott, who takes the slightest interest in our membership of the Customs Union Study Group.[30]

On 23 March 1948, after reading the letter to Johnson, Woods tried to reassure Kahn by explaining why, despite the economic arguments to the contrary, the British government supported the customs union on realpolitik grounds.

> [Y]ou have a hunch against a Customs Union, at any rate as the notion is being pursued. So have I. [...] But surely the general answer is this. Given the United States views on the subject one cannot just drop it. Some months ago when Oliver Franks was over here from Paris, he pressed very strongly, against Board of Trade scepticism, that we must show some degree of forthcomingness on this subject. [...] I do not myself believe that the time has yet come when we can walk out in the open and say "all this is nonsense and we undertook it because we feared we might not get Marshall Aid (or adequate and acceptable Marshall Aid) without going through the motions". [...] This is in other words just one of those crosses which have to be borne by the patient administrator. Will not the impatient academic put his shoulder under one of these crosses? Frankly, while believing you are completely right on the merits, I don't think that politics whether international or our own, will stand your solution.[31]

Kahn's response to Woods, on 27 March 1948, reveals less political naivety on his part and awareness about different positions within the British cabinet. He warns Woods that US support for a customs union may not be shared by other Western countries lobbying against it. Ignoring this fact in order to secure a fair share of the Marshall Plan risks leaving Britain in the lurch. Not to mention the ground Britain loses with the Commonwealth and other countries by pursuing the customs union and the risk, that if this pursuit continues, the Foreign Office 'are likely to take the line that it is

[30] Kahn to Johnson, 13 March 1948 (RFK/7/3/1572–3).
[31] Woods to Kahn, 23 Mar. 1948, (RFK/7/3/1566–7).

too late to go back, whatever the Board of Trade may say'. Moreover, Kahn observes that the Ministries of Agriculture and Industry 'are likely to make a pretty good stink about the whole business when they realise (poor boobs, they are pretty slow in doing so) what is afoot, and the Government will probably have to climb down in a very undignified manner'. With this in mind, Kahn's recommended course would be to put the case 'fairly and squarely' to the ministers, without hiding the case against customs union, and then let them decide. However, aware that these considerations would not convince Woods, Kahn informs him of his and Habakkuk's decision to quietly resign from the UK Study Group.[32]

Despite his resignation from the Study Group, Kahn continued to receive documents and other relevant material, which led him to make one last attempt to turn the course of events in what he believed to be the right direction. This happened in the summer of 1948, when Marcus Fleming (Cabinet Office) sent him a Memorandum on the Economic Corollaries of a Customs Union by the Economic Section of the Cabinet secretariat with a request for comments.[33] In his reply to Fleming, dated 7 August 1948, Kahn insisted on the need for each member of a customs union to retain the ability to impose barriers to control capital movements between member states and on the need for each country to retain control over the totality of its currency reserves.[34] Kahn passed the letter on to Robertson, who wrote to Fleming three days later, expressing a qualified support for Kahn's views.[35] Fleming's reply to Kahn, on 13 August 1948, put an end to the matter and to Kahn's attempts.[36]

Kahn's involvement in the Economists' Group and the British Study Group on Customs Unions exemplifies his commitment to safeguarding Britain's interests in relation to all other countries, without showing any particular preference for Western Europe or a sense of subordination to the United States. Like many of his generation, Kahn does not seem to consider the possibility that Britain has lost the ability to independently determine its own economic destiny. When it came to pursuing Britain's economic interests, Kahn adopted a non-dogmatic approach, viewing the customs union issue for what it was: barriers, tariffs and conflicting

[32] Kahn to Woods, 27 Mar. 1948, (RFK/7/3/1563–5).
[33] Fleming to Kahn, 22 Jul. 1948, (RFK/7/3/1513–4).
[34] Kahn to Fleming, 4 Aug. 1948, (RFK/7/3/1507–9).
[35] Robertson to Fleming, 7 Aug. 1948, (RFK/7/3/1505–6).
[36] Fleming to Kahn, 13 Aug. 1948, (RFK/7/3/1502–3).

interests. This was in contrast to an ideal laissez-faire situation, which does not involve any customs union. Kahn's preference for discretionary management of international trade is part of the same attitude, based on the use of all the instruments at the government's disposal.

This is consistent with Kahn's belief in the limited virtues of laissez-faire and with the idea, inherited from Keynes, that government should seek to maintain as wide a margin of manoeuvre as possible in the pursuit of its internal objectives, using direct discretionary controls to this end and circumventing external constraints as much as possible. It is in the combination of these elements, in which the Keynesian legacy is combined with a certain inclination of Kahn's (which perhaps Keynes would not have shared) towards the use of direct controls in the management of economic affairs, that we identify the main features of Kahn's intellectual profile in his mature years.

Obviously, by 1947–1948 these positions were no longer entirely consistent with the official line of the British government,[37] with the result that Kahn's ability to exert any significant influence on major decisions was limited. The same desire to be 'useful' and to influence policy decisions that he had shown during his six years in the Civil Service animates Kahn's repeated persistent attempts to be heard, but not to the point of abandoning his deeply held convictions. The inevitable result was that, after his unsatisfactory experiences with the Economists' Committee and the British Study Group on the Customs Union, Kahn never returned to the fray, either with the Attlee government or with the Conservative governments of Churchill, Eden, Macmillan and Douglas-Home in 1950s with whom he was politically distant. It was only when Wilson's Labour Party was returned to power, in 1964, that Kahn retraced his steps and tried again, with limited success, to exert his influence on economic policymaking in Britain.

[37] On the Labour Party's external economic policy in the 1940s, see Toye (2000b) and more recently Thackeray (2021, pp. 28–30).

4.4 Tariffs and the Terms of Trade

Kahn's first theoretical article after the interruption of the war years was devoted to the problem of determining the value of the optimal tariff in relation to the terms of trade (1947).[38] We can surmise that the choice of this topic reflected in part Kahn's commitment, as agreed with Woods in February 1947, and in part his interest in the effects of restrictions on international trade, a subject which was evidently highly topical in Britain in the early post-war years.

> Until recently economists were content to state the proposition that a tariff, if it is not too large, will benefit a country in terms of a "small" tariff. They did not concern themselves very much with the question how big a "small" tariff can be. (Kahn, 1947, p. 14)[39]

Kahn's article, similar in content and form to those of the 1930s, starts by analysing two articles by C.F. Bickerdike (1906, 1907) and how they treat the problem of identifying the conditions under which the introduction of a small tax on imports (or exports) leads to an increase in the welfare of the community, distinguishing between direct effects (on the country that imposes the tariff) and indirect effects (on the country that is affected by the tariff). Taking both effects into account, Bickerdike derives a formula for calculating the change in a country's net benefit from international trade and concludes 'rather strong assumptions have to be made as to the elasticity of foreign supply and demand if the rate of the tax affording maximum advantage is to come below 10 per cent' (1907, p. 100).

This is the result that Kahn proposes to 'revive', following a mathematical approach, to quantify the optimal tariff and to show that, under plausible assumptions about the elasticities of foreign import supply and foreign export demand, the optimal tariff is not as low as might be expected. In arriving at this result, Kahn assumes an initial situation in which the country under analysis, having imposed an ad valorem tariff on imports from another country in the past, decides to reduce it. Kahn

[38] In studying this problem Kahn obtained a result that continued to be mentioned in the literature on the positive and normative effects of tariffs for years to come. See, for example, Graaff (1949), Johnson (1950, 1953), Bardhan (1965), Hamilton and Whalley (1983).

[39] The economists that Kahn mentions in relation to this are Edgeworth, Pigou, Kaldor, Joan Robinson, Scitovsky and Lerner.

assumes that the target country of the tariff has not reacted in the past and will not react when the tariff is reduced.

On the basis of these premises and a number of other assumptions (full employment in the country that reduces the tariff, no possibility of foreign borrowing, equivalence of imports and exports in terms of value, homogeneity of labour supply, same degree of competition between different sectors of the economy at home and abroad, free movement of factors from one sector to another), Kahn derives the optimal tariff as follows (Kahn, 1947, pp. 15–16):

- I= Quantity of imports by the country imposing the tariff
- E=Quantity of exports by the country imposing the tariff
- p=Price of imports (without the addition of the tariff), measured in overseas wage units
- q=Price of export measured in overseas wage units

Following the reduction in tariffs, and taking into account the previous hypotheses, imports and exports will increase in value and volume by the same amount, as Eq. (4.1) indicates

$$\partial(pI) = \partial(qE) \quad or \quad p\partial I + I\partial p = q\partial E + E\partial q \tag{4.1}$$

Indicating with η the 'elasticity of foreign supply of imports' and with ϵ the 'elasticity of foreign demand for exports', we have

$$\frac{\partial p}{p} = \frac{\partial I}{I}\frac{1}{\eta} \quad and \quad \frac{\partial q}{q} = -\frac{\partial E}{E}\frac{1}{\epsilon} \tag{4.2}$$

Taking (Eq. 4.1) and (Eq. 4.2) into account, we obtain

$$p\partial I\left(1+\frac{I\partial p}{p\partial I}\right) = q\partial E\left(1+\frac{E\partial q}{q\partial E}\right) \quad or \quad p\partial I\left(1+\frac{1}{\eta}\right) = q\partial E\left(1-\frac{1}{\epsilon}\right) \tag{4.3}$$

Assuming full employment in the country, the increase in exports $q\partial E$ (consequent on the increase in imports facilitated by the lower tariff) requires an equal reduction, in volume and value, in the production of domestic goods for the internal markets, which are now replaced by imports of equal value. By evaluating these goods in terms of the all-inclusive price (relevant price on the domestic market of the country in question) and assuming that these changes in the composition of production do not have a significant impact on wages, either in the country imposing the tariff or abroad, and neglecting second-order effects, we have

$$q\partial E = p(1+t)\partial I \; or \, (1+t) = \frac{q\partial E}{p\partial I} = \frac{\left(1+\frac{1}{\eta}\right)}{\left(1-\frac{1}{\epsilon}\right)} \tag{4.4}$$

From which the optimal tariff is

$$t = \frac{\left(\frac{1}{\eta}+\frac{1}{\epsilon}\right)}{\left(1-\frac{1}{\epsilon}\right)} \tag{4.5}$$

Commenting on (Eq. 4.5), Kahn observes how the ability of a foreign country to significantly increase its exports towards the country that has lowered the tariff is increased by the ability of the country that has lowered the tariff to increase its exports to the foreign country, thus allowing it to devote more resources to exports. In other words, the two elasticities influence each other and in the same direction.

> As ordinarily understood, the elasticity of foreign supply of imports would show the relationship between an increase in the volume of production by foreigners of the commodities in question and the rise in prices (measured in terms of overseas wage units) required to elicit such an increase in production. But the responsiveness of foreigners' production to a rise in prices will be increased if it is accompanied by an increase in the supply to foreigners of the goods exported by the country under review: an increase in England's exports of cotton-goods will assist the process of diverting foreign labour from foreign cotton-mills to foreign wheat-fields, with the result that the relevant elasticity of foreign supply of wheat will be greater than it would be if measured in the ordinary way. For a similar reason, the relevant elasticity of foreign demand for exports is greater than the same elasticity measured in the ordinary way. (Kahn, 1947, p. 17)

Based on this consideration, Kahn proposes some numerical examples to show that, under plausible assumptions, the optimal tariff ranges between 5% and 50%.

> Sufficient has been said, in this very rough and ready kind of way, to demonstrate that the optimum tariff will often be far from being "small" and in the case of some countries (large countries and countries which are idiosyncratic in the nature of their exports or imports) the optimum tariff will be surprisingly great. (Ibid., p. 17)

Therefore, for larger countries, which are relatively less dependent on international trade than smaller countries, both elasticities will be relatively low and the optimal tariff correspondingly high. All the more so in a realistic situation where all countries that have already introduced a tariff (perhaps in response to other countries' tariffs) that raises domestic prices and reduces quantities find themselves on the inelastic part of their respective supply and demand curves and therefore have a limited capacity to change their internal production structures. To the prevailing view that the starting point of reasoning is the assumption of perfect generalised competition, Kahn counters an appeal to realism and common sense. To reason about the effects of tariff variation and the concept of the optimal tariff, one must assume that tariffs already exist and are applied by all countries.

> In the real world a country does not have to ask itself whether, by putting on a tariff, it may be endangering the structure of universal free trade. Most other countries will already be protectionist, and what it has to ask itself is how far, by becoming protectionist, or more protectionist, itself, it will cause other countries' trade barriers to be raised still further. The word "retaliation" is not necessarily applicable. [...] What this amounts to is that in practice a country would usually be foolish to remain free-trade simply on account of the effects of its own tariff on the tariffs maintained by other countries. But in calculating its optimum tariff it should (as in the theory of oligopoly) take account of the effect of its own tariff in altering the levels of optimum tariffs of the others. (Ibid., p. 18)

This last quotation provides an ideal link between Kahn's article on the duopoly and that on the optimal tariff. In both cases, as in others which we will discuss later, the final outcome of the action taken by an economic entity depends on the combination of objective elements (number and size of competing units, size and bargaining power of the entity taking the action in relation to competing entities, characteristics of the market and the products traded) and subjective elements (conjecture about the possible reaction of competitors, attitude to risk, quantity and quality of available information).

Moreover, it is hard not to see a link between the theoretical conclusions reached by Kahn in his 1947 article and the positions he supported as a member of the Committee of Economists and the UK Study Group on the Customs Union in the same years. In a world where all nations are still adopting protectionist measures, a large economy like the United Kingdom, with a relatively inelastic production structure, which is slowly adapting to the new reality of peacetime and even more slowly overcoming supply-side bottlenecks and restrictions, may have an interest in maintaining relatively high barriers to international trade and in gradually reducing them only after some elasticity has been restored to its production structure and after other nations have done the same. Acting unilaterally in the name of a general appeal to the benefits of free trade, perhaps to set a good example, may prove counterproductive to the national interest. On the contrary, maintaining in peacetime some of the protectionist barriers and discretionary direct controls on resource allocation that were tried and tested during the war years is more beneficial to the national interest than too rapid a liberalisation based on a trust in laissez-faire and price mechanisms.

The choice between liberalisation and the maintenance of direct controls on international trade returns in an important article that Kahn devoted to commenting on a book by James Meade on *Planning and the Price Mechanism* (1949). The importance of this article lies in what it reveals partly about Kahn's economic vision in the immediate post-war years and partly about the differences between this vision and that of Meade, despite the common reference to a Keynesian approach. As is well known, James Meade occupies a prominent place among twentieth-century British economists, not only for his contributions to economic theory and applied economics but also for the role he played in affirming Keynesianism in the United Kingdom.[40] He is also an important figure in

[40] On Meade's lifetime contributions, see Howson (2000) and Atkinson and Weale (2000). On Meade's specific contribution between the 1930s and the 1940s in elaborating and spreading the message of *General Theory* among Labourites and Neo-Fabians, see also Durbin ([1985] 2019, pp. 138–142 in particular).

the intellectual biography of Richard Kahn. In the 1930s, Meade contributed to the formulation of the multiplier as a member of the Cambridge Circus, and he began a close personal and intellectual relationship with Kahn that would last fifty years. As the following section documents, between the 1940s and the 1950s, Meade and Kahn had different ideas about how to organise the British economy in peacetime, and how to reconcile full employment with stable prices and a balanced balance of payments. The existence of this difference, in turn, is indicative of the fact that even after the war, when the memory of Keynes was still vivid, the front line of Keynesian economists in Britain, represented here by two of its leading exponents, was already divided in ways that would become more apparent in the years to come and that would ultimately prove detrimental to the continued influence of Keynesianism in the country where it had originated.

4.5 Varieties of Keynesianism: Kahn on Meade, Planning and the Pricing Mechanism

Upon resigning from the Economics Section in the summer of 1947, after three years of exhausting activity and struggles within the government, James Meade had accepted Lionel Robbins's offer of a Professorship of Commerce with special reference to international trade at the LSE. At the same time, he continued to participate actively in the theoretical elaboration and political debate on how to reorganise the British economy after the war and how to consolidate its achievements (full employment, welfare state, reduction of inequality), while striking a compromise between liberalism and the socialism of the Labour Party. Meade's main contribution in this respect was a book published in 1948 and entitled *Planning and the Pricing Mechanism* (1948a).

In this book Meade recognises the importance of planning, especially in addressing problems of equity and market failure, but stresses its limitations in terms of inefficiency, bureaucratic rigidity, difficulty in responding quickly to changes in consumer preferences and in promoting innovation. Hence his liberal-socialist proposal, based on the one hand on the restoration of the pricing system, in which prices guide allocation by responding to individual preferences, and on the other hand on public intervention to correct market failures, promote a more egalitarian distribution of income and wealth, and maintain full employment.[41]

In 1949 Kahn devoted a lengthy review to Meade's book (1949), reflecting the disagreement between the two that had arisen in February 1946 over the role of direct sectoral controls versus macroeconomic regulation in maintaining full employment and reconciling it with internal and external equilibrium. For Meade this objective should be pursued by using budgetary policy and automatic stabilisers to maintain aggregate demand at the level of full employment, leaving the task of allocating resources between different sectors of the economy to market mechanisms, which were gradually being re-established after the war.

After noting that Meade's proposals depend on the realisation of three conditions—(a) maintaining aggregate demand at a level compatible with full employment, (b) achieving a tolerably equitable distribution of income and wealth and (c) limiting market power by private companies—Kahn expresses his doubts regarding each of them in turn, beginning by criticising the lack of guidance as to what a reasonably and tolerably fair distribution means and how it can be achieved once the direct controls, and in particular rationing, are removed and replaced with incomes taxes and subsidies to narrow down the gap between rich and poor.

> What is at issue is how wide the gap would still be after Professor Meade had had his way. And it is clear enough that perforce the gap would still be wide. If this is true the money and pricing system would still be an election machinery where some people are given more votes than others, and Professor Meade's analysis breaks down on a fundamental point—unless it can be maintained that greater equality brought about by methods involving direct Government control was equally intolerable, inequitable or inexpedient. (Kahn, 1949, pp. 3–4)

[41] A useful supplement to Meade (1948a) is Meade (1948b), where Meade comments on three lectures on economic planning given by Oliver Franks (see Appendix C) at the London School of Economics in 1947 (Franks, 1947). Meade points out that Franks's idea of overcoming the contingent difficulties of the British economy through a system of planning and direct controls, capable of creating the right economic incentives without reference to the price mechanism, but relying on a flexible state apparatus and the same spirit as during the war years, raises serious doubts. Meade's objections in this respect are particularly interesting in view of the similarity between Franks's vision of planning and direct controls and that of Kahn, who had worked under Franks in the Ministry of Supply on the management of raw materials.

Kahn is unconvinced by Meade's proposal to combat inequality through inheritance taxes and capital levies rather than direct controls on the allocation of essential goods. The details provided are too few and contradictory, and the effect of the measures he proposes is too uncertain. Similar doubts arise regarding Meade's proposals for tackling monopolies. On the one hand, Meade 'is only really happy' where there are many competing producers each producing a small proportion of the total supply of a fairly standardised product, and each employing a small proportion of a fairly homogeneous type of labour (ibid., p. 5). On the other hand, Meade is aware of the numerous cases where monopoly is not merely inevitable 'but is desirable if the maximum wealth is to be produced' (public utilities, but also some branches of the iron, steel and coal industry). Where Meade sees the right balance between competition and regulated monopoly is not clear to Kahn.

Kahn sees a similar problem in Meade's treatment of the labour market and in his recommendations that firms must be free to hire the workers they need without fear of having to pay higher wages due to the full employment conditions prevailing in the economy. For Kahn, this may be impossible to achieve as long as labour shortages persist in some industries, especially shortage of skilled labour, and labour surpluses in other industries, unless the average unemployment rate is high, a risk that Kahn, with his insistence on full employment, is particularly sensitive to.

> Indeed, Professor Meade does have to postulate the maintenance of some unemployment to make his system of ideas work. But his reason is a different (though by no means negligible) one. What Professor Meade is worried about is the danger of "an inflationary upward movement of money wages, money costs, and money prices." While "some 4% unemployment may well be the technical minimum to allow for the necessary turnover of jobs in a dynamic society," compared with actual unemployment of 1 1/2% to-day, a very much higher percentage of unemployment (by way of illustration, Professor Meade mentions the figure of 10%) may be required "so to reduce the bargaining position of the Trade Unions that the general level of money wage-rates was not pushed up by more than the tolerable" amount per annum, which Professor Meade suggests might be 2% (p. 71). It would then be a matter of choosing between deliberately inflicting more than the necessary technical minimum of un-employment and suffering a continuous rise in money costs and prices at an excessive rate. (Ibid., p. 7)

Meade believes that strengthening the welfare state and introducing progressive income and inheritance taxes would persuade workers and trade unions to accept moderate unemployment. This increase is necessary to make the economy more flexible and to prevent wages and prices from rising too quickly. However, Kahn doubts that the unions would agree to a return to relatively high unemployment. He also questions the idea of leaving the reallocation of labour between different sectors of the economy and regions of the country to price signals reflected in wage differentials agreed upon by unions and employers.

Meade argues that, in addition to allowing for flexibility in wages, trade unions should accept that increases in the cost of living, such as those caused by rising import prices, are fully reflected in lower real wages, without the need for direct compensatory measures, such as food subsidies. Instead, he suggests that compensation should take the form of indirect income support, such as higher child benefits or pensions, which would allow households to choose how to spend the additional funds. Kahn challenges this, arguing that direct controls offer greater flexibility and responsiveness. These permit timely and targeted intervention and can be more easily adjusted; indirect measures, on the other hand, risk becoming permanent and distorting the economy. The same applies to export policy: if resources are to be reallocated towards exports without causing unemployment, direct instruments, such as licencing and the allocation of raw materials, are preferable to general macroeconomic tools, such as monetary tightening.

Kahn's concluding words, as well as praising Meade's value as an economist and his intellectual integrity, allow us to grasp the essence of the distance between Kahn's and Meade's approaches to the problem of finding the right balance between planning and deregulation.

> [Meade's book] is not likely to persuade the "anti-planners" to re-examine the foundations of their belief in "the miracle of a properly working pricing system." On the other hand, it is those who do not believe in the miracle who have most to learn about the operations of the pricing system. But to these, prices are, or should be, a servant. A book which makes prices out to be a master, and which might, read superficially, be regarded as an attack on all those who believe in controls or who administer them, is ill designed to introduce more sense into the designing and operation of controls. This is a great pity. For more sense is certainly needed. And prices should play a more important part. It is not a matter of either black or white (any more than the

> obvious impracticability of free trade as an objective for the next few years justifies our Government's policy of extreme autarchy). The system of controls and their administration could be usefully transformed if economists who understood the operations of the pricing system—both its virtues and vices—would address themselves to the problems involved. (Ibid., pp. 15–16)

In Kahn's review, which Meade regarded as fair and perceptive, there is no animosity but an underlying disagreement about economic planning and liberalisation, which Meade acknowledged with grace.

> My dear Richard, what a tremendous honour to have (i) a review article (ii) by you (iii) in the first place in the E.J.! Very many thanks for such a fair, flattering and searching criticism. I realise that what I want is rather an extensive change in present arrangements; but I am not yet convinced that we cannot fruitfully proceed by some moderate movements in the direction I advocate on all fronts simultaneously. (RFK/14/81/76)

Despite their shared commitment to full employment and the reconciliation of internal and external equilibrium, the exchange between Meade and Kahn highlights a fundamental divergence in their approaches. As was evident from the earlier distinction between 'Thermostatters' and 'Gosplanners', Meade favours the rapid dismantling of wartime controls and a return to private-sector autonomy. He relies on macroeconomic tools, such as automatic fiscal stabilisers and flexible monetary policy, to maintain stability. For Meade, full employment is defined more loosely (i.e. as being above the wartime and early post-war unemployment rate of 1.5%). He also emphasises the importance of the welfare state and progressive taxation in addressing inequality. By contrast, Kahn advocates a more gradual and selective withdrawal of controls, as well as a more dirigiste approach. He supports continued state intervention at the sectoral level to pursue efficiency and equity. His vision of full employment, maintained at an unemployment rate of 1–1.5%, rests on a combination of direct controls, cheap money and fiscal policies aimed at stimulating investment and moderating private consumption.

4.6 Physical Controls

Further evidence of Kahn's attitude to direct controls as a policy tool, and the possibility of maintaining some of them in peacetime, can be found in an unpublished essay entitled *Physical Controls*. The essay, dated 1953, was intended to form part of a second volume of *New Fabian Essays*, but was never published.[42] In his interview with M.C. Marcuzzo Kahn recalled:

> Shortly after the War I was a member of a group of economists, most of them friends of mine, who hoped to publish a volume of New Fabian Essays. In the outcome this hope was not realised, as a result of failure to secure agreement. Among the members were Hugh Gaitskell, Douglas Jay and Nicholas Kaldor. We used to meet at a country house near Oxford. My contribution was a paper in which I tried to answer the question whether it was possible and desirable to apply in peacetime some of the controls of the economy which proved so valuable during the War. My answer, given with reluctance, was that even under a Labour Government controls would be regarded as intolerable. Unfortunately I gave my only copy to Harold Wilson. It would be quite impossible for me today to worry him about it. I do not believe that he has kept it or, if he has, that he could possibly lay his hands on it. (2020, p. 23)

In possible contradiction to this statement a typed essay entitled 'Physical Controls' is preserved among Kahn's papers (ref. RFK/2/19). While it is not certain that this is the same paper mentioned in Kahn's interview with Marcuzzo, it is a possibility. According to the caption below the title, the paper was read at the Fourth Buscot Park Conference, held on 16 and 17 May 1953. Before outlining the content of this paper, it is interesting to reflect briefly on the names that Kahn mentions in his recollection, for they are nodes in a network that stretched across the British Labour establishment; a network that, combined with his increasingly prominent

[42] On the first volume of New Fabian essays, the links between Fabian economics and Keynesian ideas in the 1930s and 1940s, see Durbin ([1985] 2019). Two letters addressed by H. Gaitskell to Kahn and preserved in the Gaitskell archive (UCL Special Collections) provide a clue as to why the second edition of essays was not published. In the first letter, dated 4 May 1954, Gaitskell writes: 'I enclose a copy of a letter received from Nicky Caldor [sic]. I am afraid this places us all in a very difficult position', and goes on to ask Kahn if, in his opinion, anything can be done. In a second letter, dated 13 May, Gaitskell thanks Kahn for his suggestion and proposes to 'drop the idea of a coherent plan of policy and simply publish a collection of separate essays'. In the end, this project also failed.

position at Cambridge University, was the main channel through which Kahn exerted his influence on British post-war economic policymaking.

Part of this network had been formed in the 1930s and 1940s, when some young economists active in the Labour Party and the New Fabian Movement had taken an interest in Keynes's ideas, about which the party leadership had some reservations, and sought to combine them with their strong aspirations to create a social democratic economy.[43] After the war, these economists, especially H. Gaitskell and D. Jay, gained important positions within the Labour Party, and in this way some of their own ideas entered the British political mainstream, contributing to the emergence of a mixed economy based on a compromise between private capitalism, nationalised industries and the welfare state. In this context, the issue of direct control discussed by Kahn retained its legitimacy, even if, as Kahn himself suggests, his ideas did not seem to be entirely in line with the Labour Party mainstream at the time.[44]

With this issue in mind, Kahn begins by discussing negative controls and in particular the measures for withholding investment through licences, particularly in the construction sector, and the granting of the right to carry out new share issues. The use of these instruments, which Kahn would like to make permanent, would make it possible to direct resources precisely to the sectors to be supported and to create a queue of investment projects which could be accelerated or slowed down according to the needs of the economy and the objective of maintaining full employment. On the other hand, the highly discretionary nature of these controls and the pressure they place on administrators and ministers lead Kahn to recommend that the right of outright veto should be limited to cases where the government has planned a comprehensive development programme for a sector with which individual initiatives not included in this plan could conflict, or where it is deemed unnecessary or harmful to the overall economic plan, or where the resources are better allocated to public rather than private use.

[43] On the formation of this network and the penetration of Keynesian ideas into the economics of democratic socialism developed within the Labour Party, with particular reference to the names mentioned by Kahn, see Durbin ([1985] 2019). See also Toye (2003).

[44] On direct controls in Britain at the beginning of the 1950s, see Worswick (1952). On Hugh Gaitskell, see Appendix C, Saville (1980) and Williams (1982). On Douglas Jay, see Appendix C, Schuster (1955, pp. 25–30 in particular) and Toye (2002) for a focus on Jay's economic views. On Gaitskellism, favouring mixed economy and welfare reform over socialist nationalisation, see Thompson (2006).

> But it is important that a shortage of productive labour in a prosperous area should not be readily regarded as a reason why the building of a new factory ought to be banned if efficiency would at all seriously suffer from its being built in a less prosperous area, particularly if the project might then be abandoned altogether. The manning of new factories may entail denuding less efficient factories of their manpower and so compelling them to close down. That is the nature of economic progress under conditions of full employment, and we must beware of full employment establishing a barrier to further process. (RFK/2/19/202)

More complicated is the case of direct control (rationing) over the production of machinery and/or the allocation of the raw materials needed for it, especially in the case of steel.[45] In this case, the main problem is how to establish objective criteria to ensure that scarce raw materials reach the most efficient firms, especially in the export industry. Since it is unrealistic to think that civil servants can successfully carry out this activity in peacetime, given the complexity of anticipating the specific and changing needs of different industries and sectors, it would be preferable to intervene downstream with measures to restrict the sale of consumer goods manufactured using the scarce raw materials (e.g. through limitations on hire-purchase), as was successfully done in the case of the motor industry. Alternatively, if conditions warrant, the government should build up buffer stocks to ensure a regular flow of strategic raw materials to strategic industries, without leaving the task of regulating these stocks (as part of the investment) to monetary policy.

> The fact is that the problems of checking fluctuations in stocks is not one to which there is any adequate solution. Monetary policy can be applied only by risking adverse effects on productive investment. Fluctuations in stocks, associated with errors in forecasting on the part of business men, will always have to be reckoned with. In so far as the direct impact is on the demand for imported raw material the remedy really is to have an adequate monetary reserve and to be prepared to see it fluctuate without resulting, on the one hand, in panic or, on the other hand, in profligacy. To lessen the impact on domestic production and employment, "buffer-stock" holdings of certain

[45] For the history of the British steel industry in the post-war period as an example of the difficulties of simultaneously managing the expansion of production capacity and the modernisation of a sector that is strategic for the development of the economy and the maintenance of external equilibrium within the mixed economy referred to in Kahn's analysis, see Blair (1997).

> standard materials would be a great help, e.g. of coal, pig iron, grey cloth, staple rayon fibre. (RFK/2/19/204)

An alternative to restricting private consumption, other than rationing and strategic buffer stocks, is to resort to the purchase tax,[46] a high sales tax levied at the wholesale stage on all non-essential goods to reduce the purchasing power of domestic consumers across the board, allowing businesses to adapt to changing domestic and international demand patterns and tax revenues to rise in line with consumption. These advantages should be weighed against the limited flexibility of the purchase tax, which can be changed only once a year when the budget is discussed, in comparison with direct controls on the allocation of raw materials that can be changed at short notice. Only in an emergency, such as a shortage of foreign exchange reserves so severe that the country's ability to meet international payments is threatened, can rationing and direct allocation of resources be justified in peacetime.

> The engineering industries present a particularly likely case for such temporary re-imposition of control. They have suffered and are likely to continue to suffer, from fluctuations in overseas demand which are perversely correlated with fluctuations in domestic demand. [...] Monetary restriction is the "natural" means of resolving the conflict but it discourages domestic demand without an eye to the strength of overseas demand for individual products, and by lightening the pressure on the resources of the building industry it helps only indirectly to facilitate exports of machinery. In other words, it is patchy, wasteful and capricious in its operations. The physical controls can be applied in a highly discriminatory manner. For such temporary and exceptional machinery licensing would be best of all. (RFK/2/19/206)

Another field in which negative controls can operate effectively, in Kahn's opinion, is the engagemnt of labour. After the Attlee government had done away with the Control of Engagements in 1950, something similar re-emerged with the Conservative governments under the name of Notification of Vacancies. This measure, which was meant to operate in synergy with the Labour Exchanges,[47] required employers to notify the

[46] On the purchase tax in Britain in connection with wartime controls, see Soloway (1954).

[47] Labour Exchanges were government-run offices that facilitated the matching of workers with available jobs. Initially established under the Labour Exchanges Act of 1909, their pur-

Ministry of Labour of any job vacancies they had before those vacancies could be advertised or filled. The idea was that the Ministry of Labour could then help direct suitable candidates to these vacancies, ensuring that jobs were filled efficiently and that labour was allocated in line with national priorities.

The main obstacle to the use of these controls may be workers' fears and resentment at being forced to take one job rather than another. On the other hand, it is important to have instruments to facilitate the direct assignment of workers for two reasons. The first is that these controls can be applied to the service sector as well as to industry, thereby strengthening the government's ability to steer the economy in the desired direction. The second reason is that under conditions of full employment, bottlenecks and shortages are very likely to arise at the sectoral or regional level, and these are easier to deal with by controlling employment than by relying on other mechanisms, such as the flexible wage differentials as envisaged by Meade in *Planning and the Price Mechanism*, or through fiscal measures.

> All this means that if manpower is not to be wasted and if the social evils of unemployment are not to be incurred, there will have to be much shifting about of labour from industry to industry. To attempt to achieve this exclusively by means of fiscal measures designed to operate on consumption as a whole, or even on the consumption of particular goods, will mean waste of resources and partial failure. But control of engagements will not be necessary everywhere and all the time. There are likely to be long periods in which there is sufficient slack for the control to be disposed with. At other times it might be imposed in certain areas only, or on employment of certain industries and trades only, or on employment of certain classes of labour only. (RFK/2/19/208)

Whereas, in arguing the merits of labour controls, Kahn feels compelled to limit their applicability, aware of the hostility they can generate and the difficulty of applying them continuously in peacetime, his attitude to import controls is different.

pose was to help reduce unemployment by matching job-seekers with employers who had vacancies. By the early 1950s these exchanges had become an important part of the post-war welfare state, playing a crucial role in managing employment in the economy. Their key functions included job placement, provision of unemployment benefits, nationalised employment services, training and support.

> Then there is quantitative control of imports. This is a negative control retention of which will be necessary for an indefinite future. There may conceivably be times when it can be completely withdrawn but in such an unlikely event it would be essential to retain the fabric against a subsequent deterioration of the balance of payments. (RFK/2/19/208)

Kahn is more cautious and less dogmatic about direct price controls, where the risk of removing any incentive to innovate and improve efficiency is high, especially in those cases where the domestic market is small and the British companies must compete with foreign firms that can achieve much greater economies of scale. There are various ways of correcting the competitive disadvantage, that derive from a limited domestic market, ranging from the use of public purchasing agencies for the purchase of imported raw materials, to the promotion, under government auspices, of inter-industry cooperation in the organisation of activities of common interest, such the creation of agencies to promote cooperative selling overseas. In this type of activity, which mainly benefits smaller firms rather than larger ones, the role of government as a catalyst is essential. This type of activity, like the creation of state-owned enterprises, falls within the sphere of positive control, to which Kahn devotes the second part of his essay.

> When everything possible has been done by the Government to encourage, induce, coerce industry to seek extra efficiency in all possible ways, there will still remain several gaps between what the Government deems desirable and what capitalists feel that they are justified in taking on, after considering the prospects of profit and the risks involved. The physical controls, negative in their operation, can do something to cover such gaps but, under the conditions likely to prevail over the coming years, not very much. Initiative by the Government on the positive task has to be devised. (RFK/2/19/213)

Between the two extremes of totally private and totally public industry, there are intermediate forms of intervention, such as the activation of programmes to expand the private firm with public support, or the acquisition by the State of individual firms, inevitably the least efficient, within an industry that remains private. Kahn is not particularly favourable to these hybrid solutions, preferring others such as public support for research and development, where positive externalities are strong, or guaranteeing certain firms that they can sell at a minimum price. In any case, whatever the structure chosen for the various industries, the basic problem of ensuring an adequate level of investment remains.

> The defects of capitalism are particularly apparent when it is a matter of carrying out bold expansionist plans, going far beyond anything which seems reasonable to a capitalist interest in fulfilling his natural role in the system. Even when his own view of the future is sufficiently expansive to provide an economic basis in his own mind for the Government's plan of expansion, he cannot disregard the view of the Stock Exchange. This is often more cautious and shows itself in an unduly low market price of his company's shares, which fixes the terms on which part at any rate of the capital required for the expansion will have to be raised. (RFK/2/19/217)

Reading these words brings to mind the words Keynes used in the *General Theory* to describe the ambivalent influence of the Stock Exchange on investment. On the one hand, the possibility of liquidating shares encourages the desire to buy them and thus to invest. On the other hand, large speculative fluctuations can distort the allocation of resources, diverting them from sectors where they would be most profitable in the long run. In addition to this problem, Kahn discusses the underlying risk aversion that characterises many investors, an attitude that depresses the price of securities, thereby holding back investment and capital accumulation. Among other reasons that limit the accumulation of risk capital, Kahn cites the high taxation of personal income (which, by penalising the wealthy, penalises the savings that flow into the stock market, while small investors prefer government securities) and the competition between public and private companies to raise funds on the stock market. In order to overcome the scarcity of risk capital, in addition to a system of initial allowances,[48]

> [t]he State must be prepared to provide equity capital and to do so on a heroic scale. This proposal is not aimed at helping the State, without resort to full-blooded nationalisation, to secure control over sections of industry. In fact the whole object is to avoid exercising control to retain the advantages of private enterprise in terms of initiative and decision-making and at

[48] The expression initial allowances referred to a form of tax relief granted to businesses on capital expenditures, such as investments in plant, machinery or industrial buildings. These allowances were designed to encourage investment in the post-war economy by allowing businesses to write off a portion of their capital costs against their taxable profits, thereby reducing their tax liability.

> the same time to liberate it from the cramping influence exercised by the shortage of suitable finance. It is like a sleeping partner in this particular context that the State should come in. This proposal must be kept completely clear of any proposal for mixed enterprises. [...] And if both proposals are adopted they should be carried out through quite separate organisations. (RFK/2/19/219)

Kahn is aware of the difficulties of implementing this and the other direct controls, both from an administrative point of view and because of the obstacles that can arise from the hostility of the regulated parties, but he does not seem to attach undue importance to these difficulties. Kahn's stance reflects his belief in the impartiality of the civil service, as well as his conviction that rational argument is the most effective means of defending public control against policies that risk sacrificing full employment in order to combat inflation, external deficits and declining competitiveness. In this respect, he was particularly critical of restrictive monetary policy, warning of its detrimental effects on employment and growth.

4.7 Inflation and the Balance of Payments: Kahn on the Dangers of Monetary Restriction

In the early 1950s the United Kingdom experienced inflationary pressures, balance of payments difficulties, severe tensions in the foreign exchange market and a temporary rise in the unemployment rate.[49] Many of these problems were due to the outbreak of the Korean War, the resulting rise in the price of raw materials and food (of which the United Kingdom was a net importer) and the need to increase defence spending.[50] Beyond these, however, there remained the fundamental problem of a mature economy struggling to reconcile full employment, price stability and external balance and growth, not least because of a production system

[49] Inflation rose from 3.1% in 1950 to 9.2% in 1952, before falling back to 3.1% the following year. Unemployment rose from 1.6% in 1951 to 2.4% in 1952, gradually falling back to 1.6% in 1955. (The current account balance, which had improved in the post-war years from –£380 million in 1947 to +£358 million in 1950, turned negative in 1951 (–£369 million), putting pressure on sterling and UK official reserves for the fourth time since the end of the war (Thirlwall & Gibson, 1992).)

[50] On the impact of the Korean War on the British economy, see Geiger (2004, Chapter 8).

in need of investment and modernisation.[51] Whereas the Attlee government had kept inflationary pressures and the balance of payments in check through voluntary wage restraints, fiscal restraint and import controls,[52] the new Conservative government led by Churchill adopted a different approach. In October 1951, the Chancellor, R.A. Butler, reactivated a restrictive monetary policy with the dual aim of reducing inflation and strengthening sterling.

The new monetary policy was characterised an increase in the Bank Rate for the first time in 12 years (from 2% to 2.5%), followed by increases in the rates of interest on loans to local authorities, on gilt-edged securities and on time deposits. In parallel, the new policy entailed a change in the relationship between the Bank Rate and money market rates as the prices of Treasury bills were no longer stabilised. This removed the assurance of a permanent secure cheap source of liquid funds for commercials banks. In the same spirit, a funding operation in which a large block of Treasury bills was replaced by longer-term securities and new instructions to the Capital Issues Committee to freeze some of the new lending to the private sector while the Chancellor exerted strong moral suasion to persuade the banks to reduce their lending to the private sector.[53] Thus came to an end the long period of 'cheap money' that had characterised the war years and those of the Attlee government, together with the idea that the monetary authorities could control short- as well as long-term interest rates by combining monetary operations and government debt management.[54]

In this context, British economists, including Richard Kahn, questioned the merits and possible effects of the new monetary policy. An early occasion in this respect was a Symposium, coordinated by G.D.N. Worswick and published in 1952 in the *Bulletin of the Institute of Statistics at Oxford University* (Nos 4 and 5 and 8). The Symposium opened with two papers,

[51] For a contemporary description of these problems in the context of an analysis of British economic policy 1945–1958, see Shonfield (1958).

[52] See Kahn (1948) for a criticism of the measures adopted by Stafford Cripps in the 1948 Budget, in particular with regard to the size of the Budget surplus, which Kahn would have liked to be larger so as to reduce inflation and the cuts in the capital investment programmes.

[53] In March 1952 the Bank Rate rose to 4% and new restrictions on hire purchase were introduced. On the reactivation of monetary policy by the Conservative government, see Sayers (1952) and Allen (2014, pp. 19–31), among others.

[54] The classic studies on the origins of cheap money in the 1930s and early 1940s and on British monetary policy between 1945 and 1951 are Howson (1975, 1993).

one by Harry Johnson, then a young colleague of Kahn's at Cambridge,[55] and the other by Charles Kennedy (Queen's College, Oxford).

As Johnson (1952) observes, the partial reversion to monetary orthodoxy in 1951–1952 remained heavily reliant on wartime regulatory mechanisms, particularly those governing bank liquidity and credit controls. This dependence raised doubts about whether a genuine return to orthodox monetary policy has taken place. Johnson also questions the effectiveness of Bank Rate increases in strengthening sterling, asking whether they truly promoted more efficient resource allocation or simply restrict credit without strategic direction. He further considers whether similar anti-inflationary outcomes could be achieved through alternative methods with lower fiscal costs. Kennedy (1952) addresses these concerns and offers an ambivalent assessment. While higher interest rates and tighter credit strengthen sterling and dampen investment—both directly, by raising borrowing costs, and indirectly, by increasing uncertainty—he argues that comparable results might be achieved more effectively through direct controls or fiscal restraint. Such alternatives, Kennedy contends, avoid the rigidity and delayed transmission of monetary policy and its negative impact on public debt management.

The papers by Johnson and Kennedy were commented on by Frank W. Paish, Robertson, Harrod, Kahn, Thomas Balogh and John R. Hicks, who were divided between those in favour of the new monetary measures as a matter of principle (Paish and Robertson), those moderately in favour on contingent grounds (Harrod and Hicks) and critics (Kahn and Balogh). The greatest distance between the six commentators emerged on three issues: (1) the appropriateness of adopting restrictive monetary policy to respond to the contingent difficulties of the British economy; (2) the effectiveness of this policy as opposed to direct controls; (3) the negative consequences of monetary restriction as opposed to the possible benefits. On the first point, Kahn observes:

> Nobody can predict the degree of success of a given restriction. There is a serious danger that undue reliance will be placed on the adequacy of a modest restriction of credit, and that the need for other measures—more effective, less disadvantageous and more rapid—will not be sufficiently realised. [...] Here experience has little, or nothing, to teach us. Nostalgic references

[55] On Johnson's years at Cambridge, see Moggridge (2011, pp. 93–160; see in particular pages 132–134 for a reference to the Monetary Policy Symposium).

> to 'all the delicate mechanisms of financial control which the experience of ages was gradually fashioning' do not really help: they refer to conditions [...] which to-day would be regarded by almost everybody as unthinkable. (Kahn, 1952a, p. 147)[56]

Under normal circumstances, monetary policy should not be conducted in a countercyclical manner, not least because its effects are delayed and tend to be unpredictable. Better to pursue a monetary policy that is favourable to investment and, if necessary, to intervene with restrictive measures of a different kind.

All the other commentators, with the exception of Balogh, argue against this position and in favour of an anti-inflationary monetary policy (Paish, Robertson) which contributes to strengthening sterling and reducing the pressure on aggregate demand by reducing investment (Harrod). The six commentators agree that controls are not perfect, but while Kahn and Balogh stress the positive aspects of controls (greater effectiveness compared with changes in the Bank Rate, greater possibility of modulating restrictive interventions on a sectoral basis rather than indiscriminately across the economy), the others emphasise their downside (distortionary effects, possibility of circumvention, ineffectiveness). When it comes to assessing the effects of raising official interest rates, the sides are reversed. While Kahn and Balogh focus on the increase in the cost of public debt, the depressing effect on stock market prices and the increase in uncertainty for companies investing, the others praise the greater flexibility of the Bank Rate manoeuvre compared to direct controls (which must in any case be authorised by law) and the ability of this manoeuvre to stabilise entrepreneurs' expectations with regard to price and exchange rate developments. In addition, Kahn points out how a restrictive monetary policy can prejudice the future use of 'cheap money' in the event of a new phase of economic depression.

> This argument—overlooked by Mr. Johnson and Mr. Kennedy—has to be based on one or other (or both) of two assumptions, both of them highly reasonable. The one is that there is a 'bottom stop' to the rate of interest [...] the height of which depends on people's expectations of the possibility

[56] The reference to the 'delicate mechanism of financial control' is found in the Stamp Memorial Lecture on the Balance of Payments given by L. Robbins in 1951. As we will see below, Kahn will return to Robbins's lecture critically in an essay shortly after the one on which we are commenting.

> of a rise in the rate of interest as coloured by past history. The alternative assumption is that although open-market operations, carried on *à outrance*, could, given a reasonable period of time, bring the rate of interest down to any desired level [...] various irrational fears connected with the idea of inflation will interfere with an unlimited expansion of the quantity of money. (ibid., pp. 147–148)

Thus, backward-looking expectations and/or the belief that vigorous monetary expansion will inevitably lead to inflation (and higher nominal interest rates) may make it impossible to implement this expansion when needed. In both cases, the obstacle is subjective rather than objective, and its removal requires a systematic exercise in persuasion of the kind that Kahn would engage in almost to the end of his life, as the following chapters show.

A comparison of the various opinions expressed in the Symposium reveals a certain closeness of Kahn and Balogh to the positions of the 'young' Johnson and Kennedy, from which Paish and Robertson are more distant, with Hicks and Harrod in the middle position. This difference, almost of a generational nature, is recognised by Robert V. Roosa (Federal Reserve Bank of New York), whose contribution opens a second Symposium, which was published in the August issue of the *Bulletin*, together with commentaries from Robert Frost, Victor Morgan, Joan Robinson, E. Nevin and, again, Hicks and Kahn. In this second Symposium a number of themes emerged which would be the focus of the Radcliffe Committee a few years later.

Roosa, supported by Morgan, focuses on the need to control the entire supply of money and credit, through banks and non-bank financial intermediaries, and not just bank credit. To do this, the government must abandon the policy of stabilising interest rates on government debt, fix the quantity of base money and let interest rates reach the level necessary to balance the supply of and demand for credit. From this perspective, direct controls have at best a subsidiary effect and should be used sparingly because of their distortionary effects. Both Frost and Hicks dwell on the reluctance of British governments to see the rising cost of public debt as an obstacle to higher interest rates, which are nevertheless recognised as having the capacity to dampen investment and aggregate demand.

Kahn (1952b) dwells on this possibility, criticising Harrod's argument in the first Symposium and elsewhere about the desirability of reducing private investment in order to increase resources for exports and reduce inflationary pressures.[57] From here, Kahn's critique shifts to an article, published anonymously and entitled 'Can Monetary Policy Carry the Load', *The Banker*, No. 316, May 1952. The article supported the idea that raising interest rates would lead to an increase in investment by creating a temporary excess of productive capacity and savings in the short run. For Kahn, this idea is difficult to accept, except in relation to the effect of rising interest rates on the reduction of inventories held by producers. Moreover, with London's reduced ability to attract capital from abroad, with full employment as the primary objective of economic policy, and with a high public debt exposed to the risks of rising interest rates, an appeal to traditional monetary mechanisms is risky and based on a misdiagnosis of the underlying problem.

> I had already in my contribution to the earlier Symposium suggested that if the Government think clearly about the matter, they must realise that their monetary policy is not the traditional monetary policy but is simply something temporary forced on them by the shortage of steel. [...] To my mind the overwhelming question is what the Government will do when more steel could be secured (if necessary by paying dollars for it). If we are then still in balance of payments difficulties will the Government drift into behaving as though it was after all the traditional monetary policy to which they were desperately clinging? That is the great danger, entailing a continued discouragement of industrial investment. [...] I have been labouring this confusion of thought, partly because this article in *The Banker* really does deal with the mechanics of monetary policy and does not simply take refuge, like most published articles on the subject, in sanctimonious claptrap about the virtues of 'monetary discipline' and 'flexibility of interest rates', partly because any article in *The Banker* is authoritative and influential (unlike, I fear, the Oxford Symposium, which has been subject to what looks almost like conspiracy of silence on the part of the press). (Kahn, 1952b, p. 280)

Once again, these words reflect Kahn's concern—already evident during the war—to build the right public conviction for policies capable of

[57] These ideas were fully articulated in Harrod (1958), where the author analyses the strategies for controlling inflation in post-war Britain and argues that curbing excessive private investment, rather than restricting consumption, is a more effective way of controlling inflation without damaging living standards and balancing economic growth with price stability. The book reflects Harrod's Keynesian perspective, which differs from Kahn's, and contributes to the wider debate on inflation control in the 1950s, to which we return in the next chapter.

sustaining government activity in support of employment and growth against the alternative of laissez-faire and austerity. The same concern animates Kahn's many interventions in the press. From 1946, when he left the civil service, Kahn was constantly present in the quality press (*The Times*, *The Economist*, *The Financial Times*, *The Listener*) with short letters and articles reiterating his convictions on the benefits of direct control, the need to increase investment and exports and the possibility of tackling the British economy's problems without resorting to disinflation. Some examples will suffice to document this activity. Kahn (1951) opposed *The Economist*'s call for disinflation to address labour shortages, arguing it would increase unemployment, reduce consumption and cause labour hoarding. He defended targeted controls, blaming shortages on poor enforcement rather than the policy itself. Kahn (1954) argued that in a low-unemployment economy, balancing consumption and investment required more than just taxation adjustments. He favoured an expansionary monetary policy ('cheap money') to boost industrial investment without harming consumption while keeping government debt costs low. He dismissed inflation fears, asserting that demand and wages could be managed, and defended cheap money for its role in economic stability and growth.

Finally, Kahn ([1952c] 1972) focuses on the transmission mechanism by which a monetary restriction can lead to an improvement in the balance of payments. Kahn's polemical target here is the price-specie flow mechanism and the traditional idea that when a country runs a trade deficit, the resulting outflow of money leads to a fall in domestic prices and a rise in foreign prices, causing the deficit to disappear without any government intervention. Against this idea, which Kahn traces to Lionel Robbins's 1951 Stamp Memorial Lecture (Robbins, 1951), Kahn asks:

> But is it so simple? Even in the illustrative case from which the argument starts of currency systems based on convertible metal coinage, is it really just the waving of a magic wand? Suppose that in such a case a country lost ground in export industries to competitors. [...] But why should prices fall? [...] 'There is always a level of internal prices and incomes at which the balance of payments would tend to equilibrium'. But how is it established? (1952c 1972, p. 62)

Kahn's answer, based on Keynes's authority, is that the decrease in exports will cause employment and output to fall, with depression and unemployment spreading to other industries. This will reduce the demand for money for transactional purposes, freeing up monetary resources that will flow abroad. At the same time, the trade contraction and unemployment will cause prices and wages to fall (first-round effect), although Kahn thinks it unlikely that this alone will be sufficient to obviate the need for further coinage to finance the external deficit. This additional outflow will come from the decumulation of domestic hoards and the decline in private investment caused by the rising interest rates and tighter credit conditions that accompany the initial outflow of money (second-round effect).

The second point Kahn makes is that relying on monetary restraint to reduce domestic inflation and thus improve the current account is not always the right approach, although domestic inflation can worsen and in some cases even lead to a balance of payments crisis. Resorting to measures that curb inflation by dampening domestic demand is appropriate in the presence of severe labour shortages, fierce competition for labour among employers (causing wages to drift above the levels negotiated with the unions) and strong pressure from the unions to secure further increases in nominal wages. In this case, the restrictive measures will not only remove excess inflationary pressures but also help to free up labour and goods used domestically for additional production of goods for export. Even in this case, however, it should be recognised that monetary policy may not be the appropriate instrument to achieve this result:

> The economic system is a sticky and patchy affair—very far from the ideal world of perfect mobility and foresight beloved of theoretical economists. If waste is to be avoided and efficiency defended, the operation of blind economic forces has to be tempered by intervention which is discriminatory in character, in the sense in which monetary policy is not, but a discriminatory purchase tax, allocations of output backed by steel allocation, and building licencing are, particularly if they are combined with a real readiness to influence the movement of labour from one job to another by making full use of the Notification of Vacancies Order. [...] The object should be to release labour at points at which it can effectively be reabsorbed in useful production. (Kahn, 1952c 1972, p. 68)

Ignoring this fact and relying solely or primarily on monetary policy because of its supposed neutrality and greater effectiveness against inflation and external deficits risks having the only long-term effect of structurally reducing that part of private investment which is most sensitive to interest rates and credit conditions and on which the rate of productivity growth depends. In criticising monetary restriction as a response to inflation and external deficits, Kahn—drawing on his scepticism of the Quantity Theory of Money and his faith in direct controls—develops arguments, later reiterated before the Radcliffe Committee.

References

Allen, W. A. (2014). *Monetary policy and financial repression in Britain, 1951–1959*. Palgrave Macmillan.

Atkinson, A. B., & Weale, M. (2000). James Edward Meade. 1907–1995. *Proceedings of the British Academy, 105*, 473–500.

Bardhan, P. K. (1965). Optimum accumulation and international trade. *Review of Economic Studies, 32*(3), 241–244.

Barker, R. S. (1986). Civil service attitudes and the economic planning of the Attlee government. *Journal of Contemporary History, 21*(3), 473–486.

Bickerdike, C. F. (1906). The theory of incipient taxes. *Economic Journal, 16*(64), 529–535.

Bickerdike, C. F. (1907). Protective and preferential import duties, by A.C. Pigou. *Economic Journal, 17*(65), 98–102.

Blair, A. M. (1997). The British iron and steel industry since 1945. *Journal of European Economic History, 26*(3), 571–581.

Booth, A. (2001a). New revisionists and the Keynesian era in British economic policy. *Economic History Review, 54*(2), 346–366.

Booth, A. (2001b). Britain in the 1950s: A 'Keynesian' managed economy? *History of Political Economy, 33*, 283–313.

Cairncross, A. (1985). *Years of recovery: British economic policy 1945–51*. Methuen.

Cairncross, A. (1992). *The British economy after 1945*. Institute of Contemporary British History.

Cairncross, A. (1993). *Austin Robinson; The life of an economic adviser*. Palgrave Macmillan.

Cairncross, A., & Watts, N. (1989). *The economic section 1939–1961: A study in economic advising*. Routledge.

Chick, M. (1998). *Industrial policy in Britain 1945–1951*. Cambridge University Press.

Cohen, R., Kahn, R. F., Reddaway, W. B., & Robinson, J. V. (1964). Statement submitted to the Lloyd Jacob Committee on resale price maintenance. *Oxford Bulletin of Economics and Statistics, 26*(2), 113–121.

Deane, P. (2018). Cohen, Ruth Louisa (born 1906). In *The New Palgrave dictionary of economics (1763–1764)* (3rd ed.). Palgrave Macmillan.

Dow, J. C. R. (1964). *The management of the British Economy*. Cambridge University Press.

Durbin, E. ([1985] 2019). *New Jerusalems. The Labour Party and the economics of Democratic Socialism*, Routledge and Kegan Paul. New edition 2019, Routledge.

Franks, O. (1947). *Central planning and controls in war and peace*. London School of Economics and Political Science (University of London). Longmans, Green and Co.

Gardner, R. N. (1956). *Sterling-Dollar diplomacy: Anglo-American collaboration in the reconstruction of multilateral trade*. Oxford University Press.

Geiger, T. (2004). *Britain and the economic problem of the cold war: The political economy and the economic impact of the British defence effort, 1945–1955*. Ashgate Publishing.

Graaff, J. de V. (1949). On optimum tariff structures. *Review of Economic Studies, 17*, 47–59.

Hamilton, B., & Whalley, J. (1983). Optimal tariff calculations in alternative trade models and some possible implications for current world trading arrangements. *Journal of International Economics, 15*(3–4), 323–348.

Hancock, W. K., & Gowing, M. M. (1949). *British war economy*. HMSO.

Harrod, R. F. (1958). *Policy against inflation*. Macmillan.

Holmans, A. E. (1999). *Demand management in Britain 1953–58*. Institute of Contemporary British History.

Howson, S. K. (1975). *Domestic monetary management in Britain 1919–1938*. University of Cambridge Department of Applied Economics Occasional Papers, No. 48. Cambridge University Press.

Howson, S. (1993). *British Monetary Policy 1945–51*. Clarendon Press.

Howson, S. (2000). James Meade. *Economic Journal, 110*(461), F122–F145.

Howson, S., & Moggridge, D. (Eds.). (1990). *The collected papers of James Meade, Vol. IV, The Cabinet Office Diary, 1944–46*. Unwin Hyman.

Hutchison, T. W. (1968). *Economics and economic policy in Britain, 1946–1966: Some aspects of their interrelations*. Allen and Unwin.

Irwin, D. A., Mavroidis, P. C., & Sykes, A. O. (2009). *The genesis of the GATT*. Cambridge University Press.

Johnson, H. G. (1950). Optimum welfare and maximum revenue tariffs. *Review of Economic Studies, 19*, 28–35.

Johnson, H. G. (1952). The new monetary policy and the problem of credit control. *Bulletin of the Oxford University Institute of Statistics, 14*, 117–131.

Johnson, H. G. (1953). Optimum tariffs and retaliation. *Review of Economic Studies, 21*, 142–153.

Johnson, H. G. (1978). Ruth Cohen: A neglected contributor to contemporary capital theory. In E. S. Johnson & H. G. Johnson (Eds.), *The shadow of Keynes:*

Understanding Keynes, Cambridge, and Keynesian economics (pp. 167–180). University of Chicago Press.

Kahn, R. F. (1947). Tariffs and the terms of trade. *Review of Economic Studies, 15*(1), 14–19.

Kahn, R. F. (1948). The 1948 budget: An economist's criticism. *The Listener*, May 6, 738–739.

Kahn, R. F. (1949). Professor Meade on planning. *Economic Journal, 59*, 1–16.

Kahn, R. F. (1951). Manpower control. *The Economist*, December 15.

Kahn, R. F. (1952a). Comments (on monetary policy and the crisis). *Bulletin of the Oxford University Institute of Economics and Statistics, 14*, 147–153.

Kahn, R. F. (1952b). Comments (on monetary policy again). *Bulletin of the Oxford University, 14*, 278–280.

Kahn, R. F. (1952c). Monetary policy and the balance of payments. *Political Quarterly, 23*(3), July, 250–261. Reprinted in R.F. Kahn (1972), *Selected Essays on Employment and Growth* (60–71). Cambridge University Press.

Kahn, R. F. (1954). The case for cheap money. *The Financial Times*, June 3–4.

Kennedy, C. (1952). Monetary policy and the crisis. *Bulletin of the Oxford University Institute of Statistics, 14*, 132–140.

Lidbury, C. (1947). Great Britain in relation to the world's trade situation. *Journal of the Royal Society of Arts, 95*(4736), 160–173.

MacDougall, D. (1987) *Don and Mandarin: Memoirs of an economist.* John Murray Publishers Ltd..

Marcuzzo, M. C. (2020). Richard F. Kahn: A disciple of Keynes. *History of Economics Review, 76*(1), 2–57.

Meade, J. E. (1948a). *Planning and the pricing mechanism.* Macmillan.

Meade, J. E. (1948b). Planning without prices. *Economica, 15*(57), 28–35.

Meade, J. E. (1950). Review of *A charter for world trade*, by C. Wilcox. *Economica, 17*(66), 215–218.

Middleton, R. (1998). *Economists and the British economy from Marshall to Meade.* Edward Elgar.

Moggridge, D. E. (2011). *Harry Johnson. A life in economics.* Cambridge University Press.

Peden, G. C. (1990). Old dogs and new tricks: The British Treasury and Keynesian economics in the 1940s and 1950s. In M. O. Furner & B. Supple (Eds.), *The state and economic knowledge: The American and British experiences* (pp. 208–238). Woodrow Wilson International Center for Scholars and Cambridge University Press.

Peden, G. C. (2003). New revisionists and the Keynesian era in British economic policy: A comment. *Economic History Review, 56*(1), 118–124.

Robbins, L. (1951). *The balance of payments (stamp memorial lecture).* Athlone Press.

Robinson, A. (1986). The economic problems of the transition from war to peace: 1945–49. Review of the book *Years of recovery: British Economic Policy 1945–51*, by A. Cairncross. *Cambridge Journal of Economics, 10*(2), 165–185.

Robinson, A. (1992). My apprenticeship as an economist. In M. Szenberg (Ed.), *Eminent economists: Their life philosophies* (pp. 203–221). Cambridge University Press.

Saville, J. (1980). Hugh Gaitskell (1906–1963): An assessment. *Socialist Register, 1980*, 148–169.

Sayers, R. S. (1952). The development of British monetary policy, 1951. *Banca Nazionale del Lavoro Quarterly Review, 5*(20), 3–9.

Sayers, R. S. (1956). *Financial Policy, 1939–45* (Vol. 1). HM Stationery Office.

Schuster, G. (1955). Richard Stafford Cripps, 1889–1952. *Biographical Memoirs of Fellows of the Royal Society, 1*, 11–32.

Shonfield, A. (1958). *British economic policy since the war*. Penguin Books.

Silberston, A. (1973). Price behaviour of firms. In *Surveys of applied economics* (pp. 45–114). Palgrave Macmillan.

Soloway, A. M. (1954). Economic aspects of the British purchase tax. *Journal of Finance, 9*(2), 188–208.

Taylor, R. W. (1954). Central economic coordination in British government. *Social Research, 21*(2), 179–203.

Thackeray, D. (2021). Britain's turn towards Europe, 1947–75. In The British Academy (Ed.), *Trade Policy History, The British Academy* (pp. 27–35).

Theakston, K. (1999). 'Otto' Clarke. In *Leadership in Whitehall* (pp. 148–172). Palgrave Macmillan.

Thirlwall, A., & Gibson, H. (1992). A history of the UK balance of payments. In *Balance-of-payments theory and the United Kingdom experience* (4th ed., pp. 219–271). Macmillan.

Thompson, N. (2006). *Political economy and the labour party: The economics of democratic socialism 1884–2005* (2nd ed.). Routledge.

Thorpe, A. (2015). *A history of the British labour party* (4th ed.). Red Globe Press.

Tomlinson, J. (1987). *Employment policy. The crucial years 1939–1955.* Clarendon Press.

Tomlinson, J. (1991). The Attlee government and the balance of payments, 1945–1951. *Twentieth Century British History, 2*(1), 47–66.

Tomlinson, J. (1997). *Democratic socialism and economic policy. The Attlee years 1945–1951.* Cambridge University Press.

Tomlinson, J. (2000a). Marshall aid and the 'shortage economy' in Britain in the 1940s. *Contemporary European History, 9*(1), 137–155.

Tomlinson, J. (2000b). Review of *Demand management in Britain, 1953–1958*; *Demand management, 1958–1964*; *Diaries: The Radcliffe Committee and the Treasury, 1961–1964*, by A. E. Holmans, R. F. Bretherton, and A. Cairncross. *Economic History Review, 53*(4), 833–835.

Toye, R. (2000a). Gosplanners versus Thermostatters: Whitehall planning debates and their political consequences, 1945–49. *Contemporary British History, 14*, 81–106.
Toye, R. (2000b). The Labour Party's external economic policy in the 1940s. *The Historical Journal, 43*(1), 189–215.
Toye, R. (2002). The gentleman in Whitehall' reconsidered: The evolution of Douglas Jay's views on economic planning and consumer choice, 1937–47. *Labour History Review, 67*, 187–204.
Toye, R. (2003). *The Labour Party and the planned economy, 1931–1951*. Boydell Press for the Royal Historical Society.
Wilcox, C. (1947). The London draft of a charter for an international trade organization. *American Economic Review, 37*(2), 529–541.
Williams, P. M. (1982). *Hugh Gaitskell: A political biography*. Oxford University Press.
Worswick, G. D. N. (1952). Direct controls. In G. D. N. Worswick & P. Ady (Eds.), *The British economy 1945–1950* (pp. 278–312). Oxford University Press.
Worswick, G. D. N., & Ady, P. H. (Eds.). (1952). *The British economy 1945–1950*. Oxford University Press.

CHAPTER 5

Professor Kahn

5.1 Kahn, Keynesianism and the British Economy in the 1950s

During the 1950s, the Conservative governments of Churchill (1951–1955), Eden (1955–1957) and Macmillan (1957–1963) focused on reconciling high and stable employment with containing inflation and achieving equilibrium in the balance of payments. They also aimed to comply with the new Bretton Woods rules and preserve the UK's international economic and geopolitical status. In tackling this complex task, British policymakers were able to draw on Keynesian ideas, which had gained political traction.[1] These included the idea of countercyclical management of aggregate demand through fiscal policy; the acceptability of a budget deficit in the event of a recession; and the notion that inflation depended on demand pull as well as cost-push factors. While these ideas had largely become part of the mainstream of British economic policy, the Keynesian theory was the subject of reflection and controversy among economists.

[1] On the development and influence of Keynesianism in British economic policy in the 1950s, see Hall (1986, especially pp. 69–99). On the association between Keynesianism and Conservative governments in Britain, see Tomlinson (1995), Booth (2000, 2001) and the references therein. On the limits of the idea of continuity and consensus between the Labour and Conservative governments of the 1950s (Butskellism), see Rollings (1996).

P. Paesani, *Richard F. Kahn*, Great Thinkers in Economics,
https://doi.org/10.1007/978-3-032-09123-9_5

Although the debate was complex and multifaceted, two distinct and opposing viewpoints emerged. On the one hand, there were those who sought to play down the innovative scope of the *General Theory* on a theoretical level, while still believing in the positive role of public intervention in the spirit of Keynes for pragmatic reasons. Conversely, others were convinced that the Keynesian theoretical framework—including effective demand, a theory of investment under conditions of uncertainty, the idea that money is not neutral and a non-monetary theory of inflation—could be developed from the short to the long term. This would generate a new theory of growth and distribution, offering an alternative to the neoclassical paradigm and informing policy decisions. Richard Kahn, who was elected to a personal Professorship in 1951, dedicated himself to this latter approach, as well as to consolidating economic studies at Cambridge.

> As an economist in the post-War period I was heavily involved in the work of the Faculty of Economics and Politics, on which I served as Chairman for two years. I took part in a radical reform of our examination system and the introduction of Sociology into the University. Student participation in Faculty government made rapid and successful progress. I ran a seminar held in my room consisting of the leading Cambridge economists, Nicky Kaldor and Joan Robinson, with active participation by others. We elaborated the theories of growth, distribution of income and the character of capital. Discussion on occasion became somewhat heated but we remained close friends. I took over from Keynes and Dennis Robertson the Political Economy Club. My publications, though numerous, were mainly ephemeral in character, largely concerned with the state of the economy and Government Policy. (Marcuzzo, 2020, p. 26)

In the 1950s the state of the (British) economy, to which Kahn referred, could best be described as mixed.[2] GDP growth rates averaged around 2–3% per annum, with consumer spending and living standards rising and a gradual shift from heavy industry to a more service-oriented economy.

[2] For an overview of various aspects of the British economy in the 1950s, in addition to those mentioned at the end of Chap. 4, with reference to data, see Worswick and Ady (1962), Cairncross (1992), Clarke (1996), Holmans (1999). For a lively contemporary description of British economic policy since the war, see Shonfield (1958), and for a focus on the Treasury, see Brittan (1964). For a detailed discussion of monetary policy and Britain's monetary and financial problems in the 1950s, see Allen (2014). On wages and employment policy, see R. Jones (1987, pp. 48–62). The source of the data mentioned in this section is here

In general, British economic performance was positive in itself, but less brilliant than that of other European countries, particularly West Germany.[3] Part of this prosperity came from the many jobs created by the post-war recovery, particularly in manufacturing and services, with unemployment rates averaging around 1–2%. However, there were marked regional disparities, with some areas experiencing higher unemployment than others.

Inflation was a major problem, peaking at around 9% in 1951 as a result of post-war adjustments and rising costs, as well as the pressure caused by the Korean War. With the end of the Korean War (July 1953) inflation declined, also thanks to the return of international demand to less paroxysmal levels, which lowered import prices of food and raw material in Britain, but it did not disappear. The resurgence of inflation between 1955 (4.5%) and 1956 (4.9%) brought the problem to the attention of the government and highlighted the existence of two different approaches within the Conservative government.

On the one hand there were those, like Prime Minister Macmillan, who believed that reducing inflation was a matter of containing aggregate demand through a gradual monetary restraint and the curbing of public spending, while relying on exhortations to trade unions and businessmen to moderate their demands and to let the economy take its course. On the other hand, there were those, such as Chancellor of the Exchequer Peter Thorneycroft (1957–1958), who thought it necessary to take a more aggressive stance on inflation in order to bring the rate of increase in prices below that of nominal wages. Between January 1957 and January 1958, in particular, Thorneycroft took a number of initiatives to address the problem of accelerating prices. These included a new phase of monetary restraint combined with the establishment in July 1957 of the Council on Prices, Productivity and Incomes, a group of three experts charged with assessing how full employment and rising living standards could be reconciled with reasonable stability in prices and income levels.[4]

Inflation contributed to a weakening of the UK balance of payments, which was already burdened by Britain's dependence on imports of food and raw materials, the cost of maintaining military commitments abroad

[3] Towards the end of the 1950s this difference began to be perceived as a problem, paving the way for the idea that the British economy had entered a period of relative decline, which could be reversed by a bold policy of innovation and investment (Tomlinson, 1996).

[4] On the Council on Prices, Productivity and Incomes and the context in which it operated, see Cristiano (2023).

and large foreign investments. Exports grew strongly, but not enough, while foreign exchange reserves were generally low. Partly because of this, partly because of the high level of British external debt, particularly to the United States and the sterling area, sterling often came under pressure, particularly in 1955 and again in 1957.

In this context many British economists, from Harrod and Robbins to Robertson and Paish, argued that Britain's problems were primarily due to excessive demand pressure on limited productive capacity. Unemployment rates hovering between 1% and 1.5% and shortages of some key raw materials were often cited in the debate as indicators of 'over-full employment'. This diagnosis led to a recommendation for the rapid adoption of restrictive measures. Monetary restraint was seen by many as particularly appropriate, as higher interest rates were expected to strengthen sterling and at the same time deflate excess demand. Of the British economists of the Keynesian persuasion, Harrod was the only one who really took the position that the main cause of inflation and the problems of the British balance of payments were determined by excess demand.[5] All the others, starting with R. Hall (1901–1988), head of the Economic Section after J. Meade from 1947 to 1961, had a more nuanced position, and in some respects more in line with the cost-push thesis, which was supported—as we shall see—by Kahn. The demand-pull theory was also adopted by Phillips in 1958 in connection with the problem of the empirical determination of the unemployment rate consistent with price stability.[6]

In Kahn's view the resurgence of these ideas threatened some of the achievements of post-war Britain, and in particular full employment and the possibility to promote investment, productivity and modernisation of the British economy. As such, these ideas had to be countered with rational arguments, backed up by an appeal to the intellectual and moral authority of Keynes. In the 1950s, Kahn did so on several occasions (e.g. Kahn, 1956a, 1956b). He stressed the dangers of a restrictive monetary policy which, by penalising investment and hence the possibility of increasing productive capacity and productivity, could well be counterproductive, condemning Britain to semi-permanent stagnation and un-competitiveness vis-à-vis other developed countries. To avoid this scenario, monetary policy should remain accommodative and be combined with other measures. These measures could include the regulation of planning permission and

[5] On this see, Harrod (1958). On Harrod's biography, see Caldentey (2019).

[6] On this, see Cristiano and Paesani (2018a, 2018b).

capital issues, the direct allocation of steel and other scarce raw materials and limitations on hire-purchase schemes and the purchase of durable consumer goods. This would help to remove bottlenecks, free up resources and encourage an orderly increase in investment and exports.

The insistence on investment and growth as a priority objective of economic policy was one of the few points on which Kahn's ideas aligned with those of many British economists in the 1950s, particularly the young progressives (e.g. Shonfield, 1958; Middleton, 2004). These economists believed that promoting investment, public and private, was the only way to halt and reverse the UK's relative decline compared to other developed countries.[7]

If the situation called for a dampening of aggregate demand, Kahn recommended curbing private consumption, combining an increase in income taxes with restrictions on hire purchase schemes and import controls. In addition, and most importantly, Kahn recommended that inflation should be kept under control by ensuring that money wages grew on average at the same rate as productivity. To achieve this, it was essential to make bargaining between unions and employers' organisations more orderly and less confrontational.[8] In the 1950s, characterised by a widespread desire to move on as quickly as possible from the austerity and controls of the war, by a renewed confidence in free trade and enterprise and by the government's desire not to interfere with wage negotiations, Kahn's proposals found little favour with the British governments.

Robert Hall's diaries provide evidence about this. In the first volume of these diaries, covering the period 1947–1953 (Cairncross, 1989), Kahn's name appears only three times, and in no case on any relevant issue. In the second volume (Cairncross, 1991), relative to 1954–1961, Kahn's name appears four times, where Hall reports on his disagreements with Robertson and, in particular, on Kahn's role in the OECD Committee on the Problem of Rising Prices (see below). Hall's limited references to

[7] In 1964, Wilson's Labour government adopted this thesis and acted accordingly (Pemberton, 2004). Subsequently, the theory of decline became associated with conservatism, alongside the idea that decline was due to excessive regulation and state intervention creating obstacles to free enterprise, competition and the market. For a recent reconsideration of the thesis on the relative decline of the British economy during the post-war period, see Tomlinson (2023).

[8] See, for example, Kahn ([1956a] 1972, p. 106).

Kahn are a further indication of the distance Kahn, with his links to the Labour Party, had from the policy choices of Conservative governments.[9]

In spite of this, Kahn continued to insist on what he considered essential to promote prosperity in Britain. He did so moving on three distinct but interrelated fronts: economic theory, opinion making and interaction with policymakers. Each of these activities drew strength from the other two. Extending and strengthening the Keynesian analytical framework was essential both to counter attempts to downplay the innovative scope of Keynes's thought and to give strength to the policy proposals that drew inspiration from this. Convincing the public of the validity of Keynesian policies by explaining their underlying logic in understandable terms was essential to their success. This is evidenced by a number of non-academic writings from this period, as well as his interventions in the quality press (*The Times*, *The Financial Times*, *The Economist*) and radio talks. These interventions, dealing with issues as diverse as Marshall aid (Kahn, 1950), the budget (Kahn, 1951a), manpower control (Kahn, 1951b, 1952), equipment for industry (Kahn, 1953), cheap money policy (Kahn, 1954), money wages growing faster than productivity rather than demand pressure as the main cause of British inflation in the 1950s (Kahn, [1956a] 1972), gave Kahn an opportunity to reaffirm the validity of the Keynesian perspective on Britain's economic problems, as he understood them. Equally, and perhaps more importantly, it was necessary to find a way of bringing these proposals to the attention of policymakers, so that they could be implemented effectively. Evidently, Kahn's close association with Keynes and the prestige that came with having become a professor at Cambridge were very valuable assets in this respect.

5.2 Some Notes on Liquidity Preference

In the mid-1950s Kahn participated in the theoretical debates surrounding the development of Keynesian theoretical framework, focusing on three issues: (1) liquidity preference, speculation and portfolio choice, (2) causes and remedies for inflation and (3) elaboration of a Keynesian theory of growth and distribution. The essay on liquidity preference (Kahn, 1954), which originated as a revision of two lectures given by Kahn at the University of Manchester in 1954, is Kahn's major contribution to the

[9] On the absence of Kahn's name from the accounts of economic policy in Britain, in particular in the 1950s, see also Bogdanor and Skidelsky (1970), Peden (1985), Tomlinson (2017).

first strand and more generally to the Post-Keynesian theory of money and interest rates.[10] The article revisits Keynes's theory of liquidity preference, focusing on the relationship between the demand for money for precautionary and speculative reasons, and how this relationship depends on the investment decisions made by a diverse group of investors based on their expectations and assumptions in uncertain conditions.

Kahn's *Notes on liquidity preference* provide another example of his modus operandi: starting from one theoretical concept proposed by others, developing it in an original way to obtain new ideas about the phenomenon under observation. In this case, the starting point is the Keynesian theory of interest rates as interpreted by Robinson (1951) on the background of Cambridge controversies between liquidity preference and loanable funds theory (Johnson, 1951).[11] Robinson's analysis overcomes the dichotomy between money and long-term securities and applies the theory of liquidity preference to multiple assets, taking into account different types of investors and how their portfolio choices take place in historical time.

Building on these elements, Kahn focuses on the microeconomic aspects of portfolio choice and the interplay between risk and uncertainty, and arrives at two main results: a general characterisation of investor behaviour and the conclusion that the liquidity preference function cannot be conceived as a function that inversely and unambiguously relates the long-term interest rate to the demand for speculative money, but at best has a vague correspondence. In other words, for a given interest rate structure at a given time, the liquidity preference may vary within a range whose width depends on investors' expectations of the path of interest

[10] For a formalisation and analysis of Kahn's theory of liquidity preference, see Dardi (1994), whose notation we follow in this Section. For mentions of Kahn's paper on liquidity preference in connection with Post-Keynesian monetary theory, see Wells (1983), Bibow (1998), Rousseas (1998), Cardim de Carvalho (2010), Rezende (2015), Koutsobinas (2022). See also Rochon (2001) who argues that, in the mid-1950s, both Kahn and Joan Robinson offered insights into the workings of a credit economy, in particular regarding the endogeneity of the supply of money, that have been largely ignored by Post-Keynesians and that nonetheless are consistent with Post-Keynesian monetary theory.

[11] Throughout the 1950s, the Theory of Interest Rates was the main course taught by Kahn at the University of Cambridge (see Appendix B and Sect. 6.2). For a consideration of the place of Kahn's paper within the liquidity preference versus loanable funds debates of the 1950s, and more generally between Cambridge economics and the neoclassical general equilibrium synthesis, see Bridel (2021). On Robinson's theory of the rate of interest, see Pivetti (1996).

rates at different maturities at a given time, the degree of confidence with which these expectations are held and the type of investors prevailing in the market. It follows that a given change in the money supply may have quite different effects on interest rates, depending on the contingent state of liquidity preference, which is not known a priori and which in turn depends, among other things, on the reaction of investors to the observed changes in the money supply. The main policy implication that Kahn draws from all this, and which he will return to in his testimony to the Radcliffe Committee, is that if the monetary authorities want to control interest rates, they must do so directly and not by relying on the manipulation of the money supply.

Kahn challenges the conventional theory, endorsed by economists such as Hicks (1946, pp. 164–166), Kaldor (1939, p. 13) and Kalecki (1954, pp. 81–82), which states that long-term interest rates are determined solely by current and expected short-term rates set by monetary authorities.[12] This theory downplays the influence of risk elements and uncertainty over the future course of interest rates and focuses on the relative stability of long-term interest rates compared to short-term rates. It assumes that investors make fixed choices between bonds and bills based on a shared expectation of what will happen during the bond's maturity period. Kahn argues that this assumption is flawed because investors holding short-term bills are not locked into rolling them over and may switch to bonds if market conditions change, particularly in response to changes in monetary policy. Therefore, investor behaviour is more flexible and responsive than the theory suggests.

> When a bill is bought rather than a bond the only relevant expectation determining the decision is what the bond rate will be when the bill matures. That expectation is certainly related to the expectation of what the bill rate will itself be at that same date. [...] All this is, however, a very different thing from saying that the bond rate *depends* [in the original] on expectations about the future of the bill rate itself, rather than of banking and monetary policy generally. (Kahn, [1954] 1972, p. 78)

Following this idea, Kahn restores autonomy to the long-term interest rate and to the analysis of how expectations about its future path affect its

[12] On the difference between Hicks's and Kaldor's treatment of long-term interest rates and Kahn's own, see Sardoni (2007). On the notions of risk premium and liquidity premium in Hicks and Keynes, see Fantacci et al. (2014).

current value, focusing on an individual investor choosing between money and fixed-rate irredeemable bonds, while assuming bills away. As Kahn ([1954] 1972, p. 79) explains, while this simplifying assumption departs significantly from real-world conditions, it does not undermine the core argument if the earlier reasoning holds. The short-term interest rate still plays a background role, appearing indirectly through individuals' expectations about how the long-term rate will behave. However, these expectations are highly subjective and shaped by uncertainty and risk. He further clarifies that the long-term interest rate should be understood as a blend of returns on perpetual financial instruments, such as irredeemable bonds and preference shares.

The investor bases her decision on two elements: the current long-term interest rate i, and the rate at which she expects i to rise (or fall) over the relevant investment horizon. On the assumption that the coupon paid to bond holders is equal to 1 euro, the current price of the bond p is equal to the reciprocal of the long-term interest rate ($p = 1/i$). Defining v as the expected price of the bond at maturity of the first coupon, the investor will be indifferent between bonds and money, whose return is equal to zero, when

$$1 + v - p = 0 \tag{5.1}$$

Dividing both sides by p and isolating i, Eq. (5.1) becomes

$$i = v\left(\frac{1}{v} - \frac{1}{p}\right) \tag{5.2}$$

where $v\,(1/v - 1/p) = g$ represents the expected rate of variation in the long-term rate of interest. As long as v is unique and held with complete certainty, the investor's speculative demand for money will be equal to zero if $g < i$ and to her entire portfolio if $g > i$. In this case, the precautionary motive is inoperative and only marginal investors, whose expectations are consistent with Eq. (5.2), will hold both money and bonds. On the assumption of heterogeneous agents—each of them holding unique expectations with absolute certainty—the aggregation of individual positions yields the market demand for securities and its obverse, the speculative demand for money.[13] However, when heterogeneous investors hold expectations with less than perfect confidence, uncertainty and the precautionary demand for money enter the analysis. To understand this point, it is necessary to consider two distinct and interacting elements: first, the different degrees of confidence with which each investor formulates her expectations of the long-term interest rate; and second, the impact that financial risks of a different nature have on different categories of investors.

Regarding the first element, some investors have certain expectations about the future path of long-term interest rates and are therefore 'absolute' bulls (bears), placing all their assets in securities (money) when they expect long-term interest rates to fall (rise). At the other extreme are those investors who remain in their current position, either because they have no clue about the future path of interest rates or because they are extremely risk-averse. In between these two extremes are those investors, the majority, who have some idea of the direction in which interest rates will move (the speculative component) but are aware of the possibility of being wrong and therefore, with varying degrees of risk aversion, take precautions by holding part of their assets in securities and part in money (the precautionary component). In defining this balance, the second factor mentioned above comes into play, the impact that risks of different types have on different economic agents.

Favouring money over securities exposes the investor to the loss of the income associated with holding those securities (income risk), while the opposite choice exposes the investor to the risk of losing capital (capital risk).[14] Some investors ('widows and orphans') perceive income risk more strongly than capital risk, and this leads them to prefer securities to money and to resist the temptation to sell these securities unless there is a certainty of a significant capital loss or the income received is close to zero. In their case, a strong perception of income risk works in the same direction as bullish sentiment. Other investors ('bankers') perceive capital risk more strongly than income risk and therefore prefer money to securities and resist the temptation to buy securities unless there is a certainty of a capital

[13] The same result obtains if individual expectations are not unique but still held with complete certainty. The only difference with the respect to the case of unique expectations is that each agent, as long as she is sufficiently risk averse, will hold both money and bonds. On this and related aspects, see also Tobin (1963).

[14] For a definition of these two types of risk, which Kahn draws from Hawtrey, see Kahn ([1954] 1972, pp. 81–82). See also Robinson (1951).

gain or the income associated with owning those securities is very high. In their case, a strong perception of capital risk works in the same direction as bearish sentiment. Each investor chooses how to allocate his or her assets on the basis of an ideal internal dialogue between a speculator, who urges the investor to take action by moving into bonds or money, as the case may be, and the hedger, who urges the investor to be cautious and not to put all his or her eggs in one basket.[15]

> Risk, and uncertainty, attaching to the behaviour of the rate of interest, by bringing into play the precautionary motive, create intensive margins, one to be imagined inside the mind of each person concerned, which operate along the extensive margin. Lack of conviction on the part of individuals has the same effect on the shape of the liquidity preference curve as heterogeneity among them. The elasticity of the demand for money is a function of both. It is as though 'two views' operated inside each person's mind, one being responsible for holding securities and one for holding money. (Kahn, [1954] 1972, p. 88)

Aggregating individual choices, where most investors, with the exception of extreme bulls and bears, end up holding both money and securities in variable proportions depending on their idiosyncratic aversion to different risks and on their lack of conviction about their own expectations, speculative and precautionary demand for money become almost indistinguishable from one another. In this way, the financial markets imagined by Kahn are populated by different categories of investors, who act on the basis of discontinuous orders of preference, different types of risk aversions and different capacities to process relevant information. This introduces an element of indeterminacy in the relationship between money and interest rates, which renders Kahn's liquidity preference function different from what Keynes writes about the schedule of liquidity preference in the *General Theory* and very different from the versions of this function transposed by the models of the neoclassical synthesis of Keynesian thought à la Hicks, Modigliani and Tobin.[16]

[15] On the 'two views' and the notion of multiple-self underlying Kahn's theory of liquidity preference, see Dardi (1994, pp. 94–95).

[16] For an analysis of how the leading exponents of the neoclassical synthesis of Keynesian thought distorted the original Keynesian monetary theory, see Chick and Tily (2014) who, however, do not cite Kahn.

Whereas in the *General Theory* (Keynes, 1936, pp. 154–164), Keynes concentrates on the behaviour of expert financial agents (Kahn's bankers) who, again on the basis of this experience, tend to have relatively well-defined expectations about the trend of long-term interest rates (albeit varying between them and subject in any case to the problem of uncertainty), Kahn introduces other categories of much less sophisticated and much more uncertain investors, for whom the fear of capital loss, which leads to a preference for money over securities, is intertwined with the fear of losing coupon and dividend income, which leads to a preference for securities over money.

Moreover, while the expectations that guide Keynesian speculators are strongly influenced by the state of the news and the attempt to anticipate market movements, in the world imagined by Kahn it is possible that these attempts are frustrated by the presence of a large mass of inexperienced operators who oscillate between inaction and sudden movements in one direction or another dictated by herd behaviour.

> Sufficient has been said to demonstrate the unsuitability of thinking of a schedule of liquidity preference as though it could be represented by a well-defined curve or by a functional relationship expressed in mathematical terms or subject to econometric processes. Keynes himself often gave way to the temptation to picture the state of liquidity preference as a fairly stable relationship, despite his intuitional horror of undue formalism, but his treatment at least can be justified by the need at the time for a forceful and clear-cut exposition if it was to carry any weight at all. (Kahn, [1954] 1972, p. 90)

The margin of indeterminacy makes it impossible to know in advance the measure of the variation in money supply required to bring about a certain variation in interest rates. This leaves as an alternative for the monetary authorities the possibility of setting interest rates at different maturities directly according to the needs of the moment and enforce them by varying the supply of short-, medium- and long-term securities and money on the basis of the demands that investors make on these interest rates. This approach allows for a synergistic management of monetary policy and public debt, offering the monetary authorities the possibility of keeping interest rates and the cost of government financing under control.

This was the policy followed by the British government in the war years, on the recommendation of Keynes, and in the years of the Labour government, in connection with the phase labelled 'cheap money policy'.[17] In contrast, the conservative governments of the 1950s had reactivated restrictive monetary policy against inflation with technical support and advice from the Economic Section under Robert Hall,[18] but with limited success.[19] Against this backdrop, Kahn's ideas on monetary policy, the non-monetary nature of inflation and the possibility of controlling it without monetary restrictions became relevant, influencing British political thinking, particularly in relation to the works of the Radcliffe Committee.

5.3 Radcliffe Committee: Memorandum and Testimony

The Radcliffe Committee, formally known as the Committee on the Working of the Monetary System, was set up by the Chancellor of the Exchequer, Peter Thorneycroft, in 1957 to assess and recommend changes to monetary policy in the context of the resurgence of inflation in Britain and the limited success of monetary restriction in combating it. By 1957, this had become a serious policy problem for the Conservative government of Macmillan, as it sought to consolidate an economy and a currency that were fragile and severely downsized after the loss of the Empire. At the same time, the apparent ineffectiveness of monetary restraint in controlling inflation posed a challenge to the traditional (and resurging) economic doctrine that saw inflation as a monetary phenomenon and the price level as the primary concern of the monetary authorities.

The Committee on the Working of the Monetary System, chaired by Lord Radcliffe, comprised eight members, including Richard S. Sayers and Alec Cairncross, professional economists with a Keynesian orientation.

[17] On this, see Dalton (1954, pp. 234–240 in particular) and Howson (1993). See also Howson (1988) for an analysis of the cheap money policy from 1932 to 1951.

[18] Since 1947 Robert Hall had led the Economic Section and, when the Economic Section moved into the Treasury in 1955, Hall served as the chief economic advisor to the Chancellor (Cairncross & Watts, 1989, Ch. 9; Peden, 2000, p. 483). Hall believed that keeping aggregate demand below 'over-full employment' was necessary for price stability, but not sufficient on its own. Once the economy reached or exceeded full employment, inflation depended on wage bargaining. He argued that even at this level of unemployment, an income policy was needed to prevent inflation driven by wages. In 1957 Hall proposed raising unemployment slightly and introducing a wages policy tied to productivity growth, a concept later known as the 'guiding light to prices' (Jones, 1987). On Hall, see K. Jones (1994).

[19] On the difficult reactivation of monetary policy in the United Kingdom between 1948 and 1957, see Cairncross (1996).

The Committee was asked to review how monetary policy could be used to manage inflation, promote economic stability and support full employment. This included analysing the effectiveness of tools like interest rates, credit controls and the role of the money supply. The Committee also examined how banks, financial institutions and the broader financial system influenced the economy and the flow of credit.

It fell upon Sayers and Cairncross to draft the final version of the Report, with Sayers concentrating on the theoretical part and Cairncross on the introduction, capital markets, external relations and statistics (Cairncross, 1999). The Radcliffe Report (Committee, 1960a) was regarded as one of the most important documents in Keynesian monetary economics (Chick, 1973; Cobham, 1992). Indeed, the Radcliffe doctrine continued to be the primary source of inspiration for British policymakers until the early 1970s.[20]

The Radcliffe Doctrine, as summarised by some of the early readers of the Radcliffe Report,[21] combined several ideas: (1) that interest rates have some, albeit limited, influence on aggregate demand and saving; (2) that the management of public debt is important and forms an integral part of monetary policy; (3) that the idea of limiting the task of monetary policy to the control of the money supply by banks, without taking account of non-bank financial intermediaries and all sources of credit to the economy, risked creating inefficiencies in the organisation of finance without having any significant impact on the control of aggregate demand; (4) that the monetary authorities should concentrate on the control of general liquidity rather than on money supply only; (5) that this control should be exercised by steering the entire term structure of interest rates, thereby influencing the propensity of banks and non-banks to hold assets and lend; (6) that monetary policy can help, but should play a subsidiary role to budgetary policy and direct controls.

General liquidity was defined as the overall access to spending power available to the private sector, not just in the form of money (cash or bank deposits), but also including credit facilities, near-money assets and the ability to borrow. Based on this definition the Radcliffe Committee posited that monetary policy works not through changes in the quantity of

[20] The Committee met on 59 occasions to hear oral evidence, which is documented in the Minutes of Evidence (Radcliffe Committee, 1960b). In addition, the written evidence is presented in three volumes (Radcliffe Committee, 1960c).

[21] On this, see Arndt (1962), Gurley (1960), Kaldor (1960), Jasay (1960), Katz (1960).

money but through its impact on liquidity and the willingness of institutions and individuals to hold assets or spend. For example, in a period of strong credit expansion, the rise in interest rates and the consequent fall in the price of securities would have made banks and the non-bank financial institutions reluctant to sell the securities they held in the secondary market in order to raise the liquid reserves needed to continue the credit expansion. This would have favoured a slowdown in the supply of credit, even in the presence of a low interest rate elasticity of investment.

Kahn participated in the work of the Radcliffe Committee by sending a lengthy memorandum (Kahn, [1958a] 1972) and agreeing to answer the Commission's questions (Kahn, 1960). In their final report, the members of the Radcliffe Committee wrote:

> We therefore follow Professor Kahn, in the evidence which he submitted to us, in insisting upon the structure of interest rates rather than some notion of the "supply of money" as the centre-piece of monetary action; this does not however imply an absence of special interest in the activity of the banks. (Radcliffe Committee, 1960a, p. 134)

While Cristiano and Paesani (2018c) have reconstructed how Kahn's influence on the Radcliffe doctrine was not as relevant as this quote suggests, his memorandum and testimony represent a central contribution to Kahn's scholarly work as well as a synthesis of his economic credo, a credo that had taken shape between the 1930s and 1940s and to which Kahn remained faithful to the end. The key message of Kahn's memorandum is that monetary policy should be directed primarily towards supporting investment, both because it is on investment that monetary factors have the greatest influence and because supporting investment is functional to promoting employment and increasing productive capacity and productivity, external competitiveness and living standards.

> It will be clear that I attribute to monetary forces a substantial influence on investment, though I regard it as slow in coming into effect and unpredictable in its results. At the same time I certainly take the view that there are other methods of influencing investment when it needs to be influenced. While considerable reliance should be placed on these other methods, this

> does not mean that monetary forces should remain completely impassive in the face of changing circumstances. (Kahn, [1958a] 1972, p. 128)[22]

Limiting monetary policy to the secondary role of regulating (supporting) investment leaves open the question of what instruments should be used to control inflation directly. Kahn's solution to this problem is based on his view of the price formation process.

> The level of prices at any moment of time can be regarded as mainly the outcome of three factors:—the level of money wages, the state of productive equipment and technical knowledge and efficiency, and the level of demand. Demand is in a direct sense an unimportant influence on prices unless it is so high as to strain the available productive resources and to result in scarcity prices. [...] The *movement* [in the original] of prices, as opposed to the actual level of prices in relation to money wages, depends on how money wages move. Broadly speaking, the price level will rise to the extent that money wages rise faster than productivity, as determined by improvements in the state of productive equipment and technical knowledge and efficiency. (Kahn, [1958a] 1972, p. 137)

In this view, controlling inflation requires aligning nominal wage growth with productivity. Under conditions of full employment and fragmented union bargaining, as in 1950s Britain, this necessitates reforming the wage-setting process to reduce conflict and introduce mechanisms, such as an incomes policy, to manage wage growth and differential adjustments in a coordinated and stable manner. In making these recommendations, Kahn is aware that the wage issue is outside the remit of the Radcliffe Committee. But this does not prevent him from raising it, both on the basis of his convictions and to emphasise that, in the absence of a coordinated solution to the wage problem, the only solution left to control inflation is to increase unemployment, a solution which Kahn rejects as ineffective (unless unemployment is raised to socially unsustainable levels) and unfair. Kahn's recommendations are based on a clear rejection of the idea that inflation is a monetary phenomenon, as well as an equally clear

[22] The monetary forces to which Kahn refers are primarily the long-term interest rate together with bank advances. The other methods include the control of capital issues to discriminate between one project and another, building licences, investment allowances and the direct allocation of scarce resources (Kahn, [1958a] 1972, pp. 151–152).

rejection of the distinction between demand and cost inflation, which Kahn considers to be 'unhelpful and misleading'.[23]

> It is the rise in wages which is the cause of prices rising. In that sense all price inflations are 'cost inflations' (or wage inflation). But the speed at which wages, and therefore prices, rise is likely in some degree to depend on demand. In that sense there is nearly always some measure of 'demand inflation'. (Ibid., p. 138)

Based on this view, Kahn's memorandum treads a fine line between recommending that inflation be fought because of the risks that can arise from the consolidation of an inflationary mindset, and recognising the ex-post benefits of moderate inflation for the economy.

> The really important thought which underlies advocacy of price stability relates to the harm which is done to the economic system once it becomes generally recognized *as a certainty* [in the original] that the price level will go on progressively rising without interruption and without limit. It is continuous and complete confidence in that *expectation* [in the original] which does the harm. But to break that confidence it is not necessary to achieve absolute price stability. Provided that there are periods of time during which process of considerable number of commodities fall somewhat in a manner that cannot altogether be foreseen, so that the direction of the course of prices at each moment of time cannot be predicted with certainty, it will not seriously matter if it turns out *ex post* that over a number of years the trend of prices has been upward. (Ibid., pp. 144–145)

Ensuring that inflation expectations remain anchored while the economy develops at full employment is a complex task requiring the combination of monetary measures to support investment, budgetary measures to restrain private consumption (and, as far as possible, defence spending), direct controls on imports and the allocation of some key raw materials (e.g. steel), and the regulation of wages as discussed above. Monetary authorities must be prepared to extend their control from short-term interest rates alone to the entire term structure, and in particular to

[23] For a review of inflation theories shortly after the publication of the Radcliffe Report with reference to the demand-pull/cost-push distinction, see Bronfenbrenner and Holzman (1963), Johnson (1963) and Hutchison (1967). Among the main British supporters of the demand-pull thesis, with references to a pre-Keynesian and proto-monetarist point of view, we find Lionel Robbins (1963, pp. 197–226) and Frank W. Paish (1962).

long-term interest rates, without worrying about the consequences for the money supply, which must adapt endogenously to the quantity demanded on the basis of income, interest rates and prices.[24] On this point, as on the existence of an inverse relationship between interest rates and investment, the doctrine set out in Kahn's memorandum departs significantly from mainstream opinion as is evident from the answers to the questions that the members of the Radcliffe Committee put to him during his testimony of 23 October 1958 (Kahn, 1960).

The inverse relationship between interest rates and investment, which had been the subject of debate in Britain in the 1950s between those (e.g. Wilson & Andrews, 1951) who doubted its existence and those, like Kahn, who continued to believe in it, is the first issue addressed in Kahn's testimony.[25] Pressed on the matter of the response of investment to a change in long-term interest rates, Kahn reiterates his belief in the existence of an inverse relationship between the two variables, operating primarily through the cost of finance. For a change in interest rates to have an effect on investment, this change should be substantial and its impact would not be felt immediately, but with a lag of about two years. The existence of this lag, and the slow adjustment of profit expectations in the face of changing circumstances, entails the risk that the monetary authorities will act at the wrong time in the face of unforeseen events. For this reason, the ideal monetary policy, in Kahn's view, must remain as accommodative as possible and move in a restrictive direction only in those rare occasions in which the monetary authorities anticipate the emergence of 'pure demand inflation', in which the demand pressure on productive resources is very strong and there is an acute general shortage of labour.

[24] On the possibility of interpreting Kahn's position and the ensuing conclusions of the Radcliffe Committee in the light of the Post-Keynesian concept of endogenous money supply, see Sawyer (2002) and Vernengo and Rochon (2001).

[25] In his contribution to Wilson and Andrews (1951), Sayers reflected on the belief that changes in the rate of interest could significantly influence economic activity. He noted that this idea had reached its peak in Keynes's *Treatise on Money* (Sayers, 1951, p. 1). Sayers also referenced the Oxford Economists Research Group's investigation into the relationship between the rate of interest and investment decisions, which was published in *Oxford Economic Papers*. The results of this inquiry showed that changes in the rate of interest had little to no effect on investment. Although the inquiry was based on limited empirical evidence, it had a significant influence on the field, as Sayers's survey reveals. In his own paper, Sayers approached the issue cautiously, though he expressed surprise at the simplicity and confidence of Keynes's argument (ibid., pp. 1–2).

From the relationship between investment, expected profits and long-term interest rates, the members of the Radcliffe Committee, in particular Franks, Sayers and Cairncross, move on to the notion of the monetary 'mystique', the term used by Kahn to refer to and criticise the idea that control of the money supply should be regarded as the main objective of monetary policy, given the direct link between the money supply and the macroeconomic variables in which the monetary authorities are interested (price level, exchange rate). Against this idea, Kahn reiterates his conviction that if the monetary authorities really want to influence spending (and in this way inflation) they should concentrate on controlling interest rates at different maturities and leave the money supply to take care of itself, that is to adjust to the demand for money.

> Money is a stock, it is not a flow. The things which influence people's conduct are flows, profits, incomes, that sort of thing: things you measure as rates per unit of time; not a stock which is simply a matter of how at any particular moment people decide to dispose of their personal wealth and companies of their liquid assets. (Kahn, 1960, p. 742, § 10986)

Against the observation that it is equivalent to control the money supply and short-term interest rates while leaving the market to determine long-term interest rates, as had always been done, or to control long-term and short-term interest rates while leaving the market to determine the money supply, as he recommended, Kahn returns to the ideas he had expressed in his 1954 article on liquidity preference. He insists on the need to abandon the concept of a causal relationship from short-term rates (both current and expected) to long-term rates, potentially incorporating a risk premium. Instead, he proposes a model in which interest rates at various maturities influence one another and, within certain limits, operate independently. Based on this vision, Kahn argues that long-term interest rates should be directed mainly at controlling investment, while short-term interest rates should be moved mainly by paying attention to the foreign exchange market and international capital flows.

Based on this, Kahn recommends that the monetary authorities equip themselves with a mechanism for controlling interest rates at different maturities—in other words, term structure control. This should be achieved by applying the desired interest rates to government securities of different maturities issued on tap, as was done during the war and in the early post-war period. According to Howson (1988, p. 250), the origin of the idea of controlling savings and investment through direct control of interest rates of different maturities by the monetary authorities, combined with the use of controls on new stock issues and physical controls on the allocation of resources, can be found in a memorandum sent by Keynes to the Chancellor of the Exchequer and the Governor of the Bank of England (Catto) on 28 May 1939. In the years that followed, this proposal was successfully implemented (also thanks to the introduction of new instruments for financing government expenditure, such as Treasury Deposit Receipts) as part of the effort to keep short- and long-term interest rates low in order to reduce the government's borrowing costs during the war years (cheap money policy). The same policy was continued in the early years of the Attlee government, in line with the ideas of the Chancellor of the Exchequer, Hugh Dalton, the young Labour economists (Gaitskell, Jay, Meade, Clark) who supported him, and also Joan Robinson.[26]

If the interest rates set by the authorities are acceptable to investors, the issuance of government bonds will proceed smoothly and the chosen maturity structure will become effective. If not, the monetary authorities must be prepared to intervene with open market operations of different maturities, potentially without limits (à outrance) in order to achieve their objectives. The idea of using potentially unlimited open market operations to push interest rates in the direction desired by the government, even in the presence of recalcitrant investors, was first formulated by Keynes in the *Treatise on Money* and later in the *General Theory* (Keynes, 1936, pp. 205–208), despite his awareness of the likely reluctance of monetary authorities to conduct open market operations in the long-term securities sector. It is precisely this reluctance that would stand in the way of full acceptance of Kahn's proposals to the Radcliffe Committee.[27]

The control of the interest rate structure thus obtained implies the abandonment of control over the quantity of money and, within certain limits, over the maturity composition of the government debt, which adapts to the preferences of investors, given the interest rates set by the monetary authorities. The success of the policy recommended by Kahn to the Radcliffe Committee requires unity of purpose and close coordination

[26] On this, see Howson (1988, pp. 259–279) and, for a more detailed account, Howson (1993).

[27] Recently, the topic of open market operations à outrance has been revived in the context of the use of unconventional monetary measures (Kregel, 2013; Cristiano & Paesani, 2018c) and a broader reconsideration of Keynes's theory (Tily, 2010).

between the Treasury and the Bank of England, plus the ability of both to steer investors' expectations in the desired direction. In response to Lord Radcliffe's perplexity about the possibility that this could be perceived as deliberate and sustained manipulation of the financial markets, Kahn replies:

> Yes, but how much the authorities have to do depends on the state and the responsiveness of the market. If the market likes to help by altering its expectations, because it thinks this is the way the cat is jumping, then the authorities will not have to do so much. If the market proves very obstinate and does not believe that they are going to succeed in doing what they are trying to do, then they will have to do much more. (Kahn, 1960, 743, § 10988)

In the strategic game between markets and monetary authorities, Kahn believes that the latter will always come out on top, provided they have clear ideas and are prepared to take the necessary measures to implement those ideas, even if this means altering the money supply to an extent that could seem imprudent. Determination on the part of the monetary authorities and a commitment to see their policies through are crucial elements in ensuring the success of the measures proposed by Kahn, as is close coordination between monetary policy, public debt management and budgetary policy, and the use of direct controls on share issues, investment grants and building permits to steer the level and composition of investment precisely in the desired direction (Kahn, 1960, pp. 744–745). On the issue of coordination between monetary and budgetary policies, careful not to tread on political turf, Kahn argues that the overall direction of economic policy should remain in the hands of the Treasury rather than the Parliament, whose role is to take the basic demands of society and translate them into objectives that the technical structures of the civil service can implement.

In a non-mechanical vision of the economy such as that of Kahn (and Keynes), in which fundamental economic decisions, in particular investment and portfolio choices, are strongly influenced by subjective elements (expectations, opinions, prejudices), some of which are volatile, some of which are rooted in past experience, gradual but determined action to manage expectations is crucial to the success of the government's manoeuvres. With regard to Kahn's political attitude and his views on the role of government in the economy, the memorandum and his testimony to the

Radcliffe Committee provide additional evidence that Kahn was neither seeking political expediency nor overly concerned with pleasing his interlocutors when he came into contact with government circles. For example, when he recommended that certain elements of wartime regulation be maintained (and in some cases reactivated), or when, to the perplexity of the members of the Radcliffe Committee, he insisted on the irrelevance of controlling the money supply. Fidelity to his own convictions, and the firmness with which he stood by them even when his political interlocutors had different ideas, combined with Kahn's idea of government as an entity capable of directing the economy as a conductor, would direct his orchestra.

The success of the performance depends in equal measure on the skill of the conductor and the willingness of the orchestra to follow him. Clear direction from the government and a willingness to cooperate from the various relevant economic actors are crucial to the success of economic policy and the progress of the economy. Without this combination the alternative is a situation in which each component pursues its own goals selfishly, without regard to the impact of its decisions on the others, leading inevitably to conflict and instability. To avoid this risk, it is necessary for the government to place full employment and the improvement of living standards at the centre of its strategy, combining strong support for investment and aggregate demand with measures capable of preventing this strong support from causing inflation and balance of payments deficits, which would in turn justify the adoption of restrictive measures.

On these points, and in rejecting the idea of an inverse and stable relationship between unemployment and inflation (the Phillips curve) and that monetary restraint was the best anti-inflationary remedy, Kahn found himself before the Radcliffe Committee on the same side as the Cambridge Keynesians, Henry Phelps Brown and Thomas Balogh,[28] just to name two prominent British economists with whom Kahn was in contact, and on the opposite side from Harrod, Meade and the LSE economists.

This is the essence of the ideas that Kahn expressed before the Radcliffe Committee. One year after participating in its work Kahn had a second important opportunity to express the same ideas, when he participated as a member and de facto chairman in the work of an international commission of experts on the problem of rising prices, convened within the

[28] On Ernest Henry Phelps Brown, see Appendix C and Hancock and Isaac (1998). On Thomas Balogh, see Appendix C and Morris (2007).

Organisation for Economic Co-operation and Development (OEEC) in 1959–1960.

5.4 The OEEC Report and Wage-Wage Inflation

In the early years of the post-war recovery, the United Kingdom was not alone in experiencing high levels of employment and mounting inflationary pressures. In some of the larger developed economies, including the United States, the United Kingdom and France, the defence sector continued to absorb substantial resources, adding to demand pressures and diverting resources from civilian uses. The conversion of production systems from a wartime to a peacetime order required considerable investment. At the same time, private consumption increased, fuelled by the mass of liquid assets that many households had accumulated during the war and by the expansion of welfare states. The resumption and rapid expansion of international trade encouraged the simultaneous growth of exports and imports, which occasionally led to balance of payments problems. Workers and trade unions, especially in the more dynamic sectors, pressed for wage increases, which employers could afford thanks to the generally favourable economic climate.[29] By the end of the 1950s, the problem of wage and price inflation had become a major concern for economists and policymakers.[30]

In this context the Council of the Organisation for European Economic Cooperation (hereafter OEEC), created in 1948 to coordinate economic recovery in Europe and a precursor to the OECD, decided on 12 June 1959 to convene an international group of experts to study the problem of rising prices. The Group was composed of William Fellner (Professor, Yale University), Milton Gilbert (Director of Economics and Statistics, OEEC), Bent Hansen (Professor and Director of the Konjunktur Institutet, Stockholm), Friedrich Lutz (Professor, University of Zurich), Pieter de Wolff (Professor of Econometrics and Director of the Central

[29] For a comparative long-run analysis of growth and labour income share in the United Kingdom, France, and the United States, see Charpe et al. (2019).

[30] For an analysis of post-war inflation and related problems from the different perspectives of developed, planned and developing countries, see Hague (1962). For an example of a comprehensive analysis of the economic and institutional links between wages and prices in the years covered by this section, see Bowen (1960).

Planning Bureau, The Hague) and Richard Kahn, who acted as de facto Chairman of the group.[31]

This episode marks the high point of Kahn's participation and influence on the international debates on post-war inflation. The Report of the Group (Fellner et al., 1961), which was published in 1961, attracted some attention at the time of its release.[32] It consists of seven chapters that document the behaviour of prices between 1953 and 1960 in a selected group of developed countries and analyse the role of demand, wages, monopolistic pricing and external considerations that influence them.[33]

The members of the Group, with the notable exception of Kahn,[34] agreed on the role of demand as a driving force behind price increases, particularly in 1955–1957, and on the appropriateness of the use of fiscal and monetary restraint by many countries. However, the Group stressed that wage inflation, rather than demand-driven inflation, was a major and persistent problem. The six experts agreed that wages are largely the result of collective bargaining, which can only be partly influenced by demand conditions. They also agreed that wage policies and reforms to the bargaining mechanism, designed to enhance coordination and cooperation between trade unions, would be more effective in curbing inflation than restrictive measures. To implement this strategy, the authorities would need to define and clearly communicate an acceptable average wage increase, and gain the support of the relevant parties.

To oversee this process, a public sector body should be tasked with managing it, and government officials should participate in key wage

[31] On this, see Marcuzzo (2020, p. 30).

[32] Smithies (1962) highlights the different economic perspectives on inflation and the policy recommendations of the report's six authors, as well as questioning some of their conclusions. In the same vein, see also Weise (1961) and Dow (1965). Lerner (1962) focuses on the group's analysis of the roles of wage negotiation and of monopolistic pricing in the inflationary process and the unacceptability of the idea of rising unemployment to reduce inflationary pressure. On this, see also Kindleberger (1967, p. 217). In later years, Romanis (1986, Chapter 4) highlighted the importance of the Group's ideas on wage inflation.

[33] The countries are Austria, Belgium, Canada, Denmark, France, Germany, Greece, Iceland, Ireland, Italy, Netherlands, Norway, Portugal, Spain, Sweden, Switzerland, Turkey, United Kingdom, United States.

[34] The chapter devoted to demand opens with the following statement: 'One of us (Professor Kahn) does not believe that the concept of "excess demand" provides a satisfactory method of analysing the processes of inflation. He does not, however, feel that this difficulty has prejudiced the formulation of the recommendations' (Fellner et al., 1961, p. 33). On Kahn's dissociation, see Romanis (1986, p. 78).

negotiations to safeguard public interests. Additionally, significant updates to wage bargaining structures are necessary, as many existing models still reflect outdated, pre-war approaches. The merits of a national wage policy were disputed by Fellner and Lutz, who expressed concern about the degree of regulation that the introduction of a wage policy might entail, and who advocated the decentralisation of bargaining from the national level to those of individual firms. In spite of this, 'the main achievement of the report was to make the idea of a "wages policy" intellectually respectable'.[35]

From an analytical point of view, the proposal to introduce a national wage policy was based on the idea that, apart from any demand-side impulses, nominal wages can rise as result of reasons internal to the bargaining mechanism: (1) the impact of wage bargaining in key sectors of the economy on the wage structure; (2) the price-wage spiral (compensatory increase in wages caused by a previous increase in prices, particularly noticeable in the case of extreme excess demand); (3) monetary illusion (defined as the expectation on the part of the unions that monetary wages should rise anyway in conditions of economic prosperity) and, above all, (4) the wage-wage spiral, Kahn's preferred explanation (Marcuzzo, 2020, pp. 29–32).

The wage-wage spiral, also labelled 'leapfrogging effect', originates from efforts by individual trade unions to surpass the existing wage structure to secure higher pay for their members, both in comparison to other workers and in real terms. This leapfrogging is particularly prominent when industries negotiate wages independently, but also occurs within industries and firms, including between skilled and unskilled workers. Wage disparities, especially between those with standardised pay and those whose wages are negotiated more freely, can intensify competition to maintain wage differentials. Unlike the price-wage spiral, triggered by price increases that lead to delayed wage adjustments, the wage-wage spiral results from sectoral wage increases that alter the pre-existing structure and trigger compensatory wage increase in return, causing widespread and swift inflationary effects. In this way the competition between trade unions, in the absence of agreement on relative wages, is a permanent source of inflation.

[35] On the influence of this relationship in facilitating the introduction of incomes policy in the United Kingdom, see Backhouse and Forder (2013, 30).

Adopting restrictive monetary and fiscal measures helps to temporarily moderate the wage-wage spiral by creating a climate of concern and alarm, but does not resolve the problem satisfactorily. To achieve this, it is necessary to introduce institutional mechanisms that can encourage trade unions to coordinate with each other and within different sectors of the economy when negotiating wage levels and differentials. In parallel, measures must be adopted to prevent the opportunistic deviations by employers from agreed wages and national wage and income policies must be implemented with the aim to define a framework within which the complex problem of wage differentials is to be addressed, compatibly with the general macroeconomic situation and the goals of the government.

The main legacies of the OEEC experts' report on the problem of rising prices are the rejection of the idea that there is a mechanical and unambiguous relationship between aggregate demand and the development of money wages, the appeal to find ways of reducing inflation without jeopardising investment and employment and the invitation to governments to adopt a wage policy and mechanisms to encourage trade unions and employers to act cooperatively. The influence of Kahn, who puts the concept of the 'wage-wage spiral' and the conflicts that this spiral reflects at the basis of his Post-Keynesian analysis of inflation, cannot be ignored behind these legacies.[36]

5.5 Exercises in the Analysis of Growth

Kahn's ideas on liquidity preference, monetary policy and inflation in the 1950s are intertwined with his reflections on extending the Keynesian theoretical framework from the short run to the long run. The main result of this reflection can be found in Kahn (1959), a work inspired by a set of concepts developed by Joan Robinson in *The Accumulation of Capital* (Robinson, 1956). This book, a fundamental step in the development of a Post-Keynesian theory of distribution and growth at Cambridge, was the main result of her attempt, with some help from Kahn himself, to extend the Keynesian theoretical framework from the short run (static) to the

[36] As Destefanis (1999, p. 486) observes, 'The relevance of wage relativities for the determination of money wages has always been of paramount importance in Post-Keynesian economics. Indeed, in his recent and thoughtful survey, Lavoie (1992, ch. 7) emphasises that conflict over the distribution of income, originated by requirements of equity and fairness, is the core of the Post-Keynesian theory of wage inflation'.

long run (dynamic), an area already explored by Harrod (1939, 1948) and in a different context by Kalecki (1954).

According to Robinson, Kahn's contribution to the writing of *The Accumulation of Capital* was evident both at the initial stage, when the two of them, together with Sraffa, studied Harrod's *Towards a Dynamic Economics*, and at a later stage, on a specific point relating to the formulation of the production function (Robinson, 1956, pp. xxxii–xxxiii). The book concludes with a contribution by Champernowne and Kahn, who offer a formula for analysing the cost of capital goods, incorporating the element of interest under certain assumptions. Apart from this, the extent of Kahn's contribution to *The Accumulation of Capital* remains unclear, and it should be noted that Kahn may not have agreed with everything in the book, believing that it needed more time for development.

The Accumulation of Capital is divided into eight books, with Book II presenting the central thesis on long-run accumulation and the theoretical framework underpinning it.[37] Robinson designs an economy closed to the rest of the world and divided into two classes: entrepreneurs, who save and invest all their income, and workers, who consume their entire wages. Workers are homogeneous, and both consumption goods and production processes follow rigid, fixed proportions. There are no scarce natural resources, as all equipment is produced and reproducible. Technical progress is defined solely by improvements in production methods, and constant costs are assumed, meaning no economies of scale exist. The economy evolves in a state of tranquillity, with expectations about the future being fulfilled. Accumulation and labour force growth are independent and may not always align. Finally, laissez-faire capitalism is firmly established, with governments playing no role in economic affairs. Initially, Robinson assumes a fixed production technique, where employment levels are determined by the available stock of equipment. Later, technical progress is incorporated, maintaining the assumption that each stage of technological development corresponds to a single production method for each commodity and type of equipment. Finally, the discussion expands to consider the choice between different production techniques.

Given these hypotheses, and assuming that the degree of competition in the two sectors of the economy and the bargaining power of unions and

[37] On *The Accumulation of Capital*, see Harcourt and Kerr (2009, pp. 76–100), Marchionatti (2024, pp. 284–292). See also the essays contained in Part IV of Marcuzzo, Pasinetti and Roncaglia (1996).

entrepreneurs are given, the rate of accumulation is equal to the rate of profit. To illustrate this result, we can use the notation proposed by Lancaster (1960) and adopted by Findlay (1963):

$$Y = rPM + wL \tag{5.3}$$

$$Y = P\Delta M + C \tag{5.4}$$

By measuring all quantities in terms of consumer goods, Eq. (5.3) expresses the distribution of income between total wages (equal to the unit wage rate w times the number of workers L, determined on the basis of the number of entrepreneurs) and total profits (equal to the profit rate r times the value of capital goods M measured in terms of consumer goods P).[38] Equation (5.4), on the other hand, expresses the equivalence between product and aggregate demand, which is obtained by adding consumption C to investment measured in terms of consumer goods. By equating (Eq. 5.3) and (Eq. 5.4), on the assumption that ($wL = C$), we obtain the equality between the rate of profit and the rate of accumulation (Eq. 5.5).[39]

$$r = \frac{\Delta M}{M} \tag{5.5}$$

Equation (5.5) embodies the idea of a reciprocal influence between the rate of profit and the rate of accumulation. On the one hand, investment decisions are based on the profit that entrepreneurs expect to make; on the other hand, without profit, that is without a surplus of production over what is needed to pay workers and reintegrate the means of production, accumulation is impossible. As Robinson (1956, p. 76) put it: 'If they have no profit, the entrepreneurs cannot accumulate, and if they do not accumulate they have no profit'.

In considering this problem, Robinson first assumes that the rate of accumulation is constant and equal to the rate of growth of population and labour, and that the rates of profit and wages are also constant. In this case, capital accumulation can continue indefinitely in a steady state, and the supply and demand of goods and labour grow harmoniously. Robinson

[38] Lancaster shows that P is a function of the technological coefficients and the wage rate. See Findlay (1963, p. 2).

[39] Assuming that capitalists and workers are free to move from one sector to another, the rate of profit will be the same in both sectors, as will the wage rate.

then considers two departures from this equilibrium. If population grows faster than capital accumulation, unemployment rises and money wages fall. The outcome depends on entrepreneurs' reactions: if they maintain a fixed accumulation rate and competitive conditions hold, falling prices may keep real wages stable. However, since capital accumulation does not adjust to absorb the labour surplus, unemployment continues to rise. Conversely, if capital accumulates faster than the labour supply, firms struggle to find workers and compete by offering higher wages. The impact depends on how investment responds to labour shortages, leading to various possible economic scenarios. Taking the three possibilities into account,

> In an economy with only one technique, and no consumption out of profits, when the supply of labour adapts itself to demand, starting from any given situation (produced by past history), the future rate of accumulation is limited:
>
> (1) By the technical surplus available above subsistence wages for the workers employed.
>
> (2) Within that limit, it is limited by the surplus above the level of real wages that the workers are willing to accept and able to enforce (by creating an inflation barrier against a fall in real wages).
>
> (3) Within that limit, accumulation is limited by the energy with which entrepreneurs carry it out.
>
> (4) When the size of the labour force is independent of the entrepreneurs' demand for workers, a maximum is set to the possible rate of accumulation by the rate of increase of the labour force. When accumulation fails to reach this rate there is growth of long-period unemployment. (Robinson, 1956, pp. 83–84)

As these words suggest, for Robinson (as well as for Kahn, as we see below) the steady state growth rate is conditioned by the interplay of objective factors (the capacity of the technology in use to generate a surplus, the population growth rate), subjective factors (animal spirits and the propensity of entrepreneurs to invest) and institutional constraints (on the form of the minimum real wage rate acceptable to workers, which may be higher than the subsistence wage). In describing this interplay, one of the main theoretical concepts devised by Robinson is that of a Golden Age, which she defines as follows:

> When technical progress is neutral, and proceeding steadily, without any change in the time pattern of production, the competitive mechanism working freely, population growing (if at all) at a steady rate and accumulation going on fast enough to supply productive capacity for all available labour, the rate of profit tends to be constant and the level of real wages to rise with output per man. There are then no internal contradictions in the system. Provided that political events cause no disturbances, and provided that the entrepreneurs have faith in the future and desire to accumulate at the same proportional rate as they have been doing over the past, there is no impediment to prevent them from continuing to do so. As long as they do, the system develops smoothly without perturbations. Total annual output and the stock of capital (valued in terms of commodities) then grow together at a constant proportionate rate compounded of the rate of increase of the labour force and the rate of increase of output per man. We may describe these conditions as a *golden age* [in the original] (thus indicating that it represents a mythical state of affairs not likely to obtain in any actual economy). (Ibid., p. 99)

A Golden Age is characterised by five conditions: (1) steady growth rate—the economy grows at a constant proportional rate, ensuring stability in accumulation and employment; (2) neutral technical progress—productivity increases in both investment and consumption sectors at the same rate, maintaining a constant real-capital ratio and a stable profit rate; (3) constant replacement proportion—the ratio of annual capital replacements to the total capital stock remains unchanged; (4) full employment—labour supply adjusts to demand, preventing persistent unemployment, (5) no disruptions in expectations—entrepreneurs' investment behaviour aligns with the steady growth path, avoiding economic cycles and instability.[40]

The Accumulation of Capital and the notion of a Golden Age provide the basis of the second important theoretical essay that Kahn wrote in the 1950s in addition to the *Notes on liquidity preference*. The essay, entitled 'Exercises in the Analysis of Growth' appeared in 1959 in *Oxford Economic Papers* (Kahn, [1959] 1972). Kahn takes up and clarifies a number of concepts proposed by Robinson and others[41] in the context of the development of Post-Keynesian growth and distribution theory. This is the main

[40] A Static State is considered a special case of a Golden Age, where there is zero growth in the labour force and technology, leading to an economy where wages absorb the entire net output, and the rate of profit is zero.

[41] See, for example, Kaldor (1955, 1957), Champernowne (1958), Little (1957).

value of an essay in which Kahn provides another example of his usual modus operandi.[42]

> The development in the last few years of theories of economic growth has introduced new concepts and called on unfamiliar tools. In this lecture I intend no more than to take out for an airing a few of the concepts to which Mrs Robinson and others have introduced us and to try out the edge of a few of the tools. I am not attempting to build up a theory of growth and still less to arrive at any conclusions. (Kahn, [1959] 1972, p. 192)

The first concept to fall under Kahn's magnifying glass is the identity between investment and saving, and the transition from this identity to the formula that relates the rate of increase of the capital stock (measured as the ratio between investment and the value of the capital stock) to the distribution of income and the propensity to save of capitalists (α) and workers ($\beta < \alpha$). Using the notation proposed by Kahn and measuring all quantities in terms of consumer goods, as we did above and Kahn himself does, we have (ibid., fn. 1)

$$\begin{aligned} investment &= saving = \alpha\left(capitalists' incomes\right) + \beta\left(wages\right) = \\ &= \left(\alpha - \beta\right)\left(capitalists' incomes\right) + \beta\left(value\, of\, output\right) \end{aligned} \tag{5.6}$$

From this, it follows that the rate of growth of the value of the stock of capital[43] is equal to

$$\begin{aligned} \frac{investment}{value\, of\, stock\, of\, capital} &= \left(\alpha - \beta\right)\frac{capitalists' incomes}{value\, of\, stock\, of\, capital} \\ &+ \beta \frac{value\, of\, output}{value\, of\, stock\, of\, capital} \end{aligned} \tag{5.7}$$

[42] On this, see Harcourt (1991). Other authors more recently mention Kahn ([1959] 1972) as one of the earliest contributions to the post-war Keynesian theory of growth (Dutt 2017), or to the Cambridge conception that distribution depends on the rate of capital accumulation (Smith, 2012, p. 550, fn. 8). On this and related matters, see also Ciccarone (2004), Ederer et al. (2021) and Patriarca and Sardoni (2017).

[43] Setting $\alpha = 1$ and $\beta = 0$, equation (5.7) is formally equivalent to Eq. (5.5), provided that we can consider the capitalists' income equal to the profits, as Kahn specifies in the main text.

Equation (5.7) is an identity which is independent of any technical or other condition, and emphasises that it is the current income of capitalists rather than the (prospective) rate of profit which appears in this identity. However, if we assume that the economic system has settled into a long-run equilibrium characterised by a constant rate of increase in the capital stock and a low propensity of workers to save, then the ratio of capitalists' income to the value of the capital stock can also be regarded as constant over time and equal to the (expected) rate of profit. If we assume the existence of a multiplicity of techniques and the possibility of technological progress, additional hypotheses are needed in order to define the equilibrium trajectory along which the (expected) rate of profit is equal to the ratio between the (current) capitalists' income and the value of the stock of capital. In discussing these assumptions, Kahn takes a rather orthodox approach, as Harcourt (1991, p. 26) describes it, even if he qualifies it as 'heroic', not 'valid in practice' and made because, 'for my own part, I desire to learn to walk before I try to run' (Kahn, [1959] 1972, p. 195).

> First of all, I assume that the stage of technical knowledge can at any moment of time be represented by a production function. [...] Given the production function, the choice of technique depends on the expectations over the prospective lifetime of the plant of the relationship between the price of the particular product and the cost of producing it. With a rate of profit which is constant through time there is a unique relationship between the rate of profit and the techniques which are being adopted at any moment of time, in the sense of higher rates of profit being associated with lower degrees of mechanisation. [...] In the second place, I assume that the state of technical knowledge at each moment of time, as depicted by the production function, and the development of technical knowledge, as depicted by the movement of the production function through time, are independent factors, and in particular do not depend on the rate of accumulation of capital. In the third place, I assume that the progress through time of technical development is neutral. (Ibid., p. 195)

Kahn's analysis of growth therefore revolves, even if with due caution, around the hypothesis that there is an inverse relationship between the rate of profit and the degree of mechanisation of the new equipment that capitalists plan to install. On the other hand, the assumptions about technological progress allow Kahn to conclude that in a steady state with technological progress the output to capital ratio continues to be constant and with it the relative shares of income going to workers and capitalists. This ratio depends on the set of available techniques, the degree of substitutability between labour and capital and the value of the rate of profit relative to that of the wage rate. Other things equal, a lower rate of profit means a higher capital-output ratio—the greater the technical substitutability (the wider the choice of technique at a given stage of technical development) the stronger the tendency will be.

On the basis of these considerations, Kahn identifies a causal order valid in the long run among the variables under analysis. Given the rate of accumulation (historically determined, assumed to be constant over time and equal to the rate of growth of output, given the constancy of the capital-output ratio along the Golden Age trajectory) and given the propensity of capitalists to save (the propensity of workers to save is assumed to be low or equal to zero), the rate of profit is determined. Given the rate of profit and the technical conditions of production, the capital-output ratio, the wage rate corresponding to this ratio profit (all income that doesn't go to the capitalists goes to the workers) and the distribution of income between workers and capitalists (which remains constant over time in the conditions we have described) are determined. Along the equilibrium trajectory, since the rate of neutral technical progress (equal to the rate of growth of output per worker) is, by hypothesis, independent of the rate of accumulation (equal to the rate of growth of aggregate capital and aggregate income), and since

$$\textit{Rate of technical progress} = \textit{rate of accumulation} - \textit{rate of growth of employment} \tag{5.8}$$

any difference between the rate of technical progress and the rate of accumulation is reflected in the rate of change of employment. If the rate of technical progress exceeds/is equal to/falls short of the rate of accumulation, employment falls/remains constant/increases. The rate of employment, in turn, compared with the rate of growth of the population (and the labour force), determines the rate of change of unemployment. If the population grows more quickly (more slowly) than employment, the unemployment rate will increase (decrease) over time. If the population and employment grow at the same constant rate, the unemployment rate will remain constant and if this unemployment rate is so low that it can be defined as full employment, the situation will be equal to Joan Robinson's Golden Age.

In taking up this concept, Kahn insists on its unreality and on the fact that a Golden Age may not be an optimal situation. In fact, it may be that, due to a historical accident, the economy has settled on a path of equilibrium characterised by the use of techniques with a low degree of mechanisation (and therefore relatively unproductive) and accumulation (and growth) and savings rates lower than what the economy could achieve if some external factor caused them to increase (Kahn gives the example of a government investment policy financed by increasing taxation). Furthermore, and this is the case that Kahn focuses on, it is possible for the economy to settle on an equilibrium trajectory in which the rate of accumulation is higher than the rate of technical progress and therefore employment increases, but at a rate insufficient to generate full employment. Kahn defines the coexistence of balanced growth and unemployment as the Bastard Golden Age and devotes the rest of his analysis to this concept.[44]

Building on the definition of Bastard Golden Age as 'a state of equilibrium growth which has all the attributes of a Golden Age other than full employment' (Kahn, [1959] 1972, p. 200), Kahn explores the possibility that the economy will remain stuck in this position rather than move towards a Legitimate Golden Age (balanced growth with full employment).

> The possibility of a Bastard Golden Age turns on the absence of any progressive tendency towards the easing of the state of finance, and, more particularly towards a lowering of rates of interest and of yields of ordinary shares. If, for example, money wage-rates tend to fall progressively under the pressure of unemployment or the quantity of money tends to rise faster than money wages or the monetary authority in the face of unemployment

[44] If Joan Robinson had analysed the possibility of long-term equilibrium with unemployment in *The Accumulation of Capital* (Robinson, 1956, p. 79), it is to Kahn that we owe the definition of the Bastard Golden Age. Robinson takes up this concept in Robinson (1962, p. 58): 'Inflationary pressure, bringing financial checks into operation, may arise when there is no scarcity of labour—indeed a great mass of non-employment—if the real-wage rate refuses to be depressed below a particular level. A higher rate of accumulation means a lower real-wage rate. When the desired rate of accumulation is greater than the rate which is associated with the minimum acceptable real wage, the desire must be checked. A situation in which the rate of accumulation is being held in check by the threat of rising money wages due to a rise in prices (as opposed to rising money wages due to a scarcity of labour) may be described as a bastard golden age'.

> deliberately makes credit progressively cheaper, there will be such a progressive tendency and this will undermine the equilibrium of a Bastard Golden Age. (Ibid., p. 201)

There are three obstacles to the possibility that the economy will move from a Bastard to a Legitimate Golden Age, either as a result of a spontaneous adjustment or as a deliberate intervention by the monetary authorities: (1) the increase in the risks perceived by entrepreneurs, which widens the gap between the risk-free rate and the rate of return on prospective investment, discouraging entrepreneurs, (2) the fear of the monetary authorities of the possible inflationary consequences of the expansion and, above all, (3) the possibility that the temporary compression of wages (in nominal and real terms) to encourage accumulation may meet with resistance from the workers and the trade unions that represent them.

If this happens, the economy will hit the inflation barrier, which Robinson (1956, pp. 48–51) had defined,[45] and Kahn links to the Bastard Golden Age.

> The inflation barrier is the minimum real wage-rate which will be tolerated without provoking reactions inconsistent with a state of equilibrium growth. To that minimum real wage-rate there corresponds, given the technical and thriftiness conditions, a particular Bastard Golden Age, with a rate of growth just sufficiently low to secure this minimum real wage-rate for those employed. (Kahn, [1959] 1972, p. 202)

Thus the existence of the inflation barrier may frustrate attempts to permanently increase the rate of accumulation in order to bring the economy onto a full employment growth path. Attempts to expand investment will come up against rising money wages and prices and the coexistence of unemployment and inflation.[46] The possibility of circumventing the inflation barrier depends on the government's ability to persuade workers to accept a sacrifice today, in the form of a temporary reduction in current real wages, in the name of a greater benefit later. If the government is successful, the speed with which full employment is attained in the long run will thus depend on lowering the inflation barrier—the higher the

[45] On Robinson's treatment of the notion of inflation barrier, see also Boianovsky (2005, p. 93, fn. 1).

[46] On the link between the inflation barrier concept and Joan Robinson's (and Kahn's) ideas on inflation and trade unions, see also Williams (1981).

minimum real wage rate required by workers the lower the speed will be—and on the ability of policymakers to take appropriate measures to stimulate accumulation with the support of workers and trade unions.

This is one of the main messages that emerge from Kahn ([1959] 1972), along with the idea that in order to make full employment compatible with price stability and an improvement in living standards, it is necessary, on the one hand, to act on the monetary lever, maintaining as far as possible expansionary conditions, and, on the other hand, to induce the unions to moderate their wage demands. In the tense labour market of the 1950s in Britain,[47] Kahn insisted repeatedly on these ideas, not only in his academic work but also in his interventions with the public and in official forums in Britain and abroad. On a different level, the fact that, five years after the first skirmishes that would lead to the Cambridge Capital Controversy (Cohen & Harcourt, 2003), Kahn referred to the idea of a production function and of an inverse and unique functional relationship between the rate of profit (interest) and the degree of capital intensity of new production techniques while remaining aloof from the controversy is indicative of the gulf between his analytical approach, which remained tied to elements of the neoclassical Marshallian tradition, and that of many Cambridge economists, including those closest to him, who were moving in other directions.

5.6 Development, Full Employment and the Control of Inflation in Emerging Countries

Kahn's involvement in the employment and inflation debates of the 1950s was not confined to Britain. In 1957, for example, during a visit to Israel (24 June–9 July), the country where two of his sisters lived, Kahn's participation in an international conference at the Heliezer Kaplan School of Economics at the Hebrew University in Jerusalem gave him the opportunity to articulate his views on economic development and how to reconcile it with full employment and low inflation.[48]

[47] On this, see R. Jones (1987, pp. 48–65 in particular).

[48] Other speakers included Simon Kuznets and Don Patinkin, who played a major role in the development of the Department of Economics at the University (Lengyel, 1959). During the same visit Kahn met with several prominent Israeli officials, including Foreign Minister Golda Meir. For a full reconstruction of Kahn's activities in Israel as an informal adviser to the Israeli government in 1957 and again in 1962, see Schiffman (2017).

Kahn's lecture, entitled 'The Pace of Development' (Kahn, [1958b] 1972), is an underappreciated contribution to the analysis of economic planning and development economics in the Keynesian tradition, a field to which many Cambridge economists, including Kaldor (Targetti, 2005), Joan Robinson (Adelman & Sunding, 1989) and Austin Robinson (Cairncross, 1994), made notable contributions.[49] For these economists theoretical reflection on economic development was combined with direct involvement as advisers in the new international economic institutions created within the United Nations system to reconcile the needs of developing countries with those of the developed economies. In Kahn's case, as discussed below, this engagement took the form of a long association with the Food and Agriculture Organisation (FAO) in the 1950s and the United Nations Conference on Trade and Development (UNCTAD) in the 1960s.

The main value of Kahn's lecture on economic development lies in his ability to adapt his Keynesian vision of the economy and full employment without inflation to the characteristics of developing economies, taking into account their specificities, and in particular the large surplus of unemployed labour force combined with a very limited endowment of physical resources and of skills as the key element that distinguishes developing from developed countries. The strategy recommended by Kahn for transforming the difficulties associated with this situation (initial scarcity of specific productive resources and skills) into opportunities, and thus initiating a take-off in the sense of Rostow (1956), is based on a combination of direct and indirect taxes, subsidies, direct controls aimed at maximising investment and directing it to the most appropriate uses, while at the same time keeping inflationary pressures in check.

Kahn entrusts direct taxation with the task of reducing the disposable income and consumption of those who are in secure employment, before the development programme begins. This is done in order to allow consumption by the newly employed to increase without aggregate consumption increasing. In this way, investment, financed mainly by public funds, but also by the private sector, can be redeployed entirely or almost entirely in the increase of production and productive capacity giving rise to the virtuous circle and the progressive reduction of the initial surplus of the

[49] On this, see Hirschman (1982), Chakravarty (1987), Amdekar and Singh (2017). On the political context (cold war, post-colonial transition) in which the development economics took shape and on the first top-level contributions to the topic, see Alacevich (2018).

labour force. The redistribution of consumption from the better-off to the less well-off is the primary objective here rather than the reduction of inequality in income distribution per se.

To mitigate opposition to the development programme by those who may be harmed by the rise in direct taxation, Kahn recommends the introduction of subsidies to support consumption of the bare necessities of life by all. These subsidies should be implemented with great caution, so as not to divert excessive resources towards consumption and away from investment. Indirect taxation, in turn, should focus on those goods and services that are non-essential and/or characterised by a rigid supply schedule. In this way, the regressivity and distortion problems that are commonly associated with this type of taxation should be mitigated. The level of rates should be set at a level that reduces the extra profits of producers without unduly penalising them.

The objective of reducing the high surplus of unemployed labour suggests that labour-intensive techniques should be adopted, especially in construction and agriculture. In line with the recommendations of Lewis (1954) and Robinson (1956), Kahn advises against the temptation to accelerate the mechanisation of agriculture and industry in order to imitate more developed countries. It is recommended that mechanisation be implemented at a later stage, but that the problem of surplus labour should be addressed at the outset.

By promoting the initial adoption of low mechanisation, high labour-intensity techniques, which favour the absorption of previously unemployed people (whether open or disguised unemployment) into existing production circuits, a series of concomitant advantages are obtained: an increase in employment, in aggregate income, in savings to be channelled into investment (primary accumulation), the possibility of economising on the foreign exchange reserves needed to purchase imported capital goods and the possibility of absorbing into the productive circuits people (e.g. domestic servants) who lose their jobs as a result of the income compression of the better-off. Furthermore, the individual who secures gainful employment no longer relies on familial or communal support. Consequently, those who were previously employed within the family or community prior to the commencement of the development programme now possess a higher disposable income, which enables them to save more money for investment in the initiation of the take-off phase.

In advocating a development strategy based on the introduction of measures to redistribute a given level of consumption between a larger number of consumers and to promote investment and the initial adoption of high labour-intensive techniques. Promoting the adoption of labour-intensive techniques in the early stages of economic development should be done without placing undue reliance on the pricing mechanism, to the extent that observed wages do not reflect the real surplus supply of labour, confined outside formal economic circuits. Private enterprise, in its search for maximum profits, fails to make allowance for the existence of surplus labour, except insofar as this is reflected in the wage rates which are paid, and for both the foregoing reasons this failure implies that it adopts a technique which, from the social point of view, is too capital-using even if the social objective is to maximise the current rate of accumulation, that is it would be desirable to use a technique requiring more labour and less capital for a given output (Kahn, [1958b] 1972, p. 183). Having clarified this point, Kahn does not forget the risks of inflation caused by the heavy demand on the limited resources available.

> But I would not for a moment deny that a rapidly rising price level presents a serious obstacle to a country's development and that it is perfectly possible that as a result of trying to do too much a country may succeed in doing too little. Nor would I deny that, especially in underdeveloped countries, the speculative indulgence in hoarding of commodities and gold, and in wasteful forms of buildings, leads to misdirection of resources. These anti-social methods of holding private wealth call for strict controls and stringent penal measures. Their extent does also depend, among other things, on the general state of credit and on levels of rates of interest. (Ibid., p. 177)

Credit and interest rates are defined in the context of monetary policy, which is entrusted with the very delicate task of finding a compromise between the objectives of promoting investment, meeting the demand for money for transactional purposes and avoiding speculative pressures. These recommendations, although differing in detail according to the context in which they are formulated, anticipate certain elements that Kahn elaborated on in his testimony before the Radcliffe Committee in October 1958. Similar considerations apply to Kahn's assertion that there is no direct correlation between money supply and inflation, even in developing economies, depends mainly on wage developments.

> The behaviour of money wages is the key to the behaviour of the price level in Israel, as in advanced economies. In a country like India, on the other hand, the proportion of the working population which lives on wages is

> small. Even there, however, the wage system provides some sort of a base, small and uncertain though it may be, for a very large pyramid of the price structure, though obviously other elements contribute to the danger of the system of prices will move progressively higher in an unsuccessful attempt to achieve stability. (Ibid., p. 178)

This diagnosis leads to the conclusion that an anti-inflationary strategy should be based on the empowerment of trade union leaders, organised labour representatives and employers, who must be asked to exercise restraint in bidding up wages. As part of this strategy, indexing monetary wages to prices may prove counterproductive, even with a view to a selective increase in indirect taxes that would cause some prices to rise. It is preferable to utilise prudent subsidies to contain the price of essential goods with the objective of stabilising a cost-of-living index. In the event of unforeseen circumstances, such as external shocks, it may be necessary to implement price adjustments to wages as a contingency measure. Another aspect of this price containment strategy could be educational and propaganda campaigns that, by presenting the issue of inflation in a straightforward and understandable manner, may influence social psychology in a manner conducive to price stability.

Overall, Kahn's proposals for reconciling economic development, full employment and inflation control present the authorities with a choice between a rational and a less rational solution. The rational solution requires the authorities to direct resources in directions that the market, left to itself, would not go, without, however, falling prey to the temptation to imitate the more developed countries too soon by adopting techniques that are too capital-intensive, too expensive and incompatible with the rapid absorption of surplus labour. The success of this solution depends on the ability to find the most appropriate instruments to overcome the resistance of the interests harmed by the development strategy, while avoiding waste and corruption. The less rational solution to the same problem leaves the various parties involved free to act in their own interests in a decentralised manner, leaving the government with the task of solving any problems that may arise from this interaction after the event. In presenting this alternative, echoes of the ideas expressed in the article on the multiplier, in the lecture on public service to the Marshall Society, in his review of Meade's book on planning and pricing mechanisms and in his Radcliffe testimony, come to the fore. As we shall see, the same echoes can be heard in Kahn's analyses of the problems of the British and international economy in the 1960s and 1970s.

5.7 A Coherent Vision

The combined analysis of Kahn's theoretical works from the 1950s, alongside his official and unofficial statements, reveals a consistent economic vision from theoretical and methodological standpoints, as well as in terms of policy implications.

Theoretically, Kahn focuses on three key areas: the relationship between financial variables and investment decisions; the relationship between aggregate demand, wages and prices; and the relationship between investment, productivity and long-term employment. In all three cases, Kahn drew inspiration from Keynes, extending his mentor's ideas in different directions. While Keynes was cautious (and generally sceptical) about mathematical economics and gave the impression of treating the link between monetary variables, interest rates and investment in functional terms, Kahn explicitly rejected this possibility.

In the short period, 'concerned with things as they are—and, we fear, usually never should be', to quote Kahn's words at the Political Economy Club in the 1930s, the factors influencing portfolio choices and investment decisions are too numerous and complex to model with mathematical and statistical functions. Opinions, conjectures and expectations, formulated in conditions of uncertainty by heterogeneous agents who are often in possession of imprecise information and incomplete preferences, deprive the liquidity preference function of clear boundaries. The same applies to the effect of animal spirits and profit expectations, which change more or less rapidly depending on the case and are formulated by entrepreneurs who are often not very dynamic. Based on this view, Kahn conceives of the short-term link between money, financial variables and investment as an underlying trend surrounded by wide margins of uncertainty, conditioned by institutions that regulate the behaviour of monetary authorities and the functioning of financial markets and investment goods.

The same applies to the link between aggregate demand, wages and prices. In the short term, for a given level of productivity growth, this link is fairly precise. However, the same cannot be said for the determination of monetary wages. Again, little can be said in general theoretical terms here. Depending on the organisation of the labour market, the willingness of trade unions to cooperate with each other to ensure wage increases that are compatible with price stability and the willingness of employers to adhere to trade union agreements, the same pressure from aggregate demand can have completely different effects on the inflation rate in the short term. Again, in the short run, the underlying causal relationships between the variables of interest can be barely discerned against the backdrop of a changing reality that economists must investigate using all available means, without assuming that they can mathematically represent that reality. Kahn's scepticism about the Phillips curve stems from this, as well as his concern that it could be used to justify reducing inflation by increasing unemployment.

The situation changes in the transition from the short to the long term: 'When things are as they should be, and never are', to quote Kahn again from his speech to the Political Economy Club. In the long term, especially under Golden Age conditions, uncertainty and changing opinions give way to a steady state: a present that resembles the past (and the future), and fulfilled expectations. In this case, the causal links between variables become clearer, the aforementioned margins of uncertainty diminish and eventually disappear and economists are able to make more accurate judgements, for example on the relationship between the rate of profit and the capital intensity of investment processes. Kahn moves cautiously on this terrain, formulating concepts and conjectures that can be understood when considered in relation to John Robinson's theoretical framework in *The Accumulation of Capital.*

According to this view of the short and the long run, if policymakers wish to influence the economy, they must combine action with clarity of purpose. They must clarify the underlying objectives of their actions (e.g. allocating resources to investment to support employment, productivity, growth and the modernisation of the economy) and the instruments they intend to use to achieve these objectives. There are no fixed rules, only discretionary interventions and decisions, which allow for flexibility in response to unpredictable circumstances and guide economic agents in the desired direction. For Kahn (as for Keynes), economic policy is, above all, a matter of opinion. Policymakers must mould the opinions and expectations of economic agents in the desired direction, without setting themselves quantitative targets or precluding the use of all available instruments. This includes those instruments that are seemingly less favourable to free trade and corporate profits in a capitalist economy. This remains Kahn's main reference point.

If the government succeeds in steering public opinion in the desired direction with rational and sensible arguments, its actions will be effective without the need for drastic measures, provided there is social agreement. However, if the government fails to convince the public, it will have to act more decisively without allowing itself to be distracted by possible conflicts that its actions may trigger. Kahn remains convinced that, unless the government decides to let things take their course, it will prevail in any case and in this way prevent that the strongest will prevail over the weakest.

References

Adelman, I., & Sunding, D. (1989). Joan Robinson as a development economist. In G. R. Feiwel (Ed.), *Joan Robinson and Modern Economic Theory* (pp. 702–722). Palgrave Macmillan.

Alacevich, M. (2018). The birth of development economics: Theories and institutions. *History of Political Economy, 50*, 114–132.

Allen, W. A. (2014). *Monetary Policy and Financial Repression in Britain, 1951–59*. Palgrave Macmillan.

Amdekar, S., & Singh, A. (2017). Cambridge and development economics. In R. Cord (Ed.), *The Palgrave companion to Cambridge economics* (pp. 73–92). Palgrave Macmillan.

Arndt, H. W. (1962). Radcliffe monetary theory: A comment. *Economic Record, 38*, 341–351.

Backhouse, R., & Forder, J. (2013). Rationalizing incomes policy in Britain, 1948–1979. *History of Economic Thought and Policy, 1*, 17–35.

Bibow, J. (1998). On Keynesian theories of liquidity preference. *Manchester School, 66*, 238–273.

Bogdanor, V., & Skidelsky, R. (Eds.). (1970). *The age of affluence*. Macmillan.

Boianovsky, M. (2005). Some Cambridge reactions to *The General Theory*: David Champernowne and Joan Robinson on full employment. *Cambridge Journal of Economics, 29*, 73–98.

Booth, A. E. (2000). Inflation, expectations and the political economy of conservative Britain, 1951–1964. *The Historical Journal, 43*, 827–847.

Booth, A. E. (2001). Britain in the 1950s: A 'Keynesian' managed economy? *History of Political Economy, 33*(2), 283–313.

Bowen, G. (1960). *The wage-price issue*. Princeton University Press.

Bridel, P. (2021). The part played by general equilibrium in the liquidity preference vs loanable funds episode (1936–1956). *European Journal of the History of Economic Thought, 28*, 753–786.

Brittan, S. (1964). *The Treasury under the Tories, 1951–1964*. Penguin Books.

Bronfenbrenner, M., & Holzman, F. D. (1963). Survey of inflation theory. *American Economic Review, 53*(4), 593–661.
Cairncross, A. (Ed.). (1989). *The Robert Hall diaries, 1947–1953.* Unwin Hyman.
Cairncross, A. (Ed.). (1991). *The Robert Hall diaries, 1954–1961.* Unwin Hyman.
Cairncross, A. (1992). *The British economy since 1945.* Institute of Contemporary British History, Cairncross Treasury Series, University of London.
Cairncross, A. (1994). Austin Robinson. *Economic Journal, 104*(425), 903–915.
Cairncross, A. (1996). Prelude to Radcliffe: Monetary policy in the United Kingdom, 1948–57. In A. Cairncross (Ed.), *Economic ideas and government policy* (pp. 113–129). Routledge.
Cairncross, A. (1999). *Diaries: The Radcliffe Committee and the Treasury 1961–64.* Institute of Contemporary British History, Cairncross Treasury Series, University of London.
Cairncross, A., & Watt, N. (1989). *The economic section 1939–1961: A study in economic advising.* Routledge.
Caldentey, P. E. (2019). *Roy Harrod.* Palgrave Macmillan.
Cardim de Carvalho, F. J. (2010). Uncertainty and money: Keynes, Tobin and Kahn and the disappearance of the precautionary demand for money from the liquidity preference theory. *Cambridge Journal of Economics, 34*, 709–725.
Chakravarty, S., (1987). *Post-Keynesian theorists and the theory of economic development.* WIDER Working Papers No. 295551, World Institute for Development Economic Research.
Champernowne, D. G. (1958). Capital accumulation and full employment. *Economic Journal, 68*(270), 263–288.
Charpe, M., Bridji, S., & McAdam, P. (2019). *Labor share and growth in the long run.* ECB Working Paper No. 2251. European Central Bank.
Chick, V. (1973). *The theory of monetary policy.* Gray-Mills.
Chick, V., & Tily, G. (2014). Whatever happened to Keynes's monetary theory? *Cambridge Journal of Economics, 38*(3), 681–699.
Ciccarone, G. (2004). Finance and the Cambridge equation. *Review of Political Economy, 16*, 163–177.
Clarke, P. (1996). The Keynesian consensus. In D. Marquand & A. Seldon (Eds.), *The ideas that shaped post-war Britain* (pp. 67–87). Fontana Press.
Cobham, D. (1992). Radcliffe Committee. In J. Eatwell, M. Milgate, & P. Newman (Eds.), *The new Palgrave dictionary of money and finance* (pp. 265–266). Macmillan.
Cohen, A. J., & Harcourt, G. C. (2003). Retrospectives: Whatever happened to the Cambridge capital theory controversies? *Journal of Economic Perspectives, 17*(1), 199–214.
Cristiano, C. (2023). The early reception of the Phillips curve in the United Kingdom: New evidence from the papers of the Council on Prices, Productivity, and Incomes. *History of Political Economy, 55*(2), 215–248.

Cristiano, C., & Paesani, P. (2018a). Monetary policy and price stability in British post-war debate: Restatement of evidence from economists' papers presented to the Radcliffe committee. *European Journal of the History of Economic Thought, 25*(6), 1311–1341.

Cristiano, C., & Paesani, P. (2018b). Price stability and the origins and early influence of the Phillips curve on British policy debates. *History of Political Economy, 50*(3), 483–509.

Cristiano, C., & Paesani, P. (2018c). Unconventional monetary policy *ante litteram*: Richard Kahn and the monetary policy debate during the works of the Radcliffe Committee. *Cambridge Journal of Economics, 42*, 1145–1163.

Dalton, H. (1954). *Principles of public finance*. Fourth edition.

Dardi, M. (1994). Kahn's theory of liquidity preference and monetary policy. *Cambridge Journal of Economics, 18*, 91–106.

Destefanis, S. P. (1999). The wage-wage spiral and wage determination: An empirical appraisal for Italy. In C. Sardoni & P. Kriesler (Eds.), *Keynes, post-Keynesianism and political economy: Essays in honour of Geoff Harcourt* (pp. 486–509). Routledge.

Dow, J. C. R. (1965). Review of *The problem of rising prices*, by W. J. Fellner, M. Gilbert, B. Hansen, R.F. Kahn, F.A. Lutz, and P. de Wolff. *Economic Journal, 75*, 126–129.

Dutt, A. K. (2017). Heterodox theories of economic growth and income distribution: A partial survey. *Journal of Economic Surveys, 31*(5), 1240–1271.

Ederer, S., Mayerhofer, M., & Rehm, M. (2021). Rich and ever richer? Differential returns across socioeconomic groups. *Journal of Post Keynesian Economics, 44*, 283–301.

Fantacci, L., Marcuzzo, M. C., & Sanfilippo, E. (2014). A note on the notions of risk-premium and liquidity-premium in Hicks's and Keynes's analyses of the term structure of interest rates. *European Journal of the History of Economic Thought, 21*(6), 1102–1108.

Fellner, W. J., Gilbert, M., Hansen, B., Kahn, R. F., Lutz, F., & Wolff, P. de. (1961). *The problem of rising prices*. Organisation for European Economic Cooperation.

Findlay, R. (1963). The Robinsonian model of accumulation. *Economica, 30*(117), 1–12.

Gurley, J. G. (1960). The Radcliffe report and evidence. *American Economic Review, 50*, 672–700.

Hague, D. C. (Ed.) (1962). *Inflation, Proceedings of a Conference held by the International Economic Association*. Macmillan.

Hall, P. (1986). *Governing the economy. The politics of state intervention in Britain and France*. Oxford University Press.

Hancock, K., & Isaac, J. E. (1998). Sir Henry Phelps Brown, 1906–1994. *Economic Journal, 108*(448), 757–778.

Harcourt, G. C. (1991). R.F. Kahn: A tribute. *Banca Nazionale del Lavoro Quarterly Review, 176*, 15–30.
Harcourt, G. C., & Kerr, P. (2009). *Joan Robinson*. Palgrave Macmillan.
Harrod, R. F. (1939). An essay in dynamic theory. *Economic Journal, 49*, 14–33.
Harrod, R. F. (1948). *Towards a dynamic economics: Some recent developments of economic theory and their application to policy*. Macmillan.
Harrod, R. F. (1958). *Policy against inflation*. Macmillan.
Hicks, J. R. (1946). *Value and capital* (2nd ed.). Clarendon Press.
Hirschman, A. O. (1982). The rise and decline of development economics. In M. Gersovitz, C. F. Diaz-Alejandro, G. Ranis, & M. R. Rosenzweig (Eds.), *The theory and experience of economic development: Essays in honor of Sir W. Arthur Lewis* (pp. 372–390). George Allen and Unwin.
Holmans, A. E. (1999). *Demand management in Britain 1953–58*. Institute of Contemporary British History.
Howson, S. (1988). Cheap money and debt management in Britain, 1932–51. In P. L. Cottrell & D. E. Moggridge (Eds.), *Money and power* (pp. 227–289). Palgrave Macmillan.
Howson, S. (1993). *British Monetary Policy 1945–51*. Oxford University Press.
Hutchison, T. W. (1967). *Economics and economic policy in Britain, 1946–1966*. Allen and Unwin.
Jasay, A. E. (1960). The working of the Radcliffe monetary system. *Oxford Economic Papers, 12*, 170–180.
Johnson, H. G. (1951). Some Cambridge controversies in monetary theory. *Review of Economic Studies, 19*, 90–104.
Johnson, H. G. (1963). A survey of theories of inflation. *Indian Economic Review, 6*, 29–69.
Jones, R. (1987). *Wages and employment policy, 1936–1985*. Allen and Unwin.
Jones, K. (1994). *An economist among mandarins: A biography of Robert Hall, 1901–1988*. Cambridge University Press.
Kahn, R. F. (1950). Marshall aid. *The Times*, November 11.
Kahn, R. F. (1951a). The budget. *The Economist*, May 5.
Kahn, R. F. (1951b). Manpower control. *The Economist*, December 15.
Kahn, R. F. (1952). Manpower control. *The Economist*, January 5.
Kahn, R. F. (1953). Equipment for industry. *The Times*, April 20.
Kahn, R. F. (1954). Some notes on liquidity preference. *Manchester School of Economic and Social Studies, 22*(3), 229–257. Reprinted in R.F. Kahn (1972), *Selected Essays on Employment and Growth* (72–96). Cambridge University Press.
Kahn, R.F. (1956a). Lord Keynes and contemporary economic problems. *The Listener*, May 3 and 10. Reprinted in R.F. Kahn (1972), *Selected Essays on Employment and Growth* (103–123). Cambridge University Press.

Kahn, R. F. (1956b). Full Employment and British Economic Policy. *Nihon Keizai Shimbun*, 1956. Reprinted in R.F. Kahn (1972), *Selected Essays on Employment and Growth* (97–102). Cambridge University Press.

Kahn, R. F. (1958a). Memorandum of evidence submitted to the Radcliffe Committee (27 May). In Radcliffe Committee (Committee on the Working of the Monetary System) (1960b), *Principal Memoranda of Evidence* (Vol. 3, 138–146). HMSO. Reprinted in R.F. Kahn (1972), *Selected Essays on Employment and Growth* (124–152). Cambridge University Press.

Kahn, R. F. (1958b). The pace of development. In *The challenge of development: A symposium*, 163–198. Lecture delivered at the Eliezer Kaplan School of Economics and Social Sciences, Jerusalem: Hebrew University of Jerusalem. Reprinted in R.F. Kahn (1972), *Selected essays on employment and growth* (pp. 153–191). Cambridge University Press.

Kahn, R.F. (1959). Exercises in the analysis of growth. *Oxford Economic Papers, 11*(2), June, 146–163. Reprinted in R. F. Kahn (1972), *Selected essays on employment and growth* (pp. 192–207). Cambridge University Press.

Kahn, R. F. (1960). Testimony to the Radcliffe Committee (23 October 1958). In Radcliffe Committee (Committee on the Working of the Monetary System) (1960c), *Minutes* (739–746). HMSO.

Kaldor, N. (1939). Speculation and economic stability. *Review of Economic Studies, 7*, 1–27.

Kaldor, N. (1955). Alternative theories of distribution. *The Review of Economic Studies, 23*(2), 83–100.

Kaldor, N. (1957). A model of economic growth. *Economic Journal, 67*(268), 591–624.

Kaldor, N. (1960). The Radcliffe Report. *Review of Economics and Statistics, 42*(1), 14–19.

Kalecki, M. (1954). *Theory of economic dynamics: An essay on cyclical and long-run changes in capitalist economy.* George Allen and Unwin.

Katz, S. I. (1960). Radcliffe report: Monetary policy and debt-management reconsidered. *Banca Nazionale del Lavoro Quarterly Review, 13*(53), 3–36.

Keynes, J. M. (1936). *The general theory of employment, interest, and money.* Macmillan.

Kindleberger, C. P. (1967). *Europe's postwar growth: The role of labor supply.* Harvard University Press.

Koutsobinas, T. (2022). The rising importance of liquidity-premium analysis: Towards a regeneration of liquidity-preference theory? In P. Hawkins & I. Negru (Eds.), *Monetary economics, banking and policy* (pp. 160–174). Routledge.

Kregel, J. A. (2013). Was Keynes' monetary policy, à outrance in the *Treatise*, the model for ZIRP and QE? In T. Hirai, M. C. Marcuzzo, & P. Mehrling (Eds.),

Keynesian reflections: Effective demand, money, finance and policies (pp. 115–126). Oxford University Press.
Lancaster, K. (1960). Mrs. Robinson's dynamics. *Economica, 27*, 16–29.
Lavoie, M. (1992). *Foundations of post-Keynesian economic analysis.* Edward Elgar Publishing.
Lengyel, E. (1959). Review of *The challenge of development. American Economic Review, 49*, 173–175.
Lerner, A. P. (1962). The problem of rising prices. William Fellner, Milton Gilbert, Bert Hansen, Richard Kahn, Friedrich Lutz, Pieter de Wolff. *Journal of Political Economy, 70*(4), 415–416.
Lewis, W. A. (1954). Economic development with unlimited supplies of labour. *Manchester School, 22*, 139–191.
Little, I. M. D. (1957). Classical growth. *Oxford Economic Papers, 9*(2), 152–177.
Marchionatti, R. (2024). *Economic theory in the twentieth century. An intellectual history, Vol. III: 1946–mid-1970s. Economic theory in the new Golden Age of Capitalism*. Palgrave Macmillan.
Marcuzzo, M. C. (2020). Richard F. Kahn: A disciple of Keynes. *History of Economics Review, 76*(1), 2–57.
Marcuzzo, M. C., Pasinetti, L. L., & Roncaglia, A. (Eds.). (1996). *The economics of Joan Robinson*. Routledge.
Middleton, R. (2004). Economists and economic growth in Britain, 1955–65. In L. E. I. Black & H. R. Pemberton (Eds.), *An affluent society? Britain's post-war 'Golden Age' revisited* (pp. 129–147). Routledge.
Morris, J. (2007). *The life and times of Thomas Balogh: A Macaw among Mandarins.* Sussex Academic Press.
Paish, F. W. (1962). *Studies in an inflationary economy.* Macmillan.
Patriarca, F., & Sardoni, C. (2017). Distribution and growth. A dynamic approach. *Structural Change and Economic Dynamics, 40*, 1–9.
Peden, G. C. (1985). *British economic and social policy* (2nd ed.). Philip Annan.
Peden, G. C. (2000). *The Treasury and British Public Policy, 1906–1959.* Oxford University Press.
Pemberton, H. (2004). Relative decline and British economic policy in the 1960s. *The Historical Journal, 47*(4), 989–1013.
Pivetti, M. (1996). Joan Robinson and the rate of interest: An important change of view on a topical issue. In M. C. Marcuzzo, L. L. Pasinetti, & A. Roncaglia (Eds.), *The economics of Joan Robinson* (pp. 75–80). Routledge.
Radcliffe Committee (Committee on the Working of the Monetary System) (1960a). *Report*, Cmnd. 827. HMSO.
Radcliffe Committee (Committee on the Working of the Monetary System). (1960b). *Principal Memoranda of Evidence, 3 vols.* HMSO.
Radcliffe Committee (Committee on the Working of the Monetary System). (1960c). *Minutes of evidence.* HMSO.

Rezende, F. (2015). Demand for financial assets and monetary policy: A restatement of the liquidity preference theory and the speculative demand for money. *Journal of Post Keynesian Economics, 38*, 64–92.
Robbins, L. (1963). *Politics and economics. Papers in political economy*. Macmillan.
Robinson, J. (1951). The rate of interest. *Econometrica, 19*, 92–111.
Robinson, J. V. (1956). *The accumulation of capital* (2nd ed.). Macmillan.
Robinson, J. V. (1962). *Essays in the theory of economic growth*. Macmillan.
Rochon, L. P. (2001). Cambridge's contribution to endogenous money: Robinson and Kahn on credit and money. *Review of Political Economy, 13*(3), 287–307.
Rollings, N. (1996). Butskellism, the Postwar consensus and the managed economy. In H. Jones & M. Kandiah (Eds.), *The myth of consensus: New views on British history, 1945–64* (pp. 97–110). Macmillan.
Romanis Braun, A. (1986). *Wage determination and incomes policy in open economies*. International Monetary Fund.
Rostow, W. W. (1956). The take-off into self-sustained growth. *Economic Journal, 66*, 25–48.
Rousseas, S. (1998). *Post-Keynesian monetary economics* (3rd ed.). Macmillan.
Sardoni, C. (2007). Kaldor's monetary thought: A contribution to a modern theory of money. In M. Forstater, G. Mongiovi, & S. Pressman (Eds.), *Post-Keynesian macroeconomics: Essays in honor of Ingrid Rima* (pp. 127–146). Routledge.
Sawyer, M. (2002). Economic policy with endogenous money. In P. Arestis, M. Desai, & S. Dow (Eds.), *Essays in honour of Victoria Chick* (pp. 35–44). Routledge.
Sayers, R. S. (1951). The rate of interest as a weapon of economic policy. In T. Wilson & P. W. S. Andrews (Eds.), *Oxford studies in the price mechanism* (pp. 1–16). Clarendon Press.
Schiffman, D. (2017). Ex-officio adviser: Kahn in Israel, 1957 and 1962. In D. Schiffman, W. Young, & Y. Zelekha (Eds.), *The role of economic advisers in Israel's economic policy* (pp. 51–80). Springer.
Shonfield, A. (1958). *British economic policy since the war*. Penguin Books.
Smith, M. (2012). Demand-led growth theory: A historical approach. *Review of Political Economy, 24*(4), 543–573.
Smithies, A. (1962). Review of *The problem of rising prices*, by W. Fellner, M. Gilbert, B. Hansen, R. Kahn, F. Lutz, and P. de Wolff. *American Economic Review, 52*(3), 535–538.
Targetti, F. (2005). Nicholas Kaldor: Key contributions to development economics. *Development and Change, 36*, 1185–1199.
Tily, G. (2010). *Keynes betrayed: The general theory, the rate of interest and 'Keynesian' economics*. Palgrave Macmillan.
Tobin, J. (1963). An essay on the principles of debt management. In *Fiscal and debt management policies* (pp. 143–218). Prentice-Hall.

Tomlinson, J. (1995). An unfortunate alliance: Keynesianism and the conservatives 1945–1964. *History of Political Economy, 27*(Supplement), 61–85.

Tomlinson, J. (1996). Inventing 'decline': The falling behind of the British economy in the postwar years. *Economic History Review, 49*(4), 731–757.

Tomlinson, J. (2017). *Managing the economy, managing the people: Narratives of economic life in Britain from Beveridge to Brexit.* Oxford University Press.

Tomlinson, J. (2023). Imagining economic growth in post-war Britain. *Twentieth Century British History, 34*(4), 754–779.

Vernengo, M., & Rochon, L. (2001). Kaldor and Robinson on money and growth. *European Journal of the History of Economic Thought, 8*, 75–103.

Weise, H. (1961). Review of *The problem of rising prices*, by W. Fellner, M. Gilbert, B. Hansen, R. Kahn, F. Lutz, and P. de Wolff. *Weltwirtschaftliches Archiv, 87*, 81–83.

Wells, P. (1983). A post Keynesian view of liquidity preference and the demand for money. *Journal of Post Keynesian Economics, 5*(4), 523–536.

Williams, C. G. (1981). Joan Robinson on unions, distribution and inflation. *Relations Industrielles/Industrial Relations, 36*(3), 576–588.

Wilson, T., & Andrews, P. W. S. (Eds.). (1951). *Oxford studies in the Price mechanism.* Clarendon Press.

Worswick, G. D. N., & Ady, P. H. (Eds.). (1962). *The British economy in the nineteen-fifties.* Clarendon Press.

CHAPTER 6

The Keynesian Citadel

6.1 Kahn from the 1950s to the Mid-1960s

Kahn's scholarly contributions in the 1950s and 1960s were intertwined with his involvement in the activities of the Faculty of Economics and Politics at the University of Cambridge. These were intense years for Cambridge, with the number of students, courses and staff increasing to meet the growing demand for professional economists from the British government and other public and private institutions. Kahn played a key role in this process as a teacher, seminar organiser and influential member of the Faculty of Economics. Within the Faculty, the fault lines that had begun to emerge before the war between what can be conventionally defined as the Keynesian group (Kahn, Joan Robinson, Nicholas Kaldor, but also Ruth Cohen, Piero Sraffa, Brian Reddaway Kenneth Berrill, Robin Marris) and their opponents (such as Robertson and Claude Guillebaud) became more apparent, while other members of the Faculty, such as Richard Stone and James Meade, who had been close to Keynes in the 1930s and 1940s but who for various reasons remained outside the inner circle of the Keynesians, took a more reserved position. The same can be said of Austin Robinson, an ally of the Keynesians in the Faculty battles but distant from them on a theoretical level. As Robinson himself recalled in later years:

P. Paesani, *Richard F. Kahn*, Great Thinkers in Economics,
https://doi.org/10.1007/978-3-032-09123-9_6

> I came back to Cambridge with what I thought was a mission to quantify economics and move forward from the vague generalities of pre-war economics to the sort of economics that [we] were engaged in creating in Whitehall during those war years. I never persuaded Cambridge collectively to take an interest in quantification and measurement. I found Joan, Nicky Kaldor and Richard Kahn playing about with a new version of pre-war economics of their own, with a good deal of Marx and Kalecki added. I had no part in that and was not at all interested in it. But I was very much interested in the setting up of the Department of Applied Economics with Dick Stone in charge, and I took more interest in that and my own personal work than in anything else. (In Cairncross, 1993, p. 111)

In this context, as Harry Johnson, an acute if not particularly sympathetic witness,[1] observed, Richard Kahn was recognised as the leader and strategist of the group of the Keynesians, responsible for academic policy and strategies of recruitment and promotion; Joan Robinson and Kaldor focused on the battle of ideas at the theoretical level and Austin Robinson presided over *The Economic Journal* and the Royal Economic Society and was deeply involved, as just mentioned, in the establishment of the Department of Applied Economics (DAE).

The image of Kahn that emerges from this part of my reconstruction is that of a man certain of his own ideas, ready to confront his opponents, even harshly, and at the same time a dedicated if not particularly inspiring teacher, a courteous and attentive host to the participants in the Secret Seminar and fully committed to the defence and consolidation of the Keynesian citadel of Cambridge. At the same time, as we shall see, Kahn did not always promote harmony within the Keynesian group or among the Faculty in general.

During the 1960s, in contrast to the previous decade, Kahn's scholarly activity slowed down, at least in terms of his publications (see Appendix A). This slowdown appears to have been the result of a variety of factors related to his heavy academic commitments, his occasional activities as adviser to the Wilson government and a member of the National Coal Board and his participation in a number of commissions for United Nations Conference on Trade and Development (UNCTAD). However, one suspects that, at a deeper level, Kahn's absence from the theoretical

[1] On Harry Johnson at Cambridge, see Johnson and Johnson (1978). See also Turner (1989, pp. 69–73), with a comment on Johnson by Kahn, and Moggridge (2011). See also Naylor (1981) and Khatkhate (2009).

debates of the 1960s—including those in Cambridge—reflected the growing distance between his own theoretical vision and the direction in which economic theory was heading at the time as well as his gradual loss of interest in new economic theories.

Kahn did not participate in the capital controversy between the two Cambridge (Cohen & Harcourt, 2003). Although he was an admirer and friend of Sraffa, he distanced himself from his ideas. He was highly critical of the neoclassical synthesis of Keynesian economic thought, Hicks's IS-LM model and the Phillips curve. Similarly, Kahn, who was always sceptical of econometrics, chose not to get involved in the DAE's research projects based on the empirical modelling of growth and economic policy. Far removed from these new areas of research, and therefore increasingly isolated even within Cambridge, in the mid-1960s Kahn continued to focus on his pet topics: investment and its financial determinants, effects of monetary policy, how to reconcile full employment and growth with control of inflation and the balance of payments.

Relaunching investment and productivity, controlling inflation and restoring external balance were the main problems facing the British economy in the 1960s and in the transition from the Conservative governments of Macmillan and Douglas-Home (1957–1963) to Wilson's Labour government (1964–1970). Overall, the 1960s was a decade of both economic success and increasing challenges for the British economy. GDP growth averaged 3.5%, unemployment remained low at 2.7% and inflation averaged 3.5%. Real per capita disposable income increased by 25% over the decade. However, underlying problems began to surface, making the end of the decade less promising than the beginning. The decade was marked by the (failed) attempt to put an end to the 'stop-go' policies of the 1950s: periods of rapid expansion were followed by abrupt slowdowns as policymakers alternated between stimulating the economy to combat unemployment and tightening it to curb inflation and trade deficits.[2]

[2] On the British economy and economic policy in the 1960s, see Cairncross (1996) for an internal perspective from the government's point of view (Cairncross was an economic adviser to the British government between 1961 and 1964), Tomlinson (2004) for his focus on the key economic policy decision of the Wilson government, and O'Hara (2007) on the revival of economic and social planning in the 1960s after the attempts in this direction by the Attlee government. For the source of the data, see also the House of Lords Library website https://lordslibrary.parliament.uk/the-uk-economy-in-the-1960s/

The devaluation of sterling in 1967, from $2.80 to $2.40 per pound on 18 November 1967, marked a turning point in the British economy,[3] stimulating export-led growth and improving the balance of payments. Unlike in previous cycles, export-led growth during this period was undermined by rising import prices after devaluation. While restrictive fiscal policy achieved a rare budget surplus and reduced public debt, industrial competitiveness declined amid rising interest rates, labour unrest and a falling share of world exports. By the end of the decade, inflation and unemployment were rising, revealing underlying weaknesses despite favourable headline indicators.

The need to foster investment because of its positive contribution to employment, productivity and external competitiveness, and to do so while keeping inflationary pressures in check through wage and income policies, was central to Kahn's interventions in public debate, in the press and, from 1965, in the House of Lords, to which Kahn was elevated on the initiative of the Wilson government. While Kahn's reputation, his wartime record and his long association with the Labour Party favoured this appointment, it is important to note that Kahn was never one of the group of economists hired by the Labour government, among whom the names of Alec Cairncross, Nicholas Kaldor, Thomas Balogh and Robert Neild stand out.

Compared to them, Kahn maintained a position of autonomy and occasional criticism, as in the case of Britain's plans to join the EEC. Overall, both politically and academically, Kahn's decision to remain faithful to his economic vision and ideas about policy and society—formed in the 1930s and 1940s—at a time when that vision and those ideas were becoming increasingly obsolete, coupled with his reserved nature and reluctance to engage, contributed to his gradual isolation from the 1960s onwards. Although he was still consulted out of respect for his judgement, economic expertise and position, his advice was increasingly disregarded.

6.2 Teaching

In the 1950s, the University of Cambridge was one of the three most important centres of economic education in Britain, together with Oxford and the London School of Economics.

[3] On the devaluation, see Naef (2022, pp. 127–165), Cairncross and Eichengreen (2003).

> There were other institutions, but they were small in size and provincial in more than the geographical sense. Of these LSE was perhaps the most open to international influences contrasting strongly with the Cambridge habit of focusing mainly on work by other Cambridge economists. (Backhouse, 1996, p. 35)

By the academic year 1952–1953, following Kahn's election to the Chair of Economics in 1951, the Faculty of Economics and Politics, including professors and lecturers, had grown to 45 members, of which 41 were men and 4 women (source: *Cambridge University Reporter*),[4] and offered an expanded range of courses compared to the pre-war years.[5]

Until his retirement in 1972, Kahn maintained a steady teaching schedule, giving at least one course in each of the three terms: Michaelmas, Lent and Easter (see Appendix B). Between the Easter term of 1947–1948 and the Lent term of 1957–1958, except for 1955 when he was at the OEEC in Geneva, Kahn taught a course on the theory of interest rates to students preparing for Part II of the Tripos examinations every year. He combined this course with a series of classes on money, which were taught in the Michaelmas term alongside Joan Robinson and, occasionally, other lecturers: Harry Johnson (1950–1951), Richard Goodwin (1952–1953) and Robert Neild (1956–1957).[6]

[4] S. Adler, N.G. Annan, Prof. A.L. Banks, P.T. Bauer, K.E. Berrill, Prof. D.W. Brogan, A.J.Y. Brown, R.L. Cohen. P.M. Deane, S.R. Dennison, M.H. Dobb, E. Farmer, Prof. M. Fortes. R.M. Goodwin. C.W. Guillebaud, W. Hagenbuch, R.F. Henderson, E.J.E. Hobsbawm, M. Tappan Hollond, H.G. Johnson, Prof. R.F. Kahn, N. Kaldor, Prof. H.S Kirkaldy, Prof. Lauterpacht, S.Y. Mallett, R.L. Marris, R.C.O. Matthews, Prof. A.C. Pigou, Prof. M.M. Postan, A.R. Prest, W.B. Reddaway, Prof. D.H. Robertson, Prof. E.A.G. Robinson, J.V. Robinson, L. Rostas, J.W.F. Rowe, A.D. Roy, F.R. Salter, F. Sewell Bray, Z.A. Silberston, P. Sraffa, J.R.N. Stone, F. Thistlewhite, J.E.G. Uttig, J. Wishart. For essential biographical references on each one of these people, see ACAD (*A Cambridge Alumni Database*) website https://venn.lib.cam.ac.uk/Documents/acad/intro.html

[5] Over the next decades, in the context of the transformation of the British university system, the situation changed, with a significant increase in the number of courses and Faculty members. After 1960, British university education expanded significantly, becoming more inclusive and accessible. Spurred by the 1963 Robbins Report, which called for education for all qualified individuals, enrolment grew and new universities and polytechnic institutions emerged. Government investment increased, diversifying subjects and making higher education accessible to more women, working-class and minority students (Movrich, 1975).

[6] As Di Matteo and Sordi (2008) reconstruct, Goodwin was invited to apply to Cambridge by Kahn himself. On Goodwin at Cambridge, see also Velupillai (2017, p. 817, fn. 5). In 1949, Harry Johnson was invited by D. Robertson to become an assistant lecturer. The fol-

Thanks to the recent and ongoing digitalisation of Luigi Pasinetti's papers, the contents of Kahn's course on interest rates can be reconstructed.[7]

> This course will be concerned mainly with the theory of the rate of interest as developed by Keynes in the General Theory, with further generalisations. We shall not enter in the philosophy of rate of interest as Keynes did but influence of rate of interest as market determined on economic system—on actual and prospective situation. The influence of rate of interest on investments in Keynes is striking.[8]

Kahn's analysis is based on three financial assets: money (with a zero return), irredeemable bonds and ordinary shares. Physical capital belongs to companies, which in turn belong to shareholders. The expected return on shares depends on various factors, including lender risk (as defined by Keynes in *The General Theory*), the actual replacement cost (i.e. the cost of selling some shares to buy others), the interest rate (i.e. what a person could earn by investing elsewhere, such as in public debt) and the risk associated with the variability of expected returns.[9]

Kahn focuses on the difference between risk and uncertainty, and on the issue of a lack of conviction affecting investors. He also considers whether investment choices are guided by realised gains or dividends distributed to shareholders, ex post or by the expected return on the new investment or on the company's total capital. The influence of interest rates on investment is further complicated by the possibility that firms resort to bonds or self-financing as an alternative to shares, by the distinction between shareholders and managers, and the possibility that their expectations may not align. When new investments are financed exclusively through the issuance of new shares, optimism or pessimism regarding marginal investment becomes synonymous with the company's overall

lowing year, he became a lecturer and was also elected a fellow of King's College, which gave him the opportunity to meet Kahn on a regular basis.

[7] Pasinetti's notes consist of a set of 28 handwritten notes entitled 'The Rate of Interest by Prof. Kahn—Lent Term' (source: the Pasinetti Papers Archive)

[8] Source: the Pasinetti Papers Archive, Folder 1, File 2, Sub-file 3 (Faldone 1, Cartella 2, Cartellina 3), 1.

[9] Source: the Pasinetti Papers Archive, Folder 1, File 2, Sub-file 3 (Faldone 1, Cartella 2, Cartellina 3), 2.

outlook.[10] From this, Kahn concludes that Keynes's idea of an inverse relationship between interest rates and investment remains valid. However, this relationship should never be considered mechanically. Instead, it must always be considered within the relevant institutional context and with the multitude of subjective factors that can influence it in mind. These factors are often difficult to quantify and can strengthen or weaken the relationship depending on the circumstances.

Similar considerations apply to liquidity preference and the inverse relationship between interest rates and speculative/precautionary demand for money. These topics are discussed by Kahn in the second part of the course, where he compares Keynes's ideas in *The General Theory* with the interpretations of liquidity preference offered by Modigliani, Hansen and Robertson. Kahn then presents his own interpretation of liquidity preference, which reflects that outlined in his 1954 article, as discussed above. He also discusses Robertson's theory of loanable funds and Hicks's IS-LM model.

In addition to Pasinetti's notes, there are two published accounts of the course on interest rates and liquidity preference, by Harry Johnson and Geoffrey Harcourt.

> It was primarily Kahn who carried on the Keynesian tradition of liquidity preference theory. It is important for the understanding of Keynes to realize that he started his life as a lecturer—talking about the stock market and the financial markets generally—and that he kept on with these lectures through much of his career. Kahn took over from him both in lecturing on that subject and in managing the College's finances (where this analysis is really of great practical importance). Kahn was a rather peculiar lecturer. He would always spend something like twenty minutes of an hour summarizing what he had said the *last* [in the original] time and then, by the time he got through that, of course he could not finish what he was going to do *this* [in the original] time, so that he had to go into the *next* [in the original] lecture's summary. (Johnson & Johnson, 1978, p. 143)[11]

Thus, his lectures on liquidity preference theory to research students in the 1950s were well received by the (then) handful of Ph.D. students with

[10] Source: the Pasinetti Papers Archive, Folder 1, File 2, Sub-file 3 (Faldone 1, Cartella 2, Cartellina 3), 5.

[11] On the development of the Keynesian theory of liquidity preference as a theory based on the expected variations of the interest rate, and consequently on the expected variations in the capital value of financial assets, see Panico (2018).

> whom the lecturer had a friendly rapport. They sat in the front row and absorbed the argument despite the lecturer's almost complete inability to write on the board. But in discussion at the "Secret Seminar" or in smaller groups, or one to one, though he could be crusty and sometimes obscure (when his notorious anger would be used as a cover for lack of understanding), Kahn was in his element as sympathetic critic *par excellence*. (Harcourt, 1991, p. 28)

When evaluating Kahn's lecture on interest rates and liquidity preference, it is important to note that, like Keynes, Kahn had direct knowledge of how financial markets worked. This knowledge derived primarily from his activities, alongside Keynes as Second Bursar at King's College from 1935 to 1946 and then as First Bursar, formally between 1946 and 1951 and informally in the following years. Moreover, Kahn was for some years a director of the Anglo-Israel Bank (AIB), which was the UK subsidiary of Israel's Bank Leumi (Schiffman, 2013, p. 13) and his private correspondence reveals that Kahn frequently invested in his own name and occasionally sought financial advice and opinions from his colleagues, particularly Sraffa and Kaldor.[12]

In the Michaelmas term of 1958–1959 Kahn taught the course on the theory of interest rates for the last time and, after that, the focus of his teaching shifted to wage theory and wage policy, combined with occasional courses on economic development for graduate students, economic principles and problems and principles of economic planning.[13] In the last two years before his retirement (1970–1971 and 1971–1972) the title of the course became 'Prices and Income Policy'.

[12] For an account of Kahn's activities and achievements as Bursar, see Johnson and Johnson (1978, pp. 162–165). Further evidence of Kahn's direct knowledge of the world of finance and his links with it is evidenced by two reports he wrote for the financial house N.H. Rothschild and Sons. The first report, titled 'The Future of Interest Rates' and dated 20 March 1963 (RFK/2/19/348–361), contains an analysis of the relationship between the short-term rate, the long-term rate and monetary policy decisions, which broadly follows the ideas put forward in the 1954 article. The second report, entitled 'An Economic Review of the United Kingdom' and dated 2 July 1964, contains a summary analysis of the Labour government's main policy areas (RFK/2/19/399–407). This second report is preceded by a 38-page document, unsigned and marked confidential, devoted to the economic prospects under a Labour government (RFK/2/19/362–398). On Kahn as investor and man of affairs, see Samuelson (1994, pp. 60–61).

[13] For the course on the economics of government intervention, see the Pasinetti Papers Archive, Folder 1, File A2, Sub-file 7 (Faldone 1, Cartella A2, Cartellina 7).

A set of notes, collected by David Arthur Russell (later Lord Howell of Guildford) and kept at the Churchill Archives Centre, allows us to reconstruct the content of the course on wages taught by Kahn in 1959.[14] In this case, Kahn's lessons are grounded in the theoretical framework set out by Joan Robinson in her book *The Accumulation of Capital*. The first part of the course focuses on the determination of real wages in a Golden Age perspective, on the links between the rate of growth and the rate of profit, and the relationship between wages and profits per capita. Based on this and after discussing the concepts of the Bastard Golden Age and the inflation barrier, Kahn moves on to consider the relationship between changes in wages and price inflation. On the crucial point of the causes of inflation, Russell's notes indicate:

> Kahn believes that the two terms 'cost' and 'demand' inflation should be avoided. They are useful analytically only. He believes in both!! On the one hand wage negotiations are vital but the wage rates paid are not completely dictated or even 'mostly' by the T.U.s. On the contrary, most rates actually paid are determined by local 'demand' consideration. As a result the national negotiations are influenced and many other wages go up automatically. In other words some wages are demand supported, some are Union supported. The less the Union support, the wider the "wages-drift gap". Both phenomena are nevertheless interdependent. Inflation can be characterised by cost, or wage negotiation outcomes, but at the same time these outcomes are dependent on the level of demand. (Source: GBR/0014/HWLL 1/2/5)

These words echo Kahn's memorandum to the Radcliffe Committee, confirming that, when analysing the relationship between wages and prices or interest rates and investment, Kahn rejected the idea of a mechanical, functional relationship in favour of a more nuanced vision. This vision was attentive to institutional determinants, as well as the subjective factors affecting economic decisions in situations of uncertainty.

6.3 Secret Seminar and Faculty

Kahn's commitment to spreading Keynesian ideas, particularly on liquidity preference, investment and inflation, was closely related to Joan Robinson's attempt to extend the Keynesian framework from the short

[14] Ref. GBR/0014/HWLL 1/2/5. On this course, see also the Pasinetti Papers Archive, Folder 2, File A2, Sub-file 5 (Faldone 2, Cartella A2, Cartellina 5).

run to the long run as part of her efforts to establish a Post-Keynesian theory of growth and distribution at Cambridge. As Richard Goodwin recalled:

> To understand his [Kahn's] role one has to realise the fact of the degree to which his intellectual life and that of Joan were conducted in common. They met constantly, commonly discussing economics; they frequently dined together, often with other economists; they took long walks together; they travelled together; they climbed mountains together: in short it was a shared life of the spirit. Whereas Richard in public and in print spoke rarely, Joan loved nothing more than expressing her opinions and in telling others how wrong they were. The consequence was that, though in no sense was Joan simply the mouthpiece of their shared views, it was she, not he, that gave voice to what must have been much of their common economic thinking. (Goodwin, 1994, p. 75)

One of the main venues in which Joan Robinson had the opportunity to articulate her ideas on the accumulation of capital, distribution and growth was the so-called Secret Seminar, organised by Kahn in his rooms in Webb's Court at King's College.

The Secret Seminar had been started in 1949 and continued in existence until the late 1960s.[15] Its members included Jan Graaff, Joan Robinson, Austin Robinson, Nicholas Kaldor, Richard Stone (who attended it rarely), Piero Sraffa, Ruth Cohen, Brian Reddaway, Robin Matthews and Kenneth Berrill. Later members included Richard Goodwin, Aubrey Silberston and Robin Marris. Dennis Robertson was excluded, alongside other neoclassical economists such as Alan Prest, Peter Bauer, Stanley Dennison and Ronald Henderson, among others. James Meade, who had been part of the Cambridge Circus of which the Secret Seminar was a kind of development, did attend when he first arrived as Professor but then lapsed and later returned.[16] This exclusivity likely mirrored

[15] On the 'secret seminar', see Matthews (1989), Turner (1989, pp. 97–98) Moggridge (2011, p. 96) and Saith (2022, pp. 347–352).

[16] On Meade's participation in the Secret Seminar, see Silberston (2011). As Susan Howson observed in a personal communication to the author on 16 August 2024, upon his arrival in Cambridge as a professor, Meade was on cordial terms with Joan Robinson. He provided extensive feedback on the first draft of her *Exercises in Economic Analysis*, offering detailed criticisms, primarily of a technical nature. However, when she began to critique his work on growth theory, Meade became increasingly frustrated with her approach to dispute, particularly her unwillingness to concede the possibility of error in her criticisms. This led him to

Kahn's reserved personality, characterised by discomfort with large audiences and preference for small discussions, as well as his desire to protect Cambridge economics.

The practice was for one of the members to read a paper and after refreshments provided by Kahn, for the paper to be discussed. The seminar was intellectually vibrant but contentious and debates were heated, including when guests from the United States such as Leontief, Solow and Samuelson attended. Over time, tensions within the group and logistical changes, such as the opening of the Sidgwick Avenue building, diminished the centrality of the seminar. There was criticism of its exclusivity, which younger economists argued stifled participation and innovation.[17] These frustrations spurred the creation of alternative forums, such as the Queens' Economics Seminar led by Ajit Singh,[18] which embraced broader participation and became a lasting legacy. Ultimately, the Secret Seminar ceased to exist in 1969, two years before Kahn's retirement, and attempts to revive it in the 1970s were ultimately abandoned.

If the lectures and the Secret Seminar gave Kahn the chance to contribute to the development of the Cambridge Keynesian theory of growth and distribution, it was in the governing bodies of the Faculty of Economics and Politics that he exerted the greatest influence in the academic battles in support of the Keynesian position. The Faculty was marked by intense internal conflicts over institutional control, economic doctrines and political affiliations. These divisions, the origins of which can be traced back to the late 1930s, created a highly polarised environment where moderate positions were often marginalised, and political loyalty frequently outweighed academic merit. Johnson described the Faculty Board as a

stop corresponding with her altogether. Nevertheless, Meade never allowed his reaction to Robinson's behaviour to affect his enduring friendship with Richard Kahn. Over the years, Meade and Kahn met regularly, often for lunch, and corresponded on a variety of subjects pertinent to their relationship, such as commodity price stabilisation, buffer stocks and incomes policy. Meade's interest in improving mechanisms of wage determination dated back to the immediate post-war years, as reflected in numerous publications, including his Cambridge inaugural lecture, his Wincott Lecture and Stagflation, Volume I. On this matter, Kahn shared much of Meade's perspective. One further point of note concerning Meade, Robinson and Kaldor: Meade nominated Robinson for Fellowship of the British Academy in 1958, the year she was elected, and Kaldor in 1963, the year he was also elected. With Kaldor, Meade maintained an amicable intellectual exchange both in person and through extensive correspondence for many years.

[17] On Pasinetti as the youngest member of the Secret Seminar, see Garbellini (2023).

[18] On this, see Saith (2019, pp. 167–169).

'strongly political body', entangled in both academic and party politics. Faculty elections often required allegiance to either the left or the right factions, fostering bitterness and discouraging centrism. For example, in 1953, Wilfred Prest, brother of Alan Prest lecturer in Economics, documented the Faculty situation as follows:

> On the one hand there is the Robertson party comprising, in addition to Sir Dennis himself such diverse characters as Guillebaud, Richard Stone, R.F. Henderson and S.R. Dennison. This group has never quite accepted Keynes without reservations and its members are inclined to be conservative, politically and socially. On the other hand, there is the Kahn party comprising, in addition to Professor Kahn, Sraffa, Kaldor, Dobb, Rostas, Joan Robinson, Ruth Cohen and Harry Johnson [*sic*]. This group is neo-Keynesian in outlook and is well to the left politically. The conflict between the two is deep and bitter. ... In Faculty meetings I am told that squabbles develop over such things as the appointments of examiners and the arrangements of timetables. Because Dennis Robertson gives a course in interest rates, Kahn must give one too; then the timetable is mangled so that the student hears Kahn's version first. (Saith, 2022, p. 87)

Robert Neild, who returned to Cambridge as a Teaching Fellow in 1956, lamented the Faculty's environment, describing it as 'political and savage' and dominated by 'prima donnas'. In his private recollections, recorded by Hodgson (2019, p. 41), he recounted being pressured by Kahn to vote along partisan lines and feeling bullied into conformity. Amartya Sen, a Cambridge student from 1953, later noted the 'intense fights' between schools of thought (Sen, 1999). While Keynesians were generally perceived as left-leaning compared to neoclassical economists, internal divisions within the Keynesian camp were also fierce. Sen recalled Joan Robinson, his thesis supervisor, as 'brilliant but vigorously intolerant', while Kahn was described as 'bellicose'. Political divisions often overshadowed scholarly collaboration. Bliss (2010) attributed the Faculty's contentious atmosphere to a 'tradition of self-righteous intolerance' dating back to Keynes, a fact which Hodgson contests. However, broader socio-political influences and the Faculty's ideological zeal also played significant roles.

There is a significant amount of material on the life of the Faculty of Economics and Politics in the Kahn Archive (RFK/4/1–9), but most of it relates to organisational matters, recruitment, applications for research grants, CVs and letters of recommendation for potential new Faculty members. Within this material, however, some documents deserve attention for what they reveal about Kahn's views on the effectiveness of economics teaching at Cambridge and his position within the Faculty in 1962 on the eve of his election as Chairman.

The first document, signed by Kahn, is the Chairman's Report on Part II of the Economic Tripos for the academic year 1957–1958 (RFK/4/9/2–4). Kahn's report raises concerns about the decline in the quality of students and the difficulty of teaching economic theory to such a diverse group, which could result in a compromise that does not satisfy the strongest or the weakest students. Kahn laments the poor performance in the Principles of Economics exam, criticising candidates for their reliance on the rote reproduction of familiar material, and for their inability to apply their knowledge creatively to unfamiliar problems. In the field of industrial economics, with particular reference to the short run, the subject matter that Kahn himself had taught in the 1930s, the assessment is if possible even more negative.

> While the 'new stuff' has not yet got properly established (and inevitably this is partly a matter of time), it seems to have driven out the old. The old-fashioned economics of the short period has been replaced by some quite extraordinarily shoddy stuff. I should never have guessed—had I not known—that a number of these candidates had in their second year attended a course of lectures on the economics of the firm, and one wonders to what extent, with so much ferment in the third year, second-year lectures in economic theory produce any lasting impression. There was a great deal of talk about Mr Andrews but, for all the evidence that was available to me knowledge of his contribution might have been derived from a review of his book in a popular daily newspaper. His work seems, however, to have the result that the pre-Andrews short-period value theory either is ignored or is got hopelessly wrong. (RFK/4/9/4)[19]

In this passage and the subsequent handwritten notes, Kahn refers to P.W.S. Andrews and his critique of the short-run neoclassical theory of the firm—a theory to which Kahn himself had contributed. As secretary of the Oxford Economists' Research Group (1938–1952), Andrews had coordinated empirical research suggesting that firms set prices by adding a profit margin to variable average costs and maintaining prices despite demand

[19] On Robinson versus Andrews in the context of the 'Full cost' controversy, see also, Jacobsen (2019). On Andrews, see King (2021).

fluctuations—thus rejecting the neoclassical equilibrium condition. Although Kahn criticised this pricing approach in his 1952 review of *Oxford Studies in the Price Mechanism*, it is more likely that his comments pertain to Andrews's *Manufacturing Business* (1949). As Jacobsen (2017) observes, this work challenged formalist extensions of Marshallian theory and advocated empirically grounded industrial economics. However, this stance was also criticised by Austin Robinson for lacking sufficient factual basis.

The second set of documents relating to Kahn's role in the Cambridge Faculty of Economics consists of a series of letters sent to him by James Meade and Michael (Posner). The first letter, dated 20 July 1962 (RFK/4/1/1), contains Meade's proposal to put forward Kahn's candidature for Chairman of the Faculty for the year 1962–1963, following Austin Robinson's decision to stand down in view of his retirement. This letter was followed by a second one, dated 26 July 1962 (RFK/4/1/2–4), where Kahn accepted Meade's offer on condition that the length of his term of office, the relationship between the Faculty of Economics and Politics and the Department of Applied Economics (both chaired by Austin Robinson) and other minor issues were clarified. Reassured by Meade on each of these points, Kahn's candidature took shape and was formally proposed by Meade on 9 October 1962 (RFK/4/1/13). A letter from Michael Posner (Secretary of the Faculty Board), undated but probably from early October 1962, provides interesting information about the state of relations within the Faculty in the run-up to the election of the new Chairman. Reporting on a lunch with Kaldor, Posner informs Kahn that

> Nicky was concerned lest you should feel that he was hostile to your becoming Chairman. At a lunch during the Examining period, Nicky made the following three points:
>
> (a) That he thought you should be Chairman as the best candidate
> (b) He had told JEM [Meade] this, and had tried hard to quiet James' fears
> (c) That, if despite everything, there was insuperable opposition to your election he would regard WBR [Reddaway] as a good second best
>
> I recall this completely. I do hope that I have not given you the wrong impression. The only chap who was ever at all hostile [in the original] to

your election was perhaps Aubrey [Silberston], and that was in a fit of temper. (RFK/4/1/16–17)

Posner's letter sheds light on a tense period in the long and often ambivalent relationship between Kahn and Kaldor, characterised by alternating phases of disagreement and reconciliation regarding theory, faculty matters and Joan Robinson's influence. Despite their periodic estrangement, Kahn played a pivotal role in securing Kaldor's position at Cambridge and defending the university's Keynesian legacy, as the following section illustrates.

6.4 Neither with You nor Without You: Kahn and Kaldor

By the mid-1950s, Kahn and Joan Robinson had known each other for almost thirty years, while their acquaintance with Kaldor began a little later.[20] In 1940, when the LSE was evacuated to Cambridge, Kaldor and the Robinsons became neighbours and Kaldor joined a kind of 'war circus' with Sraffa, Robinson and Kahn.[21] In the subsequent years, while Kahn and Austin Robinson were occupied with their wartime activities, Kaldor and Joan Robinson participated in the wartime debate on post-war reconstruction, advocating Keynesian demand management and the welfare state. Kaldor was a contributor to the Beveridge Report, while Joan Robinson's writings emphasised welfare spending, public works and state planning. Both supported continued economic controls after the war, as discussed in pamphlets and public lectures (King, 2004). In the late 1940s

[20] See Ambrosi (2004) on the early joint commitment of Kahn, Kaldor and Robinson to develop common theories and concepts not necessarily in line with those of Keynes. See also Hayes (2010).

[21] On that occasion, Keynes had invited Kaldor to give a course on the theory of distribution, which aroused Robbins's strong resentment. On this, on the first contacts between Keynes and Kaldor in 1931, and on the origins of Kaldor's conversion to Keynesianism, see Albani (1986) with references to Cristina Marcuzzo's interview with Kaldor, published in Italian in the same year (Marcuzzo, 1986). Two letters from Kahn to Kaldor, dated 8 February 1935 (NK/3/5/88–89, as well as 90–93), reveal the beginnings of their acquaintance. In them, Kahn expresses his usual caution regarding questions of attribution related to his paper on ideal output On the war circus and the relations between Kahn, Kaldor and Robinson in the war years, see King (1998, pp. 412–416) and King (2009, pp. 56–57).

and early 1950s Kaldor and Robinson worked independently on closely related issues, while Kahn was still engaged in other activities.

Evidence of Kahn's early interest in Kaldor and his career prospects is provided by a letter from Kahn to Henry Lintott, his former boss at the Board of Trade. In this letter, dated 28 July 1947 and part of a correspondence which also involved Oliver Franks, another of Kahn's former bosses, Kahn updates Lintott on Kaldor's job prospects and mentions the possibility that Kaldor would have remained at the European Commission, where he was then in a research post, had he not been offered a permanent government post.

> My own view is that, taking the position as it is, his contribution in the international sphere will not justify the loss involved to this country.[22]

Two years later, in 1949, Kahn was instrumental in getting Kaldor a fellowship at King's College and a lectureship there.[23] Kaldor began teaching at Cambridge in 1950 and was appointed Reader in Economics in 1952.[24]

Robinson, Kahn and Kaldor's shared commitment to economic theory was intertwined with their other activities at Cambridge. The three acted in concert in the Cambridge Faculty of Economics and Politics, while the Secret Seminar, organised by Kahn, provided Robinson and Kaldor with an important opportunity to disseminate their new ideas. It is therefore not surprising that to outside observers of Cambridge, Kahn, Kaldor and Robinson might look like a compact phalanx engaged in the struggle to establish Keynesianism against the neoclassical front.

[22] Letter from Kahn to Lintott, 28 July 1947, (RFK/13/64/2).

[23] In his interview with Marcuzzo, Kaldor recalled that Kahn had seated him at the college's high table next to the Latin professor in the hope that his classical knowledge would impress the professor and secure his admission to Cambridge (Marcuzzo, 1986).

[24] Those interested in a synoptic view of the biographies of Kahn, Kaldor and Robinson can usefully consult Arestis and Sawyer (1992, pp. 286–301, 454–462) and Harcourt (2001, chs. 1, 3, 4) as well as Thirlwall (1987), and Pasinetti (1991, 2007). On the place of the three economists in the context of Post-Keynesian economics, see Hamouda and Harcourt (1988), King (2002, pp. 56–78) and Marchionatti (2024, pp. 277–299), with a focus on Kaldor (1956) and Robinson (1956). On the genesis of Robinson (1956), originating in 1937 and the ensuing discussions between Sraffa, Robinson and Kahn of Harrod's *Economic Dynamics*, see also Kregel (1983) and Harcourt (1986).

> The Cambridge (UK) economics faculty was dominated during these years by the triad of Kaldor, Kahn and Joan Robinson. [...] The ideological front maintained by these three dominated Cambridge; Piero Sraffa was a charming, but largely invisible, figure in the Marshall Library; Austin Robinson appeared a minor, self-effacing attachment; James Meade was yet to be invited to come, and Dennis Robertson had just retired; though the dominant triad managed successfully to marginalize any serious competitive challenge from these latter two. (Goodhart, 1997, pp. 389–390)

In fact, from the mid-1950s onwards, the relationship between the three, or rather between Kahn and Robinson on the one hand and Kaldor on the other, began to show signs of tension for reasons of intellectual priority, leading to a break between Kaldor and Robinson in 1956, followed by a partial reconciliation. As Marcuzzo (2005) recalls, in a letter from Kaldor to Sraffa of 19 August 1956, from Geneva, immediately after the publication of Robinson's *Accumulation of Capital*, Kaldor wrote that he did not want to return to Cambridge the following term because 'I just couldn't face being bullied by Joan and Kahn about the wonderfulness of Joan's book and how everything must be different from now on!' (SP: C/151). King (1998) reconstructs how the dispute between Kaldor and Robinson in the mid-1950s caused a deep rift which, although superficially healed, led to the progressive estrangement of their research agendas. According to King, Kahn's role in this affair would have been to inflame rather than defuse this conflict. Years later, recalling this episode, Harcourt confirmed King's reconstruction.

> He [Kaldor], Joan and Kahn worked on growth and distribution theory and, unfortunately, Nicky and Joan fell out over this in the 1950s. Nicky thought that Joan was pinching his ideas, Joan tried to calm him down but Richard, a rather naughty man in some ways, stirred them up, just when there was a terrible faction fight between the Robertsonians and the Keynesians in Cambridge. (Harcourt, 2012, p. 20)

Others, and in particular Pasinetti (2007), while acknowledging the moments of tension and differing views on specific theoretical issues, have stressed the existence of an underlying unity of purpose among Kahn, Kaldor and Robinson, based on adherence to a common theoretical paradigm and worldview.

The interpretation I propose here lies somewhere between these two extremes. On the one hand, I follow King and others in noting that the research agendas of Joan Robinson, with Kahn in the background, and Kaldor developed along different lines from the 1960s onwards, with Kaldor differing from Robinson and Kahn on specific issues and often encountering communication difficulties and misgivings with them. On the other hand, I argue that that while Kahn occasionally displayed a sense of intellectual superiority and belligerence towards Kaldor, he never gave up on him and actively worked to keep Kaldor on the Keynesian front at Cambridge, including playing a major role in dissuading him from leaving Cambridge in 1958. Kaldor, in turn, while undaunted by Kahn's occasional high-handedness, sought his opinion and continued to do so throughout the 1960s and beyond.

In general, communications between Kahn and Kaldor followed a given pattern: after an initial exchange of cordiality, a statement by one of the two provoked resentment in the other and the start of a heated debate, at the end of which each remained firm in his position. An example of this pattern is provided by a series of letters exchanged between them from May to November 1956, after the publication of both Kaldor's 1955 article and Robinson's *Accumulation of Capital*. This exchange is also important for what it reveals about the two men's different perceptions of Joan Robinson's book and how, for Kahn but not for Kaldor, the importance of this book lay in introducing new concepts in the study of distribution and growth and a new language to present them.

In a first letter dated 3 May 1956 (ref. RFK/13/55/64–65), Kahn informed Kaldor that 'your article is not yet out—there was a muddle about proofs of that number of the Review. Joan's book is not due till the end of June'. A month later, on 3 June from the Imperial Hotel in Tokyo, Kaldor asked Kahn to 'please tell Joan that I made a lot of propaganda for her new book, so she must tell the publishers to send lots of copies to Japan. […] I think I managed to convey the impression to some 6 Universities that Cambridge is still the place they got to look out for'. In the same letter, Kaldor expressed his satisfaction with the appointment as lecturer of Robin Marris, a former supervisee of Kahn, despite his earlier misgivings about Marris's work.[25] It was over Marris, and the links between his work and that of Joan Robinson, that the previously cordial communication between Kahn and Kaldor suddenly became strained. On 3 August,

[25] Ref. RFK/13/53–55. Further evidence of Kaldor's critical attitude to Marris's work can be found in RFK/13/55/41–44. On Marris and his contribution to economic theory and policy debates, see Wood (2017).

referring to an earlier letter from Kaldor dated 26 July (which contained a copy of a letter from Kaldor to Robin Marris, with the former's comments on the latter's work), Kahn accused Kaldor of ignoring Robinson's new book.

> With Joan's help I have been through your article and your Peking lecture and by translating them into terms of Joan's book I have been able to see what you are doing. I would strongly recommend you to ask yourself whether you could make it all very much easier if, as appropriate—i.e. most of the time, you talked in terms of Joan's Golden Age, making the necessary assumptions about technical progress being neutral and the expected rate of profit being constant. If you are not prepared to put in these terms there is wholly lacking from your treatment any explanation of the mechanism which causes investments to behave in the manner which you describe. [...] Please do not think that I am trying to tease you about all this, but I really am puzzled and bothered over your attitude towards Joan's book.[26]

In his reply from Santiago de Chile a week later, on 10 August 1956, Kaldor expressed his irritation at Kahn's criticism while defending both his own reasoning and his professional integrity.

> I certainly do not think that you are trying to tease me but I do think that you are in one of your rare crazy moods in which you think your friends are your enemies or the enemies of your friends. [...] If I did not refer to Joan's book more extensively in my recent article—I did refer to it and I thought rather nicely, in my Review article—it is primarily because I have not read it nor have I the means to do so as I do not possess a copy. [...] However, if you cannot read my Peking literature or my new article without Joan's help or without translation into Joan's terminology, all I can suggest is that you are in serious danger of losing your reasoning powers as an economist. [...] That is not the way to gain adherents to the new creed. When in the 1930s you were engaged in propagating the ideas of the General Theory, you did not say to people "I shall not argue with you if you persist in using this "ante-diluvian" term marginal productivity instead of calling it marginal efficiency!" So far as your letter goes this is precisely what you are doing.[27]

[26] Letter from Kahn to Kaldor, 3 August 1956, ref. RFK/13/55/21–22. The Peking lecture to which Kahn refers would eventually be published as Kaldor (1957) while the article should be Kaldor (1956).

[27] Letter from Kahn to Kaldor, 3 August 1956, ref. RFK/13/55/20.

Four days later, on 14 August 1956, Kahn replied, comparing Kaldor's attitude towards Robinson's recent work to the early dismissals of Keynes's *General Theory*.

> I had no patience with people who, after the "General Theory" appeared, took the line that they knew that it was no use and were therefore not proposing to read it. [...] Your attitude reminds me a little of that of L.S.E. at that time, except that when the book did appear they did read it.[28]

In the same letter, after noting the limited number of reviews Robinson's book had received to that point, Kahn added:

> [T]here has been what you would describe as a 'conspiracy of silence'; but which I relate to the prevalence of your own attitude i.e. not wanting to be bothered with having to adjust one's mind to new ideas, many of which one had already in some form or another thought out for oneself or in the course of conversation. [...] When you talk about my losing my reasoning powers as an economist, it is rather as though somebody wanted to discuss some of the pre-Keynesian Swedish writings with me after the "General Theory" had appeared without himself having read Keynes. [...] I do not feel at all optimistic as to the speed with which Joan's framework and ideas will be accepted. There is going to be terrific mental resistance. [...] You seem to me to be a prominent member of the resistance movement. [...] Of course I understand the deep-seated inhibitions which are particularly strong in your case. But you and Joan both are prepared to be generous about the contributions of the other. Can't you get into the state of thinking of the advance of economics in a co-operative rather than competitive spirit? I sometime think that it is my failure to show the latter spirit which leads to criticism of me. (Ibid.)

Two days after this invitation, Kahn wrote two more letters to Kaldor. In the first letter, Kahn addressed the theoretical question of the relationship between the rate of profit and the choice of technology that he had raised on 3 August.[29] Kahn's choice to frame his arguments in terms of the concept of the Golden Age seems to be an attempt to do what Kaldor had asked him to do, namely to enter into the merits of the dispute by showing Kaldor's possible error in not adopting Joan Robinson's theoretical premises and definitions. In his reply of 22 August 1956, Kaldor informed

[28] Letter from Kahn to Kaldor, 14 August 1956, ref. RFK/13/55/18–19.

[29] Letter from Kahn to Kaldor, 16 August 1956, RFK/13/55/14–17.

Kahn that he had read the first 150 pages of Robinson's book. While expressing appreciation for its style, he stated that he had found nothing particularly new in its content. Beyond this immediate point, however, Kaldor's letter revealed deeper underlying tensions and a sense of resentment towards both Joan Robinson and Kahn's approach. He also accused Robinson of unwittingly absorbing the ideas of others and presenting them as her own—an allegation he linked to what he called a 'conspiracy of silence'.

> So far from saying that "you have no patience with people" who don't acknowledge Joan's intellectual leadership you should go out of your way to explain to them where they go astray when they leave her ideas and contributions out of account. I would go further and suggest that if you really think that Joan's new book contains the same kind of revolutionary new thought as the General Theory, the best way of securing their penetration is to write an article giving a brief exposition of the central ideas, in much the same way as David Champernowne, Roy Harrod, Hicks and Oscar Lange have done for Keynes. I hope you don't regard this as an effrontery, as I realise that you are by no means so "young" in relation to Joan as David Champernowne or Roy Harrod had been in relation to Keynes. If you really think, however, that Joan's new book is a revolution in economics, the most important thing you could do is to crystallize her ideas in a semi-mathematical paper of a dozen pages or so which I should be delighted to publish in the Review. It is no good your saying that it cannot be done—iy [sic] only books without ideas which cannot be summarized. Malthus can be explained in 2 pages, Ricardo's in 4, Marx in 5 and Keynes in at most 8. Perhaps Joan requires 10.[30]

Kaldor's letter ends with this semi-serious challenge, with an indication of the addresses in Argentina to which future correspondence should be sent, and with a handwritten addendum: 'Now that I let off steam, I feel much better'. Kahn replied briefly on 28 August 1956, closing the matter in his own conciliatory tone: 'I do not think that this is the kind of argument that it would be good for either of us to carry on in the long run'. The postscript also indicates a desire for reconciliation:

> How many pages are needed to explain Kaldor's Theory of Capital? It would save a lot of time if I did not after all have to read all those articles (one of

[30] Letter from Kaldor to Kahn, 22 August 1956, RFK/13/55/11–12.

> which is with you). Incidentally, how are you getting on with your collected writings.[31]

The main consideration that emerges at the end of this first exchange is that both Kahn and Kaldor, even at the height of the conflict and despite their different characters and modes of communication (with Kahn's tone more serious and professorial and Kaldor's more direct and genial), there is respect and a mutual desire to keep a channel of communication open. Judging from this exchange, it does not appear that the 1956 episode did irreparable damage to the relationship between Kahn and Kaldor, nor to the importance the former continued to attach to the latter in strengthening the Keynesian front at Cambridge. Evidence of this comes from a second set of letters in Kahn's archives, dating from the second half of 1958, in which Kaldor is the subject of correspondence.

In a first letter dated 22 May 1958, Noel Annan,[32] Provost of King's College, informed J.E. Raven (Fellow of the same college and responsible for undergraduate supervision) and Kahn of Kaldor's request to be relieved of the directorship of studies and undergraduate teaching duties in order to concentrate on seminars for the benefit of doctoral students and on his research activities (ref. RFK/3/26/19, 20). Raven's reply the following day pointed out the exceptional nature of Kaldor's request, the economic implications of granting it and the need to submit it to the Council (ref. RFK/3/26/17, 18). The matter remained inactive until 6 December 1958, when Annan informed Kaldor that the request had been rejected, giving detailed reasons for the decision (ref. RFK/3/36/14–17). Five days later, Kaldor wrote to Kahn, who was in Paris at the time:

> This is to tell you the very sad news that Clarisse and I decided to leave Cambridge at the end of the year. The recent decision of the Council is not really the cause of this, though it may have precipitated it. […] we shall always be grateful to you (and Joan) for having brought us here but there are moments in one's life when one must face a major decision.[33]

Kahn's reply, five handwritten pages dated 26 December (RFK/3/26/10–11), opens with a series of statements that set the general tone for the rest of the letter.

[31] Letter from Kahn to Kaldor, 28 August 1956, RFK/13/55/10.

[32] For a brief biography of Noel Annan, see Appendix C.

[33] Letter from Kaldor to Kahn, 11 December 1958, RFK/3/26/10–11.

> My dear Nicky, your letter came as a great shock to me. Although in one sense your decision might be described as premeditated, in another it was obviously a sudden whim. In a fundamental sense I thought that doing the part time termers and the jointers had become easier, and indeed there is quite a lot of evidence that you were assuming that you would be staying on in Cambridge. I do hope, therefore, that—immune from the daily distractions of mundane existence—you will carefully consider Noël's letter, backed by a letter which I gather Robin had written you earlier, and reconsider your decision. If you decide that you cannot—perhaps because you are now committed (a very bad reason), it will be a terrible grief to me: I doubt whether you at all realise how much. And the loss to Cambridge is shattering to think of. This covers part of my loss as well, but in addition I have to face the thought that in some sense we have failed. Nevertheless—should you persist in your intention—the feeling here will certainly be that your sojourn with us has been tremendously to our advantage. I shall feel that particularly, for one very clear reason as well as for other only less obvious ones. And I do sincerely hope that what will survive will be a feeling of friendship rather than bitterness.[34]

On 5 January 1959, Clarisse Kaldor wrote to Kahn a long letter, which is important for what it reveals about Kaldor's perception of his position at Cambridge.

> Nicky really felt that there was hostility to him in the College, and that you would all be quite pleased if he left, and he is surprised and happy to realise that this is not so. Nicky has been increasingly unhappy in Cambridge, partly due to the atmosphere in the College and the faculty but chiefly because of the breach with Joan, which is only superficially healed. He still feels it is impossible to discuss economics with her, and this poisons everything. All his new ideas have been greeted with carping hostility (and not only by Joan) and this is not stimulating or encouraging to academic work. It was in order to write his book on growth that he was so very keen on the Californian year. We agree that serious academic work is the most important consideration: at present Cambridge doesn't provide the atmosphere favourable to it.[35]

Clarisse Kaldor went on to thank Kahn for his role in Kaldor's appointment to Cambridge, acknowledging the warmth of the friendship shown

[34] Letter from Kahn to Kaldor, 12 December 1958, RFK/3/26/5–9.
[35] Letter from Clarisse Kaldor to Kahn, 5 January 1959, RFK/3/26/1–4.

by Kahn and others on the occasion, and adding that they were considering their decision carefully and did not wish to leave hastily or on bad terms. And indeed they did reconsider. Kaldor remained at Cambridge, where, as King (2009, p. 8) recalls, he was (belatedly) given a personal chair in 1966, which he held until his retirement in 1975. And so the relationship between Kahn and Kaldor at Cambridge continued to be characterised by mutual search for approval and recognition, interspersed with the occasional incomprehension on personal and scientific matters.[36]

For example, in 1963, Kahn and Kaldor argued over Kaldor's so-called Bancor Scheme—a monetary proposal conceived by Kaldor and later developed in collaboration with Albert G. Hart and Jan Tinbergen (Hart et al., 1964). The scheme presented to UNCTAD in 1964 aimed to address growing concerns about exchange rate instability and deteriorating terms of trade for developing countries that relied on commodity exports. Based on earlier proposals for an international commodity reserve currency, Kaldor, Hart and Tinbergen set out a detailed plan to stabilise exchange rates and commodity prices, which could be refined in the future.

Drawing inspiration from Keynes's original vision for the Bretton Woods system, the proposed Bancor system would entail the IMF issuing a new international currency backed by gold and a basket of standardised, durable commodities. This currency would be convertible only by central banks and would serve as a global settlement medium. The initial issue would be $30 billion. Through buffer stock management, the IMF would counteract commodity price volatility, thereby benefiting primary producers and enhancing international liquidity. The scheme attracted the attention of Kahn, who, as we shall see, was an expert in commodity price stabilisation and buffer stocks.

In a first letter dated 16 August 1963, Kahn, also writing on behalf of Joan Robinson, made two main criticisms of Kaldor's scheme. The first concerned Kaldor's analysis of the terms of trade, defined as the ratio between the price of manufactured goods sold by developed countries to developing countries and the price of primary goods sold by developing countries to developed countries. With regard to the latter, Kahn argued that it was essential to introduce a distinction—which Kaldor had omitted—between 'traded primary products' and 'locally consumed primary products'. Given the significant weight of locally consumed primary

[36] See NK/3/30/120/2–4 for a letter from Kaldor to Kahn, dated 15 June 1962, which shows that the dispute between the two over Joan Robinson's ideas was still ongoing.

products in the consumption basket of developing countries, Kahn argued that these countries would benefit most from a simultaneous reduction in the prices of manufactured goods and, to a lesser extent, traded primary products. This, he argued, would encourage the development of local primary production without adversely affecting the balance of international trade. The second, more fundamental criticism concerned Kaldor's proposal that all currencies be simultaneously devalued against the Bancor, allowing the IMF to carry out large-scale purchases of commodities to support their prices. Kahn was not convinced by this idea—or at least not by the reasoning Kaldor used to justify it.

Kaldor's reply, dated 28 October 1963, was sent on his return from the Bellagio conference, where the Bancor paper had taken shape.[37] In this letter, Kaldor informed Kahn that he had misplaced the file containing the comments of various economists (including Kahn) on the Bancor Scheme. Kahn responded on 6 November.

> You mention that the file contains a letter from me. This is your first reference to my letter. I wonder whether you ever read it. You are always pressing me to write to you about your various memoranda, but perhaps this was not the kind of letter that you wished to receive.[38]

Kaldor's conciliatory reply began with an assurance that he had read Kahn's letter and wished to respond calmly. Kahn replied on 21 November, indicating that he was unconvinced by Kaldor's arguments for non-response to the observations Kahn had raised in August, regarding Kaldor's Bancor paper. Despite this, the general tone of the letter remained friendly, and it included, as usual, details of Faculty life.

[37] Letter from Kaldor to Kahn, 28 October 1963, RFK/3/24/31. The Bellagio Conference, held from 16 to 24 September 1963, was a Chatham House conference focused on 'New Directions for World Trade'. The conference was organised by the Royal Institute of International Affairs and sponsored by the Carnegie Endowment for International Peace, with the aim to discuss and explore the changing dynamics of international trade, particularly in relation to the industrialisation of developing countries in view of the first meeting of the United Nations Conference on Trade and Development that would take place in Geneva in the spring of 1964. On the Bellagio conference, Kahn's initial role in promoting its organisation, Kahn's replacement by Kaldor among the participants and the links between the conference and the Bancor paper, see Paesani and Rosselli (2014, pp. 22–26).

[38] Letter from Kahn to Kaldor, 6 November 1963, RFK/3/26/29–30.

> If I remember rightly there was a period of several weeks during which you and I were both in Cambridge and I was very hurt that you did not refer to it. I cannot suppose that you really want me to send you a copy of it.[39]

The three letters that conclude this exchange show how both Kaldor and Kahn want to have the last word.[40] On 27 November Kaldor replied on both points, stating that he did not understand the point of the first objection and that he saw the devaluation of all major currencies against gold as the way to encourage a general rise in commodity prices, rather than relying on the coordinated action of a buffer stock system. In his reply Kahn succinctly reiterated his objection on the main point of devaluation without changing Kaldor's position.

While we have examined a series of letters testifying to moments of tension between Kahn and Kaldor, we cannot ignore other exchanges in which the tone is more relaxed. I refer, in particular, to a long series of letters dated February–December 1955, during which time Kahn was working at the OEEC in Geneva and contributing to the drafting of the Economic Survey for Europe. These letters, which are preserved in the Kaldor Papers (NK/3/30/119/46–113), cover a variety of topics. Kahn asks Kaldor for information on short-term business cycle indicators (e.g. new share issues and the relationship between self-financing and external funds in the financing of investments by European companies), various aspects of life at the Faculty (Kahn is keen not to be kept in the dark, and Kaldor is committed to updating and reassuring him), requests for information on King's College investments (e.g. NK/3/30/119/91–94) and personal matters (e.g. the investments of Rachel Rostas, the widow of the Hungarian economist László Rostas, who died in Cambridge in 1954 and was Kahn's companion in his final years). The main result of Kahn's work during the months he spent in Geneva as a consultant in 1955 is a long document entitled Short-Term Business Indicators in Western Europe (Kahn, 1955) for the Research and Planning Division of the Economic Commission for Europe (ECE), of which Kaldor was one of the first directors (Berthelot & Rayment, 2007).[41]

[39] Letter from Kahn to Kaldor, 21 November 1963, RFK/3/26/26–27.

[40] Ref. RFK/3/26/21–25.

[41] For a reconstruction of the ECE's research activities between 1947 and 1957 with the support of the Rockefeller Foundation, see ECE (1957, Chapter XIV).

6.5 The 'Stone Affair'

By 1955, the year Kahn spent in Geneva, Richard (Dick) Stone had been Director of the Department of Applied Economics at Cambridge for ten years.[42] From 1931 to 1935 he had attended Gonville and Caius College, initially studying law but switching to economics after two years. As Caius College had no resident economics fellow, Stone had been supervised by Richard Kahn at King's and J.W.F. Rowe at Pembroke in his first year and by Gerald Shove at King's in his second year. Despite obtaining a First in economics, he initially opted not to pursue research but joined a Lloyd's brokerage firm in the City. In 1939 Stone was recruited by the Ministry of Economic Warfare (MEW). In August 1940, Austin Robinson, a member of the Central Economic Information Service (CEIS) of the War Cabinet, had Stone transferred from the MEW to the CEIS to assist James Meade who had been working at CEIS since early June 1940 and had already devised the new national accounts. Meade needed help calculating the figures for the accounts, so Stone was recruited for this purpose. In the same year the idea of establishing a Department of Applied Economics (DAE) in the University of Cambridge, as a research wing for the Faculty of Economics, was put forward by a committee composed of Keynes (Chairman), David Champernowne, Austin and Joan Robinson, Gerald Shove, Piero Sraffa and Dennis Robertson (coopted). The war delayed the founding of the DAE, but in November 1944 the University set up a Steering Committee, chaired by Keynes, which met and offered the Directorship, at the time the equivalent of a University Lectureship, to Richard Stone as a lifetime appointment (Newbery, 1998, p. xx).

Between 1945 and 1955 the DAE, under Stone's leadership, became one of the leading research centres in the field of econometrics and applied economics, according to many on a par with the Cowles Commission. Stone himself continued to work on the improvement of the national accounting system, both British and American, and on the econometric analysis of market demand. Despite these successes, as Pesaran and Harcourt (2000) recall, there were elements in the Faculty of Economics at Cambridge, including Kahn and Joan Robinson,[43] who felt that the more limited original aim of the DAE had not been stressed enough by

[42] On Richard Stone, see Appendix C, Deaton (1993), Pesaran and Harcourt (2000) and Barker (2017).

[43] Goodwin noted that '[...] though Stone had been taught as student by Kahn, the two had grown apart because of Kahn's active hostility to econometrics'. Goodwin (1995, p. 17).

Stone as Director and who also felt that his work on demand analysis was not what should have been emphasised, or even done.

For these reasons, when an offer was made in 1955 for Stone to take up the P.D. Leake Chair of Finance and Accounting, members of the Faculty Board who were unhappy with Stone's work took this as an opportunity to impose a new condition of incompatibility between the directorship of the DAE and the professorship. As Barker (2017, p. 840) recalls, 'Stone strongly objected, arguing that he would not have accepted the post under this condition. He was forced to choose between remaining Director and taking the Chair'. In the end, he gave up the Directorship while maintaining a cordial working relationship with the new director, Brian Reddaway, and leading a major research group—the DAE growth project with Alan Brown (Cambridge Growth Project).

A series of letters from Joan Robinson to Kahn, written between November and December 1955 and preserved in Kahn's archive,[44] offer an important inside perspective on the context in which the 'Stone affair' and the ensuing rift between Stone and the Keynesians developed.[45] Reading these letters is important both as another example of the tense climate within the Faculty of Economics at Cambridge in the 1950s and for what they reveal about Kahn's role and character in this context.

In November 1955, with the elections to the Faculty Board coming up, the strategy devised by Joan Robinson and proposed to Kahn as leader was a compromise whereby the Keynesians would propose a single candidate (Kenneth Berrill) to the Faculty Board, leaving the others free to nominate the other candidate (identified as Alan Prest).[46] However, Stone had disrupted the arrangement by unexpectedly nominating A.D. Roy in addition to Prest.[47]

> We made out a plan for the Faculty elections whereby we offer peaceful coexistence but fight if it is not accepted. [...] I managed to catch Piero in a cooperative mood. Nicky is rather difficult as his only contribution is to ask

On statistical and econometric studies at Cambridge during the Stone and Reddaway years, see Harcourt and Kitson (1993).

[44] There are no answers from Kahn in Joan Robinson's archive.

[45] For more on the 'Stone affair' and the need to consider caveats when assessing the rift between Stone and the Cambridge Keynesians, see Saith (2022, pp. 422–423).

[46] On Alan Prest, see Appendix C.

[47] On A.D. Roy, see Appendix C.

when he can be elected. May I have your formal consent to be put on the appointments committee in place of Nicky?[48]

We decided to offer peaceful coexistence i.e. to nominate only Ken if no one else except Prest was nominated. […] But, if you please, Dick Stone nominated Prest and Roy. He disappeared to Paris and was out of touch. It is not known whether he has made an unholy alliance with Denison or if he is trying to form a 3rd party of statisticians. Reddaway is in general sympathetic to us and said he thought Ken [Berrill] should and would get in.[49]

On 21 November 1955 Robinson sent a gloomy report on the results of the Faculty Board elections, along with some comments on the tone of some of Kahn's letters, which had obviously not helped to calm the climate within the Faculty and attract supporters to the Keynesian party.

The situation in the Faculty is even worse than you expected. Not only did we lose the election (Prest 28, Roy 27, Berrill 20, Gilbertson 15) but we are out of control of the Board. […] This is very bad, as two lectureships are to be filled up shortly, one with preference for history. […] What you say in jest about your nasty letters is only too sadly true. It is like putting in a tariff to redress the balance of trade. No doubt writing them relieves your feelings, but you should take into account the consequences of dis-relieving other peoples.[50]

Two days later, Robinson adds:

I feel very sick about the Faculty, especially as you will feel, quite rightly, that we have let it get into a mess in your absence. […] You will have to get onto terms with Stone when you come back. I think he is actuated entirely by spite and revenge and hasn't any particular policy in view (except to boost Statistics or perhaps not even that as it would be pouring water on Reddaway's nutt [slang for head] rather than his own).[51]

Three days later, in response to a letter from Kahn asking about the results of the Faculty elections, apparently because he had not received the letter of 18 November, Robinson summarised the situation by adding

48 Letter from JVR to Kahn, 7 November 1955, RFK/13/90/5/208–209.
49 Letter from JVR to Kahn, 18 November 1955, RFK/13/90/5/201.
50 Letter from JVR to Kahn, 21 November 1955, RFK/13/90/5/195–196.
51 Letter from JVR to Kahn, 23 November 1955, RFK/13/90/5/187–188.

some remarks about 'young phoneys', an expression referring to the young lecturers hired to teach courses in applied economics and econometrics 'lined up against us by Dick to satisfy his spite'.[52] On 28 November 1955, two letters sent a few hours apart show how Joan Robinson, Kaldor and Sraffa were trying to redefine a strategy to overcome the situation created by Stone's hostile actions, starting with an acknowledgement of their own mistakes. The letter is also interesting for what it reveals about the Keynesians' attitude to econometrics and statistics, and for the frankness with which Robinson acknowledges the validity of the motives of Stone, to whom it was decided to send Kaldor as a messenger of peace.

> Nicky, Piero and I had a "criticism and self criticism" meeting yesterday. I think Piero is sending you the voting analysis. [...] The upshot of out confab was a [sic] our chief mistake has been to be too high-handed—what people like is to be consulted and brought in at an early stage. (2) Dick was completely shocked at our not backing him against Austin [Robinson] over the professorship and is now venting his rage. Nicky has promised to have a heart to heart with him and try to re-establish good relations. (3) Reddaway is now the rising star and our line is not anti statistics as such but anti phoneys. Reddaway is of the same opinion + our alliance with him can be quite genuine. [...] On the latter point I have been talking to him about the idea of having small high-power discussion groups on particular projects with a view to evolving ideas about what can and cannot be done with figures getting the phoneyness out of the statistical [?rot] and at the same time finding how to frame theory in terms that can be given a meaning. On all this he is extremely sympathetic. They have a project on Stock exchange prices where you + Nicky should figure.[53]

> Stone's rage is easy to understand. He wanted to be Prof and Director. We all lined up against him on this and he made matters worse by publicly expressing himself. Then Austin let him know that in future Directors were to be for 10 years only and must have made him feel that the Chair was an excuse to cut him down to this period.[54]

As December progressed, Robinson's letters revealed her renewed complaints about the tone of some of Kahn's letters, which were seen as demoralising. She pointed to the danger that his inflexibility could create

[52] Letter from JVR to Kahn, 26 November 1955, RFK/13/90/5/183–186.
[53] Letter from JVR to Kahn, 28 November 1955, RFK/13/90/5/176–177.
[54] Letter from JVR to Kahn, 28 November 1955, RFK/13/90/5/180.

further divisions, undermine morale and make it harder for the Keynesians to regroup. Nevertheless, there were attempts to mend fences, as Kaldor's heart-to-heart with Stone showed signs of progress.

> I have now had a report from Nicky of his interview with Stone. N. took the line what's the trouble Dick, why have you turned against your old pals? Dick in his usual smooth way pretended innocence + said he meant no harm, the idea he was allying himself with Dennis was laughable etc. Nicky, I think rightly, avoided a breach and left it that in future we must keep in touch and consult. [...] As for your "public Richard" letters the point is that you give the appearance of mixing up the question of what is the best thing for the cause under discussion with the collection of evidence for your general thesis that everybody except you is an imbecile. This is bad for morale because it makes it much harder for the imbeciles to admit mistakes and find out how to do better in future.[55]

> Dick is a nice boring subject. [...] For heaven's sake don't go and have a feud with him. The only way is to adopt his own smooth manners and discuss future moves with him. You give us sermons on how to behave and then fly off the handle yourself.[56]

The year ended on a cautious note. Although animosities remained, there was a recognition of the need for unity. The battle was not one of ideology but of approach—forthrightness versus compromise. With a renewed commitment to working together and a pragmatic view of alliances, the group entered the new term determined to rebuild and face the challenges ahead.[57]

6.6 Work in Progress

Kahn's scholarly production came to a virtual standstill during the 1960s. The only exception is a thick 37-page typescript entitled 'Work in Progress', which Kahn sent to a number of colleagues in September 1964, asking for their comments and suggestions (ref. RFK/2/16/1–49). This document, which remained unpublished until 1971 and was included in Kahn (1972)

[55] Letter from JVR to Kahn, 5 December 1955, RFK/13/90/5/166–167.
[56] Letter from JVR to Kahn, 3 December 1955, RFK/13/9/5/162–163.
[57] Letter from JVR to Kahn, 12 December 1955, RFK/13/9/5/160.

under the title 'Notes on the Rate of Interest and the Growth of Firms',[58] stems from Kahn's attempt to rework the concepts proposed by Robin Marris in his theory of managerial capitalism (Marris, 1964),[59] and by Joan Robinson in her reconsideration of imperfect competition in the context of a Keynesian analytical framework extended from the short to the long run. Managerial capitalism describes a situation in which control of large companies shifts from owners (shareholders) to professional managers who pursue their own objectives—mainly the growth of the company—rather than strictly maximising shareholder profits. Marris argued that managers seek to balance growth in the size of the firm (which gives them prestige, power and job security) with the need to keep shareholders happy enough to prevent them from interfering. Thus, the firm's objectives are a trade-off between maximising growth and ensuring financial performance.

Kahn's 'work in progress', elaborated two years before Kaldor (1966), provides one of the earliest Cambridge analyses of the valuation ratio, the ratio of the market value of a company's shares to the value of its assets, best known in later years as Tobin's q. His analysis is based on the idea that ownership and management of a firm are separate, and that crucial decisions regarding the firm's development (and the economy as a whole), that is investment decisions, are made by managers based on subjective and objective factors. Kahn attempts to provide a realistic description of the cognitive processes underlying these decisions, combining the Keynesian concept of 'animal spirits' with an examination of the factors that drive and restrain managers' behaviour, as well as the constraints imposed on their actions by demand for the company's products and the characteristics of their sector. In analysing these aspects, the 'work in progress' addresses many of Kahn's long-standing concerns, including the impact of interest rates, shares prices and business expectations on investment; the relationship between wages and prices in explaining inflation; and the constraints imposed on the domestic economy by external factors.

[58] On Kahn's essay, see Harcourt (1993, p. 26) and Eatwell (1992, p. 291).

[59] For a contextualisation of Marris's theory in relation to the managerial theories of the enterprise developed starting in the late 1950s, see Weinstein (2012). As a student in Cambridge, Marris was first supervised by G. Shove in 1941 and after the war by Kahn in 1945. For a discussion of the link between Marris's theory of managerial capitalism (taken up by Kahn) and Marshall's theory of the firm developed by Edith Penrose in Penrose (1959), see Loasby (1991, pp. 59–60).

> Basic to the analysis of this article, and to the demonstration of the stability of the system, is the concept of an economic system as an organic structure, consisting of companies the managements of which have personalities and propensities. The limited elasticity relating the rates of growth of any individual company to the difference between its rate of profit and the rate of interest provides the clue to much that is puzzling if an attempt is made to generalise in long-period form the analysis of the determination of investment contained in Keynes' General Theory. Acceptance of the view that the behaviour of the system is not insensitive to the rate of interest carries with it the implication that serious disturbance is liable to be caused by the state of the balance of payments on income account and the international mobility of capital funds. What is apt to happen is that in a country like Britain the rate of interest, instead of being set at a low level so that the flagging spirits of her businessmen are stimulated, is set nearer to the level called for in order to restrain the buoyancy of the businessmen of, say, Germany. The disharmony is aggravated if, as a result of the higher rate of technical progress in Germany, the balance of payments on income account is favourable for Germany and unfavourable for Britain. (RFK/2/16/38)

In the economic system devised by Kahn, managers choose how much to invest and must find ways to finance it while maintaining the confidence of shareholders/savers. By assumption, managers and savers hold expectations about future profits and growth with certainty and the average rates of profit and growth at the aggregate level are assumed to be constant. Uncertainty is ruled out of the analysis and the economy finds itself in a state of tranquillity that approximates the conditions of Robinson's Golden Age.

Corporate investment is financed by managers combining the company's retained profits with shareholder funds obtained by issuing new shares. Corporate bonds are not considered. The return on shares comprises two components: the dividend yield and the rate at which the value of the shares appreciates. As shareholders are only concerned with the total rate of return on their investment, they are indifferent between dividends and capital appreciation. Assuming the capital market is perfect, the rate of return on all shares will be equal. In general, the returns on shares can be described, following Kahn, as the interest rate, represented by i, whereas the value of each company's capital assets is indicated by C. The number of shares issued by the company is represented by N, and the price of each share is represented by p. Thus, Np is the market valuation of the shares, and the valuation ratio is defined as

$$v = \frac{Np}{C} \tag{6.1}$$

Indicating a company's profit (net of depreciation) by *P*, under conditions of tranquil growth, the rate of current and prospective profit π is equal to *P*/*C*. Profits are made up of distributed profits (dividends) and retained profits, where *r* is the retention ration $D = (1 - r)P$. Based on Eq. (6.1), we can express the return on the shares issued by each company as the sum of the current dividend yield (D/Np) plus the rate of appreciation of the shares $\dot{p}/p$

$$i = \frac{(1-r)P}{Np} + \frac{\dot{p}}{p} = \frac{1}{v}(1-r)\pi + \frac{\dot{p}}{p} \tag{6.2}$$

Deriving Eq. (6.1) with respect to time and assuming that under Golden Age conditions the valuation ratio is constant, the rate of growth of capital assets, that is the rate of investment (defined as the rate of change in the value of the company's assets $\dot{C}/C$), will be equal to

$$\frac{\dot{C}}{C} = \frac{\dot{N}}{N} + \frac{\dot{p}}{p} \tag{6.3}$$

Bearing in mind that by assumption investment ($\dot{C}$) is financed either with retained profits or by issuing new shares

$$\dot{C} = rP + p\dot{N} \tag{6.4}$$

Dividing both sides of (6.4) by C and taking Eq. (6.1) into account and the previous definitions into account, we obtain:

$$\frac{\dot{C}}{C} = r\frac{P}{C} + \frac{pN}{C}\frac{\dot{N}}{N} = r\pi + v\frac{\dot{N}}{N} \tag{6.5}$$

Finally, indicating the rate of growth of capital assets by $g\left(\frac{\dot{C}}{C} = g\right)$ and substituting Eqs. (6.2) and (6.5) into (6.3), we obtain the following relationship between the valuation ratio v, the rate of profit π and the rate of interest i.

$$v = \frac{\pi - g}{i - g} = \frac{\pi}{i} \frac{\left(1 - \frac{g}{\pi}\right)}{\left(1 - \frac{g}{i}\right)} \tag{6.6}$$

Based on (6.6), three cases are possible. In the first case, the value of the shares is equal to the replacement cost of the capital assets which underlie them ($v = 1$), and the rate of return on the shares (i) is equal to the current rate of profit of the company ($\pi = i$). The market value of the company will not change regardless of the growth rate chosen by the managers and regardless of the mix of retained earnings and new share issues chosen to finance the company's growth.[60]

As Kahn points out, (RFK/2/16/8), '[A]ll this is empty formalism, as we have done nothing more than state identities which are derived from our definitions of a constant rate of profit, to which the rate of interest is equal. The question is what, in this simplest of possible cases, is responsible for determining growth'. Kahn's answer to this question is based on the identification of the propulsive and retroactive forces that influence the managers' investment decisions.

> The propulsive factors take the form of the ambition and creative urge of the management, expressing itself through the physical development of the company to which they are committed, as well as to some extent the inducement of higher emoluments. [...] The retroactive factors are partly psychological. A higher rate of growth comes up against inertia and resistance to change: it means more onerous tasks for the management and longer hours of work. [...] The retroactive factors are also economic in character in so far as a higher rate of growth entails higher costs and so, with a given behaviour of the economy, a lower rate of profit for the individual firm. [...] The propulsive factors are weaker as the rate of growth is higher and the retroactive factors are stronger. Subject to the rate of interest being equal to the actual rate of profit, the sustained rate of growth adopted by management can be regarded as a point of balance between the two sets of opposite pressures. (RFK/2/16/9–11)

[60] For a proof, see Kahn (1972, pp. 213–215).

This description, somehow reminiscent of marginal reasoning, is followed by an analysis of the case in which the rate of profit is less than the rate of interest $\pi < i$ and therefore the valuation ratio is below 1, that is investors value the firm at less than the value of its assets. In this case, based on a series of numerical examples, Kahn highlights the existence of an inverse relationship between the rate of asset growth g and the valuation ratio v, which becomes more pronounced as the interest rate i rises (RFK/2/16/14). As the company acquires capital assets which cost more than the value placed on them by shareholders, the shares trade at a discount $(1 - v)$, which is equal to

$$1 - v = \frac{i - \pi}{i - g}; \tag{6.7}$$

In this case, the discount is lowest when the company is not growing at all ($g = 0$). On the other hand, if the managers choose a positive g, that is if they choose to invest, this will reduce v, causing an absolute loss to the company's original shareholders and depriving them, as well as any new shareholders, of the potential gain they would receive if the managers chose $g = 0$. The existence of this loss, which Kahn quantifies as $g(1 - v)C$, constitutes a further brake on investment by managers, either out of loyalty to existing shareholders, whose opinions managers must always bear in mind, or out of fear of possible takeovers, which are all the more likely the higher the discount on shares. Hence the conclusion that in less dynamic sectors, where the profit rate is lower than the average (which as we shall see later coincides with the interest rate set by the monetary authorities), management is unlikely to adopt innovation and growth policies.

The opposite occurs when the rate of profit exceeds the rate of interest $\pi > i$, the valuation ratio exceeds unity ($v > 1$, i.e. investors value the firm at more than the value of its assets). In this case, the company's shares trade at a premium $(v - 1)$, which increases with the rate of growth of the company's assets g. Again, Kahn uses numerical examples (RFK/2/16/23) to show how the positive relationship between g and v becomes more intense as the interest rate falls. Growth now entails the acquisition of capital assets which shareholders value above their cost. The larger the scale on which this operation is conducted the greater the premium. In this case, loyalty to the shareholders will induce the managers to pursue a rate of growth above the one they would pursue if the rate of profit were equal to the rate of interest. Moreover, whereas in the case $\pi < i$, fear of 'take-over' restrained managers to pursue high growth strategies, nothing of the sort occurs in this case. In this sense there is an asymmetry between the opposite influences on growth of a rate of interest above or below the rate of profit.[61]

From here, the analysis moves to the level of the economy as a whole, conceived as a set of industries within which each firm produces a heterogeneous set of commodities, similar to the imperfect competition imagined by Robinson (1953). Each industry is associated with a different average elasticity of demand to income; the higher this elasticity, in an economy growing at a uniform rate, the higher the growth of demand for the sector's products and the higher corresponding rate of profit. Consequently, the different industries in the economy can be ordered according to their respective rates of profit, from highest to lowest. The position of the interest rate relative to the sequence of profit rates will determine the boundary between industries whose managers have an incentive to pursue a high growth rate ($\pi > i$) and those where prudence suggests the opposite ($\pi < i$). The growth rate of the economy will be equal to the average of the growth rates of the different industries multiplied by the respective income elasticities of demand.

The different industries grow at different rates depending on the income elasticity of demand for their products. In industries where the profit rate is higher and/or barriers to entry are lower, new companies are attracted. In industries where the profit rate is lower and/or barriers to entry are higher, the opposite occurs. In this way, over time the dispersion of profit rates across sectors should diminish. Moreover, differential profit rates instigate a progressive process of product diversification as companies associated with lower rates of profit diversify their output, pushing it into more profitable markets to the extent that managers succeed in overcoming the economic and psychological barriers to change. Finally, the fear of takeovers has the effect of slowing down growth in those industries where income elasticity of demand and profits are lower. The combination of these three elements serves to reduce the dispersion of sectoral profit rates without eliminating it.

[61] The importance of the monetary authorities keeping interest rates low is implicitly reiterated.

The relationship between profits, savings and investments at the aggregate level on the assumption of a closed economy can be defined as follows. Aggregate demand consists of consumption A and investment $\dot{C}$ $\left(Y = A + \dot{C}\right)$; income is divided between labour income W (wages and salaries) and rentiers' income R ($Y = W + R$).[62] Rentiers' income includes both dividends received D and the capital appreciation due to retentions ($R = D + rP$). Consumption comes from both wage earners and rentiers ($A = A_w + A_r$). Wages are spent entirely on the purchase of consumer goods ($W = A_w$). Capital income is only partly spent on the purchase of consumer goods and partly saved. Investments are financed partly through retained profits (rP), partly through external finance (EF) $\left(\dot{C} = rP + EF\right)$. When all these assumptions, with their clear links to Post-Keynesian distribution theory, are taken into account, we obtain:

$$A_w + A_r + \dot{C} = W + R \tag{6.8}$$

From which

$$R = A_r + \dot{C} = A_r + rP + EF \tag{6.9}$$

From which

$$EF = D - A_r \tag{6.10}$$

In this way, the amount of financial resources that companies have to raise on the Stock Exchange to finance the part of investment that is not covered by self-financing is equal to the difference between dividends and the consumption of the recipients of financial income. Thus, the savings of rentiers/shareholders are transferred to companies.

The system is closed with the determination of the interest rate i, which is expressed in monetary terms and determined by the balance between the supply of money (which by assumptions consists of bank deposits only) and the demand for money, which in a state of tranquillity reflects the transaction purposes only, while the precautionary and speculative

[62] The model does not explicitly explain how income is determined at the aggregate level, but Kahn clearly refers to the principle of effective demand and investment, determined at the sectoral level and then aggregated, as the main determinant of income (given the propensity to consume and the multiplier).

motives remain inoperative (RFK/2/16/33, fn. 2). As such money demand can be conceived as a function of aggregate income Y expressed in nominal terms. The money supply comes from a banking system that finances enterprises by granting them short-term money advances, providing temporary finance for the whole of the excess of each company's investment over its retained profits. The banks operate by deciding at what intervals of time companies shall pay off their overdrafts by issuing new shares ($EF = p\dot{N} =$ paid-off overdrafts).

> The strictness of monetary control is indicated by the length of the interval between new issues. The shorter the interval the smaller, ceteris paribus [in the original], are the amount of bank advances and the stock of money and the higher is the rate of interest. (RFK/16/2/34)

In order for the interest rate to remain constant, as is appropriate in the state of tranquillity to which the entire analysis refers, the growth of the money supply must be equal to the growth of money demand, which in turn is equal to the rate of growth of aggregate income in nominal terms. This latter rate is equal to the growth rate of the economy in real terms, which is in turn equal to the average rate of investment across the different industries, plus the rate of inflation h. The rate of inflation is equal to the difference between the increase in nominal wages and the rate of labour productivity growth.

> The behaviour of the price-level depends on the behaviour of money wages. The price-level rises if money-wages rise faster than productivity. [...] The behaviour of money-wages depends mainly on the degree of shortage of manpower. To a much lesser extent it depends on the degree of any surplus of manpower over what can be employed. It is possible to establish sustained growth equal to the natural rate with a constant proportion of surplus manpower. [...] It may [in the original] be possible but not necessarily, with a sufficiently high proportion of surplus manpower, to achieve a constant price-level with money wages rising no faster than productivity. In any case considerable skill must be imagined on the part of the banking system to get the economy settled down at a growth rate equal to the natural rate with substantial though constant proportion of surplus manpower. (RFK/2/16/35)

Given the foregoing, it is interesting to note that Kahn introduces an element of asymmetry in describing the relationship between nominal wages and inflation. While a shortage of labour can cause wages, and therefore prices, to rise, the opposite situation, a surplus of labour, does not cause wages to fall. It almost seems, but this is pure conjecture, that Kahn wants to introduce a kind of downward rigidity of monetary wages to fit the context of his model, while he chooses not to mention trade unions. The other important element that emerges from the last passage concerns the role of 'orchestra conductor' that Kahn assigns to the monetary authorities, in concert with the banking system, to steer the economy towards balanced growth by controlling interest rates and the money supply. If the actual growth rate is initially lower than the natural rate, increasing it requires a reduction in the real interest rate. Therefore, having reduced the monetary interest rate as far as possible, the monetary authority must insist on an expansionary policy, even though this may lead to inflation.

Kahn sent his manuscript to a number of colleagues for comments and suggestions. The list of recipients, all of them at Cambridge and from various generations, is interesting for what it tells us about Kahn's closest academic contacts in the mid-1960s. The list included Cristopher Bliss (in 1964 a PhD student), David Champernowne (Professor of Economic Statistics), Charles Goodhart (PhD student), Frank Hahn (Lecturer and then Reader), Robin Marris (Lecturer), Jan Kregel (graduate student), James Meade (Professor of Political Economy). James Mirlees (postdoctoral student), Joan Robinson (Reader), Jan Graaff (lecturer), Robert Rowthorn (graduate student). As is clear from the more than two hundred pages of material that follow Kahn's typescript, this article was read and commented on by these and other people. Taken together, their comments, formulated between October 1964 and August 1965, provide an interesting example of the theoretical debate that was taking place in Cambridge, informally but no less intensely, as well as marking the distance between Kahn's way of doing economics in 1964 and the way of doing economics of his interlocutors.

The first comments came from four of Cambridge's youngest economists. On 2 October 1964, Goodhart urged Kahn to consider the disadvantages as well as the advantages that a dynamic and highly profitable firm might suffer by acquiring a less dynamic firm. Goodhart also asked Kahn to introduce at least a second interest rate (on bank loans) to the general return on shares i, to specify the transmission mechanism linking one to the other 'in a series of Robertsonian steps' and to deepen the empirical dimension of the analysis.[63] On 5 October, Champernowne confined himself to a few formal remarks, inviting Kahn to clarify, with the aid of appropriate graphs, the relationship between the income elasticity of demand for a company's product in different sectors and the corresponding valuation ratio.[64] Kregel, on 19 November, noted how the case where the valuation ratio is greater than 1 looked implausible to him, as it was difficult to believe that in a world of perfect foresight managers could be clever enough to raise the valuation ratio above unity without shareholders noticing, by adjusting the value of *C*.[65]

Three long mathematical notes, written by Jan Graaff, Hahn and Rowthorn (RFK/2/16/48–76), reformulated Kahn's analysis in terms of differential equations and analyse the conditions under which Kahn's state of tranquillity might be plausible. The intensity of the objections to his treatment of this possibility raised by the three led Kahn to turn to Francis Bretherton, the mathematician at King's College, who prepared a long note devoted to the analysis of the stability conditions of *v* (RFK/2/16/83–89). On 3 February 1965 Kahn sent this note to nine people: Bliss, Champernowne, Hahn, Marris, Meade. Mirlees, Robinson, de Villiers Graaff and Rowthorn, enclosing the following words:

> In circulating the attached note by Francis Bretherton, King's mathematician (son of R.F. the economist and civil servant), prepared after Graaff's talk to us, I am very conscious that Champernowne, Graaff himself, Hahn and Rowthorn, and probably others, all produced results sometime ago for the rate of change of v, and that I have been very remiss in failing to respond and that it was only on Monday evening when Meade showed me his results expressed in terms of a stability condition that I appreciated the significance of all this. I throw Bretherton's note into the arena. At this point I would only add this. The stability of the share price must depend on how shareholders' (including those who do not yet own the share) expectations about the future of the price are influenced by any deviation in its current behaviour. There is, I suspect, a missing equation. (RFK/2/16/82)

From here the debate continued with contributions from Joan Robinson, Bretherton again (with two further notes), Meade with a long handwritten note dated March 1965 (RFK/2/16/114–119), which

[63] Letter from Goodhart to Kahn (RFK/2/16/39–42).
[64] Letter from Champernowne to Kahn (RFK/2/16/43–44).
[65] Letter from Kregel to Kahn (RFK/2/16/46–47).

Kahn sent Bretherton with a request for help (RFK/2/16/113). Bretherton's reply was followed by further comments from Meade and Joan Robinson between March and May 1965.

In June of that year, Kahn sent an eight-page typewritten note to the recipients of Bretherton's first note, excluding Villier Graaff and adding Luigi Pasinetti. In this note Kahn dealt with the problem of the dynamics of v and the identification of the conditions of divergence and convergence of this variable to steady state values (RFK/2/16/158–165). The note was commented on by Champernowne and Meade and prompted a new reply from Kahn on 31 August 1965 (RFK/2/16/183). In September 1965 Joan Robinson intervened again, followed by Mirlees and again by Champernowne. The final relevant documents in this exchange consist of two handwritten notes by Kahn, dated 1 and 5 September 1965, addressed to Marris, Williamson, Ajit Singh, Geoffrey Harcourt. The two notes deal with the inverse and concave relationship between the rate of profit π and the rate of growth g, and the calculation of the value of g which maximises v (RFK/2/16/249–254).

Comparing the text of the typescript 'Work in Progress' with the final text published by Kahn in his collection of writings (Kahn, 1972), with the title 'Some Notes on Interest and the Growth of Firms', little of the intense exchange of ideas and opinions that we have documented emerges. The published text is more compact than the original, but the structure, numerical examples and conclusions are the same. References to dynamic adjustment problems are present in the notes, but the text contains no explicit references to dynamic analysis. Kahn must have found it too much trouble to change a text on which he himself had not worked for a long time.[66]

On the other hand, Kahn's decision not to publish his work on the valuation ratio when he actually conceived it, but only eight years later and

[66] Following their publication, Kahn's *Notes* attracted limited attention from the secondary literature. One exception is Vianello (1988). In this essay, Vianello (1939–2009), a fine interpreter of the economics of Ricardo, Keynes and Sraffa, refers to Kahn's theoretical framework, particularly the idea that monetary authorities determine the interest rate. This, in turn, determines the return on shares, the average rate of profit and therefore the distribution of income. Vianello uses this idea to support his criticism of Goodwin's critique of the hypothesis of an externally determined rate of profit, as introduced by Sraffa in *Commodity Production by Means of Commodities*. In recent years, few works mention Kahn's *Notes* in connection with the reconsideration of Tobin's q in historical perspective (e.g. Kurose, 2003; Franke & Yanovski, 2016).

without making any substantial changes, prevented him from claiming priority in the treatment of the valuation ratio and its macroeconomic implications within the Cambridge Post-Keynesian model,[67] leaving this priority to others, notably Kaldor (1966). Abraham-Frois, comparing Kaldor's and Kahn's approaches to corporate behaviour, the valuation ratio and macroeconomic analysis, observes:

> In his 'Notes on the rate of interest and the growth of firms' (1972) [...] (Kahn) refers to Marris, Marris and Wood, Robinson, Penrose, but not to Kaldor. (Abraham-Frois, 1991, p. 197)

The fact that the version of the work published by Kahn in 1972 coincides with the 1965 text, apart from minor textual differences, suggests that he did not revisit the work during the seven-year period between these two dates. This appears to explain why Kahn's text does not reference Kaldor (1966), instead citing other works by Kaldor written before 1965. On the other hand, Kaldor's absence from the list of persons among whom the original manuscript of the *Notes* was circulated suggests the possibility that either he was unaware that Kahn was working on the same subject o he preferred not to mention an unpublished manuscript.

Overall, Kahn's work on the valuation ratio appears to represent a significant culmination of the key elements that shaped his economic vision. These elements include investment and its financial determinants, the heterogeneity of economic agents and the role of psychological factors, conjecture and marginal reasoning in determining their actions. At the macroeconomic level, economic growth depends on investment, and thus on monetary policy, stock exchange performance and banking decisions. Inflation, meanwhile, depends directly on wage and productivity dynamics, and indirectly on demand. While Kahn's initial intentions were ambitious, as evidenced by the interaction with the other Cambridge economists over his Work in progress, the final outcome was not successful. Once again, as on other occasions, Kahn's reluctance to publish worked against him and against the possibility of having any real impact on the theoretical debate.

For Kahn, the decision to remain anchored in a qualitative analytical approach, after experimenting with the quantitative approach in the early

[67] Marris (1971), who had been aware of Kahn's work since its inception in 1964, was the first to trace the origin of the valuation ratio formula to Kahn's manuscript.

part of his career as an economist, may well have reflected his conviction that economic theory should confine itself to identifying certain underlying causal relationships, to be understood as trends rather than mathematical functions, even given the margins of indeterminacy surrounding these relationships due to uncertainty, the influence of a multitude of subjective factors that cannot be mathematised, not to mention the influence of institutions. This conviction, never explicitly and systematically articulated in a methodological paper, is nevertheless evident in the evolution of Kahn's scientific output as reconstructed so far. On the other hand, macroeconomic theory had by then taken a different path, the path of theorems, functions, the mathematisation of expectations, the transformation of uncertainty into risk, the transition from static to dynamic models and econometrics. In the mid-1960s, Kahn left this path for good and, as we shall see, devoted the last fifteen years of his intellectual life to defending the Keynesian legacy as he understood it in other ways.

6.7 House of Lords: Debut and Defence of Keynesianism

The year 1965, that saw Kahn busy reworking his essay on the valuation ratio and interest rates, was also the year in which he was created a life peer, with the title of Baron Kahn of Hampstead, in recognition of his services to the British government.

> With this distinguished record of service to national and international institutions, there was no surprise, in 1965, when in the first honours list of Harold Wilson's new Labour Government, Richard Kahn appeared among the Life Peers. Harold Wilson, himself a convinced Keynesian, was an admirer of Kahn's academic work. But Kahn was never part of the group of Labour Party counsellors; he always kept a detached attitude. In the House of Lords, he sat on the cross benches. (Pasinetti, 1991, p. 430)[68]

In his new role Kahn gained an important new forum from which to defend his ideas in support of a Keynesian view of the economic problems

[68] Crossbench Peers are non-party political and by tradition sit on the benches that cross the chamber of the House of Lords (source: the UK Parliament Glossary website https://www.parliament.uk/site-information/glossary/crossbench-peers/).

of the day. In keeping with his character, he did so discreetly, limiting his interventions in the 1960s to four.

To understand the context in which these discourses took shape, it is worth recalling that at the beginning of their mandate, the Wilson Government had introduced relatively large tax increases, coupled with an emergency increase in the Bank Rate to deal with a crisis of confidence in sterling between October and November 1964.[69] In 1965, as O'Hara (2006) reconstructs, facing renewed pressure on the pound, the UK government slightly eased monetary policy but maintained tight credit controls and cut public spending. Seeking to curb demand without stalling economic growth, it introduced the Selective Employment Tax, targeting service industries. Though private consumption was checked, investment continued to surge, particularly in public sector projects and council housing, exacerbating balance of payments pressures and triggering a sterling crisis. In response, further credit restrictions, interest rate hikes and deeper public spending cuts were implemented. In July 1966, Prime Minister Harold Wilson announced sweeping measures to combat rising inflation, including a wage and price freeze (standstill),[70] despite concerns over their impact on workers and productivity. Over six million workers were affected by halted wage increases, while businesses retained profits and dividends were only loosely regulated. Although intended to allow productivity to catch up with income growth, critics warned that suppressed production and investment could worsen economic stagnation.

In this context, Kahn took advantage of his maiden speech, delivered on 28 July 1966 in a session devoted to the economic situation, to reflect on the necessity for balance in economic policy and express his concerns about the impact of recent government measures on investment, labour markets and economic growth. While acknowledging the need for fiscal restraint, he stressed the importance of fostering investment and avoiding policies that could slow down growth or exacerbate unemployment. As he had done on several previous occasions, Kahn insisted that action should be taken to redeploy productive resources, and in particular labour, from the consumption to the investment goods sector, without compromising high levels of employment in the name of disinflation. To achieve this, Kahn recommended avoiding further credit restrictions or selective

[69] On this, see Naef (2022, pp. 128–135).

[70] On the wages and employment policies of the Wilson government, see Jones (1987, pp. 66–83).

employment taxes, and instead relying on labour exchanges and the identification of a system of national priorities in labour allocation, which the exchanges would be tasked with implementing.[71]

> In putting forward this indication to your Lordships' House I appreciate that I shall be accused of trying to invoke one form of war-time legislation, the Control of Engagement Orders. Taken by themselves—I am not harking back to any other form of war-time control of labour—that was a purely negative control. […] I am relying far more on what happened in this context in the decade after the war. (Ibid.)

In 1947, for example, as Kahn reminded the Lords, amid a precarious balance-of-payments situation, the Control of Engagements Order had been introduced and maintained until 1950. By 1952, facing another balance of payments crisis, the government reintroduced a similar labour control system under the Notification of Vacancies Order to address rearmament challenges. However, neither the Attlee government nor the Conservatives in the 1950s had enforced these controls with notable rigour. In proposing the reactivation of this type of control, therefore, Kahn was simply appealing to a well-established and proven practice of both parties when confronting a similar emergency situation.[72]

In his second speech on 3 August of 1966, delivered during a session devoted to *The Prices and Incomes Policy*, Kahn addressed several critical points regarding the standstill and its broader implications, focusing on

[71] Ref. UK Parliament, Hansard, Lords: 28 July 1966, Lords Chamber, *The Economic Situation*, Volume 276, Column 938, debated on Thursday 28 July 1966.

[72] Prior to this speech, on 16 July 1966, Kahn wrote to Sir Eric Roll, Permanent Secretary of the Department of Economic Affairs, anticipating the content of the speech, particularly in relation to Kahn's desire to 'come out with an old idea of mine', to restore wartime controls on deployment orders, aimed at concentrating the use of labour in key sectors, by adapting them to the peace context and to raise a number of related issues (RFK/11/6/32–33). On 18 July 1966, after consultation with the Chairman of the House, Kahn wrote directly to the prime minister, who was in Moscow at the time, requesting the same information (RFK/11/6/34). It was Thomas Balogh who replied to Kahn on 25 July 1966, anticipating a telephone reply (RFK/11/6/35). Kahn's letter of 23 July to the Office of the Government Chief Whip shows his concern that, in the absence of direct measures to contain the pressures on prices and sterling through a direct reallocation of labour from the consumer goods sector to the capital goods sector, the only course open to the Government would be to tighten monetary policy (RFK/11/6/36–37). A letter of a different tenor was sent by Kahn to Chancellor Callaghan (RFK/11/6/39–40).

prices and incomes policy.[73] A key concern was the legal and ethical implications of asking employers to delay wage increases already agreed upon, which could undermine trust. Kahn stressed the importance of balancing wage and price freezes, arguing that one cannot be effective without the other. However, he warned that the standstill must be used as an opportunity to re-evaluate and improve income policies, as in the absence of careful planning the temporary freeze might not lead to sustainable economic progress. Kahn also discussed the complexities of productivity agreements,[74] cautioning against wage increases that may outpace productivity or create wage disparities across industries. Kahn's main concern in this respect was the possibility that sectoral wage increase, granted on the basis of a productivity agreement, could trigger a wage-wage spiral.

> What we call the leapfrog effect, the competitive struggles of workers in each industry to keep up with workers in other industries, is perhaps the most important cause of the unduly rapid rise of wages in this country.[75]

In addition to the leapfrog effect, Kahn identified 'wage drift', where wages increase outside formal bargaining, as another factor that could undermine price stability, and urged the government to address both factors in a clear and transparent manner, focusing on long-term economic competitiveness and a stable external surplus. While supporting the need for tough decisions in times of emergency, Kahn's speech concluded by stressing that success depended on attention to detail and the ability to mobilise support even in the face of unpopularity (ibid.).

With his third speech, delivered on 8 May 1967, in the context of the debate on Britain's entry into the European Economic Community (EEC)

[73] In a letter dated 30 July 1966, anticipating the Leader of the House and Lord Privy Seal, the Earl of Langford, to seek advice on whether to intervene again in the economic situation, Kahn wrote: 'I take a very great interest in incomes policy and I believe it to be vital. I can claim to some extent to be a pioneer, as a member of the O.E.C.D. Group on the problem of rising prices, which reported in 1961'. (RFK/11/6/189).

[74] 'Under the Wilson government, productivity agreements aimed to align wage increases with measurable productivity gains as part of a broader anti-inflation strategy.' However, these agreements were ultimately undermined by weak enforcement and economic pressures, especially after the 1966 sterling crisis. On this and on productivity agreements, see Tomlinson (2002).

[75] Ref. UK Parliament, Hansard, Lords: 3 August 1966, Lords Chamber, *The Prices and Incomes Policy*, Volume 276, Column 1365, debated on Wednesday 3 August 1966.

and the European Coal and Steel Community (ECSC),[76] Kahn had a chance to express his critical perspective on the implications of the United Kingdom joining the EEC, focusing on constitutional, economic and social concerns, starting with the observation that, differently from other international agreements, the Treaty of Rome lacked provisions for a member state's withdrawal. Kahn went on to emphasise disparities in tariff structures and noting that while reducing the UK's higher tariffs could eliminate barriers to EEC trade, it would have also lowered tariffs for non-EEC countries, making it doubtful whether the benefits of such reductions would have outweighed the uneven impacts on various industries. Broadly, Kahn questioned whether the economic benefits of EEC membership justified the associated obligations. He suggested that alternatives, such as a Free Trade Area encompassing EEC and EFTA members, might provide similar advantages without the drawbacks of the EEC's policies, particularly the Common Agricultural Policy. Overall, he concluded that the potential benefits were marginal and outweighed by significant social and economic costs, especially for poorer households, casting doubt on the value of joining the EEC.[77]

Kahn's fourth speech on 24 January 1968, during a debate on Britain's economic position following the devaluation of sterling in November the previous year, was similarly critical of the government. Focusing on incomes policy, Kahn drew attention to the Prime Minister's Statement on Incomes Policy, which proposed that excessive wage increases should be countered by additional taxation. Kahn questioned the effectiveness of this approach, arguing that extra taxes would exacerbate the problem by increasing production costs and reducing competitiveness and expressing concern that the benefits of devaluation could be squandered within a few years if wage increases were not kept in check. Kahn also criticised the government's reliance on cooperation between the Trades Union Congress

[76] During Wilson's first government (1964–1970), Britain's approach to the European Economic Community (EEC) was cautious and politically constrained. Although initially sceptical, Wilson came to recognise the potential economic benefits of membership as Britain's growth slowed. In 1967 his government formally applied to join the EEC, but the application was vetoed by President de Gaulle, who doubted Britain's European commitment. Wilson thereafter maintained a pragmatic but non-committal approach to Europe, navigating a divided Labour Party with some members strongly opposed to EEC membership and others in favour.

[77] Ref. UK Parliament, Hansard, Lords: 8 May 1967, Lords Chamber, *The European Economic Community*, Volume 282, debated on Monday 8 May 1967.

(TUC) and the Confederation of British Industry (CBI) in managing the prices and incomes policy, expressing scepticism about the TUC's ability to meet this target without stricter oversight or intervention. Kahn warned that disparities in wage negotiations across sectors could undermine the overall goal, with some agreements exceeding the proposed limits and others failing to offset the excesses.[78] Taken together, Kahn's parliamentary speeches in the 1960s provide additional evidence of his economic vision. This vision and its implicit defence of Keynesianism include confidence in the possibility of reconciling full employment, inflation control and balance of payments through direct controls and income policy. They also include a call for countries to adopt economic measures to maintain autonomy and independence from external constraints, and above all, a call for the general interest to be kept in mind by all economic actors when formulating their demands and strategies.

6.8 The Kahn-Berrill Memorandum on Incomes Policy

In 1966 Kahn and Kenneth Berrill, then at King's College and one of Kahn's close associates,[79] were commissioned by the newly established Department of Economic Affairs (DEA) to write a report on prices and incomes policy.[80] The report was written at a time when the Wilson government was imposing a freeze on wages and prices, as mentioned above, with the stated goal of giving the economy 'a breathing space of twelve months in which productivity can catch up with the excessive increases in incomes which have been taking place'.[81]

The report, a version of which exists in the Kahn archive (RFK/10/1/2–49), consists of two parts. The first part, which is longer,

[78] Ref. UK Parliament, Hansard, Lords: 24 January 1968, Lords Chamber, *The Economic Situation and Public Expenditure*, Volume 288, Column 361–364, debated on Wednesday 24 January 1968.

[79] On Kenneth Berrill, see Appendix C and Brewerton (2009).

[80] As Blick (2007, p. 41) recalls, the DEA was established in 1964 as a rival to the Treasury. Its primary function was to devise and then implement a National Plan for economic growth, which was published in 1965 The Plan was abandoned, however, with the deflationary measures taken during the sterling crisis of July 1966. The DEA, which had lost its raison d'être, was finally wound up in 1969. On the DEA, see MacDougall (1987, pp. 149–175).

[81] Source: *Prices and Incomes Policy: An 'Early Warning' System*, Cmnd. 2808, November 1965. Paragraph 2.

contains proposals for the conduct of price and income policy in the long run (1970 and beyond), assuming that the emergency situation that necessitated the imposition of the freeze has passed and the economy has settled into a new equilibrium. The second part analyses the short-term situation, the impact of the freeze on public opinion and the concrete possibilities of implementation.

The long-term scenario outlined in the first part is based on the assumption that both the physical capacity of plant and equipment and the labour force are employed at normal levels, without unexpectedly large amounts of idle capacity and/or unemployment, and generally without exceptional pressures on resources. Labour shortages, if any, are primarily the result of bottlenecks in particular regions or particular industries and occupations and should not generally be related to total employment or total unfilled vacancies.

> In particular we do not accept the view of Professor Phillips and his followers which makes increases in wages and prices depend largely on average unemployment. Still less do we accept the related contention of Professor Paish that, year in year out, it is desirable to maintain a margin of unused physical capacity as well as of unused labour. [...] We do not believe that one can calculate from past cyclical data an unemployment level which will give stable prices, with the inference that lower unemployment makes prices and incomes policy unworkable and higher unemployment makes it unnecessary. We thus reject the Phillips-Paish calculations. (RFK/1/10/6)

This rejection stems from the consideration that there is nothing 'natural' about the relationship between unemployment and wages, but that it depends on a variety of changing and contingent factors.[82] This belief is intertwined with Kahn's long-standing refusal to conceive of unemployment as a weapon against inflation, all the more so if, at the same time, he thinks he wants to keep the economy on a growth path.

> We do not, therefore, believe that in the 1970s one should try to avoid the need for a prices and incomes policy by having a high level of unemployed labour. Still less do we believe that the objective should be surplus plant as

[82] For more information on the emergence of the Phillips curve in 1958 and the subsequent challenge of determining an unemployment rate that is consistent with price stability, refer to Cristiano and Paesani (2018). For an analysis of the early reception of the Phillips curve in the United Kingdom, see Cristiano (2023).

> well as surplus labour. This might possibly achieve a measure of price stability but it would certainly achieve stagnation. Nor do we believe that the 1970s should see further attempts at prices and incomes policies which are as unsuccessful as those of the past, so that the stop-go cycle remains both repetitive and expected. This achieves neither price stability nor a reasonable rate of economic growth. We are looking for a process and incomes policy, radical if it has to be, which will permit high and stable employment and which will encourage the greater investment and faster productivity growth on which the long-term rise in real incomes depends. (RFK/10/1/6)

With regard to the employment target, Kahn and Berrill put the range of 1.5–1.75% as the value of the unemployment rate below which tightness in the labour market would create tensions, even in the presence of price and incomes policies. This estimate, with all due caution, is based on the assumption that incomes policy has been successfully implemented and that at least some of the bottlenecks in the UK labour market have also been removed by the introduction of measures to encourage retraining and geographical and sectoral mobility of workers. The target unemployment rate is combined with the assumption of an average annual productivity growth rate, measured as output per hour worked, of 3.5% over a relatively long period, obtained as an average between past values and a hypothetical future trend once income and price policies have come into effect. With this rate of productivity growth and an inflation target of 2%, the average rate of increase in hourly earnings for a normal working week to which the government should aim is 5.5% (net of one-off increases in indirect taxes or exceptional increases in the prices of imported goods). On the inflation target, Kahn and Berrill note:

> It must be remembered that a 2 per cent rise in the cost of living would mean a rise of less than 2 per cent in the average costs of manufactured goods, for rents and the charges of services normally rise more than the prices of manufactures. Within the manufacturing field the costs and prices of many categories would be stable or falling and the prices of some individual items would have to fall significantly. However, wage negotiations would take place within the context that the government was aiming at relative, but not absolute, price stability. (RFK/10/1/8–9)

Aiming for a positive inflation target, rather than zero inflation, serves to provide the economy with the flexibility needed to maintain full employment. Moreover, with observed inflation close to 5%, the proposal to move to zero would hardly be credible, which could undermine the government's move towards price stabilisation. Kahn and Berrill do not rule out the possibility that the 2% can be reduced over time, but this depends on the success of price and income policy.

Finally, it is important to note that for Kahn and Berrill the inflation target does not have to be officially announced. The government need only announce that it is committed to achieving price stability, leaving a margin of uncertainty as to the actual inflation rate it wishes to achieve. The purpose of this margin of uncertainty is to leave the public, and especially the trade unions and firms on which wages, profit margins and prices depend, in doubt that if there is behaviour inconsistent with the government's overall objectives, the government may decide to punish that behaviour with particularly restrictive measures. To avoid this risk, unions and firms should moderate their demands at the outset, creating the conditions for the ideal situation of full employment, moderately positive ex-post inflation and zero or near-zero inflation expectations to be realised.

As we will see in the next chapter, a similar idea underlies Kahn's proposals for stabilising commodity prices and exchange rates. This idea reflects Kahn's belief that uncertainty causes economic agents to hold their positions or to move less abruptly than they would if they could accurately predict market movements. If the government's objective is to stabilise some quantity (general price level, commodity price, exchange rate) without specifying it, then announcing its intentions without committing to a numerical target is the right way to combine flexibility in economic policy with the management of expectations. If, on the other hand, the objective is to determine exactly the numerical value of a variable, provided that it is realistic, the authorities must be prepared to take measures to the bitter end until the objective is achieved.

Kahn and Berrill argue that price and income policy should be evaluated in the medium to long term, as they have limited effectiveness in addressing external imbalances or promoting social justice. Without such policies, however, the risk of persistent inflation under a fixed exchange rate triggering stop-go cycles that hinder productivity growth increases. Excluding the determination of rents and dividends from the scope of their proposals, Kahn and Berrill propose three qualifying measures to implement incomes and price policy: (1) the establishment of a permanent system to control prices and profit margins, (2) the definition and implementation of a standard for the rate of wage increases of 4% per annum and (3) a radical change in the mechanisms of wage bargaining from the status quo.

Implementing a comprehensive system of inspection and price control across the entire economy would present significant administrative challenges. It would require expert knowledge, sustained effort and a large, trained workforce. Such systems are generally resisted by administrators and industrialists alike due to their complexity and intrusiveness. Nevertheless, some degree of price and margin control is deemed vital for an effective incomes policy. Politically, wage regulation is more acceptable when accompanied by visible efforts to contain prices and profits. From an economic perspective, reducing prices in key sectors helps curb overall inflation, and margin controls limit the risk of generous wage settlements in high-productivity industries triggering wage spirals across the economy.

A wage increase norm of around 4% per year has been proposed—below the projected monetary income growth—to account for labour market realities. This norm is intended to act as a ceiling, though in practice it risks becoming a de facto floor. It also allows for wage drift, which is the unpredictable result of local bargaining exceeding national agreements. Enforcement mechanisms would need to address excessive drift while allowing for upward adjustment where wages have lagged behind the norm.

A third key reform centres on restructuring the wage bargaining process to shift influence from local to national negotiations. Ideally, this would be achieved through synchronised bargaining between unions and employers, based on a model similar to those in Scandinavian countries. This approach aims to prevent leapfrogging and wage escalation driven by local settlements. To this end, emphasis would be placed on sectoral productivity agreements, and government institutions would play a more central role, particularly the Ministry of Labour in national negotiations and the Ministry of Economic Affairs in overseeing overall wage and income policy coordination.

The presence of the Ministry of Labour at the wage bargaining table should serve to bring the general interest to bear on these negotiations and should be backed up by giving the government the necessary statutory powers to prevent an agreement between the social partners from leading to a rate of wage increase incompatible with the general interest. Kahn and Berrill are aware that the introduction of the wage freeze has created the right psychological conditions in public opinion and among the various actors involved to introduce radical changes in price and income policy. On the other hand, without the willingness of unions and business to cooperate with the government, incomes and prices policies are doomed to failure, leaving only two alternatives: voluntary agreements, which past experience has shown do not work, and a return to stop-and-go policies. Kahn and Berrill conclude their interim memorandum by writing:

> The governess-like tone of our Memorandum may have given the impression that we regard the position of Her Majesty's Government of the United Kingdom as tantamount to that of a dictator. Such an impression is the result of an attempt to achieve brevity but we are anxious to correct it. [...] There can be no delusions as to the possibility of success in the absence of support from the populace at large. But this support can be secured for a reasonably devised prices and incomes policy. There must, however, be protection against the selfishness and irresponsibility of recalcitrant minorities. Attitudes of individual trade unions, and perhaps attitudes of individual employers' associations, will vary. But we are under no delusion as to the vital importance of securing the cooperation of the T.U.C. and the C.B.I. [...] It must be made clear to them that the Government have to maintain a central role but that this is not feasible without their co-operation. If the policy is not feasible, the Government will have to govern as best as it can—with stop-go and what have you. (RFK/10/1/48–49)

Despite these assurances, Kahn and Berrill's fears that they would not win the favour of those involved in the planned price and incomes policy soon materialised. As Tomlinson (2004, pp. 137–139) reconstructs, the Kahn-Berrill report raised (though did not answer) all the strategic questions about income policy. Its proposals, and others from the DEA, were debated in the winter of 1966.[83] However, neither the proposal for the

[83] Evidence of this from the Kahn archives includes the following relevant documents. The draft of a DEA paper, dated 6 January 1967 and entitled 'Future Development of the Productivity, Prices and Incomes Policy' with emphases by Kahn on points of agreement and disagreement with his proposal (RFK/10/3/99–156). Three set of notes of meetings at the DEA in which Kahn's attempts to support his and Berrill's point of view in front of government representatives are highlighted (10 January 1967—RFK/10/3/93–97, 16 January 1967—RFK/10/3/83–87, 18 January 1967—RFK/10/3/77–82). A note from the Chairman of the Official Steering Committee on Prices and Incomes Policy comparing the Kahn-Berrill memorandum with a paper prepared by the DEA (RFK/10/3/90–92). One note signed by Berrill and Kahn, dated 15 February 1967 on the norm for July 1967 to July 1968, where the two authors raise grave objections to the 'nil-norm' that would eventually be adopted (RFK/10/3/2–4).

Ministry of Labour to be present at every wage negotiation, described by Alec Cairncross (quoted by Tomlinson) as 'totally unrealistic',[84] nor the 2% inflation target were considered.

The new policy announced in March 1967 provided for a 'zero norm', the continuation of productivity agreements and the reduction of statutory powers to the government's prerogative to delay wage and price increases for a maximum of seven months. Despite this, the unions remained strongly opposed to the idea of incomes policy, while the CBI was more open. With the gradual marginalisation of incomes policy by the Wilson government, Kahn began to distance himself from the Labour Party, with which he had never been organically associated, if not from the intentions of the official reports. As we shall see, this distance deepened in the 1970s and led to Kahn's departure from the Labour Party to join the British Social Democratic Party.

More generally, and in a somewhat symmetrical way, if the work on the valuation ratio represents Kahn's last attempt at original theoretical elaboration, the report written with Berrill represents his last attempt to influence British economic policy directly. In both cases, the failure of Kahn's attempt can be linked to his desire to remain consistent with a vision of the economy that by the mid-1960 was becoming increasingly marginalised. It was a Keynesian vision in the highest and noblest sense of the word, in which government acted as the guarantor of the country's material well-being, freedom, social stability and economic independence, and citizens, workers and businesses recognised this commitment and accepted government leadership, working together to achieve common goals. While in the 1950s, with the memory of the war still fresh, this vision had some chance of success, by the 1960s, even with Britain governed by the Labour Party to which Kahn belonged, this was clearly no longer the case.

References

Abraham-Frois, G. (1991). Corporate behavior, valuation ratio and macroeconomic analysis. In E. J. Nell & M. Semmler (Eds.), *Nicholas Kaldor and mainstream economics* (pp. 190–205). Palgrave Macmillan.

[84] This proposal in particular was very strong and almost revolutionary in the context of British industrial relations, which have traditionally been based on the freedom of trade unions and employers' organisations to negotiate without government interference.

Albani, P. (1986). Nicholas Kaldor (1908–1986). *Quaderni di Storia dell'Economia Politica, 4*(1/2), 3–21.

Ambrosi, G. M. (2004). *Keynes, Pigou and Cambridge Keynesians: Authenticity and analytical perspective in the Keynes-classics debate*. Palgrave Macmillan.

Andrews, P. W. S. (1949). *Manufacturing business*. Macmillan.

Arestis, P., & Sawyer, M. (Eds.). (1992). *A biographical dictionary of dissenting economists*. Edward Elgar.

Backhouse, R. E. (1996). The changing character of British economics. *History of Political Economy*, Annual Supplement to Volume *28*, 33–60.

Barker, T. (2017). Richard Stone (1913–1991). In R. Cord (Ed.), *The Palgrave companion to Cambridge economics* (Vol. 2, pp. 835–855). Palgrave Macmillan.

Berthelot, Y., & Rayment, P. (2007). *Looking back and peering forward. A short history of the United Nations economic Commission for Europe, 1947–2007*. United Nations.

Blick, A. (2007). Harold Wilson, labour and the machinery of government. In G. O'Hara & H. Parr (Eds.), *The Wilson governments 1964–1970 reconsidered* (pp. 40–59). Routledge.

Bliss, C. (2010). The Cambridge post-Keynesians: An outsider's insider view. *History of Political Economy, 42*(4), 631–652.

Brewerton, D. (2009, June 26). Obituary: Sir Kenneth Berrill. *The Guardian*. Available online.

Cairncross, A. (1993). *Austin Robinson: The life of an economic adviser*. Palgrave Macmillan.

Cairncross, A. (1996). *Managing the British economy in the 1960s*. Macmillan.

Cairncross, A., & Eichengreen, B. (2003). *Sterling in decline: The devaluations of 1931, 1949, 1967*. Palgrave Macmillan.

Cohen, A. J., & Harcourt, G. C. (2003). Retrospectives: Whatever happened to the Cambridge capital theory controversies? *Journal of Economic Perspectives, 17*(1), 199–214.

Cristiano, C. (2023). The early reception of the Phillips curve in the United Kingdom: New evidence from the papers of the council on prices, productivity, and incomes. *History of Political Economy, 55*(2), 215–248.

Cristiano, C., & Paesani, P. (2018). Price stability and the origins and early influence of the Phillips curve on British policy debates. *History of Political Economy, 50*(3), 483–509.

Deaton, A. (1993). Richard Stone, 1913–1991. *Proceedings of the British Academy, 82*, 475–492.

Di Matteo, M., & Sordi, S. (2008). Un pioniere nel campo della dinamica economica: le scelte di Goodwin nel periodo 1949–52. In P. Barucci, L. Costabile, & M. Di Matteo (Eds.), *Gli archivi e la storia del pensiero economico* (pp. 201–231). Il Mulino.

Eatwell, J. (1992). Kahn, Richard (1905–1989). In P. Arestis & M. Sawyer (Eds.), *A biographical dictionary of dissenting economists* (pp. 286–292). Edward Elgar Publishing.
ECE – European Commission for Europe. (1957). *ECE. The first ten years. 1947–1957*, United Nations. Available online.
Franke, R., & Yanovski, B. (2016). On the long-run equilibrium value of Tobin's average Q. *European Journal of Economics and Economic Policies: Intervention, 13*, 103–113.
Garbellini, N. (2023). Luigi Pasinetti 1930–2023. *Review of Political Economy, 35*(2), 582–585.
Goodhart, C. A. E. (1997). Whither now? *Banca Nazionale del Lavoro Quarterly Review, 50*(203), 385–430.
Goodwin, R. M. (1994). Kahn and economic dynamics. *Cambridge Journal of Economics, 18*(1), 73–76.
Goodwin, R. M. (1995). In memory of sir Richard stone. In E. Giovannini (Ed.), *Social statistics, National Accounts and economic analysis: International conference in memory of sir Richard stone* (pp. 17–20). *Annali Di Statistica*, *X*(6)). Istituto Nazionale di Statistica.
Hamouda, O. F., & Harcourt, G. C. (1988). Post-Keynesianism: From criticism to coherence? *Bulletin of Economic Research, 40*, 1–33.
Harcourt, G. C. (1986). On the influence of Piero Sraffa on the contributions of Joan Robinson to economic theory. *Economic Journal, 96*, 96–108.
Harcourt, G. C. (1991). R.F. Kahn: A tribute. *Banca Nazionale del Lavoro Quarterly Review, 44*(176), 15–30.
Harcourt, G. C. (1993). *Post-Keynesian essays in biography*. Macmillan.
Harcourt, G. C. (2001). Joan Robinson and her circle. *History of Economic Ideas, 9*(2), 59–71.
Harcourt, G. C. (2012). Keynes and his Cambridge pupils and colleagues. *Meiji Journal of Political Science and Economics, 1*, 12–23.
Harcourt, G. C., & Kitson, M. (1993). Fifty years of measurement: A Cambridge view. *Review of Income and Wealth, 39*, 435–447.
Hart, A. G., Kaldor, N., & Tinbergen, J. (1964). The case for an international commodity reserve currency. In N. Kaldor (Ed.), *Essays on economic policy* (Vol. II). Duckworth. (originally 1963 as a memorandum submitted to UNCTAD).
Hayes, M. G. (2010). The fault line between Keynes and the Cambridge Keynesians: A review essay. *Review of Political Economy, 22*(1), 151–160.
Hodgson, G. M. (2019). *Is there a future for heterodox economics? Institutions, ideology and scientific community*. Edward Elgar.
Jacobsen, L. (2017). P.W.S. Andrews' manufacturing business revisited. *Review of Political Economy, 29*(2), 190–208.
Jacobsen, L. (2019). Robinson, Andrews and Marshall: A case of arguing at cross purposes? *History of Economics Review, 72*(1), 35–58.

Johnson, E. S., & Johnson, H. G. (1978). *The shadow of Keynes: Understanding Keynes, Cambridge and Keynesian economics*. Basil Blackwell.

Jones, R. (1987). *Wages and employment policy. 1936–1985*. Allen Unwin.

Kahn, R. F. (1955). Short–term business indicators in Western Europe. *Economic Bulletin for Europe, 7*(3), 34–78.

Kahn, R. F. (1972). *Selected essays on employment and growth*. Cambridge University Press.

Kaldor, N. (1956). Alternative theories of distribution. *Review of Economic Studies, 23*, 83–100.

Kaldor, N. (1957). A model of economic growth. *Economic Journal, 67*(268), 591–624.

Kaldor, N. (1966). Marginal productivity and the macro-economic theories of distribution: Comment on Samuelson and Modigliani. *Review of Economic Studies, 33*, 309–319.

Khatkhate, D. (2009). Harry Johnson: Portrait of a polymath [Review of *Harry Johnson: A life in economics*, by D. Moggridge]. *Economic and Political Weekly, 44*(51), 27–33.

King, J. E. (1998). Your position is thoroughly orthodox and entirely wrong: Nicholas Kaldor and Joan Robinson 1933–1983. *Journal of the History of Economic Thought, 20*(4), 411–432.

King, J. E. (2002). *A history of post Keynesian economics since 1936*. Edward Elgar.

King, J. E. (2004). Planning for abundance: Nicholas Kaldor and Joan Robinson on the socialist reconstruction of Britain, 1942–45. In I. Barens, V. Caspari, & B. Schefold (Eds.), *Political Events and Economic Ideas* (pp. 306–326). Edward Elgar.

King, J. E. (2009). *Nicholas Kaldor*. Palgrave Macmillan.

King, J. E. (2021). P.W.S. Andrews (1914–1971). In R. A. Cord (Ed.), *The Palgrave companion to Oxford economics* (pp. 395–415). Palgrave Macmillan.

Kregel, J. A. (1983). Post-Keynesian theory: An overview. *The Journal of Economic Education, 14*(4), 32–43.

Kurose, K. (2003). The reconsideration of 'valuation ratio' from the contemporary perspective. *Economic Journal of Hokkaido University, 32*, 123–139.

Loasby, B. J. (1991). *Equilibrium and evolution: An exploration of connecting principles in economics*. Manchester University Press.

MacDougall, D. (1987). *Don and mandarin: Memoirs of an economist*. John Murray.

Marchionatti, R. (2024). *Economic theory in the twentieth century. An intellectual history. Volume II 1946-mid-1970s*. Palgrave Macmillan.

Marcuzzo, M. C. (Ed.) (1986). Nicholas Kaldor. In *Ricordi di un economista*. Garzanti.

Marcuzzo, M. C. (2005). Piero Sraffa at the university of Cambridge. *European Journal of the History of Economic Thought, 12*(3), 425–452.

Marris, R. (1964). *The economic theory of managerial capitalism*. Macmillan.

Marris, R. (1971). An introduction to theories of corporate growth. In R. Marris & A. Wood (Eds.), *The corporate economy* (pp. 1–36). Palgrave Macmillan.

Matthews, R. C. O. (1989). Joan Robinson and Cambridge—A Theorist and her milieu. In G. R. Feiwel (Ed.), *Joan Robinson and Modern economic theory* (pp. 911–915). Palgrave Macmillan.

Moggridge, D. E. (2011). *Harry Johnson. A life in economics.* Cambridge University Press.

Movrich, R. F. (1975). The foundation and growth of the new British universities. *Western European Education, 7*(3), 5–29.

Naef, A. (2022). *An exchange rate history of the United Kingdom: 1945–1992. Studies in macroeconomic history.* Cambridge University Press.

Naylor, R. T. (1981). Johnson on Cambridge and Keynes. *Canadian Journal of Political and Social Theory/Revue canadienne de théorie politique et sociale, 5*(1–2), 214–229.

Newbery, D. M. (1998). Foreword. In I. Begg & B. Henry (Eds.), *Applied economics and public policy* (pp. xix–xxii). Cambridge University Press.

O'Hara, G. (2006). 'Dynamic, exciting, thrilling change': The Wilson government's economic policies, 1964–70. *Contemporary British History, 20*(3), 383–402.

O'Hara, G. (2007). *From dreams to disillusionment: Economic and social planning in 1960s Britain.* Palgrave Macmillan.

Paesani, P., & Rosselli, A. (2014). The case for a supra-national control on commodities in the post WWII world: Novel perspectives from FAO and Kaldor archives. *History of Economic Thought and Policy, 1*, 5–30.

Panico, C. (2018). Liquidity preference. In S. N. Durlauf & L. E. Blume (Eds.), *The new Palgrave dictionary of economics.* Palgrave Macmillan.

Pasinetti, L. L. (1991). Richard Ferdinand Kahn 1905–1989. *Proceedings of the British Academy, 76*, 423–443.

Pasinetti, L. L. (2007). *Keynes and the Cambridge Keynesians: A 'revolution in economics' to be accomplished (Federico Caffe lectures).* Cambridge University Press.

Penrose, E. T. (1959). *The theory of the growth of the firm.* Basil Blackwell.

Pesaran, M. H., & Harcourt, G. C. (2000). Life and work of John Richard Nicholas stone 1913–1991. *Economic Journal, 110*, F146–F165.

Robinson, J. V. (1953). Imperfect competition revisited. *Economic Journal, 63*, 579–593.

Robinson, J. V. (1956). *The accumulation of capital.* Cambridge University Press.

Saith, A. (2019). *Ajit Singh of Cambridge and Chandigarh: An intellectual biography of the radical Sikh economist.* Palgrave Macmillan.

Saith, A. (2022). *Cambridge economics in the post-Keynesian era: The eclipse of heterodox traditions.* Palgrave Macmillan.

Samuelson, P. (1994). Richard Kahn: His welfare economics and lifetime achievement. *Cambridge Journal of Economics, 18*(1), 55–72.
Schiffman, D. (2013, December 31). *Richard Kahn and Israeli Economic Policy, 1957 and 1962*. Available online.
Sen, A. K. (1999). Amartya Sen—Biographical. In T. Frängsmyr (Ed.), *Les Prix Nobel. The Nobel prizes 1998*. Nobel Foundation.
Silberston, A. (2011). Ken arrow, James Meade and the secret seminar. *Cambridge Economics, 4*(Autumn), 4.
Thirlwall, A. P. (1987). Nicholas Kaldor 1908–1986. *Proceedings of the British Academy, 72*, 517–566.
Tomlinson, J. (2002). The British 'productivity problem' in the 1960s. *Past and Present, 175*(1), 188–210.
Tomlinson, J. (2004). *The labour government 1964–1970*. Manchester University Press.
Turner, M. S. (1989). *Joan Robinson and the Americans*. M.E. Sharpe.
Velupillai, K. V. (2017). Richard Murphey Goodwin (1913–1996). In R. A. Cord (Ed.), *The Palgrave companion to Cambridge economics* (pp. 815–834). Palgrave Macmillan.
Vianello, F. (1988). A critique of Professor Goodwin's 'critique of Sraffa'. In G. Ricci & K. Velupillai (Eds.), *Growth cycles and multisectoral economics: The Goodwin tradition (Lecture notes in economics and mathematical systems)* (pp. 111–119). Springer.
Weinstein, O. (2012). Managerial theories: Baumol and Marris. In M. Dietrich & J. Krafft (Eds.), *Handbook on the economics and theory of the firm* (pp. 89–95). Edward Elgar.
Wood, A. (2017). Robin Marris (1924–2012). In R. A. Cord (Ed.), *The Palgrave companion to Cambridge economics* (pp. 893–914). Palgrave Macmillan.

CHAPTER 7

In the Spirit of Bretton Woods

7.1 Kahn, Keynes and the Spirit of Bretton Woods

An interest in international economic problems is a constant feature of Kahn's intellectual biography. In the 1930s, this interest led him to study the transfer problem, the newly established Bank for International Settlements, and the possibilities of persuading the United States to support the recovery of the world economy. In the 1940s, Kahn's main concern was to organise the supply of raw materials between the United Kingdom and the Middle East. He read and commented on Keynes's proposals for an International Clearing Union.[1]

At Bretton Woods, Keynes argued for multilateral rules on international trade, exchange rates and capital movements that would reconcile the freedom of individual nations to pursue their own domestic economic objectives with the gradual and regulated liberalisation of trade in goods and currencies. In particular, no country should ever again be forced to choose between full employment at home and balance of payments equilibrium, as Britain and other countries were forced to do in the 1920s. To

[1] On Kahn's comments on the Clearing Union see the *Collected Writings of John Maynard Keynes* (Moggridge, 1980, pp. 40–42). See also Cesarano (2006, pp. 136–137). In 1978, Kahn devoted a long and detailed essay to Keynes's contribution to the creation of the Bretton Woods system, which I take up again in Chap. 8. Pressnell (1986) provides a comprehensive reconstruction of Keynes's role in shaping Britain's foreign economic policy from the outbreak of the Second World War to 1947.

P. Paesani, *Richard F. Kahn*, Great Thinkers in Economics,
https://doi.org/10.1007/978-3-032-09123-9_7

this end, and with a view to facilitating the expansion of international trade with a limited amount of official reserves, Keynes recommended the use of multilateral clearing wherever possible, combined with the application of rules to contain external deficits and surpluses simultaneously. Exchange rates should be fixed, but adjustable in the face of structural external imbalances, and adjustment should be the result of an orderly process conducted by monetary authorities rather than the outcome of speculation and financial crisis. Liberalisation of international trade should be gradual and countries should retain controls on imports, exports and capital movements until they could safely dispense with them.[2]

These were the main features of Keynes's approach to the regulation of international trade and finance in the years leading up to Bretton Woods, together with a special attention to the economic interests of Britain. The same features, and the same 'spirit of Bretton Woods' characterise Kahn's own approach to the analysis and regulation of international economic problems in the four decades after Keynes's death. While Kahn continues in the tradition of Keynes, we can also identify significant elements of originality in his 'international writings'. In particular, this concerns the way in which Kahn extends his ideas on the role of speculation in organised markets to the study of different problems, ranging from the role of buffer stocks in stabilising commodity prices to the reorganisation of foreign exchange markets following the 1971 Bretton Woods crisis. Kahn's writings also demonstrate originality in the field of payment clearing at the European level, a fact that has not yet been sufficiently recognised.

The post-war decades were characterised by full employment, strong growth and rapid economic and social development in the capitalist world (*Les Trente Glorieuses*),[3] the Cold War and NATO, the emancipation of former colonial countries, and the division of the world into three blocks. In this context, and amidst daunting domestic challenges (reconstruction, creation of the welfare state, modernisation of industries), the United Kingdom had to come to terms with the end of the Empire, to be replaced by the Commonwealth, the declining international role of London as one

[2] For an introduction to Bretton Woods and more generally to the issues discussed in this chapter, see Eichengreen (2008, pp. 86–126) and Amato and Fantacci (2012, pp. 121–145), among many other sources. On Keynes at Bretton Woods, in addition to the sources cited on the previous page, see Steil (2013).

[3] *Les Trente Glorieuses*, a term coined by Jean Fourastié, refers to the period of exceptional economic growth in Western Europe from 1945 to 1973, driven by Marshall Aid, workforce expansion and technological advancements, ending with the 1973 oil crisis (Fourastié 1979).

of the world's leading financial centres, and most importantly the beginning of European economic integration in the wake of the Marshall Plan.[4]

Reflecting on these subjects, Blank (1977) suggests that two sets of constraints, internal and external, affected the performance of the British economy in the early post-war decades. Internal constraints included archaic industrial structures, low levels of investment, outdated industrial relations systems, and trade union and management practices that were not conducive to industrial modernisation and economic expansion. External constraints stemmed mainly from the vulnerability of Britain's international financial position, a balance of payments that was often under pressure, and extensive external financial and economic constraints partly deriving from Britain's attempt to maintain its international economic, financial, military and geopolitical role. The perception of Britain's international commitments as external constraints limiting her ability to invest domestically can be seen in Kahn's work, as well as in that of other authoritative observers, particularly Shonfield (1958).[5]

In general, Kahn's writing on international economic problems reflects his commitment to finding solutions that allow for gradual (and managed) multilateral liberalisation of international trade and capital mobility while leaving each country, Britain in particular, with the autonomy to reconcile internal and external goals. In this vein, Kahn favoured a gradual, regulated liberalisation, whereby each country could reintroduce selective restrictions on imports or capital movements, in case these were needed, while coordinating with other countries as much as possible to avoid conflict.

He believed that regulated international trade was superior to both autarky and complete liberalisation, the latter of which very few countries,

[4] On the Marshall Plan and its implications for European economic integration from the perspective of Anglo–American relations and Britain's attempts to strike a difficult balance between its special relationship with the United States, assuming leadership in Western Europe (in competition with France) and maintaining leadership of the Commonwealth and the sterling area, see Hogan (1987) and more recently Entrikin and Agnew (2004).

[5] More recently, Schenk (1994, p. 7), reviewing Blank (1977) in conjunction with Shonfield (1958) and other important contributions to the analysis of Britain's foreign economic policy and sterling (e.g. Strange, 1971), has argued that 'over the past thirty years there has been a broad consensus that the external position of the British economy has inhibited domestic growth and foreign economic policy'. Schenk herself, and other authors she refers to (e.g. Milward), does not entirely agree with this position and emphasises how the Commonwealth and the sterling area were also used as sources of leverage, to be preserved for political and strategic motivations.

and certainly not post-war Britain, could afford. This explains Kahn's lack of sympathy for permanent European economic and financial integration, a view he expressed on several occasions. Similarly, Kahn never fully abandoned the idea that London should retain control over its interest rates, sterling, and monetary and financial autonomy. In this spirit, he called for the full application of the Bretton Woods rules, including the possibility of varying official parities relatively frequently and in a concerted manner when necessary, without idolising those parities. In dealing with these issues, Kahn emphasised the vital role of policymakers in not only setting economic parameters, but also shaping expectations. He argued that effective policy requires strategic flexibility, sometimes involving broad commitments (such as stabilising commodity prices) without rigid targets, and at other times establishing and defending benchmarks (such as official exchange rates), but without turning it into a fetish and always maintaining ample margins of discretion.

7.2 Britain's Post-War Problems: Dollar Shortage, Devaluation, Overspill

After the Second World War, Britain was still a heavily regulated economy. In 1939 the United Kingdom introduced exchange controls that were not lifted until 1979. Imports were limited by quotas and licences. The monetary authorities oversaw all foreign exchange transactions. In 1947 the Exchange Control Act formalised capital controls and divided the world into four main currency areas: the sterling area,[6] the dollar area centred on the United States,[7] the transferable-account countries including West Germany, Italy, Scandinavian and other European countries but also the USSR,[8] and the bilateral countries (including France, Belgium, Argentina,

[6] Sterling area members, including India, Pakistan, Australia, New Zealand and South Africa, all pegged their exchange rates to the pound, 'maintained a common exchange control against the rest of the world while enjoying free current and capital transactions with the UK', and kept their central bank reserves in sterling (Schenk, 1994, p. 8).

[7] Dollar area sterling was held by 'residents of the United States, Canada, the Philippines, Liberia, and thirteen Latin American countries' who were free to exchange their sterling earnings for dollars and vice versa or to use sterling in payment to transferable accounts or to the sterling area (Schenk, 1994, p. 8).

[8] Countries using transferable-account sterling followed specific rules: transfers were freely allowed between transferable sterling accounts and between those and sterling area accounts,

Switzerland, Israel, China and many others),[9] plus a number of unclassified-account countries. Each area had its set of rules regarding convertibility and capital controls. The Bank of England oversaw the exchange rate, and only authorised banks were allowed to deal in foreign currencies, within narrow official bands. The sterling area exchange controls were fairly complex. Their main purpose was to restrict convertibility of sterling into dollars in the context of the post-war dollar shortage (see below) and generally to conserve foreign exchange.

The post-war sterling area system was characterised by three main features.[10] First, participating countries fixed their exchange rates to the British pound. Second, they implemented joint exchange controls in relation to non-member countries, while allowing unrestricted current and capital transactions with the United Kingdom. Third, they held their national reserves in the form of sterling balances, which involved the collective management of foreign exchange earnings. Although many members had historical political or economic ties to Britain, such connections were not essential for inclusion in the system.

Sterling balances refer to the holdings of sterling by foreign governments, central banks and institutions—mainly within the British Empire and Commonwealth—accumulated through trade surpluses or war payments.[11] These balances were typically held in accounts in London and could be used for trade within the sterling area. However, they represented a potential liability for the United Kingdom, as they could be converted into other currencies or used to demand goods and services, threatening Britain's post-war financial stability.[12] At the end of the war,

but transfers from transferable accounts to bilateral or American accounts were prohibited (Schenk, 1994, p. 8).

[9] Transfers among bilateral countries were allowed only by 'administrative transferability', which required the express permission of the Bank of England. Generally, these countries ran balance of payments surpluses with the sterling area and were unwilling to accumulate sterling beyond a certain level, so their sterling transactions were most closely controlled. With the development of the EPU in 1950, administrative transferability for bilateral OEEC countries became virtually automatic (Schenk, 1994, p. 9).

[10] For an introduction to the main features of the sterling area, see A.J.B. (1944) and Gaitskell (1952), and for an introduction to the problem of sterling balances see P.B. (1946). For a detailed analysis of the functioning of the sterling area in the post-war world see Bell (1956) and more recently Schenk (1994, pp. 1–16).

[11] On sterling balances see Schenk (1994, pp. 17–52).

[12] In 1947, Britain implemented sterling convertibility under US pressure as a condition of the Anglo-American Loan. However, the rapid depletion of reserves forced its suspension

these liabilities amounted to five times the level of British foreign exchange reserves, so they could obviously not be liquidated immediately. By the first quarter of 1950, the level of sterling area sterling balances was £2541m, or slightly more than the 1945 level. The central reserves, meanwhile, amounted to only £900m.[13]

The other side of the British (and Western Europe) monetary problem in the second half of the 1940s was the dollar shortage problem. As Eichengreen (2008, p. 96) recalls: 'Post-war Europe had immense unsatisfied demands for foodstuffs, capital goods and other goods produced in the United States, and only limited capacity to produce goods for export; its consolidated trade deficit with the rest of the world rose to $5.8 billion in 1946 and $7.5 billion in 1947'. The resource allocations, and in particular the allocation of gold and dollars, made at the time of the creation of the International Monetary Fund to help countries with balance of payments difficulties fell far short of their actual needs. Britain, which could count on its former colonies and on a productive apparatus in better condition than that of other European nations (starting with Germany), was no exception to this state of affairs.[14]

In the fifteen years following the Second World War, the concept of a global 'dollar shortage' became a central issue in international economic debates (Dellas & Tavlas, 2025). As the war was drawing to an end, some economists, like Gottfried Haberler, downplayed the problem, viewing it as temporary and arguing that the responsibility for correction lay with deficit countries through orthodox fiscal and monetary policies. In contrast, others—such as Seymour Harris, Charles Kindleberger, Balogh, Hicks and Paul Samuelson—considered the dollar shortage a symptom of

within weeks, highlighting sterling's fragility in the post-war period. Amid economic strain and global imbalances, the United Kingdom devalued the pound by 30.5% in 1949 to address persistent trade deficits and speculation. These crises both underscored the structural weaknesses that complicated post-war monetary recovery, namely, sterling balances and a dollar shortage. On the 1949 sterling devaluation, see Naef (2022, pp. 8–34) and the reference cited therein.

[13] As Schenk (1994, p. 17) observes, 'Britain's accumulation of enormous sterling liabilities to the Commonwealth and colonies profoundly affected the post-war configuration of the sterling area system'. Post-war sterling history is a story of progressively phasing out these foreign balances.

[14] In a 1947 memorandum to the US State Department, the British Embassy in Washington detailed the United Kingdom's worsening currency position following the 1945 Anglo-American Financial Agreement and the onset of the global dollar shortage (ref. US State Department historical documents website).

structural imbalance rooted in the US economy, and thus called for more unorthodox, systemic responses. In 1947 Harrod had expressed the opinion that the 'dollar famine' was 'one of the most absurd phrases ever coined', adding that the 'allegation of a "world dollar shortage" is surely one of the most brazen pieces of collective effrontery that has ever been uttered' (Harrod, 1947, pp. 42–43). Six years later he had undergone a change of mind and published a study that affirmed the existence of a dollar shortage the causes of which he sought to diagnose (Harrod, 1953).[15]

In the aftermath of the 1949 sterling devaluation, Kahn also wrote an article published in the Italian journal *Economia Internazionale* (1950a) in which he elaborated on the views of Haberler (1948), Machlup (1950), Ellis (1948) and Graham (1949) on the definition of the concept of dollar shortage, its measurement, and the possibility of eliminating it through a compensatory change in the official exchange rates. In a world slowly returning to multilateral free trade, this essay offers valuable insights into Kahn's cautious stance on the matter.

Displaying his usual confidence in the effectiveness of direct controls and discretionary selective measures, Kahn argues for the need to strengthen trade between countries experiencing a shortage of dollars. This is defined as a situation in which a country is obliged to counter a balance of payments deficit by resorting to one or more of the following remedies: (1) import restrictions; (2) restrictive measures that lower output and increase unemployment, while reducing demand for imports and increasing the supply of exports relative to conditions of full employment; (3) loss of official reserves to countries with a stronger trade position; or (4) emergency borrowing on particularly onerous terms ('distress borrowing').[16] Measures capable of promoting international trade between

[15] Many believed that countries outside the United States consistently spent more than they earned, leading to a chronic lack of dollar and gold reserves needed for trade. The IMF addressed the issue through its 'scarce currency' clause, and leading economists such as Paul Samuelson highlighted it as a major unresolved problem. Charles Kindleberger's 1950 book *The Dollar Shortage* reinforced the idea. However, several economists, including Milton Friedman, Frank Graham, Henry Hazlitt and Raymond Mikesell, rejected the notion, arguing instead that fixed exchange rates, not real scarcity, caused the problem. They maintained that allowing the dollar's value to float would resolve the issue rapidly, casting doubt on the widespread belief in a genuine shortage. In the early post-war years, two views existed as to the nature of the dollar shortage (Blair, 1961, pp. 168–169).

[16] In a footnote, Kahn acknowledges that his definition is similar to one of the three definitions proposed by Machlup (1950), but points out that Machlup's article had been published after Kahn had composed his article (Kahn, 1950a 1972, p. 36, fn. 1).

countries experiencing a dollar shortage, and in parallel limit imports from dollar-countries, would mitigate the scope of the problem and allow these countries to continue participating in international trade under acceptable conditions. Countries subject to discrimination—those with dollar surpluses—must bear this in mind when considering retaliatory measures.

The partial selective restriction of free trade is a necessary condition for achieving both internal and external objectives, such as full employment, investment support and balance of payments equilibrium—at least until the productivity of countries with dollar shortages (starting with the United Kingdom) rises to the level of surplus countries. Kahn (1950a) is sceptical about the possibility of reducing the dollar shortage by devaluation, because of the limited effect of this manoeuvre in the case of low import and export price elasticities and the negative impact of devaluation on the terms of trade of the devaluing country. In addition, devaluation can redistribute income towards export sectors and trigger wage-wage and price-wage spirals that threaten economic stability. This does not mean that devaluation should be ruled out in all cases, but discretionary direct controls on international trade, if properly calibrated, can be a viable and, in Kahn's view, superior alternative.[17]

In Kahn (1951a), direct controls and measures to promote intra-sterling area trade are presented as vital instruments for stabilising the sterling area and supporting Britain's recovery, even if it involves slight discrimination against the dollar area. These measures address post-war constraints, including substantial external debt and mounting sterling balances that London is unable to convert into dollars or gold. Despite limited UK production capacity and intensifying global competition, strengthening trade within the sterling area is considered a way to reduce pressure on the currency and prevent unproductive capital outflows.[18] The effectiveness of promoting trade in the sterling area relies on Britain's supply capacity and the competitiveness of its exports in a recovering global

[17] Another example of Kahn's confidence in direct controls can be seen in his correspondence with Harrod, who favoured the rapid elimination of direct controls as part of the implementation of the Marshall Plan in Great Britain. In a letter exchange in *The Times* at the start of November 1950, Kahn (1950b) defended the continued use of import controls and questioned how Britain would finance additional imports once Marshall Aid ended. Harrod (1950) countered that future trade conditions were uncertain and likely to improve. He contended that maintaining restrictions as a precaution would impede liberalisation, whereas easing them could mitigate domestic inflation and yield broader European benefits.

[18] For an introduction to these problems see Shonfield (1958, pp. 66–159 in particular).

market. Due to production limitations, redirecting exports to the sterling area decreases dollar earnings, highlighting the importance of gradually liberalising trade alongside implementing targeted controls to maximise economic and monetary returns.

The idea of using direct controls on private consumption and international trade as an alternative to devaluation, rather than letting the market decide, reappears in Kahn's reflections on the distinction between those who saw exports and domestic production as influenced by the same determinants (overspill thesis), and those who saw them as an autonomous factor (Kahn, 1951b). Proponents of the first thesis called for government to support domestic consumption by creating the conditions for an overall increase in output which, by reducing fixed unit costs, would enable British entrepreneurs to export at more competitive prices. Advocates of the opposite view, and Kahn with them, argued for the containment of domestic consumption to free up production capacity for exports and force entrepreneurs to conquer new foreign markets and sell there what they could not sell at home.

In the short term the containment of domestic consumption would lead firms to reduce the prices of their products and to try to offset, at least in part, the worsening prospects on the domestic market by stimulating exports. Under full employment and in the presence of bottlenecks, like those prevailing in the United Kingdom in 1951, there is little doubt that curbing domestic demand, and in particular private consumption (e.g. by introducing a sales tax with differentiated rates),[19] will reduce the absorption of goods by the domestic market and lead to an equal increase in exports. The alternative, and apparently less painful, way of achieving the same result as resorting to selective controls and taxation (devaluation) is, in Kahn's eyes, second-best because it is likely to be inflationary and to encourage other countries to devalue in turn.[20] For Kahn, devaluation is the carrot and indirect taxes (and other forms of internal market

[19] Acquisition taxes and sectoral restrictive measures are superior to a general recourse to an increase in direct taxes, both in terms of the ability to discriminate between different situations/taxpayers/goods and in terms of the general depressive effect of an increase in indirect taxes, and because devaluation entails an undue redistribution of income in favour of the export sector, which the tightening of acquisition taxes does not entail.

[20] On the possibility of using devaluation to make foreign markets more attractive without depressing consumption and the domestic market, Kahn remained ambivalent. In 1949, '…it would have been madness not to have devalued in September 1949 and to have relied instead on a drastic curtailment of consumption', but at the same time 'it would also be madness to

restrictions) are the stick. These are two different ways to motivate British entrepreneurs, about whom Kahn does not express a particularly favourable opinion, as on other occasions.

In some ways the stick is more effective than the carrot. The businessman is not always interested in making the maximum profit, least of all with present rates of taxation. The opening up of a hitherto undeveloped export trade makes heavy demands on his energies. It is not only a matter of working up new contacts through intractable channels, but of devising special selling methods and special types of products, and often, if real and permanent success is to be achieved, of organising the supply of spare parts and servicing facilities. Although the calculation, which must, of course, allow adequately for the expenses and risks involved, may point to a financial advantage to be secured by diverting to overseas markets, all too often mental inertia will determine the issue the other way. But this psychological barrier to enterprise, which is not easily overcome by the lure of additional profit, is far less effective when it is a question of keeping the businessman's works occupied and his labour force employed. Faced with the prospect of loss of trade, involving not merely a decline of profits but a reduction of output, the businessman will be much more ready to seek alternative outlets (Kahn, 1951b, p. 283).

In the longer term, the picture changes. The curtailment of private consumption and the consequent persistent depression of the domestic market, motivated by the need to free up resources for exports, can have a threefold negative effect on exports: (1) if it forces individual firms or entire industries to close (in which case exports disappear), (2) if it distracts from the need to adapt production to the needs of the foreign market, and (3) if it reduces the incentives for product innovation, since it is more difficult to use the domestic market as a reserve market. Therefore, even the policy of restraining domestic demand should be used with restraint.

In 1952, on the occasion of a lecture delivered at the Fifth International Banking Summer School at Christ Church (University of Oxford),[21] Kahn

carry the devaluation so far as to make the curtailment of consumption unnecessary' (1951a, p. 282).

[21] The International Banking Summer School (IBSS), established in 1948, was an annual event aimed at fostering the study of major developments in banking. During the 1950s the IBSS was notably held at Christ Church, Oxford University. These sessions featured a series of lectures and discussions on topics pertinent to international banking and foreign trade. The 1952 session included lectures compiled in the publication *Banking and Foreign Trade*,

returned to the qualifying points of his vision of international economic problems, the reasons for maintaining or at least reactivating direct import controls, and the need to take into account the heterogeneity among nations and among the objectives that guide their actions (Kahn, 1952).

Until 1931, free trade was closely linked to confidence in the gold standard. While this supported multilateral trade, it also forced deficit countries to make painful deflationary adjustments. The Bretton Woods system emerged as a compromise, favouring fixed but adjustable exchange rates to enable freer trade without requiring such sacrifices, particularly for countries with weak external balances. Kahn argued that, while free trade promised efficiency, its universal application overlooked legitimate reasons for maintaining trade barriers, such as protecting vulnerable industries, addressing inequality and managing external shocks. He criticised the moralistic and retaliatory arguments for liberalisation, noting that they lacked credibility in poorer nations and failed to account for the uneven distribution of gains and losses.

Trade liberalisation often risked worsening terms of trade, particularly for large economies whose actions affected world prices, making protectionism a rational choice in some cases. Kahn proposed a more nuanced, context-sensitive approach involving pairing tariff reductions with currency devaluations. However, these measures had complex effects, including reduced government revenue and potential consumer harm. Furthermore, discriminatory trade practices, though criticised, had facilitated trade growth in ways that full convertibility and floating rates might not have. Consequently, unilateral liberalisation remained implausible; only coordinated multilateral action, sensitive to structural imbalances and the risks of liberalisation, could ensure that free trade was genuinely beneficial and sustainable.

Commenting on these conclusions, Gibson (1954) is ambivalent, highlighting an aspect that recurs in Kahn's approach to direct controls and economic policy measures in general: the lack of clear and unambiguous indications of the limits within which the proposed measures should be applied. In fact, the absence of guidelines lamented by Gibson can be interpreted as reflecting Kahn's belief that economic policy authorities should always retain as much discretion as possible in order to respond in the best way to changing circumstances.

which addressed issues such as commercial policy and the dynamics of international trade (Gibson, 1954).

In the 1950s, political and social consensus in Britain oscillated between two extremes. On the one hand, there was an urgent need to support exports and contain balance of payments imbalances, and a certain reluctance towards full trade liberalisation. On the other hand, there was growing confidence in widespread prosperity and a desire to increase private consumption after years of austerity, which radically changed the British way of life. Consequently, international trade was perceived as an essential lever of economic policy, while consumption became a symbol of modernity and social advancement. Regarding the advisability of rapidly removing restrictions on private consumption, Kahn recommended caution. Priority should be given to private investment and increasing productive capacity. Only then would it be possible to make the British economy more competitive and increase exports without compromising domestic demand.

These reflections must be considered in light of the complex and frequently conflicting challenges that the Labour government faced between 1948 and 1951. Domestically, the government was engaged in an ambitious project of national reconstruction, centred on modernising British manufacturing, enhancing industrial productivity and establishing the welfare state through initiatives like the establishment of the National Health Service and the expansion of social security. On the international stage, Britain had to perform a delicate balancing act. It aimed to maintain a central role within the Commonwealth, particularly as custodian of the substantial sterling balances amassed by its colonies and dominions during the war. This placed constraints on British economic sovereignty. At the same time, the government sought to preserve and strengthen its 'special relationship' with the United States, viewing it as a source of economic support and a geopolitical ally in the emerging Cold War order. Alongside these efforts, Britain was also committed to the economic integration of Western Europe, using Marshall Plan aid to fund domestic recovery and shape the emerging European economic architecture. Balancing these overlapping priorities—Commonwealth obligations, Atlantic ties and European commitments—proved to be a major strategic challenge, especially as Britain's global position weakened and its economic vulnerabilities became more apparent.[22]

[22] On this see Hogan (1987) and Pelling (1988) among many others.

7.3 Perspectives on the Marshall Plan and European Monetary and Economic Integration

On 5 June 1947, US Secretary of State George C. Marshall announced the broad outlines of a US government aid plan for war-ravaged European countries. On the basis of a unified plan for the economic reconstruction of Western Europe presented by a committee representing sixteen European countries, the US Congress authorised the establishment of the European Recovery Programme (ERP), which became law on 3 April 1948. The Marshall Plan provided substantial financial assistance to European countries, with the aim of stabilising their economies, stimulating production, employment and the resumption of international trade, promoting the gradual return to convertibility of European currencies, and providing an economic and financial bulwark in Europe against the spread of Communism.[23]

The Economic Cooperation Administration, a specially created agency, distributed some $13 billion in economic aid between 1948 and 1952, partly in the form of grants and partly in the form of loans. As Eichengreen (2008, p. 96) observes, comparing the amounts of the Marshall Plan with the financial support provided under the newly established International Monetary Fund: 'This was more than four times the drawing rights established on Europe's behalf and more than six times the maximum US obligation under the Articles of Agreement'. The dollar shortage, although alleviated by the launch of the Marshall Plan, had not been eliminated. In the first half of 1950, the US current account surplus was still $3 billion a year. It was by no means clear that other countries, with limited reserves and substantial deficits, would be able to complete the transition to convertibility within two years, as envisaged in the US programme. Intra-European trade was still stifled by a number of restrictions on current account transactions. In this context, part of the Marshall Plan funds was used to set up the European Payments Union (EPU).

The EPU, in operation from 1950 until 1958, aimed to restore the convertibility of current accounts between its members in line with the

[23] After the withdrawal of the Eastern European countries occupied or under the influence of the Soviet Union, the list of participants in the Marshall Plan included Austria, Belgium, Denmark, France, Greece, Iceland, Ireland, Italy, Luxembourg, the Netherlands, Norway, Portugal, Sweden, Switzerland, Turkey, the United Kingdom and West Germany. The United Kingdom was the main beneficiary of the Marshall Plan (or European Recovery Plan, ERP). For a recent political history of the Marshall Plan see Steil (2018).

Bretton Woods principles.[24] EPU members agreed to apply trade restrictions in a fair manner and to reduce them progressively, first by 50%, then by 60% and finally by 75%. In particular, the EPU was based on the principle of multilateral clearing for intra-European trade balances. Before the EPU, most trade in Europe was settled bilaterally: each country had to settle its trade balance individually, which usually required scarce dollar reserves. The EPU centralised this process with the aim of reducing the problems caused by dollar shortages and stimulating intra-European trade and economic integration. Member countries submitted data on their imports and exports with other member states.

At the end of each month the EPU calculated a net position (surplus or deficit) for each country. These imbalances were partially offset at the multilateral level, which meant that one country's deficit could be offset by another's surplus, reducing the need for hard currency. Only net imbalances were required to be settled, and even these were partly financed through credit mechanisms within the EPU, rather than requiring immediate payments in dollars or gold. The EPU offered automatic credit lines to deficit countries, allowing them to run temporary trade deficits within agreed limits. These credit lines were backed by ERP funds, which made the system more credible and stable. This gave countries time to adjust their economies without having to impose trade restrictions or devalue their currencies. At the time of its dissolution, loans of almost $3 billion remained outstanding, about 50% more than the original quotas.

Projects for the organisation of an intra-European multilateral clearing system had been discussed since the start of the Marshall Plan (see Hirschman, 1951). In this context, Kahn proposed the creation of an intra-European discount system (Kahn, 1949), a regional version of the Keynes plan presented at Bretton Woods according to Kregel (2017a). Kahn's plan was based on a consideration of the difference between the transferability and convertibility of drawing rights on ERP funds. Transferability referred to the ability of a country holding a certain amount of drawing rights on ERP funds to transfer part of them to another country participating in the Marshall Plan to offset a bilateral trade deficit with

[24] On the European Payments Union in the context of the evolution of international monetary institutions see Amato and Fantacci (2012, pp. 110–120). See also Eichengreen (2008, 104–107) for a discussion of how the EPU departed from the Bretton Woods model and challenged its principles and institutions. For a detailed history of the EPU, with a reference to Kahn as discussed below, see Kaplan and Schleiminger (1989).

that country. Convertibility allowed creditor nations to demand gold and convertible currencies (dollars) from debtor nations, with the risk of putting them into difficulty and forcing them to adopt restrictive measures to reduce imports or devalue their currency.

To avoid this risk and to promote the recovery of international trade, Kahn argued that it was necessary to encourage transferability as much as possible, while limiting convertibility, given the small size of European countries' currency reserves. In order to achieve this objective, he proposed the creation of a multilateral compensation mechanism which would allow participating countries to settle their credit and debit positions as far as possible in a definitive and mutually satisfactory manner. To this end, the proposal provided for the settlement in convertible currency (or gold) of the net balance recorded at the end of each six-month period. However, this settlement would not be at parity, but on the basis of a European discount in dollars, to be determined and reviewed every six months through a process of trial and error.

> This discount, the same of course for all the European currencies involved, I shall call the "European Discount." It would be altered from period to period according to need, but it would be fixed at the beginning of each settlement period (or, perhaps better, a couple of months before) for the whole of that period, so that the authorities of each country could operate their economies with full knowledge of the value of intra-European exports, and of the cost of intra-European imports, passing between their own country and the other participants. The European Discount would not of course in any way apply to the rates of exchange at which transactions were effected between traders in the various countries. It would apply only to the settlement of net balances arising from intra-European trade. And such settlement would be definitive—the liquidation in dollars, on the basis of the Discount, would be complete. (Kahn, 1949, p. 297)

The principal advantages of this scheme were associated with the re-establishment of the principle of multilateral clearing. It preserved the opportunity for countries to earn dollars through exports, particularly within the dollar area, and facilitated the resumption of normal economic relations between states—an important step towards eventual full convertibility. Additionally, the scheme supported the integration of new nations into the system, helped to overcome the limitations of bilateral settlements between creditor and debtor countries, and fostered an implicit preference for European goods, which were generally less expensive than their

American counterparts. At the same time, it introduced a restraint on excessive import growth, which still required financing.

Kahn's proposed scheme thus offered a rational, flexible and selective solution to imbalances within the intra-European payment system, providing an alternative to unilateral devaluation by deficit countries. Under this scheme, governments and monetary authorities were responsible for determining the size of the discount and managing the settlement of net balances. Creditor nations, receiving a lower dollar amount than they would have in the absence of the European discount, were required to obtain the difference from their national treasuries in order to settle the actual balance. This mechanism had a restrictive effect on their domestic economies. Conversely, debtor nations, paying a reduced dollar amount under the European rebate, experienced a corresponding budget surplus, thereby diminishing the need for additional restrictive fiscal measures.[25]

In 1950, a second article was published before the details of the EPU had been finalised. This gave Kahn the opportunity to denounce what he perceived as fundamental flaws in the EPU project compared to his own scheme (Kahn, 1950c).[26] His first objection concerned the lack of symmetry in the treatment of debtor nations in relation to creditor nations, particularly given that the EPU anticipated that a persistent deficit position would require increasing compensation in gold (Kahn, 1950c, pp. 306–307). The second criticism concerned the excessive emphasis placed by the EPU on balancing creditor and debtor positions on a regional rather than an international basis, together with the imposition of a rigid and non-extendable ceiling on the total amount of resources available to indebted countries.

> My main quarrel with the E.P.U. arises from the concept of "creditor" and of "debtor" countries. A "creditor" country is a country which has a favourable balance of payments *with the other members* [in the original], even though its over-all balance is adverse. A "debtor" country has an unfavourable balance with other members, but might conceivably have an over-all favourable balance. The philosophy of the E.P.U. is based on the view that

[25] A recent revisiting of Kahn's discount scheme is by Kregel (2017b), who applies it to the analysis of financial imbalances within the euro area. This analysis is taken up by Carabelli (2021, p. 146) in the context of a discussion of the relevance of Keynes's thought to the analysis of global financial imbalances.

[26] Kahn's article was written in August, while the EPU was signed in September 1950 with retroactive effect to July.

> there is something wrong—in the sense of departure from equilibrium—in a country being either in a "creditor" or in a "debtor" position with the rest of Western Europe. The latitude which the Union will provide in either direction is represented by an aggregate lump sum, the amount of which is fixed irrespective of the period of time over which the Union has operated. If this ceiling had been conceded as an annual rate, the amounts of the possible credits and debits being renewed year by year, much of my objection would have disappeared, since a "departure from equilibrium" in the E.P.U. sense could then be financed under conditions which could remain steady through time. But the ceiling is a cumulative aggregate and not an annual rate. Once the ceiling has been reached the Union can offer no further help. (Ibid., p. 307)

In contrast to the EPU approach, Kahn's discount scheme, meant to be permanent and extended worldwide (and not just to Western Europe) and not tied to a pre-determined amount of ERP funds, emphasised the definitive settlement of creditor balances and the symmetrical treatment of creditor and debtor positions without any implicit bias in favour of the creditor countries as was the case with the EPU.[27] The presence of this bias, together with the other features of the EPU, risked discouraging the recovery of intra-European trade. The widening of creditor/debtor positions would lead to the exhaustion of EPU-guaranteed credit lines, necessitating the settlement of balances in gold. This would make debtor/creditor nations more cautious about importing and exporting than they would otherwise be. Conversely, countries with a balanced trade would demand more imports than they would otherwise, creating inflationary conditions in exporting European countries and reducing exports to the dollar area. Some countries might find themselves pushed into an extreme creditor/debtor status unintentionally.

As with Keynes's proposal for an International Clearing Union, Kahn's discount scheme, although based on the objective of promoting the gradual restoration of free trade and convertibility and providing a permanent structure for the realistic and joint reconciliation of the interests of creditor and debtor countries, without necessarily depending on US support, did not find favour with the British government. During the negotiations which led to the creation of the EPU, as Hirschman (1951, pp. 50–52) recalls, the Chancellor, Sir Stafford Cripps, refused to accept a scheme which would replace the existing bilateral arrangements, which also

[27] On this implicit bias see Eichengreen and Braga de Macedo (2001).

included significant restrictions on the transferability of sterling and its convertibility into gold. Instead, he favoured a system that would operate only after bilateral credit lines had been exhausted, thus overlapping with the bilateral arrangements as a 'lender of last resort'. At the same time, Sir Stafford Creeps stated that the United Kingdom could not agree to limit its action on quantitative trade restrictions.

Kahn's proposal for the system was therefore at odds with the first instance, though not necessarily with the second, given Kahn's views on the usefulness of direct controls. Conversely, there is no evidence that Kahn exerted any particular pressure to promote his ideas on how to regulate intra-European payments, as was so typical of him. Furthermore, given his challenging experience with the ITO group between 1947 and 1948, it is unlikely that Kahn had much support or influence within the British government at that time.[28]

This does not mean that Kahn lost interest in the question of the reorganisation of the European economic area, in connection with proposals to create a European Free Trade Area (EFTA).[29] This proposal took shape in the year following the 1956 Suez crisis, against the background of Britain's growing difficulties in competing with Germany as a manufacturing power and the other macroeconomic problems (low investment, low productivity growth, inflationary tensions). The underlying tension between loyalty to the Commonwealth (and the special relationship with the United States) and the desire to remain associated with (and, as far as possible, to govern) the process of European economic integration had influenced the British position since the negotiations for the Marshall Plan and then the EPU (Hogan, 1987). Overall, Britain had managed to maintain special treatment both in the EPU and in its relations with the United States, while deciding not to join the European Coal and Steel Community and continuing to refuse to subordinate its policy choices to the will of any supranational body, whether European or international.

[28] The only evidence of a potential influence can be found in the correspondence between Robert Hall and James Meade, in which Hall mentions having discussed the United Kingdom's economic situation with Kahn in 1951, when Gaitskell was Chancellor of the Exchequer. I am grateful to Susan Howson for drawing my attention to this.

[29] On the political context in which the Free Trade Area proposal took shape, see Young (1993), among others. On the economic problems associated with this proposal from Britain's point of view and beyond the essays included in the Symposium, see Meade (1957), with its focus on financial issues and the possibility of reconciling full employment and external equilibrium.

Echoes of these problems can be found in the Symposium, published in the Bulletin of the Oxford Institute of Statistics in 1957, in which Kahn participated with J. Black (Magdalen College, Oxford), author of the introductory essay with statistics and data on Britain's economic position compared to European countries, the United States and the Commonwealth, and the commentators including Harry Johnson (Manchester University), Thomas Balogh (Balliol College, Oxford), Roy Harrod (Christ Church, Oxford), J.R. Sargent (Worcester College, Oxford) and David Worswick (Magdalen College, Oxford), who was responsible for the conclusions of the Symposium.[30] The Symposium highlighted divergent views on the EFTA, with Kahn and Balogh standing on the same side, as had been the case in the Symposium on monetary policy in 1952.[31] While on that occasion Kahn and Balogh shared the view that restrictive monetary policy to combat inflation had negative aspects, which most of the other participants at the symposium downplayed, here the issue was the possibility of maintaining direct discretionary controls on imports as an alternative to gradual and irreversible liberalisation of international trade.

Harrod cautiously supported free trade but advocated the implementation of stabilising mechanisms such as automatic credits to manage fluctuations in the balance of payments. Johnson, by contrast, argued that national economies possessed untapped potential for economies of scale and questioned the immediate benefits of tariff removal. He called for careful, quantitative analysis before any major liberalisation. Balogh, taking a more sceptical stance, warned of potential economic imbalances, expressing concern that Germany's position as a creditor and its superior productivity could undermine weaker economies. He therefore emphasised the need for equitable development mechanisms to accompany integration. Sargent proposed practical innovations, such as the strategic use of stockpiles to address short-term fluctuations, and underlined the importance of distinguishing between structural and cyclical challenges in economic management. These varied contributions collectively illustrated the complexity of the prospective Free Trade Area (FTA) and the multifaceted nature of its potential impacts.

Kahn's assessment of Britain's potential membership in the FTA reflected both his rejection of an ideologically rigid commitment to free

[30] The Symposium was republished in Worswick (1960).

[31] See above Sect. 4.7.

trade and his confidence in the possibility of managing international economic relations in a way that preserved national autonomy. This led him to adopt a stance that fluctuated between cautious endorsement and reserved scepticism. One source of this ambivalence lay in his recognition that 'the tide [had] turned strongly against closer affiliation with the Commonwealth and Sterling Area countries', and that 'in the next few years economic statesmanship [was] likely to be severely strained by the wholly negative task of curbing the rate of utilisation of Sterling balances held within the Sterling Area' (Kahn, 1957, p. 63). In the light of such constraints, Kahn viewed European economic integration as a pragmatic, albeit second-best, alternative. He was particularly attentive to the role of institutions such as the Organisation for European Economic Co-operation (OEEC), which he believed offered promising mechanisms for the centralised coordination of import controls—an element he deemed essential for reconciling full employment with external balance. For such coordination to be viable, however, the cautious realism of critics such as Balogh would need to temper the support of advocates like Harrod.

A further advantage deriving from closer cooperation with Western Europe concerned the possibility of managing exchange rate adjustments in a more orderly and coordinated manner, particularly in response to prolonged and significant balance of payments imbalances. Khan's thinking on this issue appeared to have evolved over time. During the early 1950s, especially in the context of debates following the 1949 devaluation, he had been wary of advocating further exchange rate changes, though he did not dismiss the possibility outright. By the time of the 1957 symposium, however, his position had softened. Whether this shift reflected growing doubts about the efficacy of direct controls or increasing confidence in the responsiveness of trade flows to relative price changes remains open to interpretation.

On the other hand, Kahn continued to insist on the importance of preserving a degree of national policy autonomy—particularly in sensitive areas such as the regulation of working hours or wage policy. He maintained that such matters must reflect domestic conditions and values, warning against what he described as the 'stupidity' of attempting to impose absolute harmonisation through supranational legislation. For Kahn, the success of economic integration hinged not only on coordination but also on a commitment to institutional flexibility and respect for national diversity. The same approach, as the following section shows, characterised Kahn's analysis of buffer stocks as a means to stabilise commodity prices.

7.4 Buffer Stocks, Commodity Prices and Speculation

Kahn's approach to the analysis of international economic problems finds an important application in his work as an advisor to the Food and Agriculture Organization (FAO) on the problem of stabilising commodity prices through the use of buffer stocks.[32] This part of Kahn's work has been reconstructed in full by Rosselli (2017),[33] an essay from which this section draws extensively. Thinking about the role of buffer stocks in commodity stabilisation allowed Kahn to combine his ideas about investor psychology and the benefits of setting limits to laissez faire with some ideas that Keynes had formulated in the interwar years and more systematically at the Bretton Woods Conference (Fantacci, 2017).

During the interwar years Keynes turned his attention to the problem of commodity price volatility, attributing it to the absence of mechanisms for storing surplus stocks and to the specific characteristics of raw materials and foodstuffs that made them fundamentally volatile. Unlike financial assets, commodities are unappealing to private investors because they generate no returns and come with significant storage costs. To address insufficient private storage and create a buffer to stabilise production, supply, consumption and demand, Keynes advocated for publicly managed commodity buffer stocks under the oversight of a transnational organisation. Between 1942 and 1944 his ideas for a Commodity Control system underwent extensive discussion and multiple revisions, only to be abandoned in the end.[34]

[32] The term 'buffer stock' refers to a large supply of a commodity, either agricultural or mining, which is bought and stored when there is a surplus in the international market and sold when there is a shortage, in order to stabilise its price and quantity.

[33] On Kahn and buffer stocks, see also Palma (1994), whose reconstruction, however, 'is flawed by an incorrect understanding of the chronological order in which it was produced' (Rosselli, 2017, p. 484).

[34] In recent years Keynes's ideas on speculation in financial and commodity markets and the role of buffer stocks in mitigating commodity price volatility have been the subject of intense research by a group of Italian scholars. Important contributions to this line of research include Fantacci et al. (2010), Fantacci et al. (2011), Marcuzzo (2012) and Paesani and Rosselli (2014). See also Mini (1996) and Ussher (2016).

In the early 1950s the question arose as to how international commodity markets could be organised in such a way as to support producer countries, many of which were less developed emerging economies undergoing development processes, while at the same time ensuring demand from developed countries. The FAO, established after the 1943 Hot Springs Conference, sought to stabilise primary product prices to support developing countries and ensure food security. However, lacking political power, its major post-war projects, like the World Food Board and International Commodity Clearing House, failed. By the 1950s the FAO had shifted to an advisory role, monitoring commodity agreements often criticised for prioritising surplus allocation and producer interests over price stability and food shortages.

In this context, Gerda Blau,[35] chief of the Commodities branch of the Economic division of the FAO, contacted Kahn, whom she knew from her Cambridge days, and asked him to research buffer stocks. Kahn spent nearly nine years, between 1952 and 1961, working on a book about the fluctuations in commodity prices of primary products, their causes and consequences, and how to curb them, but the book was never published.[36] In this work, Kahn advocated for the creation of buffer stocks for each commodity, managed by a supranational authority with suitable financial backing to buy when prices were low and sell when they were high.

The story of Kahn's unpublished book on buffer stocks can be summarised following Rosselli (2017). In 1952 Blau persuaded Kahn, who had gained considerable experience in commodities during the war years,

[35] On Gerda Blau see Appendix C and FAO website https://www.fao.org/4/p4228e/P4228E12.htm.

[36] In Kahn's archives there is a wealth of material on buffer stocks and related subjects. RFK/2/10 contains drafts of chapters I–III and V of 'Buffer stocks', made up of autograph manuscript and copy typescript, mostly in the hand of J.V. Robinson. RFK2/11 contains some draft chapters headed 'for cutting up', with an article on buffer stocks by B. Swerling for the *Economic Journal*, Dec. 1953, and a covering note from Roy Harrod, 29 Oct. 1953. RFK/2/12 contains typescripts comprising: (1) 'short version', (2) 'long version'; (3) contents page and chapters III–VI. RFK/2/13 contains research correspondence and notes. RFK/2/14 includes FAO publications, 1950s; lecture notes by RFK, 1956; undated autograph manuscript notes by J.V. Robinson; autograph letters signed from St Clare Grondona, 1958–9; and comments by J.E. Meade on the manuscript, 26 May 1958. RFK/2/19 includes two reports on 'The buffer stock under the International Tin Agreement' and 'Multilateral options for sugar', written by Kahn for the United Nations, September 1959. The correspondence with Gerda Blau is in RFK/13/13. References to Gerda Blau can also be found in the correspondence between Kahn and Joan Robinson, RFK/13/90/5–6.

to write a report on the subject. The project for a monograph under Kahn's name was initiated in 1952 but encountered delays due to academic commitments and difficulties in accessing relevant documentation. Blau provided substantial support, though by 1953 disagreements emerged regarding agricultural market intervention policies, particularly the use of buffer stocks. Despite the submission of revised chapters by 1954, shifting international political conditions reduced the FAO's interest. Kahn resumed work in 1956 at Cambridge, with additional input from Joan Robinson, but the prospects for publication had significantly diminished.[37]

Aside from the troubled history of the buffer stock book, the qualifying points that Kahn discusses concern the analysis of the causes and consequences of commodity price volatility, the role of speculation in mitigating or exacerbating it, and the technique of buffer stock management. Regarding the causes of commodity price volatility, Kahn, echoing Keynes (1938), argues that the market for primary products fails to reach stable equilibrium, causing a persistent mismatch between supply and demand. Kahn explains that low elasticities in supply and demand lead to significant price fluctuations. Primary commodities have inelastic demand due to their small share in final goods' costs, and producers face inelastic supply due to high specialisation.

While this explains short-term fluctuations, Kahn adds that expectations under uncertainty prevent prices from stabilising. High prices lead to overinvestment, while low prices cause neglect, resulting in slow recovery when demand picks up, as illustrated by the 'cobweb' effect. Private speculation can help stabilise prices by moving commodities from periods of abundance to scarcity, but several factors hinder its effectiveness. High storage costs, risk, and borrowing expenses prevent speculators from providing the necessary stabilising service, particularly during times of depression. Moreover, speculators often face limited borrowed funds, making them cautious about investing heavily in a single commodity. Additionally, during price drops they become reluctant to buy, as the price may fall further due to large stock sell-offs. Futures markets exacerbate this, increasing negative market sentiment.

Kahn believes that buffer stocks can solve these problems and benefit producing and consuming countries alike. Unlike quotas, which favour producers at the expense of consumers by restricting supply artificially, the

[37] Full details can be found in Rosselli (2017).

buffer stock system stabilises prices. It helps producers avoid catastrophic losses in the event of excess supply while preventing excessive price fluctuations that harm consumers. In this way, buffer stocks facilitate the progressive expansion of production capacity for the mutual benefit of producers and consumers.

Although Kahn's arguments were not entirely novel from a theoretical standpoint, his views on managing buffer stocks certainly were. Kahn recognises the challenges of operating in a market with both individual buyers and speculators. Speculators, relying on the buffer stock to defend a price floor, may profit from stabilisation without contributing to its costs. Conversely, if speculators expect the floor to drop, they will offload stocks, forcing the buffer stock to absorb losses or abandon price stability. To reconcile price stability with limited resources, Kahn proposes setting wide-ranging indicative dealing prices, managed by expert judgement rather than automatic rules or political bargaining. In the same vein he advocates strategic interventions: delaying purchases to allow markets to self-correct and selling early during price rises to moderate increases and generate small profits. This approach minimises resource use while managing market expectations.

Unpredictability in price adjustments prevents the market from accurately forecasting buffer stock actions. Unexpected interventions discourage speculative certainty and reinforce the buffer stock's stabilising role. Kahn argues that stability arises paradoxically from discretionary and seemingly arbitrary behaviour, which shapes both the content and confidence of market expectations. Drawing parallels to his liquidity preference theory, Kahn noted similarities between commodity and financial markets, where both professional speculators and less informed participants shape price movements. In both cases, uncertainty about the direction in which prices will move can stabilise them to the extent that operators prefer to maintain their positions, limiting purchases and sales, and thus avoiding sharp market fluctuations. In the case of buffer stocks, administrators can deliberately create this uncertainty. At the same time, the mere existence of these stocks and the knowledge that they will stabilise the market should reassure private operators, thereby helping to stabilise commodity prices.

Despite the setback in publishing his book on buffer stocks, Kahn remained interested in the subject. In 1958 he corresponded with James Meade, who had reviewed parts of Kahn's manuscript on buffer stocks and expressed hope for its eventual publication. In a letter of 26 May 1958,

Meade thanked Kahn for sending him the manuscript on buffer stocks.[38] In this letter Meade commented on the limitations he saw in Kahn's proposal, while agreeing with him that 'Harrodry and Grondonary should be abandoned in favour of less ambitious projects, managed on a discretionary basis, so that they enter the market (finally for the most part) only rather late in the downturn, and with the intention of covering their costs and, if possible, building up a substantial reserve fund'.

The reference is to the proposal for the creation of a buffer system put forward by L. St Clare Grondona in a book entitled *Utilising World Abundance* (1958), with a preface by Harrod and Graham Hutton. The essence of Grondona's proposal was the idea of setting an initial 'index' price for a commodity, calculated based on a prescribed formula, typically slightly below the prevailing market price. An upper selling price and a lower buying price are then set at 10% above and below this 'index' price. The managing authority would have unlimited borrowing capacity to purchase the commodity at the lower buying price and sell it at the upper selling price, provided it has stock. The 'index' price, along with the buying and selling prices, would automatically adjust on a sliding scale: decreasing when the authority's buffer stock increases due to more purchases, increasing when the buffer stock diminishes as a result of resales. Additionally, if the authority holds no stock and the market price remains above its buying price for an extended period and by a significant margin, the 'index' price would automatically rise under a formula. Meade notes how the Grondona proposal has the merit of providing a strong countercyclical impulse in general downturns. Hence the call for Kahn to clarify that his buffer stock proposal, unlike Grondona's, is primarily aimed at stabilising commodity prices and not economic activity in general.

[38] Most of Meade's comments relate to Chapter VI of Kahn's manuscript (short version). The location of the letter in Meade's archive is MEADE/4/8. In the same file there are a number of letters from Meade to St Clare Grondona (see below) which are relevant to the subject discussed here. See also Meade (1958, 1964). Susan Howson recalls that Meade was particularly interested in commodity schemes in the summer of 1958 (personal communication to the author, 15 July 2024). This was because he had been asked to work with Haberler and Tinbergen on a report on the trade of developing countries, which had been commissioned by the authorities in charge of the General Agreement on Tariffs and Trade (GATT). Meade wrote the section of the report on commodity schemes, which reviewers noted reflected his in-depth knowledge—he had drafted the 1949 International Wheat Agreement in 1947. There was also some correspondence between Kahn and Meade at the end of 1957/beginning of 1958 regarding a letter Meade had written to *The Times* concerning commodity prices.

The second point raised by Meade concerns the suggestion to stress more that 'the advantage of buffer stocks over restriction schemes is that they can be operated efficiently by a limited number of countries, whether producing or consuming, or indeed by a single country. Their effectiveness will, of course, be greater the more countries take part'. Meade is more sceptical than Kahn about the possibility of organising a buffer stock system on a supranational basis, and even more sceptical about the possible participation of the United States. Hence the invitation to discuss 'how much one might hope to get out of purely national schemes and of the various implications of such national stocks'. Finally, Meade's main objection concerns the so-called neutrality principle, the idea that the operations of the buffer stock should not have a significant impact on the balance of payments of the countries in which the buffer stock operates. Meade urges Kahn to reconsider this idea and to distinguish more clearly between the case where the objective of the financing of the buffer stock itself is not to change the balance of payments from what it would have been in the absence of the buffer stock, and the case where the objective of the financing of the buffer stock itself is to counteract (in whole or in part) the change in the balance of payments caused by the shock that the buffer stock is intended to neutralise.

In 1959 Kahn was also in contact with Leo St Clare Grondona and mentioned his intention to revisit his project that summer. However, instead of continuing with the book, Kahn focused on individual commodity schemes, applying his ideas to specific cases. He worked with the International Sugar Council and wrote a report advocating for a buffer stock scheme for sugar, and also completed a report on the International Tin Agreement. Possible further evidence of Kahn's involvement in related commodity stabilisation issues is provided by Nelson (2009) in his reconstruction of Milton Friedman's activities in the United Kingdom. In 1954 Kahn had a debate with Milton Friedman and Frank Paish on the 'Stabilization of Commodity' prices on the radio.

> The radio program was entitled 'Stabilization of Commodity Prices,' and probably covered the general subject of inflation rather than commodity prices narrowly interpreted. The participants were Friedman, Kahn, and the London School of Economics' Frank Paish. The three participants happened to represent the three major positions that emerged in the economics profession in the debates over the following decades. Friedman took a monetary view of inflation and rejected any long-run unemployment/inflation

trade-off; Kahn took the cost-push line; and Paish, the view that inflation responded to aggregate demand in a manner that implied a permanent inflation/unemployment trade-off. (Nelson, 2009, p. 51)

In Kahn's ideas on buffer stocks we find an important element of continuity with his general view of the economy and economic policy. In this view, what happens in reality as a result of the interaction between different groups of economic agents depends on the combination of objective and subjective elements. The objective elements include the institutions within which economic agents operate and the rules that condition their choices. The subjective elements, are associated with the opinions and expectations that guide the decisions of economic agents in an environment characterised by risk and uncertainty.

On this basis, the policymaker, be it the buffer stock manager, the central bank or the Treasury, must design (and manage) institutions in such a way as to give economic agents as much freedom as possible, consistent with the composition of the various interests at stake in the general interest. To do so, the policymaker must provide general indications of his intentions without tying his hands too tightly with publicly declared rules or numerical targets. Sometimes meeting the policymaker's goals may require all-out action and direct control; sometimes it may require discreet and flexible action. In any case, this view is based on the profoundly Keynesian idea that the policymaker has more and better information than private economic agents and a greater capacity to manoeuvre his instruments in the overriding interest of the community he is called upon to govern. As we shall see, Kahn remained committed to this vision of economic policy, which I will attempt to explain, even when it became the subject of increasingly intense criticism from monetarists, starting in the 1960s.

7.5 UNCTAD

In the course of the years 1965–1969 Kahn served as a member of four groups of experts for the United Nations Conference on Trade and development (UNCTAD). The UNCTAD was established in 1964 to address global economic disparities and promote equitable trade and development for the Global South. It emerged as a platform for developing countries to advocate for reforms in international trade and finance. UNCTAD shared (and shares) strong ties with the Food and Agriculture Organization

(FAO), particularly on issues like commodity markets and food security. Drawing on the FAO's expertise in agricultural development and price stabilisation, UNCTAD expanded its focus to include broader trade and development concerns, with a focus on food security, rural development and commodity market volatility.

The intellectual history of UNCTAD (2004) helps to define the context in which the collaboration between Kahn and the newly established institution took shape. In 1963 the IMF Compensatory Financing Facility (CFF), established in part due to UN advocacy, aimed to provide short-term, quickly disbursable loans to commodity-exporting developing countries to offset temporary export-earning shortfalls caused by volatile commodity prices. By isolating fluctuations in the current account beyond a country's control, the CFF maintained conditionality while offering relatively low conditionality for developing nations, making it highly valued. The UNCTAD secretariat consistently pushed for greater accessibility to the CFF for these countries. In parallel, to address the 'Triffin Dilemma' [39]—the tension between the global need for US dollar liquidity and confidence in the currency—Professors Hart, Kaldor and Tinbergen proposed at UNCTAD I (1964) a scheme for an international commodity reserve currency.

UNCTAD I adopted several recommendations concerning the international monetary system, including proposals to expand the IMF's compensatory financing allocation from 25% to 50% of a member country's quota and to examine supplementary financing measures to align monetary reforms with the needs of developing nations. Another recommendation emphasised studying payments arrangements to address systemic issues. To further these goals, the UNCTAD Secretary-General convened an expert group led by the economist Gamani Corea,[40] later UNCTAD's third Secretary-General, to assess how developing countries might be impacted by the G-10's plans to create additional international reserve assets. The expert group, chaired by Gamani Corea, included Richard Kahn, Tibor Scitovsky, Trevor Swan, Pierre Sanner, the governor of the African Development Bank, Mamoun Beheiry (Sudan), Octavio A. Dias Carneiro (Brazil) and Rodrigo Gomez of the Bank of Mexico. Although he approved the selection of experts, Kaldor believed that their remit was 'completely hopeless (from the point of view of getting anywhere)' (source

[39] On Robert Triffin, see Maes and Pasotti (2021).

[40] On Gamani Corea and his connection with Cambridge University, see Kohr et al. (2014).

UNCTAD, 2014, p. 37). The group focused on aligning international monetary reforms with the trade and development needs of what today we would call the Global South.

> Due to his intellectual stature and to the close relations between academia and public administrations in the UK (Coats, 1981), Kahn was a major political asset for UNCTAD. Even though Corea presided over the group, the British economist's fame was such that it would sometimes be called "the Kahn Committee". (Orange-Leroy, 2023, p. 12)

On the first of the four reports edited for UNCTAD with Kahn's contribution, and entitled *International Monetary Issues and the Developing Countries* (1965),[41] Kahn has this recollection:

> [W]e considered the need for reform of the International Monetary System, which would make it responsive to the need for economic growth of both developed and developing countries. We had useful discussions with the Board of the International Monetary Fund in Washington and meetings with the Board of UNCTAD in New York. We advocated that part of the additional international liquidity created by the IMF in the form of Special Drawing Rights should be placed at the disposal of the International Bank [for Reconstruction and Development]—the famous Link. Although this proposal was not adopted in the precise form in which we formulated it, its essence has been accepted. (Marcuzzo, 2020, p. 35)

The 1965 report *International Monetary Issues and Developing Countries* (UNCTAD, 1965) marked a pivotal moment in shaping the North–South debate on reforming the international monetary system to better address global growth needs, particularly those of developing countries. It emphasised that developing nations required additional unconditional liquidity, not merely more aid. The report argued that G-10 countries should not unilaterally pursue changes in the international monetary system that could affect others. It proposed reforms to the IMF CFF, suggesting its use should be decoupled from gold and credit tranches, allowing such drawings without impacting a member's capacity for ordinary withdrawals.

[41] Located in the UNCTAD archives: *International Monetary Issues and Developing Countries: Report of the Experts* (1965), TD/B/32—TD/B/C.3/6.

A central innovation of the report was the introduction of the 'link' concept, proposing a mechanism to connect the creation and allocation of international reserve assets with the transfer of resources to developing nations, aligning reserve accumulation with development finance needs. Variations of the link schemes generally minimised reliance on national wealth (or its proxies) as the primary criterion for allocating Special Drawing Rights (SDRs). Despite these proposals, IMF CFF drawings did not grow as expected. Subsequent improvements in 1966 (and later in 1975) expanded drawing rights and broadened the scope of shortfall definitions, gradually enhancing the facility's operational range. On the other three reports prepared for UNCTAD, Kahn recalled that

> Our report on *Trade Expansion and Economic Cooperation among Developing Countries* dealt with the possibilities of expansion of trade among developing countries by commercial measures with coordination of investment programmes and a regional integration of national markets. Looking back I feel somewhat sceptical as to the usefulness of this report. In our report on *Payments Arrangements among Developing Countries* (1966) we considered the contribution which could be made towards the expansion of trade among developing countries by payments arrangements, clearing arrangements, credit arrangements and monetary unions. This report resulted in the creation of a number of economic regions in Africa and Latin America. In our report on *International Monetary Reform and Cooperation for Development* (1969) we developed the ideas put forward in our earlier report for a Link. We also made proposals about the shares of developing countries in IMF quotas. This report can be claimed to have exercised some useful influence. For me it was a wonderful experience to serve on these groups together with the representatives from the Third World. (Marcuzzo, 2020, pp. 35–36)

On the issue of the link between development aid and the issuance of Special Drawing Rights, which Kahn would return to in the early 1970s, as Orange-Leroy (2023, p. 25) notes, UNCTAD had no official views, while Prebisch and Sidney Dell (British economist, head of the UNCTAD secretariat) shared the ideas set out by Kahn, I.G. Patel (Indian economist and a Cambridge graduate)[42] and Trevor Swan. Patel worked under Gerald Shove's supervision on the relationship between trade and development in

[42] Source: https://www.ralphbuncheinstitute.org/un-intellectual-history-project/PDFs/Patel%20IG.pdf

Japan and Argentina. After these formative years, Patel oscillated between the Indian Ministry of Finance (1954–1958, 1961–1967), where he was involved in the country's planning, and the IMF (1950–1954, 1958–1961). At first a member of the Fund's Research Department, where he perfected his skills in applied economics with Bernstein and Polak, Patel came back to Washington as the Indian representative at the IMF Board. In front of the IMF Board, Patel put the emphasis on a solution, later called 'organic link', by which developed countries would automatically transfer a share of their SDRs allocation to development banks.

This idea was supported by the UNCTAD Secretariat but led the experts to split. Kahn considered the negotiations too tense for the argument not to be a disruption in the attempt to create SDRs. As the reform was voted, the 'organic link' proved ultimately too complex to even be promoted with the developed countries that opposed it.

7.6 Reforming Bretton Woods: Floating vs. Fixed Exchange Rates, SDRs and Development Aid

In 1973 an invitation to deliver a lecture at the 85th annual meeting of the American Economic Association (Kahn, 1973a) gave Kahn the opportunity to reflect on the prospects for the international monetary system two years after the declaration of the dollar's inconvertibility into gold, which had effectively ended the Bretton Woods system.

In December 1971 the Smithsonian Agreement had been reached, which devalued the dollar by about 8% and set new exchange rate targets for major currencies. However, this attempt to stabilise the system was short-lived, and by 1973 most major currencies had shifted to floating exchange rates. Against this background, Kahn began by noting that the smooth functioning of the international monetary system had required mechanisms capable of regulating exchange rate changes in an orderly fashion. In the case of Bretton Woods, these mechanisms had not worked as expected, and changes in official parities—at least in the case of industrial countries—had been infrequent and delayed, driven more by speculation than by the intention of monetary authorities to correct structural external imbalances. Therefore, the flaw lay not in the Bretton Woods rules, but in the reluctance of the monetary authorities to devalue or revalue. It was as if fixed parities were a fetish that could only be abandoned in an emergency, when mounting international speculation forced the issue. Faced with this problem, proponents of flexible exchange rates had recommended relying on markets and the free negotiation of exchange traders.

For Kahn, who remained an advocate of fixed but adjustable exchange rates, the weakness of this position was that it failed to account for the mismatch between the short-term focus of traders and the longer period required for exchange rate changes to correct the imbalances they had caused. This mismatch had greatly reduced the possibility that flexible exchange rates could exert a stabilising effect on prices. For example, a devaluation triggered by a balance of payments deficit would not immediately lead to a reduction in the deficit but rather to an increase, due to higher import values for the same volume (which changed more slowly). The overshooting of the exchange rate relative to this new parity could also have been aggravated by the inflationary response of wages and prices and the possible reaction of other countries, which might have felt compelled to devalue in turn. Thus, far from facilitating the rebalancing of exchange rates and balances of payments, flexibility could have made it more difficult.

To avoid these problems, fixed but adjustable exchange rates had to be maintained but made more flexible than they had been in the past, taking into account the effects of the recent liberalisation of short-term capital movements and the increasing use of derivatives for hedging and speculative purposes. The latter factor had increased the risks of instability and the emergence of herd behaviour by speculators moving in only one direction, forcing the monetary authorities to engage in costly hedging operations which often resulted in large losses for the authorities and substantial gains for the speculators. To avoid this risk, the monetary authorities had to act without following pre-established patterns and, if possible, in ways that surprised traders.

> Once it becomes reasonably evident to the authorities that the competitive position is becoming unduly unfavourable or favourable, it is important to act with speed before large bear or bull positions have built up. Best of all is to take the markets by surprise. Markets are very difficult to handle when considerable unanimity of view has become established—what is sometimes called "sellers only" or "buyers only." Markets exercise some stabilizing influence when there is a wide dispersion of views (what Keynes called "two views"). A small change in the exchange rate—within the permissible spread—will then bring considerable recuperative pressure into being. And

> if some fresh piece of news happens somewhat to strengthen bearish sentiment and weaken bullish sentiment throughout the market, the number of actual bulls who become bears will be small and vice versa. (Kahn, 1973a, pp. 183–184)

We find in these words a correspondence with the ideas that Kahn had proposed twenty years earlier when reflecting on the modus operandi of buffer stocks to stabilise commodity prices. The creation of a margin of uncertainty about the market prices to be stabilised leads private financial operators to act cautiously, reducing the size of purchases or sales to take into account the possibility that prices will move in a different direction from that expected. This facilitates the task of the authorities who have to stabilise those prices, especially when their resources are limited.[43] From a theoretical point of view, this idea has its roots in the 1954 essay on liquidity preference and in the description of the decision-making processes underlying portfolio choices under conditions of uncertainty, as opposed to the idea of efficient markets,[44] invoked by proponents of flexible exchange rates with reference to developed countries in particular.

In the case of less developed countries, Kahn's analysis shifted to the potential role of the International Monetary Fund (IMF) and Special Drawing Rights (SDRs) in supporting them, particularly during periods of economic stagnation in industrial nations. Kahn referred to the establishment of a 'link' between the issuance of SDRs and financial aid to developing countries, wherein industrial nations would allocate a portion of their SDRs to the International Development Association (IDA). The IDA would then use these funds to assist developing countries, with the expectation that industrial nations would eventually recoup their allocations through increased exports to those countries. The Link scheme had the dual merit of supporting the development of emerging economies while alleviating economic stagnation in industrial countries by creating an outlet for their underutilised resources.

Orders from developing countries stimulated economic activity in the developed world, reducing unemployment and encouraging growth and

[43] If resources are not constrained, monetary authorities can go a long way in pursuing their stabilisation objectives. This, as will be recalled, is Kahn's recommendation to the Radcliffe Committee.

[44] On Kahn's interpretation of Milton Friedman's arguments for exchange rate flexibility, see Endres (2005, p. 137). On Kahn's rejection of freely floating exchange rates, see also Pippenger (1973).

investment. Moreover, this arrangement improved the balance of payments and monetary reserves for industrial countries, since SDRs did not count negatively against their balance of payments, unlike traditional bilateral aid. The Link, owing to its multilateral structure, enabled rapid adjustments in industrial economies, particularly by providing a more immediate and direct boost to exports and economic activity. It allowed for the swift mobilisation of necessary resources through the IDA, avoiding the prolonged delays typically associated with government aid programmes. In evaluating the advantages of the Link system, Kahn combined one of his earlier ideas—on using taxes and subsidies to improve resource allocation and achieve ideal output—with his confidence in the IMF and IDA's capacity to implement such a system.

> I would like in passing to put forward a suggestion of mine that is bound to receive an incredulous reception. So far I have relied on the normal competitive processes of the market to steer the additional orders from developing countries towards the industrial countries that need them—countries suffering from adverse balances of payments and underutilization of productive capacity. But my audience will remember that I said that competitive forces act in this way only to a partial extent. My suggestion is that IDA should supplement the operation of market forces by taxing orders that are placed with the more successful industrial countries and subsidizing those placed with the less successful countries. The rates of tax and subsidy would be determined by the IMF and would reflect the economic position of each industrial country. Over a period the aggregate taxes would be equal to the aggregate subsidies. The rates could be altered fairly frequently so as to take account of the changing economic pattern in the industrial world. Of course the rate would not be altered on an order for which tenders had already been invited or which had already been placed. The adoption of my suggestion would arm the IMF with a powerful weapon for improving the adjustment process. (Ibid., pp. 187–188)

In making this suggestion, Kahn gives us another example of his general approach to economic policy. Faced with the objective of improving the allocation of resources, economic policy authorities must use the instruments at their disposal in a discretionary manner to steer market forces in the desired direction. This requires a degree of trial and error and a considerable capacity for sudden and decisive action on the part of the authorities themselves. The extent to which this was possible in the complex context of the post-Bretton Woods world is a question on which Kahn remains silent.

Kahn revisited the analysis of the Link scheme in an article for the *Lloyds Bank Review* (1973b), using as a starting point an article by P. Bauer published in the same journal (1973). In that article, Bauer had expressed concern that the Link system would lead to a dissociation between donor countries and the additional demand for their resources created by the transfer of new SDRs to developing countries, thereby encouraging global inflation. In response, Kahn developed a series of counterarguments in which theoretical reasoning was interwoven with an analysis of the institutional and political constraints shaping the implementation of the system, grounded in a basic awareness of the limited scale of development aid relative to the needs of recipient countries.

The differences between Kahn and Bauer lay in their assumptions about the degree of utilisation of productive resources, the underlying causes of inflation, and the impact of international aid on the balance of payments of donor countries. Bauer assumed that full employment was the normal state of affairs in developed economies, viewed inflation as the result of excessive demand for limited productive capacity, and saw a crucial asymmetry between development aid financed by direct transfers and that financed through the issuance of SDRs. In the case of direct transfers, donor countries were obliged to consider the effects of aid on their economies, including its financing and its impact on exports, aggregate demand and official reserves. When aid was financed via SDRs, however, this obligation was removed, as there was no immediate or direct impact on the donor country's economy. As a result, Bauer warned of a risk that donor countries might become unaccountable, leading to excessive inflationary pressures on a global scale.

Against this approach, Kahn argued that it was not necessarily true that donor countries operated at full employment, and that increased exports from recipient countries did not inevitably lead to higher wages and prices in donor economies. The risk of such inflationary effects, he contended, could be mitigated through discretionary and relatively frequent (e.g. biennial) reviews of the number of SDRs created and allocated under the Link scheme. Furthermore, he emphasised that decisions regarding the creation and distribution of SDRs were made at the political level—not by international organisation officials. The voting mechanisms governing IMF decisions remained firmly under the control of the finance ministers and central bank governors of developed countries. As such, the likelihood that less developed countries represented in the IMF Governing Council could force the hand of developed nations, or that the latter would pursue inflationary excesses, appeared remote.

> The representatives of the Western European countries were, and are, much obsessed with the dangers of adding to inflationary pressure, in the same way as is Professor Bauer. They have been in a good position to appreciate these dangers because the pressures on the productive resources of their own economies have been heavy. The very favourable state of their balance of payments and the very high level of their monetary reserves have meant that they have to be persuaded that the SDR scheme would be beneficial to countries other than their own. (Kahn, 1973b, p. 6)

The idea of persuading developed countries of the benefits of giving up some of their SDR allocations to developing countries, based on the recognition that their economic conditions would allow them to do so without making particularly heavy sacrifices, is part of the usual approach of Kahn. The element of persuasion and the need for all those involved in the application of an economic policy measure to recognise that it is in their own interest to give up something for the benefit of their counterparts is an essential part of Kahn's way of arguing, whether he is talking about how to reconcile full employment and price stability at the domestic level or, as in this case, discussing SDRs allocation. The same arguments, without any critical reference to Bauer, reappear in the text of a paper entitled 'The Link between the Creation of Special Drawing Rights and Aid to Developing Countries', read by Kahn at the Christ Church Conference, presumably held in Oxford from 7 to 11 January 1974. On that occasion, Kahn explained how

> It constitutes no part of my case for the operation of the Link that it is a magic wand which enables aid to be given to developing countries without involving the sacrifice for the donor countries entailed in alternative methods of providing aid. The extent of the sacrifice obviously depends on the extent to which the productive potential of the industrial countries is being fully utilised. Under modern conditions it is on the whole fully utilised. But slack does develop, though in a very patchy way [...]. It is part of the argument for the Link that it is a mechanism which does, to some limited extent, take up slack which would not be taken up by other methods. (RFK/4/25/6)

On the basis of these ideas, the description of the modus operandi of the Link and the decision-making processes underlying the distribution of SDRs follow what Kahn wrote in the 1973 articles. To these considerations, the 1974 text adds others concerning alternatives to the Link. The first alternative concerns the possibility for developing countries to receive a larger number of SDRs relative to their IMF quotas than that allocated to industrial countries. This would require a change in the decision-making process underlying the issuance of SDRs, which would lead those authorities concerned about excessive liquidity to argue that the allocation of SDRs to industrial countries should be reduced to the extent that the allocation to industrial countries is increased, making opposition from industrial countries highly likely.

The idea of directly increasing the assistance provided through the IDA runs up against the difficulties of any multilateral negotiation, which could be circumvented by the automaticity of the link. Finally, the possibility of groups of industrialised countries organising to provide additional development aid in lieu of the link clashes with the neo-colonial character of much existing aid. The fact that at least two-thirds of Britain's official aid in 1972 went to Commonwealth countries, and that the same is true in the case of France or the EEC more generally, is, in Kahn's eyes, all the more reason to support the Link scheme. Eventually, and in spite of Kahn's and others' best efforts, the Link proposal faced significant challenges and was ultimately not implemented. One major concern was the potential for excessive SDR creation, which could lead to inflationary pressures and destabilise the global economy. Additionally, there were procedural objections, as the establishment of the SDR facility itself was the result of long, difficult international negotiations and compromises among countries. Many parties were hesitant to alter the system so soon after its creation.

References

A. J. B. (1944). The sterling area. *Bulletin of International News, 21*(24), 1000–1005.

Amato, M., & Fantacci, L. (2012). *The end of finance*. Polity Press.

Bauer, P. (1973). SDR, inflation and aid. *Lloyds Bank Review, 27*(109), 31–35.

Bell, P. W. (1956). *The Sterling area in the postwar world*. Clarendon Press.

Blair, A. R. (1961). The dollar shortage in retrospect. *Review of Social Economy, 19*(2), 166–187.

Blank, S. (1977). Britain: The politics of foreign economic policy, the domestic economy and the problem of pluralistic stagnation. *International Organisation, 31*(4), 673–727.

Carabelli, A. M. (2021). *Keynes on uncertainty and tragic happiness.* Palgrave Macmillan.

Cesarano, F. (2006). *Monetary theory and Bretton Woods: The construction of an international monetary order.* Cambridge University Press.

Coats, A. W. (1981). Britain: The rise of the specialists. *History of Political Economy, 13*(3), 365–404.

Dellas, H., & Tavlas, G. (2025). *The great dollar shortage debate: A modern perspective.* Bank of Greece Working Paper No. 339. Bank of Greece.

Eichengreen, B. (2008). *Globalizing capital: A history of the international monetary system* (2nd ed.). Princeton University Press.

Eichengreen, B., & Braga de Macedo, J. (2001). The European Payments Union: History and implications for the evolution of the international financial architecture. In J. Braga de Macedo, D. Cohen, & H. Reisen (Eds.), *Fragility of the international financial system: How can we prevent new crises in emerging markets* (pp. 25–42). Presses Interuniversitaires Européennes.

Ellis, H. S. (1948). The dollar shortage in theory and fact. *Canadian Journal of Economics and Political Science/Revue Canadienne d'Economique et de Science Politique, 14*, 358–372.

Endres, A. M. (2005). *Great architects of international finance.* Routledge.

Entrikin, J. N., & Agnew, J. (Eds.). (2004). *The Marshall Plan Today: Model and metaphor.* Routledge.

Fantacci, L. (2017). Reconciling money and goods: Keynes's commodity and currency plans for the postwar world. *Annals of the Fondazione Luigi Einaudi, 51*, 149–176.

Fantacci, L., Marcuzzo, M. C., & Sanfilippo, E. (2010). Speculation in commodities: Keynes' 'Practical Acquaintance' with futures markets. *Journal of the History of Economic Thought, 32*(3), 397–418.

Fantacci, L., Marcuzzo, M. C., Rosselli, A., & Sanfilippo, E. (2011). Speculation and buffer stocks: The legacy of Keynes and Kahn. *European Journal of the History of Economic Thought, 19*(3), 453–473.

Fourastié, J. (1979). *Les Trente Glorieuses, ou la révolution invisible de 1946 à 1975.* Fayard.

Gaitskell, H. (1952). The Sterling area. *International Affairs, 28*(2), 170–176.

Gibson, J. D. (1954). Review of *Banking and Foreign Trade*: being the lectures delivered at the Fifth International Banking Summer School, Christ Church, Oxford, July 1952. *Canadian Journal of Economics and Political Science/Revue Canadienne d'Economique et de Science Politique, 20*(2), 264–266.

Graham, F. D. (1949). *The cause and cure of 'dollar shortage'*. International Finance Section, Department of Economics and Social Institutions. Princeton University.

Grondona, L. S. C. (1958). *Utilising world abundance*. George Allen and Unwin.

Haberler, G. (1948). Dollar shortage? In S. E. Harris (Ed.), *Foreign Economic Policy for the United States* (pp. 426–445). Harvard University Press.

Harrod, R. F. (1947). *Are these hardships necessary?* Rupert Hart-Davis.

Harrod R. F. (1950). Dollar imports benefits of eased restrictions. *The Times*, November 7.

Harrod, R. F. (1953). *The dollar: Sir George Watson lectures*. Macmillan.

Hirschman, A. O. (1951). Negotiations and the issues. *Review of Economics and Statistics, 33*(1), 49–55.

Hogan, M. J. (1987). *The Marshall Plan: America, Britain, and the reconstruction of Western Europe, 1947–1952*. Cambridge University Press.

Kahn, R. F. (1949). A possible intra-European payments scheme. *Economica, 16*(64), 293–304.

Kahn, R. F. ([1950a] 1972). The dollar shortage and devaluation. *Economia Internazionale, 3*(1), February, 89–113. Reprinted in R. F. Kahn (1972), *Selected Essays on Employment and Growth* (35–59). Cambridge University Press.

Kahn, R. F. (1950b). Marshall aid. *The Times*, November 7.

Kahn, R. F. (1950c). The European Payments Union. *Economica, 17*(67), 306–316.

Kahn, R. F. (1951a). The balance of payments and the sterling area. *District Bank Review, 100*, 3–17.

Kahn, R. F. (1951b). Home and export trade. *Economic Journal, 61*(242), 79–289.

Kahn, R. F. (1952). International regulation of trade and exchanges. In *Banking and Foreign Trade, Lectures delivered at the Fifth International Banking Summer School, Oxford* (pp. 1–18). Europa Publications for the Institute of Bankers.

Kahn, R. F. (1957). A positive contribution? *Bulletin of the Oxford Institute of Statistics, 19*, 63–68.

Kahn, R. F. (1973a). The International Monetary System. *American Economic Review, 63*(2), 181–188.

Kahn, R. F. (1973b). SDR and aid. *Lloyds Bank Review, 28*(110), 1–18.

Kaplan, J. J., & Schleiminger, G. (1989). *The European Payments Union: Financial diplomacy in the 1950s*. Oxford University Press.

Keynes, J. M. (1938). The policy of government storage of food-stuffs and raw materials. *Economic Journal, 48*(191), 449–460.

Khor, M., Yu III, V. P. B., & Timossi, A. J. (2014). *A tribute to Gamani Corea: His life, work and legacy*. South Centre.

Kregel, J. A. (2017a). What would Keynes have thought of the European crisis? *Annals of the Fondazione Luigi Einaudi, 51*, 107–120.

Kregel, J. A. (2017b). *A two-tier Eurozone or a Euro of regions? A Radical Proposal Based on Keynes's Clearing Union*. Public Policy Brief No. 144. Levy Economics Institute of Bard College.

Machlup, F. (1950). Three concepts of the balance of payments and the so-called dollar shortage. *Economic Journal, 60*(237), 46–68.

Maes, I., & Pasotti, I. (2021). *Robert Triffin: A life*. Oxford University Press.

Marcuzzo, M. C. (2012). *Speculation and regulation in commodity markets: The Keynesian Approach in Theory and Practice*. MPRA Paper No. 44131. University Library of Munich.

Marcuzzo, M. C. (2020). Richard F. Kahn: A disciple of Keynes. *History of Economics Review, 76*(1), 2–57.

Meade, J. E. (1957). The balance-of-payments problems of a European Free-Trade Area. *Economic Journal, 67*, 379–396.

Meade, J. E. (1958). Review of *Utilizing world abundance*, by L. St. Clare Grondona. *Economic Journal, 68*(271), 550–554.

Meade, J. E. (1964). International commodity agreements. *Lloyds Bank Review, 73*(July), 28–42.

Mini, P. V. (1996). Keynes on markets: A survey of heretical views. *American Journal of Economics and Sociology, 55*(1), 99–111.

Moggridge, D. (Ed.) (1980). *The collected writings of John Maynard Keynes*: Volume XXV. *Activities 1940–1944. Shaping the post-war world: The Clearing Union*. Macmillan.

Naef, A. (2022). *An exchange rate history of the United Kingdom, 1945–1992*. Cambridge University Press.

Nelson, E. (2009). Milton Friedman and U.K. Economic Policy: 1938–1979. *Federal Reserve Bank of St. Louis Working Paper* No. 2009-017. Federal Reserve Bank of St. Louis.

Orange-Leroy, R. (2023). *UNCTAD experts as an intellectual basis for developing countries' involvement in the reform of the international monetary system*. Paper presented at the Summer Institute of the Center for the History of Political Economy, Duke University, June 19–22.

P.B. (1946). The sterling balances: Britain's debts to the sterling area countries. *World Today, 2*(8), 353–362.

Paesani, P., & Rosselli, A. (2014). The case for a supra-national control on commodities in the post WWII World: Novel perspectives from FAO and Kaldor archives. *History of Economic Thought and Policy, 1*, 5–30.

Palma, G. (1994). Kahn on buffer stocks. *Cambridge Journal of Economics, 18*(1), 117–127.

Pelling, H. (1988). *Britain and the Marshall Plan*. Springer.

Pippenger, J. E. (1973). The case for freely fluctuating exchange rates: Some evidence. *Economic Inquiry, 11*, 314.

Pressnell, L. S. (1986). *External economic policy since the war*. HMSO.

Rosselli, A. (2017). Richard Kahn and the stabilization of commodity prices. *Journal of the History of Economic Thought, 39*(04), 483–501.
Schenk, C. R. (1994). *Britain and the sterling area: From devaluation to convertibility in the 1950s*. Routledge.
Shonfield, A. (1958). *British economic policy since the war*. Penguin Books.
Steil, B. (2013). *The battle of Bretton Woods: John Maynard Keynes, Harry Dexter White, and the making of a new world order*. Princeton University Press.
Steil, B. (2018). *The Marshall Plan: Dawn of the Cold War*. Simon and Schuster.
Strange, S. (1971). *Sterling and British Policy: A political study of an international currency in decline*. Oxford University Press.
UNCTAD. (2004). *Beyond conventional wisdom in development policy: An intellectual history of UNCTAD 1964–2004*. UNCTAD. Available online https://unctad.org/system/files/official-document/edm20044_en.pdf
UNCTAD. (2014). *UNCTAD at 50. A short history*. UNCTAD. Available online https://unctad.org/system/files/official-document/osg2014d1_en.pdf
Ussher, L. (2016). International monetary policy with commodity buffer stocks. *European Journal of Economics and Economic Policies: Intervention, 13*, 10–25.
Worswick, G. D. N. (Ed.). (1960). *The free trade proposals*. Basil Blackwell.
Young, J. W. (1993). Macmillan, the Free Trade Area and the first application, 1957–63. In I. J. W. Young (Ed.), *Britain and European Unity, 1945–1992. British history in perspective* (pp. 57–85). Palgrave.

CHAPTER 8

Prejudice and Pride

8.1 Keynesianism and the UK Economy in the 1970s

In 1972, Richard Kahn retired and became an Emeritus Professor. Free from the heavy academic engagements of the previous decades, the 1970s were a very important period in Kahn's intellectual life. He undertook new studies, participated in international conferences and frequently spoke out in defence of the Keynesian perspective on contemporary economic issues. Kahn's intellectual activity in the 1970s should be understood in the context of growing criticism of Keynesianism, in both theory and policy. By this time, monetarism and rational expectations were gaining ground, and Keynesianism was beginning to be regarded as an outdated and flawed economic doctrine. Many regarded it as unable to explain current economic issues or offer effective solutions. This was particularly evident in its apparent inability to explain or solve the stagflation that many developed countries faced during that period. Although Keynesianism remained prevalent in British policy during the decade, it was also becoming associated with inefficiency and stifling public intervention against economic freedom.

Between 1970 and 1979 growth in the United Kingdom oscillated between 6.5% in 1973 and −2.5% one year later (average 2.7%). Inflation rose from 6.4% in 1970 to 24.2% in 1975 and then slowed down to 13.4% in 1979. The unemployment rate went from a five-year average of 3.9%

P. Paesani, *Richard F. Kahn*, Great Thinkers in Economics,
https://doi.org/10.1007/978-3-032-09123-9_8

(1970–1974) to 5.3% in 1975–1979. Private investment as a percentage of GDP fell from an average of 14.3% (1970–1974) to 12.8% (1975–1979), matching the fall in the rate of return on capital.[1] The UK current account deteriorated steadily from a surplus of £315 million in the first quarter of 1970 to a deficit of £878 million in the fourth quarter of 1974, recovering over the next four years, partly thanks to North Sea oil revenues, to fall back to a deficit of £332 million in the fourth quarter of 1979. Problems that had first emerged in the 1950s and 1960s in milder forms, such as inflation, an external deficit and a weak pound, resurfaced in a striking manner within an increasingly unstable macroeconomic framework.

In 1971 the Conservative Government, led by Edward Heath, elected on a platform of lower taxes, fiscal responsibility, liberalisation, the promise to abolish the incomes policy and reform of the welfare state, implemented two measures that would soon become the catalyst for a deterioration in industrial relations and an enhanced inflationary pressure.[2] The first was the Industrial Relations Act of 1971, which was vehemently opposed by the trade unions, and was enacted with the objective of stabilising industrial relations by concentrating bargaining power and responsibility in the formal union leadership, with the courts playing a pivotal role.[3] The second measure was a major reform of banking regulation named *Competition and Credit Control*. This ended the inter-bank interest rate cartel, reduced bank reserve requirements, shifted from quantitative to qualitative credit controls (while extending them to a wider range of financial institutions) and ended the practice of the Government Broker—the Treasury's agent in the gilt-edged markets—stabilising government bond prices and long-term interest rates. These measures, the implementation of which marked the end of the regulatory regime that had evolved since the publication of the Radcliffe Report in 1959,

[1] Source of the data: https://lordslibrary.parliament.uk/the-uk-economy-in-the-1970s/. For an overview of the British economic and political landscape in the 1970s, see the chapter on the United Kingdom in Flanagan et al. (1983) dealing with unionism, economic stabilisation and incomes policy. On the same subjects, see also Smith (1987) and Hall (1992), among others.

[2] On the Heath Government see Ball and Seldon (1996) and Roe-Crines and Heppell (2021).

[3] For a recent re-appraisal of the Industrial Relations Act, see Warner (2021).

contributed to a sharp increase in the domestic supply of money and credit and fuelled inflationary pressures.[4]

As these and other measures were being implemented, unemployment began to rise from 3.8 percent in 1970 to 4.3 percent in 1972. The government's response was to adopt a highly expansionary monetary and fiscal stimulus, which revived growth and employment in the short term (the Barber Boom), but at the cost of further increases in inflation and balance of payments difficulties. In response, a new Statutory Incomes Policy was introduced, marking a U-turn. This attracted considerable criticism from hard-line Conservatives and some sections of the trade union movement, but also support from those on the opposite side of the political spectrum, including Kahn.[5] The Heath Government prioritised securing the United Kingdom's membership of the European Economic Community (EEC), reflecting Heath's pro-European vision. Through determined negotiations, the government overcame domestic opposition, culminating in the United Kingdom joining the EEC on 1 January 1973. While membership was seen as a step towards economic and geopolitical strength, it sparked enduring controversy over sovereignty and the costs of integration, shaping decades of debate about Britain's role in Europe.

In 1972, following the Smithsonian Accords, the government decided to float the pound in the hope that this would ease balance of payments tensions. The first OPEC shock in 1973 dashed these hopes. As the pound plummeted, raising the cost of imports and adding to inflationary pressures, the Heath Government was forced to tighten monetary and fiscal policy, thus exacerbating an economic climate already tense due to conflicts with unions, particularly in the coal industry. The 1974 general election, called by Heath to resolve a standoff with striking miners, resulted in a narrow Labour victory under Harold Wilson, which was solidified in a second election later that year. Labour initially pursued an ambitious economic strategy, combining expansionary fiscal policies with a Social Contract to encourage voluntary wage restraint by trade unions, while repealing the 1971 Industrial Relations Act. However, these efforts unravelled in 1975, as economic pressures mounted, with deteriorating public

[4] On Competition and Credit Control, see Goodhart (2015) and Copley (2017), among others.

[5] For an overview of incomes policy in Britain, in addition to the source mentioned in footnote 3, above see Soskice (1983) and Backhouse and Forder (2013).

finances, mounting inflation and a worsening balance of payments. In response, Labour shifted its priorities.[6]

Under James Callaghan, who succeeded Wilson as Prime Minister in 1976, and Chancellor of the Exchequer Denis Healey, Labour adopted policies focused on fiscal restraint, monetary targets and inflation control, marking a significant shift in British economic policy. This became particularly apparent in 1976 when Callaghan announced that full employment would no longer be the focus of British policymaking, despite downward pressure on aggregate demand, and that deficit spending would no longer be regarded as a legitimate means of achieving it. To many, Callaghan's words signalled the end of the mixed economy, Keynesian welfare state in Britain.[7] By 1978, however, the economy had stabilised, with improvements in the balance of payments and public borrowing. Despite these positive outcomes, Britain's economic and social situation began to deteriorate amid intensifying trade union demands and a growing sense of political paralysis. In this context, Callaghan's decision to delay a general election proved costly. The 1978–1979 'Winter of Discontent' marked by widespread public sector strikes and disruptions, eroded public confidence and paved the way for the Conservative victory in 1979, ushering in the era of Thatcherism.

In the 1970s, inflation became the central issue of economic policymaking and one of the main points of contention between British economists along the Keynesian versus monetarist divide, with the former committed to supporting different versions of the idea that inflation is determined by the interaction of demand pull and cost push factors, and the latter focused on reviving the idea of inflation as a monetary phenomenon.[8]

[6] For an overview of the Labour governments in the 1970s see Morgan (2021, pp. 423–512). On the Social Contract in connection with incomes policy and inflation, see Tarling and Wilkinson (1977). On the 'Winter of Discontent' and the crisis of British Keynesianism, see Hay (2010).

[7] On this and on several matters discussed in this chapter, see Murphy (2025). On the collapse of Keynesian welfarism in Britain in 1970–1979, see also Byrne et al. (2020, pp. 51–84).

[8] For an overview of the divergent macroeconomic performance of the main industrialised countries from the 1960s to the 1980s and a discussion of different approaches to modelling stagflation, see Boltho (1982) and Halliwell (1988), among others. For an example of a comparative analysis of British and Italian inflation in the 1970s, with references to Kahn, see Willett and Laney (1978). On inflation as a contentious issue of debate in Britain, see Tomlinson (2014) among others. For a survey of the main inflation theories in the 1970s,

The Keynesian front, which enjoyed a considerable degree of support in both academic and public institutions in Britain, was divided into three main groups (Coddington, 1976; Cobham, 1984). The first group included economists who were open to find a common ground with monetarism based on empirical evidence (e.g. Michael Artis, William Buiter, David Currie, Charles Goodhart, Marcus Miller).[9] The second group included economists such as James Meade and his associates, who were willing to debate with monetarists but more reluctant to reach a compromise with them. Finally, there were those who were opposed to monetarism altogether, many of whom were based in or influenced by Cambridge. On the monetarist front, the International Monetary Economics Research Programme at the London School of Economics, led by Harry Johnson and Alexander Swoboda, and the Inflation Workshop at the University of Manchester, led by David Laidler and Michael Parkin, were the two main fora for nascent British monetarism.[10] Other important names in the field of emerging British monetarism were those of Alan Walters, Brian Griffiths and Patrick Minford. This group could include the names of some distinguished elderly British economists, such as Paish and Morgan. In the 1950s and 1960s, they had opposed Keynesianism and its influence on the Radcliffe Doctrine (Seldon, 1960). Although not monetarists, these economists held a pre-Keynesian view of inflation as a monetary phenomenon associated with excessive demand for available resources.

During the debates on inflation in Britain between Keynesians and their opponents, Kahn was a key target of monetarist criticism due to his focus on wage–price spirals and cost-push inflation. As we shall see, Kahn's defence of his views on inflation was closely linked to his rejection of the idea that post-war Keynesian policies had ultimately caused inflation through excessive and inefficient state intervention, which stifled

see Trevithick and Mulvey (1975) and Laidler and Parkin (1975). See also Trevithick (1976) with a reference to Kahn.

[9] Many young UK economists used inflation data to compare Keynesian and monetarist theories beyond theory alone. On this topic, see Johnson and Nobay (1971) and Henry et al. (1976), among others.

[10] A substantial literature exists on the emergence of monetarism in the United Kingdom and its subsequent influence on academic and policymaking circles. For an introduction to this literature see Griffiths and Wood (1984), Smith (1987) and Davies (2012), among others. On the influence of Milton Friedman on UK economic policy see Nelson (2009). On Kahn's own ex-post recollections on the rise and fall of monetarism see Marcuzzo (2020, pp. 39–44).

economic growth. Furthermore, the 1968 publication of Axel Leijonhufvud's book *Keynesian Economics and the Economics of Keynes* (Leijonhufvud, 1968) prompted macroeconomists, particularly those of the younger generation, to reconsider the approach of the first generation of Keynesian economists and recognise that alternative methods were feasible (De Vroey, 2016, p. 115).[11]

In this context, safeguarding the Keynesian approach as understood by Kahn was of the utmost importance to him. After all, he had devoted his entire life to developing and defending that approach within the Cambridge citadel and beyond. Depending on how he perceived the threat, Kahn employed various defence strategies against critics of Keynesianism. While he engaged in academic debate with British monetarists, occasionally taking a jab at an opponent, he adopted a more resolute and aggressive stance in response to criticism of Keynesianism from former Cambridge graduates or from within Cambridge itself. In such cases, he sought the help and advice of the few younger economists close to him, both privately and publicly. Modest yet self-assured, Kahn emerged from these battles embittered and weary. This, as well as a series of health problems, led him to withdraw from public debate in the late 1970s, in order to devote himself to a final re-evaluation of Keynes's intellectual legacy, and his own role in relation to it.

8.2 Kahn at Cambridge in the 1970s: Retirement, Work Programme and Faculty Life

As Saith (2022a) has reconstructed with admirable meticulousness, economic studies at Cambridge in the 1970s were highly fragmented. On the one hand, a variety of approaches emerged, including Post-Keynesian, Kaleckian, and neo-Ricardian, which are now classified as heterodox. Conversely, the initially minor but increasingly strong influence of general equilibrium, econometrics and mainstream economics more broadly emerged. Amidst clashes between the various components of the Faculty of Economics and Politics, the heterodox components were progressively marginalised in the context of the neoliberal turn in economics and politics.

[11] For a recent assessment of Leijonhufvud (1968) in reference to Kahn's work on involuntary unemployment, see Clerc and Dos Santos Ferreira (2020).

In this context, Saith identifies the appointment of Frank Hahn, best known for his work on general equilibrium and monetary theory, upon Kahn's retirement and on Kahn's Chair, as a crucial moment in the eclipse of economic heterodoxy at Cambridge.[12] Among the various questions raised by this appointment is the support that this was given by Kahn himself, despite the fact that from a theoretical point of view he would seem to be at the opposite end of the spectrum from Hahn. In reality, while the difference between the two was undeniable, perhaps it was not as significant as one might think,[13] being mitigated by mutual respect and the occasional dialogue.

Indeed, as Newbery (2017, pp. 491–492) recalls, it was Kahn who brought Hahn to Cambridge as a lecturer in 1960 'to continue the faculty's standing as a world-class economics faculty, despite his scepticism and even hostility to mathematical economics'. In 1964, as seen above, Frank Hahn had been one of those to whom Kahn had sent his 'work in progress' on the valuation ratio, which Hahn had read and commented on. Ten years later, in 1974, this situation was to be repeated in connection with Kahn's lecture on Keynes at the British Academy. An additional indirect indication that Kahn did not perceive Hahn as a particular threat in the 1970s can be found in a letter that Joan Robinson wrote to him in 1974 from Stanford, where she was giving a lecture series. The letter, dated 8 May, contains the following sentence: 'Hahn for EJ would be a first class disaster. The end of Cambridge economics. I don't understand how you can write about it so calmly' (ref. RFK/13/90/9/50).

Reading Newbery (2017) alongside Saith (2022a) allows us to understand the context of Hahn's appointment to Kahn's Chair. A major controversy had erupted over the appointment of Robert Neild to succeed Joan Robinson in 1971, which was orchestrated by Nicholas Kaldor in an attempt to block Frank Hahn, whom Kaldor opposed for methodological and personal reasons.[14] Aubrey Silberston, Chairman of the Faculty Board of the Faculty of Economics, strongly objected to this, which led to a heated conflict with Kaldor. The backlash was so intense that, when Kahn retired shortly afterwards, Hahn was elected in his place. In this context,

[12] On this see Saith (2022a, pp. 129–138). On Hahn's arrival at Cambridge, and on his scholarly contributions, see Dasgupta (2013), Newbery (2017), Solow (2017) and Backhouse (2020).

[13] This is especially true in the field of economic policy, where Hahn and Kahn were united by a strong anti-monetarist stance.

[14] On Neild see Hodgson et al. (2018).

Hahn's appointment without any apparent remonstration from Kahn can be interpreted as a reflection of the latter's tension with Kaldor. Moreover, Hahn's appointment was also endorsed by Brian Reddaway, a long-standing friend of Kahn's from the war years and whom Kahn had supported for the position of Head of the Department of Applied Economics (DAE).[15]

Beyond the personal aspects, about which one can only speculate, the question of Kahn's support, or at least non-hostility, towards Hahn's appointment has to be placed in the more general context of his activities in Cambridge in the 1970s and of the development of his own economic ideas. On the former aspect, Saith (2022a, pp. 444–453) documents how Kahn managed to remain on good terms with orthodox economists, particularly Michael Posner and other critics of the Department of Applied Economics,[16] directed by the Keynesian Wynne Godley (recruited to that post by Kaldor in 1970). Meanwhile, Kahn did not support the establishment of the *Cambridge Journal of Economics*, which was promoted by a group of young, heterodox, left-wing Cambridge economists, including John Eatwell, Mario Nuti and Ajit Singh. Kahn refused to figure as one of the patrons of *Journal*, alongside Joan Robinson, Richard Goodwin and Luigi Pasinetti.[17]

> [A]t the very outset when he [Kahn] was the very first "great" to be approached by the pioneering group for advice and to be a patron, he had attacked the idea and the group on account of its declared leftist predilection; this matter had ostensibly, but obviously not really, been cleared, and some combination of some or all of the above considerations would go into explaining this very "Cambridge" oddity. (Saith, 2022b, p. 43)

Beyond the personal tensions, theoretical controversies and political disagreements on which Saith focuses—to which we will return—this research suggests adding a further element to explain the 'Cambridge oddity'. While Kahn's economic ideas distanced him from the neoclassical synthesis of Keynesian thought and its reinterpretation in terms of general

[15] On Reddaway's support for Hahn's election see Singh (2009, p. 371). On the relationship between Reddaway and Kahn see Tribe (1997, pp. 71–85) and Kahn's own testimony in Marcuzzo (2020, pp. 14–16).

[16] On Michael Posner see Appendix C and Wade (2006).

[17] On the founding of *The Cambridge Journal of Economics* and Kahn's opposition to this project, see Saith (2022a, pp. 305–319) as well as Saith (2022b).

economic equilibrium—placing him at odds with the small but vocal orthodox faction in Cambridge—they were perhaps even further removed from the main currents of heterodox economic thought gaining ground there.

By the 1970s, Kahn's approach, which emphasised the influence of psychological factors and risk perceptions on investment and portfolio decisions, and occasionally referenced marginal productivity, the aggregate supply curve in relation to marginal costs and the idea that profit maximisation explains firms' behaviour, was far removed from the grand synthesis between Keynes, Kalecki, Marx and Ricardo via Sraffa that attracted many young Cambridge economists. Kahn did not participate in the capital controversy (Harcourt, 1972; Cohen & Harcourt, 2003) or the subsequent debates following the publication of *Production of Commodities by Means of Commodities* (Sraffa, 1960). The same is true of strands of Cambridge economics interested in Marxism, socialism and economic philosophy. Even in the area of Keynesian growth models and the link between growth and distribution, Kahn did not make any significant theoretical contributions after 1964, preferring to focus on policy and applied issues. In the map of Post-Keynesianism drawn by Hamouda and Harcourt (1988), Kahn is virtually absent.

A long handwritten note dated 19 June 1975 and entitled 'My Work Programme' provides important evidence of Kahn's loyalty to his preferred theoretical framework and his lack of interest in the new ideas being discussed in Cambridge.[18] Addressed to Joan Robinson, Kenneth Berrill, Michael Posner, Donald Moggridge and John Eatwell, the document contains a detailed outline of the areas on which Kahn intended to work, together with a request for suggestions and advice.[19]

1. Vol. 2 of Collected Works. Here there is a heavily overdue debt to Donald [Moggridge] and John [Eatwell]. They took a great deal of trouble, and the contents were settled in June 1973. They were to consist of (a) Extracts from the Fellowship Dissertation, and possibly from the draft of

[18] I would like to thank Susan Howson for helping me in deciphering Kahn's handwriting and commenting on the content of the note, especially the absence of work relating to points (7) and (8) of his programme (Communication with the author on 2 January 2025).

[19] This handwritten note is reproduced by kind permission of Professor David Papineau. Kahn's archives contain the replies of Posner (RFK/12/2/62/8) and Moggridge (RFK/12/2/62/9).

my abortive book, on the Economics of the Short Period. (b) Early articles in the micro-economic field. [...]

2. A volume of recent articles, papers and lectures. This might be of some interest. Over the last 2 or 3 years I have accumulated material for a fair-sized book, especially if Michael [Posner] were willing to include our joint names over articles, letters etc. about the New Cambridge School. I might add a couple of new papers — on the New School and one over the present day U.K. problem of inflation.
3. A treatment of the incidence of taxation and public expenditure. If I launched out on this it would keep us busy for some time. It would amount to too much for a journal article. Possibly a journal would publish it in two instalments. But I might publish it as a pamphlet without any previous publication. I should have to consider the interests of Adrian Wood and discuss the project with him. Some considerable time ago Joan and I read part of the draft of his book on distribution of income. In the course of discussion with Adrian [Wood], the ideas of Joan and myself developed considerably. Adrian has rather conspicuously refrained from asking for any further attempt to help him. I suspect that — very justifiably — our intervention introduced confusion rather than clarification. The problem of how prices are fixed would play an essential part. Both the short and the long period would be dealt with and both the effects through time of changes and comparisons of equilibrium paths.
4. A defence of Walras against Garegnani. I spent quite a lot of time on the subject in the course of preparing my submission to our Appointments Committee over John's [Eatwell] candidature. Here everything turns on John's attitude. If he wants my help in converting his Harvard Dissertation into a book — at any rate over the relevant chapter or chapters — I ought to get on with my study. If he would prefer to be left to publish, it would be much better to postpone my study. The difficulty at the moment is that the only published work that I can comment on (apart from Morishima's Appendix) is Garegnani's Italian book of the early 1960's. This is substantially the same as his Cambridge PhD Dissertation. I could read the Dissertation in the U.L., and get some Italian friend to amend my references, so as to make them applicable to the Italian book. Garegnani has provided me with an unpublished paper of 1962, which — I understand — is similar to one of the chapters in his book. He intends to publish this, but will not embark on a revision of it until late this summer.
5. A study of the part played by the Treasury over defence expenditure in the late 30s. [...]
6. My own personal account of the Economists Committee of the Economic Advisory Council. This was suggested some time ago by Colin Clark. It is

rather important to prepare it while Lionel Robbins is still compos mentis. [...]

7. The preparation of a draft of the famous Cambridge-LSE week-end which started the conversion of LSE to Keynes. [...]
8. A personal view of Keynes as a man (rather than as an economist) [...] But although I saw only part of Keynes' life in the thirties, I saw more of it than anybody else other than Lydia. I feel that I have a duty to print something on paper (?). It would not be very long. (Ref. RFK/12/2/62/2–7)

As this work programme suggests, Kahn intended to engage with both economic orthodoxy and heterodoxy—particularly the Sraffian school, led by Pierangelo Garegnani and influential among young economists in Cambridge and beyond—in order to reaffirm the validity of Keynes's legacy. This would involve reconstructing key moments in the affirmation of Keynesian doctrine in Britain, as well as examining the origins of Keynesianism rather than its future. It would also entail reconsidering the essence of Keynes's economic thought, rather than reinterpreting it in light of the revival of classical political economy, as Joan Robinson had done.

Kahn only partially succeeded in completing his programme. The Mattioli Lectures on *Keynes and the Making of the General Theory*, which Kahn delivered in Milan in 1978 and published in 1984, and which we discuss below, gave him the opportunity to address the last three points. The Fellowship Dissertation on the *Economics of the Short Period* was published first in Italian in 1983 and then in English in 1989, while the second volume of Kahn's collected works, which combines some microeconomic writings from the 1930s with articles and lectures from the following decades, did not appear until 2022 (Marcuzzo & Paesani, 2022).

Regarding point five, Kahn sought to investigate what he believed to be a tacit effort within the British government and civil service to resist increased arms expenditure despite the urging of both Keynes and the Permanent Secretary to the Treasury. Kahn's 'conspiracy' thesis did not imply a formal plot, but rather a network of politically and administratively motivated resistance, which was rooted in fiscal conservatism, appeasement or opposition to deficit financing. According to Kahn, these factors hindered Britain's war preparations at a critical historical juncture. His interest was sparked by Stephen Roskill's biography of civil servant Maurice Hankey, and was further fuelled during his preparations for a lecture on

Keynes at the British Academy. Correspondence from 1974 reveals Kahn's growing commitment to this line of inquiry, despite counterarguments from Playfair and subsequent scholarly work by G.C. Peden, whose doctoral thesis on British rearmament and the Treasury Kahn admired. Kahn pursued the topic rigorously until 1979, when Moggridge convinced him to abandon it due to a lack of conclusive evidence (RFK/12/2/55).

Similarly unsuccessful were Kahn's efforts on the front of analysing the effects of taxation and public spending on prices, according to Kahn the most difficult part of his work programme.[20] In this case, the opportunity to work on this topic was linked to the application for and award of a research grant from the Leverhulme Foundation in 1976/1977. After a considerable initial effort, also with the support of Lionel Robbins and Kenneth Berrill, Kahn realised that he would not be able to complete the assignment due to the concurrent commitments and repaid the funds received in full (ref. RFK/12/2/49). On point four there is currently no evidence of further commitment by Kahn.

After retiring, Kahn continued to participate in the life of the Cambridge Faculty of Economics, albeit from an increasingly isolated position. For example, at the end of 1975, J. Eatwell—an Assistant Lecturer in the Faculty of Economics and Politics at the time, and a close associate of Joan Robinson—organised a round-table discussion on various topics in economic theory and policy in which Kahn participated (ref. RFK/12/2/81). The round table, planned for 21–22 February 1976, was a follow-up to a similar event held in Florence two years earlier between English and Italian economists: Joan Robinson, B. Schefold, L. Pasinetti, L. Spaventa, P. Garegnani, M. Dobb, M. Nuti, Kaldor and B. Rowthorn.

As can be seen from a series of handwritten notes that are difficult to decipher (ref. RFK/12/2/82/71–80), Kahn's talk on inflation was based on the theoretical framework that we are already familiar with (interdependence of cost and demand components, wage-wage dynamics and the leapfrogging effect) and on a comparison of the British experience with that of other European countries.[21] As for the results of the round table, a

[20] The correspondence with Adrian Wood referred to by Kahn can be found in RFK/12/2/22, while that relating to point six of Kahn's work programme can be found in RFK/12/2/35.

[21] In addition to this paper, RFK/12/2/81 contains a copy of Pierangelo Garegnani's paper entitled 'On a Change in the Notion of Equilibrium in Recent Work on Value': a comment on Samuelson, Joan Robinson's comment on Garegnani, Ian Steedman's paper on

letter from Kahn to Kaldor, dated 3 March 1976, gives a measure of Kahn's state of mind and his feelings towards his young colleagues.

> Mario [Nuti] was quite unnecessarily abusive to Joan. The discussion of my paper on inflation was completely ruined by constant reiteration of nonsense by Bob [Rowthorn] and Ajit [Singh]. [...] I was very fed up, and I very much wished that I had not attended the Conference at all.[22]

A second piece of evidence of Kahn's limited patience with his young Cambridge colleagues and his attempts to exert influence in increasingly difficult conditions comes from an exchange of letters with A. Singh, who was organising the Queens' College economic seminar at the time.[23] On 12 November 1975, Kahn wrote to Singh.

> Dear Ajit, I hope that you will not regard it as impertinent if I ask to be given or to be lent a copy of the invitation list to your Monday seminar. I may be wrong, but I have a feeling that the composition of the group has considerably altered. I am of course all if favour of people like the majority of those who attended last Monday being given a Seminar in addition to the Joint Faculty D.A.E Seminar and the Research Students Seminar. At the same time, some of us are rather anxious that there should once again be a Seminar more on the lines of the one which I used to conduct.[24]

Six days later, Singh's short response to Kahn's concerns is indicative of the state of affairs within the Faculty:

> Dear Richard, thank you for your letter of 12th November. The only people excluded from our seminar are those known extremists in the Faculty such as Frank Hahn, David Newbery and Gordon Hughes. If you wish some

'Thoughts on Joint Production', a text by Joan Robinson entitled 'The State of the Play the closing of JVR' and Bertram Schefold's paper on Energy Prices.

[22] Letter from Kahn to Kaldor, 3 March 1976, ref. RFK/ 12/2/86/4. Further evidence of the relationship between Kahn and Kaldor in the early 1970s can be found in their correspondence, which is preserved in Kaldor's archive (NK/3/30/119/2–30). These letters cover various topics, including life at the Faculty of Economics (e.g. RFK/3/30/119/13–19), Kaldor's publications (e.g. RFK/3/30/119/6–9), the publication of Keynes's *Collected Writings* (NK/3/30/199/24–30), and Kaldor's work as an advisor to Callaghan and the Labour government.

[23] On this seminar, with reference to Kahn's rather bellicose attitude, see Saith (2019, pp. 167–169).

[24] Letter from Kahn to A. Singh, 12 November 1975, ref. RFK/12/2/38/2.

> others to be added to this exclusion list please let me have their names and I shall inform them of your objections.[25]

Kahn's reply to this is self-explanatory:

> Dear Ajit, in your letter of the 18th, replying to mine of the 12th, you deal neither with the financial question which I raised nor with the question of the clash with the Churchill Seminar. You go out of your way to disregard the wording of the rest of my letter. I was not suggesting that people should be excluded from the seminar. What worries me — and still does worry me — is that people are being excluded other than the "non-extremists." I wonder how many of them are. You mention three, but your use of the phrase "such as" indicates that you want to maintain the whole thing a mistery. […] It does seem to me that something is very wrong somewhere.[26]

These exchanges, and others to be found in Kahn's archive and in Saith (2022a), further show how in the 1970s Kahn often did not see eye to eye with some of the young heterodox Cambridge economists who were more active on the academic side. In addition to the differences in age, character, basic theoretical approach and political vision, there were also significant differences on specific theoretical and policy issues, as the diatribe between the New and Old Cambridge Schools reveals.

8.3 Cambridge Controversies: The New vs. Old Cambridge School

In 1974, one year before drawing up his work programme, Kahn, together with Michael Posner, became involved in a bitter controversy with a group of Cambridge economists associated with the DAE and the Cambridge Economic Policy Group.[27] The group, which would soon be labelled the New Cambridge School (henceforth NCS) in opposition to the 'Old Cambridge School' represented by Kahn and Posner, included Wynne Godley and Francis Cripps, (both advisers to the new Labour government that took office in 1974 after the defeat of Heath's Conservatives) as well as Robert Neild. The story of the NCS and of its disagreements with Kahn

[25] Letter from A. Singh to Kahn, 18 November 1975, ref. RFK/12/2/38/4.

[26] Letter from Kahn to A. Singh, 24 November 1975, ref. RFK/12/2/38/5.

[27] On the DAE and the Cambridge Economic Policy Group in the 1970s, see Saith (2022a, pp. 439–516).

and Posner has been told many times and from many different perspectives.[28] Here we recall the essentials of that story, focusing then on the theoretical propositions that Kahn and Posner defended and on the echoes of the Cambridge controversy at the institutional level, in particular during the work of the House of Commons Expenditure Committee in the summer of 1974.[29]

The NCS first manifested itself in a series of articles in *The Times* by Godley, Cripps and Neild (Godley & Cripps, 1973a, 1973b, 1974a, 1974b; Neild, 1974), written in the wake of the Barber boom and the devaluation of the pound. The main doctrine of the NCS consisted of five propositions, which can be summarised as follows with the help of a paper by M.G. Phelps (University College, Cardiff) preserved in Kahn's archives (RFK/12/2/133/8–35).[30] First, 'Thus a single (necessary and sufficient) condition governs equilibrium in the balance of payments [...] that the volume of total domestic expenditure, including investment, should fall short of (or exceed) the real national income by exactly the amount of the target surplus (or deficit) on current account'. Second, '...other than in the short term, the private sector shows a small and stable surplus (of receipts over expenditure) (which) implies that the public sector's budget deficit fully determines the current balance of payments'. Third, 'Given the size of the budget deficit, changes in exports, import prices, etc., make a lot of difference to real income and output, but none at all to the balance of payments'. Fourth, '...the Budget should be used to determine the foreign balance and the exchange rate to determine the level of activity [...] (contrary to) [...] the Keynesian orthodoxy that the Budgets should be used to determine the level of employment and the exchange rate to regulate the foreign balance'. Fifth, 'The Balance of Payments is no harder to forecast and control than domestic output' (Godley & Cripps, 1974a).

[28] See, for example, Mata (2012), Smith (2016), Saith (2022a) and more recently Murphy (2025).

[29] On the relationship between the British Treasury and the New Cambridge School in the 1970s, see Maloney (2012). For a simple formalisation of the main propositions of the School see Dixon (1982).

[30] The paper is entitled 'More Cambridge Controversies — the Balance of Payments' and contains a trenchant criticism of the New Cambridge School, which, in the author's view, amounts to a repetition of the absorption approach combined with the theoretically unattractive assumptions of near-equivalence of saving and investment and the budget behaviour of governments. On the analytical premises and economic policy implications of the New Cambridge School see also Barca (1977).

Added to these propositions was the idea that prices are directly dependent on nominal wages, the behaviour of which was explained by the real wage resistance theory. This theory explains why it is difficult to reduce real wages, even in times of unemployment. Trade unions oppose accepting wage settlements that do not at least compensate for price increases since the last agreement. Employers also know that workers dislike reductions in their real incomes. They believe that wage offers involving real reductions are bad for morale, so they are reluctant to make them. Real wage resistance hinders necessary adjustments to the structure of relative wages and makes it difficult to end an inflationary spiral.[31] Hence the idea that devaluation does not lead to significant improvements in the balance of payments because, by pushing up import prices and the cost of living, it raises wages without leading to lasting gains in competitiveness and the proposal to use direct controls on exports and imports to contain that balance of payments deficit.

The policy proposals emanating from the NCS faced significant resistance and scepticism in Treasury, notably from Kenneth Berrill, Kahn's close associate and the government's Chief Economic Adviser, with whom Kaldor clashed bitterly (King, 2009, pp. 108–109). The Treasury was dismissive of New Cambridge ideas, describing them as overly reliant on media exposure rather than rigorous academic publication and suggesting they were an unproductive diversion. A concerted Treasury critique targeted Wynne Godley, with accusations levelled before he, Francis Cripps and Martin Fetherston even testified before the Public Expenditure Committee (Maloney, 2012).

Although formulated within a Keynesian analytical framework consistent with a cost-push view of inflation, the proposals of the NCS, in particular the criticism of discretionary fiscal policy and the usefulness of devaluation as a remedy for balance of payments deficits as an alternative to austerity, could, perhaps unintentionally, have served as weapons against Keynesianism, as Kahn (1976b) and others (e.g. Bishpam, 1975) would note in the years following the outbreak of the controversy. This risk must have seemed serious enough to prompt Kahn, with the help of Michael Posner, to intervene immediately. He did so with two articles, first published separately in *The Times* and then collected in one article published in the *London and Cambridge Economic Bulletin* (Kahn & Posner, 1974a).

[31] See Eichengreen (1983) and Wright (1984) for an early exposition of the real wage resistance theory.

Kahn and Posner show how the NCS proposals depend on the assumption that the propensity to import is very high and the other parameters defining the multiplier very low.[32] Under these assumptions, saving, investment and the net acquisition of financial assets are indeed stable functions of private sector disposable income and the government balance is directly proportional to the balance of the current account. Under the same assumptions, any change in exports (and income) induced by a change in the exchange rate will, after an adjustment period, lead to a change in imports of the same magnitude without significantly affecting the balance of payments. Accepting these conclusions is tantamount to assuming that every change in private sector saving is offset by changes in the same direction and of roughly the same magnitude in investment.

Contrary to the conclusions of the NCS, so Kahn and Posner continued, it can therefore be argued that a devaluation, by increasing exports, income and savings more than investment, will also have a positive effect on the balance of payments. On the other hand, a sufficiently restrictive fiscal policy can serve to improve the balance of payments, but while for the NCS the sacrifice in terms of income is minimal, given the expected sharp reduction in imports as aggregate demand falls, Kahn and Posner are much less optimistic. Hence the invitation to formulate their hypotheses more clearly and to be wary of 'certain dangers arising from the methods of presentation employed by the New School' (Kahn & Posner, 1974a, p. 28), avoiding the impression of treating private investment as a residual variable and supporting a bias in favour of private consumption. Hence the conclusion: 'While we agree that there are occasions when such a bias is justified, the New School fails to recognise that the "main cause of Britain's post-war economic difficulties" is not, as Professor Neild claims, "Keynesian orthodoxy", but too high a share of consumption in national output and too low a share of productive investment' (ibid., p. 29).

In the spring and summer of 1974 Godley, Kahn and Kaldor exchanged a series of letters. This correspondence, which Mata (2012) has carefully reconstructed and contextualised, reveals the strong initial differences of opinion and the attempt on both sides to find a common denominator, partly because Godley and Cripps were eager to reach an agreement with Kahn and Posner and benefited from Kaldor's disinterest in continuing

[32] These parameters are the propensity to save in relation to the desire to buy new property, the response of profits and investment to changes in income, and the response of tax receipts, government expenditure and losses of nationalised firms to changes in aggregate income.

the argument. Wynne Godley expressed dissatisfaction with the prospect of a public dispute and advocated for private discussions within Cambridge. Cripps eventually convinced Kahn that such debates risked misrepresentation and that it would be more productive to await empirical results from the Department of Applied Economics (DAE) on the contested issues. Godley and Cripps intentionally framed their approach as a 'hypothesis' or 'equation' rather than a new school as a strategic choice that emphasised continuity with Cambridge's Keynesian legacy while showcasing its ongoing intellectual vitality.

Kahn and Posner's critique dovetailed with criticism of the same tenor by officials in the British Treasury in the context of the work of the Commons Public Expenditure Committee (PEC), which in May 1974, under the leadership of Tory MP Michael Alison, had set up an inquiry into the impact of public spending on the balance of payments (Maloney, 2012, pp. 1004–1006). This Committee became the arena in which economists with different ideas confronted each other and their position of fine tuning, inflation, fiscal and monetary policy and devaluation.[33] Kahn and Posner were summoned to a hearing before the PEC, where they had the opportunity to expand on the criticisms of the NCS that they had made a few months earlier (Kahn & Posner, 1974b).

In their memorandum to the PEC, Kahn and Posner argued that economic instability can be caused by both the public and private sectors, but that public spending plays a vital stabilising role, particularly when private investment is low. They argued that cuts to public spending are only warranted when demand puts pressure on resources, which could lead to inflation. The United Kingdom's key structural issues were low investment and productivity. Tight labour markets amplified inflationary pressures, and overly restrictive policies during periods of high unemployment could exacerbate labour unrest. In connection with this observation, Kahn and Posner claimed to

> [H]ave no belief in the notorious Phillips Curve. If the ideas embodied in the doctrine commonly attributed to Professor Phillips ever had any validity, they were relevant only to the cyclical experience of the past, and not to any

[33] For a reconstruction of the political circumstances which led to the House of Commons Expenditure Committee's Inquiry into Public Expenditure, Inflation and the Balance of Payments, and for a lively and rather critical account of the Keynesian position expressed in different ways by Kahn, Posner and Berrill (representing the Treasury) and the New Cambridge School, see Bruce-Gardyne (1976).

> longer-term more stable relationship between the rate of increase of money-wages and the level of unemployment, maintained fairly steadily over a considerable period of years. But this denial of the explanatory power of the pressure of demand leads us inevitably to stress the other causes of cost inflation. We believe that normally the main cause is the character of wage settlements in industry as a whole. [...] To cope with the problem of cost inflation, [...] and with the consequent problem of the balance of payments, we regard statutory control of money wages (as well as other incomes and prices) as absolutely vital. (Kahn & Posner, 1974b, pp. 73–74)

The only reasons to believe that high public deficits generate inflation and balance of payments deficits are linked to persistent pressure on aggregate demand from public spending, combined with the government's reluctance to raise interest rates or accompany deficit monetisation with compensatory sterilisation measures to control the growth of base money. Kahn and Posner did not intend to endorse the monetarist hypothesis that inflation was a direct consequence of government deficit monetisation, which accounted for only a small proportion of the overall public deficit. Instead, they aimed to highlight the choice between supporting aggregate demand and full employment through consistent fiscal and monetary policies and incomes policy as an alternative to monetary restriction as recommended by Friedman and the British monetarists. This would involve trusting in a rapid adjustment of inflation without lasting negative consequences for employment, an unlikely scenario according to Kahn and Posner.

> We do however agree that there should be a limit to the period of time over which a large borrowing requirement builds up a high degree of liquidity. [...] The question is whether it is feasible to nudge the economy into Professor Milton Friedman's state of tranquil growth. [...] Our answer is that such a happy state of affairs would be achieved only if there was a revolutionary change in our system of wage-settlement, if the trade-union leaders were replaced by civil servants, and if a statutory wage policy were firmly enforced. We do not believe that a devastating slump would prove in any way conclusive to the establishment of Professor Milton Friedman's happy state. (Ibid., p. 79)

The criticism of trade unions and the appeal to the reform of the wage-setting mechanism tally with similar considerations from Kahn's writings on monetarism and inflation. It is likely that Kahn's positions on British trade unions, while consistent with his theoretical views on inflation, did not increase Kahn's chances of influencing the debate in which he had engaged with Posner at a time when the Labour Party, through its proposal for a social contract, was seeking to obtain the unions' consent to voluntary wage restraint rather than on statutory incomes policy.[34]

At the beginning of 1976 the dispute between Kahn and Kaldor over the issues raised by the NCS was not entirely over, as evidence from Kahn's papers shows.[35] In the first letter, dated 23 January 1976, Kahn thanked Kaldor for sending two papers on the New Cambridge Approach to Bryan Hopkins, Chief Economic Adviser to the Treasury under the Labour Chancellor Denis Healey, while also formulating a number of criticisms. These criticisms concerned the way in which Kaldor had treated the multiplier in both his 1939 article on speculation and the aforementioned papers. Kahn accused Kaldor of ignoring some of the leakages that he had analysed in his 1931 article, as well as making assumptions about firms and their ability to save that were difficult to substantiate. Kaldor's pointed reply of 9 February 1976 (RFK/12/2/132/3)—'I don't think you ever understood my 1939 article on speculation, either then or now'—and the arguments he used to dismiss Kahn's remarks were rather abrupt. The same was true of Kahn's reply (RFK/12/2/132/2). This short but tense exchange, like so many before it, seems to have had no lasting impact on their relationship, which was characterised by constant ups and downs, as well as mutual respect and recognition.[36]

Between 1975 and 1977 the doctrine of the NCS was discussed in a series of seminars organised by the Treasury (Maloney, 2012, p. 1006), which initiated a gradual rapprochement between previously disparate positions. Concurrently, Cripps and Godley (1976) furnished an analytical illustration of their model, delineating the assumptions on which it is based. This paved the way for its endorsement by the Cambridge Economic Policy Group (CEPG) in 1977. In 1978, a seminar was held at Carnegie-Rochester, which brought together Godley, Featherstone and Posner with some prominent American monetarists. As Godley relocated to the United

[34] For a recent summary of the positions and relationship of trade unions with British governments during the 1970s, see Whitton (2016), among many others.

[35] Ref. RFK/12/2/132/2–19. See also NK/3/30/122/27–64.

[36] The final letters exchanged between Kahn and Kaldor from 1979 to 1983, preserved in the Kaldor papers (NK/3/30/122/2–26), bear witness to this. In these letters, Kahn compliments Kaldor on a couple of parliamentary speeches and the two exchange organisational information. Kahn also mentions the obituary he wrote for Sraffa for the King's annual report.

States, the tradition of the NCS merged with the research activities of the Levy Institute (Smith, 2016). When asked to share his views on a political issue once again, Kahn remained consistent with his beliefs, even if this meant disagreeing with the current thinking of the Labour Party, which he considered as his own until at least the mid-1970s. The same attitude, as we shall see, characterised Kahn's interaction with the British monetarists as well as his speeches in the House of Lords.

8.4 Kahn vs. the Monetarists on Inflation in Britain

The core of the monetarist analysis of post-war inflation in Britain, as set out by Harry Johnson, David Laidler and Michael Parkin, among others, was to view it as the consequence of poorly designed policies based on a misconception of how the economy functioned (see Friedman, 1975; Johnson, 1975a, 1975b, 1976; Laidler, 1976a, 1976b; Parkin, 1974a, 1974b, 1975). According to this explanation, the fundamental mistake made by post-war British governments and their Keynesian advisers had been to pursue an unrealistically low rate of unemployment (overfull employment) through expansionary fiscal policies. This had led to an increase in the public sector borrowing requirement, combined with attempts to keep nominal interest rates low through monetary expansion and direct controls. This combination had resulted in persistent structural inflationary pressures, as the monetary authorities had validated all wage and price increases, which were occasionally exacerbated by external factors such as the devaluation of sterling and the rise in oil and other commodity prices.

Therefore the wage and incomes policy advocated by the Keynesians, and by Kahn in particular, to keep inflation at bay was wrong, both because it was geared towards treating the symptoms and not the causes of the problem and because it was proposed without concern for the fact that 'its implementation becomes embogged in the effort to correct real distortions in the operation of the competitive system, or even more hopelessly in the effort to distort the workings of competition in order to secure a more ethically satisfactory distribution of income' (Johnson, 1975a, p. 202). This criticism led the British monetarists to regard incomes policy as a damaging waste of time and to recommend the rapid adoption of measures to curb public spending and the growth rate of the money supply, in order to reduce inflation and inflation expectations and bring the unemployment rate down to its natural level. At the same time, economic liberalisation, reduced public spending and taxation, and an end to attempts to regulate prices and wages would restore competition and freedom of enterprise.

In this context, Kahn—identified as a leading proponent of the Keynesian view on wage-driven inflation and the need to control it through incomes policy—responded. Three of his writings are particularly notable in this respect: an essay published in *The Banker* defending incomes policy against the monetarist critique (Kahn, 1975a)[37]; a second essay in the *Lloyds Bank Review* (Kahn, 1976a), written at the editor's invitation in response to Michael Parkin[38]; and a contribution to a symposium in the *Scottish Journal of Political Economy* (Kahn, 1976b).[39] By reading these essays together, the main differences between Kahn's analysis of inflation and that of the monetarists can be identified, as well as some common ground.

Kahn is willing to concede that a steady increase in the money supply is a concomitant factor in inflationary processes, and that under certain conditions, monetary restriction can reduce inflation. Furthermore, he agrees with monetarists in recognising the importance of inflation expectations in determining the behaviour of workers and businesses when setting wages and prices. However, while monetarists base this concept on formal models of adaptive expectations, Kahn attributes it to institutional and historical dynamics in wage bargaining. Apart from these shared features, however, Kahn's analysis of inflation differs profoundly from that of the monetarists.[40]

Regarding the causes of rising prices, Kahn rejects the monetarists' idea that inflation is determined by demand pressure during periods of economic slowdown, as experienced by the United Kingdom and other developed countries in the 1970s.

> To anybody who has not been led astray by the monetarists, it is surely obvious that, at times when there is a certain amount of slack in the use of the

[37] The text of the article and related correspondence can be found in RFK/12/2/65.

[38] Letter from J.R. Winton to Kahn, 23 July 1975, RFK/12/2/63/2.

[39] For details see RFK/12/2/67/12–17.

[40] Retrospectively, in his interview with Cristina Marcuzzo, Kahn reiterated his criticism of monetarism (a great scourge from which the whole world has been suffering for many years) as well as of some propositions of the New Cambridge School (Marcuzzo, 2020, pp. 39–44).

> country's productive potential, the *direct causal* [in the original] influence which determines the rate of increase in prices is the rate of increase in money costs, which is *determined* [in the original] by the rate of increase in wages, less the rate of growth of productivity — together with the rate of increase in prices of imported goods in terms of domestic currency. (Kahn, 1975a, p. 1169)

In a context where inflation and unemployment occur together, the observed increase in the money supply (and credit) results from the banking system's response to the increased demand for money for transaction purposes caused by rising wages, prices and incomes.

> I now come to what many of us regard as the correct formulation of the Quantity Theory of Money. As prices and incomes rise, more money is needed as a means of exchange. If this rising demand for money is not met by a rising supply of it — resulting from a rising volume of bank credit — credit will become tighter, rates of interest will rise, equity prices will fall. [...] It is not that an excessive rate of growth of the quantity of money is the *cause* [in the original] of rising prices. The *cause* is rising wages. But an adequate rate of growth of the quantity of money is a *necessary* [in the original] condition for avoiding a progressively deepening slump. [...] Moreover, experience in this country since the end of the War demonstrates that the slump would have to become catastrophic before the excessive upward movement of money wages was halted. [...] Meanwhile the country would have permanently suffered serious economic losses — not only loss of potential output but loss of productive investment, resulting in an even lower rate of economic growth. The heavy unemployment would not only have incurred much misery but it would result in serious embitterment. The purpose of incomes policy is to avoid these horrors. (Ibid.)

According to this view, the main causes of inflation, especially in Britain, are excessive wage demands, unrealistic expectations and poor coordination between trade unions, accused by Kahn of 'astonishing stupidity' (Kahn, 1976a), the sluggishness of entrepreneurs, and the acquiescence of the government, particularly in the presence of weak productivity and investment growth, as in the United Kingdom.

This naturally leads to a call for incomes policy as the only solution to inflation, in which all parties involved (trade unions, employers' organisations and monetary authorities) would be obliged to openly assume their responsibilities. In the absence of this, the alternative was the deflationary policies proposed by monetarists, which appeared painless and politically neutral.

> This is the political virtue of the monetarist case — it specifies responsibility in a single place. That is precisely what monetary restraint does *not* do. It operates through the "hidden hand". That is why it appeals to politicians and bankers. No particular individuals can be shown to be responsible for the damage which it inflicts. To stand up to the trade union movement is the courageous line. It is the line from which Mr Harold Wilson, encouraged by Mrs Barbara Castle [First Secretary of State and Secretary of State for Employment and Productivity in the Wilson government], ran away in the late "sixties". It is the cowardly monetarist line on which Mr Heath and his supporters won a General Election. Mr Heath had the courage, together with other members of his Cabinet, to repudiate his election pledge, and resorted, faced by acceleration of the upward movement of wages, to incomes policy. (Kahn, 1975a, p. 1170)

Part of the apparent neutrality of the monetarist diagnosis of inflation and how to cure it is linked to the concept of the natural rate of unemployment: the rate determined by the structural conditions of the economy, below which it is not possible to go without triggering inflation. For Kahn, the natural rate of unemployment is an artificial and politically insidious concept. Artificial because it is subject to very large margins of error and variability, and because it is conceived as an objective quantity that can be determined independently of the changing attitudes of trade unions. Politically insidious because it serves to present the choice between reducing inflation through monetary restraint and increasing unemployment as a restoration of the 'natural' conditions of the economic system by a responsible government, rather than the result of a deliberate choice to the detriment of workers.

> The real trouble about the concept of a 'natural unemployment rate' is two-fold. It is not explained what determines the rate of inflation when the level of unemployment lies at the natural rate; secondly, it fails to explain why the natural rate, if indeed there is one, appears to vary so much from one period to another period for any country and appears in any one period to vary so much between different countries. (Ibid., p. 1170)

Kahn rejects the idea of considering the control of inflation as a technical problem. Instead, he considers it a political issue to be resolved through negotiations and institutional adjustments. Relying on monetary discipline to restore price stability, as the monetarists recommended, obscures responsibility for the human and economic costs of deflation, such as unemployment, loss of investment and industrial unrest. This approach risks worsening the situation rather than improving it. A better approach, albeit a more difficult one, would be to introduce measures to increase productivity, and in this way improve living standards and industrial relations, rationalise wage-setting institutions, to prevent the leapfrog effect, improve industrial relations, and promote cooperation agreements between the government, employers and trade unions (Kahn, 1976b).

In early 1975, Kahn had a chance to express some of his views on inflation and monetarism while lecturing in various Italian cities, including Turin, Genoa, Rome and Bari.[41] Two identical typescript copies of the text of this lecture, dated 22 February 1975, survive among Kahn's papers. This lecture is of interest for what it adds to Kahn's ideas on inflation, in particular on the international dimension of inflationary processes and the positive contribution that cost-of-living wage indexation clauses can make to slowing down the inflationary spiral. Basing his exposition on the view that inflation 'is directly caused by rising wages, while at the same time there is a feed-back reaction — in the form of the well-known vicious spiral — of rising cost of living on the rise of wages [...] (and also) in part to rising process of imported raw materials, foodstuffs, and manufactured goods', Kahn adds:

> It spreads partly because one country's rise in costs and prices becomes another country's rise in the prices of imports. Another reason is that when costs in an industry in one country rise ahead of costs in the same industry in another country, the two industries being competitive, in the course of wage negotiations the trade-union leaders are in a stronger position in the latter than in the former country to secure substantial wage increases and the employers are readier in the latter country than in the form to grant substantial increases. There is thus a tendency for some uniformity in the rate of increase in unit labour costs — the excess of the increase of wages over the increase of productivity, or output per head — after adjustment is made for changes in exchange-rates. (RFK/2/19/559–560)

[41] The text of the lecture on inflation can be found in RFK/2/19/556–583. Evidence of Kahn's trip to Italy in February 1975 can be found in two letters addressed respectively to Luigi Pasinetti (RFK/12/2/9/2–3) and Austin Robinson (RFK/12/2/9/4–5).

Kahn attributes the spread of inflation across Europe to the dismantling of income policies, which began in the Netherlands in 1959, followed by France and Italy. He emphasised the impact of unjustified wage disparities and union militancy in triggering wage explosions. Meanwhile, countries such as Germany and Switzerland managed to avoid such inflation thanks to union restraint. Although rising oil and commodity prices contributed to inflation in the early 1970s, Kahn observes that their impact was both delayed and transient. Contrary to popular belief, he argued that wage indexation mechanisms helped contain inflation by clarifying wage dynamics and reducing conflict. Apart from this, the most effective way to control inflation is through a coordinated wage-setting process involving the government, unions and employers. If this is unachievable, however, reliance on monetarist austerity could lead to recession, unemployment and long-term economic damage.

> No doubt there would come a point at which wages would cease to rise at an unacceptable rate. But what price to pay for that outcome? It is not easy, as the monetarists themselves admit, once an economy is in a state of serious depression and a financial crisis prevails, to bring about a recovery, which at best will be achieved only after a period of years. Meanwhile much potential output and additions to productive equipment will have been lost for ever, and much misery entailed and much indignation provoked. It is unlikely that any Government would allow such a situation to develop, least of all in a country like Italy in which any Government is unstable. If the Government did not fairly readily capitulate, the result in most countries would be a revolution. (RFK/2/19/569)

8.5 Eltis and the Attack on the Conventional Keynesian Doctrine

The monetarist analysis of post-war inflation against the opinion of the Keynesians in Britain was occasionally intertwined with the claim that Keynes's disciples, including Kahn, had distorted the master's ideas after his death to create a conventional Keynesian doctrine that Keynes would not have never endorsed. This doctrine, in turn, would have influenced UK policymaking in the 1960s and 1970s, causing many of the country's economic problems. Walter Eltis, a former Cambridge academic, was one of these critics (Eltis, 1976).[42]

Tracing this doctrine back to Harrod, Kaldor and Kahn, Eltis questions the belief that expansionary fiscal policy, especially public investment, reliably boosts employment, output and savings. He also criticises the notion that increasing the money supply invariably leads to lower interest rates without causing inflation, particularly in an open economy such as the United Kingdom's, where such policies can lead to crises in the balance of payments and cyclical instability. He highlights the impracticality of proposed solutions such as protectionism or global policy coordination to maintain full employment and balance of payments equilibrium internationally. Finally, he claims that Keynesian models overlook important factors such as the behaviour of firms, profits and the role of savings in driving investment. Eltis singles out Kahn for dismissing the possibility that monetary expansion could lead to higher interest rates due to inflationary expectations and for treating government deficits as irrelevant to macroeconomic outcomes.[43]

As Kahn prepared his reply to Eltis, he was not alone, as archival evidence suggests. The first relevant document is a letter from Joan Robinson to Eltis,[44] dated 14 October 1976. Joan Robinson, who had supervised Eltis at Cambridge, recalls that 'vulgar Keynesianism did not come out of Cambridge. It came in theory from Hicks and in policy from Harrod'. She

[42] In 1976, Walter Eltis became prominent in British policy debates, as co-author of a book entitled *Too Few Producers* with R. Bacon (Bacon & Eltis, 1976). The main thesis of the book was that in the 1960s and early 1970s the growth of the public sector in Britain had diverted resources from the private sector, contributing to falling growth, rising inflation and unemployment. This thesis, apart from the problematic aspects that were soon highlighted (e.g. Ietto-Gillies, 1978; Hadjimatheou & Skouras, 1979), had great resonance and influence on both the Conservative and Labour parties in government. On Eltis and his contribution, see Appendix C and Dimsdale (2019).

[43] With regard to this issue, Eltis's criticism of Keynesian doctrine is associated with a standard monetarist argument, at least since Friedman (1968). Conversely, Eltis is not considered one of the recognised exponents of UK monetarism (e.g. Davies, 2012), nor is he known for actively promoting monetarist ideas (Middleton, 1998, pp. 288–311). As we shall see, Eltis himself rejected the monetarist label attributed to him by Kahn, despite clear similarities between his views and those of the monetarists, for example on the damage caused by excessive public spending and taxation, or on the need to free productive forces from excessive regulation.

[44] Letter from J. Robinson to Eltis, ref. RFK/12/2/72/11–12.

goes on to accuse Eltis of deliberately misreading Kahn, regarding his opinions on the budget deficit.

> He was talking about above the line and below the line budget and saying that government investment (below the line) has the same direct effect as private investment. The difference in the way it is financed affects money and this should be either offset or supplemented if changes in the quantity of money are desirable. No good Keynesian could possibly say that the budget deficit (above the line) is not important. (RFK/12/2/72/11)[45]

In his reply, dated 26 October 1976,[46] Eltis reiterates that vulgar Keynesianism, 'taught to tens of thousands of students in British, Australian and Canadian universities', has done far too much damage and should be 'crushed as hard as possible'. Against Robinson's opinion of Hicks and Harrod, Eltis points to Keynes's favourable reaction to the IS-LM model and Harrod's importance as an official government adviser to Macmillan. As for Kahn and the question of the government budget deficit, his reply, while courteous, leaves little room for compromise:

> I am puzzled by what you say about my "wilfully" misreading Kahn. I am sure you know that I would not "wilfully" misread anyone, and I am extremely sorry if I inadvertently did so, but I do not accept that a budget deficit below the line is without significance, and to believe that its monetary effect can be offset or supplemented as desired is precisely one of the parts of the "Keynesian conventional wisdom" that I was criticising. [...] It is precisely the supposition that increasing the money supply tends to lower the rate of interest that I have been attacking. As it raises portfolio prices in general, it tends to raise actual (and thence expected) rates of inflation [...] and therefore to make bonds still less attractive in relation to other portfolio assets. I therefore stand by my argument, and my view that the quotations make a point that needs to be made, namely that the most rigorous "Keynesian" with probably the most sophisticated understanding of

[45] In the context of British budgetary policy, the terms 'above the line' and 'below the line' have historically referred to different components of the government's accounts. 'Above the line' denoted current revenue and expenditure, such as tax receipts, welfare payments and interest on debt, reflecting the government's fiscal stance. By contrast, below the line captured financial transactions such as lending to public corporations or capital investment, which were considered outside the scope of day-to-day fiscal policy. This distinction enabled policymakers, particularly during the post-war period, to justify borrowing for investment purposes while maintaining a balanced current budget.

[46] Letter from W. Eltis to J. Robinson, ref. RFK/12/2/72/9–10.

> portfolios of anyone in 1958 (he was publishing and I assume thinking about them a great deal about that time) still drifted into the position that extra money will not depress bond prices. [...] I am sure Kahn would see the argument much as I do in broad terms today, and put it far more elegantly, but it is of historical significance that he got it wrong in 1958. (RFK/12/2/72/9)

A second document on the 'Kahn–Eltis' issue is an exchange of letters between Kahn and Laurie Tarshis, who was then Head of the Division of Social Sciences at Scarborough College, University of Toronto, and who had spent some years at Cambridge in the 1930s.[47]

In a first letter, dated 3 January 1977, Tarshis announces to Kahn his intention to write an article in response to Eltis, entitled 'The Failure of "The Failure of Keynesian Contemporary Economics" doctrine'.[48] The article was never published, but in a ten-page typewritten letter dated 14 January 1977, Tarshis gives Kahn a preview of its contents that helped Kahn to draft his own reply to Eltis. This letter, which may have been annotated by Michael Posner, challenges Eltis's assumptions and interpretations. It argues that Eltis's numerical examples misrepresent the open economy multiplier and are based on flawed assumptions. The letter also criticises his portrayal of Keynesian views on monetary policy as a simplification that ignores Keynes's own nuanced treatment of the effect of money on interest rates and asset substitution. While acknowledging that inflationary expectations may have affected interest rates more in the 1970s than in the 1930s, the letter emphasises the need to consider broader inflationary pressures, such as oil shocks and wage-driven costs. These are issues that Eltis fails to address adequately.

Bearing in mind the exchange between Eltis and Robinson and Tarshis's arguments, Kahn (1977a) also replied to Eltis at the invitation of Cristopher Johnson, the journal's editor. Kahn accused Eltis of misrepresenting Keynes by suggesting that he (and the Keynesians) viewed full

[47] Letter from L. Tarshis to R. Kahn, ref. RFK/12/2/72/14–29. On Tarshis as an early Post-Keynesian economist see Harcourt (1993, pp. 69–82).

[48] In the same letter Tarshis sent Kahn a second, longer article on Keynes's aggregate supply function. The article, published in a volume in honour of Scitovsky (Tarshis, 1979), is important for what Tarshis writes about the connection between the aggregate supply function proposed by Keynes in the *General Theory* and the content of Kahn's lectures on short-run economics, which Tarshis had taken at Cambridge in 1932 and on which he had made a series of notes which he later sent to Kahn, who had asked for them.

employment as a precise, quantifiable target, rather than a matter of degree. Kahn also rejects Eltis's assertion that Keynesians ignored the complexities of balancing full employment with external equilibrium and the influence of global interest rates. Eltis's analysis of money and interest rates is also flawed because it disregards the implicit assumption of zero inflation expectations. Finally, Kahn sarcastically dismisses Eltis's idea that inflation might be triggered by monetary expansion through rising real estate prices, investment and bottlenecks in domestic supply chains. In his reply, Eltis (1977) welcomes Kahn's acknowledgement that a rising money supply can lead to higher nominal interest rates, and hopes that this insight will enter mainstream teaching. He also criticises the tendency among Keynesians to advocate controls similar to those in Eastern Bloc economies in order to maintain full employment. Eltis also rejects the 'monetarist' label, criticising Kahn for overlooking the role of real estate in household portfolios and its macroeconomic significance.

Taken as a whole, the exchange between Kahn and Eltis illustrates the extent to which two men of different generations, but educated in the same ideas, could end up on opposite sides of the fence in their views of economic mechanisms in the 1970s. On the one hand we have Eltis, born in Czechoslovakia and emigrating to the United Kingdom, with his liberal-conservative outlook, his belief in the validity of certain basic propositions of classical political economy (particularly with regard to saving, profit and competition), and his belief in the deleterious effects of applying a simplified Keynesianism and the Radcliffe Doctrine to British economic policy. On the other hand, we find Kahn willing to accept some specific points of Eltis's critique, even at Tarshis's suggestion, but decidedly affirming the validity and subtlety of Keynes and his doctrine over Eltis's crude treatment. The same firmness appears in a second episode of a similar kind, which pitted Kahn against T.W. Hutchison.

8.6 'A Dreadful Piece by Hutchison'

In one of the letters to Tarshis, Kahn refers to being engaged in formulating a response to a 'dreadful piece by Hutchison'. The piece to which Kahn refers is contained in a pamphlet entitled *Keynes v. the 'Keynesians' ...?* written by T.W. Hutchison.[49] In this pamphlet, published as Hobart

[49] On T.W. Hutchison, historian of economics and methodologist, see Appendix C and O'Brien (2009). On Hutchison's Cambridge education with references to Kahn see Tribe (1997, p. 127).

Paperback No. 11 by the Institute of Economic Affairs,[50] Hutchison analyses Keynes's ideas on full employment, price stability and free trade by examining his writings and statements in the years after 1936, with the aim of highlighting a fundamental incompatibility between Keynes's views and those of Kahn, Joan Robinson, Harrod, Kaldor and Balogh, whom Hutchison calls the pseudo-Keynesians, in the 1950s and 1960s (Hutchison, 1977).

Drawing on the arguments of the monetarists and Eltis, whom he quotes, Hutchison sets out to show how much of the criticism of Keynes should be directed at his disciples, who were guilty of turning the master's subtle and changing ideas into rigid dogmas, and of putting these dogmas at the service of policies of full employment and growth that were beneficial to politicians and trade unions, but deeply damaging to Britain and other countries where they were applied, as a cause of inflation and over-regulation. This frontal attack on the pseudo-Keynesians and on Kahn in particular is combined with Hutchison's attempt to show the compatibility of some of Keynes's ideas with those of Pigou, Robertson, Lionel Robbins and to some extent even Milton Friedman. A daring attempt favoured by the rediscovery of Keynes's minor writings, which in those years were being edited by Donald Moggridge (several times mentioned by Hutchison), and by the possibility, underlined by Moggridge himself, of finding 'more than enough ammunition in Keynes for many varied points of view, especially if .... [one] wishes to lift it out of context' (Hutchison, 1977, p. 48).

Specifically, Keynes would have anticipated a natural rate of unemployment of around 10–12% in 1937 and 3–4% in the post-war period. He would also have recommended caution against inflation and expressed scepticism about controls that could disrupt the efficient operation of markets. Notably, he reiterated the long-term benefits of free trade in his

[50] Founded in 1955, as a research educational charity, to study the role of 'markets and pricing systems as technical devices for registering preferences and apportioning resources', The Institute of Economic Affairs (IEA) provided a consistent alternative analysis to the macroeconomic hegemony of the 1950s to 1970s (Muller, 1996). During the 1970s, as politicians and public opinion began to question the economic role of the state, the IEA and its publications gained increasing recognition and success. It was one of the main venues in Britain for the popularisation of monetarist ideas (e.g. Walters, 1969; Friedman, 1975) and the criticism of Keynesianism. One of the IEA's series, the Hobart Paperbacks, launched in 1971, was particularly important in this respect, with contributions from S. Brittan, F.A. Hayek, W.A. Niskanen and G. Tullock, among others.

final article, published in the *Economic Journal* in 1946. In contrast, the pseudo-Keynesians of Cambridge (Kahn, Robinson and Kaldor) and Oxford (Harrod and Balogh), having disregarded Keynes's caution, recommended economic doctrines that bore little resemblance to those of Keynes. These included pursuing over-full employment through demand expansion, maximising the growth rate as the primary policy objective, downgrading price stability as an economic policy objective, referring to incomes policies to stop inflation, and taking an overly optimistic view of public spending.

Kahn in particular is accused of misreading Keynes's thinking on the British unemployment rate in 1937, attributing Keynes's apparent acceptance of a rate of 10–12% to an implicit desire to maintain a reserve margin to be exploited once rearmament entered an accelerated phase. A second charge concerns Kahn's reading of Keynes's views on post-war problems, where he had expressed his optimism in the face of the dollar shortage problem, his appeal to the 'wisdom of Adam Smith' regarding the long-term advantages of free trade, and his impatience with some modern developments in Keynesian theory that had become 'sour and silly'. The third charge relates to Kahn's testimony to the Radcliffe Committee, which, in Hutchison's view, demonstrates his lack of understanding of the monetary nature of inflation, as evidenced by his recommendation of a wage policy to combat it (Hutchison, 1977, pp. 28–30). Finally, the fourth charge concerns the inconsistency between Kahn's attack on the British trade unions of the 1970s and his calls on the same unions to follow the example of their German counterparts and moderate their wage demands, thereby helping to contain inflation (ibid., pp. 33–34).

Kahn starts with these words to accuse Hutchison of piecing together a series of sentences chosen to support a preconceived thesis. In doing so, Hutchison ignores the context in which those sentences were uttered, the circumstances that might justify them, and the presence of other sentences by Keynes that support positions identified by Hutchison as pseudo-Keynesian (ibid., pp. 48–57). Regarding the role of trade unions in influencing wages and inflation, and Keynes's refusal to use unemployment to control trade union demands, Kahn references extracts from *How to Pay for the War*, as well as unpublished correspondence from Keynes, from which 'the beginnings — but no more than the beginnings — of an incomes policy, under which the rate of increase of wages and prices is largely determined by negotiations at a political level', emerge (ibid., p. 52). Kahn is scathing in his criticism of Hutchison's attempt to attribute to Keynes the anticipation of the concept of a natural rate of unemployment, and he also criticises Hutchison for ignoring the evidence of the fiscally prudent attitude of British governments in the post-war decades, as documented by Matthews (1968), and for overlooking the circumstances, which justified Kahn's words while testifying before the Radcliffe Commission, at a time when inflation and inflation expectations were still substantially under control.

A reading of Kahn's reply to Hutchison and of the latter's rejoinder (Hutchison, 1977, pp. 61–64) reveals a deep incommunicability between the two.[51] Hutchison and Kahn stick to their respective positions, trading accusations of misusing sources and distorting Keynes's words to suit their own worldviews. What is at stake is Keynes's intellectual legacy, of which Kahn was a natural repository and which clearly remained important to British economists of Hutchison's generation. Again, as in his response to the criticisms of the monetarists and Eltis, Kahn sought the support of the economists among those younger and closer to him. Evidence of this can be found in a letter from J. Trevithick to Kahn dated 1 June 1977 (one month before the publication of Hutchison's pamphlet and Kahn's reply and rejoinder) and in some typed notes entitled 'Rough comments on Hutchison's paper' and Kahn's reply, which refer to Trevithick's own work (RFK/12/2/69/110–115).[52]

8.7 Kahn as a Public *Persona*: House of Lords, Political Views and Public Debate

During the 1970s Kahn occasionally intervened in the political debate, both through his speeches in the House of Lords (seven in all during the decade) and through articles and letters in newspapers and magazines. He did so to reiterate his belief in incomes policy, the contention that austerity could exacerbate inflation rather than tame it by generating frustration in the trade unions, and the need to direct private and public resources

[51] The same applies, in a minor key, to Austin Robinson's brief comment on Hutchison (1977, pp. 58–60) and Hutchison's rejoinder. For A. Robinson's negative reaction to Hutchison's paper, see also RFK/12/2/69/116, which contains a letter from A. Robinson to A. Seldon of the Institute of Economic Affairs where Robinson laments Hutchison's choice to refer to Joan Robinson as Lady Robinson as a deliberate insult.

[52] On James Trevithick see Appendix C, Harcourt and Palma (1994) and the University of Cambridge website https://www.econ.cam.ac.uk/news/2025/remembering-james-trevithick-1945-2025

towards investment. These interventions are notable for the vehemence with which Kahn presents his ideas, as well as for an attitude that leads him to put consistency with his own economic beliefs above party loyalty.

Between 1973 and 1977, Kahn's interventions in the House of Lords consistently prioritised rational economic management over party allegiance. Notably, in 1973 he praised the Conservative Heath government's counter-inflation strategy of combining demand stimulation with statutory price and incomes policies. However, he also urged further restraint on private consumption and targeted state controls to address labour and supply bottlenecks (Kahn, 1973a). He warned Labour peers that wage inflation had already accelerated under the Wilson government due to the abandonment of incomes policy, marking the beginning of his public criticism of Labour's economic stance. In later speeches, Kahn urged his party not to oppose statutory wage controls, criticising the reliance on industrial strife as a mechanism for wage moderation and stressing the need for coordination over conflict (Kahn, 1973b).

During the miners' strike, he cautioned against conceding to sectoral wage demands and predicted inflationary leapfrogging (Kahn, 1973c). In February 1974, he proposed amending the Counter-Inflation Act to allow limited exceptions while preserving the broader framework (Kahn, 1974a). While Wilson's Labour government was in power (1974–1976), Kahn remained sceptical of high-unemployment strategies and monetarist prescriptions. While he supported the Labour Chancellor Dennis Healey's initial counter-inflation budgets (Kahn, 1974b), he objected to the over-reliance on monetary targets and criticised the empirical weakness of the Phillips Curve in explaining wage trends (Kahn, 1974c). Rejecting the monetarist claim that monetary restraint could sustainably reduce inflation without permanent negative effects on employment levels, he argued that this approach would worsen recession and discourage investment (Kahn, 1975b).

Kahn also opposed proposals from the New Cambridge School for import controls and fiscal austerity. Instead, he called for a credible incomes policy and productive investment to address inflation without economic stagnation (Kahn, 1975b, 1975c). In his July 1975 speech in support of the Labour government's *Attack on Inflation* White Paper, he expressed renewed optimism in incomes policy provided that the targets were realistic and would not deter investment (Kahn, 1975c, 1975d). In his final address in 1977, Kahn again emphasised the importance of increasing productive investment and argued for reducing public expenditure as a proportion of national income in order to reallocate resources towards long-term growth and industrial renewal (Kahn, 1977b).

Kahn's criticism of Labour's economic policy in the 1970s was linked to his growing intolerance of what he saw as the maximalist and, to him, destructive attitude of many trade union representatives. This was one of the main reasons why Kahn left the Labour Party and joined the Social Democratic Party in the early 1980s, following James Meade.

The Social Democratic Party (SDP) was founded in 1981 by a group of senior Labour politicians—Roy Jenkins, David Owen, Shirley Williams and Bill Rodgers—who had become disillusioned with the Labour Party's shift to the left. The SDP sought to occupy a centrist position in British politics, advocating moderate social democracy, support for the mixed economy, European integration and constitutional reform. Initially enjoying significant public support, it contested elections in alliance with the Liberal Party as the SDP-Liberal Alliance. Despite its early electoral success, the party failed to challenge the dominance of the Labour and Conservative parties. By 1988 it had merged with the Liberals to form the Liberal Democrats. However, a small breakaway faction of the SDP continued under David Owen for a few more years.[53]

In his public statements in the 1970s, Kahn emphasised the importance of supporting investment, often combining this with appeals to British trade unions to opt for wage moderation and collaboration with employers and the government within an incomes policy framework, rather than pursuing conflict and demanding excessive wage increases. When the unions refused this invitation, Kahn responded angrily, making comments that did little to enhance his popularity among the Labour Party, of which he was a member, or among the young radical economists of Cambridge. For example, in his response to Parkin from 1976, which was discussed above, we read:

> Our central employer (CBI) and trade-union (TUC) organizations are very feeble bodies and the men who run them are sadly lacking in intelligence. [...] One serious aspect of the astonishing stupidity of our trade-union leaders, and of our unofficial labour leaders, is their complete failure to take a long-sighted view. Their sole concern is with the level of the real wage in the

[53] As Susan Howson recalls in her personal communication with the author on 16 August 2024, both Meade and Kahn joined the SDP at its inception. Meade was, in fact, more heavily involved in the party than Kahn, having served on its Economic Policy Committee from the outset. Reference to the SDP and Meade in Kahn's papers is RFK/11/5.

immediate future, as opposed to the rate of increase in the real wage. By insisting on unduly high wage increases, they force the government and the central bank to adopt restrictive measures and they undermine the confidence of employers. [...] The result is not only unemployment and surplus physical capacity, but a low rate of productive investment, resulting in a low rate of growth of productivity and a low rate of increase in the real wage. [...] Our trade-union structure is quite extraordinarily intricate and irrational. We have far too many trade unions. [...] Our basic trouble is that trade-union leaders naturally want to be seen to be earning their salaries. This is the main reason for what otherwise would be quite unintelligible insistence on the virtues of our traditional system of collective bargaining. It is easy to see how easily the laws of the jungle can result in an accelerating upward movement of wages. (Kahn, 1976a, pp. 4–5)

These words immediately attracted the attention of the press, as evidenced by two articles in *The Financial Times* of 5 January 1976 (RFK/12/2/63/62–63) and *The Sunday Times* of 11 January 1976 (RFK/12/2/66), which recalled the adjectives 'feeble and stupid' used by Kahn to describe the behaviour of the trade unions. In a letter of 17 January 1976 to the financier Sir Hugh Weeks, in response to his own letter of 13 January, in which Weeks praised Kahn's article, Kahn replied:

What I find particularly irritating is being regarded as a "Union basher." I devoted quite a lot of space to the narrowing of differentials [...] and to the dangers involved. Any serious Trade Union official should have been interested in this. [...] All experience shows that narrowing differentials over a period of years leads to a wage explosion as a result of the better paid workers insisting on restoring their differentials. I have not heard a word on this important issue. [...] When I come, on page 4, to discuss why our country is so heavily subject to inflation, my very first reason is the low rate of growth of productivity. I have been given no credit for this at all. Nor have I been given any credit for arguing against the danger of a large Public Sector financial deficit.[54]

British entrepreneurs were not immune to Kahn's criticism, either. Kahn was quick to criticise businesses for their negligence in cooperating with the government to implement wage and income control policies, as well as for their failure to respond promptly to economic adversity. For

[54] Letter from Kahn to Woods 17 January 1976 (RFK/12/2/63/28–29).

example, in a short 1975 article written for a symposium on the effects of the first oil crisis, Kahn wrote

> There is every sign that our industrialists are letting us down very badly indeed. [...] The hideous fact is that, on present form, the UK is one of *the* least successful industrial countries — almost certainly *the* least successful industrial country — in securing the orders which the oil producing countries are placing at a rapidly increasing rate. (Kahn, 1975e, pp. 36–37)

Once again, behind the criticism of trade unions for their stubbornness in pushing for unrealistic and unacceptable wage demands, of entrepreneurs for their short-sightedness and slowness in responding to current difficulties, and of Labour governments for being willing to abandon incomes policy and full employment, Kahn's underlying economic vision emerges: that full employment should be the primary goal of economic policy, together with implementing shared measures (and sacrifices) to keep price dynamics and the balance of payments under control. In the 1970s, Kahn reacted strongly and vehemently against the selfishness and short-sightedness of trade unions and employers, something he had rarely done in previous years.

All the themes Kahn touched on in his public interventions on inflation, unemployment and the balance of payments in the 1970s return in Kahn and Posner (1977). The article was written as Britain began to enjoy the fruits of the discovery of North Sea oil. The external deficit of the early 1970s had turned into a surplus, the pound was strong again, and inflation was gradually falling. A lively controversy developed over how to manage the exchange rate and the balance of payments. On the one hand, there were those who welcomed the surplus, the appreciation of sterling, and the continuation of restrictive fiscal and monetary policies because of their positive contribution to further reducing inflation and strengthening the United Kingdom's international financial position. On the other hand, there were those who argued for an end to austerity and a return to a policy of stimulating employment and investment, even if these stimulus measures might partially reduce the external surplus, which they believed should not be reversed anyway. Kahn and Posner supported the second position on the basis of two main arguments.

The first argument revolves around analysing the impact of the policies of developed countries, producers of manufactured goods, on less developed countries, producers of raw materials. When developed countries opt for austerity, they not only reduce employment, profit expectations and domestic investment, but also create the conditions for the same effects to occur in less developed countries. Reducing the rate of growth of productive capacity in the less developed countries helps to restrict the supply of raw materials and sets the stage for a sharp rise in commodity prices, with all the negative consequences that entails, as soon as the international economy improves. The second argument, which echoes some of Kahn's classic themes, revolves around the fallacy of relying on rising unemployment to defeat trade union demands and thereby reduce inflation. For Kahn and Posner, the opposite effect is far more likely.

> Levels of unemployment of the order of the one and a half million cause resentment against authority (including trade union leaders as well as the government). This resentment takes a number of forms. Trades union leaders are subject to strong pressure to make larger demands for wage increases than they think desirable in the interests of the country or of their members, taking the trade union membership as a whole. Shop stewards are encouraged to take independent action, and demands of which the trades union leader disapprove are put forward at the establishment, plant and shop-floor levels. Generally, unions discipline is undermined. As a result of all this the rate of increase of money earnings may rise while the level of unemployment rises as well. Even monetarists agree that those two statistics can increase together, at any rate for a period. (Kahn & Posner, 1977, p. 33)

On the basis of this diagnosis, and their scepticism about the attempt to control prices without controlling wages, as the Callaghan Government was trying to do, Kahn and Posner called on the government to take measures to support employment and to use the slowdown in inflation to reopen the issue of wage differentials. All this must be done to avoid the risk that the government, by relying on the dwindling oil surplus and the temporary strength of the pound, creates the conditions for a progressive and permanent reduction in British productive capacity and a state of stagflation and semi-permanent stagnation.

By the second half of the 1970s, Kahn's public presence gradually diminished. He stopped delivering public speeches in the House of Lords and to the press in 1977. It was now clear that Kahn's vision, forged in the 1930s and 1940s, of a government acting in the national interest with the help of impartial civil servants and academic advisors, and social bodies coordinating their decisions based on government strategies, was obsolete. Faced with the decline of his physical and intellectual strength and aware of his limited ability to influence government decisions indirectly through his contacts with Berrill and Posner, Kahn gradually withdrew from public debate. He devoted the final years of his intellectual career to rethinking and re-evaluating the Keynesian legacy and his own contribution to economic theory. In 1981, Kahn signed an appeal against Mrs. Thatcher's monetarist policies alongside more than 300 British economists, including Neild. This can be considered his final public statement on British economic policy.[55]

References

Backhouse, R. (2020). Economic theory in an imperfect world: Frank Hahn, general equilibrium and Keynesian economics. *Oxford Economic Papers, 72*(4), 1091–1107.

Backhouse, R., & Forder, J. (2013). Rationalizing incomes policy in Britain, 1948–1979. *History of Economic Thought and Policy, 1*, 17–35.

Bacon, R., & Eltis, W. (1976). *Britain's economic problem. Too Few Producers.* Macmillan.

Ball, S., & Seldon, A (1996). *The heath government 1970–74: A reappraisal.* Longman.

Barca, F. (1977). Premesse analitiche e politica economica della 'Nuova Scuola di Cambridge'. *Note economiche, 10*(5/6), 115–140.

Bishpam, J. A. (1975). The new Cambridge and 'monetarist' criticisms of 'conventional' economic policy making. *National Institute Economic Review, 74*, 39–55.

Boltho, A. (1982). *The European economy: Growth and crisis.* Oxford University Press.

Bruce-Gardyne, J. (1976). *Myths and magic in economic management: An analysis of the evidence given to the house of commons expenditure committee in the summer of 1974 on public expenditure, inflation and the balance of payments.* Barry Rose for the Centre for Policy Studies.

Byrne, C., Randall, N., & Theakston, K. (2020). The collapse of Keynesian welfarism 1970–1979: Heath, Wilson, Callaghan. In C. Byrne, N. Randall, & K. Theakston (Eds.), *Disjunctive prime ministerial leadership in British politics* (pp. 51–83). Springer.

[55] See Neild (2014) for more information on this appeal. The text of the letter, which had been prepared by Robert Neild and Frank Hahn, and the full list of signatories, including Kahn, are available in the Thatcher Archive: see online https://archive.margaretthatcher.org/doc02/FECEBF1EA893413EB9D3FA246218F30A.pdf.

Clerc, P., & Dos Santos Ferreira, R. (2020). On *Keynesian economics and the economics of Keynes* after fifty years. *European Journal of the History of Economic Thought, 27*(6), 919–937.
Cobham, D. (1984). Convergence, divergence and realignment in British macroeconomics. *Banca Nazionale del Lavoro Quarterly Review, 37*(149), 159–173.
Coddington, A. (1976). Keynesian economics: The search for first principles. *Journal of Economic Literature, 14*(4), 1258–1273.
Cohen, A. J., & Harcourt, G. C. (2003). Whatever happened to the Cambridge capital theory controversies? *Journal of Economic Perspectives, 17*(1), 199–214.
Copley, J. (2017). Financial deregulation and the role of statecraft: Lessons from Britain's 1971 competition and credit control measures. *New Political Economy, 22*(6), 692–708.
Cripps, F., & Godley, W. (1976). A formal analysis of the Cambridge economic policy group model. *Economica, 43*, 335–348.
Dasgupta, P. (2013, April). Obituary: Frank Hahn. *Newsletter, Royal Economic Society*. https://res.org.uk/newsletter/april-2013-newsletter-frank-hahn/
Davies, A. (2012). *The evolution of British monetarism: 1968–1979*. Oxford economic and social history working papers no. 104. University of Oxford, Department of Economics.
De Vroey, M. (2016). *A history of macroeconomics from Keynes to Lucas and beyond*. Cambridge University Press.
Dimsdale, N. (2019, November). Walter Eltis: A creative economist of genuine originality. *Newsletter Royal Economic Society*. https://res.org.uk/newsletter/november-2019-newsletter-walter-eltis/
Dixon, R. (1982). On the new Cambridge school. *Journal of Post Keynesian Economics, 5*(2), 289–294.
Eichengreen, B. J. (1983). Protection, real wage resistance and employment. *Weltwirtschaftliches Archiv, 119*(3), 429–452.
Eltis, W. (1976). The failure of the Keynesian conventional wisdom. *Lloyds Bank Review, 32*, 1–18.
Eltis, W. (1977). Reply to Kahn. *Lloyds Bank Review, 33*.
Flanagan, R. J., Soskice, D. W., & Ulman, L. (1983). *Unionism, economic stabilization, and incomes policies: European experience*. Brookings Institution.
Friedman, M. (1968). The role of monetary policy. *American Economic Review, 58*(1), 1–17.
Friedman, M. (1975). *Unemployment versus Inflation?* IEA occasional paper no. 44. Institute of Economic Affairs.
Godley, W., & Cripps, F. (1973a, January 9). Need for unconventional methods. *The Times*.
Godley, W., & Cripps, F. (1973b, September 6). Drastic steps to restore the balance. *The Times*.

Godley, W., & Cripps, F. (1974a, January 22). Why Britain needs a fresh set of principles to manage the economy. *The Times*.

Godley, W., & Cripps, F. (1974b, January 23). Payment deficits: The strategic options. *The Times*.

Goodhart, C. A. E. (2015). Competition and credit control: Some personal reflections. *Financial History Review, 22*(02), 235–246.

Griffiths, B., & Wood, G. E. (1984). Monetarism in the United Kingdom. In B. Griffiths & G. E. Wood (Eds.), *Monetarism in the United Kingdom* (pp. 3–12). Palgrave Macmillan.

Hadjimatheou, G., & Skouras, A. (1979). Britain's economic problem: The growth of the non-market sector? *Economic Journal, 89*, 392–401.

Hall, P. A. (1992). The movement from Keynesianism to monetarism: Institutional analysis and British economic policy in the 1970s. In S. Steinmo, K. Thelen, & F. Longstreth (Eds.), *Structuring politics: Historical institutionalism in comparative analysis* (pp. 90–113). Cambridge University Press.

Halliwell, J. F. (1988). Comparative macroeconomics of stagflation. *Journal of Economic Literature, 26*(1), 1–28.

Hamouda, O. F., & Harcourt, G. C. (1988). Post Keynesianism: From criticism to coherence. *Bulletin of Economic Research, 40*(1), 1–33.

Harcourt, G. C. (1972). *Some Cambridge controversies in the theory of capital*. Cambridge University Press.

Harcourt, G. C. (1993). An early post-Keynesian: Lorie Tarshis. Or: Tarshis on Tarshis by Harcourt. In *Post-Keynesian essays in biography: Portraits of twentieth-century political economists* (pp. 69–82). Macmillan.

Harcourt, G. C., & Palma, G. (1994). Introduction. *Cambridge Journal of Economics, 18*(1), 1–2.

Hay, C. (2010). Chronicles of a death foretold. The winter of discontent and construction of the crisis of British Keynesianism. *Parliamentary Affairs, 63*, 446–470.

Henry, S. G. B., Sawyer, M. C., & Smith, P. (1976). Models of inflation in the United Kingdom: An evaluation. *National Institute Economic Review, 77*(1), 60–71.

Hodgson, G. F., Gagliardi, F., & Gindis, D. (2018). From Cambridge Keynesian to institutional economist: The unnoticed contributions of Robert Neild. *Journal of Institutional Economics, 14*(4), 767–786.

Hutchison, T. W. (1977). *Keynes v. the 'Keynesians' …?*. Hobart paperback no. 11. Institute of Economic Affairs.

Ietto-Gillies, G. (1978). Britain's economic problem: The growth of the non-market sector? *British Review of Economic Issues, 1*(1), 1–11.

Johnson, H. G. (1975a). The problem of inflation. In H. G. Johnson (Ed.), *on economics and society* (pp. 197–211). University of Chicago Press.

Johnson, H. G. (1975b). World inflation: A monetarist perspective. In H. G. Johnson (Ed.), *On economics and society* (pp. 239–247). University of Chicago Press.
Johnson, H. G. (1976). What is right with monetarism. *Lloyds Bank Review, 120*, 13–17.
Johnson, H. G., & Nobay, A. R. (1971). *The current inflation*. Macmillan.
Kahn, R. F. (1973a, November 6). *Economic and industrial affairs*. Address to the House of Lords.
Kahn, R. F. (1973b, November 20). *Counter-inflation (prices and pay code) (no. 2)*. Address to the House of Lords.
Kahn, R. F. (1973c, December 18). *Economic policy and fuel supplies*. Address to the House of Lords.
Kahn, R. F. (1974a, February 6). *Industrial and economic situation*. Address to the House of Lords.
Kahn, R. F. (1974b, July 28). *The mini-budget and the crisis*. The Sunday Telegraph.
Kahn, R.F. (1974c, July 30). *The economic position*. Address to the House of Lords.
Kahn, R. F. (1975a, August). Monetarism and incomes policy. *The Banker*, 1167–1170.
Kahn, R. F. (1975b, March 5). Erosion of UK competitive position. *The Times*.
Kahn, R. F. (1975c, July 4). Reducing the rate of inflation. *The Times*.
Kahn, R. F. (1975d, July 30). *The attack on inflation*. Address to the House of Lords.
Kahn, R. F. (1975e). Oil and the crisis. In J. Hicks et al. (Eds.), *Crisis '75…? IEA occasional papers special No. 43* (pp. 34–38). Institute of Economic Affairs.
Kahn, R. F. (1976a). Thoughts on the behaviour of wages and monetarism. *Lloyds Bank Review, 119*, 1–11.
Kahn, R. F. (1976b). Inflation: A Keynesian view. *Scottish Journal of Political Economy, 33*(1), 1–16.
Kahn, R. F. (1977a). Mr. Eltis and the Keynesians. *Lloyds Bank Review, 124*, 1–13.
Kahn, R. F. (1977b, January 26). *The economic situation*. Address to the House of Lords.
Kahn, R. F., & Posner, M. (1974a). Cambridge economics and the balance of payments. *London and Cambridge Economic Bulletin, 85*, 19–32.
Kahn, R. F., & Posner, M. (1974b). The effects of public expenditure on inflation and the balance of payments. In *Public expenditure, inflation and the balance of payments: Ninth report from the expenditure committee (HC328)*. HMSO.
Kahn, R. F., & Posner, M. (1977). Inflation, unemployment and growth. *National Westminster Bank Quarterly Review, 10*, 28–37.
King, J. E. (2009). *Nicholas Kaldor*. Palgrave Macmillan.
Laidler, D. (1976a). Inflation in Britain. A monetarist perspective. *American Economic Review, 66*(4), 485–500.
Laidler, D. (1976b, April). Letter to the editor: Lord Kahn on monetarism. *Lloyds Bank Review*, 47–48.

Laidler, D., & Parkin, M. (1975). Inflation: A survey. *Economic Journal, 85*, 741–809.

Leijonhufvud, A. (1968). *On Keynesian economics and the economics of Keynes*. Oxford University Press.

Maloney, J. (2012). The Treasury and the new Cambridge school in the 1970s. *Cambridge Journal of Economics, 36*, 995–1017.

Marcuzzo, M. C. (2020). Richard F. Kahn: A disciple of Keynes. *History of Economics Review, 76*(1), 2–57.

Marcuzzo, M. C., & Paesani, P. (2022). *Richard F. Kahn: Collected Economic Essays*. Palgrave Macmillan.

Mata, T. (2012). Godley moves in mysterious ways: The craft of economic judgment in post-war Britain. In D. B. Papadimitriou & G. Zezza (Eds.), *Contributions to stock-flow modelling. Essays in honor of Wynne Godley* (pp. 12–35). Springer.

Matthews, R. C. O. (1968). Why has Britain had full employment since the war? *Economic Journal, 78*, 555–569.

Middleton, R. (1998). *Charlatans or Saviours? Economists and the British Economy from Marshall to Meade*. Edward Elgar.

Morgan, K. O. (2021). *The people's peace: Britain since 1945* (4th ed.). Oxford University Press.

Muller, C. (1996). The Institute of Economic Affairs: Undermining the post-war consensus. *Contemporary British History, 10*(1), 88–110.

Murphy, C. (2025). The political crisis of British Keynesianism, 1973–1983. *Past and Present*, gtaf012. https://doi.org/10.1093/pastj/gtaf012

Neild, R. (1974, February 26). Reversing Keynes on budgetary policy. *The Times*.

Neild, R. (2014). The 1981 statement by 364 economists. In D. Needham & A. Hotson (Eds.), *Expansionary fiscal contraction: The Thatcher government's 1981 budget in perspective* (pp. 1–9). Cambridge University Press.

Nelson, E. (2009). *Milton Friedman and U.K. economic policy: 1938–1979*. Economic research, Federal Reserve Bank of St. Louis working paper, 2009–017.

Newbery, D. (2017). Frank Horace Hahn 1925–2013. *Biographical Memoirs of Fellows of the British Academy, XVI*, 485–525.

O'Brien, P. (2009). Terence Wilmot Hutchison 1912–2007. *Proceedings of the British Academy, 161*, 179–203.

Parkin, M. (1974a). Inflation: Causes, effects and cures. *Economic Papers, 1*(45), 17–25.

Parkin, M. (1974b). United Kingdom inflation: The policy alternatives. *National Westminster Bank Quarterly Review*, 32–47.

Parkin, M. (1975, July). Where is Britain's inflation going. *Lloyd's Bank Review*, 1–13.

Roe-Crines, A. S., & Heppell, T. (Eds.). (2021). *Policies and politics under prime minister Edward heath. Palgrave studies in political leadership.* Palgrave Macmillan.

Saith, A. (2019). *Ajit Singh of Cambridge and Chandigarh: An intellectual biography of the radical Sikh economist.* Palgrave Macmillan.

Saith, A. (2022a). *Cambridge economics in the post-Keynesian era.* Cambridge University Press.

Saith, A. (2022b). The Cambridge journal of economics — A forum of one's own. *Review of Political Economy, 35*(1), 28–49.

Seldon, A. (1960). *Not unanimous: A rival verdict to Radcliffe's on money.* Institute of Economic Affairs.

Singh, A. (2009). Better to be rough and relevant than to be precise and irrelevant: Reddaway's legacy to economics. *Cambridge Journal of Economics, 33*(3), 363–379.

Smith, D. (1987). *The rise and fall of monetarism.* Penguin books.

Smith, G. (2016). *The new Cambridge school: Contribution and legacy.* https://cpes.org.uk/wp-content/uploads/2016/07/Graeme_Smith.pdf

Solow, R. (2017). Frank Hahn (1925–2013). In R. Cord (Ed.), *The Palgrave companion to Cambridge economics* (pp. 915–927). Palgrave Macmillan.

Soskice, D. (1983). The United Kingdom. In R. J. Flanagan, D. Soskice, & L. Ulman (Eds.), *Unionism, economic stabilisation, and incomes policies: European experience* (pp. 363–446). The Brookings Institution.

Sraffa, P. (1960). *Production of commodities by means of commodities: Prelude to a critique of economic theory.* Cambridge University Press.

Tarling, R., & Wilkinson, F. (1977). The social contract: Post-war incomes policies and their inflationary impact. *Cambridge Journal of Economics, 1*, 395–414.

Tarshis, L. (1979). The aggregate supply function in Keynes's general theory. In M. J. Boskin (Ed.), *Economics and human welfare* (pp. 361–392). Academic Press.

Tomlinson, J. (2014). British government and popular understanding of inflation in the mid-1970s. *Economic History Review, 67*(3), 750–768.

Trevithick, J. A. (1976). Inflation, the natural unemployment rate and the theory of economic policy. *Scottish Journal of Political Economy, 23*(1), 37–53.

Trevithick, J. A., & Mulvey, C. (1975). *The economics of inflation.* Martin Robertson.

Tribe, K. (1997). *Economic careers. Economics and economists in Britain 1930–1970.* Routledge.

Wade, R. H. (2006, October 6). Obituary: Michael Posner (1931–2006). *The Guardian.*

Walters, A. A. (1969). *Money in boom and slump.* Hobart Paper 44. Institute of Economic Affairs.

Warner, S. (2021). Industrial relations: Reappraising the industrial relations act 1971. In A. Roe-Crines & T. Heppell (Eds.), *Policies and politics under prime minister Edward heath. Palgrave studies in political leadership* (pp. 115–140). Palgrave Macmillan.

Whitton, T. (2016). Strife, beer and sandwiches: British trade unions and industrial action during the seventies. In G. Leydier (Ed.), *Le Royaume-Uni à l'épreuve de la crise 1970–1979* (pp. 47–65). Ellipses.

Willett, T. D., & Laney, L. O. (1978). Monetarism, budget deficits, and wage push inflation: The cases of Italy and the U.K. *Banca Nazionale del Lavoro Quarterly Review, 31*, 315–331.

Wright, J. F. (1984). Wage resistance: Eighty years of the British cost of living. *Oxford Economic Papers, 36*, 152–167.

CHAPTER 9

The Remains of the Day

9.1 Keynesian Reminiscences

The defence of the Keynesian point of view in the British debates of the 1970s, against monetarists and those who accused Kahn and the other Keynesians of betraying their master's ideas, is connected, in Kahn's case, with an in-depth re-examination of those ideas. While involved in the publication of Keynes's *Collected Writings*, edited by Elizabeth Johnson and Donald Moggridge,[1] Kahn read the *General Theory* for the first time in many years,[2] alongside Keynes's other published and unpublished works, correspondence, official documents and dispatches. This offered him the opportunity to revisit Keynes's past, as well as his own.

Moreover, in the 1970s, Kahn's testimony was in high demand at symposiums and conferences, at a time when Keynes's ideas were the subject of much debate and controversy. The opportunity to question one of the

[1] For more on Moggridge's acquaintance with Kahn in the context of a reconstruction of his own life and career, see Moggridge (1997). See Cox (1995) for more information on the construction of Keynes's Archive, which is preserved at King's College. For more information on Kahn's role as Keynes's literary executor and his important role in the publication of Keynes's collected works, together with Geoffrey Keynes, Austin Robinson and Roy Harrod, see O'Donnell (1995).

[2] An account of this, together with an appreciation of Kahn by the Japanese economist Uzawa, can be found in Okuno-Fujiwara and Shell (2009). I thank Giacomo Gabbuti for pointing this out to me.

P. Paesani, *Richard F. Kahn*, Great Thinkers in Economics,
https://doi.org/10.1007/978-3-032-09123-9_9

protagonists involved in the Keynesian Revolution was not one that anyone wanted to miss. Despite his declining strength, Kahn responded to these requests with his usual modesty and meticulousness, combined with a novel and perhaps justifiable desire to see his own merits acknowledged. This commitment resulted in a series of essays on Keynes, biographical and analytical in nature.

Kahn (1976a), for example, reconstructs Keynes's role during the negotiations that led to the establishment of the International Monetary Fund and the World Bank.[3] By following Keynes's transatlantic travels, his moments of satisfaction, despair and anger, the difficulties of a complex negotiation conducted by the British delegation at Bretton Woods, Keynes's tense relations with Dexter White, with the Americans and with part of the British delegation, and his supreme effort to persuade the House of Lords not to oppose the American loan in December 1945, Kahn sketches a memorable portrait of Keynes. Memorable for his ability to bring out the strengths and weaknesses of a great man, his unflagging optimism coupled with the fatigue of an exhausting negotiation in extremely poor health, and his ability to persuade and convince his compatriots to accept what could not be changed after trying to do so to the last.

In his analytical essays on Keynes, of the 1970s, Kahn reaffirmed his commitment to the Keynesian theoretical framework as set out in the *General Theory*, at the same dwelling on some of its limitations. These were either issues that had escaped his attention as a young man or issues that he had not wanted to point out to Keynes. For example, in the spring of 1974, participation in a conference organised by G.D.A. Worswick and devoted to the concept and measurement of involuntary unemployment (Worswick, 1976) allowed Kahn to note that this concept was initially proposed by Pigou and Robertson (Kahn, 1976b, pp. 227–228), rather than Keynes. He also argued that the definition of involuntary unemployment used by Keynes in the *General Theory* was inadequate. It was overly

[3] Kahn prepared this paper for the Second Keynes Seminar at the University of Kent. Between 1972 and 1991 the University of Kent at Canterbury hosted a series of biennial Keynes Seminars organised by A.P. Thirlwall at Keynes College. The seminars were established to honour the legacy of Keynes, by exploring various aspects of his life and work in economics, philosophy and public policy. Each seminar featured prominent scholars and practitioners, and the proceedings were published in volumes that made a significant contribution to Keynesian scholarship. Kahn participated as a speaker in the second and sixth seminars.

complex and based on the assumption of an inverse relationship between real wages and labour productivity. This corresponded to the idea that there was a direct relationship between output and prices for a given money wage rate—an idea that had been empirically disproven by L. Tarshis and J.G. Dunlop shortly after the publication of the *General Theory* (see Dunlop, 1938, 1939; and Tarshis, 1938, 1939). Reflecting on this issue, Kahn comments how

> The *General Theory* is based, on the whole, on the economics of the short period. It was assumed that short-period supply curves were rising curves. Work done by J.G. Dunlop and Lorie Tarshis threw doubt on this assumption. Keynes rightly attributed his error to me and pointed out that, if in fact the real wage remains constant when the demand for labour rises, "it would be possible to simplify considerably the more complicated version of my fundamental explanation". (Kahn, [1976b] 2022, p. 229, fn. 13)

These words, and Kahn's decision to relegate them to a footnote, hint at the complexity of his stance on Keynes's *magnum opus* when he revisited it in the 1970s. By acknowledging one significant flaw of the theoretical apparatus of the *General Theory*, Kahn generously attributes it to himself. At the same time, stating that the *General Theory* is based on the economics of the short period—the title of Kahn's fellowship dissertation and his first significant contribution to economic theory—allows Kahn to reiterate the importance of his contribution to Keynes's intellectual endeavour.

Having spent a lifetime fighting the Keynesian battle, however, Kahn could not shy away from continuing to do so. An example of this is his indirect dispute with Sir Keith Joseph, a Conservative politician and economist who mentored Margaret Thatcher. On 5 September 1974, during an important speech, Joseph had cited Kahn's comments at the Worswick RES conference on Keynes's cautious approach to high unemployment in 1937. This was intended to suggest that Keynes's understanding of unemployment and how to address it was more nuanced than that of his supporters. In his response, published on 22 September, Kahn explained that Keynes's caution in 1937 was driven by the strategic necessity of preparing for the impending rearmament and belief in the necessity of maintaining a reserve of unemployed workers to meet the demands of rearmament and military recruitment.[4]

About two months after his exchange with Joseph, Kahn delivered his lecture, 'On Re-reading Keynes', at the British Academy on 6 November 1974, at the invitation of Alec Cairncross, at the time Fellow of the British Academy.[5] The lecture was published the following year (Kahn, 1975) and enabled Kahn to propose a complete revision of Keynes's *magnum opus* and the process that had preceded it.[6]

Kahn's narration of Keynes's transition from the *Tract* and the *Treatise on Money* to the *General Theory* is a tale of emancipation from the quantity theory of money in favour of a theory of simultaneous determination of employment, output and prices, in which inflation is the consequence of the interplay between demand and cost factors. Two concomitant motives can be discerned behind this narrative choice. Firstly, by describing Keynes's abandonment of a theory Kahn himself had been sceptical of since the early 1930s, Kahn reinforces his ideal bond with Keynes, bringing him, so to speak, onto his own ground. Secondly, Kahn's choice reflects the urgency to reaffirm the fallacy of the quantity theory of money at a time when this theory was experiencing a resurgence. In this sense, Kahn's lecture must be read in connection with the battles he was waging with monetarists in the 1970s.

In Kahn's account of Keynes's emancipation from the quantity theory of money, the first crucial step is Keynes's discovery of the concepts of income and profit inflation, as set out in the *Treatise on Money*. Income inflation mainly depends on the increase in money wages relative to labour productivity. In contrast, profit inflation depends on the difference between aggregate demand and supply, as reflected in the gap between investment and savings. By identifying these elements, Kahn situates Keynes's contribution alongside that of Wicksell, an author whom Keynes had been able to explore in greater depth with Kahn's assistance.[7] The

[4] The text of Keith Joseph's speech, delivered at Preston on 5 September 1974, can be found here https://www.margaretthatcher.org/document/110607. The text of the *Sunday Times* article can be found in Kahn (1974).

[5] For initial correspondence and guest list see RFK/12/2/87/23–26.

[6] For the text of these and other Keynes lectures see on the British Academy website https://www.thebritishacademy.ac.uk/events/lectures/listings/keynes-lectures-economics/.

[7] In 1929, Keynes had commissioned Kahn to translate Wicksell's work *Interest and Prices* from German (Kahn's family language) into English. As Moggridge (1994, pp. 107–108) reconstructs progress was intermittent, and although Keynes occasionally urged Kahn to

second step, logically consequential to the discovery of income inflation, can be traced to the idea that

> The money-wage is the fulcrum on which rests the whole structure of everything expressed in terms of money—all prices, incomes of every kind, and all money values. [...] The one important exception is the quantity of money. If it is held constant, a higher money-wage means that in real value—in terms of its purchasing power over labour and goods—the quantity of money is reduced. The only important influence on the real state of the economy of a higher money-wage takes the form of the higher rates of interest, and the general tightening of credit, which result from a reduction in the real value of the quantity of money, [...] I am of course abstracting from effects on exports and imports. The basis of the fundamental role of the money-wages in determining all prices, money-incomes, and money values is that money wages not only form part of costs of production but, because they are to a large extent spent, they form part of total purchasing power expressed in terms of money. (Kahn, 1975, pp. 16–17)

The recognition of the dual role of money wages in price determination allows Kahn to invoke Keynes's authority in support of the idea, 'which many of us have held for some years', that the leapfrogging effect (wage-wage spiral), the endogenous rise in nominal wages triggered by rivalry between the trade unions, rather than the adjustment of wages to prices (wage-price spiral) is the main cause of the rises in one and then the other. This view of inflation assumes that, in the face of rising wages and prices, the monetary authorities will adopt an accommodative stance to preserve high employment. Otherwise, the spiral would be doomed to die out because an increase in money wages and prices that is not matched by a corresponding increase in the money supply will generate a tightening of financial conditions, resulting in a slowdown in aggregate demand, lower output and employment, and in the end lower inflation. Once again, as in his debate with the monetarists, Kahn does not dispute the assertion that tightening monetary policy can reduce inflation. However, he argues that this cannot happen without lasting negative consequences in terms of lower investment, higher unemployment and reduced productivity.

continue, sustained pressure did not emerge until 1934–35. Kahn completed the translation in August 1935, and Keynes finalised the proofs the following month, praising the work as remarkably fluent. Published in 1936, the translation was widely celebrated for its clarity and literary quality.

Similarly, Kahn argues that when analysing the impact of anti-cyclical fiscal policies on unemployment, it is crucial to differentiate between their real and monetary effects. The former depend on the influence of government spending and taxation on available resources, while the latter depend on the balance between the securities and money used to finance the government budget deficit. When the economy is close to full employment, an increase in the budget deficit intended to reduce unemployment can cause inflation to rise, even if the government chooses not to monetise it. Conversely, when the economy has plenty of spare capacity, an increase in the budget deficit that is fully financed by money will not lead to inflation, provided that an effective incomes policy is in place.[8]

Read as a whole, Kahn's lecture at the British Academy contains no surprising revelations. Nor would it have been reasonable to expect any from someone as cautious and prudent as Kahn. His account moves on two levels. Firstly, Kahn traces the evolution of Keynes's thinking, meticulously drawing on published and unpublished documents from that period, particularly focusing on Keynes's involvement in the policy debates of his time. Secondly, towards the end of the lecture, Kahn emphasises the importance of linking the account of the development of Keynesian ideas to current problems, referencing the serious issue of inflation, the foolishness of trade unions demanding unrealistic wage increases, and the error of the International Monetary Fund in treating official exchange rates as untouchable idols. As on other occasions, it is Kahn's interest in concrete problems that fuels his interest in economic theory here.

On the issue of the real versus monetary effects of a fiscal expansion to reduce unemployment, Kahn had a brief correspondence with Victoria Chick, one of the attendees of his lecture. In the first of three letters, dated 12 November 1974 (RFK/12/87/57), Chick invites Kahn to reflect that even die-hard Keynesians would agree that a government deficit financed by money has greater expansionary effects than one financed by issuing securities. She also raises the issue of the impossibility of distinguishing the real effect from the financial effect of the deficit, as she illustrated in her 1973 work (Chick, 1973, pp. 131–139). Kahn partly accepts Chick's

[8] This is the starting point of an essay published in the *Journal of Economic Literature* in 1978 (Kahn, 1978), the contents of which closely reflect those of the lecture at the British Academy. This reveals Kahn's sense of urgency in clarifying Keynes's thinking at a time (the mid-1970s) when Keynesian economic policies were being criticised by monetarists committed to revitalising the quantitative theory of money.

suggestion, while politely reiterating his view on the importance of distinguishing the two effects and expressing his 'allergy' to the IS-LM-based analysis she proposes (RFK/12/87/58). In her reply, dated 5 December 1974 (RFK/12/87/80), Chick rejects the notion that she is an advocate of the IS-LM model and restates her belief in the inseparability of the real and financial aspects of deficit analysis. Nevertheless, she expresses satisfaction with the final formulation adopted by Kahn and voices her gratitude for his citation of her work in the published text of his lecture (Kahn, 1975, p. 9, fn. 2) (RFK/12/87/100).

Among the many letters of congratulations received by Kahn after his lecture (ref. RFK/12/72/87), the exchange with Goodwin deserves special attention for the analytical points it raises. Goodwin's first letter to Kahn, dated 3 July 1975, links the absence of a treatment of the problem of inflation under full employment, in the *General Theory* and the early theoretical contributions following it, to Keynes's failure to fully emancipate himself from traditional economic theory.

> In spite of your skilled defence of your Master, I think the fault lies squarely with him. The message of the G.T. is plain—output expands up to full employment and then prices as output becomes increasingly inelastic. This clearly uses the types of analysis, though not the details, of the quantity theory of money—it is market-clearing, competitive theory. And it is wrong on a number of points. 1) it is aggregative, and that cannot do for "leap-frogging". 2) it is competitive, ignoring (fair enough for its times) mark-up pricing, 3) it makes an implicit direct connection between full employment and inflation and this is, I suspect, connected with K's confusion about Say's law and full employment. [...] True he had got the right idea (but not very well expressed or analysed) in his argument about a general reduction of money wages. But he only worked it downward and not upwards. [...] But he missed the boat in not presenting a neat little analysis showing why, though wages are not the only costs, they would nonetheless control prices.[9]

In his reply, dated 11 July 1975, after expressing great appreciation for his letter, Kahn refutes the link Goodwin makes between Keynes's

[9] From Goodwin to Kahn, 3 July 1975, RFK/12/2/87/107–108. This letter is followed by a postscript in which Goodwin refers to Joan Robinson and how she had confided in him how Keynes was not too keen on the idea that prices were simply proportional to wages and 'that he had to be nudged to get him to put it into the G.T.'

exposition of the relationship between output and prices in proximity to full employment and the quantitative theory of money.

> His [Keynes's] ideas that the short-period supply curve is a rising one is one for which I have to accept responsibility. It was disputed on statistical grounds by Dunlop and Tarshis, in whose work you can really see the first indication of mark-up pricing. Keynes's idea that a rise in demand will result in a rise in the price-level meant that, when given money wages, it was a once-and-for all rise. On the other hand, in-so-far as a low level of unemployment and scarcity of labour results in rising money wages, the rise is a continuing one. This is a very important distinction. I think that you go too far in saying that Keynes failed to show how wages control prices.[10]

Kahn sees no contradiction between a one-off increase in output and the general price level (for a given level of monetary wages) and a continuous increase in both, provided one remains firm on the idea of the joint determination of output (employment) and the price level, along a rising aggregate supply function. There is also no contradiction in considering nominal wages to be a variable determined at the institutional level, while also assigning them a causal role within the theoretical framework of the *General Theory*.[11]

Another exchange between Kahn and Frank Hahn is important for what it adds to Kahn's assertion at the end of his lecture to the British Academy that, for Keynes (and the Keynesians), the problem of wage determination is political rather than economic and could never be modelled theoretically. Hahn raises two objections to this idea. The first concerns Kahn's use of the phrase 'logically impossible' for a theory of wages. According to Hahn, Kahn himself contradicts this idea when he refers to the link between past and present wages, and to the response of wages to demand pressure, sectoral bottlenecks and the wage-wage spiral as the main determinants of current wages (Kahn, 1975, p. 30).

> The view that a theory involving history, or what types like me pretentiously call, initial conditions, is not a theory seems to me odd. In any case I think philosophers would find your claim puzzling. What does it mean to assert

[10] From Kahn to Goodwin, 11 July 1975, RFK/12/2/87/110.

[11] For Keynes's 'Marshallian' view of the labour market between the 1920s and 1930s, and the influence of this view on *The General Theory*, see Lawlor (2006, pp. 35–92).

that a theory of such + such is logically impossible? Perhaps you had simple causation à la Hume in mind.[12]

The main point raised by Hahn, however, concerns the use of the adjective 'political' with respect to the nature of the inflation problem.

The interpretation which I put on the phrase is essentially inflation can neither be understood nor contained by economic theory + policies. Something else called "politics" must be invoked. I am a great deal more Marxian than that! The separation of problems into "economic" and "political" seems to me bogus. It is also a hangover from 19th century orthodoxy. The latter dealt with the individual and the circumstances that there are also coalitions of individuals was handed over to "politics". But we can study economics with coalitions and study them in a way which is far superior to anything a political scientist leave alone a politician can do. The insight of economics is that people + groups of people by and large will act in their own self-interest. The expertise of economists in the study + devising of institutions where the conflicts which arise are more or less contained and to some extent made beneficial. Inflation seems to me to be at the centre of our subject precisely because it signals a failure of some of these institutions in what are their prime concern.[13]

To this proud claim of the economist's task, Kahn responds in the following terms:

What is your theory about the determination of the rate of increase in money wages? If it is simply the quantity theory then I think I have dealt with it in my lecture. I think we are at cross purposes about the use of the word "political." What could be more political than discussions at the present time about how to deal with inflation? Not only is there intense political dissension within both the Labour Party and the Conservative party but also within the Trade union movement.[14]

To which Hahn replied

Dear Richard, let us talk in the autumn. I do not believe that wages are determined by the Quantity theory; indeed I do not believe in the quantity

[12] From Hahn to Kahn, 24 June 1975, RFK/12/2/87/118.
[13] From Hahn to Kahn, 24 June 1975, RFK/12/2/87/119.
[14] From Kahn to Hahn, 4 July 1975, RFK/12/2/87/120.

> theory! My point was simply your contention that it is "logically impossible" to have any theory of the matter. On the other issue I may be changing my mind a little largely as a result of a conversation with James [Meade?]. He offered a definition of "essentially politically" which goes some of the way to convincing me that it may be given a proper meaning in the context in which you used it. I gave a lecture in India on inflation which has been printed but they only sent me one copy. If I ever get more I shall send you one. Ever, Frank.[15]

Beyond the question of merit, the brief exchange between Kahn and Hahn highlights how, even in 1975, the two maintained a tone of cordiality and open dialogue despite their differing approaches to economic analysis.

9.2 Mattioli Lectures: *The Making of Keynes' General Theory*

The same narrative structure chosen by Kahn to describe the evolution of Keynes's thinking in his lecture at the British Academy forms the basis of the six lectures given by Kahn between 5 and 14 June 1978, at Bocconi University in Milan, as part of an initiative entitled Raffaele Mattioli Lectures, organised in collaboration with the Mattioli Foundation, created by Banca Commerciale Italiana. The initiative aimed to establish a link between research in the field of the history of economic thought and current debates in economic theory and policy, as was in the spirit of Raffaele Mattioli, an influential Italian banker and intellectual.[16] The Mattioli Archive (Folder 144, File 12) contains correspondence between Kahn and Mattioli, which is evidence of their relationship.

The first group of letters, dating from August 1952, concerns the mountain accident that befell Piero Sraffa, a close friend of Mattioli's, on 1 August 1952, while he was in Norway. While in Oslo with Kaldor and his wife, Clarisse, among others, Kahn kept Mattioli updated on Sraffa's health and progress, even after the latter returned to Cambridge. Seven years later, in March 1959, Kahn informed Mattioli of his imminent visit to Rome with Joan Robinson, mentioning their joint work as consultants to the FAO (see Sect. 7.4 above). This is followed by two letters in 1962

[15] From Hahn to Kahn, 25 July 1975, RFK/12/2/87/124.

[16] On Raffaele Mattioli see Appendix C.

devoted again to Sraffa's health problems, a short letter from Mattioli congratulating Kahn on his appointment to the House of Lords, an exchange of letters concerning a short essay by Kahn on the gold price trend written for the Rothschild Bank, and two final letters.

The first, dated 1 September 1965, sees Mattioli inform Kahn that he had learned from Marcello de Cecco[17] 'that you are on the way of a tract on the theory of interest. Trusting you will forgive my indiscretion, please send me confidentially a copy of your essay'. Kahn replied on 9 September as follows: 'I am afraid there is some misunderstanding about the character and the progress of the work in which I am engaged. I have started in a very preliminary way, a study of the ways in which the state of finance—and in particular the return on ordinary shares—might influence the rate of growth. I am hoping to get some preliminary results, based on very unreal assumptions, written up, and I will certainly let you see them'. Here Kahn refers to the notes on interest rates and growth of firms elaborated between 1964 and 1965 and published seven years later.[18]

In the Mattioli lectures, published in 1984 under the title *The Making of Keynes' General Theory* (Kahn, 1984), Kahn begins with a brief overview of the pillars of pre-Keynesian economic theory, Say's Law (Lecture 1) and the quantity theory of money (Lecture 2), making passing references to Smith, Ricardo, Mill, Marshall, Pigou and Robertson. This part is rather conventional and, as Moggridge observes (1994, pp. 109–110), it is difficult to relate Kahn's discussions directly to the modern literature on both subjects, for he made no reference whatsoever to any of the secondary interpretative literature, limiting himself to giving large blocks of quotations from the relevant classics accompanied by brief comments and little in the way of context. Keynes appears at the end of the second lecture as the author of *Tract on Monetary Reform*. This is followed by the *Treatise on Money*, in which the direct link between the quantity of money and the price level is replaced by an indirect link mediated by financial variables and balance between investment and savings. From here Kahn moves on to the British policy debates of the 1930s (Lecture 3), the article on the multiplier and the activities of the Cambridge Circus. Here, in response to Patinkin's (1978) criticism of the absence of a discussion of the dynamics underlying the multiplier, Kahn offers his characteristic understatement.

[17] On Marcello de Cecco see Appendix C and Paesani (2016).

[18] Other references to Kahn in the Mattioli archive, all related to Sraffa's mountain accident, can be found in Folder 268, file 11.

> Don Patinkin is fully justified in criticizing the presentation of the argument in my article for failure to make it clear that it was, in effect, an exercise in comparative statistics and not in sequence analysis. [...] My failure to enlarge on this issue would have led to endless trouble had not Keynes come to the rescue. In the course of the article of the American edition of *The Means to Prosperity,* published in the middle of 1933, Keynes, in a section on the multiplier, estimated the time-lags, and concluded that: it will be seen that seven eighths of the total effects come from the primary expenditure and the first two repercussions, so that the time-lags involved are not unduly serious. (Kahn, 1984, pp. 102–103)

Kahn rejects Robertson's attempt to reinterpret the multiplier using the quantity theory of money. He argues that increased employment resulting from public investment occurs even without monetary expansion. However, he acknowledges that debt-financed investment may raise interest rates unless offset by accommodative monetary policy. These reflections set the scene for Kahn's fifth Mattioli Lecture, in which he presents his interpretation of the *General Theory*, assessing its key strengths and limitations (Lecture 5).

Lecture 5 is the most important part of *The Making of Keynes' General Theory*, in which Kahn focuses on what he identifies as the heart of the *General Theory*: the theory of investment and the principle of effective demand (ibid., pp. 142–157). When dealing with this topic, Kahn emphasises the importance of Keynes's contribution while at the same time highlighting some relevant limitations. Once again, we see Kahn wavering between criticism and praise.

> Keynes' basic chapter on the determination of the rate of investment is Chapter 11 on "The Marginal Efficiency of Capital". The subject is the most important one in the *General Theory.* But this chapter is one of the most confused. [...] Keynes emphasised that he was basing his treatment on the *prospective* yield of capital and not on its *current* yield. Even to-day the confusion to which Keynes referred between three meanings of the terms 'profit' and 'rate of profit' prevails. (Ibid., pp. 145–146)

Taking into account the uncertain and fluctuating margin separating the risk-free interest rate from the expected return on new capital goods, and the fact that investment decisions are influenced by the 'state of finance' (i.e. credit supply and stock market prices), it is clear that the relationship between financial variables and investment cannot be analysed in functional terms. However, it is true that a tightening (or loosening) of financial conditions, if persistent enough and in the absence of counteracting factors, will be followed by a fall (or rise) in investment. Kahn highlights the absence of a systematic analysis of the relationship between share prices and investment decisions in the *General Theory*, as well as Keynes's difficulty in fully clarifying the relationship between the expected profits from new capital goods and the dividends paid on the shares representing those goods, as reflected in share price movements.

In a sense, Kahn takes the chapters Keynes devotes to investment as examples of what is good and bad in the *General Theory* as a whole. The good is Keynes's attempt to construct a new theory of how the economy functions, which is firmly grounded in reality and common sense, a term that recurs occasionally (and with a positive connotation) in Kahn's writings. However, the bad—and perhaps inevitable—aspect is Keynes's decision to oversimplify his reasoning, paving the way for the trivialisation of the *General Theory* within a simplified model such as the IS-LM model.

> In his burning anxiety to convince, he [Keynes] did enormously oversimplify. This statement will be ill-received by those who find the book difficult and believe that the essence of it can be presented by some simple geometry or algebra. That is the great tragedy. The behaviour of the economy is an immensely complicated subject. The diagrams and bits of algebra in the text-books up to the present day have often led to the difficulties being submerged, and incidentally to Keynes being discredited. For example, both in his exposition of the liquidity preference theory of the rate of interest and in his exposition of the inducement to invest, Keynes made use of schedules—simple relationships between two parameters, one the rate of interest in both cases—which could be represented by a curve or by a piece of algebra of the type $y = f(x)$. And yet Keynes' insistence on the overwhelming importance of expectations, highly subject to risk and uncertainty, was one of his biggest contributions. This completely undermines the prevalent idea—for which Keynes' attempt at simplification is responsible—that such schedules can be regarded as stable relationships handed down from heaven. (Ibid., p. 159)

> The result has been that the elementary teaching of Keynesian economics has been the victim of *IS-LM* and related diagrams and algebra. It is tragic that Keynes made no public protest when they began to appear. (Ibid., p. 160)

A brief discussion of the finance motive as an additional reason behind the demand for money closes the analytically relevant part of Kahn's fifth Mattioli Lecture. The finance motive refers to money held in advance to meet future payment obligations arising from investment decisions. Money held for this reason lies halfway between active and inactive monetary balances. The introduction of the finance motive reduces the importance that the interest rate plays in determining investment in favour of a more general notion of liquidity that is highly dependent on what banks and other lending institutions do, as Kahn and others had already argued in front of the Radcliffe Committee.

In order to understand the finance motive and its macroeconomic implications, we must follow Kahn and immerse ourselves in the reality of managerial capitalism, in which shareholders own companies and employ managers, driven by conflicting forces, to run them. The desire to maintain and increase share value, as well as loyalty to shareholders, leads managers to limit dividend payments and finance investments through self-financing. However, when the main shareholders are pension funds, insurance companies, investment trusts, or individual income-seeking investors, managers must pay more generous dividends. This limits self-financing and the company's growth potential. There are also risks associated with hostile takeovers if the share price is significantly lower than the value of the underlying assets. Furthermore, there is the possible market reaction to the annual publication of various companies' results, as well as the link between equity price and earnings yields (rather than dividend yield).

> For these various reasons the management are subject to strong pressure to avoid growing so fast as seriously to prejudice the rate of growth of earnings and the price of the shares. The result is that, indirectly if not directly, pressure is exercised on them to take account of their shareholders' interests. The prospective earnings yield per share, both on the real assets of the company (the internal rate of return) and on its shares, must not fall below the rate generally prevailing in the country. This factor acts as a restraint on the rate of growth of the company rather than Keynes' rate of interest. This is why the price of a company's shares matters to its management even if there is no question of making an issue of shares. (Ibid., p. 167)

The result is that it is the average rate of return on shares that determines the level of investment, rather than the risk-free interest rate on money. This serves as a benchmark for managers, who must balance the different and changing needs of their shareholders, the risk of hostile takeovers and their desire to expand the company—thereby increasing their status and economic position—when deciding how much to invest and how to finance it. As in his lecture at the British Academy, here too Kahn chooses to bring Keynes onto his own turf—a turf with which he was very familiar, having devoted a significant part of his research as a theoretical economist to reflecting on the link between monetary policy, portfolio choices and investment decisions in conditions of uncertainty. The same applies to what Kahn writes in the fifth Lecture on the relationship between wages and prices. By adopting this interpretative approach, Kahn achieves twofold results. Firstly, he reaffirms the harmony between his own thinking and that of Keynes. On the other hand, he implicitly suggests that to truly understand Keynes, one must understand those who took up and developed his ideas—starting with Kahn himself, of course.

Overall, *The Making of Keynes' General Theory* is an important and complex book. Published in 1984, five years before Kahn's death, it encapsulates his intellectual legacy and approach. There is a sense of latent tension throughout the book between Kahn's loyalty to Keynes and the Keynesian cause, and his desire for his own contributions to be recognised. On the one hand, Kahn praises Keynes as a person and an economist, emphasising his generosity, intuition and courage in proposing new ideas. However, he also criticises Keynes for the limitations and ambiguities he perceives in the *General Theory*, issues which Kahn and the other Keynesians addressed in their own work. When discussing his contribution to Keynes's *magnum opus*, Kahn exhibits the same attitude, oscillating between playing down his role and reaffirming the uniqueness of his closeness to Keynes. He portrays himself as Keynes's sparring partner, yet also takes credit for the aggregate supply curve and adapting the supply and demand model from micro to macroeconomics to determine output and the general price level simultaneously.

In hindsight, Moggridge provides a critical evaluation of Kahn's Mattioli Lectures. He suggests that, in the first two lectures, during which Kahn discusses periods prior to his own involvement, Kahn acts as a conventional historian of economic thought, albeit unsuccessfully. From 1930 onwards, however, Moggridge believes that Kahn's work is better understood as the reflections of a contemporary and close Keynesian collaborator, offering valuable insights to historians. Despite having the advantage of direct experience, Kahn does not exploit it fully, perhaps due to doubts about the reliability of his memory, even when supported by documents, or because he is ultimately more interested in economic outcomes than the historical process itself (Moggridge, 1994, p. 115). My interpretation of Mattioli's lectures is in line with Moggridge's on this point.

From a purely theoretical perspective, Kahn's interpretation in *The Making of Keynes' General Theory* is fairly standard. Kahn emphasises the elements of continuity between the *General Theory* and pre-Keynesian theory at several points. We see this, for example, when he interprets Keynes's theory of liquidity preference as a development of Cambridge pre-Keynesian monetary theory (Kahn, 1984, pp. 137–141), when he dismisses the marginal propensity to consume and the fundamental psychological law—which Keynes considered very important—in a few words (ibid., pp. 134–136) or when he chooses not to discuss connections between imperfect competition and the *General Theory*. The innovative element in Kahn's interpretation of Keynes is his attribution of the ability to combine knowledge of the real world with the capacity to solve contemporary economic problems by intuiting relevant causal links and later connecting them in a comprehensive theoretical framework.

Once published, *The Making of Keynes' General Theory* failed to generate much interest beyond Kahn's inner circle. Although it received positive reviews, in the United Kingdom and abroad, the book did not stimulate any significant debate. After all, by the early 1980s, the non-mathematical, non-econometric Keynesianism that Kahn espoused was far removed from the dominant strands of economic thought, whether critical of Keynes or seeking to reformulate his views along orthodox or heterodox lines. Thirlwall (1984) observes that *The Making of Keynes' General Theory*, although interesting and valuable as evidence, does not contain any significant new revelations, partly due to Kahn's evasive approach, which was typical of his modus operandi.[19] Kregel (1984) focuses on the fact that although Keynes was already aware of the need to consider the joint variation of prices and output in response to changes in aggregate demand it was thanks to his interaction with the Circus, and in particular with Kahn, that he succeeded in this endeavour, going beyond the assumption of inelastic supply.

[19] Annan (1984), Tarshis (1985), Howson (1985) and Klamer (1986), discussing in more or less detail the contents of the book, take a similar stance.

> Clearly, the framework that Kahn adopted was that of the analysis of Marshallian "short-period" supply that he had worked out in his Fellowship dissertation. This was precisely the area that Keynes mentioned as requiring development in any analysis of changes in output in his memorandum to Hawtrey, and precisely the form Keynes uses in setting out his "principle of effective demand." Unfortunately Kahn does not discuss the importance of his analysis of short-period supply in providing the "aggregate supply and demand structure," except for the throwaway comment in respect of his dissertation 'I did not realise when I made my choice—nor did Keynes when he approved it—that my work would turn out relevant in the radical restructuring of the shape of Keynes' own work."' Reading through the understatement it is clear that the framework of the *General Theory* owes much to Kahn's method in resolving the "indirect employment" problem, if not to the solution itself in the form of the multiplier. (Kregel, 1984, p. 509)

Barens (1984) dwells on Kahn's choice to emphasise radical uncertainty as the basis for a reading of Keynes that differs from the neoclassical synthesis, which he finds unconvincing. Hagemann (1985) emphasises that one limitation of an otherwise insightful analysis of the genesis and content of the *General Theory* is Kahn's omission of certain points, particularly with regard to Kaldor and Kalecki's views on profits and accumulation. Federico Caffè (an important Italian scholar who made significant contributions to the spread of Keynesian thought in Italy) speaks of Kahn's scholarly caution, his role in the Cambridge Circus, and his work with Keynes to bring Pigou and Robbins closer to Keynes's ideas in the years following the publication of the *General Theory*.[20]

Austin Robinson (1985) commends Kahn's historical approach to monetary theory, his defence of Keynes and his emphasis on the influence of supply and demand on price levels as an alternative to simplistic monetarist interpretations. Robinson also agrees with Kahn that the *General Theory* should not be treated as dogma. His main difference with Kahn concerns the Cambridge Circus years. While Kahn seems to have come to believe in 1979 that Keynes had already considered the possibility of a

[20] On this see Caffè (1985). Evidence of a possible meeting between Kahn and Caffè can be found in a letter dated 18 May 1976 and addressed to one of Caffè's student, Maurizio Franzini (graduated in Rome, specialised at Cambridge, and then Professor of Economic Policy in Siena and Rome Sapienza). In this letter, Caffè offers a brief account of the seminar held by Kahn at the Institute of Economics of the Faculty of Statistics, directed by Sylos Labini at the invitation of Luigi Spaventa.

variation in output in response to a variation in savings relative to investment in his *Treatise*, Robinson does not share this view.

> I have read and re-read the relevant passage in the Treatise. I am unrepentant. I think the Kahn of 1930 and the rest of us in the Circus were right (at the very least partially right) and the Kahn of 1979 is wrong. If the profits were spent on services which were absolutely and completely contemporaneous with and essentially a part of the transaction of spending the profits, I still think that one cannot argue that the whole expenditure adds nothing to output. By pure chance I argued at the time from such a case. I do not think that such cases are so exceptional that they should be disregarded. (Robinson, 1985, p. 207)

9.3 Patinkin, Tarshis and Austin Robinson on Kahn and the Cambridge Circus

The publication of *The Collected Writings of John Maynard Keynes* provided an opportunity to revisit not only Keynes's work, but also the activities of the Cambridge Circus—the group of young economists who reviewed and criticised *A Treatise on Money*, thereby influencing the development of Keynes's ideas.[21] Among those who were particularly active on this front we find D. Patinkin, at the time Professor of Economics at the Hebrew University of Jerusalem and a renowned theoretical monetary economist with important contributions to the neoclassical synthesis (and reconstruction) of Keynes's thought.[22]

In 1974, as Patinkin was working on a monograph on Keynes's monetary thought (Patinkin, 1976), he contacted Kahn, with whom he was on first name terms.[23] In a letter of 25 February 1974, Patinkin asked Kahn (a) to clarify what he saw as the primary importance of his 1931 article on

[21] On this see Kahn (1985) and Moggridge (1978, pp. 337–43). Marcuzzo (2023) offers a novel presentation of the Cambridge Circus.

[22] On the evolution of Patinkin's interpretation of Keynes's principle of effective demand in connection with the publications of volumes XIII and XIV of the *Collected Writings of J.M. Keynes* see Hartwig (2022). For a recent overview of Patinkin's contribution in connection with Keynes see Rubin (2008) among others.

[23] On the relationship between Kahn and Patinkin, dating from 1951, in the context of Kahn's connections with Israel see Schiffman (2014) and Schiffman and Zelekha (2014). Apart from the two letters mentioned in the main text, the rest of the correspondence between Kahn and Patinkin can be found in RFK/12/72/19 in the Kahn Archive and in the Patinkin Papers at Duke University, US, boxes 28 and 65. Among the arguments Kahn raises

the multiplier in relation to the development of Keynes's thought, (b) what he knew about Keynes's presidency of the Econometric Society in 1944–1945, (c) whether it was correct to describe himself, Meade, Sraffa, Joan and Austin Robinson as Keynes's pupils, and (d) what Keynes meant when he thanked Kahn for helping to avoid errors in the *Treatise on Money*.[24] Leaving the question about the Econometric Society (b) to Moggridge,[25] Kahn answered the other three questions as follows.

> (a) I regard the main importance of my 1931 article as (I) finally disposing of the "Treasury view" that, at a time of unemployment, an increase in one kind of investment will be at the expense of another kind. I demonstrated how the whole of the necessary finance is provided in the form of an increase in saving. The point is that in Can Lloyd George Do It?, Keynes and Hubert Henderson seem to imply that only part of the additional finance would be provided as a result of the investment. I did not actually express the identity between saving and investment until in a later number of the Journal I replied to a comment on my article by Warming, a Danish economist. In my article, the identity appears in the rather clumsy form of "Mr Meade's Relation." (James Meade was spending a year in Cambridge while I was completing my article, and I had a lot of talk with him). Finally disposing of the idea that the price level is determined by the quantity of money. I never had been able to understand the quantity theory. What I explained in my article is that the price level is determined by the conditions of demand and supply in much the same way as the price of an individual commodity. I took it for granted that the supply curve of consumption goods as a whole was, in the short period, a rising one. Later statistical work by Dunlop and Tarshis threw doubt on this assumption and seemed to indicate perfectly elastic supply under conditions of heavy unemployment. In his comment of Dunlop and Tarshis, Keynes pointed out that this assumption gave a fortiori force to his argument. (III) I had not altogether escaped from Keynes's Treatise, and I thought it necessary to translate my ideas into terms of the Treatise. Although I was not conscious of that at the time, the effect was to demonstrate how unsuitable the terminology and assumptions of the Treatise were.
>
> (c) At the time of the Circus, neither Joan Robinson nor I had yet been made University Lecturers, though I think we were both giving some lectures [...] I was the only one who had actually been a pupil of Keynes as an undergraduate. [...] Piero Sraffa had been brought over to Cambridge from

with Patinkin in a series of letters in 1975 is his desire that Austin Robinson's role as general editor of Keynes's *Collected Writings* be properly recognised.

[24] Letter from Patinkin to Kahn, 25 February 1974, RFK/12/2/19/5.

[25] Letter from Moggridge to Patinkin, 7 March 1974, RFK/12/2/19/4.

> Italy, and was a close friend of Keynes, but Piero was never very successful in discussing Keynes's ideas with him. Although Austin Robinson knew Keynes very well—partly because Austin was Secretary of the Faculty Board—the only member of the Circus who at that time was actively discussing Keynes' ideas with him was myself. As Moggridge brings out, I was the link between the Circus and Keynes.
>
> (d) I did not complete my Fellowship dissertation on The Economics of the Short Period, which had nothing to do with Keynes, until December 1929, having started on it in the Autumn of 1928. Keynes did not want to divert me from writing my dissertation, and it was only after December 1929 that he started giving me for comments the proofs of the Treatise. As the Treatise was finished in September 1930, I did not really have much opportunity for exercising an influence on it. I may have persuaded Keynes to alter a few passages, and no doubt I discovered a number of misprints.[26]

Parts of the Patinkin–Kahn correspondence were published as an appendix to the proceedings of a conference on *Keynes, Cambridge and the General Theory*, organised by Patinkin and J. Clark Leith and held at the University of Western Ontario in October 1975 (Patinkin & Leith, 1977). During this conference, which Kahn did not attend, his role in the Cambridge Circus and more generally at Cambridge in the 1930s and in subsequent years was discussed at length, in particular by Patinkin, Austin Robinson, Moggridge, Samuelson, Johnson and Tarshis. Rereading their testimonies is important for what they add to our knowledge of Kahn's scientific contribution as well as his *modus operandi* as an economist.

Patinkin's assertion that 'the received version of the transition from the *Treatise* to the *General Theory* assigns too large a role to the discussion of the Cambridge Circus, and correspondingly too small a one to the criticisms of such individuals as Hawtrey, Robertson, and even Hayek' (Patinkin, 1977, p. 6) set the stage for the first day of debate. Patinkin went on to argue that the essential ingredient of the *General Theory*, the principle of effective demand, was not really developed until 1933, and that there was little written evidence of any subsequent direct influence of the members of the Cambridge Circus, and of Kahn and Joan Robinson in particular, on the development of Keynes's thought. Commenting on Kahn's 1931 multiplier article, the importance of which he did not deny, Patinkin noted that the main thrust of Kahn's dynamic analysis of the

[26] Letter from Kahn to Patinkin, 19 March 1974, RFK/12/2/19/2–3, reproduced by kind permission of Professor David Papineau.

effects of increases in public investment on employment and expenditure contained in his article was to show that the expansionary process converged to a finite limit, rather than in the direction of anticipating effective demand. In reply to Patinkin, Austin Robinson remained 'completely convinced—as is James Meade—that by the end of the academic year 1930–31 the essentials of the *General Theory* were known in outline' (Robinson, 1977a, p. 36).

> We had [...] very ready at hand the necessary tools, several of them evolved or first known to us in Cambridge during the previous few years. We had Richard Kahn's new work on the multiplier, giving greater precision to earlier ideas about the total extent of the effects of public works expenditure. We had his initial work, still unpublished, on short period pricing and other work was going on to refine this. (Ibid., p. 34)

Robinson's indication that Kahn's ideas on pricing and the effects of spending in the short run should be regarded as one of the foundations of the *General Theory* was echoed in Tarshis's recollection of his years as a student at Cambridge in the 1930s.[27] In documenting the development of Keynes's thought as reflected in the content of his lectures, Tarshis (1977) emphasised the links of Keynes's progress in developing his own ideas, with Kahn's lectures on the *Economics of the Short Period*. According to Tarshis, this was particularly true of the overcoming of the separation of the theory of value and relative prices (micro) from the monetary theory of the general price level (macro) in favour of the idea that prices and quantities are determined simultaneously at the macro and the individual industry level, more or less on the basis of the same principles.

> As a result of this change, Keynes was led to introduce the notion of effective demand—with its twin determinants, the aggregate demand function and the aggregate supply function. [...] to economists who had been brought up by Marshall to think always in terms of "other things being equal"—this new approach of Keynes seemed to mark a forward step because in a way it meant a partial return to Marshall. (Ibid., pp. 53–54)

Recalling how Keynes, despite his reluctance to accept part of Marshall, had derived much value from it, Tarshis dwelt on the aggregate supply function, one of the most important and misunderstood parts of the

[27] On this see also Dimand (2019, p. 424).

General Theory—according to Tarshis—and one of the elements in which the link between Keynes's and Marshall's (also via Kahn) thought is strongest.

> Obviously, a good deal remains in modern Keynesian analysis of the aggregate demand function; by way of contrast, not much more remains of the aggregate supply function than the eerie grin of the disappeared cat which usually does not even rate mention in the index. Yet it is through the aggregate supply function that Keynes is most closely related to Marshall, and it is through it too that many of the bridges between micro- and macro-economics can be found, or to put this differently, where the micro-foundations of macro-economics are located. (Ibid., p. 54)

The main responsibility for building this bridge, bringing the idea of the aggregate supply function and the simultaneous determination of prices and quantities associated with supply and demand patterns into the *General Theory*, rests primarily with Kahn.[28]

> I have located lecture notes made whilst attending lectures on "The Short Period" given by R.F. Kahn in the autumn of 1932. It is perfectly clear that even then, in November 1932, Richard Kahn with Joan Robinson, had gone as far as was needed to provide the basis for Keynes's aggregate supply function [...] But how can we know that Keynes went along with them, or understood them? [...] Of course, I cannot know how much communication there was between Kahn and Keynes between say, 1931 and 1935, but my impression is that there was a great deal and I would be very surprised if Kahn would have allowed Keynes to submit to publisher a concept of the aggregate supply function that was notably deficient and primitive as compared to what Kahn (and some others in the 'Circus') had developed as early as November 1932. (Ibid., p. 62)

These words, which corroborate what Kahn himself wrote to Patinkin, move the influence of Kahn on Keynes forward in time, beyond the end of the Cambridge Circus in 1931.

> The main burden during this period fell on Richard Kahn, who was formalising and constraining the product of Keynes's intuitive and impressionistic

[28] On Kahn's persuasiveness in convincing Keynes to introduce increasing cost curves into the theoretical apparatus of the *General Theory*, see in particular Tonveronachi (1983, pp. 84–86, 92, 154–156). I am grateful to A. Roncaglia for this suggestion.

> intellect—although Joan Robinson also had a role in this process. It was at this stage that the "stiff supervisions" from Kahn had perhaps their greatest importance, as the truth, intuitively perceived in 1932, moved closer to a proof fit for the outside world of economists, undergraduates and policy makers. By the end of the summer of 1934, events moved towards the final stage. (Moggridge, 1977, p. 68)

The importance of Kahn as a disciplining factor of Keynes's insights and creativity, and as a critical but constructive and sympathetic reader of the drafts of the *General Theory*, returned to the centre of the debate that followed the presentation on the second day of the conference, devoted to the development of Cambridge economics. According to Austin Robinson,

> Richard Kahn's part in all this was tremendously large, and it has always seemed to me a crucial part in one sense. We, all of us in Cambridge at that time, when we had written something, submitted it to Richard Kahn to see if it was all right; and one always (if it was me) got it back with all my logical errors pointed out. [...] He did this for all of us, and he was involved in a great deal of Cambridge work of that time. If you take the imperfect competition work, I have no doubt at all in my mind that this started as a joint game between Joan and Richard Kahn. They were trying to use the marginal revenue technique to solve problems which we had not been able to solve before, or which we in Cambridge had not solved before. His part in it was enormously large. But I think at the same time (and if you know Richard Kahn, I think you would agree with me) it was not equally easy to get constructive published work of his own out of him. The best way to use Richard Kahn's gifts was, I think, to take advantage of his meticulous criticism which would turn an inadequate initial effort into something that was really satisfactory. Without Richard Kahn, in many cases, we could not have done what was done. (Robinson, 1977b, p. 80)

These words are important not only as a personal tribute to Kahn, but also as further testimony to his *modus operandi* as an economist from someone, Austin Robinson, who by then had known Kahn for almost fifty years. Robinson's impression was confirmed by Moggridge when he claimed

> If I was going to sum it up on the basis of almost ten years of working with Richard Kahn, I would put it this way: Richard is very important. However, in many respects he is the perfect foil. Without Keynes's drive and Keynes's constant flow of new ideas it would not have happened. For Richard is fan-

> tastic if he has something to react to, but the impetus is coming from outside. If he has something to react to he is spurred on. If you have what you think is a good idea and want to see if it runs, Richard is superb, but it is less certain if one wants to work the process the other way around. (Ibid., p. 81)

The portrait of Kahn that emerges from the recollections of Austin Robinson and Moggridge is that of a scholar with great attention to detail and an iron logic at the service of others. At the same time, both accounts suggest a certain lack of initiative on Kahn's part. He was always ready to respond to requests for help from members of his inner circle, but he was not particularly proactive. A final important testimony regarding this aspect of Kahn's personality in relation to his activities in the Cambridge Circus and during the war years once again comes from Austin Robinson. In 1992, when complimenting Luigi Pasinetti on his obituary of Kahn written for the British Academy, Robinson observed that

> My dear Luigi,
>
> I have been reading more carefully the article that you have written on Richard Kahn.
>
> I am full of admiration of what you have done. I think you have got him exactly right. But I hope you will forgive me if I raise one or two points.
>
> First, regarding Richard himself. My reading of him is that he was a person of infinite critical capacity, who could pick out a mistake that one had made in anything one had written. On the other hand, I think that he was a person of rather limited initiative. He did not go round creating institutions or groups of people. He waited for people to come to him. My doubts at one or two places about what you have written derive from my reading of his character. May I try to deal with the one or two places about what you have written where I am not quite sure whether you are right, and where my instinct makes me think you may be wrong.
>
> I am absolutely certain that Richard Kahn did not propose and organise the Circus. I am quite sure that it was Joan and myself who wanted his help in understanding Keynes' Treatise. We drew in first Piero Sraffa and then James Meade. I do not think you are right in seeing him as chairman and organiser of the Circus. I feel sure that we had no chairman and no formal organisation. Richard was the line of communication with Keynes because they were both fellows of King's, and he had access to Keynes very much more readily than any of the rest of us.
>
> We did not start the Circus with any clear objective other than understanding the book. We never regarded ourselves as trying to formulate the content of the new book. I cannot remember when it became clear that

Keynes was going to write the General Theory. But we certainly never regarded ourselves as having any formal relation to the birth of the General Theory.

There is one other thing about the Circus. We discussed informally during the October and January terms. By the end of that time we had questions to ask and discuss and we organised a seminar for a limited number of selected graduate students and people taking Part II, in one of the common rooms of Trinity during the May term. Thereafter the Circus came to an end. James Meade went back to Oxford. I dropped out because I was busy with a book of my own. Joan, Richard and Piero continued to advise Keynes when he asked them to. But that was no part of the Circus proper.

I said earlier that Richard had great critical power but little initiative. He was not ordinarily a very good civil servant. He did not regard the function of making things happen as being part of his makeup. He was a very great success with advising people in Egypt. But when he came back to the Ministry of Production he contributed very little. I had not remembered that he had a short time in the Board of Trade in 1945. He left no traces behind him.

I have been fascinated by the comments of various people, including Schumpeter, about his contribution to the General Theory. I feel certain that they were criticisms of Keynes's initiative. I do not believe that left to himself Richard would ever have produced the General Theory. But I am quite prepared to be told that his criticisms of Maynard's attempts to ask questions and answer them were an essential part of the process. Whether they ought to have been more formally acknowledged I leave to others.

Once again, thank you for a splendid piece of work.[29]

The most interesting part of this letter is Robinson's observation that Kahn was neither a promoter of projects nor a builder of groups or institutions, suggesting a reactive rather than proactive disposition. In terms of economic theory, this attitude, alongside other factors that will be discussed later, helps to explain Kahn's gradual disappearance from the forefront of economic theory at least until, in the 1970s, numerous requests to provide direct testimony on Keynes forced Kahn to return to the subject. Something similar happened when Kahn decided to confront two theories that had the potential to obscure the centrality and essence of Keynes's message in the 1970s: Malinvaud's reinterpretation of the *General Theory* from the perspective of general economic equilibrium with

[29] Letter from Austin Robinson to Pasinetti, 1 April 1992, ref. EAGR/6/4/60–61, reproduced by kind permission of the Marshall Librarian.

rigid prices and wages, and Sraffa's new theory in *Production of Commodities by Means of Commodities.*

9.4 Kahn on Malinvaud

In the 1970s, stagflation challenged the macroeconomic wisdom of the 1960s, amidst new interpretations of the Phillips curve by Neo-Keynesians and monetarists (Forder, 2014, pp. 81–106) and the critique of Keynesian economics and econometrics coming from New Classical macroeconomics (e.g. Goutsmedt, 2017). In parallel, new interpretations of the *General Theory* emerged, focusing on the possibility of integrating Keynesian unemployment and Walrasian general equilibrium via money in the utility function (Patinkin, 1956) and the dual decision hypothesis (Clower, 1965), or, alternatively, explaining involuntary unemployment as the result of information, signalling and coordination problems in a decentralised economy (Leijonhufvud 1968).

As de Vroey (2016, p. 123) observes, Patinkin's book (with some delay), Clower's article and Leijonhufvud's book triggered a stream of new work that initially formed what is now known as the 'disequilibrium macro' school. An important contribution to this stream is Malinvaud (1977). In this book, based on the text of his three Yrjo Jahnsson Lectures, Malinvaud tried to bridge the gap between real-world problems of the 1970s and the general equilibrium models, *à la* Barro, Grossman, Drèze and Benassy, which aimed to replicate Keynesian results in a micro-founded environment with rigid or sluggish prices.

Malinvaud develops a macroeconomic model involving households, firms and the government under conditions of short-run price and wage rigidity. Households supply labour, demand goods and services, and hold money as their sole financial asset. They aim to maximise their utility within market constraints. Firms aim to maximise profits by using labour, capital and technology. Government spending is autonomous, unproductive and financed by money creation. The model identifies three possible short-run equilibrium states: Keynesian unemployment, where there is excess supply in both the labour and goods markets; classical unemployment, where there is excess labour supply but demand for goods is insufficient; and repressed inflation, where there is excess demand in both markets. Keynesian unemployment, which is caused by insufficient demand, can be alleviated by increasing public spending or by simultaneously reducing prices and wages to stimulate demand via real-balance effects. In contrast, classical unemployment results from high real wages and weak profits, and cannot be solved by demand-side policies alone. Instead, nominal wage cuts or price increases are needed, which are the opposite of Keynesian remedies. Repressed inflation requires either restrictive fiscal policy or a shift to open inflation through rising wages and prices, which erode real balances and dampen excess demand.

In the only article he wrote for the *Cambridge Journal of Economics*, Kahn (1977) critically analyses Malinvaud's model, focusing on the incompatibility between Walrasian and Keynesian models in general, and between the assumptions underlying Malinvaud's model and the real world in particular. For Kahn (as for Keynes), economic theory must be based on realistic assumptions, starting with the fact that in the real world the level of employment is unilaterally determined by employers, as is the number of working hours per unit of time and the organisation of labour. The workers do not have a choice in the matter. At most, their preference for leisure may influence union demands, but it never directly affects the individual or aggregate supply of labour. Ignoring this fact and relying on ad hoc assumptions about behaviour blurs the line between unemployment and leisure, and is both inconsistent with how people behave in practice, and contrary to common sense.

Moreover, in a world in which profit-maximising firms produce homogeneous goods and operate with upward-sloping marginal costs and supply curves, excess demand for their products, as in the case of classical unemployment, would lead these firms to raise prices and supply, causing real wages to fall until unemployment disappeared. To justify an equilibrium with sticky prices, unemployment and excess demand for goods, one must move to a world in which firms produce heterogeneous goods and operate with horizontal or downward-sloping cost and supply curves. In this case, however, an increase in output from a situation of excess demand entails an increase, not a decrease, in profits, and so again classical unemployment cannot be maintained.

Methodologically, it is interesting to note that, in order to reconstruct and then refute Malinvaud's arguments, Kahn chooses to use a graphical apparatus consisting of supply and demand curves relating aggregate employment in the consumption sector to the corresponding price index. This is similar to what Kahn had done many years earlier in his article on the multiplier. The choice to relegate the mathematical treatment of the problem to an appendix also echoes Kahn's Marshallian imprinting.

Revisiting Kahn's analysis of Malinvaud, Schefold (1983) notes the existence of a strong link between the demand and supply functions presented by Keynes in Chapter 3 of the *General Theory* and Kahn's interpretation of Malinvaud.[30] In this paper, part of a broader reflection on the links between Keynesian theory and the classical theory of value and distribution, Schefold clarifies Kahn's argument by simplifying it and removing an inconsistency between Kahn's treatment of the demand for and supply of consumer goods. He also extends Kahn's argument to the case of falling average costs, again showing the inconsistency of Malinvaud's concept of classical unemployment. Commenting on these contributions, Schefold observes

> Keynes was, at the time of writing the *General Theory*, still a Marshallian, Malinvaud is a Walrasian, and Kahn is, in so far as he represents a later development of Cambridge economics, close to the classical theory of value and distribution. (Schefold, 1983, p. 229)

This characterisation is broadly correct, but in the light of the results of this research it seems to me necessary to supplement it by pointing out that Kahn was also a Marshallian at the time of the composition of the *General Theory* and that, thanks to his contribution, important Marshallian elements entered the *General Theory*. At the same time, while there are some evident similarities between Kahn's thinking and classical political economy, our reconstruction of Kahn's intellectual trajectory suggests relating them to his Marshallian imprinting rather than to any direct engagement with classical political economy or Sraffa's interpretation of it. In particular, I refer to the three categories of income recipients (workers, capitalists and owners of natural resources), to the dynamic nature of the accumulation process, to the possibility of determining the prices of consumer goods solely on the basis of cost conditions, and of the political nature of the wage-setting determination process.

The evidence proposed in this study suggests that, among Keynes's epigones at Cambridge, Kahn more than others, remained attached to the original approach of the *General Theory*, with its Marshallian roots, to the focus on the short run, on partial equilibria, on the influence of subjective

[30] For a review of Kahn's and Malinvaud's contributions, as well as Schefold's contributions on Kahn and Malinvaud, in the context of a reconsideration of the supply side of the Keynesian theoretical framework, see Skarstein (1992).

factors (conjectures, opinions, expectations) on economic decisions under conditions of uncertainty. These elements greatly diminish the possibility of including Kahn among those who, from the 1960s onwards, argued for a re-evaluation of classical economic theory in opposition to marginalism.

9.5 'You Are a Complete Cipher to the Outside World': Kahn on Sraffa

> Dear Kahn, I think a plausible case can be made for inefficient firms having a higher demand curve for their products. In the state of equilibrium, before the depression, when all firms were earning normal profits, only those technically inefficient firms could have survived which had marketing advantages. The typical case would be that of an old established firm which could hold its own, notwithstanding its out of date plant, thanks to its solid trade connection. Inefficiency in production and advantages in marketing may often go together, being appendages of old age. I forgot to tell you to-day that Maurice Clark in an article on Economics + Psychology in the Journal of Pol. Sc. for 1918 deals with matters connected with the limited market; from my notes I find that, had I known about it when I wrote the article for the E.J., it would have been useful to me. Yours sincerely, Piero Sraffa.[31]

This letter is one of the earliest pieces of evidence of the life-long relationship (and friendship) between Kahn and Sraffa.[32] In the 1930s the relationship between Kahn and Sraffa, both junior members of the Cambridge Faculty of Economics and Politics with a strong association with Keynes and both members of the Cambridge Circus, gradually developed into a close acquaintance. For example, in a letter from Kahn to Sraffa dated 17 February 1933 and sent from the United States, after thanking Sraffa for his letter and 'all the gossip' in Cambridge, Kahn expresses his concern for Sraffa's professional position and prospects and adds: 'Nearly everybody I meet asks about you. You are a complete cipher to the outside world'.[33]

[31] Letter from Sraffa to Kahn, 13 March 1929, ref. RFK/3/13/149. The letter is followed by notes from Sraffa to Kahn concerning the latter's Fellowship Dissertation, Kahn's comments on Sraffa's 1926 *Economic Journal* article and treatment of imperfect competition.

[32] For evidence that Kahn considered Sraffa his oldest friend see Harcourt (1984, p. 406). Sraffa at Cambridge see also Marcuzzo (2005, pp. 292–308). On Sraffa at the University of Cambridge, with references to Kahn, see Marcuzzo with D. Besomi & F. Ranchetti (2005).

[33] Letter from Kahn to Sraffa, 17 February 1933, ref. SP C/150.

In the second half of the 1930s, up to the outbreak of war, both Kahn and Sraffa 'pursuing their own thoughts' moved away from their early shared interest in imperfect competition. Kahn, while assisting Keynes in the gestation of the *General Theory*, chose to return to the terrain of perfect competition in the short-run, diminishing returns to labour, rising and convex supply functions, and the multiplier. On the other hand, Sraffa continued along the path of rediscovering classical political economy, while exerting a very limited influence on the *General Theory*.[34] It seems fair to say that by the end of the 1930s the intellectual paths of Sraffa and Kahn diverged, never to cross again, although their personal relationship remained strong. Their shared 'loyalty to Cambridge', as a place and as a way of life, was the basis of this relationship.

Apart from this, and in spite of Kahn's great admiration for Sraffa's work on Ricardo and, more generally, for his value as an economist, there are no significant points of contact between the two in the post-war decades on the analytical level. There are no references to Sraffa in Kahn's post-war scholarly production and the distance between Sraffa's revaluation of classical political economy and the critique of marginalism, and Kahn's interest in the contingent problems of the British economy, analysed within a non-formalised Keynesian framework, does indeed seem profound.

Evidence of this distance can be found in a correspondence between Kahn and Robert Solow, which opens with Solow thanking Kahn for sending him a copy of the *The Making of Keynes' General Theory*. On 14 August 1984, Solow thanks Kahn for warning his readers about the risks of the return of 'bad habits of thought in our profession', in particular with regard to market-clearing macroeconomics, but disagrees with Kahn's criticism of the IS-LM model, which Solow instead welcomes as a 'neat vehicle' to represent Keynes's conclusion, a routine application to be used in the context of non-exceptional circumstances (RFK/13/106/1–2). In thanking Solow for an earlier letter of 20 September, where he had encouraged Kahn to focus on developing the role of finance in Keynesian economics and expressed his doubts about the possibility to introduce saving and investment in the Sraffian model (ref. RFK/13/106/4), Kahn writes

[34] On this limited influence see Grieve (2012) among others. On Sraffa and Cambridge economics between 1928 and 1931 see Marcuzzo (2001). On Sraffa's diminishing interest in imperfect competition and marginalism in favour of an altogether different approach see Roncaglia (1983, particularly pp. 342–345).

> Would you agree that few people realise that what is fundamentally wrong with Sraffa's book is that he makes the ridiculous assumption that all profits however large are individually spent and none saved. That assumption through a circular argument leads to Sraffa's system being in a stationary state. But in terms of the theory of growth, he gives no reason why his economy is stationary. The assumption of zero saving is not a sufficient condition. The trouble is that Sraffa never understood the general [sic] Theory. What I am doing is to introduce growth theory into the Sraffa model.[35]

Solows's reply, written on 27 November 1984, is as follows

> I think I understand exactly what you mean about the Sraffa model. He is so intent on reproducing the circular flow of goods and the regeneration of value that he has no room for saving and therefore no room for effective demand. It comes from thinking too much about Ricardo and not enough about Keynes. There is certainly room for introducing growth theory into that sort of model. But I am hoping you will go further. If it were simply a matter of allowing for saving automatically matched by investment, I presume you will be led to a steady state generalizing Sraffa's stationary state. (What will you do about population and labour force, by the way?) But if you would like to introduce Keynesian economics into the Sraffa model, then I think the consequences will be much more drastic. When there is a genuine problem of effective demand failure, so the future is not just an extrapolation of the past, there is not much reason to expect relative values to follow simple rules either. That is what I meant in my earlier letter by saying that you were threatening to explode the whole model. The first step is certainly the introduction of growth theory anyway.[36]

The sense of these words, and of Kahn's attempt to insert a dynamic element and money within Sraffa's model, can be grasped by reading a paper written at the end of the 1970s, when Kahn's analytical skills had partially faded, and which remained unpublished at Kahn's own wish.[37] Notwithstanding the limitations of a work that remained at a preliminary stage of elaboration, this paper is nevertheless interesting for what it

[35] Letter from Kahn to Solow, 12 November 1984, ref. RFK/13/106/3.

[36] Letter from Solow to Kahn, 27 November 1984, ref. RFK/2/20/244.

[37] On this decision, see the interview with M.C. Marcuzzo in Chap. 10 below. The paper can be found in RFK/2/20.

reveals about the profound difference in his analytical approach from that of Sraffa.

The paper is entitled: 'The Sraffa System: (1) A difficulty, (2) Introduction of growth'. In setting out his analysis, Kahn refers to the concepts of equilibrium, steady state and Golden Age: 'accumulation has taken place in the past so to bring the stock of capital per man employed at its equilibrium value'. Technological progress is neutral, the available labour is fully employed and the nominal wage rate is used as the numeraire, 'and so avoid the complications which would result from assigning this function to Sraffa's composite commodity'.

Based on these premises, the first part of Kahn's essay is devoted to a critique of the idea that the system determining the relative prices of goods, the rate of profit and the wage rate is indeterminate, and that only by fixing one of the two distributional variables from the outside is it possible to break the deadlock. For Kahn, given technical and thriftiness conditions: 'there is only one possible set of values for the share of profits in income, the rate of profit, the value of capital per man employed, the real wage and the system of relative prices of commodities, which will result in zero net savings'. If Sraffa and his followers can argue, to use Kahn's words, that the system defining relative prices and the two distributive variables is indeterminate, it is because they do not explicitly consider the growth rate, nor its relation to investment, the propensity to save and the profit rate corresponding to that growth rate. Actually

> The reason is that Sraffa implicitly does discuss the rate of growth: more or less tacitly, he slips in the assumption that it is zero. But he and his followers have failed to realise that this assumption deprives the system of any degree of freedom—it is fully determined by technical and thriftiness conditions and by a zero rate of growth. (RFK/2/20)

Based on this observation and a rereading of section 81 of *Production of Commodities by Means of Commodities*, in the second part of the essay Kahn attempts to introduce a positive growth rate into Sraffa's model in the form of positive net investment. Echoing ideas expressed in his own 1964 essay on the valuation ratio, Kahn regards the value of investment as depending on the combination of animal spirits (defined as the 'Napoleonic urge for physical expansion') and the expectation of a rate of profit. This attempt, together with considerations of the problems of integrating money, monetary interest rates and a plausible description of wage determination, shows the difficulty of integrating Kahn's Keynesianism with Sraffa's system.

Kahn's Keynesianism is based on the consideration of the psychological dimension, the opinions and the uncertainty underlying individual decisions, especially in the spheres of real and financial accumulation, on the concepts of equilibrium (static and dynamic), on the non-neutrality of money and monetary policy, on the idea that it is possible for there to be a definite, if not mechanical, relationship between investment, savings, profits and growth, and on the consideration of time as a crucial factor in economic analysis. In Kahn, more than in other exponents of the Cambridge post-Keynesian school, and in particular Joan Robinson, the reference to these categories and theoretical concepts, rooted in post-Marshallian marginalism and enriched by the thought (and realism) of Keynes, prevails over the rigorous theoretical approach of the Sraffian school with its radical critique of marginalism in the name of the recovery of classical political economy.

Highlighting this fact is a further element in reconstructing the last part of Kahn's intellectual path. In the Cambridge of the 1970s, which was dominated by interest in the thought of Sraffa and his critique of marginalism and by attempts to synthesise Sraffa and Keynes from a neo-Ricardian and radical perspective, the space for Kahn's Keynesianism was rapidly shrinking. From this perspective, both the 1964 essay on the rate of interest, equity prices and the growth of firms as well as the unfinished essay on Sraffa's system can be read as an attempt by Kahn to resist this marginalisation and to reaffirm the validity of his point of view and analytical approach.

9.6 Shove and the Publishing of Kahn's Fellowship Dissertation

If the preparation of *The Making of Keynes' General Theory* led Kahn to reassess the life and contributions of Keynes something similar, albeit on a much smaller scale, happened with G. Shove, to whom Kahn devoted an entry in the *Palgrave Dictionary of Economics*, edited by J. Eatwell, M. Milgate and P. Newman (Kahn 1987a).[38] In describing Shove as a shy

[38] The other *Palgrave Dictionary* entry written by Kahn is dedicated to Laslo Rostas (Kahn, 1987b), a Hungarian economist brought to England by Nicholas Kaldor and an expert on industrial productivity. His expertise led to his appointment at the Board of Trade and later

and studious boy who chose economics after being placed in the Second Class in Part I of the Classical Tripos, and in recalling how

> His fastidious self-criticism explains why he rarely published his results and never wrote a book [...] He wrote much but published little [...] His determination not to publish anything until it seemed to say exactly what he meant—just that, and not another thing—sprang ultimately from a deep indeed religious, fealty to truth. (Ibid., p. 327)

One almost gets the impression that Kahn is talking about himself, or at least that he is trying to establish a strong connection between himself and his former supervisor. This impression is reinforced by what Kahn, writing about himself in the third person, adds immediately afterwards

> Indeed, although the name Richard Kahn is associated with that of Keynes, it was to Shove's encouragement that Kahn owes his career as an economist. Kahn's performance in Part II of the National [sic] Sciences Tripos in Physics, in 1927, was disappointing—he was placed only in the Second Class. Encouraged by his father he felt a desire to try his hand at a fourth year on Economics, aiming at Part II of the Economics Tripos. The College tutor was most discouraging. [...] But Shove was most encouraging and won the day. While Kahn in his fourth year owed much to Keynes, he owed far more to Shove, as a teacher; his successful Fellowship Dissertation owed much to Shove (and also to Piero Sraffa), little to Keynes. (Ibid., p. 328)

In formulating this tribute to Shove (and Sraffa), Kahn's recollection concludes with a description of the participation of both in the debates on increasing and decreasing returns and imperfect competition, and in particular in the symposium on Increasing Returns and the Representative Firm published in 1930 in the *Economic Journal.* Re-reading this symposium, Kahn identifies the fundamental distinction between external and internal economies, beyond the vagueness in which Marshall (and Pigou after him) had left it, as Shove's main contribution. Commenting on these words, Sardoni (2004, p. 362) observes how Kahn may have underestimated his influence on the theory of imperfect competition. While there is no direct evidence of Shove's involvement in the Keynesian revolution, Kahn may also have overlooked the similarity between Shove's and

as a Research Officer in the Faculty of Economics at Cambridge, where he influenced colleagues until his untimely death in 1954.

Keynes's perspectives on the Marshallian legacy. Both economists sought to preserve the depth and realism of Marshall's approach, while recognising the need to move beyond it.

The memory of Shove and Sraffa returns in Kahn's Introduction to the Fellowship Dissertation on *The Economics of the Short Period*, which was published first in Italian in 1983 and then in English six years later. The project to publish the dissertation in Italian began in the late 1970s, stemming from the friendship between Kahn and Giacomo Becattini. The two men had first met in Geneva in 1955, and Becattini then became a frequent visitor to Kahn at Cambridge from 1976–77 onwards.[39] Becattini greatly admired Kahn, believing his contributions to extend beyond his role as guarantor of the logical and mathematical accuracy of Keynes's work and his famous 1931 article on the theory of the employment multiplier. The two men discovered that they shared a common interest in Marshall and the Marshallians, particularly Shove. Kahn referred to Shove as his true teacher of economics even in conversation with Becattini. During one of Becattini's visits to Cambridge, he obtained a copy of Kahn's Dissertation and, after receiving Kahn's assent, entrusted his colleague Marco Dardi with editing the Italian edition.

Referring to Dardi's testimony, at the end of the following chapter, for the details of this story, we focus here on what Kahn has to say in the introduction to his dissertation, rereading it for the first time many years after it was written. Recalling the Marshallian origins of the concept of the short period ('one of Marshall's most fruitful contributions'), Kahn dwells on the arbitrary and dichotomous nature of the distinction between the short and the long run, relating it to the distinction between fixed and circulating capital. It is up to the economist to decide, on the basis of his knowledge of reality, beyond mere logical reasoning, which elements should be included in the category of 'fixed capital', considering that they remain unchanged during the period of production of final goods, and which elements should be excluded.

Defined in this way, the boundaries that define short period become blurred and uncertain. Depending on whether entrepreneurs or managers decide to modify the production capacity and organisation of businesses based on their perception of the economic situation in which they operate, it can last for a very short time or a long time. Thus, Kahn reiterates that, in the economic sphere, observed reality fundamentally depends on how

[39] On the acquaintance between Becattini and Kahn, see also Bellanca and Raffaelli (1999).

it is perceived and understood by the economic agents operating within it. In this context, direct knowledge of economic agents and the mental mechanisms that guide their actions is essential for an economist to do their job well. In the case in question, the alternative to making a clear distinction between the elements that make up fixed capital from the other means of production is to follow Mill and Marshall in distinguishing circulating capital 'which fulfils the whole of its office in the production in which it is engaged, by a single use', from fixed capital 'which exists in a durable shape and the return from which is spread over a period of corresponding duration'.

Drawing inspiration from Sraffa's approach to this distinction in *Production of Commodities by Means of Commodities*, Kahn seizes the opportunity to take credit for identifying and correcting a serious error made by Sraffa in his 1926 article for the *Economic Journal.* The point of contention concerned the properties of equilibrium under conditions of imperfect competition. Whereas for Sraffa even the slightest deviation from perfect competition would lead to monopoly equilibrium, for Kahn this was not the case. In the case of imperfect competition, equilibrium quantity prices would lie somewhere between the corresponding values of monopoly and perfect competition, depending on the degree of imperfection and, above all, on the assumptions that guide each firm's decisions about the response of competing firms to its actions.

Comparing his conclusions on this point with those of Sraffa and Chamberlin Kahn claims credit for his analysis of the duopoly, the definition of equilibrium based on the asymmetry between price leader and price follower, and the anticipation of the notion of the 'kinked demand curve'. Again, as with the identification of the foundations on which the economics of the short run must be built, it is direct knowledge of reality that suggests the explanation of why, under certain conditions, businessmen prefer not to change prices, even though this may seem convenient in the abstract.

> Conversations with business men lead me to think that this conclusion—absurd though it may appear—has some bearing in practice. It applies more particularly in those industries where policy determines the price that a firm shall charge rather than the level of its output, where the price is fixed for fairly long periods at a time, where custom or convenience dictate that a change of price shall be substantial in amount, and where the number of firms is not too large [...]. But it is important to note that while there can

be equilibrium in any position, the equilibrium is unstable for changes in a downward direction. (Kahn, 1989, p. xix)

It is the same analytical approach, rooted in observation of the reality under study, that had allowed Kahn to explain why firms in the cotton-spinning industry prefer to produce at full capacity only a few days a month, while keeping the mills closed on the other days and not adjusting the price of their product, even when it would appear to be cost effective to do so. In explaining these phenomena and formulating the concept of the inverted L-shaped prime cost curve, Kahn drew on his interviews with businessmen and his knowledge of the production statistics of the Lancashire cotton industry provided by Keynes.

There is nothing in itself original in the importance which I attach to imperfection of the market. My debt to Sraffa—both to him personally as a friend and to his article—is made clear. I feel that I should have written more about Shove, one of my teachers. And I referred to Marshall (§ 2 of Chapter 7). The importance of the dissertation rests largely on the analysis of the influence of imperfection of the market on the manner in which, at a time of depression, an industry's output is distributed between the individual firms. (Ibid., p. xx)

Dardi (1983) focuses on this aspect, and on Kahn's ability to link the microeconomic problem (determining the equilibrium of an industry characterised by a limited degree of imperfect competition) with the macroeconomic problem (depression of demand) as the main contributions of Kahn's dissertation. Reread today, Kahn's analysis appears as an attempt to develop concepts that are only hinted at in Marshall's *Principles*, combining the analytical precision that can result from the use of a mathematical and graphical apparatus with constant attention to the data of reality, to the interdependence of supply and demand factors (which are difficult to grasp in mathematical analysis) and to the elements of a subjective, conjectural and conventional nature that guide the choices of economic agents. In reality these elements give rise to the margin of indeterminacy that surrounds economic relations, a margin that the young Kahn set out to explore in his Dissertation, but then abandoned to immerse himself in the Keynesian revolution.

In my Preface I wrote that

> It is on widening the conclusions [mathematical] of Chapters 8, 9 and 10 and on furthering their practical verification, with which a very small beginning is made in this dissertation, that I place the greatest hope for further development.
>
> I am inclined to the view that while further development would have proved fruitful, it is fortunate from my own selfish point of view that I did not make the attempt. (Ibid., p. xxi)

Kahn, always hovering between reticence and desire to be recognised, does not discuss the reasons that led him to abandon the theory of imperfect competition in the early 1930s. He also says nothing new about the reasons that prompted him to suggest to Keynes, while he was developing the *General Theory*, that he should remain within the realm of perfect competition, with diminishing returns to labour, rising supply curves and anti-cyclical real wages. Marris (1991) offers a fresh perspective on this matter, based on the incompatibility between these hypotheses and the concept of involuntary unemployment as an equilibrium state. According to Marris, as long as there are unemployed workers, it is always possible, at least in theory, to maintain constant labour productivity and move along horizontal unit cost curves, as Kahn had done in his Dissertation with L-shaped cost curves and demand-determined output and employment.

During his early years within the Cambridge economic circle, Marris recalls how the young Kahn, though intellectually brilliant, showed little inclination towards developing broad theoretical systems. He developed the multiplier in response to practical concerns about the impact of fiscal policy, rather than as part of a unified economic vision. Personal relationships also shaped the trajectory of his economic thought: his associations with Keynes and Joan Robinson may have limited the reach of his ideas on imperfect competition. In a letter dated 2 May 1987, quoted by Marris, Kahn suggests that Keynes's decision to base *The General Theory* on perfect competition may have been tactical, aligning it with the dominant economic view. However, other factors likely contributed to the omission of imperfect competition from Keynes's framework, including the challenges of incorporating it into macroeconomic models, and the marginalisation of economists such as Kalecki, who had effectively managed to do so.

The same silence on the lack of connection between imperfect competition and *General Theory* characterises Kahn's recollections in a biographical interview he gave to Cristina Marcuzzo in 1987, published first in

Italian (Kahn, 1988) and only many years later in English (Marcuzzo, 2020).[40] This interview gave Kahn the opportunity to clarify, point out and claim the terms of his own contribution and emerge from the cone of shadow in which he had chosen to remain for so long. The fact that in carrying out this operation Kahn chose to justify the Marshallian origins of his first contributions, as well as to mark the distance from Keynes on some qualifying analytical points, without in the slightest way undermining his esteem towards the man and the economist with whom his name is most closely associated, seems an important fact to underline.

Equally interesting in terms of what it reveals about Kahn's limited engagement with post-war theoretical debates is his decision to dedicate relatively little space to economic theory in his interview with Marcuzzo, and instead focus on practical issues and his views on economic policy, such as the benefits of incomes policy and the importance of coordination between fiscal and monetary policy at national and international levels. The fact that more than a third of the interview is devoted to the war years, the immediate post-war period, and the debate on nationalisation indicates the importance of this phase in Kahn's development as an economist. For Kahn, economic theory is valuable not for its elegance or as a mental exercise, but for the concrete improvements it can offer to humanity's living conditions. The influence of Marshall, through Pigou, Shove and Keynes on Kahn is clearly evident here, too.

Both Dardi (1990) and Marcuzzo (2012) acknowledge the importance of this influence, albeit in slightly different ways. Dardi highlights the profound continuity in Kahn's thinking with Marshallian ideas developed in Cambridge at the start of the twentieth century, emphasising Kahn's commitment to the analysis of supply and demand, as well as his creativity. This is particularly evident in Kahn's early macroeconomic analysis of the multiplier and his subtle reworking of the theory of liquidity preference to account for investor motivations. It is also evident in his social philosophy and views on economic policy. Here, Kahn's policy approach is guided by the belief that outcomes depend not only on the policy itself, but also on how it is perceived and communicated. Dardi provocatively links this feature to modern ideas such as rational expectations. Marcuzzo also recognises Kahn's Marshallian roots, which are particularly evident in his price theory and his conception of profit maximisation as a process of trial and

[40] For an account of how the idea for the interview came about, how it unfolded and how it was presented in Bologna in 1988, please refer to the next chapter.

error. In general, she refers to this as benign marginalism, and expression introduced by Mongin (1990) and discussed in more detail below. However, unlike Dardi, Marcuzzo identifies a more radical departure from Marshallian orthodoxy in the 1930s, and notes Kahn's increasing focus on national and international monetary issues from the 1950s onwards, particularly the role of uncertainty and institutions.

References

Annan, N. (1984). Testing the sphinx. *The Observer*, October 7.

Barens, I. (1984). Review of *The making of Keynes' General Theory*, by R. F. Kahn. *Contributions to Political Economy, 3*(1), 105–108.

Bellanca, N., & Raffaelli, T. (1999). L'economista DOC: Intervista a Giacomo Becattini. *Il Pensiero Economico Italiano, 7*(1), 157–217.

Caffè, F. (1985). Tutti gli amici di Lord Keynes. *Il Sole 24 Ore*, April 7, 808.

Chick, V. (1973). *The theory of monetary policy.* Basil Blackwell.

Clower, R. W. (1965). The Keynesian Counter-Revolution: A theoretical appraisal. In F. H. Hahn & F. P. R. Brechling (Eds.), *The theory of interest rates* (pp. 103–125). Macmillan.

Cox, J. (1995). *Keynes: An archivist's view.* In A. Cottrell & M. Lawlor (Eds.), *New perspectives on Keynes* (pp. 163–176). Duke University Press.

Dardi, M. (1983). Introduzione. In R. F. Kahn (Ed.), *L'economia del breve periodo* (pp. 9–30). Trans. P. Cecioni. Bollati Boringhieri.

Dardi, M. (1990). Richard Kahn. *Studi Economici, 41*(2), 3–86.

De Vroey, M. (2016). *A history of macroeconomics from Keynes to Lucas and beyond.* Cambridge University Press.

Dimand, R. W. (2019). Lorie Tarshis. In R. W. Dimand & H. Hagemann (Eds.), *The Elgar companion to John Maynard Keynes* (pp. 424–428). Edward Elgar Publishing.

Dunlop, J. T. (1938). The movement of real and money wages. *Economic Journal, 48*(191), 413–434.

Dunlop, J. T. (1939). Price flexibility and the degree of monopoly. *Quarterly Journal of Economics, 53*(4), 522–534.

Forder, J. (2014). *Macroeconomics and the Phillips Curve Myth.* Oxford University Press.

Goutsmedt, A. (2017). *Stagflation and the crossroad in macroeconomics: The struggle between structural and New Classical macroeconometrics.* CES Working paper No. 2017-43. Chaire Énergie and Prospérité, Centre d'Économie de la Sorbonne, Université Paris 1 Panthéon-Sorbonne. Available online https://shs.hal.science/halshs-01625188/document

Grieve, R. H. (2012). Keynes, Sraffa and the emergence of the General Theory. *Review of Political Economy, 24*(1), 51–67.

Hagemann, H. (1985). Review of *Keynes and the modern world*. Proceedings of the Keynes Centenary Conference, King's College, Cambridge; *The Making of Keynes' General Theory*, by D. Worswick, J. Trevithick, and R. F. Kahn. *Weltwirtschaftliches Archiv, 121*(3), 596–601.

Harcourt, G. C. (1984). The end of an era: Joan Robinson (1903–83) and Piero Sraffa (1898–1983). *Journal of Post Keynesian Economics, 6*(3), 446–470.

Hartwig, J. (2022). The evolution of Patinkin's interpretation of Keynes' principle of effective demand. *European Journal of the History of Economic Thought, 29*(3), 505–522.

Howson, S. (1985). Review of *The making of Keynes' General Theory*, by Richard F. Kahn. *Journal of Economic History, 45*(4),1023–1024.

Kahn, R. F. (1974). What Keynes really said. *Sunday Telegraph*, September 22.

Kahn, R. F. (1975). *On re-reading Keynes*. Fourth Keynes Lecture in Economics, November 6, 1974, *Proceedings of the British Academy, 60*. Oxford University Press.

Kahn, R. F. (1976a). Historical origins of the International Monetary Fund. In A.P. Thirlwall (Ed.), *Keynes and international monetary relations* (pp. 3–35). Macmillan. Reprinted in M.C. Marcuzzo and P. Paesani (Eds.), (2022), *Richard F. Kahn: Collected economic essays* (pp. 191–221). Palgrave Macmillan.

Kahn, R. F. (1976b). Unemployment as seen by the Keynesians. In G.D.N. Worswick (Ed.), *The concept and measurement of involuntary unemployment* (pp. 19–25). Allen and Unwin. Reprinted in M. C. Marcuzzo & P. Paesani (Eds.) (2022), *Richard F. Kahn: Collected economic essays* (pp. 225–239). Palgrave Macmillan.

Kahn, R. F. (1977). Malinvaud on Keynes. Reviewing: Edmond Malinvaud, In *The theory of unemployment reconsidered*. Basil Blackwell; three lectures delivered for the Yrjö Jahnsson Foundation. *Cambridge Journal of Economics, 1*(4), 375–388.

Kahn, R. F. (1978). Some aspects of the development of Keynes's thought. *Journal of Economic Literature, 16*(2), 545–559. Reprinted in M.C. Marcuzzo and P. Paesani (Eds.) (2022), *Richard F. Kahn: Collected economic essays* (pp. 97–118). Palgrave Macmillan.

Kahn, R. F. (1983). *L'Economia del Breve Periodo*. Transl. by P. Cecioni. Bollati Boringhieri.

Kahn, R. F. (1984). *The making of Keynes' General Theory* (Raffaele Mattioli Foundation Lectures). Cambridge University Press.

Kahn, R. F. (1985). The Cambridge 'Circus'. In G. Harcourt (Ed.), *Keynes and His Contemporaries. The Sixth Centennial Keynes Seminar held at the University of Kent at Canterbury, 1983* (pp. 42–51). Macmillan.

Kahn, R. F. (1987a). Shove, G.F. In J. Eatwell, M. Milgate, & P. Newman (Eds.), *The New Palgrave: A dictionary of economics* (Vol. IV, pp. 327–328). Macmillan.

Kahn, R. F. (1987b). Rostas, L. In J. Eatwell, M. Milgate and P. Newman (Eds.), *The New Palgrave. A dictionary of economics* (vol. IV, 222–223). Macmillan.
Kahn, R. F. (1988). *Un Discepolo di Keynes.* (M. C. Marcuzzo, Ed.). Garzanti.
Kahn, R. F. (1989). *The economics of the short period.* Macmillan.
Keynes, J. M. (1937). Alternative theories of the rate of interest. *Economic Journal, 47*(186), 241–252.
Klamer, A. (1986). Review of *The making of Keynes' General Theory*, by R. F. Kahn. *History of political economy, 18*(2), 359–360.
Kregel, J. A. (1984). Review of *The making of Keynes' General Theory*, by R. F. Kahn. *De Economist, 132*(4), 506–510.
Lawlor, M. S. (2006). *The economics of Keynes in historical context: An intellectual history of the general theory.* Palgrave Macmillan.
Leijonhufvud, A. (1968). *On Keynesian economics and the economics of Keynes: A study in monetary theory.* Oxford University Press.
Malinvaud, E. (1977). *The theory of unemployment reconsidered.* Basil Blackwell.
Marcuzzo, M. C. (2001). Sraffa and Cambridge economics, 1929–1931. In T. Cozzi & R. Marchionatti (Eds.), *Piero Sraffa's political economy: A centenary estimate* (pp. 81–99). Routledge.
Marcuzzo, M. C. (2005). Piero Sraffa at the University of Cambridge. *European Journal of the History of Economic Thought, 12*, 425–452.
Marcuzzo, M. C. (2012). The elusive figure who hides in the preface of Cambridge books: An appraisal of Richard Kahn's contributions. In N. Salvadori, C. Gehrke, I. Steedman, & R. Sturn (Eds.), *Classical political economy and modern theory: Essays in honour of Heinz Kurz* (pp. 185–206). Routledge.
Marcuzzo, M. C. (2020). Richard F. Kahn: A disciple of Keynes. *History of Economics Review, 76*(1), 2–57.
Marcuzzo, M. C. (2023). Cambridge 'Circus'. In L. P. Rochon & S. Rossi (Eds.), *Elgar encyclopedia of post-Keynesian economics* (pp. 37–38). Edward Elgar.
Marcuzzo, M. C. with D. Besomi & F. Ranchetti. (2005). Kahn with Sraffa, Harrod and Kaldor. In H. D. Kurz, L. Pasinetti, & N. Salvadori (Eds.), *Piero Sraffa: The man and the scholar. Exploring his unpublished papers* (pp. 51–77). Routledge.
Marris, R. (1991). *Reconstructing Keynesian economics with imperfect competition: A desk-top simulation.* Edward Elgar.
Moggridge, D. E. (1977). Cambridge discussion and criticism surrounding the writing of *The general theory*: A chronicler's view. In D. Patinkin & J. C. Leith (Eds.), *Keynes, Cambridge and the General Theory* (pp. 64–71). Macmillan.
Moggridge, D. E. (Ed.) (1978). *The collected writings of John Maynard Keynes.* Vol. XIII. *The General Theory and after: Part I, Preparation.* Macmillan.
Moggridge, D. E. (1994). Richard Kahn as an historian of economics. *Cambridge Journal of Economics, 18*(1), 107–116.

Moggridge, D. E. (1997). Among the most fascinating of scholarly objects: a memoir. *Journal of the History of Economic Thought, 19*(1), 24–48.

Mongin, P. (1990). The early full-cost debate and the problem of empirically testing profit maximization. *Journal of Post Keynesian Economics, 13*(2), 236–251.

O'Donnell, R. (1995). Editing large unpublished writings: The case of J.M. Keynes. *History of Economic Ideas, 3*(2), 89–130.

Okuno-Fujiwara, M., & Shell, K. (2009). An Interview with Hirofumi Uzawa. *Macroeconomic Dynamics, 13*(3), 390–420.

Paesani, P. (2016). Marcello de Cecco 1939–2016. *Rivista di Storia Economica, 32*(3), 417–426.

Patinkin, D. (1956). *Money, Interest, and Prices.* Row, Peterson and Co.

Patinkin, D. (1976). *Keynes' monetary thought.* Duke University Press.

Patinkin, D. (1977). The process of writing *The General Theory.* A critical survey. In D. Patinkin & J. C. Leith (Eds.), *Keynes, Cambridge and the General Theory* (pp. 3–24). Macmillan.

Patinkin, D. (1978). Keynes and the multiplier. *Manchester School of Economic and Social Studies, 46*(3), 209–223.

Patinkin, D., & Leith, J. C. (Eds.). (1977). *Keynes, Cambridge and the General Theory.* Macmillan.

Robinson, E. A. G. (1977a). Keynes and his Cambridge colleagues. In D. Patinkin & J. C. Leith (Eds.), *Keynes, Cambridge and the General Theory* (pp. 25–38). Macmillan.

Robinson, E. A. G. (1977b). Discussion. In D. Patinkin & J. C. Leith (Eds.), *Keynes, Cambridge and the General Theory* (pp. 72–89). Macmillan.

Robinson, E. A. G. (1985). Review of *The making of Keynes' General Theory*, by R. F. Kahn. *Economic Journal, 95*(377), 206–208.

Roncaglia, A. (1983). Piero Sraffa and the reconstruction of political economy. *Banca Nazionale del Lavoro Quarterly Review, 36*(147), 337–350.

Rubin, G. (2008). Patinkin's interpretation of Keynesian economics: A genetic approach. In R. Leeson (Ed.), *The Keynesian tradition: Archival insights into the evolution of economics.* Palgrave Macmillan.

Sardoni, C. (2004). The contribution of Gerald Shove to the development of Cambridge economics. *Review of Political Economy, 16*, 361–375.

Schefold, B. (1983). Kahn on Malinvaud. In J. Eatwell & M. Milgate (Eds.), *Keynes's economics and the theory of value and distribution* (pp. 229–246). Duckworth.

Schiffman, D. (2014). Richard Kahn and Israeli Economic Policy, 1957 and 1962. *History of Economic Thought and Policy, 1*, 31–73.

Schiffman, D., & Zelekha, Y. (2014). *Do international advisers matter? Case studies of Israel's Economic Policies.* Working paper available online.

Skarstein, R. (1992). The shaky supply side: On neoclassical 'anomalies' in macroeconomic theory. *Banca Nazionale del Lavoro Quarterly Review, 45*(183), 407–430.
Tarshis, L. (1938). Real wages in the United States and Great Britain. *Canadian Journal of Economics, 4*(3), 362–376.
Tarshis, L. (1939). Changes in real and money wages. *Economic Journal, 49*(193), 150–154.
Tarshis, L. (1977). Keynes as seen by his students: (iii) Lorie Tarshis. In D. Patinkin & J. C. Leith (Eds.), *Keynes, Cambridge and the General Theory* (pp. 48–63). Macmillan.
Tarshis, L. (1985). Review of *The making of Keynes' General Theory*, by R. F. Kahn. *Journal of Economic Literature, 23*(2), 619–621.
Thirlwall, A. P. (1984). The theoretical years. Review of Richard F. Kahn. *The making of Keynes's General Theory. The Times Literary Supplement, 4*(242), 808.
Tonveronachi, M. (1983). *J.M. Keynes: Dall'instabilità ciclica all'equilibrio di sottoccupazione* [J. M. Keynes: From cyclical instability to underemployment equilibrium]. La Nuova Italia Scientifica.
Worswick, G. D. N. (Ed.). (1976). *The concept and measurement of involuntary unemployment.* Routledge.

CHAPTER 10

In My End Is My Beginning

10.1 In Memoriam: Kahn (10 August 1905–6 June 1989)

Richard Kahn passed away at Evelyn Hospital in Cambridge on 6 June 1989, aged 83, following a brief illness. He was a bachelor and did not have children. He kept his personal life and relationships strictly private until his death. Despite being modest and cautious, however, he chose to preserve a considerable amount of material about his private life among his papers. His archive contains correspondence with his parents and sisters (in both English and German), as well as with his numerous friends, correspondents and the women he was close to at various points in his life. There is also a great deal of material that is not related to economics. Examining this material reveals that Kahn's private life was far richer than his public image as an austere, aloof Cambridge don suggests. On 21 October 1989, Luigi Pasinetti, in a Memorial Service held at King's College Chapel, noted how

> This is the third time, over a short span of years, that the Congregation assembles in this Chapel to commemorate, and reflect upon, the life of a major contributor to that intellectual breakthrough that has become known in the world of economics and politics as "the Keynesian Revolution". […] If one adds that another memorial service, shortly after that of Joan Robinson, was held in Cambridge, though in another Chapel, for yet

P. Paesani, *Richard F. Kahn*, Great Thinkers in Economics,
https://doi.org/10.1007/978-3-032-09123-9_10

> another close associate of Keynes, Piero Sraffa, one cannot resist the impression that today's ceremony concludes a whole historical phase, almost an era, in the recent history of economic thought. This group of Cambridge economists had been the protagonist of one of those extraordinary and unique events in the history of ideas that decisively pushed knowledge ahead and created a break with the past.[1]

Kahn's passing presented an opportunity to reflect on his life and contributions to Keynesianism and Cambridge economics, as both Luigi Pasinetti (Pasinetti, 1991) and Geoffrey Harcourt (Harcourt, 1991) did.[2] Harcourt provides an inside interpretation of Kahn's work, emphasising his contributions to growth theory and the integration of real and financial dynamics, while acknowledging his occasional adherence to economic orthodoxy. In contrast, Pasinetti emphasises Kahn's role in shaping the *General Theory* and spearheading the Keynesian revolution, which he sees as a radical departure from economic orthodoxy.

> [The] Cambridge Keynesian school, and in particular Kahn, always took Marshall's neo-classical theory-which was the British version of that stream of economics which on the continent was associated with the names of Walras, Pareto and Menger — as precisely the theory from which the "Keynesian Revolution" broke away. For Kahn, the 'Keynesian Revolution' could not but mean what it literally says — a "revolution", a sharp breakaway from traditional neo-classical economic theory. (Pasinetti, 1991, p. 437)

Apart from the merits of this interpretation, to which I will return, the tributes paid by Pasinetti and Harcourt to Kahn, based on a long personal acquaintance, are also significant in what they reveal about his personality and some aspects of his private life that influenced his public activities.

The first relevant element in this respect concerns Kahn's Jewish identity. Kahn came from a family where strict adherence to Jewish teachings went hand in hand with a deep respect for education and culture.[3] Kahn is remembered as being particularly observant in his youth, but this aspect

[1] Source: https://www.ineteconomics.org/research/experts/lpasinetti

[2] In addition, see also Annan (1990, pp. 294–296), Brahmananda (1990), Becattini (1989), Eatwell (2000), Marcuzzo and Rosselli (2017). For more information on Noel Annan, a colleague and friend of Richard Kahn, see RFK/13/4 and Appendix C.

[3] In this vein, Pasinetti (1991, p. 431) emphasised Kahn's complete commitment to the cause of academic freedom. From 1954 to 1976, Kahn was a member of the Executive Committee of the Society for the Protection of Science and Learning, an organisation that

diminished in his later years before becoming important again towards the end of his life. He always maintained a sense of respect for his Jewish identity, evident in both the small details, such as his request to wear the kippah and swear on the Torah at his House of Lords admission ceremony, and in more significant matters. Kahn's papers contain evidence of his interest and links with various Jewish organisations and of his interest in the State of Israel, where two of his three sisters lived.[4] As Paul Samuelson recalled

> Kahn was different in being a Jew when Jews were rarer in academic life. More remarkably, he is supposed to have clung to Orthodox practices that teleologically were designed to make assimilation difficult. [...] Modern generations, attuned to anti-Semitisms that are less blatant, can hardly realise how customary it was for a Keynes or a Schumpeter or an H. L. Mencken to use language and possess attitudes that would be universally shocking today. In any case by the time of *The General Theory* Richard Kahn had worked out for himself a fellow of King's a *modus vivendi* that served well until the end of his life. Except for war and sabbaticals in public service, Richard lived in a secure cocoon. [...] I remark on this feature because one could not help but be struck with how narrowly Cantabrigian and English Richard seemed all his life. (Samuelson, 1994, p. 60)

These words suggest a tension between Kahn's desire for recognition as a practising Jew in a predominantly non-Jewish world and his desire to blend in. A similar tension runs through Kahn's intellectual life, in relation both to his contribution to the Keynesian revolution and to his attitude towards his own work, a point taken up below.

Another important aspect of Kahn's personality that deserves to be highlighted for its implications for his activities is the discrepancy between

helped refugee scholars settle in Great Britain (Baldwin, 1989). Kahn's archive contains evidence of this activity. Ref RFK/12/2/127 and RFK/12/2/130.

[4]The reference on this part of Kahn's work and life can be found in RFK/21. Here one can find assorted pamphlets on Palestine and Zionism, 'Note on short visit to Israel in December 1962, correspondence between Kahn and Rabbi Schonfeld concerning Kahn's participation in Anglo Jewry's Third Century: centenary of independent orthodoxy 1880–1980 and Golden Jubilee', Clipping from 'Jewish Chronicle', materials relative to the Conservative Friends of Israel, Britain/Israel Public Affairs Centre, the Cambridge Jewish residents association and Jewish religious education II: the jubilee book of the Jewish day school movement. In addition to this, D. Schiffman's research, referred to in previous chapters, is the main source on Kahn's contacts with Israel.

his public and private personas. This research has offered a series of testimonies on how, especially in his later years, Kahn projected a rather hard public image, combining intellectual aloofness, harshness and an unwillingness to compromise. These characteristics of the 'public Kahn', combined with his sharp criticism of mainstream economists, his invectives against British trade unions, the dryness of his press interventions and his limited participation in the activities of the House of Lords, may have reduced his ability to influence public opinion effectively. However, and in contrast with this, there was a 'private Kahn' who was very different.

> Only "the happy few" who belonged to the small group of his close friends had the privilege of appreciating the delicate sensitivity of a really exquisite personality that lay below the surface of the imposing mien of an apparently frightening authority. The warmth that was always in reserve broke loose now and then for the benefit of those who were among his guests, on the occasions of carefully prepared dinner parties, followed attendances at theatrical or musical performances, many of them at the Arts Theatre (on whose Board of Trustees he succeeded Keynes). These were normal features of his way of life. He enjoyed playing the role of the impeccable host, who cared in the most minute detail for each of his guests, including short, handwritten (almost illegible) essential biographical information about other guests. (Pasinetti, 1991, p. 431)

> To those who did not know him well, or who were from another class and/or generation, Richard Kahn must have seemed an intensely private person, certainly aloof and possibly stuck up. Also, as with many of his generation, his telephone manners were appalling, "goodbye" was not a part of his vocabulary. In his last years deafness and poor health made him a rather solitary public figure, but in private with friends he could still be stimulated into lively and acute discussion. Then it was easy to recall the vigorous rock climber and walker of youth and middle age, the person who strode ahead on Sunday walks carrying a huge knapsack which not only contained food-pubs provided drink-but also meticulous maps and details of bus timetables which would allow tired walkers a comfortable journey home; to remember the parties in his rooms at which guests were chosen with great care and sensitivity so that if people, meeting for the first time, clicked they were left alone by an ever considerate host to enjoy each other's company and to recall the man of culture, following in Keynes's footsteps, appreciating theatre, music and painting, and helping in practical manner too. (Harcourt, 1991, p. 28)

Attention to others and dedication are two traits that define Kahn's personality and have been recognised by many people. This research highlights this aspect of Kahn's character by focusing on his relationships with Keynes and Joan Robinson. In his interactions with them both, Kahn deliberately chose to remain in the background, allowing their voices and ideas to take centre stage.

Later in life, Kahn may have felt the weight of this choice more acutely, particularly with regard to Keynes. Although he remained faithful to his role as Keynes's favourite disciple and guardian of the Keynesian legacy, his later writings reveal a desire to reconsider this legacy. In these writings, particularly in the Mattioli Lectures, Kahn emphasises the strengths and limitations of the Keynesian theoretical framework. At the same time, he asserts his influence on Keynes with regard to specific theoretical points, claiming primacy in rejecting the quantity theory of money at a time when Keynes still supported it. Despite continually praising Keynes and his qualities, Kahn cites Shove, rather than Keynes, as the inspiration for his decision to become an economist and his first mentor. I see these as signs of both intellectual honesty and the unresolved tension between Kahn's loyalty to the Keynes and his desire for emancipation.

The case with Joan Robinson is different. In the 1930s, Kahn mentored Robinson as she developed her theory of imperfect competition. However, from the late 1940s onwards, their intellectual relationship became more equal and their interests gradually diverged. While Robinson continued to fight her theoretical battles, focusing on reconciling Keynes with Marx, Kalecki and Sraffa, Kahn chose a different path, while remaining close to Robinson both personally and intellectually. From the 1960s onwards, Kahn lost interest in new economic theories (except for a belated and unsuccessful attempt to confront the economics of Malinvaud and Sraffa) and, over time, expressed a desire to reconnect with his Marshallian origins. His assertion of his connection with Shove and his decision to publish his Dissertation in 1983, the year of Sraffa's and Joan Robinson's deaths, is highly symbolic in this respect. As with his re-evaluation of the Keynesian legacy, an attempt at emancipation can be discerned here, alongside the understandable desire of a scholar to have his contribution recognised and remembered.

Kahn's decision to remain in the background and avoid direct exposure can be linked to other notable aspects of his personality. As his correspondence reveals, he was and portrayed himself as a very busy man, overwhelmed by obligations, often short of secretarial assistance and often tired as a result. This attitude betrays an inability to let things go, perfectionism, meticulousness, and a desire to be useful combined with the fatigue of doing so. These elements hindered his scientific output and in general his ability to become proactive. As Austin Robinson observed in a letter to Pasinetti,[5] Kahn was neither a promoter of projects nor a builder of groups or institutions.

Evident from his youth and continuing into adulthood, this aspect of Kahn's personality goes some way towards explaining why he was at his most successful when providing expert advice to groups of peers on matters of general interest, as in the case of the Radcliffe Committee and the OEEC group of experts on rising prices. He was less successful when acting on his own behalf or within a small group that did not share his ideas. This is evident in his involvement with the 1947 group of experts on international trade, his interactions with the FAO and the Kahn–Berrill report. In these cases, Kahn presented and defended his point of view. However, when confronted with opposition, and after trying to convince his opponents, he chose to withdraw rather than insist on his ideas or try to build consensus around them. The same reluctance is evident in his limited parliamentary activity. In both cases, he failed to make the most of the opportunities afforded to him by his position and intellectual reputation.

At Cambridge, the centre of his life and work, Kahn adopted a more decisive attitude. Even there, however, he often let others take the lead, adopting a 'behind-the-scenes' leadership style that obscured the true extent of his influence on events. A similar attitude characterised Kahn's approach to the production of new economic ideas where he often showed the attitude of a 'second genius': an intellectual in possession of great skills who recognises the potential of new ideas formulated by others, subjects them to rigorous analysis and refinement, and makes them more coherent through criticism. Beyond the psychological motivations underlying this choice, this modus operandi reflects the collective way of working and reasoning typical of the Cambridge school from which he came and to which he remained loyal. As Schumpeter put it, talking about Kahn and his mentor Shove,

> Both are scholars of a type that Cambridge produces much more readily than the other centres of scientific economics or rather of science in general.

[5] Letter from Austin Robinson to Luigi Pasinetti, 1 April 1992, ref. EAGR/6/4/60–61.

> They throw their ideas into a common pool. By critical and positive suggestion they help other people's ideas into definite existence. And they exert anonymous influence — influence as leaders — far beyond anything that can be definitely credited to them from their publication (Schumpeter, 1954, p. 1152)

Kahn remained faithful to this way of doing economics and to the idea that new ideas emerge as the result of a collective rather than an individual effort, and that the reputation of a scholar is based on the quality and ingenuity of the observations he/she is able to make by commenting on the work of his/her peers.

10.2 Kahn as a Cambridge Economist

Kahn's apprenticeship at Cambridge took place between the late 1920s and the early 1930s. During this period, Marshallian studies were developing, with two notable approaches emerging: Pigou's formalised, static, policy-oriented analysis and Shove's more intuitive focus on time, demand and heterogeneity. Additionally, Sraffa critiqued Marshall (and Pigou), particularly regarding the concept of partial equilibrium, the possibility of defining a supply function in cases of diminishing returns, and the compatibility of increasing returns with competition. By analysing Kahn's Dissertation (Kahn, [1929] 1989), this research traces the influence of all three approaches on Kahn's early, and perhaps most creative work, and documents his ability to combine them in a creative and original way. The article on the multiplier (Kahn, 1931) is characterised by the same openness to drawing inspiration and new insights from the ideas of others. This is evident in its ingenious extension of the concepts of supply and demand from the micro- to the macroeconomic level, as well as in its incorporation of ideas from James Meade. His writings on ideal output (Kahn, 1935) and duopoly (Kahn, 1937) are also part of this judgement.

While the Marshallian influence of Pigou and Shove is evident in these works, Kahn's contribution to the Keynesian revolution, alongside Keynes and 'contra' Pigou, is more complicated. Much has been written on the cooperation between Kahn and Keynes in the 1930s and about Kahn's disciplining effect on Keynes.[6] This research provides two new insights into existing knowledge about this topic. Firstly, it reveals that Kahn

[6] Basic reference here is Moggridge (1985), Harcourt (1994) and Marcuzzo (2002).

engaged with the supply function and elasticity from a very early stage, despite the reservations of Keynes and Shove. Secondly, it provides new evidence supporting the view that Kahn considered the short-run aggregate supply framework, particularly the upward-sloping supply function under competitive conditions, to be pivotal to his contributions to the *General Theory*. These findings are important because of what they reveal about Kahn's transition from his Marshallian apprenticeship to Keynesianism, and his subsequent intellectual reputation.

Kahn's focus on short-run supply under competitive conditions provides a basis for analysing situations in which entrepreneurs decide not to increase their production capacity because they expect demand for their products to remain weak over a period of time.[7] Drawing this element to Keynes's attention, Kahn helped to bring a conventional view of the supply side into the *General Theory*,[8] which made it possible to focus on the main innovations of the book: effective demand, the multiplier, the theory of investment, liquidity preference, and the link between demand, wages and prices.[9]

In his mature work, between the 1950s and the 1970s, Kahn continued to refer to these elements and to an economic vision based on a non-mechanical Keynesianism, in which his early desire for exactness gave way to an awareness of margins of indeterminacy around key economic relationships, especially in the short run. The size of these margins depends fundamentally on the uncertainty surrounding economic decisions, on the subjective response of economic agents to this uncertainty, on the

[7] This conjectural dimension is an important element of Kahn's own understanding of the short run and of the interaction between demand and supply factors, as discussed by Kahn in his Dissertation. On these aspects and on the possibility of drawing an equivalence between the firm's choice to maintain a margin of unused production capacity and liquidity preference, see (Dardi, 1983).

[8] Interestingly, Shove, while sympathetic to the *General Theory*, had expressed some misgivings about this conventional view of supply. He had expressed similar views on Joan Robinson's (and Kahn's) caution against straying too far from conventional schemes in his comments on the *Economics of Imperfect Competition*. On this and on Shove's contribution to economics see Sardoni (2004). On Kahn's role in promoting a conventional view of supply and equilibrium in his contribution to the genesis of the *General Theory*, in addition to the sources quoted in the main text, see Tonveronachi (1983). On Kahn's role in the early stages of the Keynesian revolution see also Laidler (1999).

[9] By combining these elements, the link between money and prices becomes indirect and there is no place for the quantitative theory of money that Kahn had criticised long before Keynes and would continue to criticise until the 1970s.

different and changing risk perceptions of different categories of economic agents, on the incompleteness of their information and preferences, as well as on institutional factors.

Kahn argues that institutions have an important role to play in reducing uncertainty, particularly in the case of investment decisions. If the monetary authorities set targets for interest rates at different maturities and commit themselves to achieving them, as Kahn had recommended in front of the Radcliffe Committee, the uncertainty surrounding the liquidity preference diminishes, while money supply and credit become endogenous. The existence of buffer stocks, committed to stabilising commodity prices and managed at the supranational levels by expert officials, forces private speculators to be more cautious, reducing price volatility. Incomes policy, one of Kahn's pet ideas, provides a reference framework within which wages can be negotiated in an orderly fashion, reducing inflation and its volatility.

Especially in his later work, Kahn tended to represent the fundamental economic relationships between macroeconomic variables as underlying causal tendencies that should be described qualitatively rather than as mathematical functions. Kahn had an ambivalent attitude towards the use of mathematics in economics. Having studied mathematics and physics, he was well equipped to deal with functions, geometric series, integrals and differential equations. However, he always demonstrated an awareness of the limited possibility of expressing economic relationships in functional form, especially if one gives them a static and deterministic interpretation, when in reality they refer to dynamic processes subject to uncertainty. In a sense, it was Kahn's need for precision that led him to distance himself from the mathematical method, which oversimplifies and risks overlooking important elements, in a favour of a different method, which leads to the formulation of theories that are compatible, on the one hand, with the evidence suggested by common sense (a term that recurs frequently in Kahn's writings) and, on the other, with correct economic logic. The same approach underlies Kahn's rejection of general equilibrium models in favour of the analysis of short causal chains and the factors that can obscure or weaken them.

Based on these considerations, Kahn's critical attitude towards econometrics is understandable. Someone like Kahn, who did not believe in representing economic relationships as stable mathematical functions, could hardly believe in estimating those functions using econometric methods. This does not mean that Kahn did not consider data to be important; some of his studies on inflation suggest otherwise. However, his most significant contributions are undoubtedly found outside the field of empirical economics.

The essay on the valuation ratio, begun in 1964, revised during the following year and published eight years later (Kahn, [1971] 1972), is particularly significant as Kahn's last attempt to develop a comprehensive representation of the economic system in which equilibrium at the aggregate level is compatible with a situation in which individual industries, analysed in the perspective of managerial capitalism (Marris, 1964), grow and shrink according to the intensity of demand for their products with the monetary authorities setting the pace of accumulation by determining the rate of interest, the return on shares and the availability of credit. Although incomplete, this remains an important representation that is emblematic of Kahn's attempts to combine static and dynamic perspectives at individual and aggregate levels. This approach could be described as a non-formalised Keynesianism. It combines a sophisticated view of investment and its financial determinants as the core of the economy with the principles of effective demand and the non-neutrality of money. There are also echoes of Marshallian thought, particularly with regard to his analysis of managerial decisions.

On the one hand, Kahn focuses on animal spirits and the drive to expand the business and the material benefits that the managers can draw from it. On the other hand, there is the fear of exposing the firm to the risk of hostile takeovers and the costs associated with the expansion of business. When confronted with this analysis, one is reminded of what Shove (1942) wrote about Marshall and his way of interpreting the behaviour of the marketplace as 'the reflection of a balancing of divergent motives in the minds of men — "satisfactions" (or the impulse to obtain them) on the one hand, and "dissatisfactions" (or the aversion to them) on the other, "utilities" and "disutilities"'. Another instance of benign marginalism.

Part of the same Marshallian/Shovian approach to the analysis of entrepreneurial decisions is reflected in Kahn's attention to the time dimension of economic decision, to the connection between static and dynamic analysis, to the heterogeneity that characterises industries and economic sectors, to the welfare implications of this analysis. Earlier examples of the same approach characterise Kahn's analysis of investment decisions in his work on liquidity preference (Kahn, 1954; Dardi, 1994), in his works on speculation, commodity price stabilisation and buffer stocks, or when he discusses the foreign exchange market.

Throughout the theoretical debates of the 1960s and 1970s, at the time when both mainstream and heterodox economic theory were moving in very different directions, Kahn remained obstinately loyal to the position he believed to be most faithful to Keynes's ideas, which in turn had been formed in the Cambridge where Marshall, Pigou, Robertson and Shove lived and taught. The fact that these positions were contested in the 1970s by opposing fronts occupied by monetarists and rational expectations theorists, as well as young heterodox economists favouring a synthesis between Keynes, Sraffa, Kalecki and Marx, goes some way towards explaining Kahn's eclipse as an economist and the enigma surrounding his name. However, despite facing challenges from both orthodox and heterodox sources, Kahn did not change his mind. Instead, he devoted his final intellectual efforts to defending and revisiting Keynes's theoretical approach, as well as positively re-evaluating his own contribution in his Fellowship Dissertation.

> Having in 1983 read it for the first time for fifty years, I was impressed by it as a contribution made at the time — only two and a half years after I had embarked on the study of economics. Looking back, I feel that I made a mistake in failing to secure publication, in a shortened form. [...] The result is that I now strongly advise a young author of a striking but incomplete piece of work to publish it, or at least sections of it, after seeking advice, without delay. Published reviews and private comments will then be helpful in the writing of a substantial book, the completion of which is usually bogged down by teaching and administrative duties. (Kahn, [1929] 1989, p. xii)

Beyond these aspects, this research identifies investment theory as the unifying theme and core of Richard Kahn's scientific work, from his Fellowship Dissertation in 1929 to the Mattioli Lectures in 1984 (Kahn, 1984). While Kahn's early interest in investment was linked to its potential to reduce unemployment and counter stagnation, his analysis broadened from the 1950s onwards. From a medium- to long-term perspective, investment is important not only because it contributes to maintaining full employment, but also because it increases the productive capacity of the economy and productivity. This has positive effects in terms of reducing inflationary pressures and external constraints, as well as increasing real wages (which Kahn believed were linked to productivity), thereby improving the living standards of workers.

Based on these considerations, the first line of thought within Kahn's theory of investment is to analyse the obstacles that can prevent companies from engaging in this activity. In the 1930s, he identified two such factors. Firstly, current and expected stagnation made it tempting for firms to postpone investment for as long as possible, especially in the presence of unused capacity. Secondly, the Treasury and monetary authorities were reluctant to launch public investment programmes for fear that they would generate inflation, particularly if financed through monetary issuance, as well as financial instability due to a potential increase in public debt and interest rates.

In the post-war economic and social context of the 1950s, so different from that of the 1930s, Kahn identified the main obstacles to private investment in the reactivation of monetary policy against inflation and stop-and-go policies in general. Where entrepreneurs anticipate that rapid economic growth could be followed by monetary restriction to quell inflation, they will, on average, be more cautious and invest less than if they could rely on consistently favourable monetary conditions. Moreover, each phase of monetary restriction dampens profit expectations and therefore investment, and the memory of this lingers. While prioritising private consumption generates demand and upward profit expectations (with positive spillover effects on investment), it can also increase the likelihood of bottlenecks, leading to inflation and consequently monetary tightening. Even during the economic boom years, therefore, Kahn recognised latent pessimism among businesses and managers in the private sector as a structural obstacle to full employment and growth.

For this reason, governments and monetary authorities must prioritise maintaining a high and stable level of investment in their economic policy strategies to achieve full employment and economic growth. This forms the basis of the second strand of Kahn's investment theory. His preferred policy mix involves four elements. Firstly, it involves a structurally expansionary monetary policy that keeps nominal interest rates low, credit supply abundant and stock prices high. Secondly, fiscal policy should curb private consumption growth in order to leave adequate margins of productive capacity to be devoted to the production of investment goods, thereby increasing productive capacity, competitiveness and productivity over time. Thirdly, an incomes policy should be implemented to keep wage and price inflationary spirals under control, including through direct government involvement in trade union–business negotiations, thereby anchoring inflation expectations. Fourthly, Kahn advocates occasional, discretionary and flexible direct controls on the allocation of certain strategic resources in peacetime to prevent bottlenecks, as well as controls on international trade and exchange rates, at least until capacity and productivity have increased sufficiently in light of demographic trends. This combination requires strong control and guidance from governments and monetary authorities, as well as the willingness of various private sector components to limit their demands within the boundaries set by government authorities committed to acting in the general interest.

Finally, the third line of thought within Kahn's investment theory concerns the influence of monetary policy on financial variables and investment decisions, as well as the relationship between profit expectations, stock prices and investment. When addressing these topics, Kahn assumes an inverse relationship between investment and the 'state of finance'. The more accommodating the 'state of finance', the greater the investment, income and employment, other things being equal. Here as in other cases, Kahn identifies a general causal relationship without specifying its magnitude or sign. This is partly because the effectiveness of monetary policy on investment, and therefore on the economy, depends greatly on the attitudes of investors, markets and banks towards the actions of the monetary authorities, all of which cannot be modelled exactly and change constantly and in unpredictable ways. If private individuals are willing to change their behaviour as desired by the monetary authorities, relatively little will be needed for monetary policy to have the desired effect. However, if this does not happen, the monetary authorities must strengthen their intervention. Kahn seems certain that this will have the desired effect, especially if it is restrictive.

10.3 Kahn as a Teacher and His Views on Teaching Economics

With the exception of the war years and 1955, when he lived in Geneva, Kahn lectured with remarkable consistency from 1930 until his retirement in 1972. Teaching was a central part of his life, even though, as we have seen, Kahn does not seem to have been a particularly engaging lecturer, especially in his later years. In addition to the testimonies on this aspect reported in the previous pages, we can add here what Luigi Pasinetti replied on this subject in an interview with Kahn conducted in Italian and never published.[10]

> Kahn had both direct and indirect pupils. His influence is widespread, both directly and indirectly. His direct pupils included everyone who had him as a supervisor at Cambridge. There are also quite a few in Italy. Those who had this experience with Kahn all became his admirers precisely because, although he never appeared in the foreground officially or explicitly and hid behind the positions of other economists, he never skimped on time or effort when it came to reading his students' work, proposing solutions, and helping to develop the ideas that they submitted to him. It is perhaps also an opportunity to mention that, especially in the latter part of his life, Kahn was open about his disappointment and disillusionment regarding the development of economic theory. This is an interesting point because he opposed not only the monetarists, whom he considered a disaster, but also Keynesian thinking. The question that can be asked is whether the developments that Keynesian theory underwent, i.e. its absorption into traditional economics, were appropriate. For Kahn, Keynesian theory was a scientific revolution and therefore represented a break with the past, both in his opinion and in Keynes's. However, Keynesian theory, as it spread in macroeconomic texts, did not follow this line. It always tended to reconcile new developments with orthodox theory. Kahn was disappointed with the way Keynesian theory developed, and perhaps he also felt guilty for not following Keynes, who was always concerned with placing his students in prominent positions. By the end of Kahn's life in Cambridge, true Keynesian economists had almost disappeared. We are therefore left with a rather disturbing question because Kahn himself did not answer it, preferring to remain silent: was the Keynesian revolution really a paradigm shift with respect to traditional theory, or was it a temporary storm, albeit a violent one, destined to be reabsorbed by orthodox theory? No one can yet answer this question. Kahn remained silent. He could have said something, but he chose not to. Events may provide us with an answer as they unfold, especially if scholars persist in seeking it. (Pasinetti, recorded interview, my English translation)

While Kahn remained silent on the state and prospects of Keynesianism, this was not the case for his views on teaching economics and the role of

[10] I am indebted to Cristina Marcuzzo for providing me with a copy of this interview. The interview was conducted, on 10 May 1998, in the context of a project, which involved a number of prominent Italian and foreign economists who were interviewed on the leading economists of the past. In Kahn's case, the two economists interviewed were Marco Dardi and Luigi Pasinetti.

textbooks. He set out his ideas on this subject in a short essay entitled "Political Attitudes in Teaching Economics", which was published in the *Oxford Review of Education* in 1976 as part of a symposium on education and politics.[11] The article opens with a provocative statement that combines an intellectual elitism, which, at this point, we recognise as one of the hallmarks of Kahn's way of participating in public debate, with an acknowledgement that formal and informal discussion is a fundamental part of learning, which ideally takes us back to the world of the Marshallian Cambridge oral tradition.

> It is my basic contention that far too many students read economics. I believe that if many of the less able read other subjects, it would be good for them. It would also be good for the subject. The number of able students reading the subject would increase as a result of teaching resources being less heavily concentrated on the attempt-far too often remarkably unsuccessful-to teach a difficult subject to the unintelligent, and as a result of greater ease of establishment of lively and productive discussion groups, both formal and informal. I have, of course, in mind partly the intrinsic difficulty involved in understanding the subject. The adoption of mathematical methods of teaching for even those who are mathematically well qualified is more apt to conceal the processes of thought than to elucidate them. But the major consideration which arises in my mind are the perils of a political character which beset the path of a student of economics who is not, by reason of his own characteristics and upbringing or by reason of careful guidance by those members of the teaching staff who are in close touch with him, as well as by those whose lectures he attends, fully alert to the perils. They arise from the textbooks, and other books, which are read, as well as from the traditions of the subject, from which the textbooks suffer, and to which the student is directly exposed. (Kahn, 1976, p. 91)

The dangers referred to by Kahn in the above passage are of a different nature. On the one hand, he perceives the risk that favouring quantitative methods in teaching economics gives the subject a politically and socially neutral image, which encourages students to adopt a conformist attitude and substantially accept the status quo, as well as fearing to ask uncomfortable questions about what they are learning. Conversely, politically and

[11] The other participants in the symposium published in Volume 2, Number 1 of the Review were Vernon Bogdanor, Stuart Maclure, R.V. Jones, Peter Bromhead, Charles Vereker, Colin Crouch, Peter Collison and Christopher Schenk.

socially more active students, driven by strong criticism of the status quo, may reject the hard study that a good economic education requires.

This means they fail to learn how to use the analytical tools that are indispensable for developing adequate economic reasoning. The main remedy for these risks lies in the intellectual honesty of teachers, who should be willing to fairly present different points of view on a topic and allow students to form their own opinions. At the same time, teachers must encourage students who want to do well in exams to develop their critical thinking skills, rather than just memorising concepts they do not understand or agree with.

> The moral which, I hope, emerges from my tale of woe is the vital importance of intellectual integrity on the part of the teacher. A man who tries to conceal his real views, whether about economic analysis or about politics, cannot be a good teacher. At the same time, he must obviously aim at fair presentation. By all means let a man warn his audience not to be unduly influenced by his views. And if he finds it desirable-whether for the purpose of education or of success in examinations-to explain ideas in which he does not believe, he ought to be able to do so in a clear and dispassionate manner. One important lesson to convey to students is that-at any rate at the better Universities-examination success will not be achieved by professing views the basis of which the candidate does not understand-especially if he does not believe in them. (Particularly unhappy are those Universities-of which there are far too many in the United States-in which success in climbing the academic ladder depends on dishonesty in the presentation of ideas.) (Ibid., p. 92)

Turning to specific examples, Kahn focuses on two issues: the distinction between positive and normative economics, and the theory of social choice. In the first instance, Kahn notes that, although the distinction between positive statements concerning the economic sphere and normative statements concerning what should be is accepted in economic theory, it is not reflected in practice, at least judging by textbooks. Very often, behind a positive statement that appears neutral from a value-judgement perspective, value judgements are in fact made without being explicitly stated.

Referring to Arrow's impossibility theorem and Harsanyi's approach to interpersonal comparisons of utility, Kahn concludes his brief contribution by recalling Pigou, '...the great author of *The Economics of Welfare*, [who] did not falter in his stride when faced with the problem of interpersonal comparison of utility' (ibid., p. 94). With this tribute to Pigou, Kahn observes that admitting the possibility of interpersonal comparison and making one's value judgements on the matter explicit has two advantages. On the one hand, it allows us to overcome the often artificial distinction between the positive and normative planes and the real views that give rise to the way in which any economic problem is approached and resolved. On the other hand, it allows us to set out rational and reasonable economic policy strategies, in which the various parties involved give up something in the interest of the community to which they belong. As we shall see, this is an essential element in Kahn's vision of economic policy and in the advice he gave on several occasions to national and international authorities.

10.4 Kahn as a Policy Adviser

Kahn's intellectual biography and his teaching activity are intertwined with his role of adviser to domestic and international institutions and, more generally, with the parable of Keynesianism, the professionalisation of economists in Britain (Middleton, 1998; Peden, 1990; Tribe, 2021), and the concomitant expansion of state activity in the economy (Middleton, 1996).

Kahn's first formal contacts with the world of British institutions date back to the early 1930s, when alongside Keynes, he took on the role of assistant secretary of the Committee of Economists within the Economic Advisory Council. This was followed by the war years. These years were very important in Kahn's life, not only on a personal level and for the contacts he acquired in the British establishment, but also for the influence they had on his views on economic policy and the economic role of the government. In this vision, it is possible to perceive the influence of what Harrod (speaking of Keynes) defined as the 'presuppositions of Harvey Road' (Harrod, 1951) and of the idea of the economist as a civil servant evoked by A. Robinson in his obituary of Keynes (Robinson, 1947). With these expressions I want to describe the implicit assumptions held by Keynes and his Cambridge circle, particularly their belief in the duty and competence of an enlightened elite to govern society. This concept reflects the Edwardian liberal optimism that a well-educated ruling class could guide economic and political affairs for the common good.[12]

[12] On this see also Dardi (1990, pp. 61–62).

According to this vision, the main task of an economist working for the government is to find the best technical solutions to the problems of the day and to support politicians and professional civil servants by providing competent and impartial advice that considers the general interest above partisan politics. This was Kahn's approach during the war and in the twenty years that followed until the 1960s. He applied it to topics such as rationing, direct controls on imports and exchange rates, stabilising commodity prices via buffer stocks, as well as inflation, monetary, budgetary and incomes policies.

Kahn always took the same approach whenever he talked about economic policy measures. On the one hand, there is the rational solution proposed by the economist who has studied the problem in depth and has direct knowledge of the relevant causal links. This economist is also capable of formulating a solution that considers the interests of all parties involved. However, for this solution to succeed, everyone affected by it must be willing to adopt it, even if this requires them to make a sacrifice for the greater good. Trade unions must agree to moderate and coordinate their wage demands so as to avoid prioritising inflation control and the balance of payments over full employment. Commodity producers and consumers must agree on prices that consider the other party's interests, under the supervision of buffer stocks. Entrepreneurs must accept restrictions on their activities to ensure the efficient use of scarce resources. At the same time, they must avoid paying wages above negotiated levels to prevent wage drift and inflation. The same applies to banks, who must act under the expert guidance of the monetary authorities. If full employment prevails, consumers must accept a slow improvement in their standards of living to free up resources for investment, a key driver of growth and development. Without this willingness to sacrifice an immediate present and private benefit, for the sake of a larger aggregate and future benefit the status quo prevails. In this case, the strongest win and society as a whole is penalised, unless the coercive option is resorted to, which is difficult in times of peace.

If they have the strength, intention and ability, it is up to politicians to choose the first path over the second, and it is up to civil servants to assist them competently and impartially. Part of the same vision, in the field of international economic relations, is the idea, passing from Keynes to Kahn, that each nation should retain a degree of autonomy in setting its economic policy, loosening external constraints as much as possible. In Kahn's writings on the international economic problems, the logic of national interest (and of Britain's interest in particular) prevails over a preconceived and uncritical adherence to laissez-faire. Kahn is not unaware of the benefits of international trade and free trade, but he constantly urges caution and, above all, rejects the idea that external equilibrium justifies the adoption of policies that disadvantage domestic production and employment. Hence his commitment, in the spirit of Bretton Woods, to finding institutional mechanisms capable of reconciling the interests of individual nations within the framework of international cooperation.

This view on economic policy combined with Kahn's awareness of the obstacles that lie in the path of a policymaker seeking to implement a particular instrument. Kahn learnt early on that the success of a policy measure depends first and foremost on the ability to build a solid consensus around it at government level, overcoming the perplexities of those tied to the status quo or those who supported different measures. Building this consensus requires a focused effort to develop rational arguments in support of the proposed measure and to rebut the objections of those who oppose it. It is a continuous task of drafting and revising memoranda, correspondence and meetings at various levels, which Kahn undertook with technical competence, although—definitely—not with the same skill and initiative as Keynes did.

At the same time, as Dardi (1990, pp. 53–54) clearly points out, for Kahn the effectiveness of any economic policy measure depends on the public's conviction that the reasons justifying the measure are valid, and above all that the measure will achieve the desired effects. A government may implement the best measures from a technical point of view, based on a correct understanding of how economic processes work. However, in the absence of the public's conviction and willingness to adopt behaviour consistent with the proposed measures, those measures will have no effect. For the same reasons, a misguided policy based on incorrect theoretical premises can have negative effects on employment and living standards and still be accepted if the public is misled into considering it a harsh but necessary remedy. In this sense, for Kahn (as for Keynes), economic policy is primarily a matter of opinion.

After the war, Kahn actively engaged with national and international institutions. In Britain, after cooperating with the Attlee government (1945–1946), he was involved in the ITO group (1947–1948), gave advice to the Radcliffe Committee (Kahn, 1958a, 1958b), and was a member of the National Coal Board. Abroad, he worked with the FAO (1950s), the OEEC (1955), UNCTAD (1960s) and as de facto chair of the International Committee on the Problem of Rising Prices (1959–1960). Throughout this period, Kahn's actions were firmly guided by certain principles reflecting the vision he had acquired in his youth and early maturity.

Maintaining full employment was an ethical commitment to ensuring that the misery of the 1930s was never repeated. Recognising the risk that full employment poses to price stability and the balance of payments, Kahn searched for alternatives to restrictive policies, especially those implemented by raising interest rates and reducing credit: supporting private and public investment to increase productive capacity and labour productivity in order to structurally reduce scarcity and inflationary pressures; use of direct controls on resource allocation and in the financial sector; and the creation of new institutions (e.g. buffer stocks, labour market reform) to make the process of determining wages and prices more orderly.

While some of these ideas were implemented at the international level, as Kahn recalled in his interview with Marcuzzo (2020), things were more complicated at home. Even at the height of his academic prestige and visibility, Kahn had limited success in directly influencing economic policy in Britain, both when the Conservatives were in power and, more interestingly, when the Labour Party, of which Kahn was a member, governed Britain. In both cases, his main connection to British economic policy was via the Board of Trade. There were no significant direct links to either the Treasury or the Bank of England.

Kahn's views on the European Payments Union and the need to make permanent use of discretionary direct control over imports and resource allocation met with limited success in a context in which international free trade was once again becoming an obvious truth. His views on how to implement monetary policy influenced the Radcliffe Committee, but not entirely in the direction Kahn had desired (Cristiano & Paesani, 2018a, 2018b). With incomes policy, which Kahn was one of the first to advocate as his preferred alternative for controlling inflation, his direct influence was limited at best, even though some of his connections with economists working as government officials (e.g. Kenneth Berrill) gave him a chance to exert an indirect influence on this policy until the early 1970s.

After Kahn's elevation to the House of Lords in 1965, when his ability to influence economic policy as a Labour man should have been at its greatest, that influence struggled to manifest itself and indeed diminished. The 1968 Kahn–Berrill report on incomes policy had a very limited impact. In 1969, when the Labour government abandoned the statutory incomes policy to which Kahn had attached great importance, he did not hesitate to criticise it regardless of party loyalty. He did so again a few years later when Labour, back in power after the Heath years, abandoned full employment and introduced austerity measures against inflation and the balance of payments deficit. In both cases, when faced with choices seen as damaging to the economy and contrary to the general interest, Kahn prioritised loyalty to his principles and ideas over party discipline and the desire to curry the favour of his political interlocutors.

To understand this attitude, we need to go back to Kahn's vision of economic policy and of the economist as a civil servant. If this vision, forged in the years of the war, was (perhaps) still acceptable in the 1950s, when wartime memories and respect for authority were still vivid in Britain, it was no longer so by the end of the 1960s and even less so in the 1970s. The prosperity now enjoyed by large sections of the British population, the profound social changes, and the economic and social conflicts put an end to the world in which Kahn had developed his ideas and his vision of the economy and society. In the troubled context of the 1970s, Kahn's calls on trade unions and entrepreneurs to keep wage demands and wage drift under control by submitting themselves to statutory incomes policy fell increasingly on deaf ears. The same was true of his proposal to reintroduce selective controls on import or to have representatives of the Ministry of Labour participate in wage negotiations. In the 1970s, Kahn continued to be consulted because of his reputation and academic standing, but the concrete results of his actions and advice were, on the whole, limited. This did not stop him from pursuing these ideas and trying to exert his influence both among economists and in the public debate, even as his voice became increasingly muted.

10.5 The Place of Richard Kahn in the History of Economic Though (HET) and His Legacy

Today, Richard Kahn is usually placed in the pantheon of Cambridge Post-Keynesians, alongside Joan Robinson and Nicholas Kaldor, and as such classified among heterodox economists, dissenters and critics of the mainstream. My research, without questioning Kahn's Keynesian identity, suggests that this characterisation should be qualified.

Kahn's heterodoxy, if it is correct to use this term in his case, does not concern the theoretical approaches with which the term is associated today. As I document, Kahn did not take part in the capital controversy, was not particularly interested in neo-Ricardian economics, only belatedly engaged with Sraffa's system, and remained convinced of its incompatibility with Keynesian economics. Unlike Joan Robinson, he showed no interest in Kalecki or Marx or in the possibility of forging a grand synthesis between Keynesianism and classical political economy. On several occasions, as this research documents, in spite of the common Keynesian orientation, Kahn was more critical than supportive of Kaldor and did not share his desire to experiment with ideas and translate them into mathematical models and stylised facts.

Attempting to sum up Kahn's uniqueness in a concise definition, with all the risks of such simplification, I think it is possible to define him as the most Marshallian of the great Cambridge Keynesians, the one on whom Marshall's legacy, filtered through Pigou, Shove, Robertson and Keynes (as a pupil of Marshall, friend of Shove, antagonist of Pigou and mentor of Robertson), had a stronger and more lasting influence than on Joan Robinson, who came from the same tradition but decisively moved away from it, or Kaldor, who did not share the Marshallian tradition at all.

In Kahn's case, this research shows how the Marshallian imprint of his youth gradually gave way to a non-mathematised Keynesianism in which traces of 'benign marginalism', as Mongin (1990) defines it, remained evident. This is a form of marginalism that does not use utility functions, but is attentive to the subjective dimension of economic phenomena and the behaviour of individuals from different socio-economic backgrounds who act by balancing the benefits and costs of a given action at the margin. Kahn applies this paradigm to analyse the behaviour of entrepreneurs, managers, investors (from 'widows and orphans' to professional financiers), commodity producers and consumers, foreign exchange market operators, and trade union leaders at various levels. The same 'benign marginalism' can be seen in Kahn's frequent references to the concepts of elasticity of demand and (albeit in non-mathematical terms) in his adherence to the idea of an inverse relationship, albeit never mechanical, between interest rates, investment and the capital intensity of production processes, and his view that inflation, wage dynamics, and labour productivity are linked, reflecting the relationship between prices and marginal costs in the case of industrial goods. Methodologically, Kahn's approach is characterised by his early rejection of the mathematisation of economic relations, his focus on the influence of institutions on individual economic behaviour, and his insistence on common sense and realism as guiding principles in economic analysis.

As I conclude my research by proposing that Kahn is the most Marshallian of the great Cambridge Keynesians, it is important to clarify what I mean by the term Marshallian when applied to Kahn. In the 1930s, during the most creative phase of his career as an economist, this term referred not only to Kahn's training as an economist, but also to the characteristics of his early theoretical work and his contribution to the development of the *General Theory*. Specifically, I am referring to his fellowship Dissertation, which draws inspiration from Sraffa's critique of Marshall in order to create a theoretical framework that combines elements of both the Pigouvian and Shovian approaches, ultimately absorbing that critique. The Pigouvian influence is also evident in his early theoretical work. Notably, Kahn's analysis of optimal output and his concept of the short-run aggregate supply curve were suggested to Keynes as tools for solving the problem of determining aggregate output and prices simultaneously, without resorting to the quantity theory of money. While utilising Marshallian, Pigouvian and Shovian concepts to develop new ideas, Kahn nevertheless maintained his independence of judgement. From his rejection of the quantity theory of money—albeit in the flexible form of the Cambridge equation—to his scepticism towards the concept of cardinal utility and in general of utility functions, Kahn departed from the Cambridge Marshallian approach from the outset.

Then, when Keynes died and it was up to Kahn to develop the Keynesian legacy he did so in his own peculiar way. From the late 1940s to the 1960s, he focused on a number of problems that Keynes had considered but left open: the behaviour of wages and prices at full employment, the conventional nature of interest rates, the problems associated with the volatility of commodity prices, and the macroeconomic problems arising from the existence of sectoral restrictions on the supply side. In tackling these problems, Kahn adopted an approach that again refers to the Marshallian tradition. In this case, however, the ideal reference is no longer Pigou, but Shove, with his attention to the influence that subjective factors, individual socio-economic position and institutions have in conditioning the behaviour and opinions of the different categories of economic agents. This is the root of Kahn's benign marginalism, which extends from his early to his mature works.

Sometimes his analyses were accompanied by data, for example when discussing inflation and unemployment in Britain and other developed countries in the 1970s, but he did not go beyond simple descriptive statistics. On the other hand, Kahn was always careful when examining an economic phenomenon. Every time he addressed a new issue, Kahn gathered a substantial amount of related qualitative and quantitative material. This is evident in his preparatory studies for the Dissertation, for example, in his investigation of commodity markets in the 1950s and European labour markets, trade union practices and incomes policies in the 1960s. In all this we find more than an echo of his early Marshallian imprint, a tradition that already seemed outdated in the fifties and even more so twenty years later when Kahn resumed his research and publication activities in defence of Keynesianism.

Finally, in the last part of his active intellectual life, in the 1970s, Kahn's decision to republish his earlier work, and in particular his fellowship Dissertation, without distancing himself from it as Joan Robinson had done with *The Economics of Imperfect Competition*, and his willingness to revisit and praise the contribution of Shove (in his entry for the Palgrave dictionary) and to critically engage with Sraffa, seems to us to be a final testimony to Kahn's enduring connection with the Marshallian theoretical tradition in which he had been trained and which continued to exert a powerful influence on him.

Accepting Kahn's characterisation as the most Marshallian of the great Cambridge Keynesians makes it easier to explain the enigma surrounding his name. The Kahn that emerges from this research is distinct from both the neoclassical synthesis of Keynesian thought and, even more so, monetarism and rational expectations. He is also distinct from the main currents of what is now called heterodox economics, albeit less obviously. As we have seen, this distance began to emerge in the late 1950s, increased during the 1960s and became unbridgeable in the 1970s. By this time, Kahn's loyalty to a non-mathematised Keynesianism tinged with 'benign marginalism' made him too heterodox for the mainstream, which embraced mathematical economics, general equilibrium, monetarism and econometrics. At the same time, he was considered too orthodox by the Sraffians, Marxians, Kaleckians and some Post-Keynesians who rejected neoclassical economics altogether.

Something similar happened on the terrain of economic policy. By the 1970s, Kahn's approach, inspired by the mission that Marshall had imagined for Cambridge graduates, with its elitism, dirigisme and a belief in the possibility of finding solutions in the general interest, was rejected both by those who believed that such guidance was altogether unnecessary, and the economy best left to itself, and by those who believed that the capitalist system was flawed in any case. To both, Kahn's views on policy must have seemed anachronistic, politically naïve, and very conservative with his Victorian vision of full employment as a requirement of happy society,[13] his calls for wage moderation, restraint in private consumption and direct controls.

For those who wonder what Kahn's legacy is today, the answer is that it is very limited. Our attempts to trace works directly influenced by Kahn have yielded few results. On the rare occasions when he is mentioned, Kahn is almost always just one name among others in a bibliographical note. The two exceptions are the article on the multiplier and Kahn's contribution to the development of the Radcliffe doctrine and more generally to Post-Keynesian monetary theory and its critique of the quantity theory of money.[14] Recent histories of macroeconomics accord little (e.g. Snowdon & Vane, 2005) or no space to Richard Kahn (e.g. De Vroey, 2016).

Today, Kahn's name continues to resonate in the history of economic thought, as well as in a series of relatively recent works by L. Pasinetti and some of his disciples, which argue for the need to construct a classical Keynesian approach to economic theory as part of a broader reflection on the Keynesian revolution and its links and classical-Sraffian economics.[15] In his 2007 book *Keynes and the Cambridge Keynesians*, Pasinetti sets out the basis for this classical-Keynesian approach, drawing inspiration from the contributions of Kahn, Robinson, Kaldor, Sraffa and Goodwin, considering them in relation to his own analytical developments.

At the heart of Pasinetti's argument is a list of nine fundamental principles to guide the synthesis of classical (reinterpreted through Sraffa) and Keynesian economics: place concrete reality at the centre of economic theory, beyond abstract rationality; prioritise internal consistency over formal rigour alone; draw inspiration from Malthus and the classics rather than Walras and the marginalists; adopt a perspective based on non-ergodic systems rather than assumptions of stationarity; distinguish between causality and interdependence in economic analysis; prioritise macroeconomics over microeconomics; recognise imbalance and instability as normal

[13] I borrow this characterisation from Johnson and Johnson (1978).

[14] On this see Rochon (2001), Marcuzzo (2017) and Cristiano and Paesani (2018a, 2018b), among others.

[15] On this see Pasinetti (2007).

conditions of the industrial economy and develop appropriate analytical tools to study technological change and growth; and view a strong social commitment as an integral part of economic analysis.[16]

Kahn's approach to economic theory and policy is characterised by a focus on concrete reality and internal consistency, as well as causality. Kahn's social commitment—with the aforementioned nuances of elitism and social conservatism—is based on insistent references to unemployment as an economic and social evil and the need to prioritise full employment and the gradual improvement of citizens' living standards in economic policy. However, regarding other issues—notably the rejection of marginalism as a source of inspiration—my research suggests that a more cautious stance is necessary.

In addition to the field of research outlined by Pasinetti, it is possible to extract from Kahn's corpus of reflections some theoretical ideas that are of interest today, albeit in a very different context. We refer in particular to three issues: non-monetary theories of inflation, the integration of the sectoral dimension in the analysis of macroeconomic phenomena, and the analysis of speculation and conjectures in organised financial markets.

In his long-standing battle against the quantity theory of money and the idea that monetary restriction is the only remedy against inflation, Kahn highlighted an alternative vision of the causes of inflation based on three inter-related elements: the pressure of demand, supply-side constraints and bottlenecks and distributional conflicts. Kahn suggested concentrating on the second and third elements and to find ways (direct controls to ease bottlenecks, incomes policy to defuse distributional conflicts) to prevent inflation without compromising a high and stable employment. Recent research is reviving interest in this perspective.[17]

In this context, it is worth considering the idea that there is a middle ground that macroeconomists should focus on between individual (representative) agents and a fully aggregated model; a middle ground where industry and sectoral linkages are important and need to be taken into account. The difficulty that Kahn faced in trying to model this middle ground, while taking into account the interaction between the subjective and objective determinants of investment decisions and the dynamics of

[16] Exploring these points is complex but essential as Bellino and Nerozzi (2021) observe, editing a volume where scholars including M.C. Marcuzzo, A. Quadrio Curzio, B. Schefold and many others reflect and expand on Pasinetti's nine points.

[17] See, for example, Gaffard et al. (2024) and the reference cited therein.

wages and prices, prevented him from making much progress in this area. Today, the issue is back on the research agenda of both mainstream and non-mainstream macroeconomists, in the context of the analysis of inflation, sectoral supply-side shocks and wage-price spirals.[18]

The third area in which Kahn's insights can be of interest today concerns the theory of speculation and portfolio analysis. Partly on the basis of his long experience of 'playing the markets' as assistant bursar to Keynes and then Bursar of King's College, and partly on his own account, Kahn wrote perceptive analyses of how different categories of investor perceived and responded to different types of risk. He then used these ideas to make recommendations on how to stabilise commodity prices and foreign exchange markets, which still stand today.

The memory and legacy of Richard Kahn have, over the course of the past thirty years, been entrusted to a number of scholars interested in keeping alive the Cambridge tradition and the Cambridge way of doing economics. The publication of a second collection of Kahn's writings in 2022 (Marcuzzo & Paesani, 2022) has hopefully rekindled interest in a highly valued but underrated economist.[19] This intellectual biography of Richard Kahn is meant as a further step in the same direction.

10.6 Maria Cristina Marcuzzo on Kahn[20]

10.6.1 Meeting Kahn

(1) *When and under what circumstances did you first meet Kahn?*

My account of meeting Kahn begins with Kaldor. In March 1984, I interviewed Kaldor in Cambridge. The purpose of the interview was to record his recollections of Keynes, Sraffa, von Neumann and Kalecki, as well as his involvement in theoretical debates and policy choices in Britain and abroad, and his critique of monetarism. However, when I asked him to finalise the text for publication, first in Italian and then in English, he

[18] See, for example, Guerrieri et al. (2022) and Lorenzoni and Werning (2024) on the mainstream front and Stockhammer (2022) on the non-mainstream front.

[19] See Hawkins (2023), Howson (2024), Bridel (2024) and Deleplace (2025).

[20] The interview with Maria Cristina Marcuzzo took place online in May 2024. The original Italian text has been revised by Marcuzzo, as has the English translation. On Maria Cristina Marcuzzo see Appendix C.

backed out, citing concerns that it contained too much gossip. I then sent him a rather dry letter reminding him of his commitment to me. His reply was unexpected. Rather than getting angry, he agreed to revise the text for publication in Italian, but remained firm about not publishing it in English. He also informed me that he had nominated me for a place at the High Table at King's College and arranged an appointment for the following week. When I arrived in Cambridge on the evening of 30 September 1986, I discovered that Kaldor had died that very morning. Two days later, I went to the Fellows' Room at King's College, where I saw an elderly man sitting rather aloofly and looking troubled. It was Richard Kahn. As others later informed me, Kaldor's death had a profound impact on him. When I approached Kahn to introduce myself, I was somewhat surprised when he said, 'Don't worry. I will take care of you. Come and see me'. Perhaps Kaldor had told him about me, but I never found out.

(2) *What memories do you have of when you first started working with Kahn?*

A few days after our first meeting, I actually visited Kahn in his rooms at King's College, which had previously been occupied by Keynes. I was struck by the clutter and the number of objects that belonged to 'Keynes's world'. These included Lydia Lopokova's passport and a vase donated by Virginia Woolf, and lots of other memorabilia associated with Keynes. During our conversation, I mentioned that I was working on Joan Robinson at the time, which clearly piqued Kahn's interest and resulted in another invitation to meet him. It is worth noting that Joan Robinson was born on 31 October and that at her college, Girton, it had become tradition to celebrate her birthday even after her death, with a guest lecture. That year, I was invited to deliver the Joan Robinson Lecture. I suggested to Kahn, who was not going to attend, that he listen to a preview of what I was going to say. He agreed. On the day of the rehearsal, Kahn had dressed up and there was Martini on the table. I began reading my speech, monitoring Kahn's reaction. He remained impassive and silent throughout my reading, which lasted approximately half an hour. When I finished, I recall thinking: 'He didn't like it at all'. I was mistaken. The only words he uttered in a moved voice were 'It's magnificent'. Beyond the satisfaction I felt at hearing those words, their tone and expression, I had the feeling of the importance that Joan Robinson continued to have for Kahn.

(3) *What was your role in the collection of Kahn's papers?*

In November 1986, I delivered the Joan Robinson Lecture at Newnham College, where Robinson was appointed a Fellow in 1962. I also gave a speech to Girton College where Joan Robinson was made a Fellow in 1965. Afterwards, I started talking to Kahn about his work. He expressed a desire to publish a second edition of his essays and started organising his papers accordingly. However, he would occasionally reiterate, 'Don't work on me, work on Joan'. I would respond, 'Yes, I am working on Joan, but I would also like to help you organise your papers'. It is important to note that at the time (1986–1987), Kahn's papers were not archived, but instead stored in a makeshift storage area. Michael Hall, who was the King's College archivist at the time and was quite close to Kahn, told me that he would store and catalogue Kahn's papers at a later date if I provided them to him. This led to an amusing situation. Kahn and I would spend afternoons going through his drawers. I would hand him a document, and he would say, 'Throw it away', so I would put it in a plastic bag. I would then take the bag to Michael Hall, thus ensuring the preservation of many of Kahn's papers. Kahn and I met approximately three times a week for a few months. During those afternoons, I did not always manage to steer the conversation towards topics that interested me. Kahn oscillated between moments of great lucidity and moments of confusion. Before each dinner at King's College, he would give me a list of the fellows and senior guests. His speaking style was also noteworthy in that he tended to mumble, which made him difficult to understand. Our conversations were based on Kahn's sympathy for me, my interest in Robinson, and perhaps his interest in my own affairs. His partner at the time, Rachel Rostas, said that my presence helped facilitate conversation, as there was minimal dialogue when she was alone with him. Kahn's cognitive state was variable, with periods of confusion interspersed with moments of clarity.

(4) *What role did you play in the publication of Kahn's Fellowship Dissertation?*

During our conversations one day, we talked about Giacomo Becattini, whom Kahn held in high regard, and Kahn's fellowship Dissertation, which had been published in Italian by Marco Dardi a few years earlier. We agreed that it was a pity it had not also been published in English. I discussed this with Geoff Harcourt, and we decided to try to convince

Richard to publish his Dissertation in English. Robin Marris recounts this in a paper published a few years ago (Marris, 1992). Farmiloe, Macmillan's economics editor, came to King's College to discuss the matter with Kahn, and we managed to convince him with the help of Geoff Harcourt. Kahn agreed, but insisted on being the proofreader. The problem was that his eyesight was not what it used to be. He was very short-sighted, and his handwriting, which was already difficult to read, became even more illegible. As he wore large glasses that magnified the images, he believed he was writing normally, but in reality the words he wrote were very small. In short, it was impossible to make sense of it. Harcourt and I insisted on correcting the text, but it was impossible. Richard could be very stubborn.

(5) *How did the idea for the interview come about, and what memories do you have of the experience?*

The idea of the interview arose while he was putting his papers in order in preparation for the publication of the second collection of his essays. The interview was conducted over the course of several recorded sessions, each lasting approximately one hour. Kahn always began by reading me a handwritten text, interspersing it with short reflections and stories. I recall discussing these tapes with Mark G. Hayes. He told me that his son could 'burn' records and suggested that the same could perhaps be done with the tapes to make them easier to listen to. I recently found the correspondence with the King's archivist, Patricia McGuire from June 2013, in which she thanked me for receiving the tapes and CDs made by Hayes's son. These tapes are now in the King's College archive.

I would now like to return to the subject of the interview. I started transcribing them, which proved to be a challenging task. The combination of his almost illegible handwriting and his hoarse voice made transcribing the interviews particularly difficult. However, I succeeded, and today the interview is available in both Italian (Kahn, 1988) and English (Marcuzzo, 2020). During the recording, Kahn revealed that he loved Italy and would have liked to return. At the time, I was teaching at the University of Modena. I had already interviewed Kaldor at the suggestion of Guido Candela, a professor at the same university. I then suggested that Candela invite Kahn to give a lecture at Johns Hopkins University in Bologna. This was successful and, in June 1988, Kahn came to Bologna to deliver his lecture. A roundtable discussion was also held, attended by Luigi Pasinetti, Alberto Quadrio Curzio, Marcello de Cecco, Luigi

Spaventa, Jan Kregel, Carlo D' Adda, Beniamino Andreatta and many other guests.

Regarding Andreatta, I recall Carlo D'Adda telling me that, prior to Kahn's arrival, Andreatta—a full professor at the University of Bologna and former Finance Minister—had confined himself to his house for three days in order to prepare a speech that would impress Kahn. Such was his awe and admiration for Kahn, whose lectures he had attended at Cambridge. During this trip, we also managed to accomplish something quite remarkable. Kahn had told me about the Bridal Chamber frescoed by Mantegna in the ducal palace in Mantua and how much he liked the frescoes, but also how difficult it was to admire them amidst the throngs of tourists. At the time, one of my colleagues in Modena, Maurizio Zenezini, was a close friend of the mayor of Ferrara, who was in turn a friend of the mayor or museum director of Mantua. With their help, we organised a private visit to the Bridal Chamber for Kahn. We placed a small chair in the room frescoed by Mantegna and left Kahn alone for twenty minutes to quietly and calmly admire the paintings he liked so much. That was Kahn's last trip to Italy. The last things I remember are trying to proofread the drafts of his Fellowship Dissertation together with Harcourt.

I probably returned to Cambridge in late summer 1988, although the exact date is uncertain. In autumn 1988, Kahn began experiencing health issues which initially appeared non-serious. I was informed that, between late 1988 and early 1989, he had travelled to Paris for surgery. Afterwards, he told Pasinetti that it had been a mistake. However, I must stress that this is a vague recollection. By that time, the possibility of publishing a second collection of essays had been ruled out. In 1999, Luigi Pasinetti and I published a collection of essays in Italian. This was part of a series of writings by leading economists, published by Il Mulino with financial support from the San Paolo banking institution. Finally, in 2022, we were able to publish the second collection (Marcuzzo & Paesani, 2022).

10.6.2 Kahn on Sraffa, Keynes, Robinson and Cambridge

(6) *What can you tell me about Kahn's paper on Sraffa?*

While sorting through Kahn's papers, I came across a typescript entitled 'The Sraffa System'. Despite his reservations about the equations and the absence of funding, Kahn informed me of his intention to publish the paper. I read the paper and asked Luigi Pasinetti to do the same. His response was unequivocally negative: it was a poorly written text that was barely readable and not very comprehensible. Luigi Pasinetti and I agreed that we needed to persuade Kahn not to publish it in the second collection. I remember the three of us taking a long walk in the Fellows' Garden at King's College at some point in 1987 and in the end Kahn agreed.

(7) *In general, what would you say about the relationship between Kahn and Sraffa?*

Kahn held Sraffa in high regard both personally and scientifically. He greatly admired Sraffa's work on Ricardo's writings. However, he did not understand why so much emphasis was placed on *Production of Commodities by Means of Commodities.* He could not fathom why such emphasis was placed on a book in which neither money nor effective demand appeared. This attitude was not just Kahn's, though. As a true Keynesian, Kahn's reaction would likely have been similar to Keynes's if he had taken the time to read Sraffa's book—a book that remained somewhat incomprehensible to Kahn. Everything that Kahn considered relevant was missing from Sraffa's book. Conversely, Kahn had not studied the classical economists or Marx in depth. Nevertheless, there is no doubt that Kahn recognised Sraffa's genius and considered him a great friend. They had a high level of mutual respect and familiarity, but scientifically, they had little in common.

(8) *During your meetings, did Kahn share any memories of Keynes other than those in the interview?*

He never spoke to me about Keynes in any other terms than in the Mattioli Lectures, which were given in 1978 and published in 1984. I don't recall any specific details about Keynes. However, it seems that one of the objectives of the interview was to shed new light on the subject. Therefore, it is important to read the Mattioli Lectures and the interview together to gain a definitive understanding of the relationship between Keynes and Kahn as seen by Kahn.

(9) *During your meetings, did Kahn express an opinion on the future of Keynesianism?*

I believe that the interview accurately captured all of Kahn's statements regarding Keynes and Keynesianism. I also managed to elicit a significant amount of information from him. The interview was comprehensive, spanning at least a month and comprising 12 hours of recordings. Had Kahn intended to convey a definitive message on Keynes, he would have done so during this interview.

(10) *Would you like to express an opinion on the relationship between Kahn and Joan Robinson?*

Annalisa Rosselli's study of the correspondence between Kahn and Robinson formed part of the research project that resulted in the publication of Economists in Cambridge, edited by M. C. Marcuzzo and A. Rosselli and published by Routledge in 2005 (Marcuzzo & Rosselli, 2005). This study has provided valuable insights into the early stages of their relationship. From a variety of perspectives, the relationship was of great significance. Spanning over sixty years, it encompassed both intellectual collaboration and personal interaction, as evidenced by the correspondence. There were periods of disagreement and differing views between Kahn and Robinson. For example, Kahn thought that the 1956 publication of *The Accumulation of Capital* was premature. Our analysis of the correspondence concludes with Keynes's death in 1946. Subsequent developments remain to be investigated. In my view, Robinson relied heavily on Kahn during the early years of her career as an economist. Despite this, she did not always follow his advice. While Kahn was meticulous and punctilious, Robinson was often impatient. This difference between them, which was unrelated to economic theory, is evident in a letter that Robinson wrote to Kahn while she was in India. In it, she asks how much she will earn upon retirement, requesting a simple answer without additional information. Robinson was impatient with Kahn's thoroughness, as she was with everyone else she consulted. She could esteem or even admire someone, yet still act on her own accord; she was not psychologically subservient to anyone. Kahn, for his part, was concerned about Robinson throughout his life. While staying at Schumpeter's house during his trip to the United States, he woke up early every morning to find letters from Joan Robinson. He did this to ensure that Schumpeter did not form the wrong opinion of a married woman who frequently wrote to a man who was not her husband.

(11) *In the introduction to his published Dissertation, Kahn invites young people to publish their work, perhaps regretting his own decision to do otherwise. What effect do these words have on you?*

Many have recalled Kahn's perfectionism and the way it hindered his publications. Furthermore, he was heavily involved in academic politics and economic policy, acting as an advisor to the British government and international organisations, as well as participating in policy debates from the 1950s to the 1970s. These activities took precedence over his theoretical research, and it seems that he lost interest in this aspect of his work at some point. He was certainly very eager to publish the second collection of his essays, so it is a pity that he was unable to do so in his lifetime. Unlike Keynes, who could write fluently and brilliantly with ease, Kahn struggled with the written word. These things were very difficult for Kahn. Furthermore, as I have said, academic politics and participation in economic policy decisions and debates took precedence over academic publications. This attitude is exemplified by his decision to give up the Leverhulme, a highly prestigious research grant, stating that he lacked the time to devote to research. At a certain point, Kahn lost interest in developments in economic theory. For him, it was crucial to espouse and defend the Keynesian viewpoint forcefully.

(12) *Harry Johnson remembers Kahn as being reluctant to read and comment on his work. This is in contrast to what others have written about Kahn's 'generosity' as a reader of others' work. Was it just personal incompatibility, or is there more to it?*

I cannot answer this question. One would have to ask his many pupils, but unfortunately many of them, from Marcello de Cecco to Beniamino Andreatta, are no longer here.

(13) Harcourt (2012) *judged Kahn hopeless at academic politics. What are your thoughts on this? What are your general views on Kahn's role at Cambridge during the period covered by Saith's book* (2022), *and in particular, what do you think about Kahn's lack of opposition to Frank Hahn's appointment?*

I cannot answer this either. However, I would encourage anyone interested in this topic to read Saith's recent book, which is based on extensive documentation. There are also the recollections of Frank Hahn, Luigi Pasinetti and Geoffrey Harcourt to consider.

(14) *Besides you and Pasinetti, who else was Kahn connected to in Italy?*

Certainly, Giacomo Becattini and Marco Dardi, as well as all of his former students. It would be important to compile a list of Kahn's Italian students from the register of Italian students at King's College. He had ties to Israel, where two of his sisters lived and which he visited several times, as Schiffman (2013) has reconstructed.

10.6.3 Kahn as a Person and His Legacy

(15) *What do you remember about Kahn as a person?*

I remember him as a caring, kind and affectionate man. Although I first met him when he was not very elderly, I remember him as someone who occasionally experienced memory lapses and with whom it was sometimes difficult to communicate effectively. He was undoubtedly indirect, introverted and apprehensive. People like this often experience a fear of adversaries or develop fixations that could lead to paranoia. This same mental attitude also can also manifest as a tendency towards scheming and intrigue. However, I did not observe these characteristics in Kahn. I observed an elderly gentleman who was very kind and attentive to me.

(16) *What did you notice about his behaviour when you met him?*

I was impressed by his remarkable precision and meticulousness, especially given the difficulty of maintaining the same standard to which he had adhered all his life despite being 'past his prime', as the English would say.

(17) *Kahn is said to be a very private and elusive person. Do you agree with this assessment?*

Kahn never wanted to draw attention to himself. He oscillated between being very modest and having a strong sense of self. I would say that he was a very opinionated person. He held strong and determined views on people and things, and was not afraid to express them, albeit not in a conspicuous way. When it came to his scientific contributions, modesty prevailed, but a sense of self was always present. Many of Kahn's major contributions, such as his Dissertation and his article on the multiplier, came when he was still very young and just starting out. One should also not forget that, besides Keynes, his mentor at Cambridge had been Shove, whom Kahn resembled in many ways. Finally, I would like to reiterate my belief that Kahn lost interest in theoretical debates at a certain point. For example, he did not want to engage in the capital controversy. He had other priorities.

(18) *If you had to sum up Kahn's legacy in a few words, which words would you choose, and what would you say about them?*

The first element of this legacy is his lifelong commitment to preserving Keynes's ideas, particularly the notion that the primary goal of government authorities in improving people's welfare should be full employment.

The second element concerns his vision of money and the monetary system, which sheds light on a fundamental aspect of economic systems that has been overlooked by mainstream economic theory. I am convinced that much of what Kahn wrote about this subject remains valid today.

However, it is important to remember that Kahn was reasoning and writing within his own context. The role that trade unions played in determining wages and inflation in Western countries in the 1970s is irrelevant in today's market. What Kahn wrote about then cannot be reproduced in today's world. Nevertheless, his criticism of direct dependence on monetary variables remains relevant. Kahn's work deserves recognition for identifying fundamental relationships that must be adapted to the relevant context. Only by understanding this context can the relevant causal links within the general framework of Keynes's and Kahn's theory of employment, interest, and money be identified.

10.7 Marco Dardi on Kahn[21]

10.7.1 The Dissertation

(1) *When and on what occasion did you meet Kahn? Marcello de Cecco credits you with persuading Kahn to publish his Dissertation in Italian. Can you confirm this? How did the decision to publish the Dissertation in Italian come about, and what do you remember about the experience?*

I had been going to Cambridge occasionally since the early 1970s with a research programme that had no connection at all with Kahn, so that in those years I had no reason to try to contact him, nor did I have any opportunity of meeting him by chance. In fact, the story of the publication of Kahn's Dissertation in Italian began with the start, sometime around 1976, of a friendly relationship between Kahn and Giacomo Becattini, who for several years had been a regular visitor to Cambridge libraries and archives in pursuit of his personal research on Marshall and the Victorian economists. The meeting between the two was a happy encounter if ever there was one. Kahn was preparing the text of the Mattioli Lectures he was expected to give in the Milanese Bocconi University in 1978, a text that contained references to Alfred and Mary Paley Marshall's *Economics of Industry*. Becattini had just published a long essay in Italian, the title of which sounded like 'An Invitation to Read Marshall Again', which came out as an introduction to the first Italian translation of the *Economics of Industry* (Marshall & Marshall, 1975) in 1975. It was all too natural that Becattini sent a copy of his Italian essay to Kahn, who, helped by Pasinetti to overcome the linguistic barrier, managed to get some idea of the contents and responded with a letter full of praise (RFK 13/22/50). It was through this and later exchanges that Becattini became convinced that Kahn was more of a Marshallian than he himself would have admitted. This happened in the late 1970s, when I began to work on my book on the early years of Marshall's career (see Dardi, 1984). As far as I remember, it was Becattini who sparked my interest in Kahn.

[21] The interview with Marco Dardi took place on 4 July 2024 in his office at the University of Florence. The original Italian text has been revised by Dardi, as has the English translation. On Marco Dardi see Appendix C.

At one point, Becattini told me about Kahn's fellowship Dissertation. He had obtained a copy on microfilm from Kahn himself and, back in Italy, entrusted me with it. At the time we had only one microfilm reader in the Florentine Faculty of Economics, located in the rooms of the Institute of Economic History directed by Giorgio Mori, the historian of modern industry in Italy. I remember spending days and days sitting at the machine with Mori quipping that finally it was repaying its cost. The Dissertation was interesting, no doubt about that: an unknown, original piece of research by a prestigious economist, it was impossible not to propose some kind of editorial utilisation. It was so that I came up with the idea of translating it into Italian. While de Cecco is not wrong in attributing the idea of translating it to me, one must not forget that without Becattini's preparatory work that project would never have come into existence (cf. RFK 13/22/45, 46).

Kahn was not difficult to convince and the Dissertation went into production in 1981. Pierluigi Cecioni, a friend of mine who had graduated in mathematics in the US and was practically bilingual, took charge of the translation. However, as Cecioni was not familiar with the economic jargon, I revised the translation to make it more palatable to economists. I have no recollection of how it was that the publisher of the Dissertation came to be Boringhieri, at that time a prestigious, slightly old-fashioned publishing house located in Torino. Becattini had published with Boringhieri in the past and perhaps he was the one who established the connection. In any case this allowed me the pleasure of interacting briefly with Ernesto Ferrero, not an economist but a writer, literary critic, translator and a man of great culture who happened to be the chief editor of Boringhieri.

The interaction with Kahn in the phase of preparation was pleasant too. He yielded to my insistence on him writing a preface to the volume (RFK 13/22/26, 27). Aided by Pasinetti, he read the draft of my introduction in Italian and reacted to it with typically spare comments. I think we mostly understood each other, and when we didn't he was not the type who tried to prevail. The only exception to this rule happened when, at a certain point in the first draft of my introduction, I mentioned Frank Hahn on the matter of conjectural equilibria. My attempt was to establish a link between Kahn's short period and the literature of the 1970s and 1980s that proposed to construct underemployment equilibria based on systems of self-confirming beliefs. I was aware of the tensions in the Cambridge faculty of the 1970s between the original Keynesian circle and the emerging group of the neoclassical Keynesians, among whom Hahn was perhaps the outstanding personality. But, to my excuse: I had attended Hahn's lectures, I was fascinated by the perspective he applied to problems I was used to see in a different form, and I had the conviction that intelligent persons recognise each other even when they belong to different intellectual traditions and use different languages. How naïve of me all this was, I learnt when Kahn wrote to me (letter of 23 April 1982 RFK/12/2/128/23) asking me to delete the reference to Hahn, that he, convinced by Pasinetti on this point, had found 'not really compatible with my Dissertation'. At the time I offered very weak resistance (letter of 22 May 1982, RFK/12/2/128/24). Later, I suppose through some bargaining of which I have no memory, we agreed to maintain Hahn's name but to remove it from the main text to a footnote (Dardi, 1983, p. 26, fn 29).

Once published, the Dissertation received a few reviews, as did the English edition that was released shortly after Kahn's death in 1989. Of these reviews, the one by Andrea Maneschi in HOPE (Maneschi, 1988) seemed to me to engage most closely with the substance of Kahn's arguments. In general, however, the attention the Italian edition received was somewhat below my expectations. At that time, I should have known that the operation of publishing an English text in Italian ran against the trend that has made of economics an almost exclusively English-speaking discipline.

(2) *In your introduction to the Dissertation, you emphasise that the link between market imperfections and general depressed demand is the book's most striking modern element. What is your opinion on this today?*

When I wrote the introduction I was under the influence of Arrow's seminal 1969 paper on the organisation of economic activity (Arrow, 1969), in which, among other things, I found the suggestion that certain types of (imperfectly) competitive behaviour we observe in markets can be seen as responses to a variety of situations of the 'market failure' kind. In reading the Dissertation with this idea in mind I was led to interpret Kahn's situation of under-used productive capacity with suspended investment and downward rigid prices not as the usual equilibrium with capacity excess of the theory of imperfect or monopolistic markets, but as the result of a deliberate strategy of entrepreneurs, holding back from price competition in a sort of tacit non-aggression pact, and clinging to their market shares in the face of a falling demand level. At this point it struck me that there seemed to be a close analogy between this behaviour and the decision to keep the main part of one's wealth during a slump in relatively safe assets non reproducible by means of labour — which I take to be the substance of the Keynesian 'liquidity preference' doctrine. Both strategies represent effective devices to suspend decisions and fix the current situation in states of affairs so uncertain that 'wait and see' seems to be the only viable course. I thought, and still think, that this intuition, found in a text written in 1929, was definitely ahead of its time. Only later did I discover that similar ideas had been developed independently of Kahn by Josef Steindl in his 1952 book *Maturity and Stagnation in American Capitalism* (Steindl, 1952). But I must also add that Kahn, while not rejecting it, was not completely convinced by my interpretation. In a letter to Kahn dated 9 March 1981 (RFK/13/22/26), I prepared for him an outline of my argument and even ventured a hint about Kahn being a 'Keynesian before Keynes'. At the time I was unaware that also Joan Robinson used to say that Kahn was a 'true Keynesian' even before Keynes (see Pasinetti, 1991, p. 425). From the copy of my letter preserved in the Kahn archive I now see that the hint was turned down with a laconic, all too predictable 'NO' written in the margin. His reply was more diplomatic and contained the usual formulaic passage 'I should like to give more thought to your interesting suggestion of an analogy between market imperfection and liquidity preference' (Kahn to Dardi, 14 March 1981). But discussion of this issue never resurfaced in our correspondence.

10.7.2 Kahn, Cambridge and the Confrontation with Monetarists

(3) *When and on what occasion did you meet Kahn personally? What memories do you have of him in Cambridge?*

As I said before, I ended up in Cambridge in rather an unusual way. I took courses for a year without being on the PhD programme. However, from 1972 until the late 1980s I used to spend periods of variable length in Cambridge, especially in the years of my research on Marshall, which involved days and days of work on the Marshall papers in the Marshall Library of Economics. Over these years, I must have seen Kahn a few times. I first met him in person in his rooms at King's College, I think, in the summer of 1980. I remember how excited I was to be standing in front of this mythical personage of political economy. Going into the details, I was impressed by the abnormally low tone of his voice, so low that I often had difficulty in understanding him. I met him a few more times after that, but we continued to exchange letters for a long while (see, for example, RFK 13/22/4, 5 and 6).

(4) *Pasinetti wrote that there was a time when all economic thought at Cambridge revolved around Kahn, who was a professor from 1952, Dean of the Faculty, a member of the King's College committee that conferred Fellowships, and the driving force behind the secret seminar. What was left of this great influence when you were at Cambridge?*

I have no direct evidence, but my impression is that not much was left at the time of my Cambridge frequentations. There was a legend that Kahn was a 'grey eminence', someone who is rarely seen or heard from, but who pulls the strings behind the scenes. Perhaps I am wrong, and Kahn's influence on economic thought at Cambridge was stronger than I could perceive, but if so, it was very discreet. Besides, there is something that doesn't sound right in this image of Kahn the secret puppeteer. Yes, he preferred to stay behind the scenes, and in a collective situation he was the type who tends to work also for others. But the Cambridge figures with whom he interacted most of the time were strong personalities, none of them was the type willing to accept the role of the follower. Just to clarify what I mean, I refer to a letter I received from Pasinetti in 1990, after he read the article on Kahn I had written for Augusto Graziani's journal *Studi Economici* (Dardi, 1990). In that article I had noticed that in the 1960/1970s debate on 'reswitching' Kahn was conspicuous by his absence. Pasinetti agreed with this remark, but explained: 'But this is for consistency. That debate originated with Sraffa, not the Keynesians—the same could be said of Kaldor. It was Robinson who wanted to get involved in it, but wrongly and unsuccessfully' (Pasinetti to Dardi, 29 March 1990). As always, real life turns out to be more complicated than simplistic legends.

(5) *Harry Johnson described Kahn as reluctant to read his work* (Johnson & Johnson, 1978)*. Was this merely a case of personal incompatibility, or might it have indicated a broader reluctance on Kahn's part to*

engage with ideas outside the Keynesian school? For example, consider the concept of 'rational expectations' in the 1970s.

Judging by the Hahn episode that I recounted before and the dismissive comments about rational expectations found in his late writings, I would say that Kahn was somewhat closed-minded about these theoretical developments. Perhaps this attitude should be seen in the light of a broader discourse concerning the role of mathematical formalisation in economic theory. Formalisation instinctively alienates economists who see themselves as, in a strong sense, 'social' scientists—and Kahn, in spite of his excellent mathematical training, was one of these. I personally think that this attitude can be problematic because it often prevents one from recognising one's own problems expressed in other people's language. For example, one may well reject the whole formal apparatus of DSGE macroeconomics but a true Keynesian cannot reject the idea that expectations change in response to a changing economic environment or to signals such as government announcements. Of course, we must discuss the way they change. 'Rationally' means that economic agents revise their expectations in the same way as economists do, and many of us would side with Kahn in rejecting this assumption. But also the opposite assumption of a wide, constant gap between agents and economists in interpreting the available evidence is, for many reasons, too strained: people, after all, learn from experience. So, there is a serious, truly 'Keynesian' problem here, not to be dismissed. Kahn refused to come to grips with it, I suppose, because he was repelled by the mathematical wrap in which it was presented. But the question whether a theory concerning what people think is robust with respect to people learning it and becoming convinced that it is a true theory, is one that I think should have intrigued a researcher in imperfect and financial markets like him.

(6) *Harry Johnson again argued that the emphasis placed by Keynes and Kahn on full employment reflected an essentially conservative—and, underneath, classist—Victorian attitude: 'To each a secure, well-paid job, but everyone must remain in their place'. What do you think?*

This does not seem such a far-fetched idea to me. Keynes was fine with capitalism, even if he thought some of its aspects were dysfunctional and would have liked to correct them. However, he certainly did not intend to do away with it. I think the same can be said of Kahn. Yet the venom of

Johnson's remark seems to me to lie not in the suggestion of a preference for a 'reformed' capitalism, but in the innuendo that Keynes and Kahn disapproved of the idea of enhancing upwards social mobility. This is in my opinion false or in any case unproven.

10.7.3 Kahn and the Marshallian Legacy

(7) *When considering the influence of Shove and Marshall on Kahn's thinking, the following words come to mind: complexity, realism, heterogeneity and reluctance towards mathematisation. What are your thoughts on these?*

'Complexity' is too resonant a world and I prefer not to comment on it. When it comes to Kahn, I would rather speak of 'sociological sensitivity', an expression that for me captures the specific quality of his realism and attention for the heterogeneity of the human motivations that move the economy. Many of Kahn's contributions are influenced by the characteristics of English society of his time. You feel it in the Dissertation, when he enters into the corporate instincts of the British industrialists or the mentality of the Lancashire cotton spinners; and in his celebrated 1954 article on liquidity preference, in which behavioural attitudes to financial investment are related to the variety of social types operating in the market.

As to Kahn's attitude to mathematisation, we have already touched on the issue before. I would characterise it as 'caution' rather than 'reluctance'. Like Marshall, he was not against the use of mathematics per se, but viewed it as a decision to be made on a case by case basis, knowing the risk of being trapped in a chain of deductions that throw little or no light on the problem from which one has started. As Marshall said with regard to physical analogies, of which mathematical models are just an instance, they 'may help one into the saddle, but are encumbrances on a long journey. It is well to know when to introduce them, it is even better to know when to stop them off' (Marshall, 1898, p. 39). In this attitude there is of course a strongly discretionary element that exposes it to biases in opposite directions, 'too much' or 'too little' math, as I noted before. Still, I think this is preferable to the current, one-directional bias, the 'the more math the better' commandment.

In talking of 'sociological sensitivity' and 'mathematical caution' I have considered two very basic aspects of Kahn's methodology in which it is easy to recognise a distinctly Marshallian ring. But that's not surprising. Kahn liked to be remembered as 'a disciple of Keynes' (Pasinetti, 1991, p. 432), and Keynes was also, in his own peculiar way, a disciple of Marshall, as Tiziano Raffaelli argued convincingly in his reconstruction of Keynes's economic apprenticeship under Marshall's supervision (Raffaelli, 2000). Thus, it seems inevitable that something of Marshall's 'spirit' has percolated down this line of descent.

(8) *Did Kahn play a role in the development of the Marshallian school in Italy?*

If by 'Italian Marshallian school' you mean Becattini, Raffaelli, myself and the others who at various stages worked with us, I think I can answer in the negative. Recently I tried to reconstruct the long story of this research group in a paper (Dardi, 2021): in re-reading it now I realise that the name of Kahn has never been mentioned, nor is there any reason why it should have been. Among foreign scholars, the main sources of inspiration came to us from Brian Loasby and, to a minor extent, John Whitaker and Peter Groenewegen. When Becattini met Kahn in the 1970s he had already elaborated the main lines of his interpretation of Marshall; the fact that Kahn appreciated it certainly flattered him but changed nothing. Knowing Becattini very well, I am sure that in the exchanges between the two it was Becattini who tutored Kahn on Marshall and not the other way round. Considering the research on Keynes's economic apprenticeship I mentioned before, Raffaelli was perhaps the one in the group who might have benefited most from conversations with Kahn. Unfortunately, Tiziano joined the group in the late 1980s, too late for having the possibility of meeting him.

(9) *Is there anything interesting in the lecture notes by Shove that you received from and gave back to Kahn?*

The notes, that were taken by John Saltmarsh during the lectures given by Shove in 1928–1929, are mentioned in the chapter on Shove in Groenewegen's book *Minor Marshallians* (Groenewegen, 2012, p. 211). Groenewegen states that they are now (2012) preserved at King's College. The Becattini–Kahn correspondence of 1979 mentions these notes and the small 'notebook' containing them, apparently Kahn's personal property that he had lent to Becattini and now requested back (RFK 13/22/47).

Becattini passed the notes to me around 1980, along with the microfilm of the Dissertation (see my letter to Kahn of 16 May 1980, RFK/13/22/45). I certainly read them in photocopy, as by that time the original was back in Kahn's hands. As far as I remember they must have raised my curiosity and in writing to Kahn I hinted at possible utilisations. But he had already told Becattini that projects concerning Shove's lectures were not worthwhile (Kahn to Becattini, 24 December 1979).

In any case Kahn had a lot of respect for Shove, and from passages of the Dissertation I got the impression that Shove's supervision was more assiduous and thorough than Sraffa's friendly tutorship, the latter exclusively limited to technical aspects of the analysis of imperfection (but on this point see also the slightly different view of Cristina Marcuzzo in her contribution to the Kahn Memorial issue of the *Cambridge Journal of Economics*, 1994 (Marcuzzo, 1994)). Among the 'minor Marshallians', Shove was probably the most Marshallian of all. And, although the influence of Shove on Kahn and the Dissertation is yet to be analysed, this brings us back to a point we have already touched in this conversation: the features of Marshallian methodology that are recognisable in Kahn's work, be they an outcome of the Cambridge atmosphere or filtered through the teachings of such tutors as Keynes or Shove. One thing is the theory—we know that Kahn followed Keynes in rejecting whole blocks of Marshall's theory of how the economy works—quite another the method, in the basic sense of indications on 'what to look at' and 'how to elaborate the resulting observations'. On the side of method I see more continuity in Cambridge economics than the narrations in terms of the Keynesian 'break' or 'revolution' may suggest.

Incidentally, this point reminds me of the only private disagreement I had with Pasinetti, a person who was of great help in carrying out the project of publication and whom I immensely respected. In February 1991 he sent me a draft of the biographical note on Kahn that would later appear in the *Proceedings of the British Academy* (Pasinetti, 1991), inviting comments. Two points in that paper made me flinch. First, there was the idea that the Dissertation was a product of the Keynesian break from neoclassical orthodoxy under the influence of Sraffa's 1925–1926 critique of Marshall. Now, in the Dissertation Sraffa is mentioned repeatedly as the one who turned Marshall's market imperfections from 'economic frictions' into 'active forces', but is also heavily criticised for his theory of the equilibrium price as independent of the degree of market imperfection. Besides, as I have said before, I was under the impression that the influence of Shove was stronger and more pervasive than Sraffa's, and Shove was not one who wanted Marshall's theory to be trashed. The second point that disturbed me was Pasinetti's interpretation of Marshallian theory as a 'British analogue of Walrasian theory', as if the whole neoclassical tradition were reducible to a single scheme, an interchangeably Marshallian or Walrasian general equilibrium system. This was a nasty blow to all that we of the so-called Italian Marshallian school had been trying to do for years. So it was that I sent Pasinetti a lengthy letter filled with protests. I never checked whether my complaints induced any changes in the text that he eventually published in the *Proceedings*, but I appreciated the conciliatory mood of his reply. A reply that didn't even attempt to address the merits of my remarks and simply removed the whole question from the economic to the psychological plane. 'The relationship of Keynes and his young disciples with Marshall—he wrote—seems to me similar to the relationship with their father. The genetic imprint is unmistakable, but there is also the rebellion, which was traumatic and led to considerable personal tension' (Pasinetti to Dardi, 4 March 1991).

(10) *On bootstrapping and the politics of opinion do you have anything to add to the interview on Kahn that you gave to Cristina Marcuzzo in 1998?*[22]

Honestly, I remember very little of that interview so I'll probably repeat myself. I have always thought that the idea of self-confirming expectations is most important both in explaining the 'unnecessary evils' (to use Pareto's words) that market economies tend to produce and in opening new spaces for economic policy. Before this idea became commonplace with the spreading of game theory in economics, Cambridge was the place where I had found it invoked most often: Keynes, Harrod, and now Kahn's analysis of market equilibrium as mostly an 'equilibrium of theories' (I don't want to look like a provocateur but these are words I take from Hahn and that I find perfectly apt). As to the origins of the idea, I always like to refer to Marshall's own formulation, the oldest formulation that I know of, in the first edition (1879) of *The Economics of Industry* (Marshall & Marshall, 1879, p. 209), where, after claiming the status of 'moral science' for economics, he goes on to state the notion that 'in the

[22] See above footnote 10.

moral world, the belief that a change ought to occur and will occur, tends to make it occur'.

10.7.4 Kahn and Italy

(11) *Do you have particular memories of Kahn's presence in Italy?*

No, I never met him in Italy. For personal reasons that I don't recall, I couldn't attend the Mattioli Lectures in Milan nor the meeting at Johns Hopkins University in Bologna where Marcuzzo's book (Kahn, 1988) was presented.

(12) *Apart from yourself, Becattini, Cristina Marcuzzo and, of course, Luigi Pasinetti, which other Italian scholars were particularly close to Kahn?*

I don't think I can give a satisfactory answer to this question. In a letter of 4 March 1983, in which Kahn congratulated me on the completion of the volume (RFK/12/2/128/40), he enclosed a handwritten list of people living in the UK and abroad to whom he wanted a copy of the book to be sent. The section of Italian recipients included five names: Luigi Pasinetti, Luigi Spaventa, Paolo Sylos Labini, Pierangelo Garegnani and Gerda Blau (who was not Italian but at the time was residing in Rome). To this list we should add the name of Marcello de Cecco, who had been a student of Kahn's in his youth and often spoke of him in his characteristically humorous, but also affectionate, vein. Later additions to the list were Beniamino Andreatta, Augusto Graziani and Michele Salvati, but I cannot tell whether they were included at Kahn's request or for other reasons.

10.7.5 Kahn as a Person and His Legacy

(13) *What do you remember about Kahn as a person? What did you notice about his behaviour when you met him?*

I met him a few times. I remember him as a polite, attentive host, helpful and collaborative when necessary, but I sensed very clearly that I was in the presence of a reserved and private man. After the few conversations I had with him, I walked away feeling that I had not been able to hook him.

Certainly this was partly due to the speech barrier I mentioned before—his tone of voice so quiet that I could hardly understand him. The personal relationship was therefore cordial but limited. The correspondence, however, was more satisfactory and stretched over a number of years.

(14) *How would you describe your reaction to the adjective 'elusive' when Samuelson uses it to describe Kahn?*

Samuelson knew Kahn well enough and admired him for both his intellectual brilliance and his personality, all his bizarre quirks included. For this reason, I think any malign or mocking intention in alluding to Kahn's 'elusiveness' must be excluded. What Samuelson meant corresponds to what we said before: Kahn was one who worked a lot for Keynes and the other members of the 'circus' but did not like the limelight and preferred to stay in the background.

(15) *If you had to sum up Kahn's legacy in just a few words, which words would you choose, and what would your reasoning be?*

It seems to me that Kahn's legacy is by now impossible to separate from that of Keynes. This is an outcome that reflects what he was always striving for, I would say that it can be considered for the most part an achievement of his. The intellectual symbiosis between Kahn and Keynes, especially in the phase of transition from the *Treatise* to the *General Theory*, and Kahn's unwillingness to put his own mark on his contributions to the common cause, were so extreme that the two have remained indissolubly tied to each other in historical memory.

Yet we know that Kahn was not only this. The Dissertation, together with his participation in the debates of the 1930s on market imperfections and welfare economics, constitute a significant contribution, independent of Keynes, to the economic theory of the twentieth century. But I think nobody would be prepared nowadays to speak of a legacy of Kahn in these fields. When I proposed to translate the Dissertation into Italian, I found it interesting to do so because, at the time, there was a revival of interest in imperfect markets and the possibility of re-examining old problems with the new instruments of game theory. However, I myself fell inadvertently into the trap of bringing back Kahn, the innovative industrial economist of the Dissertation, to Kahn the 'disciple of Keynes', with my thesis of a resemblance between market imperfections and liquidity preference.

One more proof, if necessary, that we always end there, the Keynesian theme always ends by dominating all the others.

In any case my plan of trying to exploit the wave of interest in market imperfections to enhance a new image of Kahn among contemporary economists turned out to be based on wrong calculations. That wave was the consequence of the sudden discovery of the possibilities disclosed by a new technique, and the economists involved in the exploration of these possibilities were not interested in the search for new founding fathers. The success of the operation of publishing Kahn's Dissertation was limited to Kahn's many friends and to the historians of economic thought, as it should be. I don't think that general economists ever realised what was going on.

References

Annan, N. (1990). *Our age: English intellectuals between the world wars.* Random House.

Arrow, K. (1969). The Organization of Economic Activity: Issues Pertinent to the Choice of Market versus Nonmarket Allocation. In U.S. Joint Economic Committee, 91st Congress, 1st Session, *The analysis and evaluation of public expenditure: The PPB system* (vol. 1, pp. 39–73). U.S. Government Printing Office.

Baldwin, N. J. (1989). The archive of the society for the protection of science and learning. *History of Science, 27*(1), 103–105.

Becattini, G. (1989). Richard Ferdinand Kahn. *Il Ponte, 45*(5), 148–151.

Bellino, E., & Nerozzi, S. (Eds.). (2021). *Pasinetti and the classical Keynesians: Nine methodological issues.* Cambridge University Press.

Brahmananda, P. R. (1990). R.F. Kahn (1905–1989). *History of Political Economy, 42*, 631–652.

Bridel, P. (2024). Review of *Richard F. Kahn: Collected economic essays*, edited by Maria Cristina Marcuzzo and Paolo Paesani. *European Journal of the History of Economic Thought, 32*(1), 161–164.

Cristiano, C., & Paesani, P. (2018a). Unconventional monetary policy ante litteram: Richard Kahn and the monetary policy debate during the works of the Radcliffe committee. *Cambridge Journal of Economics, 42*, 1145–1163.

Cristiano, C., & Paesani, P. (2018b). Monetary policy and price stability in British post-war debate: Restatement of evidence from economists' papers presented to the Radcliffe committee. *European Journal of the History of Economic Thought, 25*, 1311–1341.

Dardi, M. (1983). Introduzione. In R. Kahn (Ed.), *L'Economia del Breve Periodo.* Bollati Boringhieri.

Dardi, M. (1984). *Il giovane Marshall: Accumulazione e Mercato*. Il Mulino.
Dardi, M. (1990). Richard Kahn. *Studi Economici, 41*, 3–86.
Dardi, M. (1994). Kahn's theory of liquidity preference and monetary policy. *Cambridge Journal of Economics, 18*(1), 91–106.
Dardi, M. (2021). Alfred Marshall in the lower Valdarno. In K. Caldari, M. Dardi, & S. G. Medema (Eds.), *Marshall and the Marshallian heritage: Essays in honour of Tiziano Raffaelli* (pp. 3–37). Palgrave Macmillan.
De Vroey, M. (2016). *A history of macroeconomics from Keynes to Lucas and beyond*. Cambridge University Press.
Deleplace, G. (2025). Review of *Richard F. Kahn, collected economic essays*, M.C. Marcuzzo and P. Paesani (eds.). *Cahiers d'économie politique, 86*(1), 189–202.
Eatwell, J. (2000). Richard Kahn (1905–1989). In P. Arestis & M. Sayers (Eds.), *Biographical dictionary of dissenting economists* (2nd ed., pp. 336–343). Edward Elgar.
Gaffard, J.-L., Napoletano, M., & Saraceno, F. (2024). Inflation, changement structurel et conflit de répartition: enseignements pour la politique économique. *Revue d'économie financière, 1*, 213–230.
Groenewegen, P. (2012). *Minor Marshallians and Alfred Marshall: An evaluation*. Routledge.
Guerrieri, V., Lorenzoni, G., Straub, L., & Werning, I. (2022). Macroeconomic implications of COVID-19: Can negative supply shocks cause demand shortages? *American Economic Review, 112*, 1437–1474.
Harcourt, G. C. (1991). R.F. Kahn: A Tribute. *BNL Quarterly Review, 176*, 15–30.
Harcourt, G. C. (1994). Kahn and Keynes and the making of the general theory. *Cambridge Journal of Economics, 18*(1), 11–23.
Harcourt, G. C. (2012). Keynes and his Cambridge pupils and colleagues. *Meiji Journal of Political Science and Economics, 1*, 12–25.
Harrod, R. F. (1951). *The life of John Maynard Keynes*. Macmillan.
Hawkins, J. (2023). Review of *Richard F. Kahn: Collected economic essays*, edited by Maria Cristina Marcuzzo and Paolo Paesani. *History of Economics Review, 84*, 58–59.
Howson, S. (2024). The collected writings of Richard Ferdinand Kahn. *Contributions to Political Economy, 43*, 82–93.
Johnson, E. S., & Johnson, H. G. (1978). *The shadow of Keynes: Understanding Keynes. Cambridge and Keynesian economics*. Basil Blackwell.
Kahn, R. (1976). Political attitudes involved in teaching economics. *Oxford Review of Education, 2*(1), 91–95.
Kahn, R. F. ([1929] 1989). *The economics of the short period*. Macmillan. Kahn's Fellowship Dissertation.

Kahn, R. F. (1931). The relation of home investment to unemployment. *Economic Journal, 41*, 173–198. Reprinted in Kahn, R. F. (1972). *Selected essays on employment and growth* (pp. 1–27). Cambridge University Press.

Kahn, R. F. (1935). Some notes on ideal output. *Economic Journal, 45*, 1–35.

Kahn, R. F. (1937). The problem of duopoly. *Economic Journal, 47*, 1–20. Reprinted in Marcuzzo, M. C., & Paesani, P. (Eds.), *Richard F. Kahn: Collected economic essays* (pp. 51–70). Palgrave Macmillan.

Kahn, R. F. (1954). Some notes on liquidity preference. *Manchester School of Economics and Social Studies, 22*, 229–257. Reprinted in Kahn, R. F. (1972). *Selected essays on employment and growth* (pp. 72–96). Cambridge University Press.

Kahn, R. F. (1958a). Memorandum of evidence submitted to the Radcliffe Committee (27 May 1958). In Radcliffe Committee (1960), *Principal memoranda of evidence* (vol. 3, pp. 138–146). Her Majesty's Stationary Office. Reprinted in Kahn, R. F. (1972). *Selected essays on employment and growth* (pp. 124–152). Cambridge University Press.

Kahn, R. F. (1958b). Testimony to the Radcliffe Committee (23 October 1958). In Radcliffe Committee (1960), *Minutes* (pp. 739–746). Her Majesty's Stationary Office.

Kahn, R. F. ([1971] 1972). Notes on the rate of interest and the growth of firms. In R. F. Kahn (Ed.), *Selected essays on employment and growth* (pp. 208–232). Cambridge University Press.

Kahn, R. F. (1984). *The making of Keynes's general theory.* Cambridge University Press.

Kahn, R. F. (1988). *Un discepolo di Keynes* (M. C. Marcuzzo, Ed.). Garzanti.

Laidler, D. (1999). *Fabricating the Keynesian revolution: Studies of the inter-war literature on money, the cycle, and unemployment.* Cambridge University Press.

Lorenzoni, G., & Werning, I. (2024). Wage-Price Spirals. *Brookings Papers on Economic Activity*, Fall 2023, 317–367.

Maneschi, A. (1988). The place of Lord Kahn's the economics of the short period in the theory of imperfect competition. *History of Political Economy, 20*, 155–169.

Marcuzzo, M. C. (1994). R.F. Kahn and imperfect competition. *Cambridge Journal of Economics, 18*, 25–39.

Marcuzzo, M. C. (2002). The collaboration between J.M. Keynes and R.F. Kahn from the treatise to the general theory. *History of Political Economy, 34*, 421–448.

Marcuzzo, M. C. (2017). The "Cambridge" critique of the quantity theory of money. *Journal of Post Keynesian Economics, 40*(2), 260–271.

Marcuzzo, M. C. (2020). Richard Ferdinand Kahn: A disciple of Keynes. *History of Economics Review, 76*, 1–57.

Marcuzzo, M. C., & Paesani, P. (2022). Introduction. In M. C. Marcuzzo & P. Paesani (Eds.), *Richard F. Kahn: Collected economic essays* (pp. 1–32). Palgrave Macmillan.
Marcuzzo, M. C., & Rosselli, A. (2005). *Economists in Cambridge: A study through their correspondence, 1907–1946*. Routledge.
Marcuzzo, M. C., & Rosselli, A. (2017). Richard F. Kahn (1905–1989). In R. Cord (Ed.), *The Palgrave companion to Cambridge economics* (pp. 705–721). Palgrave Macmillan.
Marris, R. L. (1964). *The economic theory of managerial capitalism*. Macmillan.
Marris, R. L. (1992). R. F. Kahn's fellowship dissertation: A missing link in the history of economic thought. *The Economic Journal, 102*(414), 1235–1243.
Marshall, A. (1898). Distribution and exchange. *Economic Journal, 8*(29), 37–59.
Marshall, A., & Marshall, M. P. (1879). *The economics of industry*. Macmillan and Co..
Marshall, A., & Marshall, M. P. (1975). *Economia della produzione* (G. Becattini, Trans. & Ed.). Istituto Editoriale Internazionale.
Middleton, R. (1996). *Government versus the market: The growth of the public sector, economic management, and British economic performance, c. 1890–1979*. Edward Elgar.
Middleton, R. (1998). *Charlatans or Saviours? Economists and the British economy from Marshall to Meade*. Edward Elgar.
Moggridge, D. E. (1985). *The making of Keynes' general theory* by Richard Kahn. *Economica, 52*, 263–266.
Pasinetti, L. L. (1991). Richard Ferdinand Kahn 1905–1989. *Proceedings of the British Academy, 76*, 423–443.
Pasinetti, L. L. (2007). *Keynes and the Cambridge Keynesians*. Cambridge University Press.
Peden, G. C. (1990). *British economic and social policy: Lloyd George to Margaret Thatcher* (2nd ed.). Philip Allan.
Raffaelli, T. (2000). Keynes's apprenticeship with Marshall in 1905. *History of Economic Ideas, 8*(2), 121–152.
Robinson, A. (1947). John Maynard Keynes 1883–1946. *Economic Journal, 57*, 1–68.
Rochon, L.-P. (2001). Cambridge's contribution to endogenous money: Robinson and Kahn on credit and money. *Review of Political Economy, 13*, 287–307.
Saith, A. (2022). *Cambridge economics in the post-Keynesian era: The eclipse of heterodox traditions*. Springer.
Samuelson, P. (1994). Richard Kahn: His welfare economics and lifetime achievements. *Cambridge Journal of Economics, 18*, 55–72.
Sardoni, C. (2004). The contribution of Gerald Shove to the development of Cambridge economics. *Review of Political Economy, 16*(3), 361–375.

Schiffman, D. (2013). Richard Kahn and Israeli Economic Policy, 1957 and 1962. *Economic History eJournal.* https://papers.ssrn.com/sol3/papers.cfm?abstract_id=2373517

Schumpeter, J. A. (1954). *History of economic analysis.* Oxford University Press.

Shove, G. F. (1942). The place of Marshall's principles in the development of economic theory. *Economic Journal, 52*, 294–329.

Snowdon, B., & Vane, R. (2005). *Modern macroeconomics: Its origins.* Edward Elgar.

Steindl, J. (1952). *Maturity and stagnation in American capitalism.* Basil Blackwell.

Stockhammer, E. (2022). Post-Keynesian macroeconomic foundations for comparative political economy. *Politics and Society, 50*, 156–187.

Tonveronachi, M. (1983). *J.M. Keynes: Dall'instabilità ciclica all'equilibrio di sottoccupazione.* La Nuova Italia Scientifica.

Tribe, K. (2021). *Constructing economic science: The invention of a discipline 1850–1950.* Oxford University Press.

Appendix A

List of Richard F. Kahn's Publications

1931

The relation of home investment to unemployment. *EconomicJournal, 41*(162), June, 173–198. Reprinted in R.F. Kahn (1972), *Selected Essays on Employment and Growth* (pp. 1–27). Cambridge: Cambridge University Press.

1932

The financing of public works: a note. *EconomicJournal, 42*(167), September, 492–495.

Decreasing costs: a note on the contributions of Mr Harrod and Mr Allen. *EconomicJournal, 42*(168), December, 657–661.

1933

Imperfect competition and the marginal principle. Translated in Italian and published in R.F. Kahn (1999). *Concorrenza, occupazione e moneta.* Ed. by M.C. Marcuzzo. Bologna: Il Mulino. Published in English in M.C. Marcuzzo and P. Paesani (2022), *Richard F. Kahn: Collected Economic Essays* (pp. 35–50). Basingstoke: Palgrave Macmillan.

Public works and inflation. *Journal of the American Statistical Association, 28*(Suppl. 181A), March, 168–173. Papers and Proceedings of the Ninety-fourth Annual Meeting of the American Statistical Association (edited by Frank Alexander Ross), held at Cincinnati, Ohio,

P. Paesani, *Richard F. Kahn*, Great Thinkers in Economics,
https://doi.org/10.1007/978-3-032-09123-9

December 28–31, 1932. Reprinted in R.F. Kahn (1972), *Selected Essays on Employment and Growth* (pp. 28–34). Cambridge: Cambridge University Press.

The elasticity of substitution and the relative share of a factor. *Review of Economic Studies*, *1*(1), October, 72–78.

Reply to J.R. Hicks, 'IV—A note on Mr Kahn's paper'. *Review of Economic Studies*, *1*(1), October, 80.

1935

Some notes on ideal output. *EconomicJournal*, *45*(177), March, 1–35.

Two applications of the concept of elasticity of substitution. *EconomicJournal*, *45*(178), June, 242–245.

1936

Review of *Soviet Money and Finance* by L.E. Hubbard (London: Macmillan, 1936). *New Statesman and Nation*, August 29, 296.

Dr Neisser on secondary employment: a note. *Review of Economics and Statistics*, *18*(3), August, 144–147.

Mr. Paine and rationalisation: a note. *Economica*, *3*(11), August, 327–329.

Review of *Works on Prosperity and Depression*, by A.D. Gayer (London: Macmillan 1935). *EconomicJournal*, *46*(183), September, 491–493.

Review of *Report of the Committee of Investigation for England on Complaints made by the Central Milk Distributive Committee and the Parliamentary Committee of the Co-operative Congress as to the Operation of the Milk Marketing Scheme* (1933). *EconomicJournal*, *46*(183), September, 554–559.

English translation of K. Wicksell, *Geldzins und Guterpreise* (*Interest and Prices: A Study of the Causes Regulating the Value of Money*. London: Macmillan).

1937

The problem of duopoly. *EconomicJournal*, *47*(185), March, 1–20. Reprinted in M.C. Marcuzzo and P. Paesani (2022), *Richard F. Kahn: Collected Economic Essays* (pp. 51–70). Basingstoke: Palgrave Macmillan.

The League of Nations enquiry into the trade cycle (review of *Prosperity and Depression: A Theoretical Analysis of Cyclical Movements*, by G. von Haberler. Geneva: League of Nations; London: Allen & Unwin, 1937). *EconomicJournal*, *47*(188), December, 670–679.

1938

Review of *Studies in the Theory of Economic Expansion* by E. Lundberg (London: P.S. King & Son, 1938). *EconomicJournal*, *48*(190), June, pp. 265–268.

A rejoinder (to some comments on Mr Kahn's Review of *Prosperity and Depression*). *EconomicJournal*, *48*(190), June, 333–336.

1939

Review of *World Economic Survey. Seventh Year, 1937–38*, by J.E. Meade (Geneva: League of Nations; London: Allen & Unwin, 1938). *EconomicJournal*, *49*(193), March, pp. 96–98.

Review of *Industrial Price Policies and Economic Progress*, by E.G. Nourse and H.B. Drury (Washington: The Brooking Institutions, 1938); Review of *Industrial Price Policies* (a summary of *Industrial Price Policies and Economic Progress*), by M.S. Stewart (New York: Public Affairs Committee, 1938). *EconomicJournal*, *49*(194), June, 321–323.

1946

Exports and manpower. *The Economist*, December 14.

1947

Tariffs and the terms of trade. *Review of Economic Studies*, *15*(1), 14–19.

Trade make-believe. *The Economist*, January 4.

The saving campaign. *The Times*, August 25.

Marshall Aid and the dollar gap. *The Times*, December 30.

1948

Civil service examination. *The Times*, March 30.

The 1948 Budget: an economist's criticism. *The Listener*, May 6, 738–739.

The volume of exports. Need to raise the level. *The Times*, October 28.

1949

Our economic complacency. *The Listener*, February 3, 166–167 and 181.

Professor Meade on planning. *EconomicJournal*, *59*(233), March, 1–16.

Disinflation continued?. *The Economist*, March 19.

Review of the *Third Annual Report of the International Bank for Reconstruction and Development, 1947–1948* (Washington, DC: IBRD, 1948). *EconomicJournal*, *59*(235), September, 445–447.

Devaluation and sterling markets. *The Economist*, October 15.

A possible Intra-European payments scheme. *Economica*, *16*(64), November, 293–304.

1950

The dollar shortage and devaluation. *Economia Internazionale*, *3*(1), February, 89–113. Reprinted in R.F. Kahn (1972), *Selected Essays on Employment and Growth* (pp. 35–59). Cambridge: Cambridge University Press.

The European Payments Union. *Economica*, *17*(67), August, 306–316.

An approach to economic development in the Middle East (review of the *Final Report of the United Nations Economic Survey Mission for the Middle East: An Approach to Economic Development in the Middle East.* London: HMSO for the United Nations, 1949). *EconomicJournal*, *60*(239), September, 634–635.

Marshall Aid. *The Times*, November 11.

1951

The Budget. *The Economist*, May 5.

Home and export trade. *EconomicJournal*, *61*(242), June, 279–289.

The balance of payments and the sterling area. *District Bank Review*, *100*, December, 3–17.

Manpower control. *The Economist*, December 15.

1952

Manpower control. *The Economist*, January 5.

Oxford studies in the price mechanism. *EconomicJournal*, *62*(245), March, 119–130. Reprinted in M.C. Marcuzzo and P. Paesani (2022), *Richard F. Kahn: Collected Economic Essays* (pp. 71–83). Basingstoke: Palgrave Macmillan.

International regulation of trade and exchanges. In *Banking and Foreign Trade* (pp. 1–18), Lectures delivered at the Fifth International Banking Summer School, Oxford, July. London: Europa Publications for the Institute of Bankers. Reprinted in M.C. Marcuzzo and P. Paesani (2022), *Richard F. Kahn: Collected Economic Essays* (pp. 163–177). Basingstoke: Palgrave Macmillan.

Review of *The Problem of Employment Stabilization* by B. Ohlin (New York: Columbia university Press, 1949). *American Economic Review*, *42*(1), March, 180–182.

Comments (on monetary policy and the crisis). *Bulletin of the Oxford University*, *14*, April–May, 147–153.

Britain's economic position. *The Listener*, July 3, 18–22.

Monetary policy and the balance of payments. *Political Quarterly*, *23*(3), July, 250–261. Reprinted in R.F. Kahn (1972), *Selected Essays on*

Employment and Growth (pp. 60–71). Cambridge: Cambridge University Press.

Comments (on monetary policy again). *Bulletin of the Oxford University*, *14*, August, 278–280.

Investment. *The Economist*, December 6.

1953

Living with the Dollar. *The Economist*, January 1.

The Dollar Gap: Our Precarious Balance. *The Times*, February 23.

Living with the Dollar. *The Economist*, March 14.

Equipment for industry. *The Times*, April 20.

1954

The case for cheap money. *The Financial Times*, June 3–4.

The convertibility risk. *The Financial Times*, September 10.

Some notes on liquidity preference. *Manchester School of Economic and Social Studies*, *22*(3), September, 229–257. Reprinted in R.F. Kahn (1972), *Selected Essays on Employment and Growth* (pp. 72–96). Cambridge: Cambridge University Press.

(With D.G. Champernowne). The value of invested capital: a mathematical addendum to Mrs. Robinson's article. *Review of Economic Studies*, *21*(2), 107–111. Reprinted as Appendix to J.V. Robinson. (1956). *The Accumulation of Capital*. London: Macmillan.

1955

Short-term business indicators in Western Europe. *Economic Bulletin for Europe*, *7*(3), November, 34–78.

1956

Lord Keynes and inflation. *The Listener*, May 3, 543–545.

Lord Keynes and the balance of payments. *The Listener*, May 10, 591–593.

Lord Keynes and contemporary economic problems. *The Listener*, May 3 and 10. Reprinted in R.F. Kahn (1972), *Selected Essays on Employment and Growth* (pp. 103–123). Cambridge: Cambridge University Press.

An answer to the capital question. *Westminster Bank Review*, August, 1–26.

Full employment and British economic policy. *Nihon Keizai Shimbun*, 1956. Reprinted in R.F. Kahn (1972), *Selected Essays on Employment and Growth* (pp. 97–102). Cambridge: Cambridge University Press.

1957

Doubts about the free trade area. *The Listener*, February 28, 331–333.

Doubts about the free trade area. *The Times*, March 21.

A positive contribution?. *Bulletin of the Oxford Institute of Statistics, 19*(1), February, 63–68.

1958

Memorandum of evidence submitted to the Radcliffe Committee (May 27). In Radcliffe Committee on the Working of the Monetary System (1959), *Principal Memoranda of Evidence* (Vol. 3, pp. 138–146). London: HMSO. Reprinted in R.F. Kahn (1972), *Selected Essays on Employment and Growth* (pp. 124–152). Cambridge: Cambridge University Press.

Evidence (October 23). In Radcliffe Committee on the Working of the Monetary System (1960), *Minutes of Evidence* (pp. 739–746). London: HMSO.

The pace of development. In *The Challenge of Development: A Symposium* (pp. 163–198). Lecture delivered at the Eliezer Kaplan School of Economics and Social Sciences. Jerusalem: Hebrew University of Jerusalem. Reprinted in R.F. Kahn (1972), *Selected Essays on Employment and Growth* (pp. 153–191). Cambridge: Cambridge University Press.

1959

Exercises in the analysis of growth. *Oxford Economic Papers, 11*(2), June, 146–163. Reprinted in R.F. Kahn (1972), *Selected Essays on Employment and Growth* (pp. 192–207). Cambridge: Cambridge University Press.

Sur l'analyse de la croissance. In *Colloques Economiques Franco-Britanniques: L'accumulation du capital* (pp. 51–69). Paris: ISMEA.

1961

Organisation for European Economic Co-operation. *The Problem of Rising Prices*, report by William Fellner, Milton Gilbert, Brent Hansen, Richard Kahn, Friedrich Lutz, Pieter de Wolff. Paris: OEEC.

The Budget I should like to see. *The Financial Times*, April 13.

A reasonable doubt: government's views on wages policy. *The Times*, October 31.

1962

Policy on wage rates: annual or actual increases. *The Times*, May 16.

1963

Economic situation. *The Times*, January 24.

1964

(With R. Cohen, W.B. Reddaway, J.V. Robinson). Statement submitted to the Lloyd Jacob Committee on Resale Price Maintenance. *Oxford Bulletin of Economics and Statistics, 26*(2), May, 113–121.

1965

The progress of the British economy in 1965. *The Financial Times*, January 1.

The progress of the British economy in 1966. *The Financial Times*, December 31.

United Nations Conference on Trade and Development. *International Monetary Issues and the Developing Countries: Report of the Group of Experts* (R.F. Kahn was one of the members). New York: United Nations.

Un confronto fra la politica inglese e quella italiana. In G. Fuà (Ed.), *Programmazioneeconomica: confronti italo inglesi* (pp. 145–150). Italian translation by G. Ascarelli-Spierer. Urbino (Italy): Argalia.

1966

The Budget I would like to see. *The Financial Times*, April 5.

The economic situation. Address to the House of Lords, July 28.

The prices and incomes policy. Address to the House of Lords, August 3.

United Nations Conference on Trade and Development. *Payments Arrangements among the Developing Countries for Trade Expansion: Report of the Group of Experts* (chaired by R.F. Kahn). Geneva: United Nations.

United Nations Conference on Trade and Development. *Trade Expansion and Economic Co-operation among Developing Countries: Report of the Group of Experts* (R.F. Kahn was one of the members). New York: United Nations.

1967

European EconomicCommunity. Address to the House of Lords, May 8.

1968

The economic situation and public expenditure. Address to the House of Lords, January 24.

1969

United Nations Conference on Trade and Development. *International Monetary Reform and Co-operation for Development* (R.F. Kahn was one of the members). New York: United Nations.

1971

Notes on the rate of interest and the growth of firms. In R.F. Kahn (1972), *Selected Essays on Employment and Growth* (pp. 208–232). Cambridge: Cambridge University Press.

1972

Selected Essays on Employment and Growth. Cambridge: Cambridge University Press.

1973

The International Monetary System, *American Economic Review*, *63*(2), 181–188. Reprinted in M.C. Marcuzzo and P. Paesani (2022), *Richard F. Kahn: Collected Economic Essays* (pp. 179–190). Basingstoke: Palgrave Macmillan.

SDR and aid. *Lloyds Bank Review*, *28*(110), October, 1–18.

Economic and industrial affairs. Address to the House of Lords, November 6.

Counter-inflation (prices and pay code) (no. 2). Address to the House of Lords, November 20.

Economic policy and fuel supplies. Address to the House of Lords, December 18.

1974

Industrial and economic situation. Address to the House of Lords, February 6.

Plans for a monetary system to replace the Bretton Woods agreement. In N.S. Fatemi (Ed.), *Problems of Balance of Payments and Trade* (pp. 199–266). New Jersey: Rutherford.

(With M. Posner). Challenging the 'elegant and striking' paradoxes of the New School. *The Times*, April 17.

(With M. Posner). Theory dogged by its assumptions. *The Times*, April 18.

(With M.V. Posner). Cambridge economics and the balance of payments. *London and Cambridge Economic Bulletin*, *85*, July, 19–32.

(With M. Posner). Why an incomes policy remains essential. *The Financial Times*, August 22.

(With M.V. Posner). The effects of public expenditure on inflation and the balance of payments. In *Public Expenditure, Inflation and the Balance of Payments: Ninth Report from the Expenditure Committee* (HC328). London: HMSO.

The Mini-budget and the crisis. *Sunday Telegraph*, July 28.

The economic position. Address to the House of Lords, July 30.

Is a dose of Sir Keith's horrible medicine the only way to bring Britain to its senses?. *The Times*, September 16.

What Keynes really said. *Sunday Telegraph*, September 22.

On re-reading Keynes (Fourth Keynes Lecture in Economics delivered on November 6, 1974). *Proceedings of the British Academy* (vol. LX, pp. 361–392). Oxford: Oxford University Press, 1975.

1975

Erosion of UK competitive position. *The Times*, March 5.

Reducing the rate of inflation. *The Times*, July 4.

The attack on inflation. Address to the House of Lords, July 30.

Inflation and the Unions. *New Statesman*, August 1.

Monetarism and incomes policy. *The Banker*, August, 1167–1170.

Oil and the crisis. In J. Hicks et al., *Crisis '75…?* (pp. 34–38). *IEA Occasional Papers Special*, no. 43. London: Institute of Economic Affairs.

1976

Thoughts on the behaviour of wages and monetarism. *Lloyds Bank Review*, 119, January, 1–11. Reprinted in M.C. Marcuzzo and P. Paesani (2022), *Richard F. Kahn: Collected Economic Essays* (pp. 241–252). Basingstoke: Palgrave Macmillan.

Inflation: a Keynesian view. *Scottish Journal of Political Economy*, *33*(1), February, 11–16. Reprinted in M.C. Marcuzzo and P. Paesani (2022), *Richard F. Kahn: Collected Economic Essays* (pp. 253–259). Basingstoke: Palgrave Macmillan.

Public expenditure cuts. *New Statesman*, February 2.

Political attitudes involved in teaching economics. *Oxford Review of Education*, *2*(1), 91–95.

Unemployment as seen by the Keynesians. In G.D.N. Worswick (Ed.), *The Concept and Measurement of Involuntary Unemployment* (pp. 19–25). London: Allen & Unwin. Reprinted in M.C. Marcuzzo and P. Paesani (2022), *Richard F. Kahn: Collected Economic Essays* (pp. 225–239). Basingstoke: Palgrave Macmillan.

Historical origins of the International Monetary Fund. In A.P. Thirlwall (Ed.), *Keynes and International Monetary Relations* (pp. 3–35). London: Macmillan. Reprinted in M.C. Marcuzzo and P. Paesani (2022), *Richard F. Kahn: Collected Economic Essays* (pp. 191–222). Basingstoke: Palgrave Macmillan.

1977

The economic situation. Address to the House of Lords, January 26.

Mr. Eltis and the Keynesians. *Lloyds Bank Review*, *32*(124), April, 1–13.

(With M.V. Posner). Inflation, unemployment and growth. *National Westminster Bank Quarterly Review*, *10*, November, 28–37.

Malinvaud on Keynes. Reviewing: Edmond Malinvaud, *The Theory of Unemployment Reconsidered* (Oxford: Basil Blackwell, 1977); three lectures delivered for the Yrjö Jahnsson Foundation. *Cambridge Journal of Economics*, *1*(4), December, 375–388.

A comment. In T.W. Hutchinson, *Keynes versus the 'Keynesians'* (pp. 48–57). London: IEA.

1978

Review of J. Hicks, *Economic Perspectives: Further Essays on Money and Growth* (Oxford: Oxford University Press, 1977). *Manchester School of Economic and Social Studies*, 46, March, 83–85.

Some aspects of the development of Keynes's thought. *Journal of Economic Literature*, *16*(2), June, 544–559. Reprinted in M.C. Marcuzzo and P. Paesani (2022), *Richard F. Kahn: Collected Economic Essays* (pp. 97–118). Basingstoke: Palgrave Macmillan.

1983

L'economia del breve periodo. Ed. by M. Dardi. Torino: Boringhieri (first publication, translated in Italian, of *The Economics of the Short Period*, Kahn's Fellowship dissertation, submitted to King's College, Cambridge, in December 1929).

1984

The Making of Keynes's General Theory: Raffaele Mattioli Lectures. Cambridge: Cambridge University Press.

'The General Theory of Employment, Interest and Money' (Fifth Raffaele Mattioli Lecture). In R. F. Kahn, *The Making of Keynes's General Theory* (pp. 119–168). Reprinted in M.C. Marcuzzo and P. Paesani (2022), *Richard F. Kahn: Collected Economic Essays* (pp. 119–160). Basingstoke: Palgrave Macmillan.

1985

The Cambridge 'Circus'. In G. C. Harcourt (Ed.), *Keynes and His Contemporaries* (pp. 42–51). The Sixth Centennial Keynes Seminar held at the University of Kent at Canterbury, 1983. London: Macmillan. Reprinted in M.C. Marcuzzo and P. Paesani (2022), *Richard F. Kahn: Collected Economic Essays* (pp. 87–95). Basingstoke: Palgrave Macmillan.

1987

Rostas, L. Entry in J. Eatwell, M. Milgate and P. Newman (Eds.), *The New Palgrave. A Dictionary of Economics* (vol. IV, pp. 222–223). London: Macmillan.

Shove, G.F. Entry in J. Eatwell, M. Milgate and P. Newman (Eds.), *The New Palgrave: A Dictionary of Economics* (vol. IV, pp. 327–328). London: Macmillan.

1988

Inflation and Commodities in the Middle East during the Second World War. *Materie prime*, 8(3), 99–101.

1989

The Economics of the Short Period. London: Macmillan (Kahn's Fellowship dissertation, submitted to King's College, Cambridge, in December 1929). Italian translation previously published (1983). *L'economia del breve periodo.* Torino: Boringhieri.

Appendix B

Courses Taught by Richard F. Kahn at Cambridge

Table B.1 Courses taught by Richard F. Kahn at Cambridge

Years	*Michaelmas term (October–December)*	*Lent term (January–March)*	*Easter term (April–July)*
1931–1932	Mr Kahn King's	Current economic problems The short period	The same continued
1932–1933	Mr Kahn King's The Short Period	—	—
1933–1934	—	The short period	The same continued
1934–1935	—	The short period	The same continued
1935–1936	—	The short period	The same continued
1936–1937	Some current economic problems	The short period	The same continued
1937–1938	Present day problems	The same continued	The short period
1938–1939	Present day problems	The same continued	The short period
1939–1940	Economics of the short period	—	—

(*continued*)

P. Paesani, *Richard F. Kahn*, Great Thinkers in Economics,
https://doi.org/10.1007/978-3-032-09123-9

Table B.1 (continued)

Years	*Michaelmas term (October–December)*	*Lent term (January–March)*	*Easter term (April–July)*
1946–1947	—	—	International trade policy
1947–1948	—	Economics of Government Intervention	Theory of the rate of interest
1948–1949	—	Economics of Government Intervention	The same continued
1949–1950	Economics of Government Intervention	The same continued	Theory of the rate of interest
1950–1951	Mrs. Robinson, Mr Kahn, Mr Johnson Discussion classes on money - Economics of Government Intervention	The same continued	Theory of the rate of interest
1951–1952	Prof. Kahn and Mrs Robinson Classes on Money - Prof. Kahn Economics of Government Intervention	Theory of the rate of interest	Economics of Government Intervention
1952–1953	Prof. Kahn and Mr Goodwin Classes on Money - Prof. Kahn Economics of Government Intervention	Theory of the rate of interest	Economics of Government Intervention
1953–1954	Prof. Kahn and Mrs Robinson Classes on Money - Prof. Kahn Economics of Government Intervention	Theory of the rate of interest	Economics of Government Intervention
1954–1955	Prof. Kahn and Mrs Robinson Classes on Money	—	—
1955–1956	—	Theory of the rate of interest	Economics of Government Intervention
1956–1957	Prof. Kahn Economics of Government Intervention - Prof. Kahn, Mrs Robinson and Mr Neild Classes in Monetary Theory	Theory of the rate of interest	Economics of Government Intervention
1957–1958	Prof. Kahn Wages policy - Prof. Kahn and Mr Matthews Classes in Monetary theory	Theory of the rate of interest	Problems of Development (primarily for research students)
1958–1959	Prof. Kahn Theory of the rate of interest - Prof. Kahn and Mr Matthews Classes in Monetary theory	Theory of Wages and Wages policy	Problems of Development (primarily for research students)

(*continued*)

Table B.1 (continued)

Years	*Michaelmas term (October–December)*	*Lent term (January–March)*	*Easter term (April–July)*
1959–1960	Prof. Kahn Theory of Economic Development - Prof. Kahn, Mr Marris, Mr Posner Current economic problems	The same continued	Wages policy and related problems of Economic policy
1960–1961	Wages Theory and policy	The same continued	The same continued
1961–1962	Economic Principles and Problems (Papers 1 and 2) - Basic principles of planning (Paper 8)	Wages policy (preliminary examination) - Prof. Kahn, Mr A.K Sen, Mr L.L. Pasinetti Seminar for research students on Under Development	EPP The same continued
1962–1963	Economic Principles and Problems (Papers 1 and 2) - Basic principles of planning (Paper 8)	Wages policy (preliminary examination)	EPP The same continued
1963–1964	Economic principles and problems (Papers 1 and 2) - Paper 4 with Pasinetti Class	Wages policy Paper 1 (preliminary examination) - Basic principles of Planning	Economic principles and problems (Papers 1 and 2) (continued)
1964–1965	Economic principles and problems (Papers 1 and 2)	Wages policy Paper 1 (preliminary examination) - Economic Principle and Problems (EPP) continued	EPP The same continued
1966–1967	Economic principles and problems (Papers 1 and 2)	Wages policy (Paper 1); EPP continued	EPP The same continued
1967–1968	Economic principles and problems (Papers 1 and 2)	Wages policy (Paper 1); EPP continued	EPP The same continued
1968–1969	Economic principles and problems (Papers 1 and 2)	Wages policy	EPP continued
1969–1970	Economic principles and problems (Papers 1 and 2)	Wages policy	EPP continued
1970–1971	Economic principles and problems (Papers 1 and 2)	Prices and Incomes policies	EPP continued
1971–1972	Economic principles and problems (Papers 1 and 2)	Prices and Incomes policies	EPP continued

Source: *Cambridge University Reporter*, various years

Appendix C

Dramatis Personae

Noel Gilroy Annan, Baron Annan (1916–2000), was an academic, public servant and writer. Educated at Stowe and King's College, Cambridge, he served in military intelligence during the Second World War before becoming Provost of King's College (1956–1966) and later of University College London (1966–1978). He was Vice-Chancellor of the University of London (1978–1981) and sat in the House of Lords as a life peer. A trustee of major cultural institutions (e.g. National Gallery, British Museum), and President of the London Library. He also authored influential works such as *Leslie Stephen, Changing Enemies: the Defeat and Regeneration of Germany* and *Our Age*.

Thomas Balogh was a Hungarian-born economist and British government adviser. He studied law and economics at the universities of Budapest and Berlin, before spending two years (1928–1930) in the United States on a Rockefeller Fellowship. During this time, he gained experience working as a financial analyst at several central banks, including the Reichsbank, the Banque de France and the Federal Reserve. With a letter of introduction from Joseph Schumpeter, he emigrated to England and secured a post with the London banking firm O. T. Falk & Co with the assistance of John Maynard Keynes, who was greatly impressed by his knowledge of banking and financial systems. Balogh was appointed lecturer at University

P. Paesani, *Richard F. Kahn*, Great Thinkers in Economics,
https://doi.org/10.1007/978-3-032-09123-9

College London in 1934 and, in 1940, became a lecturer at Balliol College, Oxford, where he was elected to a fellowship in 1945. He played a key role in establishing the Oxford Institute of Statistics, which became a haven for émigré economists from continental Europe. In later years, he served as an economic adviser to Harold Wilson during the Labour government of 1964. Keenly Keynesian, Balogh believed that sustained economic growth was the basis of sound policy. He was a vigorous critic of monetarism and an outspoken opponent of its growing influence on British economic thinking.

Kenneth Berrill (1920–2009) initially trained as a geography teacher at University College London before switching to economics at the London School of Economics, graduating in 1941. After serving in the Royal Engineers during the Second World War, he completed an MA in 1949 and began his academic career as a lecturer in Economics at Cambridge. He was a fellow and Bursar of St Catharine's before moving to King's College in 1962. Berrill gained recognition as an economic adviser, working with the World Bank, OECD, and various governments. In 1967, he became a special adviser to the Treasury, later chairing the university grants committee. By 1974 he had moved to a central government role, advising the Wilson, Callaghan and Thatcher administrations. Known for his impartiality, Berrill was respected for offering honest advice without advocating for specific policies. In 1980, he became chairman of Vickers da Costa and later led the Securities Investment Board until 1988. After retirement, Berrill remained active with public bodies, earned honorary degrees, and was knighted in 1971.

Gerda Blau entered the Food and Agriculture Organization (FAO) in 1947 and served as the Director of the Commodities Division and later the Commodities and Trade Division there from September 1951 to December 1962. She had earned her PhD from the London School of Economics (LSE), working on speculation, futures markets and commodities. Blau developed strong connections with prominent Cambridge economists, including Kahn, Joan Robinson, Nicholas Kaldor and Ruth Cohen, likely formed when the LSE relocated to Cambridge during the Second World War. These relationships continued at the FAO, where Blau invited Kaldor, Cohen and Kahn to contribute as consultants in Rome. During her tenure the Division focused on addressing challenges related to international trade in agricultural commodities, promoting cooperation, and conducting pioneering research on global commodity markets. Her leadership played a key role in shaping the FAO's efforts to balance global supply and demand for food and agricultural products, particularly in post-war periods marked by food insecurity and surplus management challenges.

Sir Otto (Richard Williams) Clarke (1906–1990) was a British civil servant and economist, known for his influential role in shaping post-war economic policy in the United Kingdom. As a senior Treasury official, he played a key part in managing Britain's economic recovery and implementing Keynesian policies. Clarke was instrumental in policy decisions related to government spending, monetary control and economic planning during the mid-twentieth century.

Ruth Cohen (1909–1991), a friend and colleague of Kahn, pursued a career as an agricultural economist after studies in the United States, later working at Oxford's Agricultural Economic Research Institute. She returned to Cambridge as a lecturer, though during the Second World War she served as an economist at the Ministry of Food and the Board of Trade. She also contributed significantly to the critique of neoclassical capital theory. In 1954 she became Principal of Newnham College, the first Jewish head of an Oxbridge college. Her principalship combined academic leadership with close involvement in many aspects of college life. She also contributed to public service, sitting on the General Medical Council, the governing body of the Hebrew University of Jerusalem, and several agricultural committees. In 1962 she chaired the Ministry of Agriculture's Provincial Agricultural Advisory Service committee and received a CBE in 1969. After retiring from Newnham in 1972, she joined the Cambridge City Council as a Labour councillor. There she chaired the Finance Committee and worked actively on development control. She continued in public service until 1987 and died in 1991.

Sir Stafford Cripps (1889–1952) was a British lawyer, politician and statesman whose adult life was characterised by intellectual rigour and public service. After establishing himself as a successful barrister, he was elected as the Labour MP for Bristol East in 1931, swiftly gaining a reputation for his socialist ideals and moral integrity. A staunch proponent of planned economics and social reform, he was expelled from the Labour Party in 1939 for advocating a united left-wing front. During the Second World War, Churchill appointed him as Ambassador to the Soviet Union (1940–1942), where he helped to strengthen Britain's alliance with Moscow. Later, as Lord Privy Seal and Minister of Aircraft Production, he proved himself to be an efficient and disciplined administrator. Following the war, Cripps became a pivotal figure in Attlee's Labour government, serving as President of the Board of Trade and subsequently as Chancellor of the Exchequer. In this role, he guided Britain's post-war recovery through austerity and financial reform. His integrity, intellect and austere dedication made him one of the most respected figures in mid-twentieth-century British politics.

Marco Dardi is Professor Emeritus of Economics, University of Florence, Department of Economics and Business. His research covers the following fields: the history of economic thought (particularly Alfred Marshall and the Cambridge school of twentieth-century economists); labour economics; decision theory; the mathematisation of political economy; and industrial districts. He is currently researching Italian economists during Fascism and Italian schools of thought after the Second World War. From 1991 to 2012, he was the co-editor, with Tiziano Raffaelli, of the online journal Marshall Studies Bulletin. In 2020, Dardi co-edited *Marshall and the Marshallian Heritage: Essays in Honour of Tiziano Raffaelli*, a collection published in the Palgrave Studies in the History of Economic Thought series. Dardi has taught at the Faculty of Economics in Florence, as well as on doctoral programmes in Florence and Siena.

Marcello de Cecco (1939–2016) was a renowned Italian economist and economic historian. After obtaining a law degree in Parma and an MA in Economics from Cambridge University in the United Kingdom, under the supervision of Kahn and M. Posner, he helped found the Faculty of Economics and Banking in Siena, where he taught from 1968 to 1979. He then taught at the European University Institute (1979–1986) and the University of Rome "La Sapienza" (1986–2003). From 2003 onwards, he was a full professor of the History of Finance and Money at the Scuola Normale in Pisa. He became a professor emeritus in November 2009 and, since 2011, has also lectured at LUISS 'Guido Carli' in Rome. He was a visiting professor at Harvard, Oxford, Berkeley and the École Normale d'Administration in Paris and was affiliated with the Institute for Advanced Study in Princeton, the Wissenschaftskolleg zu Berlin and the Institute for New Economic Thinking.

He has also collaborated with numerous other institutions, including the Historical Research Office of the Bank of Italy, the Research Department of the International Monetary Fund, Banca Nazionale del Lavoro, and the Presidency of the Council of Ministers as a member of the Council of Economic Advisers. He was a member of the board of directors of several credit institutions. Through his work as a columnist for *La*

Repubblica and other newspapers, he generously shared his knowledge and worldview with a wider audience. His research activities have focused mainly on the intersection between the theory, policy, and history of monetary and financial markets, as well as, more recently, analysing the genesis and functioning of markets. In addition to numerous scientific articles, he wrote several important monographs and collections of articles and in particular *Money and Empire: The International GoldStandard, 1890–1914* (Oxford, 1974).

Walter Eltis (1933–2019) studied Economics at Cambridge during the height of the Keynesian revolution, going on to study under Roy Harrod at Oxford, where he developed original work on capital and growth. His early research resulted in a successful textbook and a fellowship at Exeter College, Oxford. His first experience of working in policy came at the National Economic Development Office in the 1960s, where he started to question the increase in public expenditure. In 1974, he published Capital and Distribution, and he later produced influential essays on Adam Smith and other classical economists. In 1976, he co-authored *Too Few Producers* with Robert Bacon, a work that argued excessive public spending weakened productivity. This work helped shape the economic thinking of both political parties, including that of Margaret Thatcher. He also introduced elements of the Laffer Curve into British debates on taxation. In the 1980s, his focus shifted to deficits, debt and monetary policy, and he co-edited *The Money Supply and the ExchangeRate*. Returning to the National Economic Development Office as Economic Director, he advocated strict inflation control and a zero inflation target. A respected editor and organiser of economic debates, he encouraged discussion on policy issues among academics and practitioners alike. His final appointment was as an adviser to Michael Heseltine, enabling him to continue shaping British economic policy.

Oliver Sherwell Franks, Baron Franks (1905–1992), was an English civil servant, philosopher and diplomat, regarded as a key figure in shaping the post-war world. Educated at Bristol Grammar School and Queen's College, Oxford, he became a moral philosophy professor at the University of Glasgow (1936–1946) before transitioning into public service. During the Second World War, Franks played a crucial role at the Ministry of Supply, rising to permanent secretary in 1945. Knighted in 1946, he became British ambassador to the United States (1948–1952), strengthening Anglo–American relations. Returning to Britain, he chaired Lloyds Bank (1954–1962) and Friends Provident (1960–1962) while serving as a Bilderberg Group member. From 1962 to 1976 he was provost of Worcester College, Oxford, and was granted a life peerage in 1962. Frequently called upon for government inquiries, he is best known for his Falklands War report, which cleared Margaret Thatcher's government of negligence before the Argentine invasion.

Hugh Gaitskell (1906–1963) was a prominent British economist and Labour politician who devoted his adult life to public service and modernising his party. After studying at Oxford, he became an economics lecturer before being elected as the MP for Leeds South in 1945. His sharp intellect and administrative skill brought him rapid advancement in Clement Attlee's post-war government. Serving as Minister of Fuel and Power from 1947 to 1950 and subsequently as Chancellor of the Exchequer from 1950 to 1951, he managed Britain's fragile post-war economy and introduced controversial yet necessary austerity measures. Following Labour's defeat in 1951, Gaitskell became party leader in 1955, promoting a moderate social democratic vision that balanced welfare with economic responsibility. His leadership was marked by fierce internal battles, particularly over nationalisation and nuclear disarmament, as he sought to modernise the Labour Party for a changing Britain. Gaitskell's unexpected death in 1963 cut short a promising career and paved the way for Harold Wilson to become leader of the party.

Susan Howson is Professor Emeritus of Economics at the University of Toronto, where she also served as Associate Dean of the Graduate School and Vice-Dean of the Faculty of Arts and Science. After studying at the London School of Economics, where she earned a BA (1967) and an MSc (1969), she completed her MA (1974) and PhD (1975) at the University of Cambridge, where she later held a research fellowship at Wolfson College. Her research spans the history of economic thought, economic history, international economics and macroeconomics. She is widely recognised for her work on British monetary policy and on Lionel Robbins and James Meade. Key publications include *James Meade: The Utopian Economist* (2025); *Lionel Robbins* (2011); and *British Monetary Policy, 1945–51* (1993). Professor Howson has received numerous honours, including the Ellen McArthur Prize in Economic History (1975) and the T.S. Ashton Prize from the Economic History Society (1973), as well as two Connaught Senior Research Fellowships in the Social Sciences (2004 and 2007). In 2019, she was named a Distinguished Fellow of the History of Economics Society.

Terence Wilmot Hutchison (1912–2007) was an English economist and historian of economic thought who was renowned for his rigorous and methodological critiques of economic theory. After being educated at Cambridge, he went on to teach at institutions including the LSE and the University of Birmingham, where he was Mitsui Professor of Economics from 1956 to 1978. He is best known for his 1938 book *The Significance and Basic Postulates of Economic Theory*, in which he used logical positivism to challenge untestable economic frameworks. His subsequent publications, such as *A Review of Economic Doctrines, 1870–1929* (1953) and *Economics and Economic Policy in Britain, 1946–1966* (1968), provided a critical overview of economic ideas and policy recommendations in post-war Britain, prioritising empirical testing over abstract speculation.

Douglas Jay (1907–1996) was a British economist and Labour politician who advocated central economic planning and import controls to protect industry and promote social welfare. During his time as President of the Board of Trade (1964–1967), he promoted selective state intervention and industrial modernisation within a Keynesian framework.

Sir Henry J.B. Lintott (1908–1995) was a British civil servant and diplomat, best known as British High Commissioner to Canada from 1963 to 1968. He was educated at Edinburgh Academy, Edinburgh University, and King's College, Cambridge. His career in public service began in 1932 with HM Customs and Excise before moving to the Board of Trade in 1935. From 1948 to 1956 he played a key role in post-war European economic cooperation as Deputy Secretary-General of the Organisation for European Economic Co-operation (OECC). He later served as Deputy Under-Secretary of State at the Commonwealth Relations Office (1956–1963).

Oliver Lyttelton, 1st Viscount Chandos (1893–1972), was a British businessman, politician and military officer who played a key role in government and industry. Educated at Eton and Trinity College, Cambridge, he served in the First World War before joining the British Metal Corporation in 1920. He became a major figure in the global metals trade, holding key positions in various international companies. In 1940 he became President of the Board of Trade, overseeing wartime industry, and in 1941 he was sent to Egypt as Minister of State for the Middle East, coordinating military and economic policy. Returning to Britain in 1942, he served as Minister of Production, streamlining war output and strengthening Lend-Lease cooperation with the United States. Beyond politics, where he served as MP for Aldershot from 1940 to 1954, Lyttelton had a successful business career. Created Viscount Chandos in 1954, he remained a key figure in British public life until his death in 1972.

Sir George Donald Alastair MacDougall (1912–2004) attended Kelvinside Academy, Shrewsbury School, and Balliol College, Oxford. There, he switched from studying mathematics to studying politics, philosophy and economics (PPE) under the guidance of Roy Harrod. Following his early career at the University of Leeds, he joined Frederick Lindemann's (Lord Cherwell's) statistical 'S Branch' during the Second World War, where he provided economic advice to Churchill. His analyses of wartime logistics and shipping allocation were among his most significant contributions. Following the war, he returned to Oxford, holding fellowships at Wadham and Nuffield Colleges, and producing influential studies on Britain's foreign trade and comparative advantage. From 1948 to 1949, he served in Paris as the first Economics Director of the OEEC, helping to design the post-war European recovery plan. Later publications, such as *The World Dollar Problem* (1957), and his work on trade elasticities and foreign investment, further cemented his reputation. In the 1960s, he helped to establish the National Economic Development Council, and at the Department of Economic Affairs he argued for devaluation and a realistic incomes policy. From 1969 to 1973, he was Chief Economic Adviser to the Treasury and the first Head of the Government Economic Service. As Chief Economic Adviser to the Confederation of British Industry (1973–84), he advocated profitability, inflation accounting and moderation in pay bargaining. In his later years, he received many honours and chaired the 1977 MacDougall Report, which concluded that a durable European monetary union would require a federal budget of at least 7–10% of GDP. A sceptic of monetary union without such structures, he continued to advise on macroeconomic policy well into old age.

Maria Cristina Marcuzzo is Honorary Professor of Political Economy at the Sapienza University of Rome, Italy, and Fellow and Foreign Secretary of the Italian Academy of Lincei. Former President of the European Society for the History of Economics and of the Italian Society for the History of Political Economy, she is presently Distinguished Fellow and President of the History of Economics Society (United States). She has been Visiting Professor in several universities in Europe, Japan, Mexico and the United States. She has worked on classical monetary theory, the Cambridge School of Economics, and Keynesian economics. She has published more than 110 articles in journals and books, plus authoring or editing twenty-five books. Collections of her essays have been published by Routledge (*Fighting Market Failure*, 2012), by Cambridge Scholars Publishing (*Essays in Keynesian Persuasion*, 2019) and by Palgrave Macmillan (*Economics Theories, Protagonists and Facts*, 2025).

Raffaele Mattioli (1895–1973) was an Italian economist and esteemed banker who rose to become managing director and later chairman of Banca Commerciale Italiana. A committed anti-fascist, he helped save Jewish colleagues during the Racial Laws and supported cultural figures like Antonio Gramsci. Celebrated as a 'humanist banker', he championed arts, literature and economic history through extensive patronage. He also coined the term *catoblepismo* to describe problematic entanglements between industry and finance. His legacy endures via the Raffaele Mattioli Foundation and the prestigious Raffaele Mattioli Lectures.

Donald Moggridge (1943–2021) studied Political Science and Economics at the University of Toronto before completing his doctorate at the University of Cambridge under Richard Kahn. His early books on Britain's return to the gold standard established him as a leading economic historian. He was a fellow of Clare College (Cambridge) for some time before being asked to become an editor of *The Collected Writings of John MaynardKeynes*. In 1969, he became joint editor with Elizabeth Johnson, later becoming Joint Managing Editor with Austin Robinson. The publication of the thirty volumes was completed by 1989. Having taught at Cambridge, he returned to Toronto in 1974 as Professor of Economics. During his time at the University of Toronto, he also served as Associate Dean of the Graduate School, then Associate Dean of Arts and Science, and subsequently Vice Dean of the Graduate School. His major works include *Maynard Keynes: An Economist's Biography* (1992) and a biography of Harry Johnson (2008). Moggridge was President and Distinguished Fellow of the History of Economics Society.

Sir Henry Phelps Brown (1906–1994) was a prominent British economist and former president of the Royal Economic Society. He studied Modern History and later Philosophy, Politics and Economics (PPE) at Oxford, where he developed an interest in economics. Following a teaching position at New College, Oxford, he became the inaugural Chair of the Economics of Labour at the London School of Economics (LSE) in 1947. There, he made significant contributions to British labour economics. His work focused on applied economics, particularly wage trends, industrial relations and income inequality. He was renowned for his meticulous research, historical approach and emphasis on the practical relevance of economics. He also served on various government committees and commissions. His major works include *The Growth of British Industrial Relations* (Macmillan, 1959), *The Inequality of Pay* (OUP, 1977), and *Egalitarianism and the Generation of Inequality* (Clarendon Press, 1988). Phelps Brown was in contact with Kahn, in particular during the latter's engagement as an advisor to the Wilson government alongside K. Berrill.

Michael V. Posner (1931–2006) was one of Kahn's closest associates in the 1970s. A British economist, he was an influential member of the Faculty of Economics at Cambridge University. After being educated at the London School of Economics, Posner became a fellow of Pembroke College and while at Cambridge made notable contributions to international economics and innovation theory. Throughout his career, he participated in debates on economic policy, addressing issues such as the balance of payments, industrial strategy and the role of technology in economic growth. Michael Posner is considered a non-mainstream economist for his institutional and historically grounded defence of Italian public enterprises, and for his dynamic theory of international trade, which emphasises technological innovation and imitation lags over static comparative advantage. He served as Chief Economic Adviser at the UK Department of Trade and Industry, where he played a key role in formulating science and innovation policies. His academic and policy work reflected a commitment to pragmatic, empirically grounded economics, and he remained closely linked to the Post-Keynesian and Cambridge traditions.

Alan R. Prest (1919–1984) was a British economist who, in 1955, was affiliated to the Department of Applied Economics at the University of Cambridge. He collaborated with Richard Stone and Deryck Rowe on demand analysis, contributing to the development of quantitative economic research at Cambridge. Prest later became a professor at the London School of Economics and was recognised for his work in public finance.

John Primatt Redcliffe Redcliffe-Maud (later Baron Redcliffe-Maud) (1906–1982) was a British civil servant and diplomat. He was educated at Oxford, and Master of Birkbeck College (1939–1943). During the war he worked in several ministries (Food, Education, Fuel and Power) until 1946. He was High Commissioner and then Ambassador to South Africa until 1963. In 1964 he was head of the Maud Committee on management of local government. And Master of University College Oxford. In May 1944 he worked in the Office of the Minister for Reconstruction.

A.D. Roy (1920–2003) was a University Lecturer in Economics at Cambridge in 1955, affiliated to Sidney Sussex College. He is best known for the Roy Model of income distribution and early work in portfolio theory. In 1962 he left academia to become a senior economic advisor in the UK Treasury.

Sir Richard Stone (1913–1991) was a British economist. Initially studying law at the University of Cambridge, Stone was influenced by economist John Maynard Keynes to pursue a degree in economics, which he completed in 1935 (ScD, 1957). He then worked for a brokerage firm in London from 1936 to 1940, after which he joined the Central Statistical Office of the British government. Following the Second World War, he was appointed director of the newly established Department of Applied Economics at Cambridge. He held this position until 1955, when he became the P.D. Leake Professor of Finance and Accounting at Cambridge (1955–80; Professor Emeritus from 1980). In 1978, he was knighted and in 1984 he received the Nobel Prize for Economics for developing an accounting model that could be used to track economic activities on a national and, later, international scale. The first official estimates of British national income and expenditure were made using a method devised by James Meade and Richard Stone in 1941. However, the majority of Stone's work was carried out in the 1950s, when he provided the first practical statistical means of measuring investment, government spending and consumption. These models essentially constituted a national book-keeping system. He went on to adapt these models for international organisations such as the United Nations. Stone was the co-author (with J.E. Meade) of *National Income and Expenditure* (first published in 1944, with a tenth edition published in 1977 with Giovanna Stone), and the author of several other works, including *Input–Output and National Accounts* (1961), *Mathematics in the Social Sciences and Other Essays* (1966), and *Mathematical Models of the Economy and Other Essays* (1970).

James Trevithick (1945–2025) was an economist at the University of Cambridge who collaborated with Richard Kahn. He taught in the Faculty of Economics from 1976 to 2002 and became a Fellow of King's College in 1977. After studying at the LSE, he specialised in macroeconomics, with a focus on inflation and unemployment. A central figure in economics education at King's, he served as Director of Studies, Praelector and University Proctor. Following his retirement in 2002, he was elected a Life Fellow and remained closely connected to the college community. His publications include influential works such as *The Economics of Inflation* (1975), *Inflation: A Guide to the Crisis in Economics* (1977; 2nd ed. 1980) and *InvoluntaryUnemployment: Macroeconomics from a Keynesian Perspective* (1992). He also co-edited Keynes and the Modern World, reflecting his continued engagement with Keynesian ideas.

Index[1]

[1] Note: Page numbers followed by 'n' refer to notes.

P. Paesani, *Richard F. Kahn*, Great Thinkers in Economics,
https://doi.org/10.1007/978-3-032-09123-9

E

F

G

H

I

Kolibri 360 GmbH
Ferdinand-Jühlke-Straße 7
99095 Erfurt, Deutschland
produktsicherheit@kolibri360.de